Landscape of the Megaliths

excavation and fieldwork on the Avebury monuments, 1997–2003

Mark Gillings, Joshua Pollard,
David Wheatley and Rick Peterson

With contributions by
Rosamund Cleal, Nicholas Cooper, Paul Courtney, Fiona Coward,
Andrew David, Rowena Gale, Anthony Gouldwell, James Gunter, Helen Lewis, Philip Macdonald,
Andrew Mann, Louise Martin, Lorraine Mepham,
Graham Morgan, Rosina Mount, Philip Parkes, Ed Rhodes,
Vaughan Roberts, Jean-Luc Schwenninger, Nicola Snashall,
Joe White and Ruth Young

This report has been published with the support of
The Marc Fitch Fund
and the
Universities of Bristol, Leicester and Southampton

OXBOW BOOKS

First published in the United Kingdom in 2008. Reprinted as a paperback in 2010 and 2019 by
OXBOW BOOKS
The Old Music Hall, 106–108 Cowley Road, Oxford OX4 1JE

and in the United States by
OXBOW BOOKS
1950 Lawrence Road, Havertown, PA 19083

Paperback Edition: ISBN 978-1-84217-971-0
Digital Edition: ISBN 978-1-78297-523-6 (epub)

A CIP record for this book is available from the British Library

For a complete list of Oxbow titles, please contact:

UNITED KINGDOM
Oxbow Books
Telephone (01865) 241249
Email: oxbow@oxbowbooks.com
www.oxbowbooks.com

UNITED STATES OF AMERICA
Oxbow Books
Telephone (800) 791-9354, Fax (610) 853-9146
Email: queries@casemateacademic.com
www.casemateacademic.com/oxbow

Oxbow Books is part of the Casemate Group

Front cover: The Longstones, Beckhampton
Photographs: J. Pollard and M. Gillings

Contents

List of Contributors

GILLINGS, COOPER, COURTNEY, GOULDWELL, MORGAN AND YOUNG
School of Archaeology and Ancient History
University of Leicester
University Road, Leicester
LE1 7RH

POLLARD
Department of Archaeology and Anthropology
University of Bristol
43 Woodland Road
Bristol
BS8 1UU

PETERSON
Archaeology, School of Natural Resources
University of Central Lancashire
Preston
PR1 2HE

WHEATLEY, MANN, MOUNT AND WHITE
Archaeology, University of Southampton
Avenue Campus
Highfield
Southampton
SO17 1BF

CLEAL, GUNTER, ROBERTS AND SNASHALL
Alexander Keiller Museum
Avebury
Marlborough
Wiltshire
SN8 1RF

DAVID AND MARTIN
Centre for Archaeology
Fort Cumberland
Portsmouth
Hampshire
PO4 9LD

COWARD
Department of Geography
Royal Holloway
University of London
Egham
Surrey
TW20 0EX

GALE
Bachefield House
Kimbolton
Leominster
Herefordshire
HR6 0EP

LEWIS
UCD School of Archaeology
Newman Building
University College Dublin
Belfield
Dublin 4
Ireland

MACDONALD
Centre for Archaeological Fieldwork
School of Archaeology and Palaeoecology
Queens University Belfast
Belfast
BT7 1NN

MEPHAM
Wessex Archaeology
Portway House
Old Sarum Park
Salisbury
SP4 6EB

PARKES
School of History and Archaeology
Cardiff University
Humanities Building
Colum Drive
Cardiff
CF10 3EU

RHODES
Research School of Earth Sciences
Building 61
Mills Road
The Australian National University
Canberra ACT 0200
Australia

SCHWENNINGER
Research Laboratory for Archaeology and the History of Art
Dyson Perrins Building
South Parks Road
Oxford
OX1 3QY

Acknowledgements

The project was co-directed by Mark Gillings, Joshua Pollard and David Wheatley. Rick Peterson joined the team as an AHRB-funded research assistant between 2001–2003, undertaking extensive work on the antiquarian records relating to the Beckhampton Avenue, in addition to providing invaluable assistance with the fieldwork, post-excavation analysis and report preparation.

None of the work would have been possible were it not for the support and access offered by farmers and landowners in the Avebury area. Particular thanks go to Robin Butler, who put up with more disruption over five years of the project than any farmer should, yet maintained patience and interest. Likewise, we sincerely appreciate the support and co-operation of Tony and Judy Farthing. They, along with the National Trust, granted access to the West Kennet Avenue and the Falkner's Circle, and have shown much interest in the results of the project. Additional logistical support for that work came from Rob Mimmack and Rosie Edmunds of the Trust. Roger Charlton of Beckhampton Stables Ltd. kindly permitted work in Long Barrow Field, Beckhampton; and Stephen Horton, the Crown Estates and their agents Carter Jonas granted access for geophysical survey and surface collection on Firs Farm, Beckhampton.

During the 1998, 1999, 2000, 2002 and 2003 seasons much of the excavation work was undertaken by students from the Universities of Leicester, Southampton and Wales (Newport), along with volunteers from other universities, the Wiltshire Archaeological and Natural History Society and elsewhere. Glyn Goodrick was instrumental in the initial stone recording exercises carried out by the project in 1997 and 1998 and provided valuable supervisory support during the 1999 excavations. The participation of Patty Baker, Dave Bennett, Ros Cleal, Rosie Edwards, Martin Green, Lynda Murray and Mike Pitts is gratefully acknowledged. Supervisory assistance was ably provided by David Robinson, Lucy Ryder, John Tate, Paul Cripps and Lesley McFadyen. Gill and Robin Swanton provided campsite support during the early seasons, and Rosina Mount maintained excellent morale through splendid cooking and campsite management.

Pre-excavation geophysical surveys of Longstones and Long Barrow Fields and the Falkner's Circle were provided, with their usual consummate skill, by Andrew David, Louise Martin and Andy Payne of the Centre for Archaeology, English Heritage. Amanda Chadburn of English Heritage and Duncan Coe and Sue Farr of the Wiltshire County Archaeological Service gave constructive advice on project designs and fieldwork strategies.

For assistance with excavations at the Avebury Cove, we would like to thank Deirdre O'Sullivan, Jeremy Taylor and Ruth Young. The engineering contractors, Ellis and Co, and especially their site foreman, Andy, provided practical support and good humour. For their help with coordination, advice, support and assistance we would also like to thank Rob Mimmack, Hilary Makins, Rosie Edmunds and Ros Cleal of the National Trust, and Michael Heaton, the Trust's contracted archaeological consultant.

Staff at the Society of Antiquaries (especially Adrian James), the Bodleian Library, Buckinghamshire County Council (Julia Wise), the Alexander Keiller Museum, Avebury, the Wiltshire Records Office and the Wiltshire Archaeological and Natural History Society kindly assisted with archival research on antiquarian and early archaeological fieldwork in the region, and on the post-medieval sarsen industry.

For support, academic advice and other input which has made this project successful, the following deserve our grateful acknowledgement: Miranda and Stephen Aldhouse-Green, Bob Bewley, Richard Bradley, Aubrey Burl, Humphrey Case, Amanda Chadburn, Ros Cleal, Duncan Coe, Julian Cope, Chris Dyer, James Dyer, Brian Edwards, Dave Edwards, the late John Evans, David Field, Charly French, Alex Gibson, Chris Gingell, Pete Glastonbury, Jan Harding, Phil Harding, Frances Healy, Audrey Horning, Matthew Johnson, Andrew Lawson, Mike Parker Pearson, Mike Pitts, Colin Richards, Julian Richards, Paul Robinson, Niall Sharples, Colin Shell, the late Isobel Smith, Gill Swanton, Julian Thomas and Alasdair Whittle. Through their earlier work on the Neolithic of the region, John Evans and Alasdair Whittle provided much inspiration, an awareness of the unanticipated discoveries that might be made in the Avebury landscape, and a sense of what was possible. Ros Cleal should also be singled out. Not only did she provide a seemingly endless supply of tea and biscuits when we visited the Alexander Keiller Museum, and ready access to the Keiller archive, but also much invaluable local archaeological knowledge and considerable encouragement to 'keep digging'.

The work was generously funded through an AHRC (formerly AHRB) major research grant, with additional contributions by the Society of Antiquaries of London, the Prehistoric Society, and the Universities of Leicester, Newport and Southampton. Awards made as part of the AHRC Research Leave scheme enabled Gillings, Pollard and Wheatley to work on the final stages of writing and production of this volume.

Many of the illustrations within this volume are the work of Rick Peterson, with others provided by the principal authors, Anne Leaver (Chapter 6) and contributing specialists. Rosina Mount kindly took on the role of collating and formatting the bibliography. Clare Litt and Juliet Blackmore at Oxbow expertly guided the volume through production.

To all those others who we may – through lapsed memory – have forgotten to acknowledge, we extend our warmest thanks.

Every effort was made to track down the current copyright owner of the Lilywhite Ltd image reproduced as Figure 4.11. The authors are happy to respond to any enquiries from the current owner of copyright.

Note on Authorship

A publication of this kind is inevitably the work of many hands, and authorship of specialist reports is here given, following convention, at the beginning of the relevant sections of text. While the principal authors all contributed in various ways to each section of this work, 'lead roles' in the production and preparation of chapters were divided as follows:

- Chapters 1–4: Joshua Pollard
- Chapter 5: David Wheatley
- Chapter 6: Joshua Pollard
- Chapter 7: Mark Gillings and Joshua Pollard
- Chapters 8–11: Mark Gillings
- Chapter 12, Appendices 1 and 2: Rick Peterson
- Appendix 3: Mark Gillings

Summary

This volume describes the results of the *Longstones Project*, a joint-universities programme of excavation and survey designed to develop a fuller understanding of the context and dynamics of monument construction in the later Neolithic (3rd millennium BC) of the Avebury region, Wiltshire. Several elements of this internationally important prehistoric monument complex were investigated: an early-mid 3rd millennium BC enclosure at Beckhampton; the recently re-discovered Beckhampton Avenue and Longstones Cove; a section of the West Kennet Avenue; the Falkner's stone circle; and the Cove within Avebury's Northern Inner Circle.

Much of the fieldwork focussed on an area to the south-west of Avebury, close to the modern village of Beckhampton. Here, in Longstones Field, a sequence of monument building was revealed that began with the creation of a small gully-defined enclosure; perhaps of 4th millennium BC date and related to two adjacent long barrows. Around 2900–2600BC a larger, oval, earthwork enclosure was created, with a segmented ditch and a very wide eastern entrance. With the exception of a scatter of material deposited on the base of the ditch, there was little evidence of further activity at the enclosure until it was deliberately levelled in the middle of the 3rd millennium BC. The levelling of the enclosure probably corresponded to the point in time when the Beckhampton Avenue was created; this 1.3km-long setting of paired megaliths linking the erstwhile enclosure to the western entrance of the Avebury henge. Although direct dating evidence is lacking, the Beckhampton Avenue and the closely analogous West Kennet Avenue were probably constructed in the period *c.*2600–2200BC, and so were contemporary with other major monuments in the region such as the first stages of work at Silbury Hill, the complex of palisades at West Kennet and the Outer Circle at Avebury. Evidence was found of two constructional phases to the south-west terminal of the Beckhampton Avenue, the second comprising a massive four-sided cove.

Work on the central section of the West Kennet Avenue, designed to provide enhanced dating evidence, resulted in the discovery of a gap in its course and possible structural variation elsewhere. A lithic scatter and a single pit attest to earlier Neolithic activity in the area of the excavation. At the nearby Falkner's Circle traces of stone settings were revealed, associated with quantities of later Neolithic worked flint. The circle may have comprised a hybrid construction of artificially-set and natural sarsen stones, or at the very least was located on the edge of an extensive natural scatter of sarsen. Limited excavation in advance of stone stabilisation at the Avebury Cove showed the western-most stone (Stone II) to be a colossal block of sarsen in the order of 100 tonnes in weight. The work highlights the importance attached to stones within the later Neolithic of this landscape, and the reconfiguration of established geographies that their movement brought about. It is argued that the transformation to stone of Avebury, the Sanctuary, the Longstones enclosure and the avenues at the end of the region's Neolithic can be seen as a process of memorialisation, turning these monuments into 'dead' or reserved spaces rather than the locations for active ceremony, as commonly envisaged.

Following on from presentation and discussion of the excavated Neolithic monuments, the opportunity is taken to review the environmental sequence of the Upper Kennet Valley from the earliest Holocene to the late Bronze Age. A wide-ranging discussion of comparable monument complexes in lowland Britain is also provided. Here, consideration is given to the questions of how and why ceremonial centres such as that at Avebury came into being in the 3rd millennium BC. The importance of understanding the agency – the affective and perceived inherent qualities – of materials and landscapes is stressed; and the unusual character of the Wessex monument complexes is highlighted by comparison with the format and sequences of other ceremonial centres in southern Britain.

The second part of the monograph tracks the later, post-prehistoric, lives of Avebury's megalithic monuments. Evidence for later prehistoric and Roman activity focused on the Longstones Cove is discussed, with particular reference to the status of deposits of Roman and/or sub-Roman metalwork, pottery and animal bone deposited around the stones of this setting.

The project's excavations produced rich evidence of medieval and early post-medieval responses to the prehistoric megalithic settings. Several toppled and deliberately buried megaliths were discovered on the line of the Beckhampton Avenue, and one of early 20th-century date on the West Kennet Avenue. Later 17th- and early 18th-century stone destruction pits, including one of very elaborate form, were encountered on the Beckhampton Avenue, at the Longstones Cove and the Falkner's Circle. Similar burial and burning features had been reported from earlier excavations at Avebury and, combining a re-analysis of archival information with that from the recent excavations, new interpretations of stone burial and breaking are offered. The conventional view that stone burial took place over a short period of time in the 14th century and that it was a Church-sponsored activity aimed at removing 'pagan' features from the landscape is shown to be incorrect. The relationships between patterns of medieval and post-medieval boundary creation, changing agricultural activity and stone burial are explored, and the dating evidence reviewed. It is shown that stone burial was an episodic activity that lasted for several centuries, and that it was underpinned by varied motives including agricultural clearance.

The variability in practice seen in the archaeological signature of early post-medieval stone breaking is also stressed. While normally viewed as a purely economic activity, undertaken to produce building stone, and related to a major phase of rebuilding in and around Avebury during the later 17th and early 18th centuries, archaeological and historical evidence highlights greater complexity in motivation. The role of Avebury's non-conformist population in stone breaking activities is reviewed alongside a consideration of the changing status of Avebury and the avenues brought about by their recognition as antiquities during the 17th century. It is suggested that, rather than being viewed as acts of destruction, stone breaking should be understood as an important post-medieval craft tradition in its own right. A review of evidence for the medieval and early post-medieval destruction of prehistoric megalithic settings elsewhere in southern England stresses how unique the practices and events at Avebury were.

In the final section of the monograph a detailed account is provided of the early 18th-century records of the Beckhampton Avenue made by the antiquary William Stukeley.

1

Introduction: The *Longstones Project* and its context

The chalk downland of the Upper Kennet Valley of North Wiltshire, in southern England, provides the setting for one of the most impressive complexes of prehistoric monuments in Europe; an equal to the archaeological landscapes around Stonehenge, the Boyne Valley of eastern Ireland and Carnac in Brittany. Spread over an area of *c.*15km east-west by 10km north-south, centred on the village of Avebury, is a remarkable concentration of Neolithic and earlier Bronze Age funerary and ceremonial monuments (Figure 1.1). Their creation began in the second quarter of the 4th millennium BC with the con-

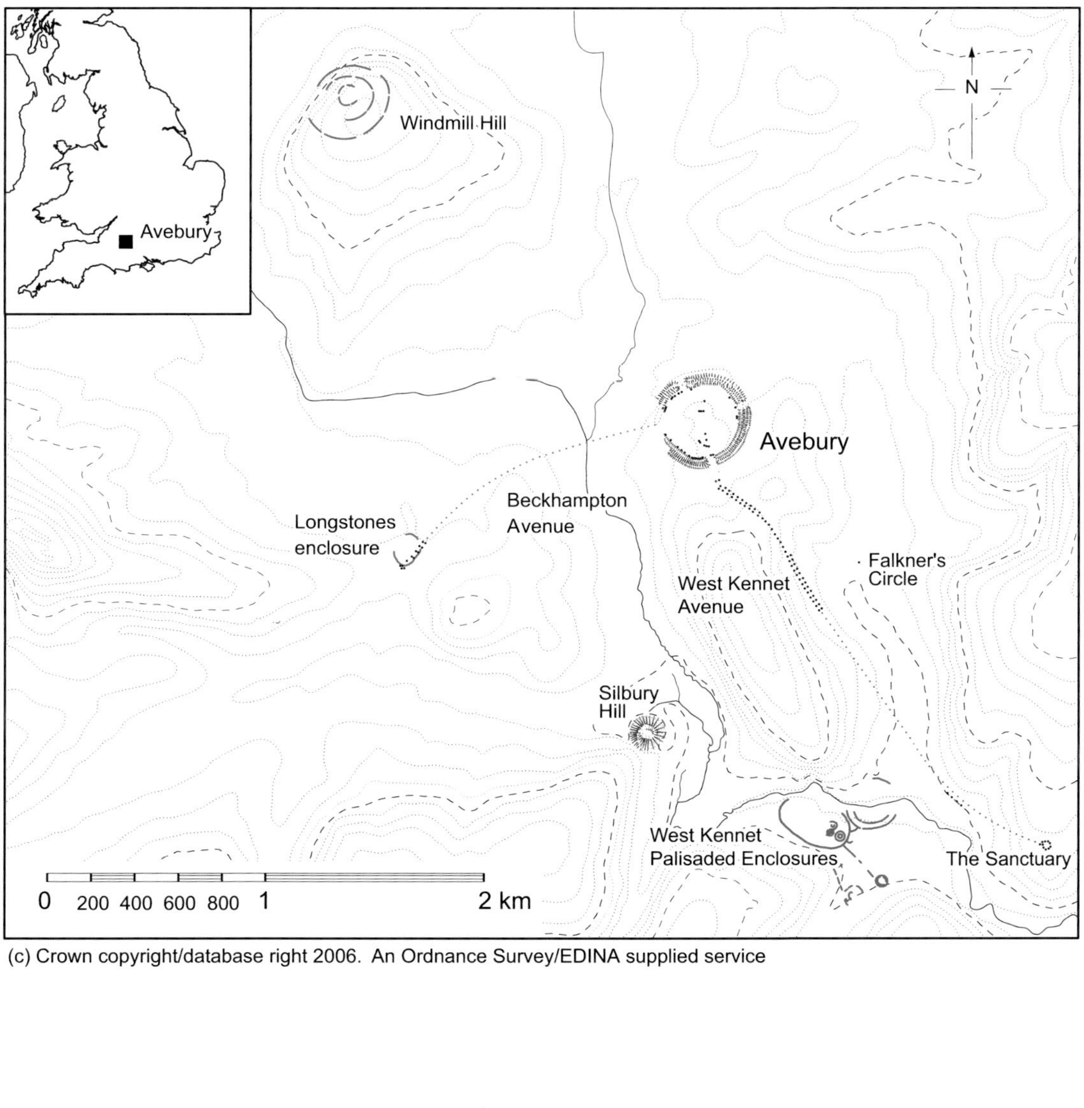

Figure 1.1. The Avebury region, showing principal later Neolithic monuments and the earlier Neolithic enclosure on Windmill Hill

Figure 1.2. Avebury henge from the east. The Longstones excavations are just visible in the far centre

struction of sites such as the Windmill Hill enclosure and East and West Kennet long barrows and, at this time, reached scales only occasionally matched elsewhere (Piggott 1962; Whittle *et al.* 1999). However, in terms of labour input, architectural complexity and visual dominance, pre-eminent status might be ascribed to the remarkable creations of the first three quarters of the 3rd millennium BC – the region's later Neolithic. These include the Avebury henge and stone circles, the West Kennet and Beckhampton megalithic avenues (Figure 1.2), the Sanctuary and, occupying the floor of the Kennet Valley, the complex of palisaded enclosures at West Kennet and the giant artificial mound of Silbury Hill (Smith 1965; Whittle 1997b). Avebury is but one of a series of great later Neolithic ceremonial centres on the Wessex chalklands, others being present in the landscapes around Stonehenge, Knowlton on Cranborne Chase, and Dorchester in Dorset. These monument complexes are exceptional in the context of the British Neolithic, yet they continue to occupy a key position in our accounts of the period because of their perceived potential to inform us of aspects of social and economic organisation, belief, ceremony and materiality. A broader, public value, as 'heritage', is reflected in the inscription of both the Avebury and Stonehenge landscapes as a World Heritage Site in 1986.

In this volume we provide the definitive report on a programme of excavation and survey on key elements of the later Neolithic monument complex, undertaken between 1997 and 2003 by a joint Universities team. Under the title of *The Longstones Project*, this programme of work was designed to develop a fuller understanding of the context, chronology and dynamics of monument construction in the later Neolithic of the Avebury region. Several elements of the late Neolithic complex were investigated: the Beckhampton Avenue, Longstones Enclosure and Longstones Cove to the west of Avebury; a section of the West Kennet Avenue and the near-by Falkner's stone circle; and the Cove within Avebury's Northern Inner Circle. Initially conceived as a small-scale, low-budget exercise in recording the extant three-dimensional components of the monument complex and the use of Virtual Reality modelling in its phenomenological analysis (see Pollard and Gillings 1998), the project rapidly developed and expanded its remit to incorporate a large programme of excavation. A highly readable account of the project's early days, its coming into being, struggles with financing, various frustrations and successes, is given in Mike Pitts' *Hengeworld* (Pitts 2001b, 178–80, 218–21). Work at the Avebury Cove was not originally intended, but a request from the National Trust for the project team to undertake excavation there in advance of stone stabilisation presented a unique opportunity to add to our knowledge of Avebury's megalithic settings and fitted well with the project's aims.

The legacy of research and how it shaped the project

It is in reaction to the exceptional nature of the Avebury monuments, their scale, their survival, and perhaps the promise they seem to hold for comprehending a distant and 'other' world of social, spiritual and symbolic relations, that many generations of antiquaries and archaeologists have been drawn to study them. The history of research on the later Neolithic complex has been long, if intermittent, and is dealt with in detail in several publications (Ucko *et al.* 1991; Cleal and Montague 2001; Pitts 2001b; Burl 2002; Pollard and Reynolds 2002; Gillings and Pollard 2004). Famously, there is the early (mid 17th century) recording by John Aubrey, credited as the 'discoverer' of Avebury, though best regarded as the first to recognise the presence of its megalithic components; and the work of William Stukeley. Stukeley, working in the region from 1719–24, produced a remarkably full written and drawn record of Avebury, the two avenues, the Sanctuary and other archaeological features, at a time when many of the surviving megalithic settings were in the process of being removed and broken-up (Ucko *et al.* 1991; see also Haycock 2002b). The publication of his fieldwork, interleaved with thoughts on pre-Roman patriarchal religion in the British Isles, in *Abury: a Temple of the British Druids* (1743) left a legacy that had to be negotiated by subsequent researchers, the authors of this volume included. Thus, Richard Colt Hoare and Philip Crocker's survey of the Avebury complex during the first two decades of the 19th century was very much coloured by Stukeley's reconstruction of its original form (Colt-Hoare 1821); much the same is true of the ambitious campaigns of excavation and restoration undertaken by Alexander Keiller at Avebury and on the West Kennet Avenue in the 1930s (Smith 1965), and Maud Cunnington's near-contemporary work at the Sanctuary (Cunnington 1931). In investigating sections of the Beckhampton and West Kennet Avenues, and Longstones Cove, we too have found ourselves influenced and guided by Stukeley's observations; the work sometimes becoming an exercise in negotiating the direct observations and interpretive 'gap filling' of this remarkable 18th-century antiquary.

A second major influence on the project has been the recent work of Alasdair Whittle and the late John Evans of Cardiff University, which has done much to elucidate details of environmental change, histories of occupation and sequences of monument construction during the region's Neolithic (Evans *et al.* 1993; Whittle 1993; Whittle *et al.* 1993; Whittle 1994; 1997b; Whittle *et al.* 1999; Whittle *et al.* 2000). In many respects, the project described within this volume continues and builds upon this work. Whittle's investigation of the complex of late Neolithic palisaded enclosures at West Kennet, under the shadow of Silbury Hill, also provided a sobering lesson. Although part of one enclosure was detected in an aerial photograph in 1950 and subject to a small-scale investigation in the early 1970s, the true date, scale and significance of the site was only revealed during Whittle's excavations between 1987–1992 (Whittle 1997b). Here was a stunning reminder of how, within such an apparently well-investigated and 'known' landscape, a major prehistoric monument could go undetected until very recently. We were to face much the same mixture of both surprise, and a reminder of the potential of what might remain 'hidden', through the 're-discovery' of the Beckhampton Avenue in 1999. Largely discredited as a figment of Stukeley's over-active antiquarian imagination, the Beckhampton Avenue was soon proved to be an archaeological reality through the relatively simple procedure of geophysical survey followed by machine-stripping of an appropriately sized and located area. At 1.3km long, this is now confirmed as one of Europe's great megalithic constructions.

The research questions

From the outset, the key aim of the *Longstones Project* was to enhance understanding of the chronology and context of monumentality during the later Neolithic of the Avebury region. Embedded within this was a series of specific questions that guided the choice of site to investigate and the way in which each would be approached through fieldwork. We wished to know the relationships between earlier and later monumental structures in the Avebury landscape, and the extent to which monument construction in the 3rd millennium BC might have served as a means of appropriating historical and mythological pasts. There was the question of whether the building of megalithic avenues reflected a development from a 'fragmented' landscape of diverse, free-standing monuments in the 4th millennium BC, to one of cohesion during the 3rd millennium BC: were the megalithic avenues a powerful material expression of a growing concern with unity and the gathering together of sacred sites? We also wished to know whether the creation of the later Neolithic monuments of the Avebury landscape took place during short bursts of constructional activity or was the result of more progressive, steady development.

While each of these research questions has been addressed with varying levels of success, the results of fieldwork forced the project to confront a broader range of archaeological issues than existed within the original, Neolithic-focussed, interpretive remit. Following the excavation of a series of medieval and early post-medieval stone burial and burning pits

Figure 1.3. Machining at the start of the 1999 excavation season in Longstones Field

during the 1999 season, and the discovery of Roman deposits associated with the Longstones Cove during 2000, it became apparent that an exclusive focus upon the region's Neolithic was inappropriate. Monuments have a tendency to retain a presence in the landscape, and that presence has to be negotiated by subsequent generations inhabiting the same space as those monuments, whether this is achieved through a process of ignoral, eradication, appropriation, mythologising, and so forth (Bradley 1993; Gosden and Lock 1998; Barrett 1999; Bradley 2002). Archaeologically, these responses are seen through the later structuring and working of the landscape in relation to the presence of pre-existing monuments, the modification of monumental constructions themselves, the occurrence of deliberate deposits in association, gradual dilapidation, or more active destruction. As a consequence of our encounter with the later lives of these constructions, particular effort was made to understand later prehistoric and historic engagements with the Avebury megaliths (here including those of the Beckhampton and West Kennet Avenues). Isobel Smith had earlier considered the mechanisms behind and motivations for the removal of standing stones within the Avebury complex (Smith 1965, 176–81), but the extra detail obtained during the project's excavations and documentary research now allows a fuller and more nuanced account to be offered (Chapters 8–10).

Organisation of fieldwork

Each season of excavation was normally undertaken over a period of four weeks during the late summer (from mid-August to late September), the work timed to fit in around the demands of agricultural schedules (Figure 1.3). The Foot-and-Mouth epidemic of 2001 resulted in the cancellation of that summer's excavation, although a limited programme of field-survey was undertaken in the autumn of that year and momentum was maintained by the inclusion of extra field seasons in Easter 2002 and Easter 2003. The progress of fieldwork was as follows:

1997 Topographic and stone survey at Avebury and the West Kennet Avenue
1998 The Longstones Enclosure
1999 The Longstones Enclosure and Beckhampton Avenue
2000 The Longstones Enclosure, Beckhampton Avenue and Longstones Cove
2001 Beckhampton Field (survey)
2002 Easter: south-west of Longstones Field. Summer: the West Kennet Avenue and Falkner's Circle
2003 Easter: the Avebury Cove. Summer: the West Kennet Avenue and Beckhampton Avenue

Landscape of the Megaliths

The title of this volume is borrowed from that of two paintings produced by the British modernist painter and illustrator Paul Nash in 1934 and 1937. These were part of a series of works both inspired by his visits to Avebury and the powerful form of its megalithic settings (lines, masses, planes and volumes), and engendered by a general fascination with antiquity and the landscape of southern England (Haycock 2002a, 54–7; Evans 2004; Smiles 2005). In his 1937 work, subsequently

Figure 1.4. Landscape of the Megaliths. *Paul Nash, 1937. Watercolour (50 × 76cm). © Albright-Knox Art Gallery*

reproduced as a lithograph, an avenue of stones is depicted running through a cultivated field, with a diminutive hedge and convolvulus in the foreground, the latter intersecting a low sun or moon (Figure 1.4). In the distance a terraced conical hill and a Silbury Hill-like mound are set within a rolling landscape. The work is explained in Nash's account of his first encounter with the Avebury landscape in July 1933:

> 'Last summer I walked in a field near Avebury where two rough monoliths stand up, sixteen feet high, miraculously patterned with black and orange lichen, remains of an avenue of stones which led to the Great Circle. A mile away, a green pyramid casts a gigantic shadow. In the hedge, at hand, the white trumpet of a convolvulus turns from its spiral stem, following the sun. In my art I would solve such an equation.'
> (Paul Nash, in Read 1934)

It is unclear whether his description relates to the West Kennet Avenue or to the Longstones at Beckhampton, around which much of our excavation work was focussed. The latter is a good candidate. Regardless of precise location, our encounters with the formal qualities of stone and chalk landscape struck a resonance with those of Nash. The 1999 excavations in Longstones Field followed immediately on from harvest, the farmer kindly leaving hay bales scattered across the field to act as a visual 'smoke-screen' to hide our presence (unsuccessfully as it turned out) from the curiosity of visitors (Figure 1.5). The combination of golden straw, soft round bales, scraped chalk and the sentinel presence of the lichen-covered grey megaliths, was quite surreal – a wonderful mixture of materials, textures and colours that seemed almost sculptural. Our thoughts were not alone, since the same scene evoked the image of Nash's stylised megalithic landscapes in the mind of the archaeologist Mike Pitts, at

Figure 1.5. A composition of stone and straw: the Longstones

that time re-excavating the Sanctuary on Overton Hill (Pitts 2001a, 218). Perhaps this was an example of what Colin Renfrew (2003) has referred to as the 'parallel visions' of artist and archaeologist: a mutual engagement with materiality and antiquity, an attempt to solve an equation.

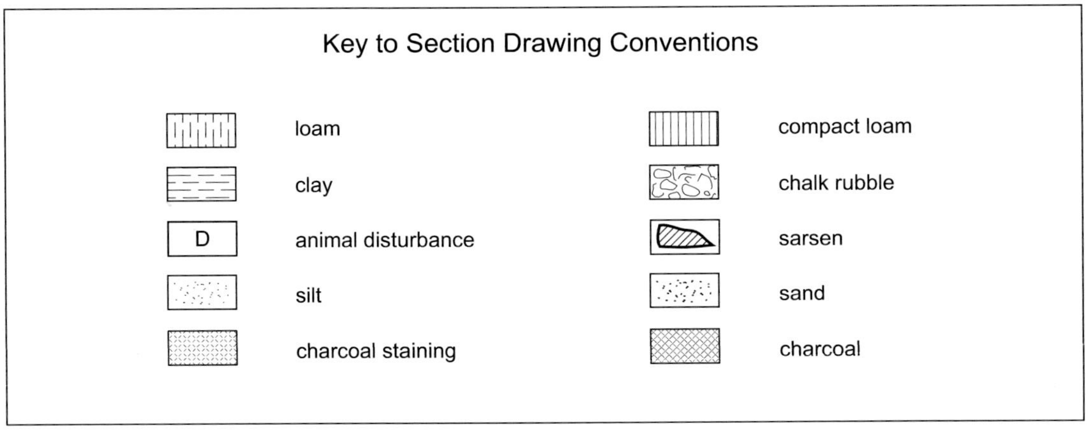

Figure 1.6. Key to sections

2

Monumentality in the third millennium BC – the Beckhampton Complex

This chapter describes the results of excavation work carried out between 1998 and 2003 in Longstones Field, Beckhampton, situated 0.9–1.2km south-west of the Avebury henge. Today, two substantial megaliths – the Longstones, known individually by their colloquial names of 'Adam' and 'Eve' – stand on a slight rise in the western corner of the irregularly-shaped field, the sole survivors of the Beckhampton Avenue and Longstones Cove (Figure 2.1). A hundred metres to the south-east of these is the heavily plough-denuded mound of the South Street long barrow, excavated by John Evans in 1966–7 (Ashbee *et al.* 1979); and 200m to the south-west, and currently hidden from the Longstones by a belt of trees, is the substantial mound of the Beckhampton or Longstones long barrow (Barker 1985, 23). These monuments are the remaining, visible elements of a more extensive complex of Neolithic and Early Bronze Age monuments sited on undulating ground to the north of the spring that feeds the Beckhampton stream. Other components include the Longstones enclosure described below, a largely ploughed-out group of round barrows, and two possible Neolithic mortuary enclosures or oval barrows on Folly Hill to the south-east (Figures 2.2 and 2.3). The latter overlook the Longstones, Avebury and Silbury Hill (Soffe 1993; Powell *et al.* 1996, 11–13). Antiquarian records also hint at the former existence of megalithic settings perhaps unconnected with the Beckhampton Avenue on lower ground to the south of the Longstones long barrow.

Taken together, these features can be seen to form a discrete group of ceremonial and funerary monuments constructed between the middle of the 4th and the middle of the 2nd millennia BC. Setting aside a limited late Mesolithic presence indicated by finds of microliths from beneath the South Street long barrow (Ashbee *et al.* 1979, 269), the early part of the sequence is represented by the two long barrows, possible mortuary enclosures or oval mounds on Folly Hill, and a small gully-defined enclosure adjacent to the Longstones (described below).

The earlier work on the South Street long barrow provided a detailed image of earlier Neolithic activity in one part of this complex. From under the mound a complex sequence of pre-barrow activity was revealed, involving cross-ploughing with an ard, and hoe or spade cultivation, followed by the construction of a fence line and a small sarsen setting (Ashbee *et al.* 1979, 282). Concentrations of knapping debris and charcoal patches, along with carinated plain bowl pottery and animal bone imply occupation of sorts. At the time of the mound's construction, probably during the third quarter of the 4th millennium BC, this area was pasture. The barrow itself comprised a complex earthen and chalk mound, internally sub-divided by fence lines. Deposits of human bone, and indeed any form of mortuary chamber, were absent; a sarsen cairn occupying a position under the proximal end of the

Figure 2.1. The Longstones, from the NW

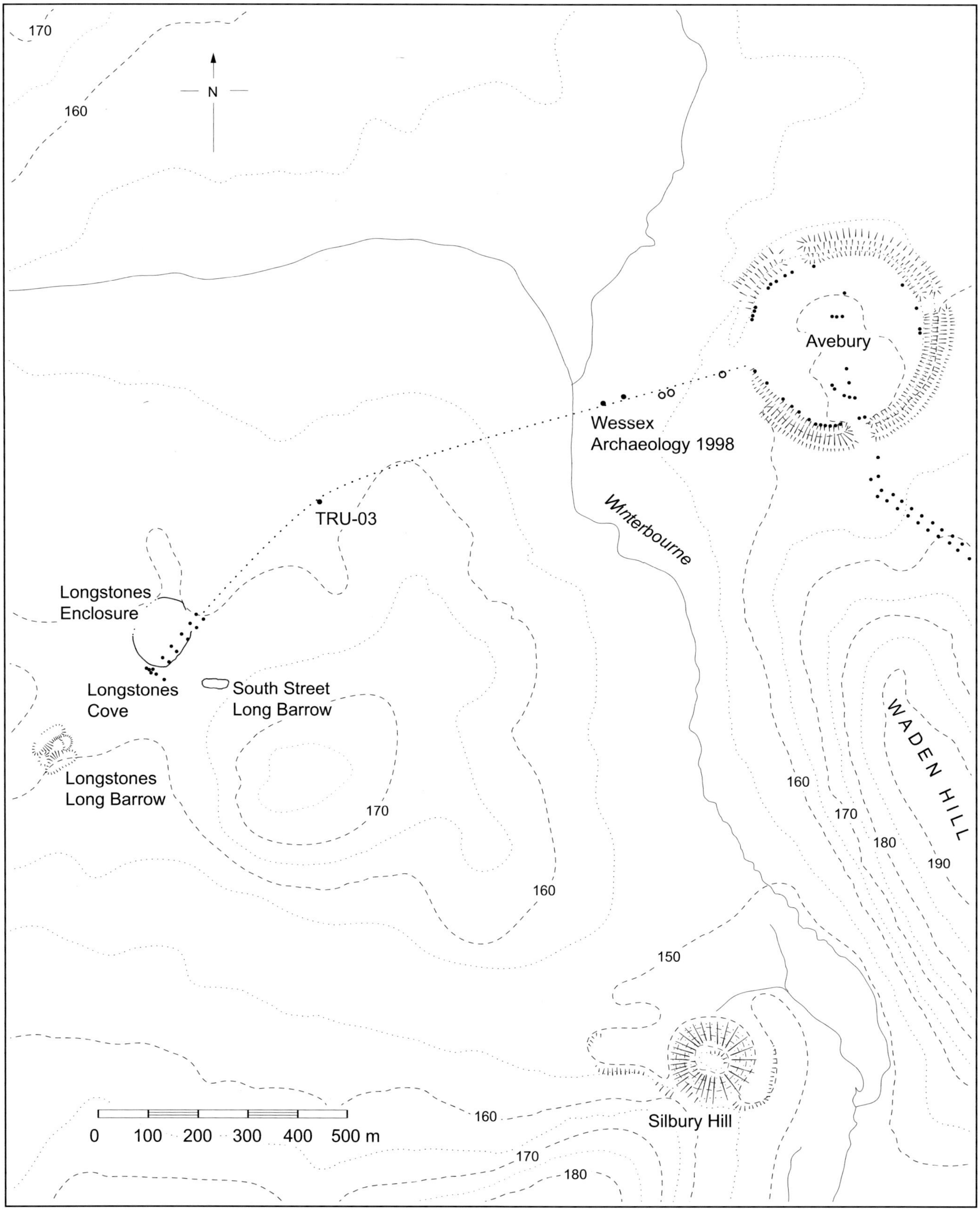

Figure 2.2. Avebury, Silbury Hill, the course of the Beckhampton Avenue and the location of the Longstones enclosure

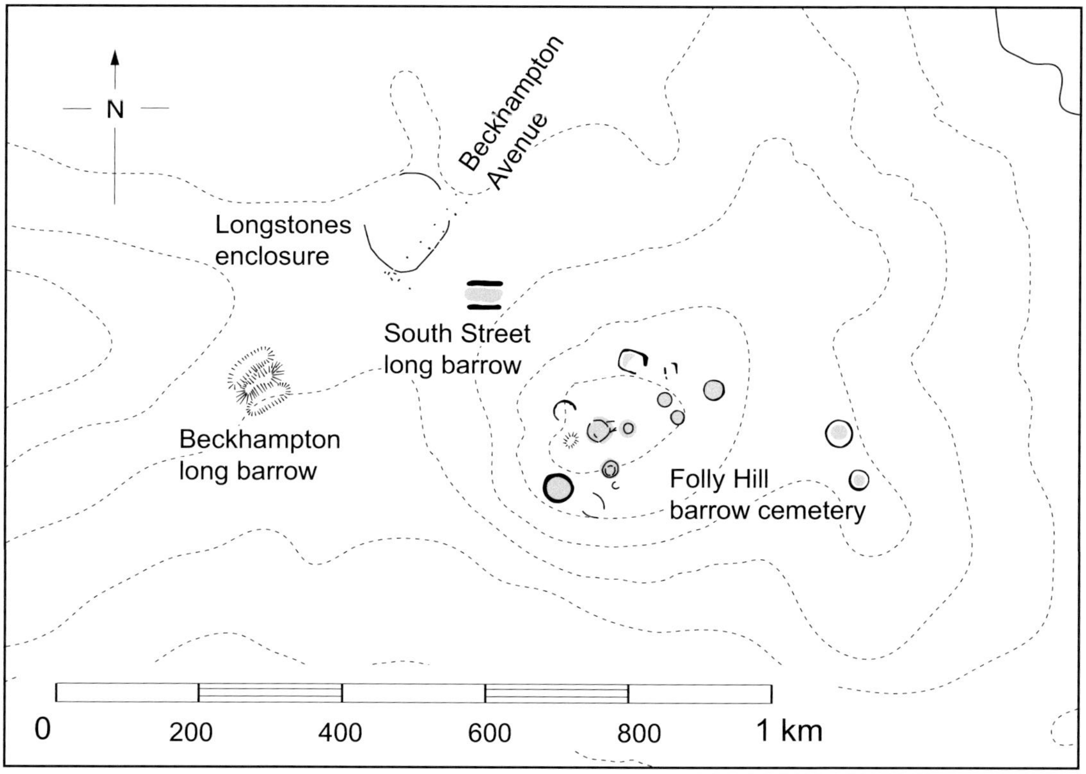

Figure 2.3. The Beckhampton complex, showing the relationship between the Longstones enclosure, earlier long barrows, and the Bronze Age round barrow cemetery on Folly Hill

mound where burials would normally be expected. The 'barrow' may never have had a funerary function as such, conceivably its purpose being to seal and mark the sarsen boulder cairn. Woodland regeneration followed as the secondary silts of the flanking ditches were forming, dated to the late 4th millennium BC by intentional deposits of Ebbsfleet pottery and lithics (Ashbee *et al.* 1979, 298; Evans 1990).

The presence of two long barrows and putative mortuary enclosures/oval barrows in this limited area to the west of Avebury is an indication of the locale's importance during the 4th millennium BC. This may well be a product of its topographic situation, being close to the source of the Beckhampton stream, and at a transitional point in the landscape marked by the confluence of a long ridge running from Knoll Down to the west, a flat, shallow valley leading from Avebury and the Winterbourne – bounded on the north by Windmill Hill – and the head of a dry valley leading to the south-west along which the Devizes road now runs. In effect, this is a natural route-way from the clay vales in the south-west to the north, and Windmill Hill, the Lower Chalk plateau, Swindon escarpment and the north-easterly continuation of the Marlborough Downs. It is perhaps this earlier Neolithic interest in the locale, brought about by its pivotal position within the landscape of the Upper Kennet Valley, that set the scene for developments in the 3rd millennium BC, which included the construction of a small earthwork enclosure, the terminal of the Beckhampton Avenue and the later establishment of a barrow cemetery on Folly Hill.

2.1 The Longstones Enclosure and associated features

Traditions of earthwork enclosure construction had been established in the Avebury region and beyond during the second quarter of the 4th millennium BC. Locally, there are three such earlier Neolithic sites, all positioned on the 'periphery' of the region as defined by the distribution of contemporary long barrows – on Windmill Hill, 2km north of the Longstones, and to the south on Knap Hill and at Rybury (Pollard and Reynolds 2002, 48–58). The Windmill Hill enclosure is a massive affair and seems to have held regional if not inter-regional pre-eminence given the level of labour input invested in its construction, and the scale of consumption and deposition evidenced by the finds from its three circuits of ditches (Whittle *et al.* 1999). From the beginning, the creation of enclosures was intimately linked to conceptions of the sacred and the performance of activities of a special or even marginal nature, including exchange and mortuary or ancestor rites (Edmonds 1999); though diversity in format and roles implies a flexible interpretation of an ultimately long-lived architectural tradition. By the mid 3rd millennium BC there was considerable diversity in the range of enclosure forms being constructed. Earth (or, more properly, turf and chalk), stone and timber were employed; scales could range from small stone and timber circles such as those at the Sanctuary (Cunnington 1931) to the massive earthwork and timber walls of the Avebury henge and West Kennet palisades (Smith 1965; Whittle 1997b); while different levels of permeability and participation are implied by both 'open' and 'closed' formats (Gibson 2004).

It was a recognition of the possibility that other Neolithic enclosures might exist within this landscape that led to the project's first excavation in 1998. Whilst undertaking stone recording work at Avebury, our attention had been drawn to aerial photographs taken of Longstones Field during a reconnaissance flight made by English Heritage in April 1997 (centred on SU 089 693). These showed a thin cropmark describing an oval and possibly discontinuous enclosure of around 1.25ha, which ran on its south-west side between the two Longstones (Crutchley 2005, 39–40). In fact this was not a wholly new discovery, since part of the enclosure's western circuit was visible on a 1989 Ancient Monuments Laboratory resistivity survey of the field (Ucko *et al.* 1991, plate 63). The thin line of more luxuriant crop that marked the enclosure circuit was reminiscent of the cropmark response produced by the trenches of the West Kennet palisades, and immediately raised the possibility that this might mark the location of another late Neolithic palisaded enclosure. There was also the issue of the relationship between the enclosure and the two Longstones, which had previously been argued to represent either the sole survivors of the Beckhampton Avenue or the remains of an independent megalithic monument (Keiller and Piggott 1936, 417). Work on the enclosure seemed imperative, both in terms of adding to existing knowledge on the repertoire of Neolithic enclosures in the region, and as an opportunity to address one of the 'big' unresolved questions relating to the Avebury complex: was the Beckhampton Avenue an archaeological reality?

Geophysical survey
Andrew David

Geophysical survey was first attempted in the vicinity of the Longstones in 1975, prompted by the late Faith Vatcher who was then the curator of the Alexander Keiller Museum. The magnetometer and earth resistance surveys were undertaken in September that year by the Ancient Monuments Laboratory of the Department of the Environment. They covered just a small area (30 × 60m) adjacent and to the south of Adam and Eve, in the hope of locating evidence for other stone settings, and to test these methods as part of a more general assessment of the value of geophysics for the detection of former megalithic features in the Avebury complex. The interest in the Longstones followed earlier discoveries of buried stones and burning pits elsewhere along the putative course of the Beckhampton Avenue (Vatcher 1969). However, and in contrast to the survey within the Avebury henge itself (NE Quadrant: Ucko *et al.* 1991, pl. 68) also conducted then, the results proved disappointing. This was not surprising, given the small area involved, the limitations of the methodology at that time, and on the evidence of what we now know of the disposition and character of features in this area (see below).

The opportunity to re-address this area did not arise until 1989 when it was stimulated by a wider reconsideration of the antiquarian record for Avebury, as a result of which a much larger survey was undertaken (Ucko *et al.* 1991). Leaving aside for now the search for the Beckhampton Avenue (see below) we will briefly review the geophysical evidence for the Longstones enclosure that resulted both from this survey, and from subsequent survey in 1999 and 2000 as part of the excavation project reported here.

The 1989 surveys included magnetometer

and earth resistance survey. The earth resistance data seemed at the time to be the more informative and the published interpretation included an outline of 'a ditched feature' just to the north of the Longstones (Ucko *et al.* 1991, pl. 63). This was 'distinguished by the alignment of its component negative anomalies at an angle to the ubiquitous ridge and furrow' and was hesitantly interpreted as 'the partial outline of a circle defined by fragmentary curvilinear anomalies' (*ibid.*, 199). Whilst this was just too tentative to dwell much upon at the time, the aerial discovery of the more distinct and larger oval cropmark enclosure in this area in 1997 re-directed attention to the earlier geophysical results. It transpired that about 18m of the earth resistance anomaly closest to the Longstones coincided with the cropmark feature, whilst the remaining components of the 'circle' did not and were therefore likely to be spurious.

The 1989 magnetometer data had at that time been dismissed as 'unproductive' (*ibid.*, 196), but now a more sensitive re-plotting of the data indicated that the survey had in fact detected an intermittent linear anomaly coinciding with over half of the cropmark circuit. This anomaly was rendered visible in the plot more on account of its continuity than on magnetic strength alone (less than 0.5nT) which could be matched widely, but less systematically, across the entire survey area. It was detected over a combined distance of about 75m. Elsewhere it faded from the image entirely and was undetectable over a distance of some 30m – an absence later confirmed by excavation, as were smaller gaps (see below). This intermittent nature, its modest dimensions (Table 2.1) and weakly magnetised filling (with much chalky rubble), help explain why the resulting anomaly is poorly defined and was not revealed in earlier and less discriminating images. Detailed earth resistance survey, in 2000, re-located the portion of the enclosure ditch immediately between and to the south of the Longstones.

Whilst both magnetometer and earth resistance surveys covered substantial parts of the interior of the Longstones enclosure no anomalies of obvious significance were detected. As stated above, it was possible to single out the enclosure ditch because of its continuity as a linear anomaly; elsewhere the survey data includes other weaker alignments and more shapeless patterns, none of which can be confidently assigned an archaeological origin. Apart from reactions to ferrous debris, the magnetic variation is both so slight and so weak that any responses from archaeological features are indistinguishable from natural variations. It is no surprise that the system of shallow gullies (F.101, F.104 and F.105: see below) found in Trench 31 were not located beforehand.

Excavation results

The first season of excavation (1998) proved unsuccessful, largely because of the restraints created by a late harvest, limited time and a very small budget. Trenches were dug by hand close to the field edge and within the trackway, but failed to locate the enclosure. With more time, resources and access to the whole of the field, work during 1999, 2000 and 2003 was successful in defining the extent and character of the monument (Figures 2.4 and 2.5). Sections of enclosure ditch were excavated in seven trenches (11, 12, 13, 14, 22, 23 and 24) and exposed and planned, but not excavated, in four others (15, 25, 26 and 31). It was most extensively sampled along the flattened south-eastern side where the line of the later Beckhampton Avenue intersected the enclosure. In total 62.5m of ditch was excavated, comprising just under 17% of the circuit. The interior was investigated by means of two 50m long trenches (20 and 21) and also in parts of Trenches 10, 22, 23 and 31, providing a roughly 10% sample of the enclosed area (Figure 2.6). By hand sorting topsoil from Trenches 20 and 21 it was possible to verify the results of an earlier surface collection, which suggested that little if any worked flint was present in the ploughsoil (Holgate 1987).

The solid geology here is lower Middle Chalk, over which is an *in situ* layer of frost-shattered chalk and remnants of solifluxed coombe rock. Peri-glacial involutions filled with a fine pale brown silty clay are present where the coombe rock has not suffered truncation, particularly in the northern part of the site. A thin lower ploughsoil is also present across the northern half of the enclosure and within the truncated bases of medieval cultivation furrows.

The enclosure describes a flattened oval,

Trench	Excavated length	Ditch width	Ditch depth	Cut	Soil on base	Primary fills	Secondary fills	Soil	Tertiary fills
11	5.0	1.4–1.7	0.60–0.75	[105]	-	[104], [107], [112], [109]	[102], [106], [111]	[103], [113]	[108], [100], [101], [110]
12	3.5	1.4–2.0	0.60–0.68	[201]	-	[210], [202]	[206], [207]	[203], *[204], *[205], *[208], *[209]	[200]
13	2.0	1.6–2.0	0.65–0.70	[304]	-	[303]	[301]	[302]	[300]
14	2.6	2.1	0.80–0.85	[500]	[507]	[506]	[503]	[504], [505]	[502], [501]
22	11.0	1.1–1.8	0.45–0.65	[620], [623], [627], [628], [629]	-	[618], [619], [622], [626], [632], [606], [608]	[617], [631], [601], [609]	[625]	[604], [621], [624], [630], [605], [607]
23	26.0	1.2–2.1	0.45–0.96	[700]	n.[721], [722], [723] [725], [726], [738], [739] c.[736], [737] s.[717], [718], [719], [720], [724], [742], [741]	n.[709], c.[735], s.[710]	n.[703], c.[734], s.[704]	n.[711], [712], [713], [714], [715], [716] c.[731], [732] s.[705], [706], [707], [708], [740]	n.[702], c.[727], s.[701]
24	12.5	1.3–2.1	0.43–0.78	[810]	[827], [848], [849]	[826], [840], [833]	[816], [836], [830]	[817], [823], [847], [828]	[811], [835], [818]

*Table 2.1 Longstones enclosure: details of ditch sections (dimensions in metres). Contexts in Trench 23 are sub-divided between the northern (n), central (c) and southern (s) sections. * = cut and fill numbers for small scoops cut through the soil over the secondary fills*

*c.*140 × 110m across and enclosing an area of approximately 1.25ha, with a 45m wide entrance on its eastern side. Defined by a shallow irregular ditch, it displays no geometric regularity and is notably flattened along its south-eastern side as if respecting an existing boundary or pathway. Its circuit has been established through geophysical survey and excavation on all but the north-western side where it runs under the grass track. Details of dimensions and contexts for the excavated sections of ditch are given in Table 2.1, while a more detailed version of the structural report is held in the archive.

Figure 2.4. Aerial view of the excavations in Longstones Field during Summer 2000, from the SE

The form of the ditch

Having been dug as a series of elongated and normally conjoined pits, the ditch (F.20) is discontinuous, with several interruptions to its circuit being discernable in both the geophysical survey and excavation. Causeways within the circuit, some no more than 0.2m across, were revealed in Trenches 22, 23 and 24, with another possibly lying just outside the southern limit of Trench 11. Otherwise, the 'pit-like' nature of the ditch was visible because of variations in its width and depth (Figures 2.7–2.20). It is perhaps more segmented along the southern part of the circuit than elsewhere, the excavated lengths in Trenches 22 and 24 being made up of five or six *c.*2–3m long sections in both instances. It may be the case that the ditch circuit comprises alternating lengths of short and long sections, as seen with the Middle Ditch at Windmill Hill (Whittle *et al.* 1999). In Trench 22, one of the pits forming the ditch [628] was off-set to the south-east of the line of the circuit, and not joined with that to the north [629], giving the impression that it may have been dug to block an original

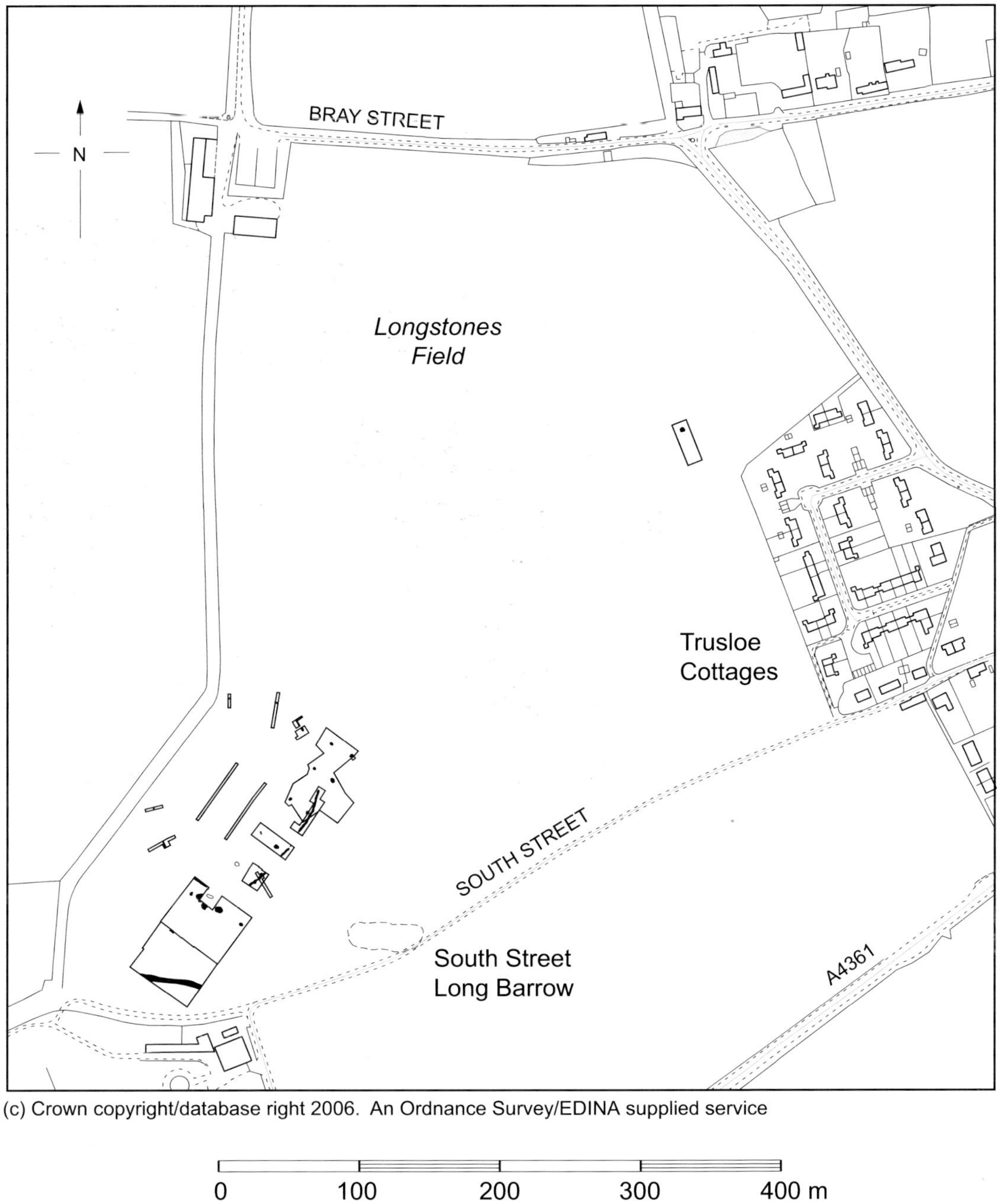

Figure 2.5. Excavations in Longstones Field: 1999, 2000 and 2003. The enclosure and avenue terminal are located in the SW corner of the field

entrance *c.*3m wide. Curiously, both [628] and [629] appeared to have been enhanced by similar lateral expansions, on their eastern and western sides respectively, and by undercutting of their sides. Though curving gently, the exposed length of ditch in Trench 23 gave the impression of three more or less equal straight lengths that had been conjoined.

In all the excavated sections the ditch was shallow, steep-sided and flat-bottomed, between 1.1–2.1m wide and 0.43–0.96m deep, being deepest in Trenches 14 and 23 where it flanked the main entrance. Shallow oval depressions (*c.*0.05m deep) were visible in the base of the ditch in Trenches 11, 23 and 24; while in Trench 23 the lower part of the ditch side was fashioned into three shallow 'steps' on the eastern edge *c.*4m back from the northern terminal.

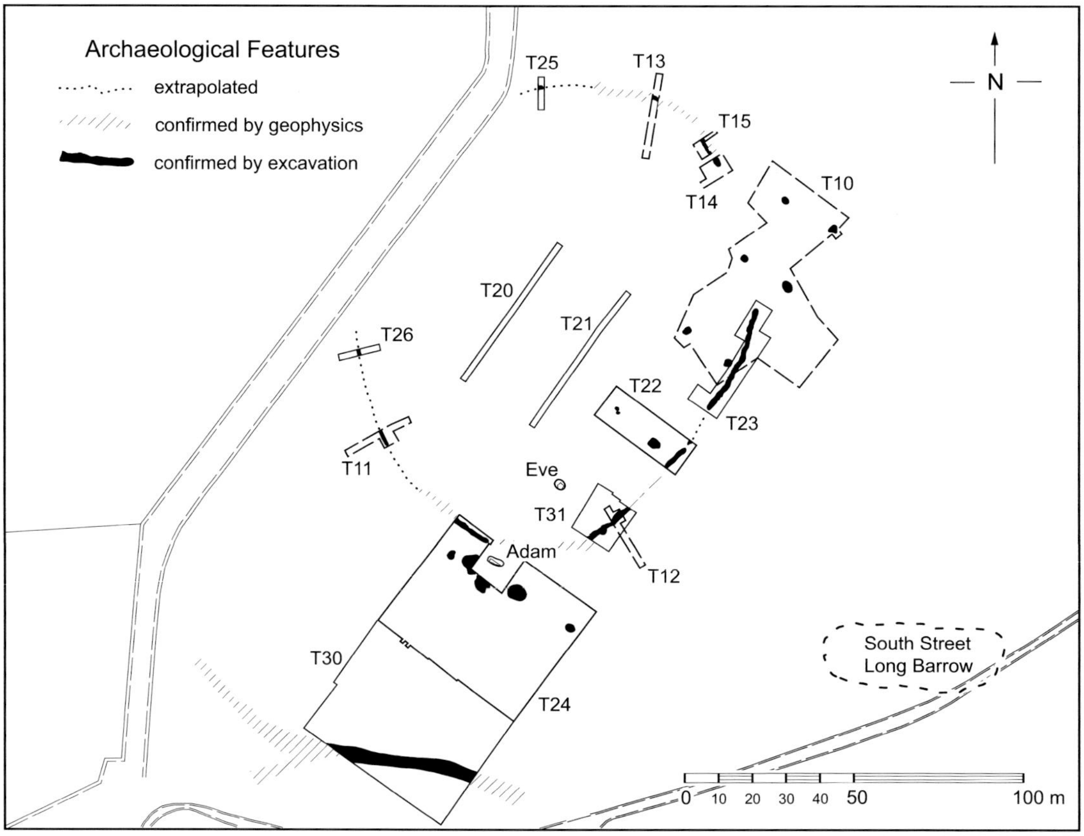

Figure 2.6. Trench locations, the Longstones enclosure, the terminal section of the Beckhampton Avenue and other excavated features in the SW corner of Longstones Field. Incorporates data © Crown Copyright/ database right 2007. An Ordnance Survey/ (EDINA) supplied service

Ditch fills

Though varying slightly in detail, a similar sequence of ditch filling was encountered in each trench (Figures 2.7–2.20). This followed a typical chalkland sequence of weathering and progressive stabilisation deposits – primary rubble, secondary silts and a soil – but with a teritary component of deliberate backfill (see Bell *et al.* 1996). In Trenches 14, 23 and 24 discrete lenses of brown clay loam lay directly on the base of the ditch, often in slight hollows. That in Trench 24 ([827], etc.) was clean, while similar soil deposits in Trench 23 ([717], etc.) contained varying amounts of charcoal, animal bone, pottery and flint. In the northern terminal adjacent to the eastern entrance was a fairly extensive lens of loam and charcoal [721]. These deposits could represent soil dumped on the base of the ditch (as seems possible in Trench 23), and/or weathered turves or lenses of topsoil that fell into the feature immediately following its digging.

Overlying these was a primary fill of variably compacted chalk rubble within a pale grey or brown silty clay, sometimes showing evidence of finer bands of silt. In places (notably within Trench 14), this contained pockets of orange-brown silty clay, not dissimilar to the material filling natural involutions in the chalk through which the ditch was cut. The primary rubble fill was usually both more chalky and compact on the inner than the outer edge of the ditch (particularly so in Trenches 12 and 22), suggesting that more material was weathering into the feature from this side, most probably from an internal bank. In Trench 11 the primary fill was overlain by a deposit of compact pale brown silty clay with fine fragmented chalk [109]. A small sarsen boulder, otherwise very rare within the ditch fills, was found within [202] in Trench 12, close to the centre of the ditch cutting.

A fine, light yellow-brown silty clay secondary fill covered the primary rubble. In Trench 12 this was thin and discontinuous, while in the deeper parts of Trench 23 it was relatively thick. This contained quantities of small chalk fragments and pockets of fine earthy rubble, and ranged from compact to moderately loose. Bands of finer material interlaced with coarser rubble, possibly indicating short periods of stabilisation or preserved annual banding, as noted at the Overton Down Experimental Earthwork (Bell *et al.* 1996), were discernable

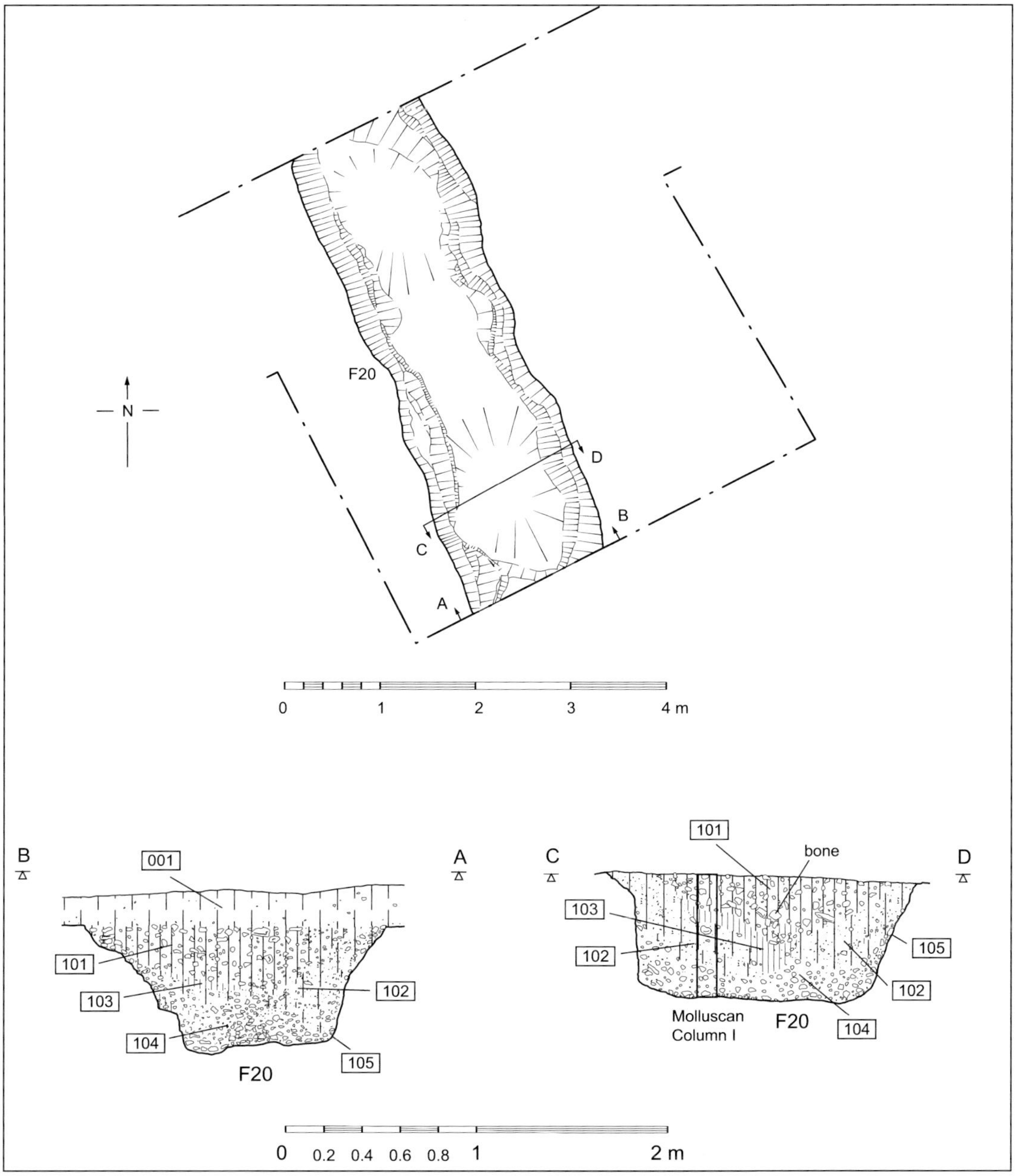

Figure 2.7. Ditch F.20, Trench 11

in some of the deeper sections of ditch in Trench 23. This was overlain by a discontinuous lens of clean brown loam with some small chalk, corresponding to a poorly developed turf- or soil-layer that had developed after initial stabilisation of the ditch fills. That in Trench 14 [505] was mixed with chalk rubble and contained occasional charcoal flecks. The soil horizon was particularly well developed in the length of ditch excavated in Trench 23, being identifiable across the entire feature, and thickest in the centre and on the eastern side. Occasionally, this became a thick, very humic loam.

Two shallow scoops, [204] and [208], were observed cutting through the soil in Trench 12. Situated at the same level and within the centre of the ditch, they were spaced c.1.5m apart, [204] clipping the south-west section. [204] was a sub-circular depression *c.*0.2m in diameter and only 0.02m deep, filled with a brown clay loam similar to the soil through which it was cut. [208] was of similar form and depth, 0.33m in diameter, with an identical fill. Within this was a substantial portion of a single Grooved Ware vessel. Although quite obvious in plan and excavated as discrete features, these were difficult to detect in section. An antler 7m from

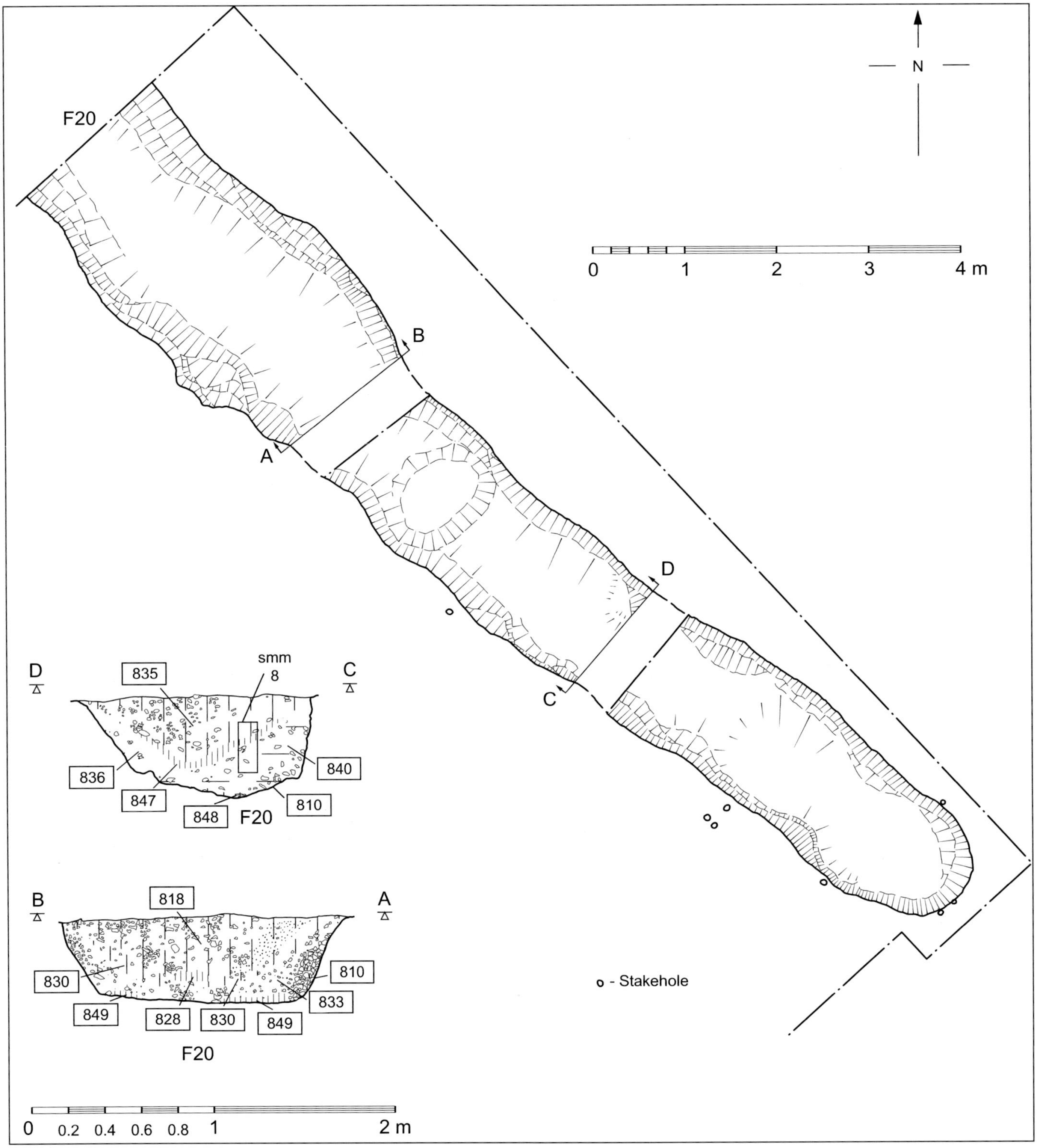

Figure 2.8. Ditch F.20, Trench 24

the southern terminal of the ditch in Trench 23 (between [706] and [707], and a cattle horncore in Trench 11 may also have been placed within shallow scoops cut from the same level.

Throughout the investigated length of its circuit the upper part of the ditch was filled with a deep layer of mixed chalk rubble and brown silty loam. The chalk rubble was poorly sorted, resting at various angles and included

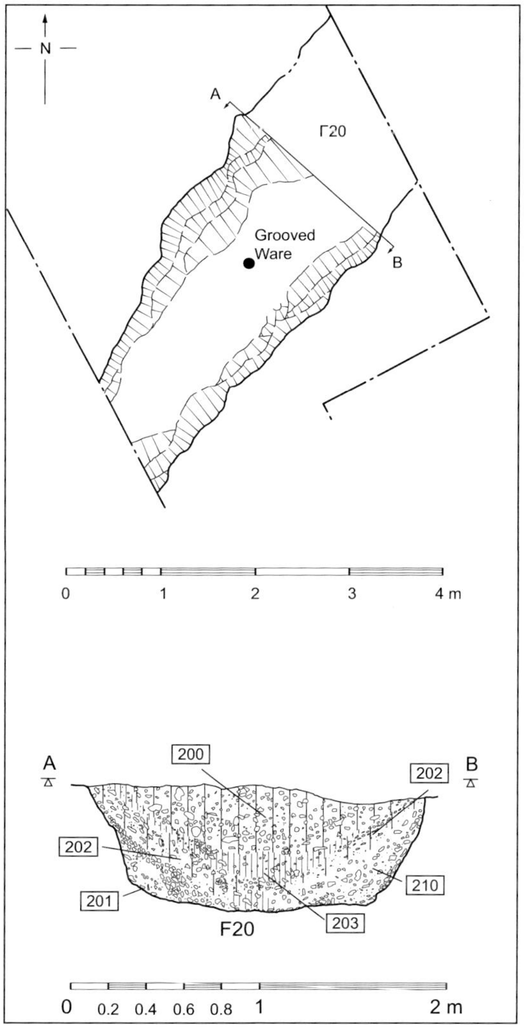

Figure 2.9. (far left) Ditch F.20, Trench 24, at the end of excavation, from the SE

Figure 2.10. (left) Ditch F.20, Trench 12

pieces up to 0.1m in maximum dimension. In places (*e.g.* Trenches 11 and 12), this deposit was very compact, with larger blocks being more frequent on the inner half of the ditch. Charcoal flecks were present within [502] in Trench 14, but not elsewhere, though it should be noted that this context and [501] were disturbed by animal burrows. Clearly the product of high-energy deposition, this is interpreted as deliberate backfill, the result of a single episode of levelling of the enclosure bank. In most cuttings, this tertiary backfill deposit was so chalky and compact that it could easily be mistaken for weathered chalk natural. In dry conditions it was only possible to distinguish it from natural coombe rock by the absence of clay involutions, although after prolonged rain the ditch fill took on a slightly darker tone and was more readily identifiable.

Figure 2.11. (above) West-facing section of ditch F.20 in Trench 12. Note chalky tertiary backfill deposit

Finds from the ditch

Very little artefactual and faunal material was recovered from the enclosure. Taken as an average, there were only 0.75 pieces of worked flint per metre of ditch and 2.9 pieces of bone; though these were not evenly distributed, with more flint occurring in Trench 11 and more bone in Trenches 14 and 23 than elsewhere. Where present, bone and artefactual material was largely restricted to two horizons: the base

Figure 2.12. Ditch F.20, Trench 22

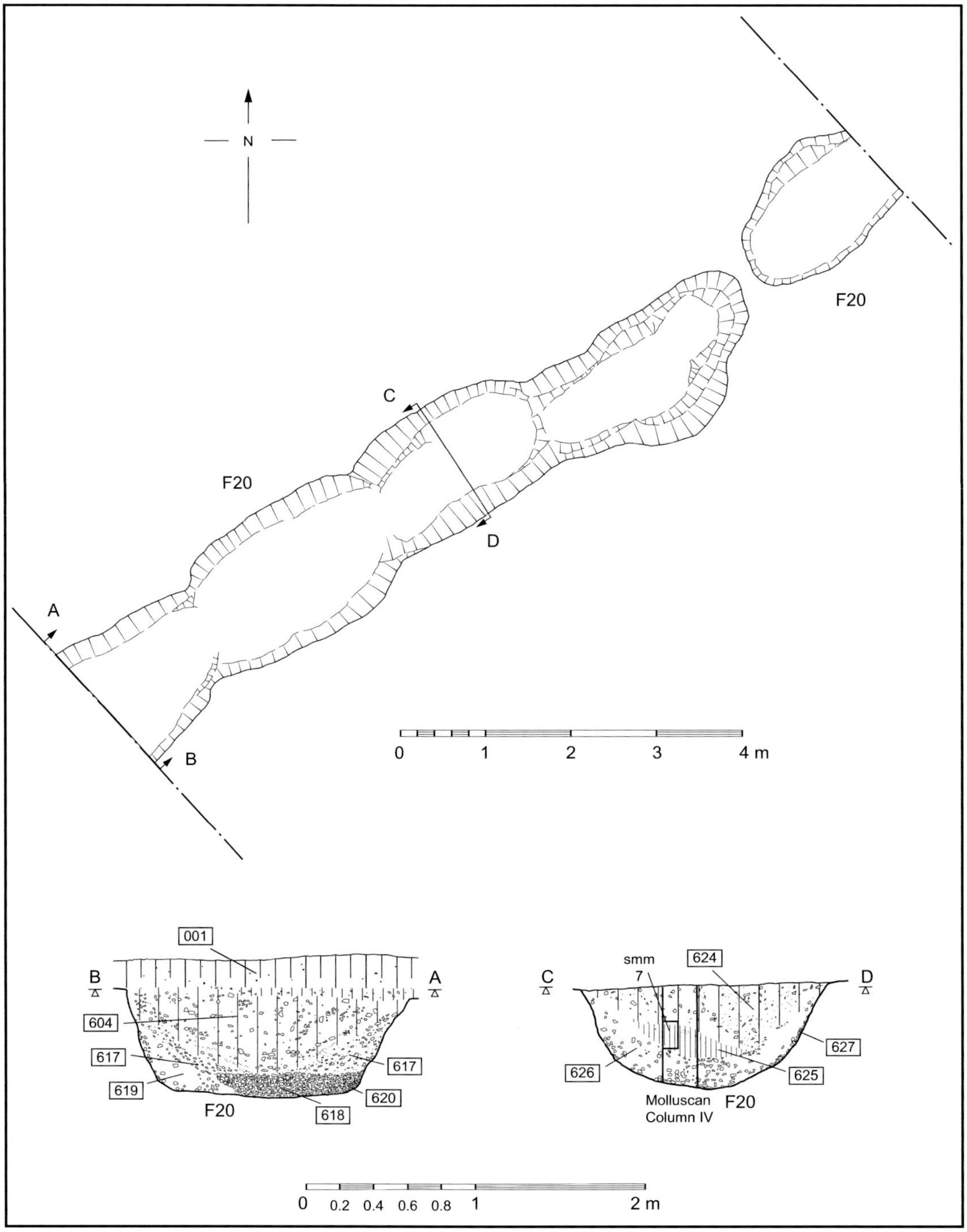

of the ditch and the level of the intermittent turf-line just below the upper layer of backfill.

On the base of the ditch, spreads of animal bone were found in several places, particularly adjacent to the terminals in Trenches 14 and 23 where numerous bone deposits were recovered. Three small sherds of Grooved Ware came from the base of the terminal in Trench 23, other small fragments from the opposing terminal in Trench 14, and a residual sherd of early Neolithic bowl from the chalk rubble in Trench 11. Pottery was otherwise absent from primary contexts. Finds from the primary chalk rubble were generally rare, though included a small amount of animal bone from Trench 14.

The greatest concentrations of finds came from the base and primary fills of the ditch on either side of the main entrance. In Trench 14 (the northern terminal) there was a small deposit of animal bone on the base that included an articulated foot and scapula of pig. In the primary fill above this [505] was a cattle vertebra. A better appreciation of the form of these primary depositions was gained through the excavation of long lengths of ditch in Trench 23. Here, a general scatter and small concentrations of fresh animal bone were found resting immediately on the base of the ditch, some within thin lenses of soil (Figure 2.21). In the southern terminal adjacent to the eastern entrance was a fairly extensive lens of loam and charcoal [721] associated with a spread of bone that included a cattle mandible and vertebra, a pig tibia and vertebra, a piece of burned sarsen and three sherds of Grooved Ware. Further bone deposits occurred throughout the length of the exposed ditch. To the south were mixed collections of pig, cattle and sheep/goat bone (including scapulae of each species, cattle vertebra, and a pig humerus and tibia), along with antler; while in the centre of

Figure 2.13. (left) Ditch F.20, Trench 22, towards the end of excavation, looking SW

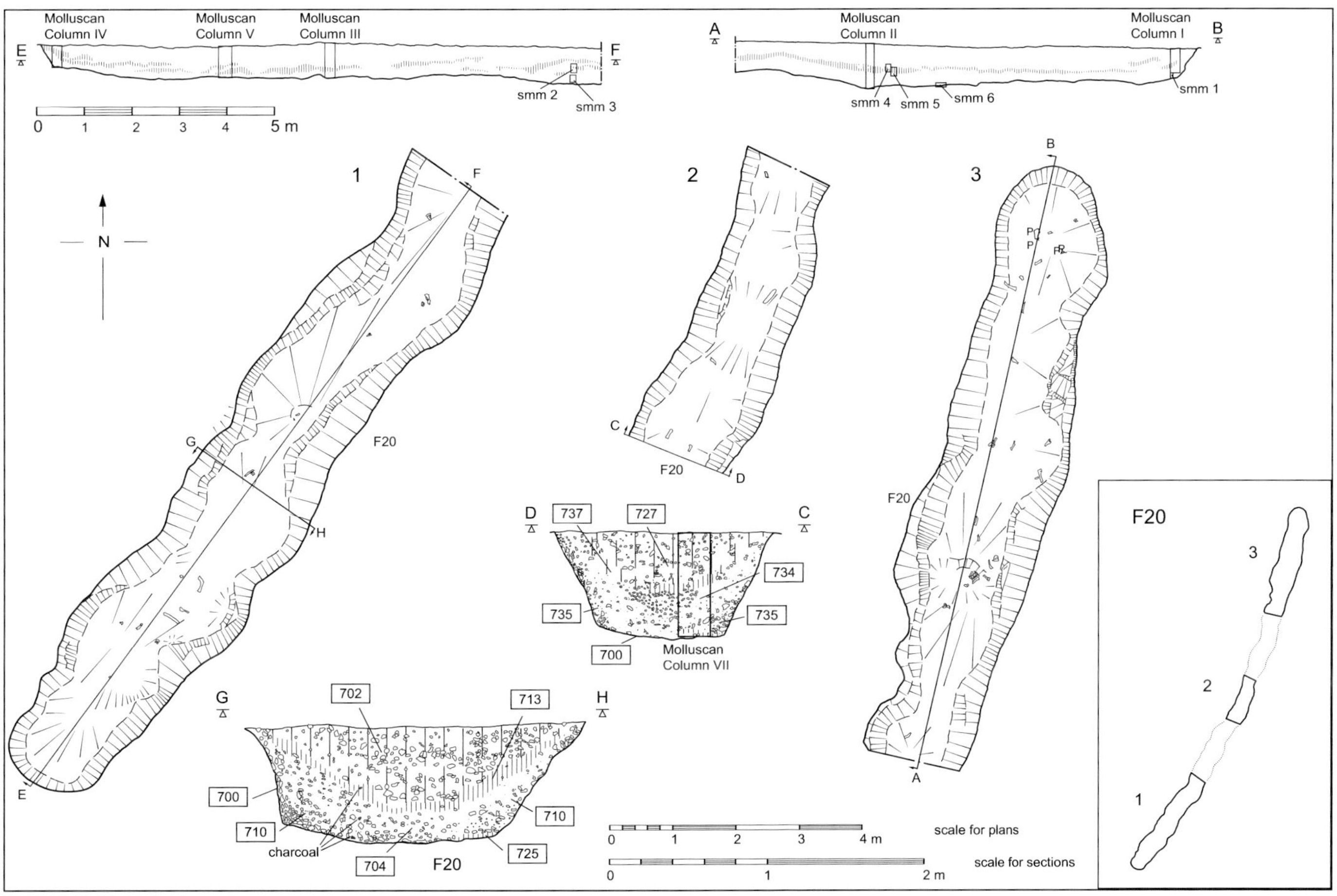

Figure 2.14. (below) Ditch F.20, Trench 23. For the plans, P = pottery, F = flint

Figure 2.15. (left) Ditch F.20, Trench 23, looking south

Figure 2.16. (right) Ditch F.20, Trench 23, under excavation

Figure 2.17. (above) Ditch F.20, Trench 23. Detail of fills in northern terminal

this segment was a scatter of ribs (species not determined). The spread of bone in the southern third of the ditch was dominated by pig (vertebrae, humeri and ulna), with single identified bones of cattle and sheep/goat (pelvis).

While the secondary silts were largely sterile, a number of animal bones, antlers, a sarsen and part of a Grooved Ware vessel came from the base of the tertiary backfill deposit, the soil below, and scoops cut through it. Given the

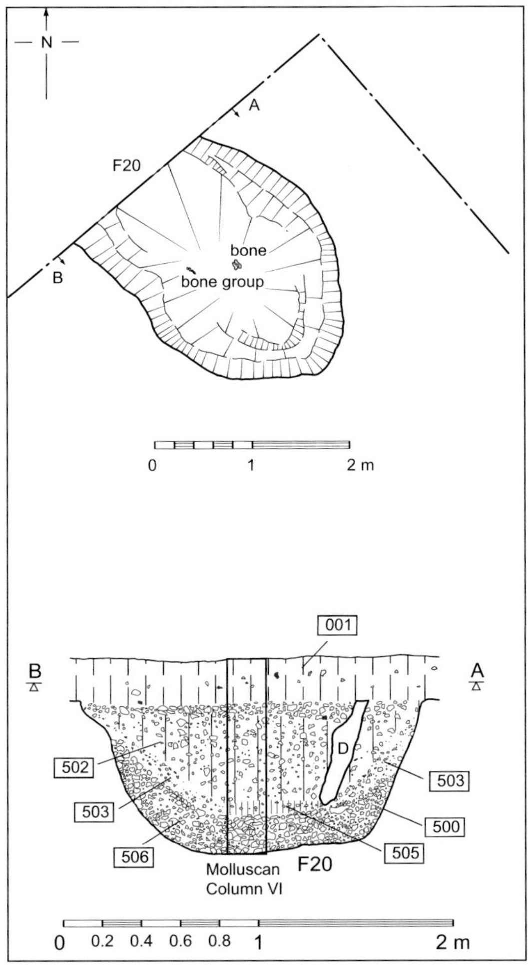

Figure 2.18. (right) Ditch F.20, Trench 14

difficulty in identifying the small scoops, it may be the case that all the material from these contexts was deposited more or less simultaneously as part of a process of 'decommissioning'. The sherds from the large portion of an unusual Grooved Ware vessel in [209] in Trench 12 must have been buried quickly since they show no sign of weathering. Other notable deposits occurred at a similar level in Trenches 11 and 22: the former comprising a substantial cattle horncore; and the latter a large antler with tines removed placed against the minor causeway. To the south a cattle long bone and large piece of haematite were recovered. Little material was present in the tertiary backfill over much of the circuit, though a number of pieces of worked flint were recovered in Trench 11 and some fragmented bone and antler in Trenches 12, 22, 23 and 24. Much of this may originally have been incorporated in the bank or in the buried soil beneath it, and can therefore be assumed to be in a derived context.

Figure 2.19. (top) Ditch F.20, Trench 14, from the SE

Figure 2.20. (above) Ditch F.20, Trench 13, east-facing section

The gully-defined enclosure

The only features encountered within the interior that may be contemporary with or earlier than the enclosure were three lengths of shallow gully in Trench 31. These made-up a small, probably sub-triangular enclosure with projected overall dimensions of *c.*10 × 10m, assuming the whole structure is symmetrical around an east-west axis. The 'back' of this mini enclosure comprised a curving length of gully, F.101, with two shorter and straighter lengths, F.104 and 105, making up a recessed 'façade' with a 0.45m-wide entrance gap in the centre (Figures 2.22 and 2.23).

Over much of its exposed 9m length, F.101 ran east-west, gently curving around to the north-west as it approached the edge of the trench. Direct dating evidence is sparse, though the base of a medieval cultivation furrow cut into the top of F.105, and several pieces of worked flint came from the gully fills, including a possible axe-thinning flake. The gully varied in width from 0.30–0.45m and ended at the east in a regular squared terminal. The sides of

Figure 2.21. (left) Animal bone on the base of ditch F.20, Trench 23

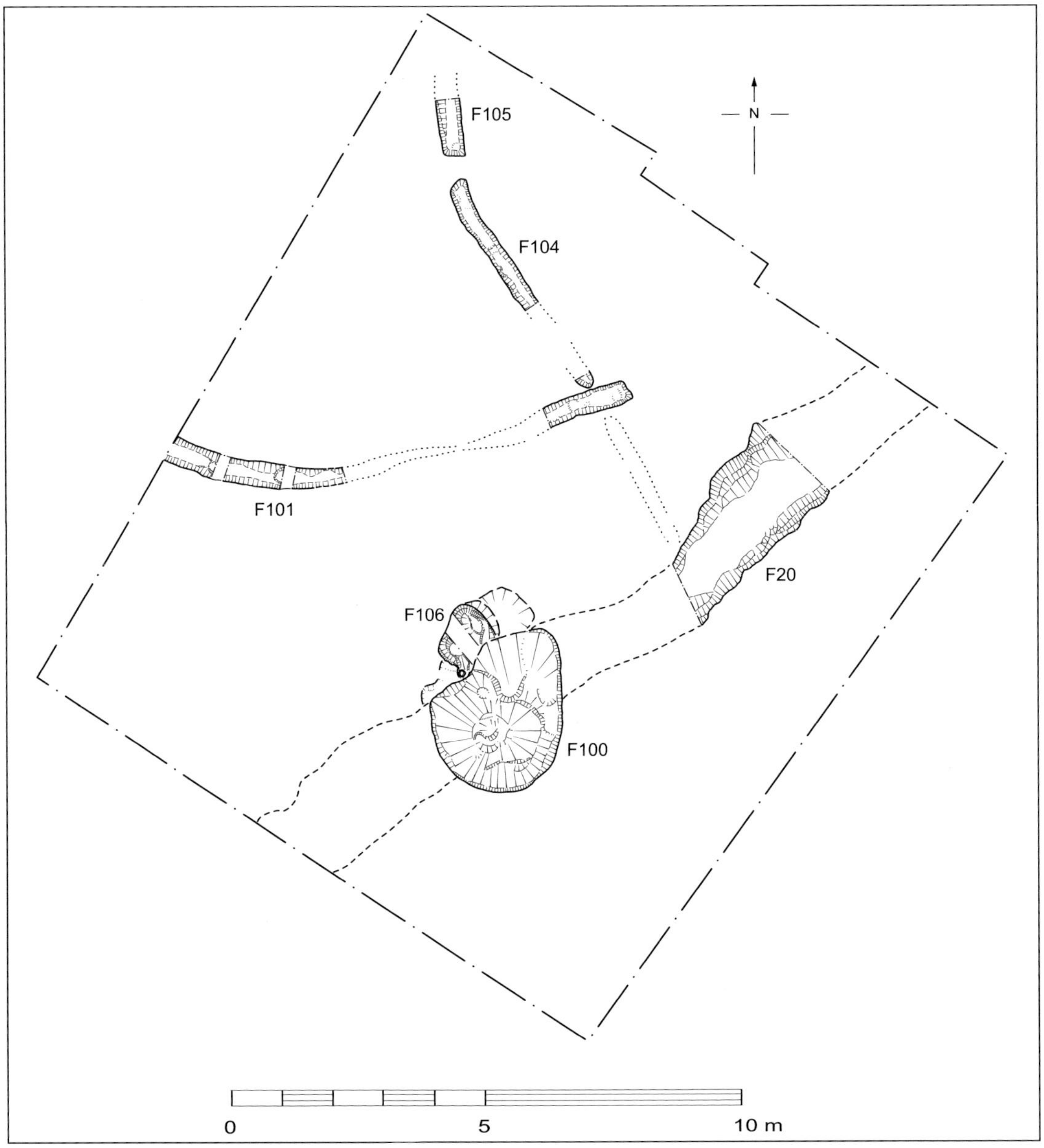

Figure 2.22. (right) The gully-defined enclosure (F.101, 104 and 105) in Trench 31. F.20 is the main enclosure ditch, F.106 a stone-hole of the Beckhampton Avenue and F.100 a post-Medieval stone burning pit

Figure 2.23. (below) The gully-defined enclosure from the east

the cut [908] were steep to moderate, and the base generally flat, though slightly irregular in places. At no point was the gully particularly deep, ranging from 0.07–0.15m and being deepest against the north-west baulk of the trench. It was filled with a brown clay loam containing varied amounts of small chalk fragments [903], the chalk content increasing markedly towards the eastern end of the feature.

The complete 4.8m length of F.104 was exposed and just over 3m excavated. At its southern end – marked by a shallow pointed terminal – the gully abutted the end of F.101, a narrow ridge of chalk being left between the two features. The northern terminal was

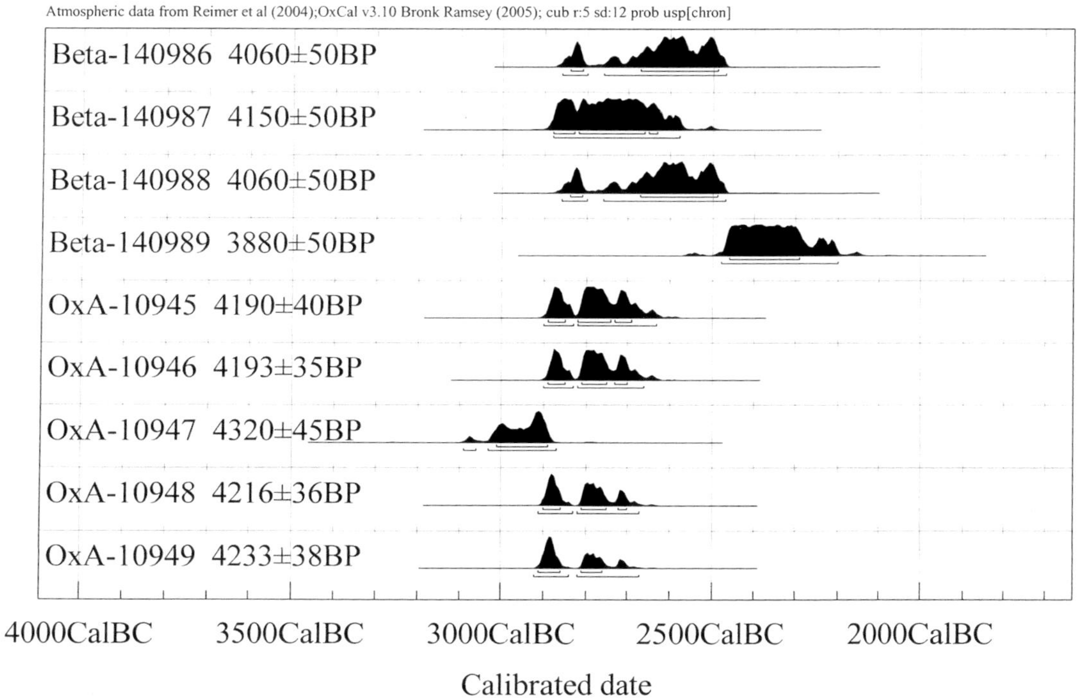

Figure 2.24. Calibrated radiocarbon dates for the enclosure ditch F.20

slightly out-turned. Here the sides of the cut [919] varied from steep to shallow and the base, which was sometimes difficult to define in excavation, rather irregular. The width of the feature ranged from 0.32–0.36m, and its depth from 0.06–0.10m. The cut of F.105, [921], was more regular and substantial than that of F.104, here around 0.45m wide and up to 0.20m deep. In general, the sides were steep and the base flat, while a neatly squared terminal defined the southern end of the gully. The fills of F.104 and 105 ([918] and [920] respectively) were identical to [903]. More chalk was noted towards the base of the fills, most likely forming an initial weathering deposit.

The character of these features – somewhat irregular, and forming a circuit described by short lengths rather than a continuous cut – hints at a Neolithic date, and the presence of fresh worked flint and the absence of later material would seem to support this. F.105 is also cut by a medieval furrow. Quite where this feature fits in the sequence – whether predating the main enclosure, contemporary with it, or relating to the avenue – could not be established through excavation, though its axis seems off-set to the south of that of the avenue line, and the south-eastern ends of gullies F.101 and 104 would, if contemporary with the main enclosure, be obscured by the bank of the latter. A shallow linear feature, originally excavated in Trench 12 and at the time interpreted as an animal burrow, may mark a south-easterly continuation of F.104 and 105; this was cut by the larger enclosure ditch. This leaves the possibility that the gullies predate the main enclosure and are of 4th or earliest 3rd millennium BC date. Cropmarks suggest there are other lengths of narrow ditch or gully extending from the western end of the adjacent South Street long barrow to the north-west and the area of the enclosure (Crutchley 2005, fig. 3:9). Given their position parallel and in close proximity to the Trench 30 features, these may be related.

Dating the Longstones Enclosure

A later Neolithic date for the enclosure was indicated by fresh sherds of Grooved Ware found on the base of the ditch in Trench 23. In order the refine the chronology of its construction and ultimate levelling, nine AMS radiocarbon dates were obtained on red deer antler and animal bone found on the base of the ditch, the primary fills, the soil horizon and tertiary fills in Trenches 13, 14 and 23. The results have been calibrated using OxCal v.3.10 and are given in Table 2.2 and Figure 2.24.

All the samples, with the exception of Beta-140987 (from the soil above the secondary silts)

Table 2.2. Radiocarbon dates from the enclosure ditch, F.20. Dates are calibrated using OxCal v.3.10

	Trench	Context	Sample type	Result	Calibrated range (Cal BC) at 95.4% confidence
Beta-140986	13	[300]	Bone (*bos*)	4060±50 BP	2840–2810, 2860–2800, 2760–2470
Beta-140987	14	[505]	Bone (*bos*)	4150±50 BP	2880–2580
Beta-140988	14	[506]	Bone (*sus*)	4060±50 BP	2860–2800, 2760–2470
Beta-140989	14	[506]	Bone (*sus*)	3880±50 BP	2480–2200
OxA-10945	23	[710]	Bone (*sus*)	4190±40 BP	2900–2830, 2820–2630
OxA-10946	23	[739]	Antler	4193±35 BP	2900–2830, 2820–2660
OxA-10947	23	[709]	Bone (*capra/ovis*)	4320±45 BP	3030–3060, 3030–2870
OxA-10948	23	[709]	Antler	4216±36 BP	2910–2830, 2820–2670
OxA-10949	23	[709]	Antler	4233±38 BP	2920–2840, 2820–2670

and Beta-140986 (from the tertiary fill), came from the base of the ditch or the lower part of the primary fills. Those from primary contexts should provide a date range for the construction of the enclosure. Beta-140987 and Beta-140986 should date the point at which the ditch fills began to stabilise and the backfilling event, respectively. The samples from the base and lower part of the primary fills are on bone that has the appearance of being deposited 'fresh', that used for Beta-140988 being part of an articulated pig foot.

The seven dates from primary contexts show good conformity, with the exception of Beta-140989, which appears too young and does not overlap with the lower range of the other dates, and OxA-10947, which is apparently too old. Some animal disturbance was noted in the section of ditch excavated in Trench 14, and it is not impossible that the bone on which Beta-140989 has been obtained was intrusive from a higher level. OxA-10947 may be on a residual or curated bone. Setting aside these two 'problematic' results, the remainder (Beta-140988, OxA-10945-6, 10948-9) fall consistently within the range 2920–2460 cal BC at 95.4% probability, with the probability range weighted towards 2820–2660 cal BC. This gives the range for the construction of the enclosure.

Significantly, the dates for the stabilisation of the ditch fills and the backfill event (Beta-140987 and Beta-140986) are indistinguishable from those obtained from material that should be closely contemporary with the initial digging of the ditch. This either indicates a short life-span for the enclosure, perhaps to be measured in a few generations, or implies that the bone and antler recovered from the upper fills is residual from the construction phase activity. Bone from these upper fills was certainly in poorer condition than that from the base of the ditch and primary fills, though this may be as much to do with *in situ* weathering and biological activity (see Lewis, below) as residuality. Whichever interpretation is favoured, a mid 3rd millennium BC date for the levelling of the enclosure is supported by the Grooved Ware 'decommissioning' deposit in Trench 12, and the reasonable assumption that the ditch and bank circuit must have been flattened prior to its bisection by the Beckhampton Avenue.

Artefactual and environmental evidence

Earlier prehistoric pottery

R.M.J. Cleal

The prehistoric ceramic assemblage from the enclosure is small, weighing only a total of 238g, the majority of which is accounted for by a large part of a single vessel. All except one sherd are clearly Grooved Ware, although only a small number of sherds are decorated. All pottery was examined by hand lens at X10 magnification and a selection, including the illustrated sherds, were examined at X20 under a binocular microscope. Percentages of frequency are estimated on surface area, using comparison charts. All sherds are plain unless noted otherwise. The pottery was recovered exclusively from the enclosure ditch, F.20.

Catalogue

TRENCH 11

EN1. [101] Depth 0.5m. One plain body sherd, weighing 20.7g, probably from an earlier Neolithic bowl. The fabric is sandy and has a compact fracture. The dominant inclusion is quartz sand, which is common (probably around 20–25% by area) and easily visible at X10. Some rare flint is also present (less than

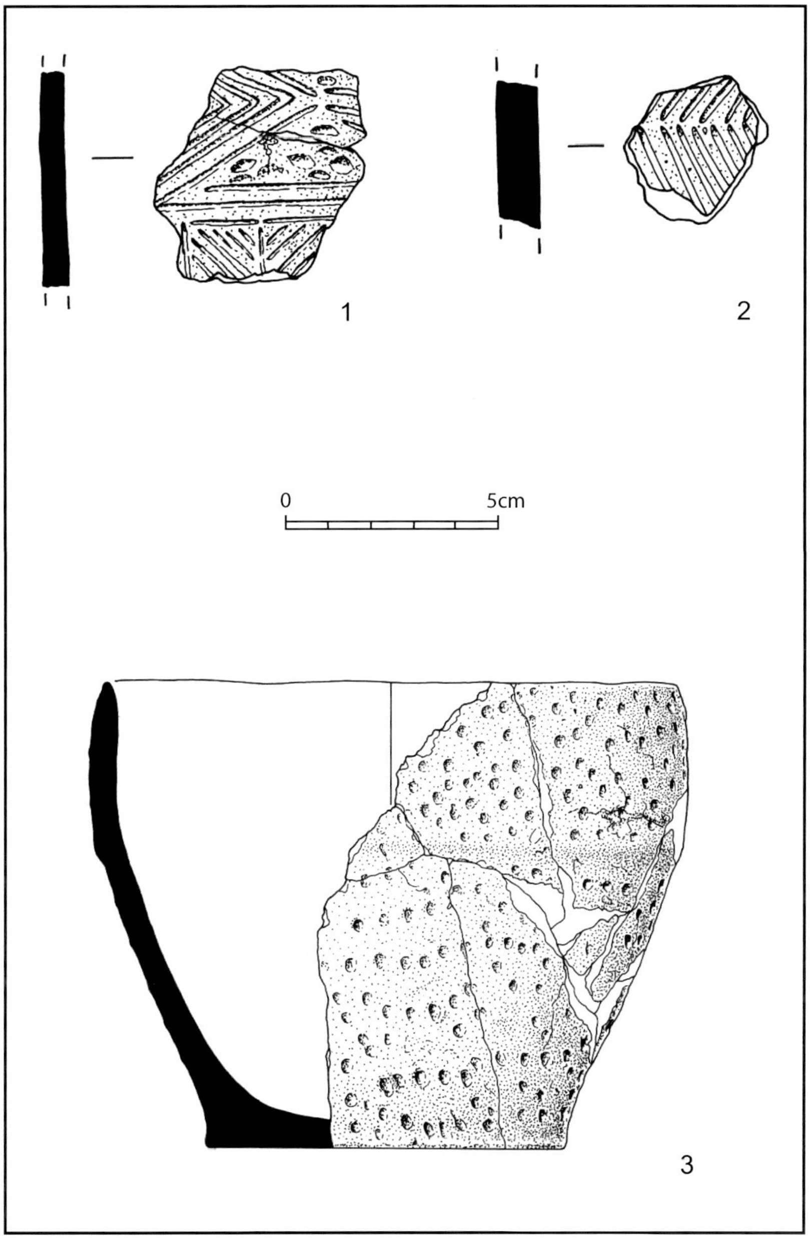

Figure 2.25. (above left) Reconstructed Grooved Ware vessel from F.20, Trench 12, [203]

Figure 2.26. (above right) Grooved Ware from F.20, Trench 23 (1 and 2, above) and Trench 12 (3, below)

1%) in fragments no greater than 3mm maximum dimension; they include both sub-angular and angular pieces; some at least appears to be heat-crackled. The surfaces are reddish brown (exterior Munsell 5YR 3/2, 3/3, 3/4 (dark reddish brown), interior 5YR 3/2). The surfaces are in fair condition with little obvious wear, while the edges are fairly worn, obscuring the core colour.

Trench 12

GW1. Base of [203], east section. Approximately one quarter to one third of a single vessel, some of the breaks clearly being ancient, some more recent, weighing a total of 169g (Figures 2.25 and 2.26.3). The fabric has a smooth, slightly soapy feel and a hackly fracture; it is moderately hard but quite brittle. The most obvious inclusion is shell, in angular plate-like fragments, up to 7mm maximum dimension; these are rare to sparse, occupying less than about 5% of the visible surface area and the sections suggest a no higher frequency than this. Fine sparse quartz grains are visible, as are fine dark grains, probably iron oxides or possibly glauconite. Given the low frequencies of the visible inclusions it is likely that there is also grog present, or the vessel is unlikely to have survived firing, but none could be identified even at X20.

The surfaces are oxidised or partially oxidised to a pale brown or buff (Munsell 7.5YR 7/6, 7/8, 6/6, 6/8, reddish yellow), although a darker patch of more orange surface suggests that the fully oxidised colour would be orange. The core in fresh breaks is black; the surface colours are very shallow, suggesting a short open firing with fairly unrestricted access to oxygen, therefore probably a bonfire firing.

The surfaces of the vessel are in fair to good condition but in one or two places the original breaks are worn, suggesting that the sherds had been weathered before they were deposited in the ditch. As the vessel has been partially reconstructed (before it was examined) it is not possible to be certain as to the number of breaks which are ancient and how many are relatively recent, but the vessel may have been deposited as more than one large sherd.

The whole exterior of the vessel appears to have been decorated with single irregular impressions. This is discussed further, below.

[203] Crumbs, probably of Grooved Ware, weighing less than 1g.

[208] One fragment of Grooved Ware in a fabric with some sand, weighing 1.7g.

Trench 13

[300] Two crumbs, probably of Grooved Ware, weighing less than 1g.

Trench 14

[503] One fragment of Grooved Ware, weighing 2g, in a fabric with some sand and grog.

[503] Two fragments of Grooved Ware, weighing 1.7g, in a fabric with some sand and shell.

[503] One fragment, probably of Grooved Ware, weighing 0.8g and containing some sand.

[503] One fragment, probably of Grooved Ware, weighing 1.8g, with a single plastic fingernail impression, in a fabric with some sand.

[503] One small sherd of Grooved Ware, weighing 1.5g, with shallow parallel grooves which seem to be discontinuous.

[503] One small sherd probably of Grooved Ware, broken into fragments weighing a total of 1.2g, in a fabric with some shell (max. dimension 3mm) and some sand.

[503] One small fragment of Grooved Ware, weighing 0.9g, with the interior surface missing. The exterior shows some curvature, suggesting that the fragment may be from just below the rim of a vessel; the fabric contains shell and sand.

[503] One fragment of Grooved Ware, weighing 0.9g, in a fabric with some shell, possibly from just above the base of a vessel; one surviving groove suggests that grooving extended to the base.

[503] Approximately eleven crumbs of Grooved Ware, weighing a total of 4.2g.

Trench 23

[709] pt 329. One small fragment, weighing 1.1g. This is harder and more compact than most of the Grooved Ware but may belong to that tradition. There are no visible inclusions and one surface is missing. The piece is dark brown.

GW2. [721] pt 349. One sherd of Grooved Ware weighing 13.5g and joining, along an ancient break, pt 354 from the same context, the latter weighing 4.2g (Figure 2.26.1). The sherds show few visible inclusions, with only fine sand, mostly quartz, but with sparse dark grains which are likely to be iron oxides or glauconite, and rare small (<3mm) shell. The exterior is reddish brown (Munsell 7.5 YR 4/3 brown), the core and interior black (Munsell 7.5YR 3/1 very dark grey), with some black residue adhering on the interior. The decoration is of incised lines which show considerable wear; there is a chalky residue trapped within the incised lines but this is almost certainly post-depositional: it does not have the appearance of the intentional white infill occasionally seen on Beakers. The edges are only slightly worn.

GW3. [723] East, pt 323. A single Grooved Ware sherd weighing 10g in a distinctive fabric with moderate finely crushed grog (sub-rounded to sub-angular <1mm, occasional pieces <2mm) and sparse small shell (<3mm, most <2mm). At X20 some of the grog can be seen to contain other smaller fragments of grog within them, and others contain coarse quartz sand and probable iron oxides (reddish grains). The decoration is of deep, well-defined grooves (Figure 2.26.2). The surface and edges show slight wear.

Discussion

The quantity of ceramics from the enclosure is small and, apart from crumbs, may represent only three Grooved Ware vessels. A single plain body sherd appears to belong to an earlier Neolithic vessel and to have been redeposited in the primary fill in which it was found. This sherd, which in fabric, firing and general appearance could be easily accommodated within the assemblage from the causewayed enclosure at Windmill Hill, will not be discussed further.

Grooved Ware from the base of the enclosure ditch (GW2 and GW3)

Although the collection of Grooved Ware from

the enclosure is a small one, it is of considerable interest. Three body sherds were found in the southern terminal of the enclosure ditch next to the eastern entrance in an extensive lens of loam and charcoal, associated with animal bone. Two of the sherds join along an ancient break, but the third belongs to a different vessel. The two conjoining sherds (GW2) seem to have entered the deposit as separate sherds as the edges are slightly worn so that the join is not a tight fit. The condition of the other edges and of the surfaces of the sherds also suggests that the sherds had weathered before they entered the ditch. The single sherd GW3 is in a distinctive fabric and is decorated with grooved herringbone or chevrons. The sherd is too small for it to be clear whether this is all-over decoration or infilling between panels, and therefore it is not assignable to a sub-style.

GW2 shows diagnostic features of two of the sub-styles defined by Ian Longworth (Wainwright and Longworth 1971). The incised panels are diagnostic of the Durrington Walls sub-style, as exemplified by, for instance, vessels at the type site (Longworth 1971), while the use of impressions as infilling in a triangular space is typical of the Clacton sub-style. In this case the infilling is almost certainly of a very small fingernail cutting into the clay to create small depressions, which is unlike the more usual rounded or irregular impressions (probably often made with a stick or wooden implement) used in the Clacton sub-style for infilling of geometric motifs, but is still quite unlike typical Durrington Walls practice. In the local area one vessel in the West Kennet long barrow infilling (NW chamber) has 'stabbed' decoration filling geometric forms probably within a design of vertical panels bounded by incision (Piggott 1962, fig. 14, R3).

Further afield, a parallel for the arrangement of the impressions and grooving above the panels on GW2 is represented by two sherds from Clacton which Longworth describes as having flag motifs (a saltire-type flag): P83 (sherd number 6, from cooking holes 4–5), and P5 (sherd number 7, from cooking hole 6) (Longworth *et al.* 1971, 103, plates XXXIV and XXXVII). Although the divergence of the grooves is not clear on one side, because the sherd has broken, it does seem likely that a similar saltire motif was present on GW2. At Clacton there are also a very few Durrington Walls sherds (P118–120), but no examples of motifs from the two sub-styles occurring on the same vessel. It is worth noting, however, that a vessel which does have a similar combination of design motifs to GW2 has been found at Wyke Down in Dorset. There, approximately one third to a half of a single vessel was found in the ditch terminal of the small Wyke Down 2 henge (Green 2000, fig. 64, incorrectly labelled Wyke Down 1), and in this case it shows a decorative scheme of incised panels with areas of infilling similar to GW2 and to the Clacton sub-style, in this case alongside herringbone, but combined with rim top pellets typical of the Woodlands sub-style and an externally decorated base which is absolutely rare in southern British Grooved Ware (and common nowhere). The motif on the base is, interestingly, a saltire (Cleal in prep.). In the case of the Wyke Down 2 vessel the deposition has the appearance of being intentional; at Beckhampton it is more difficult to argue this from the pottery alone, except to point out that even in the case of Wyke Down the vessel was not complete, and that at Beckhampton it is possible that some effort was made to include two sherds of the same pot, even though they were already separate. Both had also been used over fire, as there is visible residue on the interior of GW2 typical of the zone above the cooking liquid in a vessel and sooting on the exterior of the Wyke Down vessel. The dating of the Wyke Down vessel is less well-defined than that of the Beckhampton enclosure sherds, but both are likely to be within the first half of the 3rd millennium BC, and are therefore earlier rather than later in the chronology of Grooved Ware.

Not only do these two vessels suggest a similarity in behaviour associated with them, but they also seem to add some weight to Garwood's interpretation of 'earlier' and 'later' Grooved Ware. He points out that although the Durrington Walls sub-style has dates throughout the currency of Grooved Ware, some features, particularly applied decoration, appear more usually to be later rather than earlier, and that earlier Clacton/Woodlands and Durrington Walls style vessels appear less unlike one another than later examples of the same series (Garwood 1999, 159). Although the sub-styles might generally merit a re-examination, at present it is only possible to suggest that GW2 may be one of a small number of vessels which hint at the sub-styles being less clearly defined in the first half of the 3rd millennium BC than they may have been later.

Grooved Ware from the ditch infill (GW1)
GW1 is a strikingly unusual vessel, which on first sight presents problems in placing it within the ceramic traditions of the 3rd millennium BC. At this time (mid-millennium) the Beaker tradition was barely established, the Peterborough tradition was going out of use, and for a period of perhaps two to three centuries Grooved Ware is likely to have been the dominant ceramic almost to the point of exclusion of the others. Beckhampton falls into exactly this period. In terms of the decorative, formal and physical traits which the vessel exhibits, however, the fabric has clear similarities with both the Fengate sub-style of the Peterborough tradition, in which shelly fabrics are not infrequent (19% of 171 vessels in a study of Wessex fabrics: Cleal 1995, 159), and with Grooved Ware, in which such fabrics are common (51% of 163 vessels: *ibid.*). The decoration, of all-over impression, might be found on either Peterborough ware or on some 'rusticated' or coarse Beakers, although it is very rare for Beakers to carry random rather than linear (horizontal) impressions; but neither the fabric nor the form is at all typical of Beakers (where less than 1% in Wessex contained shell: ibid), and the form could not be accommodated within the Peterborough tradition. Overall, and although strongly atypical, it is within the Grooved Ware tradition that GW1 seems to fit. Features of the vessel which seem to support its identification as Grooved Ware (other than its fabric) are that it has a slight shoulder, with the shoulder made prominent probably by emphasising one of the coils used in its making. The effect varies even in the small amount of the circumference surviving, but it is clearly intentional and divides the pot into, approximately, one third upper:two thirds lower body proportions which are typical of the Durrington Walls sub-style.

In terms of local, regional or national parallels for the vessel, there are no close examples known to the author. Impression is, however, not uncommon on Grooved Ware, although usually combined with other decorative techniques, but it is not, even in combination, a particularly frequent feature of local Grooved Ware pottery. At Windmill Hill, for example, irregular impressions occur on one Clacton sub-style vessel from Middle Ditch II (Smith 1965, P283; Hamilton and Whittle 1999, table 165), but are absent from the West Kennet palisaded enclosures (Hamilton in Whittle 1997b). Only at Marden henge, 12 km to the south, is there anything in a Grooved Ware assemblage which has both impression, and an all over decorative scheme (Longworth in Wainwright 1971). Here, vessel P41 has irregularly spaced but roughly horizontal and diagonal irregular impressions across the exterior, with a row of impressions and stab-and-drag just beneath the rim. The form and fabric show no particular similarity to the Beckhampton pot, but there is a resemblance in that the decoration in both cases appears superficially random, but on closer inspection shows some arrangement. On GW1 this is into very vague rows, which in some cases are slightly angled and beneath the rim show just a slight suggestion of a geometric pattern as if the overall design was modelled very loosely on a geometric scheme. The form of the Marden pot, however, is not similar to GW1, nor is it in fabric. P41 from Marden cannot be dated closely, in part because the dating of the henge is uncertain, but also because it was found in a pit (Wainwright 1971, 192).

If fingernail impression is included in the discussion, two other examples occur which suggest that impressions arranged barely or very loosely in geometric patterns may be an occasional part of the repertoire within the Durrington Walls sub-style. At West Kennet palisaded enclosures vessel 16, which has Durrington Walls style applied-rib-bounded panels on the lower two-thirds of the vessel, has what appears to be very loosely geometric fingernail impression on the upper one third (Hamilton in Whittle 1997b, fig. 61). Further away, beneath the henge bank at Woodhenge, 27km to the SSW, a vessel with apparently a fairly standard arrangement of applied- rib-bounded vertical panels contains loosely horizontal to angled rows of (probably) fingernail impression (Cunnington 1929, plate 25, fig. 1).

Summary

At least two of the vessels represented at Beckhampton do not fall easily within the traditionally defined sub-styles of the Grooved Ware tradition. It should perhaps not be surprising that the ceramics are unusual, given that the enclosure from which they come is also difficult to parallel locally or regionally.

Lithics

Forty-seven pieces of worked flint were recovered from the enclosure ditch F.20, an additional three pieces from the ploughsoil over the ditch in Trenches 11 and 14, and six pieces from F.101 and 105 of the gully-defined enclosure (Table 2.3). Of these, only six are from the base and primary fills of the main enclosure, a further five from the secondary fills and soil, with the majority deriving from the tertiary backfill deposits, particularly in Trench 11. Densities are extremely low, most ditch sections producing between one and six pieces. Trench 11 is exceptional in that it yielded over 60% of the assemblage. Certainly by comparison with the quantities of lithics from other later Neolithic monuments in the region, such as the Sanctuary (Pollard in Pitts 2001b) and West Kennet enclosures (Whittle 1997b, 90–3), numbers seem low, though it should be noted that few worked flints were recovered during excavations at Avebury (Smith 1965, 227–8).

The majority of the flints are in fresh condition. Two flakes from the tertiary ditch fill in Trench 24 are rolled with spotted iron-staining and are almost certainly intrusive. Whilst a handful of pieces, such as the knife from a bone spread in [710], are almost certainly components of placed deposits, many of the flints from the tertiary layers were most probably incidentally incorporated in the ditch during the backfill event and may relate to other (even pre-enclosure) activities.

Context	Preparation flakes	Rejuvenation flakes	Flakes	Chips	Cores	Flaked pieces	Shatter fragments	Retouched / utilised
Enclosure F.20								
Tr.11								
[100]	-	3	9	3	1	-	2	3 (k, u, d)
[101]	-	1	1	-	-	-	-	-
[110]	-	-	1	-	-	-	-	-
[111]	-	-	2	-	-	-	-	-
[113]	1	-	1	-	-	-	-	-
Tr.12								
[200]	-	-	-	1	-	-	-	-
[210]	-	-	-	-	-	1	-	-
Tr.13								
[300]	-	-	-	-	-	-	-	1 (r)
Tr.14								
[506]	-	-	1	-	-	-	-	-
Tr.22								
[604]	-	-	1	-	-	-	-	-
[622]	-	-	-	-	-	-	-	1 (u)
Tr.23								
Surface	-	-	1	-	-	-	-	-
[701]	-	1	2	-	-	-	-	-
[703]	-	-	-	-	-	-	-	1 (p)
[710]	-	-	-	-	-	-	-	1 (k)
[723]	-	-	-	-	-	1	-	-
Tr.24								
[811]	-	-	2	-	-	-	-	-
[826]	-	-	-	-	1	-	-	-
[835]	-	-	2	-	-	-	-	1 (n)
Total	*1*	*5*	*23*	*4*	*2*	*2*	*2*	*8*
Gully-defined enclosure								
F.101, [903]	-	-	3	-	-	-	-	-
F.105, [920]	-	-	2	1	-	-	-	-
Total	-	-	*5*	*1*	-	-	-	-

Table 2.3. Worked flint from enclosure ditch F.20 and the gully-defined enclosure (k = knife; u = utilised flake/blade; r = retouched flake/blade; d = denticulate; p = piercer; n = notched)

The scarcity of primary/preparation flakes implies cores were brought on to the site in a prepared form, some being fully worked down and discarded. The two cores from Trenches 11 and 24 are multi-platform forms from which flakes have been removed in a fairly expedient manner. That from [826] is distinctive in being of poor quality flint with numerous internal flaws (quartz patches, thermal fracture lines, etc). No flakes struck from this are present, and it is conceivable that it, along with an unusual alternately-flaked thermal piece from a similar primary context in [210], were brought to the site for incorporation as intentional deposits.

The flake debitage displays varied modes of working. Flakes from the tertiary fill in Trench 23 are larger than average (5–7cm), broad and hard-hammer struck, one having a facetted platform. This style of working is frequently seen as characteristic of later Neolithic industries (*e.g.* Smith 1965; Holgate 1988). By contrast, flakes from Trenches 11 and 22 are smaller (<5cm), generally thin, narrow to blade-like, with signs of soft-hammer working such as diminutive platforms and diffuse bulbs of percussion. More characteristic of 4th- or earliest 3rd-millennium BC styles of working, these are from the tertiary backfill deposit, and may well represent components of a residual earlier Neolithic assemblage incidentally incorporated in the ditch fills. It was initially thought that the concentration of flakes from the tertiary fill in Trench 11 might represent debitage from a single knapping event, however attempts at refitting proved unsuccessful and it is evident that the flakes were struck from several cores.

Implements are well represented, accounting for over 17% of the assemblage. Knives, miscellaneous retouched and utilised flakes, a piercer, notched flake and denticulate are present, variously from primary, secondary and tertiary levels. Scrapers, normally ubiquitous, are absent. The piercer from [703] is unusual in being worked on a Janus flake, the point being defined by regular marginal retouch on two sides (Figure 2.27.3). The knives from [100] and [710] are on large narrow flakes/ blades with minimal modification: the former has limited marginal backing retouch and fine, regular inverse retouch along the upper half of the blade (Figure 2.27.1); the latter is naturally backed (Figure 2.27.2). Similar narrow flake knives and allied utilised flakes are known from earlier Neolithic contexts at Windmill Hill (Smith 1965, 92–3) and the later Neolithic West Kennet palisade enclosures (Whittle 1997b, 92).

Faunal remains
Fiona Coward

The majority of the faunal material recovered from this area was found on the very base of the ditch defining the enclosure, with spreads of material apparently representing deposition immediately after digging. These 'primary deposits' were sometimes found in discrete patches of darker sediment, below the primary fill, which consisted of loose chalk rubble with some animal bone. Most of the animal bone from the fill was resting on the base of the

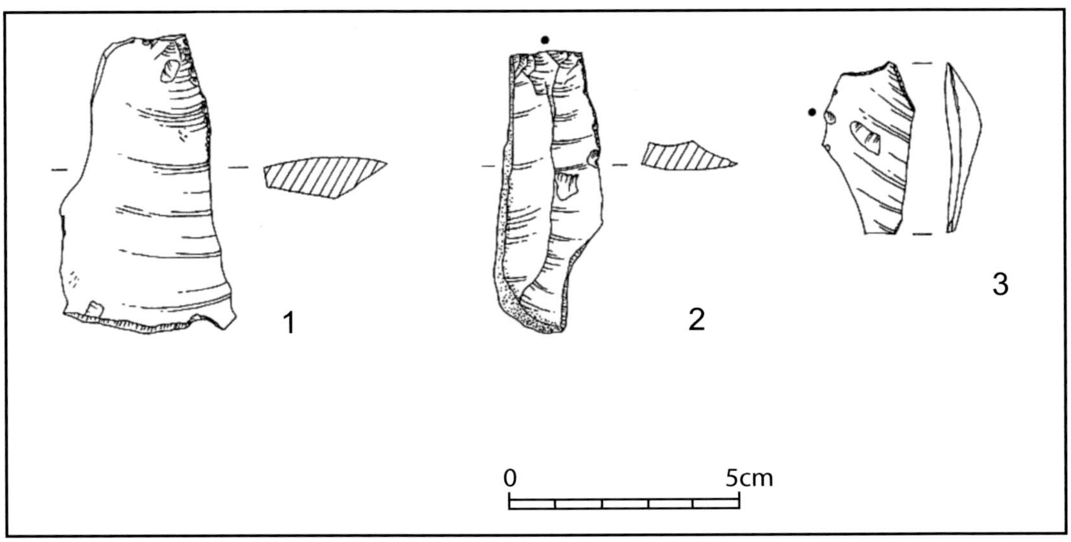

Figure 2.27. Worked flint from F.20: 1 and 2, knives; 3, piercer

ditch, contemporary but not associated with the primary deposits, while some was incorporated within the fill itself, and thus probably deposited soon after the primary deposits. For the purposes of this report, these two deposit types were amalgamated in a single category of 'primary', which appears to represent a time-span of at most a few years, and probably only a few months. Faunal material came from the primary fill, soil and tertiary backfill.

Recovery

Bone was recovered primarily by hand, with only a handful of sieved soil samples producing bone; differential recovery is thus not a significant factor.

Method

The animal bone was identified using the reference collections at the Faunal Remains Unit of the University of Southampton's Centre for Applied Archaeological Analysis.

The material from the enclosure was recorded as fully as possible. Larger bones, including the principal longbones, metapodials, scapulae and pelves were recorded by 'zone', as described by Serjeantson (1996); only fragments comprising more than half of any one zone were counted, and fragments obviously conjoining were counted as a single piece. As zones are numbered 1–8 from the proximal medial part of the bone, recording by zone also allows manipulation of the data in terms of the differential survival of various parts of individual elements as well as providing a more accurate basis for calculating the minimum numbers of individuals present. Smaller, 'unzoned' bones and fragments were recorded only when more than half of an element was present. Fragments unidentifiable to species were recorded as diaphyseal, cranial, rib or vertebral fragments, or where this was impossible simply counted and recorded as 'unidentified'.

Phalanges of the hind and fore limbs were not distinguished or sided and cranial elements used for quantification were restricted to the occipital condyles and mandibles.

Red deer bone and antler were recorded separately, as the presence of antler on a site does not necessarily imply the presence of deer. For the Neolithic in particular, where antler is often recovered in the absence of any post-cranial elements, the importance of red deer relative to other species present may be misleadingly inflated if the distinction is not made.

Distinction between sheep and goat was restricted to the range of elements for which criteria are outlined by Boessneck (1969). As no specimens were identified as goat, the ovicaprine material is simply referred to as 'sheep' throughout this report.

The total number of fragments was calculated for all material. However, NISP counts tend to be biased towards the larger species, where fragmentation may still allow identification. The minimum number of individuals (MNI) represented on the site has therefore also been calculated, using element side and zone data to determine the minimum number of individual animals that could have been responsible for the number of fragments recorded in the assemblage.

No dental eruption/wear data was available in the Neolithic assemblage. However, the fusion stage of post-cranial bones from the major domesticates was recorded and related age ranges were taken from Getty (1975).

Measurements were taken where possible following von den Driesch (1976). Unfused and fusing bones were not measured, nor were measurements made in the case of damage or burning.

Results

A total of 182 fragments were recorded. Of these, 50 (27%) were identifiable to species. The majority (54%) of material was recovered from primary contexts, 32% from backfill contexts and only 14% from the soil lenses.

The assemblage as a whole is in relatively good condition for Neolithic faunal material, although some contexts had suffered severe surface erosion, which in certain cases hampered identification and made detailed observation of surface modifications which might have aided taphonomic analysis impossible.

SPECIES REPRESENTATION

Species identified in the assemblage include cattle, sheep, pig, and red deer (mainly represented by antler).

Total numbers of identifiable fragments (NISP), percentage relative abundance and the minimum numbers of individuals (MNI) for the Neolithic assemblage as a whole and for its different deposits are given in Tables 2.4 and

2.5. Given the small size of the assemblage and of NISP/MNIs from the different deposit types, considerable caution is required in the interpretation of patterns of anatomical representation detailed below.

Relative abundance

Only four species are represented in the Neolithic material. Pig is the most numerous species in terms of NISP (44%), with cattle the second most common (38%) and sheep and red deer present in lesser numbers (13% and 7% respectively). However, the vast majority of the red deer remains are antler fragments – only a single post-cranial fragment was recovered.

In the primary deposits, pigs were the most abundant species (54%), followed by cattle (28%) and sheep (13%). Red deer (5%) is represented solely by antler fragments. Only eight identifiable bones were recorded from the backfill deposits; six identified to cattle, a single pig ulna fragment and a piece of red deer antler. Even less material derived from the soil levels; a fragment of cattle mandible, a sacral fragment identified to sheep and the only post-cranial red deer element (a calcaneum) identified in the assemblage.

In terms of minimum numbers of individuals, the faunal material may represent very few animals (Table 2.5). In the Neolithic assemblage as a whole, the major species' remains represent at least three individual animals of each, while the red deer material may have been imported to the site. Divided between the different deposits, the cattle remains could have come from just a single individual in each deposit, while a minimum of two sheep (based on two right humeri) and two pigs (based on several repeated elements) are represented in the primary levels, one sheep in the soil lenses, and a single pig in the backfill material. Given the difference in meat weight between the species it is possible that the NISP figures do not accurately reflect their relative importance. However, if we are dealing with the deliberate selection and deposition of elements rather than a straightforward reflection of an everyday subsistence economy,

Table 2.4. (below top) Neolithic species representation. Number of fragments (NISP) and percentage

	Total NISP	Total %	Primary NISP	Primary %	Backfill NISP	Backfill %	Soil NISP	Soil %
Cattle	18	38	11	28	6	75	1	33
Sheep	6	13	5	13	0	-	1	33
Pig	21	44	21	54	1	13	0	0
Red deer bone	1	1	0	-	0	-	1	33
Red deer antler	3	6	2	5	1	13	0	-
Total identified	**48**	**100**	**39**	**100**	**8**	**100**	**3**	**100**
Unidentified	**132**		**60**		**49**		**23**	
% Identifiable	**27**		**39**		**14**		**12**	
Total	**180**		**99**		**57**		**26**	

Table 2.5. (below bottom) Neolithic species representation. Minimum number of individuals (MNI)

	Primary	Backfill	Soil	Total
Cattle	1	1	1	3
Sheep	2	0	1	3
Pig	3	1	0	4
Red deer	0	0	1	1
Total	**6**	**2**	**3**	**11**

Table 2.6. (top far right) Anatomical representation by NISP: primary Neolithic contexts

Element	Cattle NISP	Pig NISP	Sheep NISP
Horncore	0	-	-
Zygomatic	0	0	0
Hyoid	0	0	0
Mandible	0	0	0
Loose tooth	2	0	0
Nasal	0	0	0
Occipital Condyle	0	0	0
Atlas	0	0	0
Axis	0	0	0
Cervical vert.	2	1	0
Thoracic vert.	0	0	0
Lumbar vert.	4	1	0
Unid. vert.	0	1	0
Scapula	1	3	1
Humerus	0	3	2
Radius	0	1	0
Ulna	0	2	0
Carpal	0	0	0
Metacarpal	1	0	0
Sacrum	0	0	0
Pelvis	0	0	1
Femur	0	0	1
Tibia	1	3	0
Patella	0	0	0
Astragalus	0	0	0
Calcaneum	0	0	0
Metatarsal	0	0	0
Tarsal	0	0	0
1st phalanx	0	2	0
2nd phalanx	0	2	0
3rd phalanx	0	1	0
Sesamoid	0	1	0
Metapodials	0	0	0
Fibula	0	0	0

Table 2.7. (bottom far right) Anatomical representation of species from Neolithic soil and backfill deposits by NISP

Species	Soil	Backfill
Cattle	1 x mandible	2 x horncore fragments 1 x mandible 1 x scapula 1 x tibia 1 x tarsal
Pig	-	1 x ulna
Sheep/goat	1 x sacrum	-
Red deer	1 x calcaneum	1 x antler fragment
Total	**3**	**8**

Element	Number un/fusing	Number fused	Age of fusion
Cattle			
Scapula	1	0	1 yr
Metacarpal	1	0	3 yrs
Tibia: distal	1	1	3 yrs
Sheep			
Pelvis	0	1	1 yr
Scapula	0	1	1 yr
Humerus: distal	0	1	1 yr
Humerus: proximal	0	1	3.5 yrs
Femur: proximal	1	0	3.5 yrs
Pig			
Humerus: distal	2	0	1 yr
Radius: proximal	1	0	1 yr
Phalanges I and II: proximal	1	0	1 yr
Scapula	3	0	1 yr
Tibia: distal	1	1	2 yrs
Humerus: proximal	0	1	3.5 yrs
Radius: distal	0	1	3.5 yrs
Ulna: proximal	1	0	3.5 yrs

Table 2.8. Bone fusion data for the Neolithic enclosure assemblage

NISP figures may be more useful than MNI (Richards and Thomas 1984, 207).

CATTLE

Wild cattle (*Bos primigenius*) were present in southern England and have been identified in some Neolithic sites, including nearby Windmill Hill (Grigson 1999). However, only a single cattle tibia from the Longstones assemblage was measurable (Table 2.9), giving a greatest distal breadth of 62.7mm, well below the measurements recorded for the Ullerslev wild cow from the Danish Early Boreal, which are often used as a standard for the wild form of the species (Degerbøl and Fredskild 1970). No unusually large specimens were noted during analysis, and the cattle represented on this site were almost certainly the domestic form *Bos taurus*.

Cattle are represented by only certain elements, including the scapula, tibia and cervical and lumbar vertebrae, two of which demonstrated ankylosing spondylitis and were pathologically fused. In addition, although cranial elements *per se* are not present, loose teeth are identified (Tables 2.6 and 2.7).

This prevalence of long bones over the more distal extremities of the skeleton could suggest differential recovery or destruction. However, many of the unidentifiable fragments recovered were much smaller than bones such as carpals/tarsals and phalanges and it seems unlikely that these former and not the latter would have been recovered. Differential survival is also unlikely given the generally good condition of even juvenile bone, particularly from the primary deposits, which also preserved more friable elements such as vertebrae and in the case of the articulated pig foot, elements *in situ*. It seems more likely that most processing occurred elsewhere and a selection of elements was brought to the site.

Four cattle bones providing fusion data were recovered – three from primary deposits and one from backfill material (Table 2.8). A single unfused scapula gives an age at death of less than one year; an unfused distal tibia and metacarpal give ages of less than 3 years at death, and there was a single fused distal tibia, indicating that at least one ox had survived beyond this age.

PIG

The identification of wild boar among the bones of domestic pigs is problematic and relies on distinctions of size and shape among a limited range of key anatomical elements or the presence of a large number of measurable bones (Serjeantson 1996, 219). Only a single measurement was obtained from a distal tibia whose greatest breadth was 28.1mm, much less than the 34.6mm recorded for present-day wild boar in Turkey by Payne and Bull (1986). As with cattle, no particularly large elements were noted during analysis, and so the material probably represents domestic animals.

Only a single ulna fragment was identified from the backfill deposits. In the primary deposits, however, the greater number of identifications reveals a particular emphasis on the long bones of the front limbs. In addition, an articulated foot was recovered from one of the terminal portions of the ditch in Trench 14. The emphasis would thus appear to be on the relatively meat-rich bones of the skeleton, and again, on-site slaughter seems unlikely.

A total of 12 bones provide epiphyseal fusion evidence. Of these, six were unfused bones giving ages at death of less than a year. Two elements fusing before 2 years of age were recovered; one fused and one unfused bone. Two unfused bones indicated slaughter before 3.5 years, and two fused demonstrate survival beyond this. It seems that most pigs were slaughtered young, with a few kept as breeding stock.

Sheep

Wild forms of sheep and goat were never native to Europe, and so this material definitely represents domesticated stock. With the exception of a sacral fragment identified from the backfill deposits, the little material identified as sheep was recovered from primary contexts. One pelvis and one femur (both from the left side), were identified together with one left scapula and two right humeri; although the material is scarce, as for cattle and pig, this suggests a narrower focus on meat bones.

Five bones provided fusion evidence. No unfused bones which would indicate slaughter at less than a year old were recovered, and three fused elements were recorded documenting survival past this. Two further fused bones indicate survival beyond 3.5 years.

Red deer

Red deer was represented in the assemblage mostly by antler fragments, with a single calcaneum recovered from the soil lenses between the secondary and backfill levels.

The antler pieces represented in the backfill contexts are small fragments; in contrast those from the primary deposits are larger pieces and relatively well preserved. One is a largely unfragmented beam and tine with coronet, probably naturally shed as the pedicle was preserved and was not attached to any cranial fragments. As such it must have been collected between March and May, although it may have been curated for some time. It represents a mature animal, and displays some probable working on the tip. The other fragment is a piece of beam only, recovered from the section near the eastern ditch terminal.

Taphonomy

Only two bones from the assemblage displayed evidence of gnawing by canids. One was recovered from primary contexts and the other from the backfill. A single unidentified diaphyseal fragment had been burnt, and no definite evidence for butchery was recorded. It proved difficult to determine whether the long bones had been smashed for marrow; the majority were fragmented to some degree, but no impact fractures or definite evidence for marrow extraction were noted.

Table 2.9. Animal bone measurements

Element	Description of measurement	Measurement (mm)
Sheep/goat measurements: primary deposits		
Pelvis	Length of acetabulum	37.5
Pelvis	Length of acetabulum on the rim	30.4
Pelvis	Smallest height of shaft of ilium	21
Pelvis	Smallest breadth of shaft of ilium	15
Pelvis	Smallest circumference of shaft of ilium	59
Scapula	Smallest length of collum scapulae	18.9
Scapula	Greatest length of glenoid process	28.9
Scapula	Greatest breadth of glenoid cavity	22.3
Scapula	Greatest length of glenoid cavity	23.6
Humerus	Greatest breadth of the proximal end	58.8
Humerus	Greatest breadth of the proximal end	43.9
Humerus	Smallest breadth of diaphysis	11.4
Pig measurements: primary deposits		
Tibia	Greatest breadth of the distal end	28.1
Cattle measurements: backfill deposits		
Tibia	Greatest breadth of the distal end	62.7

Discussion

Species representation and relative abundance

The small size of the assemblage is fairly typical of the period (although there are notable exceptions (*e.g.* Windmill Hill: Grigson 1999)), as is its domination by the three major domestic species, with the only other taxon represented being red deer – and that mainly by antler. Although occasional sites do produce some wild and 'exotic' species, (*e.g.* the Coneybury Anomaly: Maltby 1990); earlier Neolithic Windmill Hill (Grigson 1999)), the pattern of low wild species representation is the norm.

The significance of this is a question that has yet to be answered. It might reflect either a low degree of exploitation or complex forms of depositional treatment which included a deliberate exclusion of the remains of such species from certain contexts. It has been argued that at some sites these species are spatially segregated or deposited in distinct, restricted areas relative to domestic material, *e.g.* Mount Pleasant, Durrington Walls (Richards and Thomas 1984, 214) and Woodhenge (Pollard 1995b, 149).

It is possible that wild animals were perceived as 'different' to domesticates, 'holding a distinct position within Neolithic social ecologies' (Whittle *et al.* 1999, 359). The distinction between 'wild' and 'tame' animals, particularly of the same species, as for cattle and pigs, may reflect the conceptual distance of animals from humankind and thus ideas about the place of humans in nature and the world at large (Richards and Thomas 1984). Wild cattle and pig do appear in some assemblages but rarely, and are seldom treated in any distinctive way (as at Windmill Hill: Grigson 1999).

Of course this is part of a wider debate about the status of faunal assemblages recovered from such sites, and a growing acceptance that they do not necessarily reflect an everyday subsistence economy. The vast majority of Neolithic sites excavated so far appear to be more than just occupation sites and may thus be presenting 'a selective view of what was important in the sphere of subsistence, promoting the importance of domesticates and especially cattle' (Whittle *et al.* 1999, 348). However, the modern western division of 'economy' from other spheres of life such as 'ritual' or 'religion' may not be the best guide to Neolithic practices. Perhaps, as Whittle *et al.* argue, a better way to think of subsistence and human/animal interaction is 'as being contextually specific: different economies for different occasions, rather than a single monolithic "economy"' (Whittle *et al.* 1999, 349).

Species representation

Among the domesticates, the co-domination of cattle and pig seen at the enclosure is the norm for most other British Neolithic sites. Sheep/goat remains, if present, are generally represented at much lower levels. However, assemblages from sites in the Avebury area tend to incorporate sheep more commonly, and at higher frequencies, than those in the Stonehenge group. Sheep remains are thus reported in significant quantities from Windmill Hill, the long barrows at Horslip and South Street and (with pig) from pits on Roughridge Hill (Ashbee *et al.* 1979; Grigson 1999); although the West Kennet palisaded enclosures also yielded sheep only at very low frequencies (Edwards and Horne 1997). In contrast, sites such as Durrington Walls (Wainwright and Longworth 1971), the Coneybury Anomaly (Richards 1990), Woodhenge (Cunnington 1929) and Robin Hood's Ball (Thomas 1964) either yield no evidence for the exploitation of sheep/goat or contain only small numbers of bones. It has been suggested that there is a link between sites with sheep/goat remains and areas where *in situ* cereal growing has been proven (Maltby 1990); and some charred grain was recovered from the enclosure at Beckhampton (see below). This remains to be demonstrated. However, it is clear that in its relatively significant frequency of sheep the enclosure is not anomalous for the region.

It is tempting to suggest that the apparent preference for cattle and pigs stems from another source; both of these species, as discussed above, occurred in wild forms in the surrounding landscape as well as in the domestic forms husbanded by Neolithic peoples. As such, it is possible that these two species best embodied the tension between the wild and the domestic, the 'natural' and the 'human' and were preferred in these contexts for this reason.

The co-dominance of cattle and pig is thus a common phenomenon at Neolithic sites although which species is more numerous varies. Sites where cattle are more numerous than pigs include Runnymede, enclosure phase Windmill Hill, earlier Neolithic Hemp Knoll, primary contexts at Horslip long barrow and at Cherhill, and Coneybury henge and Anomaly (Ashbee *et al.* 1979; Robertson-Mackay 1980; Evans and Smith 1983; Maltby 1990; Serjeantson 1996; Grigson 1999). Pigs are more numerous at Durrington Walls, the West Kennet palisaded enclosures and Mount Pleasant in Dorset (Wainwright and Longworth 1971; Wainwright 1979; Edwards and Horne 1997). The two species are co-dominant in the 'Platform' deposits at Durrington Walls and at Marden (Wainwright 1971).

Pigs thus generally rank behind cattle on

most of the early sites, and it has been suggested that cattle dominated the earlier Neolithic, and were replaced by pigs following a later woodland regeneration (Grigson 1982). Certainly while earlier Neolithic assemblages always have more than 50% cattle, later sites have varied proportions of cattle and pig. However, the predominance of pigs may be specially related to ceremonial Grooved Ware sites where, it is suggested, they were used primarily as a feasting animal (Thomas 1999b, 26).

Intra-site species composition and anatomical representation

Some light might be thrown on the above assertion by analysis of patterns of skeletal representation. Fragment counts and percentages are given in Tables 2.4 and 2.6; however, the small sample sizes render problematic interpretations of cattle and sheep anatomical representation. Despite this, for pigs, the most numerous species, there does appear to be a general prevalence of long bones over the more distal extremities of the skeleton. This would be in keeping with patterns of anatomical element representation for other Neolithic sites, for example at Runnymede (Serjeantson 1996), the ditch assemblage at Woodhenge (Pollard 1995b), Hambledon Hill (Maltby 1990), and the West Kennet palisaded enclosures (Edwards and Horne 1997).

For cattle, the mixture of elements recovered also suggest a focus on meat. At many sites cattle and pig are not only co-dominant but treated in a similar fashion, with higher ratios of meat bearing than 'waste' bones (Maltby 1990; Thomas 1999b). However, some sites do demonstrate differences, such as the West Kennet palisaded enclosures, where cattle bones included higher frequencies of the distal extremities, and were more fragmented than pig (Edwards and Horne 1997). However, as noted above, the patterns of anatomical representation for cattle and sheep are based on only very small sample sizes.

The difficulty is compounded by the low level of butchery and burning evidence. However, this is in itself interesting. Low levels of taphonomic disturbance are noted for some other Neolithic sites such as the West Kennet palisaded enclosures (Edwards and Horne 1997) and Durrington Walls (Richards and Thomas 1984, 206) – although this has more recently been questioned (Albarella and Serjeantson 2002). However, the splitting of bone for marrow removal is relatively common. This is particularly focused on cattle rather than pig: at the West Kennet palisaded enclosures pig bones, unlike cattle, exhibit relatively few butchery marks and virtually no splitting (Edwards and Horne 1997), a pattern repeated at Runnymede where pig bones were butchered little beyond separation into joints. As at West Kennet, few pig bones (unlike cattle) had been chopped for marrow and 'some associated bones from the front leg appear to have been discarded with little modification beyond initial butchery' (Serjeantson 1996, 222). At Windmill Hill too, articulated limbs and other parts of the skeleton such as ribcages had apparently been deposited whole, although here the remains were those of cattle (the dominant species) rather than pig (Grigson 1999). In general, there is not much evidence for complex processing, marrow-splitting or butchery marks on pig bones in the British Neolithic (Thomas 1999b), and this is perhaps in itself a suggestion that feasting rather than full exploitation of the carcass was going on. Such clear examples are not apparent at the Longstones enclosure, although the articulated pig foot from the ditch terminal in Trench 14 is suggestive.

Age at death evidence adds another dimension to this picture. The evidence from the enclosure assemblage, although limited, seems to suggest the slaughter of primarily young pigs, as at other Neolithic sites from which ageing evidence is available, for example Windmill Hill, Durrington Walls and the West Kennet palisaded enclosures. At the latter, the slaughter of young pigs was on a considerable scale, with an extrapolated original total of thousands of animals (Edwards and Horne 1997).

The cattle aging evidence is slight, but indicates that although one bone came from an animal slaughtered at less than a year old and two from (an) animal(s) killed at less than 3, at least one had survived past 3.5 years. From other sites the evidence suggests older animals, often cows beyond milking age, apparently culled from much larger herds (*e.g.* at Durrington Walls, Windmill Hill and Coneybury henge), although at West Kennet, 'a significant proportion of cattle did not reach maturity' (Edwards and Horne 1997).

The aging evidence for sheep, however, indicates older animals, with no unfused bones represented. This compares well with the limited data from Windmill Hill, where it is suggested that Neolithic sheep were kept largely for secondary products such as milk and wool, or hair (Grigson 1999).

It has thus been argued that in Neolithic Wessex, and particularly later, pigs were specifically bred for feasting and sometimes slaughtered in large numbers. Of course, there may have been some reason beyond the economic for the choice of species. As Serjeantson points out, there is more than one possible reason why pigs might be more common; their meat may have been preferred; the animal may be more common because of aspects of the local ecology; or there may have been symbolic reasons for the preference (Serjeantson 1996).

It is well known that pigs are among the most 'economic' of animals to keep. They provide the best return of all domestic species when kept for meat rather than secondary products (Serjeantson 1996). They are 'remarkably fecund' (Richards and Thomas 1984, 206) as a species and easy to feed as their omnivory means they can be kept under a wide range of regimes. In addition, there is evidence both for open ground and for the woodland necessary for pannage for pigs in the Avebury area (Whittle 1993). However, given the wider Neolithic pattern and the general association of pigs with Later Neolithic sites, particularly Grooved Ware sites and henge monuments, their significance is probably not simply due to local environmental variations.

The symbolic significance of pigs has been demonstrated anthropologically, for example among the Tsembaga and Wahgi of the highlands of Papua New Guinea (Rappaport 1968; O'Hanlon 1989 cited in Edwards and Horne 1997). Serjeantson also discusses the role of pigs in Celtic societies (1996). Even in the modern world the pig is a focus of dietary taboos and often considered an anomalous and 'dirty' animal. It may also be significant that pork has often been compared to human flesh. Neolithic peoples practised complex funerary treatment of humans, probably including excarnation, and animal bones were often associated with human remains (for example the pig bones recovered from the fill of the earlier Neolithic grave of an adult male at Windmill Hill (Whittle *et al.* 1999)). Pigs may have been seen as a particularly appropriate species with which to negotiate relationships between the living and the dead.

Deliberate deposition

As Whittle *et al.* have pointed out, there are a range of ways in which artefacts and faunal remains could have arrived in the ditches, including accident, casual disposal, patterned disposal routines and intentionally 'structured' deposition (1999, 335). In many Neolithic sites there are demonstrated biases in the deposition of species, anatomical elements and even sides (as at West Kennet, where there appeared to be a preference for bones from the right side in pig pelves and femora in enclosure 1 (Edwards and Horne 1997)). This might appear to argue strongly for selective deposition. However, as Whittle *et al.* note:

> 'The term "structured deposition" is, of course, insufficiently precise, since structure will also exist within deposits that have formed through normal disposal routines, as well as through special acts. Furthermore, the definition of what is or is not a "structured deposit" remains largely undefined, and the contexts and intended outcomes of such actions may well have been very varied.' (Whittle *et al.* 1999, 356)

An association of such practices with 'ritual' may thus be a hindrance to their consideration. Nevertheless, it does appear that a certain degree of intentionality is reflected in patterns of deposition at Neolithic sites; enclosure ditches in particular have been associated with great diversity of depositional practices.

Given the small assemblage size for the Longstones enclosure, it is difficult to demonstrate spatial bias in terms of species, as has been argued for sites such as Durrington Walls, where it has been suggested that different species were clearly linked with different locales within the site (Richards and Thomas 1984). At Beckhampton, faunal remains are restricted to ditch deposits, though the absence of bones from the interior could simply relate to the absence of cut features over this part of the site. It also appears that the greatest density of faunal remains among the primary enclosure deposits came from the area of the ditch terminal, the east end of Trench 23. One of the red deer antler pieces came from here, with the pathologically fused cattle lumbar vertebrae not far away. The articulated pig foot came from Trench 14, the opposite ditch terminal.

The emphasising of ditch terminals and entrances with deposits, albeit on a much grander scale, appears to be a common theme in other Neolithic sites such as Windmill Hill (Whittle *et al.* 1999), Woodhenge (Pollard 1995b), and the north-eastern and minor southern entrances of Stonehenge (Pollard and Ruggles 2001).

There are not any self-evidently 'special' deposits found to rival those from nearby Windmill Hill, where, for example, the shaft of a child's femur was found inserted into the marrow cavity of the distal half of an ox humerus (Grigson 1999). However antler, often associated with placed deposits, was recovered from the primary deposits in quite large pieces, one with some working. Other intriguing finds from the Longstones enclosure include the fused lumbar cattle vertebrae and articulated pig foot.

Conclusion

The faunal assemblage from the Longstones enclosure fits well into the pattern of the British Neolithic in terms of its focus on domestic animals and particularly cattle and pig, mainly represented by the meat-rich anatomical elements. However, the scale of such practices is obviously much smaller here than at many other sites, where (particularly in the later Neolithic) pigs appear to have been slaughtered on a large scale for feasting and perhaps as sacrifices in their own right. This is known, for example, from the West Kennet palisaded enclosures (Edwards and Horne 1997), and with a range of animals at Windmill Hill, where the number represented probably runs into thousands (although it is recognised this probably represents repeated acts of deposition, perhaps over many generations (Whittle *et al.* 1999, 349)). In comparison with these nearby sites, the small size of the assemblage from the Longstones enclosure stands out. Very little appears to have entered the ditch of the enclosure, at least during its primary phase. It might even be regarded as anomalously 'clean'.

It has been suggested for other sites (*e.g.* enclosure phase Windmill Hill (Whittle *et al.* 1999); the West Kennet palisaded enclosures (Edwards and Horne 1997); Stonehenge I (Cleal *et al.* 1995)) that much of the material included in deposits may in fact have derived from other primary depositional contexts, perhaps even from outside the monuments themselves, having been subjected to (perhaps extended) curation or storage. Use of the monument, including depositional activity, may have extended over several generations. At Coneybury henge, for example, evidence of activity stretches over 2,000 years (Richards 1990). In this light, the monuments may refer to each other and/or to notions of time. However, at the Longstones enclosure the small scale and relatively good preservation of the deposits, coupled with the evidence of the sequence of fills implying a relatively short life for the monument in comparison with similar sites, argues rather for a relatively short-lived 'event'.

The evidence for feasting is also uncertain. Although assemblages from nearby sites such as Windmill Hill and the West Kennet palisaded enclosures demonstrate the slaughter of domestic animals on a grand scale, even here the limited butchery evidence and frequent deposition of articulated sections of carcasses have led some to argue that 'these sites appear to be characterised less by lavish consumption than by conspicuous non-consumption' (Grigson 1999, 236). The limited nature of the deposits at the Longstones enclosure suggests that any feasting would have been rather lean, although the prevalence in the primary deposits of the apparently minimally processed meat-bearing bones of pigs does link it to the nearby sites.

It is also difficult to come to any conclusions regarding the 'special' nature of the deposits at Beckhampton. The more 'exotic' aspects of the assemblage (the antler, articulated pig foot, pathological cattle lumbar vertebrae) do not approach the evidence from elsewhere. However, as Whittle *et al.* write:

> 'While articulated deposits and full burials are obvious formal deposits, we should be wary of assuming that broken and disarticulated bone simply represents "rubbish" given the evidence for selection, arrangement and the particular treatment afforded to some remains.' (Whittle *et al.* 1999, 361)

It is clear that deposition of the animal bones was to some degree deliberate; it is less clear what, if anything, it might 'mean'.

The faunal assemblage from the Longstones enclosure, therefore, demonstrates both similarities and differences with other Neolithic sites in the region and beyond. Of course we should not expect all sites to adhere to a strict template; while similar processes are obviously at work, it is also apparent that these behaviours were highly context-specific and that the practices enacted at the enclosure were both part of a wider array of behaviours, and also entirely unique.

Molluscan analysis

Rosina Mount, Andrew Mann and Joe White

This report presents the results of molluscan analysis from the ditch fill of the Longstones enclosure, undertaken over two seasons of excavation (1999 and 2000). The ditch was sampled spatially by means of columns spread over as much of its circuit as possible. Modern studies have shown Mollusca to be spatially restricted, enabling the 'mapping' of environment edges (Davies and Wolski 2001, 315). Large sections of the ditch were excavated, particularly in the 2000 season, which provided a greater choice in the siting of sample columns, making it possible to sample the deepest deposits.

Methods

Sample columns were taken from both terminals of the ditch (LSE 00 II, Trench 23, and LSE 99 VI, Trench 14), from the north of the enclosure (LSE 99 II, Trench 13), from the south-west (LSE 00 III, Trench 24), and south-east (LSE 99 IV, Trench 12).

A total of 1kg of each sample was sieved and sorted for Mollusca using standard procedures. Mollusca were then identified down to species level where possible.

Results

Results are presented below in Tables 2.10–2.14. Shell numbers were generally very low, as was diversity. All the series indicated an open country environment throughout the life of the ditch over the entire enclosure site.

Peri-glacial involutions

LSE 99 Spot Sample I was taken from the peri-glacial involutions at the base of the enclosure ditch in Trench 13.

Numbers of shells were very low, and the fauna extremely restricted (Table 2.10). This is a typical Late Glacial assemblage, similar, but less diverse and significantly lower in numbers, to the one obtained from the involutions beneath the South Street long barrow (Evans 1972, 354).

Primary fill

The primary fill from all areas of the ditch contained few shells, a characteristic of such deposits where accumulation is swift and the coarse rubbly habitat unsuitable for molluscan life.

Secondary fill and buried soil

Sample series LSE 99 II from Trench 13 contained too few shells to make analysis worthwhile. Series LSE 99 IV was also characterised by low numbers of shells and low numbers of species (14), but the dominant species in the buried soil, *Helicella itala*, *Vallonia excentrica*, *Trichia hispida*, and *Pupilla muscorum*, are characteristic of chalk grassland. *Helicella itala* in particular is characteristic of drier grassland sites, with short vegetation or bare chalk (Rouse in Bell *et al.* 1996, 146).

Sample series LSE 00 II and LSE 00 III contained slightly more diverse molluscan assemblages (17 and 19 species respectively), including some representatives of catholic species characteristic of slightly damper environments, *Vitrina pellucida*, *Nesovitrea hammonis*, *Punctum pygmaeum*, and some individuals of shade-loving species such as *Clausilia bidentata* (both series), *Oxychillus* sp. and *Discus rotundatus* (series LSE 00 III). This

Pupilla muscorum	9
Vallonia sp.	1
Limacidae	5
Helicella itala	2
Cecilioides acicula	9

Table 2.10. (left) Mollusca from series LSE 99 Spot Sample 1

Sample series LSE 99 IV
84-68cm Primary fill [210]
68-58cm Buried soil [203]
58-22cm Tertiary fill [200]
22-0cm Topsoil

Table 2.11. (below) Mollusca from series LSE 99 IV

Depth (cm)	84–75	75–68	68–58	58–48	48–38	38–30	30–22	22–11
Pomatias elegans	1	-	2	-	1	1	-	1
Cochlicopa sp.	-	1	2	1	-	1	-	1
Vertigo pygmaea	1	1	-	2	-	1	-	1
Pupilla muscorum	7	11	11	2	5	2	5	3
Vallonia excentrica	4	3	44	11	19	6	7	5
Vallonia costata	-	-	1	-	-	-	-	-
Punctum pygmaeum	-	-	-	-	1	-	-	-
Vitrina pellucida	1	1	1	-	1	-	-	-
Vitrea sp.	-	1	-	-	-	-	-	-
Limacidae	5	2	5	3	7	4	4	21
Clausilia bidentata	-	-	-	-	-	-	-	1
Helicella itala	6	4	44	10	10	7	11	9
Trichia hispida	2	4	28	12	4	-	5	-
Cepaea sp.	1	-	-	-	1	-	1	-
Cecilioides acicula	28	16	11	10	118	44	50	19

Table 2.12. Mollusca from series LSE 99 VI

Sample series LSE 99 VI
0-21cm Topsoil
21-72cm Tertiary fill
72-92cm Buried soil
92-120cm Primary fill

Depth (cm)	0–11	11–21	21–26	26–32	32–42	42–52	52–62	62–72	72–82	82–92	92–120
Carychium tridentatum	-	-	-	-	-	-	2	-	3	4	-
Cochlicopa sp.	-	-	-	-	-	-	-	2	1	3	1
Cochlicopa lubrica	-	-	-	-	-	-	1	-	2	-	-
Abida secale	-	-	-	-	-	-	-	1	-	-	-
Pupilla muscorum	-	-	-	-	1	2	3	1	4	1	1
Vallonia excentrica	-	-	-	-	1	-	6	10	41	12	3
Discus rotundatus	-	2	1	-	-	-	3	2	8	3	-
Vitrina pellucida	-	-	-	-	-	-	-	-	1	-	-
Vitrea sp.	-	-	-	-	-	1	-	2	6	11	1
Nesovitrea hammonis	-	-	-	-	-	-	-	-	2	1	-
Aegopinella pura	-	-	-	1	-	-	-	-	1	4	-
Oxychilus cellarias	-	-	-	-	-	-	-	2	3		-
Clausilia bidentata	-	-	-	-	-	1	2	2	-	-	-
Marpessa laminata	-	-	1	-	-	-	-	-	-	-	-
Helicella itala	-	3	3	-	1	2	1	1	-	3	-
Trichia hispida	-	1	-	-	-	-	1	4	1	-	-
Cepaea sp.	-	-	-	-	-	-	-	1	1	-	-
Cecilioides acicula	-	-	16	54	22	24	43	66	118	29	2

Table 2.13. Mollusca from series LSE 00 II

Sample series LSE 00 II
0-13cm Topsoil
13-49cm Tertiary fill
49-64cm Buried soil
64-90cm Primary fill

Depth (cm)	90–80	80–70	70–64	64–58	58–52	52–49	49–39	39–29	29–20	20–13
Pomatias elegans	-	-	-	1	1	1	1	2	-	-
Carychium sp.	-	-	-	-	-	-	1	-	-	-
Cochlicopa sp.	1	-	-	3	1	2	-	1	-	-
Vertigo pygmaea	-	-	-	1	-	-	-	-	-	-
Pupilla muscorum	7	1	2	2	1	3	3	2	1	1
Vallonia excentrica	1	1	1	4	15	6	10	3	-	1
Punctum pygmaeum	-	-	-	-	1	1	-	-	-	-
Vitrina pellucida	1	-	1	3	3	1	2	-	-	-
Vitrea sp.	1	-	-	-	-	-	-	1	-	-
Nesovitrea hammonis	-	-	-	1	-	1	2	-	-	-
Oxychilus sp.	-	-	-	-	-	-	1	-	-	-
Euconulus fulvus	-	1	1	2	-	-	-	-	-	-
Clausilia bidentata	-	-	-	-	3	1	1	-	-	-
Helicella itala	-	-	5	16	10	3	4	-	3	3
Trichia hispida	-	-	2	9	5	8	5	-	-	-
Cepaea sp.	-	-	1	1	3	2	-	1	-	-
Pisidium sp.	1	-	-	-	-	-	-	-	-	-
Cecilioides acicula	10	10	5	3	11	37	50	44	49	-

may be indicative of the increased lushness of the ditch-bottom vegetation at these locations in the ditch.

Sample series LSE 99 VI contained the highest proportion of shade-loving species, including the rupestral species *Clausilia bidentata* and *Marpessa laminata*, which commonly live on tree trunks. The peak of shade-lovers, in sample 82–72cm reaches over 50%, considerably higher than in the any of the series from other parts of the enclosure ditch. Even series LSE 00 III contains only 5% shade-loving species.

During the formation of the buried soil,

Table 2.14. Mollusca from series LSE 00 III

Sample series LSE 00 III
0-10cm Topsoil
10-47cm Tertiary fill
47-60cm Buried soil
60-74cm Primary fill

Depth (cm)	74–68	68–60	60–47	47–38	38–29	29–19	19–10	10–0
Succinea sp.	-	-	-	-	-	-	-	1
Pomatias elegans	1	-	3	-	-	-	-	-
Cochlicopa lubrica	1	-	1	2	-	-	-	-
Cochlicopa sp.	1	-	21	-	1	1	-	-
Vertigo pygmaea	2	-	-	1	-	1	-	-
Pupilla muscorum	-	2	-	-	-	1	-	4
Vallonia pulchella	5	-	7	4	1	2	6	-
Vallonia excentrica	1	-	14	2	-	3	1	-
Punctum pygmaeum	-	-	2	-	-	-	-	-
Vitrina pellucida	1	-	10	1	1	1	-	-
Vitrea sp.	-	-	2	-	-	-	-	-
Nesovitrea hammonis	-	-	5	1	-	-	-	-
Oxychilus sp.	-	-	1	-	-	-	-	-
Limacidae	-	-	-	-	1	-	-	-
Euconulus fulvus	-	-	-	2	-	-	-	-
Clausilia bidentata	-	-	5	1	1	-	1	-
Helicella itala	3	2	28	8	6	1	3	8
Trichia hispida	-	2	44	6	3	-	4	3
Cepaea sp.	1	1	8	2	1	-	-	-
Cecilioides acicula	43	1	8	52	121	84	44	12

therefore, when the ditch infilling had stabilised, the ditch bottom micro-environment was damper and more shaded in some parts of the enclosure than others.

TERTIARY FILL

The tertiary fill was characterised by a decrease in all species and low numbers of shells. The tertiary fill has been interpreted as re-deposited bank material and the molluscan evidence supports this conclusion.

Conclusions

The earliest evidence for the environment of the Longstones enclosure comes from the ditch fill. Unfortunately, the bank of the enclosure had been destroyed (probably deliberately levelled), so there was no possibility of the preservation of a pre-bank buried soil that would have provided information about the pre-enclosure environment.

The primary fill contains few shells, and this is consistent with its accumulation over a short time. At the Overton Down Experimental Earthwork, where the complete ditch fill only took 30 years to accumulate, the basal four samples, where the accumulation rate was very rapid, contained no apices whatsoever (Bell *et al.* 1996, 142).

The interpretation of molluscan assemblages from ditch fills must take into account the fact that once the infilling has stabilised, ditches often support longer vegetation than that of the surrounding landscape. Evans notes that 'in the absence of human interference and grazing, a rich vegetation of tall grasses and herbs becomes established' (Evans 1972, 325). This environment of lush vegetation supports a diverse molluscan fauna containing shade-loving species as well as those with open-country preferences.

However, at Longstones enclosure the ditch faunas, although showing slight spatial differences, generally contain very few shells of shade-loving species. It is therefore likely that the ditch, once stabilised, supported a short grassland habitat, as would the land immediately surrounding the enclosure. The grass would probably have been kept short by grazing. The molluscan species which characterise the assemblages from the ditch fills are those typical of grazed chalk grassland. The ditch itself would provide a micro-climate with greater moisture, shade and shelter than the surrounding land, which would provide favourable conditions for the few shade-lovers present.

Comparisons with South Street

Within the same modern field as the Longstones enclosure lies the South Street long barrow, with its long environmental sequence providing a useful correlation with the new evidence from Longstones (Evans in Ashbee *et al.* 1979).

South Street was constructed in an environment of short-grazed grassland around 3700–3100 cal BC. The pre-barrow soil shows evidence of early Neolithic woodland clearance, with the Mollusca showing a woodland to open country change, and the pollen revealing that the clearings were situated within a background of scrub.

The construction of the Longstones enclosure occurred around 2800–2700 cal BC and is associated with Grooved Ware. Unfortunately, the earliest environmental evidence comes from the ditch fill. The ditch assemblages suggest that the enclosure was constructed in an open environment. By the time the infilling stablilised and the buried soil formed within the ditch – approximately 30 years according to experimental evidence from the Overton Down earthwork (Bell *et al.* 1996, 142) – the environment was still open, but it is likely that there was woodland nearby. Radiocarbon dates suggest that the enclosure was short-lived, and deliberate backfilling of the ditch occurred a maximum of 400 years, and possible as little as 150 years, after construction. Yet the ditch environment had been colonised in some places by shade-lovers, which must have travelled from nearby refugia.

Within the South Street long barrow ditch there is molluscan evidence for a woodland regeneration phase, associated with Peterborough Ware, and dated between 3361 and 2782 cal BC. There is human activity associated with this woodland, focused on the ceremonial use of the ditch, with deposition of pottery, charcoal and animal bone. Clearance of the woodland does not occur until later in the 3rd millennium BC, perhaps coinciding with the on-set of cross-ploughing associated with Beaker pottery.

Davies and Wolski (2001, 315) have calculated the likely distance of woodland from South Street, based on the rate of colonisation of the ditch by shade-loving species, as less than 734m. The Longstones enclosure is less than 100m away from South Street, so it is possible that the source of the woodland species that colonised the Longstones ditch was the same. According to Davies and Wolski, (2001, 313) *Aegopinella pura* has the fastest migration rate (3.2–4.8m per year), then *Puntum pygmaeum* (1.6–3.2 m per year), then *Carychium tridentatum* (0.8–1.6m per year).

The Longstones enclosure ditch evidence suggests not woodland regeneration on the actual site, but the presence of woodland in the area. The ditch was open for a relatively short interval, yet there was still time for the migration of some shade-loving species. If the fastest migrating snail can move at the rate of around 4m per year, and if the minimum time from the construction of the enclosure until the introduction of shade-lovers into the buried soil is 30 years, then the woodland could have been as near as 120m away. Taking instead the maximum time between construction and introduction of shade-lovers (400 years), the woodland refugia could have been as much as 1600m distant.

Charcoal

Rowena Gale

Materials and methods

Bulk soil samples were processed by flotation and sieving. The flots were collected on a 0.5mm mesh and the residues retained on 5.6mm, 2mm and 1mm sieves. The resulting samples were scanned under low magnification and the charcoal separated from plant macrofossils. Charcoal fragments measuring >2mm in cross-section were considered for species identification.

The samples were prepared for examination using standard methods (Gale and Cutler 2000). Charcoal fragments were supported in washed sand and examined using a Nikon Labophot-2 microscope at magnifications up to x400. The anatomical structures were matched to prepared reference slides.

When possible, the maturity of the wood was assessed (*i.e.* heartwood/sapwood), and stem diameters and the number of growth rings recorded. It should be noted that measurements from charred material may be up to 40% less than the living wood.

Results

The charcoal analysis is summarised in Table 2.15 and discussed below. Group names are given when anatomical differences between related genera are too slight to allow secure

Trench	Context	Sample no.	*Betula*	*Corylus*	Pomoideae	*Prunus*	*Ulex/ Cytisus*
Tr.23	707	55	1	1	-	6	1
Tr.23	721	71	-	-	1	-	-

Table 2.15. Charcoal from enclosure ditch F.20. The number of fragments is indicated

identification to genus level. These include members of the Pomoideae (*Crataegus, Malus, Pyrus* and *Sorbus*), Leguminosae (*Ulex* and *Cytisus*) and Salicaceae (*Salix* and *Populus*). Where a genus is represented by a single species in the British flora this is named as the most likely origin of the wood, given the provenance and period, but it should be noted that it is rarely possible to name individual species from wood features, and exotic species of trees and shrubs were introduced to Britain from an early period (Godwin 1956; Mitchell 1974). Classification follows that of *Flora Europaea* (Tutin *et al.* 1964–80).

The anatomical structure of the charcoal was consistent with the following taxa or groups of taxa:

BETULACEAE. *Betula* sp., birch
CORYLACEAE. *Corylus avellana* L., hazel
LEGUMINOSAE. *Cytisus scoparius* (L.) Link, broom or *Ulex* spp., gorse. These taxa are anatomically similar.
ROSACEAE. Subfamilies:
POMOIDEAE which includes *Crataegus* spp., hawthorn; *Malus* sp., apple; *Pyrus* sp., pear; *Sorbus* spp., rowan, service tree and whitebeam. These taxa are anatomically similar.
PRUNOIDEAE which includes *P. avium* (L.) L., cherry; *P. padus* L., bird cherry, and *P. spinosa* L., blackthorn. In this instance the broad heterocellular rays suggested *P. spinosa* as the more likely.

Samples 55 and 71 were collected from contexts [707] (soil) and [721] (soil on base) of the enclosure ditch in Trench 23. The ditch contained a number of discreet deposits of brown loam, some of which included charcoal and other material (*e.g.* animal bone, pottery and flint); it is therefore probable that the charcoal originated from fuel debris, dumped in the ditch with other refuse. These deposits appeared to have been dumped in the bottom of the ditch before infilling began. The charcoal consisted mainly of shrubby species: blackthorn (*Prunus spinosa*), hazel (*Corylus avellana*), gorse (*Ulex* sp.) or broom (*Cytisus* sp.), birch (*Betula* sp.) and the hawthorn/ *Sorbus* group (Pomoideae).

Environmental evidence and fuel resources

The absence of large woodland taxa, such as oak (*Quercus* sp.), ash (*Fraxinus excelsior*) and elm (*Ulmus* sp.), could suggest either that, if present in the environment, these species were used for other purposes, or that the landscape supported a largely shrubby community at this time. Both suggestions could be relevant. Evidence from elsewhere in the wider region is indicative of extensive woodland clearance during the later Neolithic (Richards 1990). The extent of activity in or around the Neolithic enclosure at Avebury is, at present, uncertain, and no comparable data exists from the immediate vicinity. Nonetheless, charcoal analyses from sites on and around Stonehenge and Salisbury Plain recorded evidence of a broad spectrum of woodland species including oak (*Quercus* sp.), ash (*Fraxinus excelsior*) and elm (*Ulmus* sp.) (and shrubbier species) from the Coneybury Anomaly, Robin Hoods Ball, and Lesser Cursus from early Neolithic contexts, and of oak from later Neolithic sites at King Barrow Ridge and Conebury henge (Gale 1990). Oak (*Quercus* sp.), ash (*Fraxinus excelsior*) and hazel (*Corylus avellana*) were also identified from a Neolithic pit at Dunch Hill (Gale in Andrews 2006). Excavations along the site of a nearby pipeline (Kennett Valley Foul Sewer Line) produced charcoal from an old land surface beneath a Bronze Age barrow at West Overton which also included hazel (*Corylus avellana*), the hawthorn/ *Sorbus* group (Pomoideae) and oak (*Quercus* sp.) (Gale 1996).

Apart from agricultural clearance and the provision of fuel, the felling of large timbers for the construction and repair of dwellings, henges and other structures, would have made a considerable impact on the Neolithic landscape. The evidence, however, suggests that despite the comparatively widespread occupation and subsequent land clearance in many parts of the region, stands of oak-dominated woodland were still accessible in some areas during the later Neolithic (Rackham 1986; and see evidence for the extensive use of oak at the West Kennet palisades: Whittle 1997b).

Avebury developed as an important ceremonial centre during the Neolithic. The extensive layout of this early prehistoric complex, designed to encompass long-distance site-lines and viewing, may have been emphasised and enhanced by the removal of woody vegetation for some considerable radius around the structures. But, given the spiritual aspect of this environment, it is also worth considering that specific trees may have been preserved in the landscape either as way-markers or venerated as having symbolic or magical properties, or, perhaps, even as deities in their own right. The predominance of shrubby species identified from later Neolithic deposits (birch, hazel, the hawthorn group, blackthorn and gorse or broom) suggests that the contemporary landscape was probably rather open or sparsely colonised with scrub or light woodland.

Archaeobotanical material
Ruth Young

Despite an extensive sampling programme aimed at the recovery and analysis of floral macro-remains, very little plant material has been obtained from the excavated sections of the enclosure ditch. All the material discussed here was preserved through charring, although there is no evidence for domestic food processing or disposal within the complex, which strongly suggests that this is 'background' plant material of the type encountered on the majority of archaeological sites in temperate zones (Hubbard and Clapham 1992).

Methodology

The later Neolithic plant material was sampled over two excavation seasons (1999 and 2000) and processed by Wessex Archaeology, who also provided preliminary identifications. Further identification, analysis and interpretation have been carried out by Ruth Young of the University of Leicester.

From 1999 12 bulk samples of between 5 and 25 litres were collected, and from 2000 26 bulk samples of between 3 and 20 litres. These were processed according to standard flotation methods (Wessex Archaeology 2000; 2001), and it was noted that the samples from both seasons produced surprisingly small volumes of residue after the flotation process. Larger than usual amounts of weeds and uncharred weed seeds were noted however, and it is suggested that this is likely to indicate high levels of stratigraphic movement and intrusion from later contexts (Wessex Archaeology 2000; 2001).

Identifications were made using the comparative reference collection held at the University of Leicester (School of Archaeology and Ancient History), and selected reference works (Flood 1986; Schoch *et al.* 1988; Mabey 1998).

Table 2.16. Identified plant macro-remains from enclosure ditch F.20

Context	*Hodeum vulgare*	*Galium aparine*	*Chenopodium album*	*Rumex* sp.	*Corylus avellana***	*Agrostemma githago*
Soil on base						
721	2	1	2	-	-	-
723	1	2	1	-	-	-
Primary						
303	-	-	-	-	-	-
Secondary						
301	1	3	-	-	-	-
601	-	-	-	-	-	-
816	2	1	1	-	-	-
Soil						
203	-	1	1	-	-	-
302	-	-	1	1	-	-
705	3*	1	1	-	-	-
707	-	-	2	-	1	1
708	-	-	-	-	-	-
715	-	-	-	-	-	-
716	-	1	-	-	-	1
740	-	-	-	-	1	-
828	1	2	1	1	-	1
Tertiary						
300	1	1	3	1	-	-
604	3	2	4	1	-	-
702	1	-	2	-	1	-
818	1	2	1	1	-	-

* includes chaff **shell fragments

Results

Table 2.16 shows the identified material from the enclosure ditch, with the numbers of each different species or element per context. Barley (*Hordeum vulgare*) and hazel (*Corylus avaellana*) are the two food plants represented in this assemblage, and both are known to have been common since the Neolithic period, and in the case of hazelnuts, even earlier (Schoch *et al.* 1988, 65, 83). Barley is a hardy cereal crop (Thomas 1999b, 315, 317), suited to areas with cool summers (Schoch *et al.* 1988, 83). The presence of a very small amount of barley chaff suggests that it is likely to have been grown in the vicinity, and this is supported by the presence of weeds associated with arable land. Hazel is a gathered crop, and has also been identified in the wood charcoal. It is scrubby species that lends itself to management in the form of coppicing to enhance the production of nuts (Schoch *et al.* 1988, 65), and its presence here shows that gathered plant foods were of continuing importance alongside cultivated crops, and that areas of open woodland also persisted alongside areas cleared for cultivation.

Chenopodium album, or fat hen, is a very common, widespread annual weed, 'present in virtually all settlements' (Schoch *et al.* 1988, 53). *Rumex* sp. or dock is a weed of cultivation, and its presence supports the suggestion of agricultural practice in the vicinity (Flood 1986, 30; Schoch *et al.* 1988, 142). *Galium aparine*, also known as cleavers or goosegrass is another very common, widespread weed, found in both arable crops and hedgerow environments (Flood 1986, 49). *Agrostemma githago*, or corncockle, is also a weed of cereal crops, and along with dock and goosegrass strongly suggests that crops were being grown in the region (Schoch *et al.* 1988, 38). Both fat hen and dock are associated with damp or wet soils, and finding them both within this assemblage may indicate that the land used for cultivation tended towards moist rather than dry conditions.

Discussion

This is a small assemblage, which means that it is difficult to present any more than very general statements about subsistence practices in and around the enclosure, and renders any attempt at analysis beyond simple statements of presence very difficult (Pearsall 1989, 195–6). The possibility that some or even all of the material is intrusive, due to worm action, also needs to be borne in mind. There are no unusual or unexpected plant remains: all the weed seeds identified are likely to have been found in areas of cultivated or waste land, and the only cereal identified would also have been a common sight in the Neolithic landscape. Hazel shells as indicators of gathered plant foods show that the exploitation of wild plant foods continued alongside the cultivation of cereals.

Given the interpretation of the enclosure as a ceremonial monument, it should not be surprising that there is an absence of evidence for plant processing and food preparation. It is far more likely that any food consumed was prepared outside the enclosure and brought in for consumption. Other mechanisms could also be responsible for introducing the charred barley grains and chaff. They could have blown in from surrounding fields or cultivation plots after localised episodes of burning, or arrived on site via a range of animal or bird activities, thus forming part of the background 'seed rain' that we would expect in most rural areas.

Soil micromorphology

Helen Lewis

Ten micromorphology samples from ditch fill sections were taken during the 2000 excavations (Table 2.17). The samples were targeted at studying layers of soil deposition or development within the enclosure ditch fills, with the aim of examining these for indications of nearby land cover, contemporaneous land use, and information on the use of the site and the ditch histories over time. The key issue expressed by the excavation team was whether these soil layers represented stabilisation horizons (soil growth), deliberate turf deposits, or slippage of soil from the edges of the ditch or bank.

Samples for micromorphology are taken as intact blocks of soil, with the aim of examining *in situ* profiles in detail. The samples were taken with a vertical orientation, in aluminium tins *c.*6 × 12 × 6cm, and processed following the method of Murphy (1996, after Guillore 1985) at the McBurney Geoarchaeology Laboratory, Department of Archaeology, University of Cambridge. The samples were air dried, impregnated with a crystic resin mixture, and cured until hard. Thin section production entails sawing slices from the hardened blocks, mounting and grinding these down to 20–30μm, hand-finishing to a uniform thickness, and finally cover-slipping. The thin sections were described at the McBurney Laboratory and the Oxford University Research Laboratory for Archaeology and the History of Art, under plane polarised (PPL), cross polarised (XPL) and reflected (RL) light at various magnifications, following the guidelines of Bullock *et al.* (1985) and Fitzpatrick (1993). Summary descriptions are presented below and in Table 2.17 (a full report with detailed descriptions is held in archive). Micrographs of characteristic fabrics and inclusions are presented in Figure 2.28. The thin sections and resin-impregnated blocks are stored at the McBurney Laboratory.

Because segmented ditch fills regularly show

local variations both in sequence of deposition and in post-depositional processes, the deposits will be described primarily by profile. There is, however, an overall larger scale pattern seen in deposition as marked by the profiles described here: 1) final tertiary rubble backfill, over 2) stabilisation horizon or organic soil lenses, over 3) secondary chalk and soil fill or lensed soil and chalk layers, over 4) primary chalk fill. In some locations this overlies 5) thin organic soil deposits/horizons which immediately overlie 6) the surface of the chalk rock. The generalities of this sequence as seen in the thin section study, and any on-site comparability of the various contexts, will be discussed as they arise.

Thin section profiles

LSE 1

This profile contains two organic soil horizons ([721]) underlying the primary chalky fill [710], and divided by a lens of chalk. The sequence immediately overlay the chalk rock, and the impression in the field was that the lenses may represent either deposited turves or soil fallen in from the sides or the top of the ditch. In thin section the profile shows a series of alternating chalk and soil lenses, also suggestive of a sequence of dumping. The chalk lenses include a matrix of very calcareous fine soil, and are not simply stone lines sorted by earthworms, although faunal activity is seen in the organic soil fabrics. There are no indicators of surfaces, litter horizons or the presence of turves; high bioturbation could eliminate such indicators, but given the series of chalky lens deposits it is possible that the intervening soil lenses were also deposited (*i.e.* they do not represent stabilisation horizons *in situ*). There is a chance that they represent thin stabilisation horizons from a nearby location, however, such as at the edge of the ditch or on a neighbouring bank. The nature of chalky soil in the chalk lenses is similar to other deposits such as the primary 'melted' chalk fill [710]. It is likely that these lenses originated from deposits similar to these, which produce highly calcareous, chalky 'washes' in/over soil material, and frequent inclusions of 'crushed' or 'melted' chalk rock fragments. Typical locations for such fabric creation include fills comprised primarily of chalk, especially where these are relatively

Table 2.17. Micromorphology samples and field description

Sample	Location on site	Contexts (sequences from top-bottom)	Target
LSE 1	Trench 23, F20; terminus of enclosure ditch	- base of [710] - turf/thin layer of organic soil - chalky lens - [721] organic soil layer - chalk natural	Unnumbered soil layer and [721] are turves, possible dumps or slips, or stabilization layers at the ditch terminus
LSE 2	Trench 23, F.20	- base of [701] final chalk & soil backfill - [708] possible turf deposit - chalky lenses - [711] chalk and soil fill - [710] primary ditch fill	[708] is a turf deposit or possible stabilization horizon with turf on top (upper lens)
LSE 3	As LSE 2	- thin layer of topsoil material - [710] buff-coloured primary ditch fill	Thin layer of topsoil is possible turf deposit or stabilization horizon
LSE 4	Trench 23, F.20; sequence at top of ditch (stabilization horizon)	- lower [702] chalk rubble fill - upper [716] very dark brown clay-silt with chalk fragments	[716] is a stabilization horizon running along the ditch
LSE 5	Under LSE 4	- lower [716] - upper [710] primary ditch fill	As in LSE 4
LSE 6	Under LSE 5	- lower [710] - [725] turf/ thin layer of topsoil - chalk natural	[725] is a primary turf deposit or development at the base of the ditch
LSE 7	Trench 22, F.20; secondary fill of enclosure ditch	- lower [624] chalky rubble - [625] turf/topsoil - upper [626] primary ditch fill	[625] is a turf deposit or stabilization horizon
LSE 8	Trench with 'simple' enclosure ditch sequence	- lower [835] final chalk & soil backfill - [847] thin soil layer - upper [836] chalk 'cheese' layer	[847] is a possible stabilization horizon
LSE 9	Trench at side of site with no clear archaeology	- lower Ap horizon - lower Ap/incipient B horizon	Background; ridge-and-furrow runs across the site in this location
LSE 10	Under LSE 9	- incipient/upper B horizon	As in LSE 9

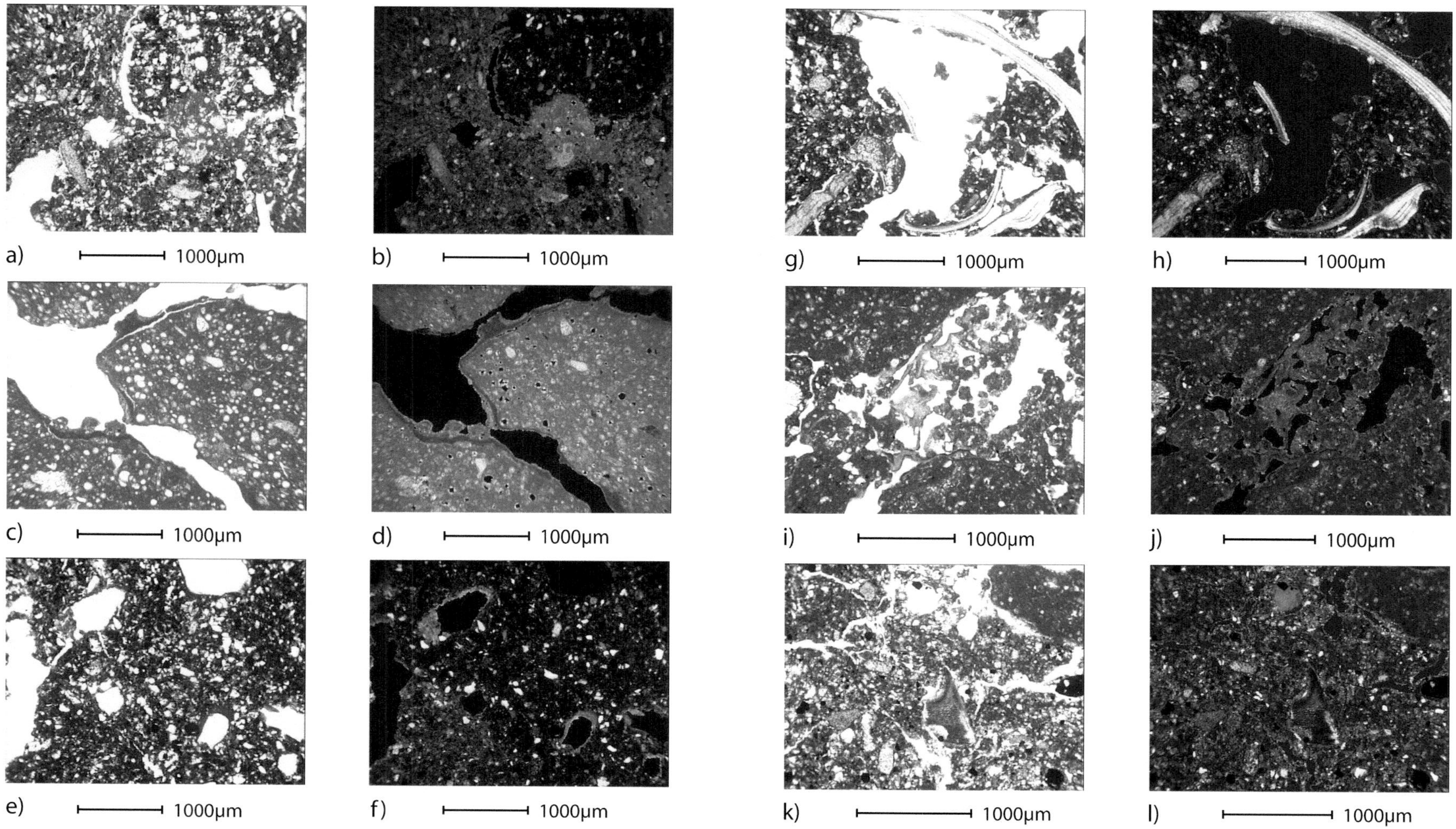

a-b) Typical [721] PPL & XPL showing calcareous fabric and depleted/organic earthworm excremental peds (LSE 1)
c-d) Clay & micrite coatings in [710] PPL & XPL (LSE 3)
e-f) Typical [716] PPL & XPL showing organic fabric and micrite coatings (LSE 5)
g-h) Typical [625] PPL & XPL with mollusc shells (LSE 7)
i-j) Typical [835] PPL & XPL with pore infills (LSE 8)
k-l) Typical modern Ap-B horizon PPL & XPL (LSE 10)

Figure 2.28. Soil micromorphology micrographs

compact and subject to leaching (*e.g.* primary chalk fills of many Neolithic and Bronze Age ditches), and weathered chalk surfaces (*e.g.* exposed chalk mound/bank capping materials, or some edges of chalk-cut features). The lenses found here could represent material slumping in from exposed upper sides of the ditch or from the surface of any surrounding bank soon after the ditch was opened. If this is the case, it would suggest this part of the ditch may have been open for some, relatively short, period of time (long enough for some stabilisation of surrounding exposed chalk) before the primary chalk backfill was deposited.

All of the layers in this profile are generally calcareous (with exceptional fabrics being directly related to earthworm excremental aggregates), with very few organic inclusions, and with frequent mixed clay and micrite infills and coatings on pores. The textural pedofeatures show the influence of leaching and illuviation of fine materials through the profile. This is a common characteristic of all of the ditch fills. The micritic nature of the main soil fabric (groundmass) and of infills and coatings represents the weathering of the chalk rock in the profile (through water action) and subsequent redeposition of calcium carbonate from solution as micrite upon drying. The small size of the crystals suggests relatively quick drying in this case (Kubiena 1938, 153). This wet-dry influence is assumed to have influenced the profile throughout its history, up to the present day. Finally, the thin layers of soil themselves fit with rendzina type profiles (thin A horizon over chalk), although one of the soil lenses in the sequence contained rare tiny clay-rich soil fragments. This suggests either inclusion of 'foreign' soil material in the layer, or, more likely, that the soil material originates from a location which at some point in the past was a thicker argillic brown earth, possibly long before its deposition in the ditch. The nature of the modern soil profile (see LSE 9–10 below) suggests that this could be on site or nearby.

LSE 2–3

These two thin sections come from the same field profile, which contained a turf deposit or stabilisation horizon associated with chalky lenses [708], immediately underlying the tertiary fill [701]. A further organic horizon underlay a secondary chalk and soil fill [711], and immediately overlay the compact primary ditch fill [710]. In this case it was difficult to separate the organic lenses from the other deposits in the thin section. The organic horizon immediately over [710], in particular, was very poorly developed and appears in thin section to be represented only by a line of earthworm excremental aggregates. These are organic stained and non-calcareous (unlike the rest of the deposits in the profile), and are also found randomly throughout the profile. Their presence as a thin line at the top of [710] would seem to have more to do the abilities or desire of earthworms to penetrate compact 'melted' chalk layers than with any other process or any cultural activity. Context [708] was thought to be a stabilisation horizon in the field, but it appears in thin section to be a mixed chalk and soil dump layer. Although there are hints of chalk rock and soil lines as described in LSE 1, there are no clear layers visible that are primarily organic soil. There are also no clear indicators of stabilisation or surfaces; nevertheless, the original nature of the horizon is not clear from the thin section. For instance, it is possible that the chalk rock fragments in [708] have been earthworm sorted to this depth, giving it a 'rubble' look that it did not originally possess.

As in LSE 1, rare fine clay-rich soil fragments were seen here, but in this case they were located in the primary chalk fill layer [710]. In addition, strongly expressed textural and crystalline pedofeatures as described above were also found in all layers in this profile. Recrystallised calcium carbonate is particularly notable in the layers overlying the primary fill, with [708] especially showing strong expression of these. Associated with the clay and micrite infills noted above, needle-like calcium carbonate crystals have formed in many pores. These 'pseudomycelia' are known to both form and disappear very quickly (Courty *et al.* 1989, 175–6) and it is likely that these formed very recently (possibly even upon drying of the samples).

LSE 4–6

This profile holds two horizons of interest. [716] is a stabilisation horizon running along the ditch, underlying a tertiary rubble fill [702], and over the primary chalk rubble fill [710]. [725] is an organic layer at the base of the ditch, under [710] and just over the chalk rock. While [725] is not distinct either macroscopically or microscopically in thin section from [710], except for a marked lack of large chalk rock fragments, the major [716] organic horizon is very evident. This appeared in the field to be an earthworm sorted 'topsoil' like layer several centimetres thick. In thin sections LSE 5–6 there is a striking change over depth in rock fragment sorting, going from an almost stone-free organic layer (lower [716]), to a layer that is rich in stones <1cm in size ([710] upper), to a very stony layer made up almost entirely of chalk rock fragments 1–3cm in size. Overlying LSE 4 shows a possible second phase of size sorting. LSE 4 comprises the lower part of [702], a chalk rubble fill, with rock fragments mainly 0.3–0.7cm in size, and the upper part of [716], which is relatively rich in rock fragments 0.5–1.5cm in size. This overlies the 'stone-free' horizon (lower [716]). The fine earth components of upper and lower [716] are virtually identical except for more strongly calcium carbonate depleted and/or organic stained fabric in lower [716]; this difference could be attributed to the influence of chalk rocks in upper [716]. Assuming the rock fragment inclusions have been sorted (downwards) through earthworm activity, it seems that [716] might have originally been a somewhat deeper organic and relatively stone-free layer than it now appears to be. Indeed, [716] is much more organic than might be expected from a ditch layer surrounded by calcareous materials. It is possible this layer was originally an organic deposit, created by rotting leaves and so forth, carried into the open ditch, which were then completely broken down and totally reworked by soil faunal activity.

It seems likely that earthworm activity is involved in at least some, if not all, of the size sorting seen. Surface-casting earthworms are known to create stone-free organic surface layers, and in the process to be responsible for the creation of stone lines or pavements at depth, as they move soil up the profile, leaving stones at the base (Atkinson 1957; Canti 2003). In the case of the underlying chalk rubble layer [710], one might wonder where they were taking the soil from; perhaps the rubble layer in this location was much more soil rich than it is now? As in other locations, [710] here is very calcareous, but it does not have the 'melted' appearance that it has elsewhere. Perhaps this location saw less compaction and less influence of chalk weathering and re-deposition of calcium carbonate than elsewhere, making it more aerobic and thus more amenable to significant earthworm activity. A further option is that the stone-free layer was not created by surface casting earthworms, but by earthworms casting at depth, thus creating, amending or sorting [716] lower. There certainly is strong earthworm activity evident in all parts of all of the profiles studied here, and some of it must be relatively recent, as well as ancient, sub-surface casting activity. However, casting at this depth would not explain the stone sorting above and below this level in the profile. Untangling the history and types of earthworm activities over time is very difficult, even in soil horizons (see Canti 2003, for example), much less in ditch deposits, but one thing is certain: this location has very significant earthworm influence.

If the argument for surface casting earthworms is accepted, this would imply that [716] was once a surface: *i.e.* that it does mark a stabilisation episode in the history of this part of the ditch. This phase obviously ended (presumably with the dumping of [702]), since lower [716] has not yet been influenced by the overlying rubble layer. The second sorting phase (of [702] into upper [716]) then follows. If surface casting was occurring, this also implies a strong possibility that artefacts in this location may have been displaced downward by this activity (Armour-Chelu and Andrews 1994; Canti 2003). This could explain the presence of what appears to be a <1cm sized fragment of iron metal in the upper part of the primary (Neolithic) ditch fill [710]. Although it cannot be confirmed from the thin section that this is indeed iron metal, the fragment does not have the appearance of iron-rich stone or iron-replaced plant remains.

Finally here, with the exception of the stone sorting seen in upper [716], most of the contexts appear to have remained relatively intact: *i.e.* there is little definite evidence of horizon 'erasing' as is often seen with strong earthworm activity; indeed, certain boundaries remain very sharp. This is not the case with the other profiles described above (with the exception of the boundary at the top of 'melted' chalk [710] in LSE 3), where there are distinctive stone and calcareous soil lines, but fairly mixed soil contexts. However, all of the contexts in all of the profiles discussed thus far do show some degree of mixing of the type expected: mixed calcareous (crystallitic) and non-calcareous (stipple speckled, organic and iron stained) groundmass types are found in all of the contexts to varying degrees. Even the dense 'melted' chalk deposits show zones of earthworm excremental aggregates (casting). So with all of this mixing activity, why have these boundaries not been erased in this profile? Canti (2003) notes that at least certain earthworms reuse deep burrows, and suggests that this is important in regard to the fact that earthworm sorted soil profiles do not necessarily become homogenised (*i.e.* there is still prehistoric stratigraphy found in earthworm-active areas), but homogenisation is still noted in areas of intense worm activity. Could lack of homogenisation be used to argue for a stabilised organic topsoil surface created through and amended by surface casting earthworm activity, suddenly interrupted by a significant dump of calcareous soil and rubble [702]? A second phase of sorting has obviously been ongoing since then; this has yet to fully influence the lower part of [716], thus preserving its stone-free nature for the time being.

LSE 7

This profile consists of one dark reddish brown organic soil layer with few rock fragments [625] between the primary [626] and tertiary [624] fills. The latter are very similar to others discussed above, being a mixture of rock fragments and calcareous soil, with earthworm and rooting disturbance, and illuvial infills and coatings. One main difference is the influence of light oxidised iron staining in this profile, which affects the general colour of these calcareous layers, and is relatively strongly pronounced in the organic soil layer [625]. Layer [624] has a 1–1.5cm sized sub-angular blocky fabric pedofeature – an inclusion of 'melted' chalk fabric, akin to that seen in LSE 3 [710]. The origin of this fragment is unclear – presumably it has been brought in from a compact chalk layer somehow, either through an original depositional event or post-depositionally.

The possible standstill or stabilisation horizon [625] does have characteristics of an organic topsoil layer, with a mixed but mainly non-calcareous, organic groundmass that has some iron staining, and is relatively stone free. Although not as distinctive as [716] in the LSE 4–6 profile, this could be argued to also represent some surface stabilisation horizon. Its location in the profile immediately overlying the primary calcareous fill also echoes the LSE 4–6 profile, where the stabilisation horizon overlies primary fill [710].

LSE 8

This profile was taken to examine a thin soil layer (context [847]) under a chalk 'backfill' layer ([835]) and over a secondary fill ([836]). Micromorphologically, contexts [847] and [835] were indistinguishable, with the exception of the inclusion of more larger chalk rock fragments. Besides this, the soil fabric is the same. Perhaps this situation similar to that in LSE 4–6 [716], where rock fragments from above have been sorted into an underlying relatively stone-free organic horizon that now appears to be very thin, but was originally somewhat more substantial. It is very difficult to decide in this case, having so little of the profile here. As with [708], there are no clear indicators of origin of the more organic layers; indeed, the layer is basically invisible in the thin section. Although the channel structure and occasional organic peds in underlying [836] shows some penetration by roots and soil fauna, the dense chalk layer and calcareous soil fabric has obviously remained a major boundary to serious bioturbation. The boundary between this and the overlying layer is sharp and strong. Even more than seen in [710] in LSE 3, this layer appears to have become cemented by calcium carbonate (mainly in the form of micrite).

LSE 9–10

Samples were taken through the modern profile as comparatives to the ditch profiles. The modern soil is a cultivated loamy brown earth (Ap-B) (after Bridges 1978). This profile also shows earthworm sorting at work, with large rock fragments primarily confined to the lowermost 5cm. The sorting is imperfect here, but shows how strongly earthworms can affect even ploughed, slightly more acidic soils such as this one. Over depth the organic-stained profile becomes increasingly red in colour ('ochreous' with iron staining), and has a stronger rooting and faunal channel structure. No increase in general clay content was noted with depth in the thin section, but fine infills and coatings similar to those seen in the ditch fills do increase in frequency with depth. A dense zone just above the B horizon is probably the main 'base of ploughing' zone, where both physical compaction and infilling with fine textured materials occur in plough soils (Jongerius 1970; Lewis 2002), although it does not contain any other distinctive characteristics. This profile also includes fine clay-rich fabric fragments as described in certain of the ditch fills. Their presence in this field suggests a local occurrence at some time of argillic brown earth profiles.

The modern soil contains some large charred plant remains and relatively frequent fine charred remains with visible structure. This is in contrast to all of the ditch fills, which are free of such inclusions, with only small possible remains ('punctuations' and tiny angular black fragments), and very few of these. If the topsoil overlying the sampled ditch fills is similar to that sampled at the edge of the site, one might expect that more charred material from that ploughsoil would be brought down into the ditch fills from above, but this does not appear to be happening. At least, any such material is not being displaced down to the depth of the samples, despite the strong earthworm mixing seen. It is possible that the charred remains in the sampled ploughsoil represent a localised deposit of material that does not extend horizontally to the other sampling locations; perhaps the material represents a localised dump, or derives from some nearby ploughed-out charcoal-rich feature.

Discussion

The general sequence, fill descriptions and variations across the segmented ditch fit well with observations made during the excavation. The idea of a relatively quick sequence of ditch construction and use, silting, and then back-filling with chalk agrees with the analysis presented here. The stabilisation episode seen (context [716] and possibly other deposits at the same point in the sequence), suggests that after the primary chalk backfill was deposited, the ditch was standing open for some time, accumulating and developing an organic soil horizon before the tertiary backfill was deposited. It is unclear how long a time period this was; it certainly was not long enough for a very thick soil profile to grow. However, it was long enough for strong sorting of particles up to at least 2.5cm in size by earthworms over a >20cm depth. Ongoing earthworm sorting is evident in overlying sediments as well. This is important in regard to interpretation of sediments and small finds across the site.

The results of the mollusc analysis, which suggest conditions of grazed grassland for the duration of the enclosure fit very well with the soil remains. It is not unexpected to find evidence for short or cropped grassland immediately in the vicinity of a Neolithic monument in England, nor to find that any soils growing on bare chalk (within the ditch, or on the bank) have grass-dominated vegetation (see Allen 2000a, for example). The general 'rendzina' like nature of the organic soil layers is also to be expected for soil growing on bare chalk or chalky deposits (*e.g.* [716]). Although rendzinas do grow under trees, they are primarily associated with grass and scrub vegetation. This picture fits that from other areas of Wessex, where combined soil and mollusc studies show maintained clearings in the locations of Neolithic monuments, both throughout much of monument history, and for a long time prior to monument construction, as evidenced by the pre-monument soils (French *et al.* 2001).

It is more difficult to find information about what is happening away from the monument over time. Buried soils can give indications of pre-monument land use history, which can be extrapolated both spatially, assuming later monument sites were not significant points in the landscape before monument construction (*i.e.* buried soils represent the general land-scape), and/or temporally. This is more difficult to do with ditch fills, as we can only be sure that they represent the landscape contemporary with their deposition. However, in this case we do have potential time depth regarding soil history. Rare microscopic indications of an earlier argillic brown earth in the rendzina soil materials found in the ditch fills suggest that, whatever the origin of the soil material in the ditch, it was once an argillic brown earth, and it had already become a rendzina by the time it was deposited in the ditch. This echoes other recent findings in the southern English chalk downlands suggesting that while thicker, clay rich brown forest soils did exist in the past in this region, they had already evolved/devolved into thinner rendzinas or simple brown earths by the early Neolithic (*e.g.* French *et al.* 2001), presumably through deforestation (cultural and/or environmental), and various land use practices that disturb the soil and affect vegetational change. Assuming this is also correct for this site, we can infer that site-specific change of this nature occurred immediately in this location. It is possible that more spatially widespread land use history can be inferred (for instance, the fine nature of soil in the primary ditch fill may show some windblown deposition from bare earth deposits), but these very disturbed ditch fills do not promote much confidence in such extrapolations. The evidence from the Longstones Enclosure ditch fills fits well with a model of stabilised shallow rendzina soils being widespread since the early Neolithic in many parts of Wessex.

Although animal bones, pottery, flint, burnt stone and charcoal remains were found in the ditch fills through excavation, the fills are markedly devoid of such remains in thin section. The absence of identifiable charcoal is particularly interesting, as it is found in the modern ploughsoil sampled, and was identified in soil deposits on the base of the ditch in Trench 23. In the thin sections, a background level of *potential* charred remains is represented in the 'punctuations' described above, but nothing identifiable optically as a plant remains survives. The occurrence of such cultural material in these primary organic soil lenses is thus variable. This suggests that they do not all originate from an occupation deposit, nor have they all seen the burning and depositional activity identified in some. This gives stronger significance to those small patches of organic soil at the base of the ditch that do contain amounts of charcoal.

Conclusions

The thin section analysis of ditch fills is always a variable exercise, especially in highly reworked contexts such as these. However, it has been possible to suggest a major hiatus in ditch infilling between the primary and secondary chalk fills and tertiary backfill, at least in some parts of the enclosure. The study has also revealed (once again) the enormous impact of earthworms on site remains in chalk downland areas; at this site earthworm sorting is particularly strong, and this must be considered in all ditch fill interpretations, and the assignation of context to artefacts. The lack of inclusions of a presumed cultural nature (*e.g.* pottery, worked or burnt stone, bone and charcoal) in the sediments examined is significant, in that it underscores the importance of a few small, spatially-distinct areas of organic soil with charcoal inclusions at the base of the ditch. These deposits are not normally seen in organic ditch fills, and are thus very interesting with regard to the history of use of the enclosure. Finally, the monument can be seen to fit well into more general models of the Neolithic landscape in the Wessex chalk downland region, at least in regard to land use indicators. As with other sites in the region, there are indications of the existence of a pre-Neolithic thicker forest brown earth which had become a rendzina soil by the time of monument construction. This is significant for our understanding not only of site-specific land use history – the immediate area, at least, appears to have been cleared of forest for a significant period of time before this monument was constructed – but the regional picture, which is more frequently showing extensive well-developed rendzina soil cover by the early Neolithic.

Discussion: location, sequence, activities and analogies

The area occupied by the western part of Longstones Field was already a significant location within the Avebury landscape by the time the enclosure was constructed in the 29th–27th centuries BC. To the south-east and south-west were two earlier long barrows (South Street and Longstones), while this locale was overlooked by the enclosure on Windmill Hill to the north and Folly Hill, with its putative Neolithic mortuary enclosures or oval barrows, to the south-east. To stand here during the early centuries of the 3rd millennium BC would to be aware of a long history of activity, earlier achievements and maybe Neolithic beginnings in the region (if such were regarded as definable historical moments). Occupation and cultivation had also taken place in this area during the earlier part of the Neolithic, as witnessed by deposits under the mound at South Street and the residual sherd and flintwork from the enclosure ditch in Trench 11, although this activity was probably small in scale and short-lived. The area was one of well-established grazed, and therefore probably managed, grassland. Both charcoal and mollusca indicate the presence of scrub or woodland in the vicinity, but perhaps at a distance. The environmental sequence obtained from mollusca in the ditches of the nearby South Street long barrow suggests that conditions of grazed grassland followed on from localised scrub and woodland re-growth that occurred during the late 4th millennium BC on the basis of associated finds of Ebbsfleet pottery (Ashbee *et al.* 1979).

Apparently also pre-dating the enclosure is the series of gullies in Trench 31, describing a small, east-facing sub-triangular setting. It is difficult to find an immediate parallel for this 'mini-monument', though analogies might be sought among so-called earlier Neolithic mortuary enclosures (Kinnes 1992, 88–89) and contemporary gully-defined 'houses' such as those at Fengate, Cambridgeshire (Pryor 1974), Gorhambury, Hertfordshire (Neal *et al.* 1990), and much further afield with recently excavated examples at Drummenny Lower, Donegal (Dunne 2003), and Enagh Townland, Derry (McSparran 2003) (Figure 2.29). This said, the former tend to be much larger, while the latter

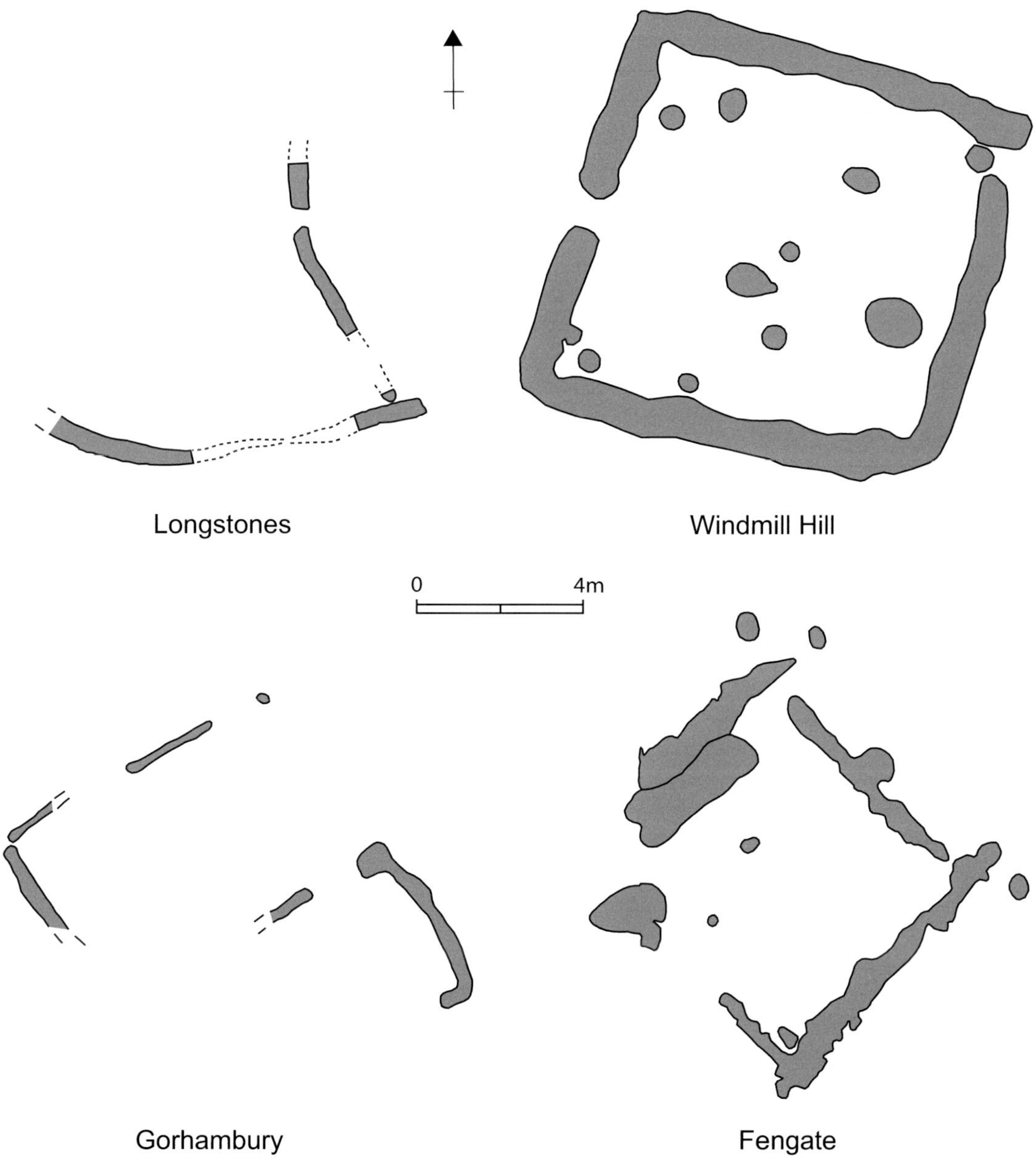

Figure 2.29. Analogies for the gully-defined enclosure

are scattered and vague analogies at best. Lacking evidence for post-settings – the gully being an 'open' feature rather than a bedding trench – it is difficult to see it as truly structural: this is more likely to have been a ditched and embanked enclosure than a palisade or building. A local context may be more useful in providing a parallel. Again associated with a larger enclosure site, the so-called Square Earthwork on Windmill Hill bears an interesting similarity (Smith 1965, 30–33). Both our 'Triangular Enclosure' and the Square Earthwork are defined by discontinuous shallow gullies, and the size of both is similar. Perhaps here we are seeing components of a local, earlier Neolithic tradition of small earthwork enclosure construction that might be allied to larger so-called mortuary enclosures of the period.

The Longstones enclosure took in and referenced, visually and morphologically, places of the past, including the earlier gully-defined enclosure. If we acknowledge that the past was important as a structuring resource to the region's Neolithic population (Pollard 2005) the enclosure's location in the landscape is not difficult to understand, but what of its role and significance? Even at 140 × 110m across, it is a modest 'monumental' statement in a landscape noted for the extreme scale of its constructions. It need not have involved many people in its creation, nor any great length of labour. Probably no more than 350 cubic metres of chalk were quarried from the ditch and dumped to form the bank; equivalent to a medium-sized long barrow or a 10m or so section of the great ditch at Avebury, though there more labour was required to remove chalk from a considerable depth (Gray 1935). Startin (1982) calculates 1560 person-hours were needed to create the inner enclosure at Windmill Hill, which, while of lesser plan dimensions, does possess deeper sections of ditch, and so could be regarded as a comparable exercise. As such, the Longstones enclosure could comfortably have been created by a group of twenty or so people over a period of two weeks. A sense of this being a 'small affair' is also provided by the quantities of fresh animal bone, worked flint and pottery making up the construction-related feasting deposits on the base of the ditch. The bones of only small numbers of cattle, pigs and sheep were present, and look to have arrived on site as joints of meat from animals butchered elsewhere. This is not debris from large-scale feasting, and compares poorly with the extensive and rich spreads of bone in the ditches of the earlier enclosure on Windmill Hill (Whittle *et al.* 1999).

There is no indication of contemporary occupation or other activity within the interior of the enclosure following its creation. The maintenance of open country conditions while the ditch fills were forming implies a continuing regime of grazed grassland, and so the presence of herbivorous animals (most likely domesticated livestock, but perhaps also deer) at least. The upper primary and secondary ditch fills were remarkably 'clean' of artefacts and charcoal. The ditch was left to silt without any intervention, the excavated sections showing a consistent pattern of primary chalk rubble, the formation a thin secondary silt and of an intermittent soil or stabilisation horizon.

There is no doubt that this is an unusual 'monument'. With an oval plan, a markedly segmentary and shallow ditch, and an internal bank, its form is reminiscent of 4th millennium BC causewayed enclosures. However, the earlier 3rd millennium BC date and Grooved Ware associations have led to the suggestion that it should be considered as separate from these (Oswald *et al.* 2001, 156). Analogies can be sought elsewhere. It has affinities, in terms of scale, method of construction, the presence of an internal bank, and the restricted access provided by a single main entrance, with the slightly earlier and more regular Stonehenge 1 and Flagstones enclosures (Cleal *et al.* 1995; Healy 1997). It is certainly a different kind of enclosure to many of the henge monuments of the later Neolithic, including the early phases of Avebury (the Avebury 1 earthwork), which must be more or less contemporary (Pollard and Cleal 2004). Its creation seems to have drawn quite actively on long standing traditions of enclosure construction, going back to the second quarter of the 4th millennium BC in Britain, and earlier still in northern central Europe (Bradley 1998). Conceivably, the Longstones enclosure was a deliberate re-creation of something of the past, and in what better location than an area of the Avebury landscape with a visibly long ancestry of monument building? Alternatively, it represents a continuation of established ways of doing things – an instance of the power of tradition

– as understood by a community who may not have engaged in the creation of similar earthworks for many generations; or it could be seen as an emulation of the not too distant enclosure at Stonehenge. If intentionally anachronistic in its form, and representing a deliberate reference to earlier sacred traditions, did its creation stand to some degree in contrast or opposition to the novel values and bodies of sacred knowledge presented by henge monuments like Avebury?

Whatever the inspiration for its form or politics behind its construction, certain features of the enclosure remain perplexing, particularly the flattening of its south-eastern side and the excessively wide eastern entrance. The flattening to its circuit might be explained by its abutting an existing pathway, the route of which would later be formalised through the creation of the Beckhampton Avenue along the same line, but off-set to the north-west. The 45m-wide entrance makes little functional sense if the purpose of the enclosure was simply to contain or exclude people or animals, which we assume it was not: the remaining circuit is too permeable for this to be the case. One possibility is that the enclosure circuit was never finished, the abnormally wide entrance being a result of terminated 'work in progress'. Against this argument is the subtle elaboration of the two flanking ditch terminals, which are wider and deeper than many other sections of the ditch, and marked by an increased scale of deposition. Such treatment suggests these sections of ditch were regarded as defining a formal entrance into the enclosure.

Although unusual in a number of respects, analogies of varying distance in time and space can be found for the Longstones enclosure amongst the wide repertoire of Neolithic earthwork monuments (Figure 2.30). Stonehenge 1 and Flagstones have already been mentioned. A sub-circular enclosure of similar dimensions, also with a slightly flattened southern side, a shallow ditch, and lacking internal features and evidence for associated occupation, has been excavated at Wasperton in Warwickshire (Hughes and Crawford 1995). Sherds of Ebbsfleet bowl from the primary fill might place its construction in the later 4th millennium BC. Perhaps because we are accustomed to the stereotyped image of henge geometry, we rarely acknowledge how common oval or irregular later Neolithic earthwork enclosures are. Examples include the site of Waulud's Bank, Bedfordshire (Dyer 1964), the major Wessex henge enclosures (Wainwright 1989), and, if of 3rd millennium BC date, the irregular oval enclosure at Long Meg, Cumbria (Soffe and Clare 1988). Wide entrances occur at the henges of Westfield, Angus (Barclay 2005), and the Great Circle at Stanton Drew, Somerset (David *et al.* 2004), as well as being a defining feature of so-called C-shaped enclosures of known or suspected 3rd millennium BC date in East Anglia, as at Broome Heath, Norfolk (Wainwright 1972), and Etton Landscape Site 3, Cambridgeshire (French and Pryor 2005, 44–5) (Figure 2.31). The latter two are of a similar scale to the Longstones enclosure, though the Broome Heath earthwork is unusual in possessing a double bank and ditch circuit on its southern side; the bank also featuring timber revetment and a possible

Figure 2.30. The Longstones enclosure and analogous monuments

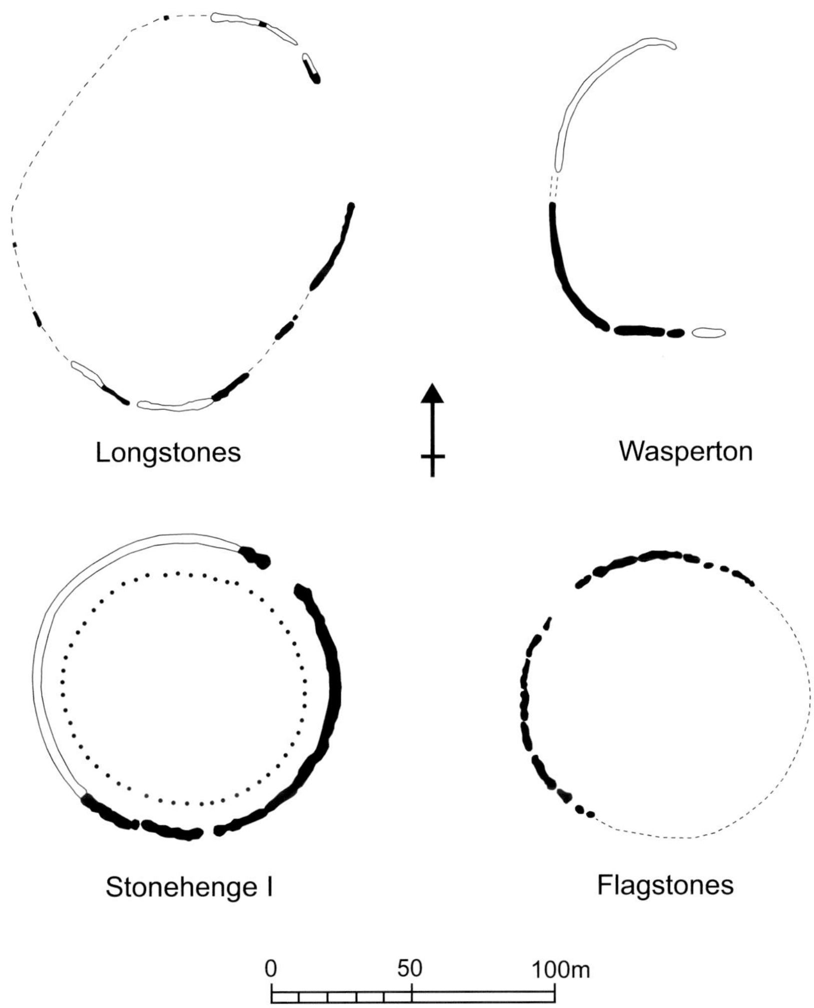

palisade. Here the enclosure surrounds an area of earlier (first half of 4th millennium BC) occupation marked by pits and surface artefact spreads, and is closely associated with a pre-existing long barrow. The association with earlier Neolithic activity and monuments, seen also at Longstones, is repeated at Etton, the C-shaped earthwork being located within close proximity to the causewayed enclosure there and the zone between the Etton and Maxey cursus monuments. A feature common to the Longstones enclosure, Broome Heath and Etton is the link to earlier long mounds, cursus monuments and mortuary enclosures; and, in general, the occurrence of wide entrance openings to the east is near consistent (Westfield, orientated to the north, being the exception). Intriguingly, a number of earlier Neolithic monuments share this feature of extremely wide easterly entrance openings. The

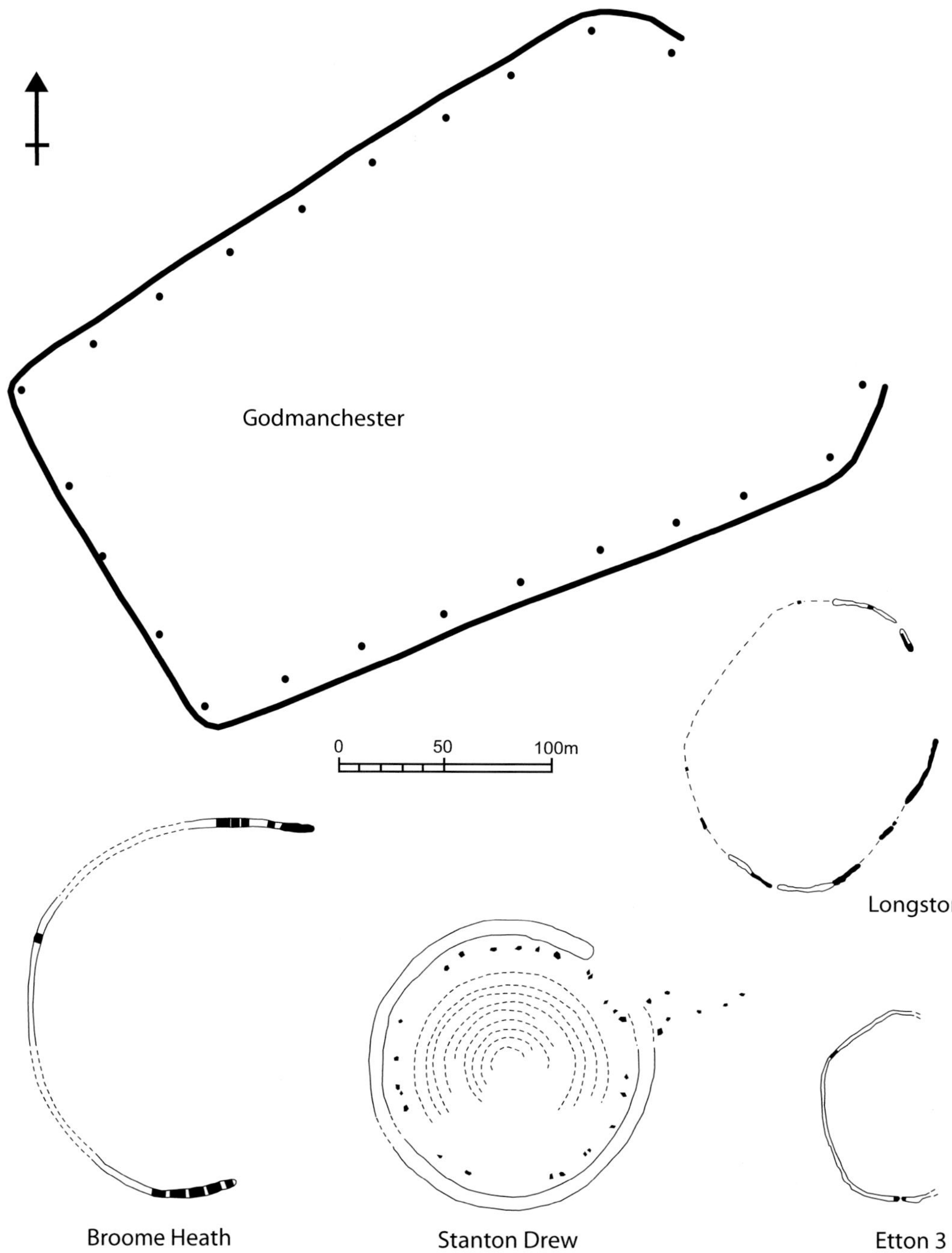

Figure 2.31. Open-sided enclosures of early and late Neolithic date

most remarkable is the massive early 4th millennium BC trapezoidal enclosure sited adjacent to the River Ouse at Godmanchester, Cambridgeshire, which surrounds a regular post setting with potential solstitial and lunar alignments (McAvoy 2000). Further upstream – and forming part of one of several regularly-spaced complexes of long mounds, long enclosures and cursus monuments along the Ouse (Malim 2000) – the middle of three cursus enclosures at Eynesbury is notable because of the absence of a substantial length of ditch on its eastern side, repeating the open format seen at Godmanchester (Ellis 2004). Further afield, there is the earlier Neolithic oblong enclosure at Church Lawford, Warwickshire, of a similar scale to that at Longstones and again with a wide eastern entrance (Stuart Palmer pers. comm.). Both the Godmanchester and Church Lawford enclosures were subsequently elaborated by the construction of cursus monuments running from their western ends.

We therefore have a series of enclosures spanning the 4th and 3rd millennia BC that, while quite disparate in geographical location and precise format, share a common feature in possessing abnormally wide eastern entrances, and which are frequently linked to linear monuments (long mounds, cursus and mortuary enclosures). Many are made up of shallow and narrow circuits of ditch, and artefact deposition within and around them was on a very limited scale. The earlier and later (carinated bowl and Beaker-associated) phases of Broome Heath aside, they did not provide a location for occupation, nor need large numbers of people have gathered at these sites once they had been created. It is not necessary to consider these enclosures as a distinct 'category' of monument, but they could have been foci for similar practices. They replicate the cosmological significance of an east-west axis, and emphasise the importance of movement (corporeal or spiritual) into, through or out of enclosed spaces. Because several are associated with long barrows and so-called 'mortuary' enclosures, it is tempting to envisage a connection with rites that involved engagements with the dead, ancestors or other spiritual agencies. A direct role in mortuary rites is, however, unlikely, since human bone is notably absent from all these sites.

Because of its scale and the relatively impoverished nature of the deposits in its ditch, it is easy to downplay the significance of the Longstones enclosure. This is surely illusory. Perhaps several generations after its construction, unusual effort was made to 'obliterate' the enclosure by levelling its bank and backfilling the ditch (at least in those parts of the circuit investigated). Whether a respectful 'decommissioning' or an active negation of the enclosure's agency and the values and beliefs it stood for, this action bespeaks of its continuing or renewed importance. As if respecting its sanctity, deposits were placed in shallow re-cuts in the ditch and incorporated into the base of the chalk backfill. The site of the enclosure was then physically linked to the Avebury henge – by this stage a pre-eminent ceremonial centre – through the creation of the Beckhampton Avenue. The context and implications of this remarkable transformation will be considered next.

2.2 The Beckhampton Avenue and Longstones Cove

By the mid 3rd millennium BC the Avebury region was already one of the most extensively transformed landscapes in north-western Europe. Over a millennium of Neolithic occupation, intermittent clearance, cultivation and livestock grazing had left very visible marks: an extensive open grassland environment on the floor of the valley (Evans *et al.* 1993), a network of pathways and areas of intermittent and more sustained settlement (*e.g.* the southern slopes of Windmill Hill: Whittle *et al.* 2000), and both actively used and 'abandoned' monumental constructions. Certain earlier Neolithic enclosures and long barrows, such as those at Horslip, West Kennet and Windmill Hill, continued to provide a focus for deposition and other rites (ancestral veneration, perhaps), others, especially on the high downs to the south, had become neglected (*e.g.* Easton Down: Whittle *et al.* 1993). Much activity was now focused on the centre of the region, the valley floor, and the Avebury henge itself. The main phase of earthwork here (Avebury 2) dates to around the 26th century BC, and the outer stone circle perhaps slightly later (Pollard and Cleal 2004). By the beginning of the second half of the 3rd millennium BC the early stages of the palisaded enclosures at

West Kennet were constructed, the timber settings at the Sanctuary and, perhaps, the primary mound of Silbury Hill (Pollard 1992; Whittle 1997b). The scale of monument building was gathering pace. Up to this point the Avebury henge, the Sanctuary and Longstones enclosure were separate sites with distinct, and in the case of Avebury quite lengthy (Gillings and Pollard 2004), histories. However, a radical transformation in the structure of the Avebury monument complex was to occur with the decision to physically link these three sites through the creation of two massive megalithic avenues: the West Kennet Avenue leading from the southern entrance of Avebury to the Sanctuary and Overton Hill, 2.5km to the south-east; and the Beckhampton Avenue from the western entrance of the henge to the site of the Longstones enclosure 1.3km to the south-west.

Sarsen

The creation of the avenues may be seen as a process of a 'lithicisation', a marking out or memorialisation of existing pathways through the erection of stone rows (Barrett 1994, 15). In this sense, it was equivalent to the transformation from timber to stone seen with the settings at the Sanctuary (Cunnington 1931), or from earthwork to stone at the Longstones enclosure (see below). While large blocks of local sarsen stone had been employed earlier in the Neolithic for the construction of chambers within several of the region's long barrows (Barker 1985), the use of stone increased considerably during the mid-late 3rd millennium BC. Taken together, the creation during these centuries of the outer and perhaps inner circles at the Avebury henge, the two avenues, the stone circles at the Sanctuary, the blocking at the West Kennet long barrow (Piggott 1962), and other, poorly understood, megalithic structures represents not just a considerable input of labour, but also a vast mobilisation of stone. In total, over 500 blocks of sarsen stone, some over 50 tonnes in weight, were prised out of the ground, dragged over distances ranging from a few to several hundred metres or more, hauled upright and set in position. At one level we are witnessing the utilisation of a readily available resource that, because of its bulk and resilience, lent itself well to the needs of monument construction. However, its employment on this scale, at this time, may also bespeak of shifting attitudes to sarsen and the natural stone fields from which it was taken. These are themes we shall return to later.

In all instances it was local sarsen stone that was employed for megalithic constructions; although small blocks of oolitic limestone were earlier used in the chambers of some of the region's long barrows. Sarsen is a highly resilient Tertiary sandstone, occurring in both boulder and tabular form. Deposited in extensive spreads along valley bottoms and sides under peri-glacial conditions during the late Pleistocene (Geddes 2000, 60–4), its distribution on the North Wiltshire Downs is now restricted to a few dry valleys that have escaped extensive post-medieval clearance (King 1968; Bowen and Smith 1977). None of the blocks used in the construction of the avenues, circles or coves during the later Neolithic were dressed, though some display evidence of prior utilisation as axe polishing stones (Smith 1965, 223; Gillings and Pollard 1999). The retention here of the stones' cortical surfaces, of their original 'identity', is in marked contrast to the extensive dressing applied to the sarsens of the contemporary phase 3 settings at Stonehenge (Cleal *et al.* 1995). We would argue that the decision not to dress stones, and so keep their original appearance and identity, was as significant as the shaping seen at Stonehenge.

The 'snake dream of the fanciful doctor': antiquaries, archaeologists and the Beckhampton Avenue

Of the two avenues leading from the Avebury henge, the West Kennet Avenue is the better known and more extensively investigated. Its enhanced state of preservation into the early post-medieval period, when the first detailed antiquarian accounts of the monument complex were being made, has facilitated a sound comprehension of its extent and format (Stukeley 1743, 28–31; Ucko *et al.* 1991, 116, 186–94). Between 1934–5 its northern third was subject to extensive excavation and restoration (Smith 1965, 185–7), a process that effectively 'ground-truthed' the earlier observations of the antiquaries John Aubrey and William Stukeley. By contrast, until the

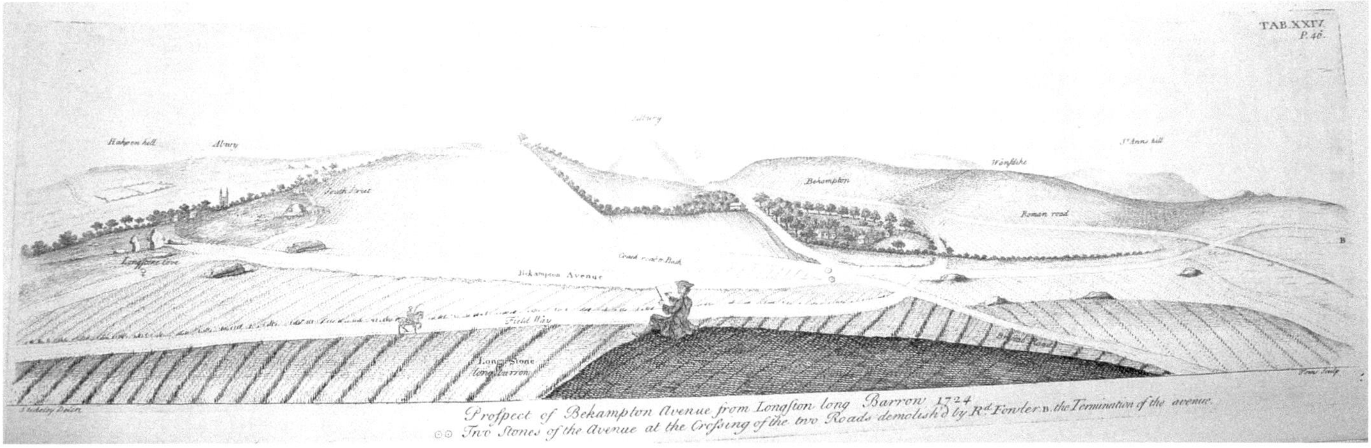

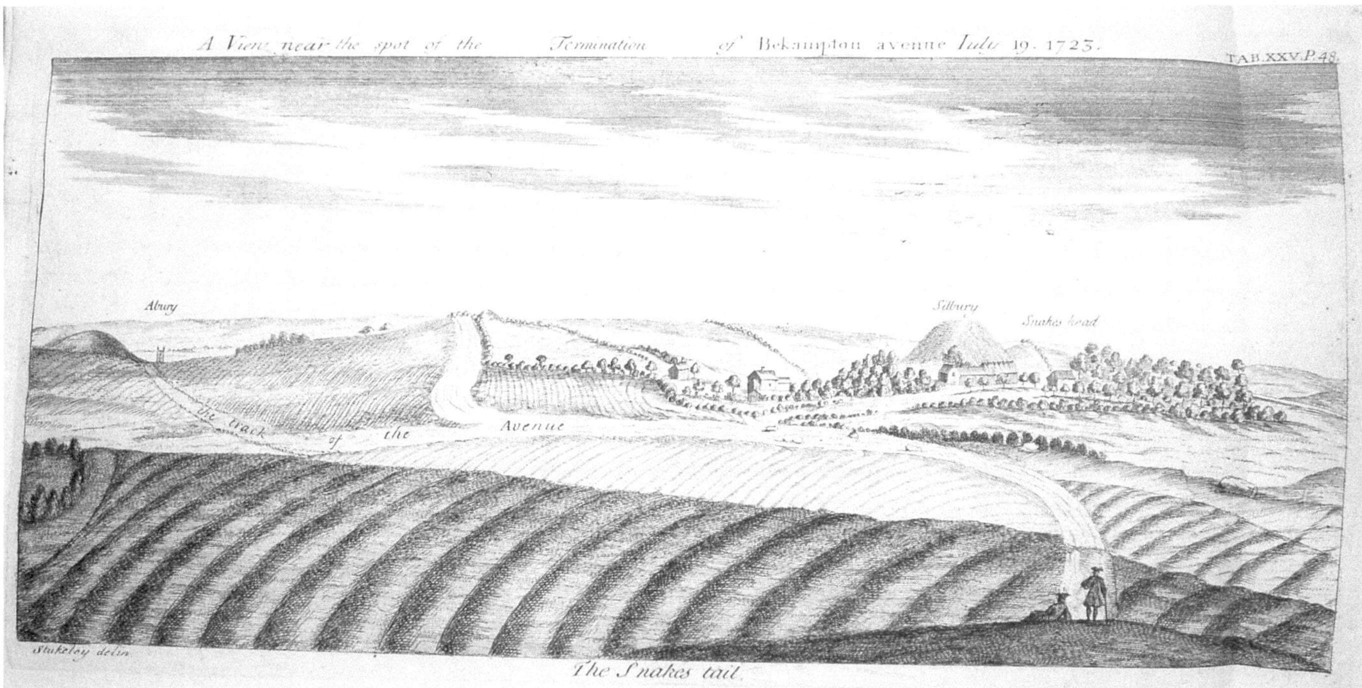

Figure 2.32. (top) Stukeley's panorama of the remains of the Beckhampton Avenue, taken from the top of the Beckhampton long barrow (Stukeley 1743, pl. XXIV)

Figure 2.33. (bottom) Stukeley's prospect of the terminal of the Beckhampton Avenue, near Fox Covert, as he erroneously envisaged it (Stukeley 1743, pl. XXV)

beginning of the work reported here, the remains of the Beckhampton Avenue were so vestigial that its former existence was a matter of personal faith, or of doubt, depending on the reliance one placed on the antiquarian record. This situation arose because only a single detailed account of the monument was produced prior to its almost total destruction in the late medieval and early post-medieval periods. This was provided by William Stukeley, and resulted from observations made by him during his visits to Avebury in 1723 and 1724 (Stukeley 1743, 34–6) (Figures 2.32 and 2.33). With one brief exception (Twining 1723), the avenue was not mentioned by earlier antiquaries such as Aubrey; even during the period of Stukeley's fieldwork it comprised an incomplete line of fallen and recently removed stones running through a patchwork of fields, paddocks, gardens and farmyards (see Appendix 1). By the late 18th century only one Avenue stone ('Eve') and one stone of the Longstones Cove ('Adam') remained upright (Figure 2.34).

Given the existence of only one detailed account of its former route and the highly fragmentary state of its physical remains, it is hardly surprising that the status of the Beckhampton Avenue should become the subject of debate following the publication of

Figure 2.34. The vestiges of the Beckhampton Avenue. Colt Hoare's view of the Longstones (Colt Hoare 1821, pl. XV)

Stukeley's *Abury* in 1743. Matters were made worse by Stukeley's conflation of his field observations with developing theories on Druidic patriarchal religion and religious symbolism. He came to envisage the whole Avebury complex as a single symbolic structure comprising a circle (Avebury) traversed by a serpent (the avenues): an abstracted representation of God's existence and creative power (Ucko *et al.* 1991, 86–91). The resulting *Dracontium* or serpent temple *required* the Beckhampton Avenue to form its tail, placing a considerable burden on a series of fragmentary archaeological traces whose interpretation as an avenue was to many equivocal. While the serpent temple format was accepted by a number of late 18th- and early 19th-century antiquaries (Figure 2.35), including Richard Colt Hoare (1821) and Henry Browne (1833; see also Gillings and Pollard 2004, 159–62), by the second half of the 19th century doubts were being raised over the reliability of Stukeley's observations. In the context of the Beckhampton Avenue, the surviving physical evidence – two standing stones in a field 1.3km to the west of Avebury – hardly provided confidence. In understated tones, William Long remarked that 'it must... be admitted that the evidence for this western avenue is of a much less decisive character than that for the eastern' (Long 1858a, 332). Canon Jackson and the Rev. W.C. Lukis went further, suggesting that Stukeley had forced ambiguous and poor quality evidence to fit his theories and that the Beckhampton Avenue had never existed (Lukis 1881–3a; b). In two papers published in 1881–3, Lukis openly attacked the legacy of Stukeley, considering the Beckhampton Avenue to be part of the 'snake dream of the fanciful doctor' (Lukis 1881–3a, 156). Lukis's skepticism arose in part because of Aubrey's silence on the matter, and also as a result of the awkward arrangement in Stukeley's scheme whereby the avenue had to cross the Winterbourne. He considered the stones making up its course to be merely 'stray' naturally occurring sarsens, while the Longstones were elements of a separate circle (Lukis 1881–3a, 155). Over the next century there followed a lengthy game of academic 'table tennis' in which opinions over the existence or otherwise of the avenue were batted back and forth with little attempt to resolve the issue through serious fieldwork.

Stukeley did have his supporters. A.L. Lewis

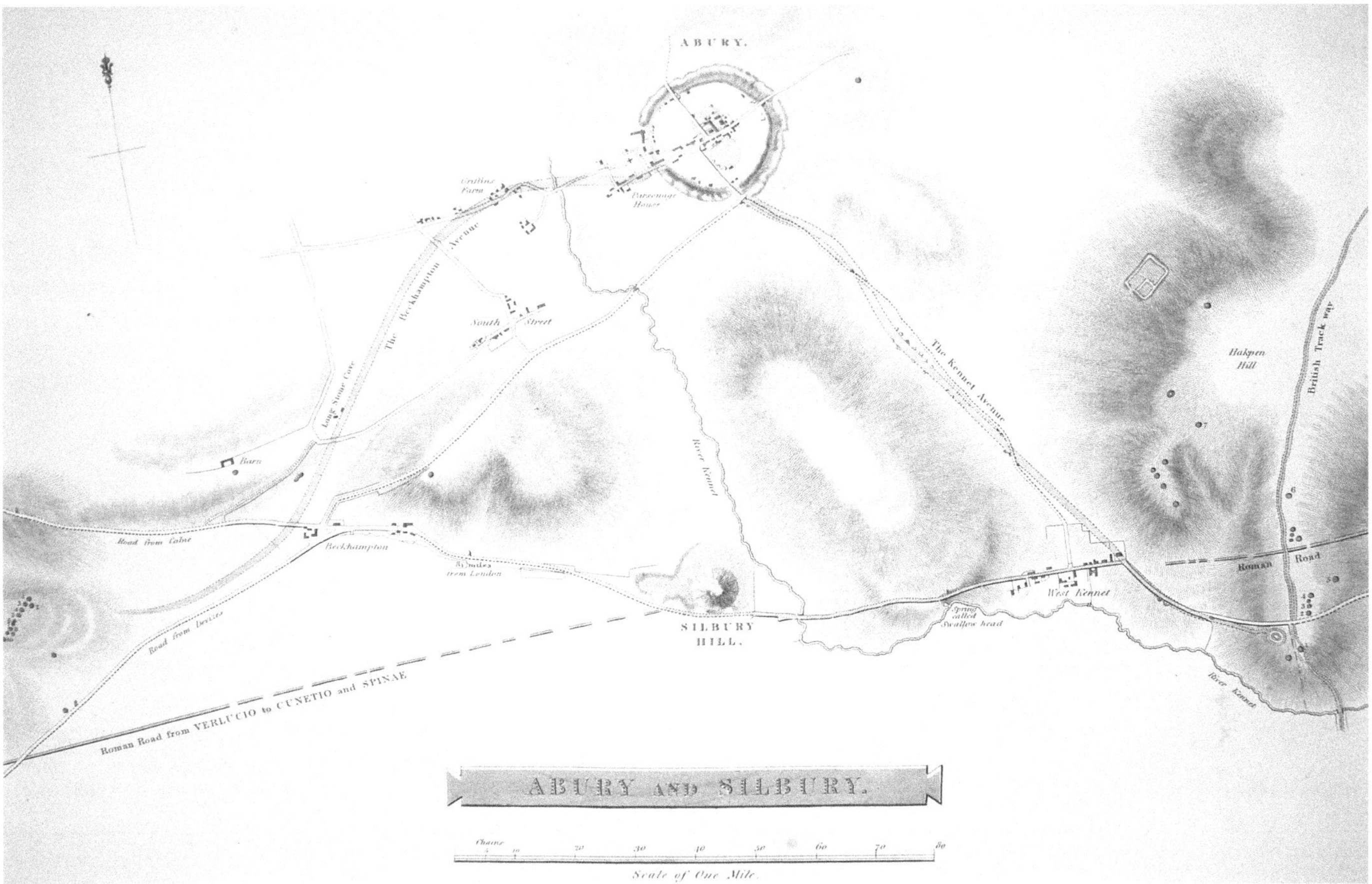

Figure 2.35. Colt Hoare's (1821) plan of the Avebury complex, much influenced by the fieldwork of Stukeley. Note the then presumed extension of the Beckhampton Avenue beyond its terminal at the Longstones (Colt Hoare 1821, pl. X)

(1891) attempted a vindication, noting how careful an observer Stukeley was; although he accepted Lukis's interpretation of the Longstones as a circle (curiously, on a similar plan to that of the Longstones enclosure), and provided a gap in the avenue where it crossed the Winterbourne (Lewis 1891, pl. XX). A notable attempt to address the issue through empirical observation rather than rhetoric was provided in the 1870s by the then vicar of Avebury, Bryan King. He noted the occurrence of patches of sarsen flakes (stone breaking debris) along the postulated avenue line in Longstones Field, and of large sarsens that could have formed components of the avenue being used as supports for the bridge over the Winterbourne (King 1879, 383). In accounting for the better survival of the West Kennet Avenue, King highlighted the discrepancy in the demand for building stone that fuelled megalith destruction between the areas to the south and west of Avebury. Since fewer cottages and property walls occurred between Avebury and Kennet than between the henge and Longstones Field, demand for sarsen as a building material was considerably less along the course of the West Kennet Avenue, and so pressure to break up megaliths less intense than along the line of the Beckhampton Avenue (King 1879, 381).

Renewed speculation over the status of the Beckhampton Avenue came in the 1930s as a direct result of a new campaign of fieldwork on the West Kennet Avenue and Avebury henge, led by Alexander Keiller (Smith 1965). Keiller had earlier purchased many of Stukeley's papers, an important source of evidence that eventually guided his excavations at Avebury (Ucko *et al.* 1991, 246). Initially, the Beckhampton Avenue was considered 'problematical' (Piggott 1935, 27). In their interim report on the West Kennet Avenue fieldwork, Keiller and Piggott followed Lukis in considering the Longstones to be part of an independent stone circle with its own short avenue, citing parallels with the circle complex at Stanton Drew, Somerset (Keiller and Piggott 1936, 417). Matters changed radically a year later with the confirmation through excavation of a western entrance into the Avebury henge.

As a result, Keiller now talked of the 'increasing probability... of the existence in some form of the 'Beckhampton Avenue'' (Keiller 1939, 232). A decade earlier, Keiller and O G S Crawford had attempted to resolve the issue of the avenue through a pioneering use of aerial photography. The results were negative, though photographs were published of its postulated course from Avebury as far as Beckhampton Field (Crawford and Keiller 1928, 209–14, pls. XXXVI–XXXVIII).

As a curious aside, the 1935 *Shell Guide to Wiltshire* included a note by the author Edith Oliver that 'the traditional Beckhampton avenue has not yet been recovered, though it was seen standing, some twenty years ago, by a clairvoyant' (Byron 1935, 41). She may have been referring to herself, for in her memoirs, published four years later, Oliver described a strange occurrence during a 'wet, dreary night' in 1916. While driving from Devizes to Swindon she left the main road at Beckhampton and found herself proceeding down the centre of an avenue of large standing sarsens heading towards Avebury. This was not the West Kennet Avenue. Upon reaching the monument she climbed the bank to observe the lights and sound of a fair in full swing. After the rain became too much to bear, she went back to her car and drove on. Nine years later she discovered that not only had the last fair taken place in Avebury around 1850, but of the section of the Beckhampton Avenue she claimed to have driven down no trace remained.

Returning to firmer ground, in publishing the results of Keiller's fieldwork, Isobel Smith cited the reliability of Stukeley as an observer and considered the grounds for accepting the existence of the Beckhampton Avenue to be strong, although remarked that 'the question of its full extent and precise relationship to the Longstones must remain open' (Smith 1965, 217). Other prehistorians, such as Aubrey Burl (1979, 191), took a similar stance.

A more guarded view was given in Ucko, Hunter, Clark and David's reassessment of the early antiquarian record relating to Avebury (Ucko *et al.* 1991, 195–9). This followed a programme of resistivity and magnetometer survey, undertaken on the avenue line in the south-west corner of Longstones Field in January 1989, by the then Ancient Monuments Laboratory of English Heritage. The results were styled as inconclusive even though stone settings were, with hindsight, detected (see below). The conclusion was that 'these findings plainly neither disprove not [sic] support Stukeley's firm assertion of the presence of an Avenue' (Ucko *et al.* 1991, 198). Noting that Stukeley saw 'only three stones standing in the entire length of the avenue between the Longstones and Avebury, in an area probably scattered with naturally occurring sarsens', they posed the now familiar question of whether these alignments were fortuitous, or even invented, or whether Stukeley's recording was 'indeed a remarkable feat of intuitive fieldwork and observation' (Ucko *et al.* 1991, 244)?

Continued uncertainty took its toll. By the last decade of the 20th century the status of the Beckhampton Avenue was so ambiguous that it was often excluded from maps and reconstruction drawings of the later Neolithic of the region (*e.g.* Whittle 1997b, fig. 87; Thomas 1999b, fig. 9.4; Parker Pearson 2000, fig. 17.5). In many respects, the problem has not been a lack of fieldwork since Stukeley's time, it is simply the kind of small-scale work that has taken place. The Rev. King's pioneering 'fieldwalking' was neither systematic, nor backed by a plan of the sarsen scatters he encountered. Maud Cunnington's excavation at the Longstones – following the fall of 'Adam' in 1911 – was limited to the clearing out of one stone-hole, and did not exploit the opportunity to further explore the putative avenue (Cunnington 1913). Observations made by the Vatcher's of a buried avenue stone and stone burning pits along and to the west of Avebury High Street in the early 1970s (Vatcher 1971a; b) were undertaken in a 'rescue' capacity. Even research excavations on the line of the avenue in Butler's Field, although undertaken with other objectives in mind, were too small to demonstrate or refute its presence (Evans *et al.* 1993).

Survey and excavation on the Beckhampton Avenue and Longstones Cove, 1989–2003

Confirmation of the existence of the Beckhampton Avenue and Longstones Cove was provided by a programme of geophysical survey and excavation undertaken over the course of three seasons (1999, 2000 and 2003). An earlier attempt to locate the avenue through

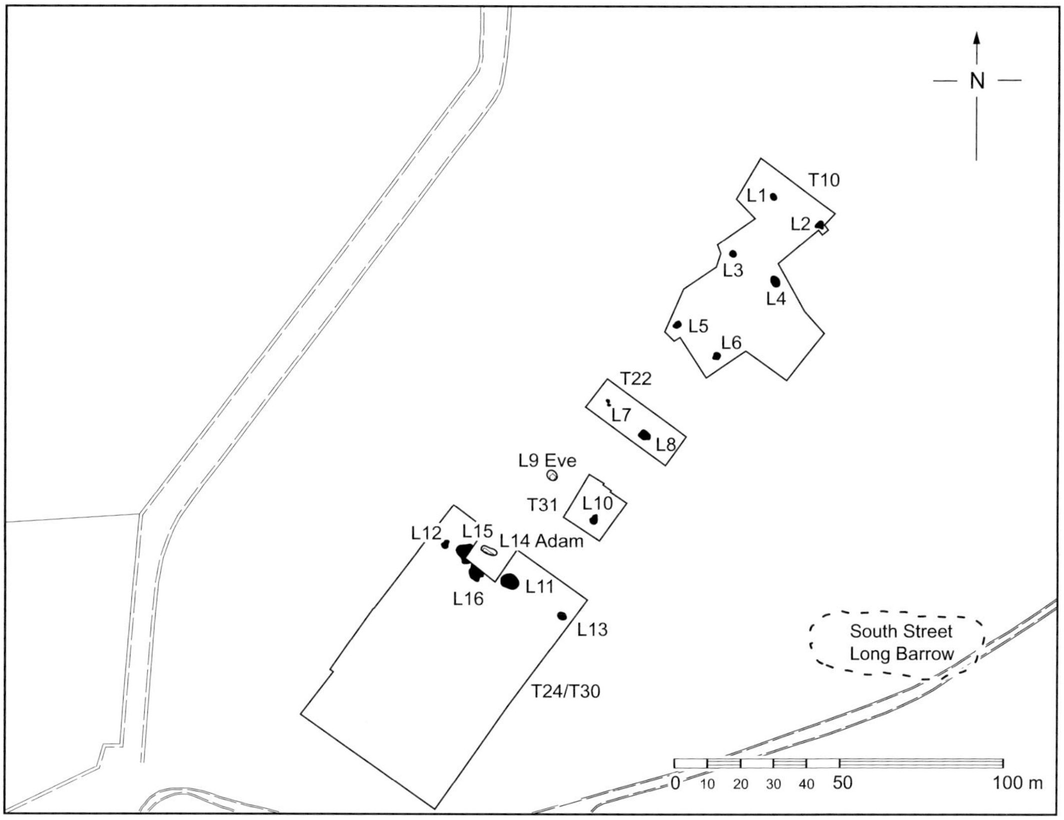

Figure 2.36. Excavated and surviving features of the Beckhampton Avenue and Longstones Cove in the SW of Longstones Field

earth resistance and magnetometer survey is reported in Ucko *et al.* (1991, 196–9) and below. The work was focused on the western half of the avenue in Longstones Field, between 0.8–1.3km to the south-west of the Avebury henge, in an area less encumbered by modern houses, farm buildings, roads and field divisions than that to the east (Figure 2.36). Much of the eastern section of the avenue is currently obscured by development along Avebury High Street and farm buildings to the west of the Winterbourne. A section of *c.*300m length does run through open ground in Butler's Field and 'Small Paddock' on either side of the Winterbourne, though is sealed by deposits of alluvium of the West Overton Formation and extensive traces of medieval settlement (Evans *et al.* 1993, 147–62).

Geophysical survey and the Beckhampton Avenue and Longstones Cove

Andrew David

The geophysical surveys of relevance here were undertaken in 1989, 1999 and 2000. Having discussed the survey results for the Longstones enclosure above, we will here concentrate on the results as they relate to the identification of stone positions, or former stone positions, in this area.

As Stukeley's depictions of the Beckhampton Avenue anchored it to the Longstones, the 1989 earth resistance survey was concentrated in this area, extending to the south-west and the north-east, in order to cover a sufficiently generous zone to try and locate further settings. The magnetometer survey results were dismissed at the time (see above), with rather more optimism placed on the earth resistance survey (Ucko *et al.* 1991, 196–9). The interpretation of the survey drew attention to 'three weak negative anomalies disposed at the corners of a suitably oriented right-angled triangle', some 90m to the north-east of Eve, and went on: 'if an avenue exists, then these anomalies, albeit very faint, might be taken to be suggestive of two stone positions on the N side of the alignment and a single one on the opposite side'. A speculative alignment for the avenue was drawn on this basis (*ibid.*, pl. 63B) but the general conclusion was reached that the 'geophysical results at present provide no support for the existence of a Beckhampton stone avenue' and went on to consider the conjecture that the Longstones might have been part of a monument unconnected with the henge (*ibid.*, 196).

The discovery of the Longstones enclosure in 1997 drew attention back to this area and it was suggested by the authors of this report that the earth resistance anomalies referred to above should be tested by excavation. In advance of this the immediate area of the anomalies was re-surveyed by earth resistance in order to confirm the presence of the anomalies and to accurately locate them for excavation. Accordingly, a 60 × 60m square was established over the area and surveyed in May 1999 with a Geoscan RM15 instrument, using the Twin Probe configuration, mobile probe spacings of 0.5 and 1.0m, and with readings taken at 0.5m intervals. The results (Figure 2.37) confirmed and amplified the previous findings. The negative anomalies were re-located with great clarity and, in addition, a positive anomaly (weakly present in the 1989 data) was located in the remaining corner of the rectangle. It was concluded that 'together, these four anomalies fall at the corners of an approximate rectangle of sides (approx 15m × 23m) roughly similar to equivalent distances between stone positions on the West Kennet Avenue (approx 17m × 24m)'… 'Taken with the fact that the north-western pair of 1999 resistivity anomalies align with Adam and Eve, it is difficult to resist the speculation that Stukeley's avenue may be a reality' (David 1999). The latter report also speculated that a pair of previously overlooked weak high resistance anomalies present in the 1989 data to the south-west 'might perhaps represent a further pair of stone positions' (*ibid.*). Happily, excavation of all six anomalies subsequently confirmed that they did indeed represent a sequence of three pairs of former uprights (L1–L6), setting the scene for returning the Beckhampton Avenue to credibility.

The four anomalies re-located in 1999 had similar shapes and dimensions, being roughly circular and with diameters of about 2.5–3.0m. The relative low resistance of the three negative anomalies (L1, L3 and L4) was consistent with the response from pits, the fill of which was relatively damp compared to the surrounding subsoil and chalk. This contrast will vary according to prevailing moisture conditions and was more accentuated in the survey data of May 1999, than that collected in January of 1989. The fourth anomaly, being high resistance, matched the type of anomaly already encountered on the line of the West Kennet Avenue (Ucko *et al.* 1991, pl. 59) and was found to be the response to a substantial buried stone [407]. The pair of high resistance anomalies at L5 and L6 were likewise found to be responses to buried stones ([424] and [435]).

Stone [407] at L2 provided an opportunity in the following year to test the response of such a target to the use of ground penetrating radar (GPR). Once its stone-hole and burial pit had been excavated and recorded these features and the stone were reburied, providing a fully documented target for the GPR. A 5 × 5m square was then centred over the site of the stone and was traversed at 0.1m intervals by a PulseEKKO PE1000 GPR using an antenna with a centre frequency of 900 MHz. A second set of orthogonal transects was also made, and the area was re-surveyed with the earth resistance meter. The GPR results are shown in Figure 2.38 in which the data is illustrated as a series of amplitude time slices which show the radar reflections from successively deeper levels (averaged within successive 2ns windows) down to approximately 1.2m. A representative profile is also shown (Figure 2.39). As might be expected, the stone is a strong reflector, with a high amplitude response clearly identifying its overall triangular shape and its tilted orientation. Such data could be used in future to provide an approximate 'virtual' three-dimensional likeness of the stone. There is some slight evidence for additional but lower amplitude reflections to the south of the stone at a depth of about 0.8m, which may be a response to the stone-hole and post-hole features here. However, the geometry of reflections from such features can be expected to be complex and obscured by the stronger response to the adjacent stone surfaces.

GPR survey using the same methodology was also undertaken over the presumed site of L10, later excavated to expose a small and shallow stone-hole (F.106) adjacent to a burning pit dug across the infilled Longstones enclosure ditch, but was unable to distinguish these features. A third 5 × 5m trial GPR survey was placed over a slight high resistance anomaly and speculative stone setting 32m south-west of L13, but a negative response here was corroborated by an absence of any features on excavation (Trench 24).

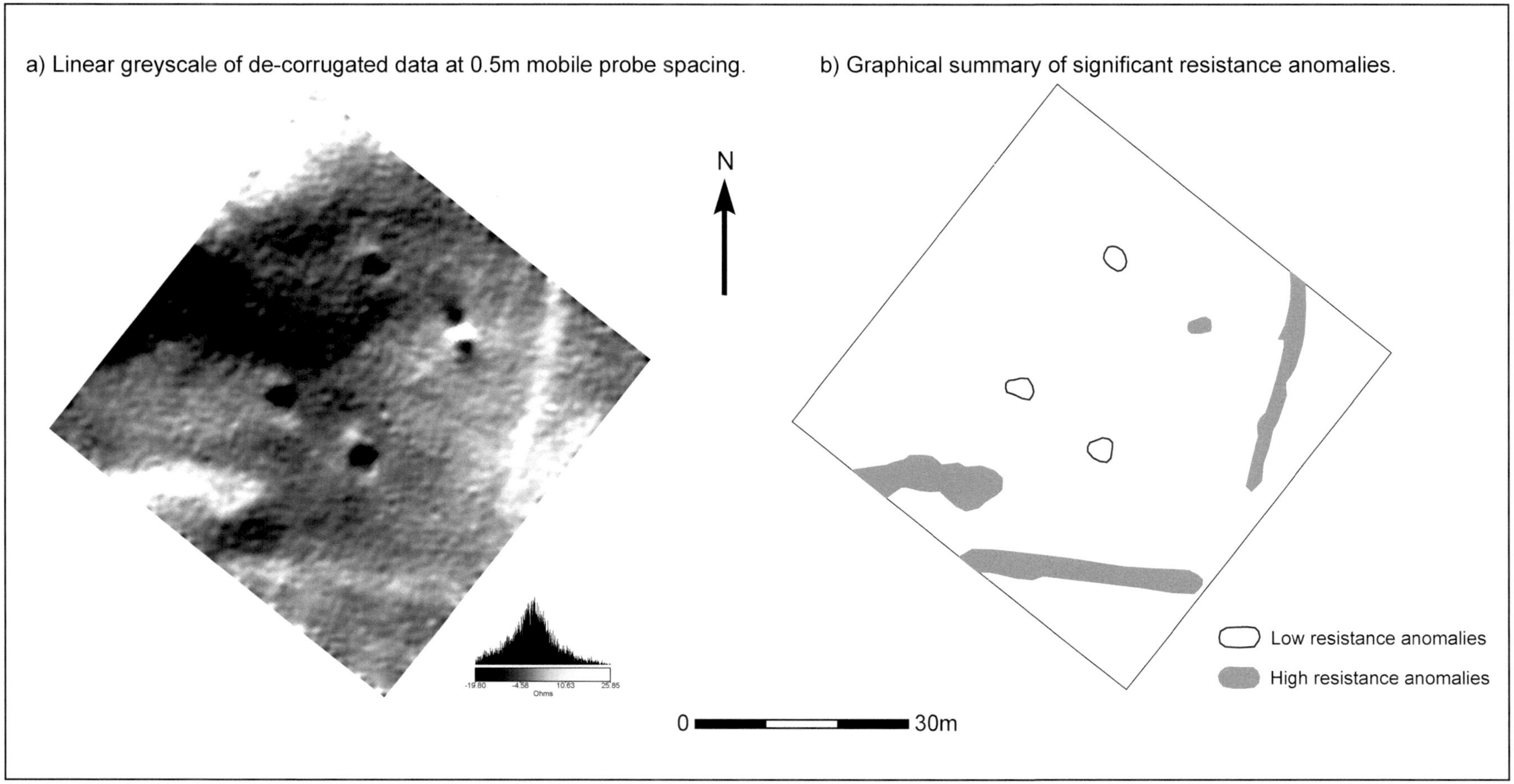

Figure 2.37. Earth resistance survey of stone placements L1–L4. Twin Electrode configuration; mobile probes spacing 0.5m; reading interval 0.5m. Directional filter

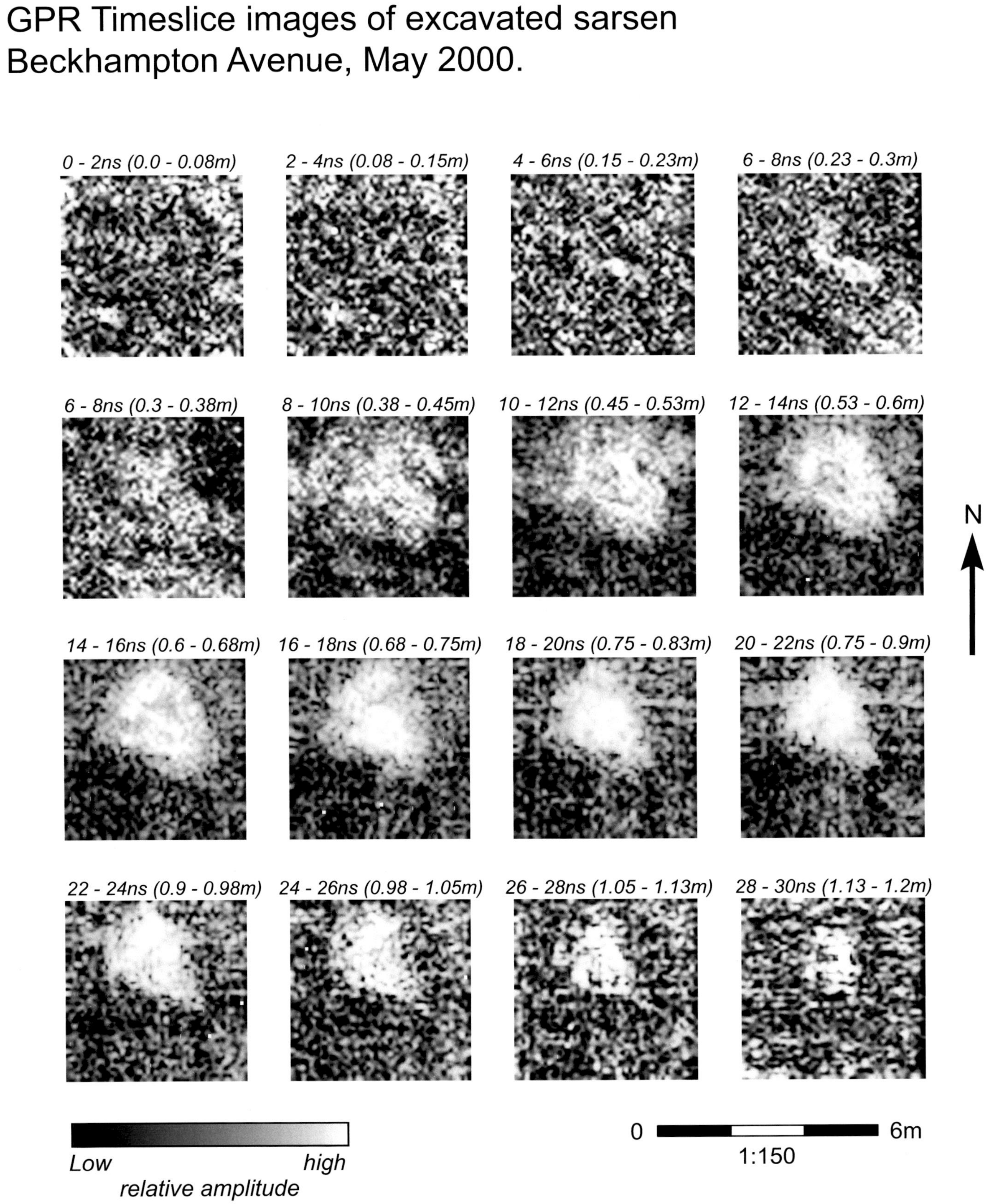

Figure 2.38. Ground Penetrating Radar survey over L2 (stone [407]): amplitude time slices

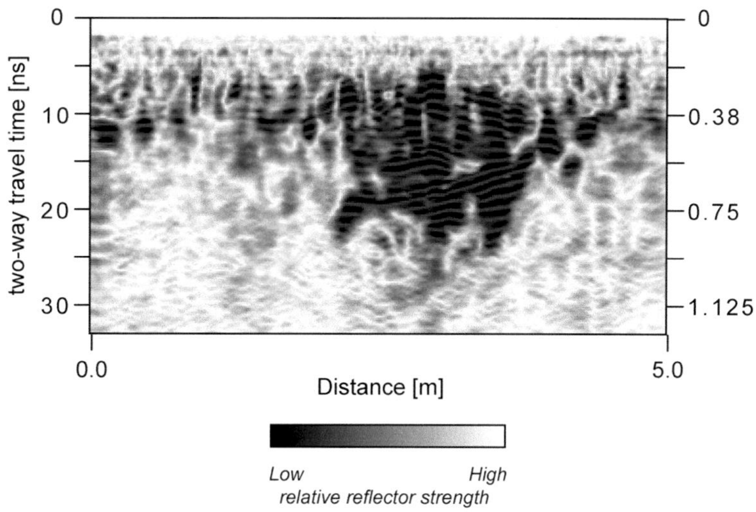

Figure 2.39. Representative GPR profile over L2 (stone [407]), illustrating reflection from the upper and lower surfaces of the stone

The GPR result over stone [407] at setting L2 clearly confirms earlier evidence from similar survey over stones on the West Kennet Avenue (Christian Pierce and Colin Shell pers. comm.) that buried megaliths in these circumstances are detectable in this way and can be crudely imaged in three dimensions.

In May 2000 the previous year's 60 × 60m grid square of detailed earth resistance measurements over settings L1–L4 was extended south-westwards to the corner of Longstones Field. The resulting 60 × 250m corridor fully encompassed the projected alignment of the Avenue up to and well beyond the Longstones to the field edge (Figure 2.40). The new survey data confirmed previous results – in particular detecting some 45m of the ditched enclosure (see above) and the lattice of former ridge and furrow, overlain by the texture of recent cultivation (trending NNW-SSE). Also, a linear low resistance anomaly parallel to and 20m out from the south-western field edge was re-located. Rather than a trackway as previously surmised (Ucko *et al.* 1991, 198; David 2000) this proved on subsequent excavation to be a 4–5m wide ditch (F.106) of complex construction and re-cutting, interpreted as a Late Bronze Age or Iron Age linear boundary (see Chapter 7). Interestingly, the May 2000 data included a new feature – a very distinct linear low resistance anomaly passing from a field entrance on South Street across the field and running on between the Longstones. This was an ephemeral anomaly caused by the access track to the previous year's excavation huts and by the recent passage of farm equipment, the resulting soil compaction raising moisture retention and electrical conductivity.

Elsewhere within this survey area there was little if any evidence for stone settings L7, L8 or L10, although the vicinity of the latter coincided with a broader area of low resistance readings (partially investigated by GPR: see above). Beyond Adam, to the south-west, no stone positions were indicated with any certainty, although at the time it was very tentatively suggested that one additional low resistance and a pair of high resistance anomalies (approximately 35m, 45m and 48m from Adam, respectively) might be significant (David 2000, fig. 2). Around the Longstones themselves, however, the response was more promising (Figure 2.41).

Both Adam and Eve were linked on their north-eastern sides to large areas of pronounced high resistance. The anomalous readings around Eve fell within a roughly circular area about 6m in diameter. The disturbance around Adam was more extensive, covering some 10 × 6m. In each case the high readings were probably the result of a number of factors – the stone footings themselves, as well as adjacent rubble (packing stones and field clearance material). The immediate surroundings of Adam, which fell in 1911, were excavated in 1912 and the stone re-erected with considerable difficulty and set in concrete (Cunnington 1913; Burl 1979, 68), activities which will also have contributed to the high resistance values here. However, these anomalies were not explored by excavation and therefore remain unexplained.

To the south-west of the high resistance readings around Eve was an amorphous area of lowered readings (approximately 10 × 5m), also seen in the 1989 data. The edges of this area were diffuse and unclear, and were also complicated by the intersection here of a former cultivation alignment as well as the vehicle track. No obvious explanation suggests itself although it is possible that some form of large and shallow pit, or undated excavation, may be responsible.

Outside the halo of disturbance around Adam, to the south-east and north-west respectively, were two distinct circular areas of low resistance readings, each about 5m in diameter. Both of these had been seen, but with less clear definition, in 1989 with the southern one interpreted then as a possible

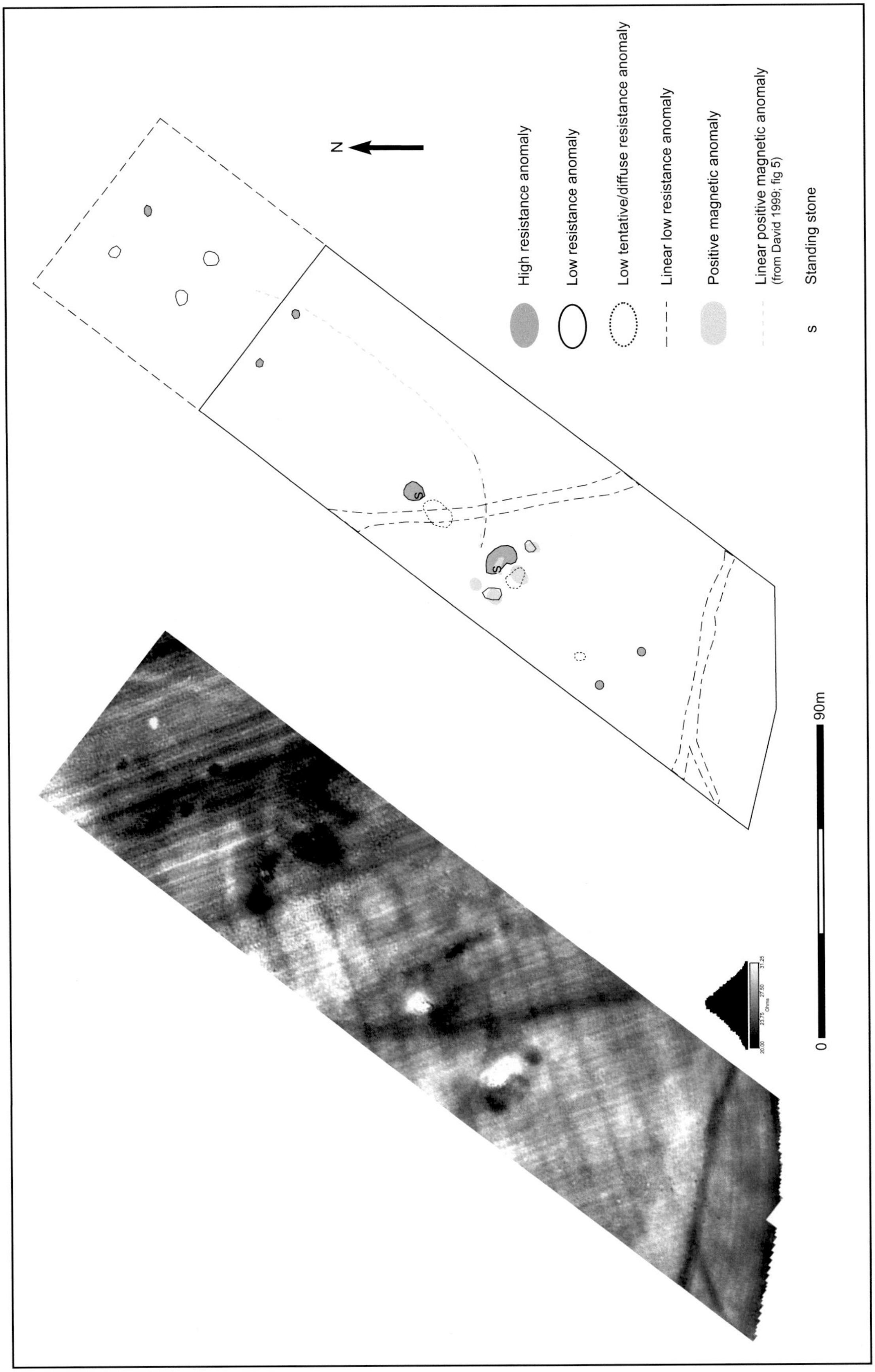

Figure 2.40. greyscale plot of earth resistance data along the avenue alignment in the SW corner of Longstones Field (covering settings L1–L16), and interpretation

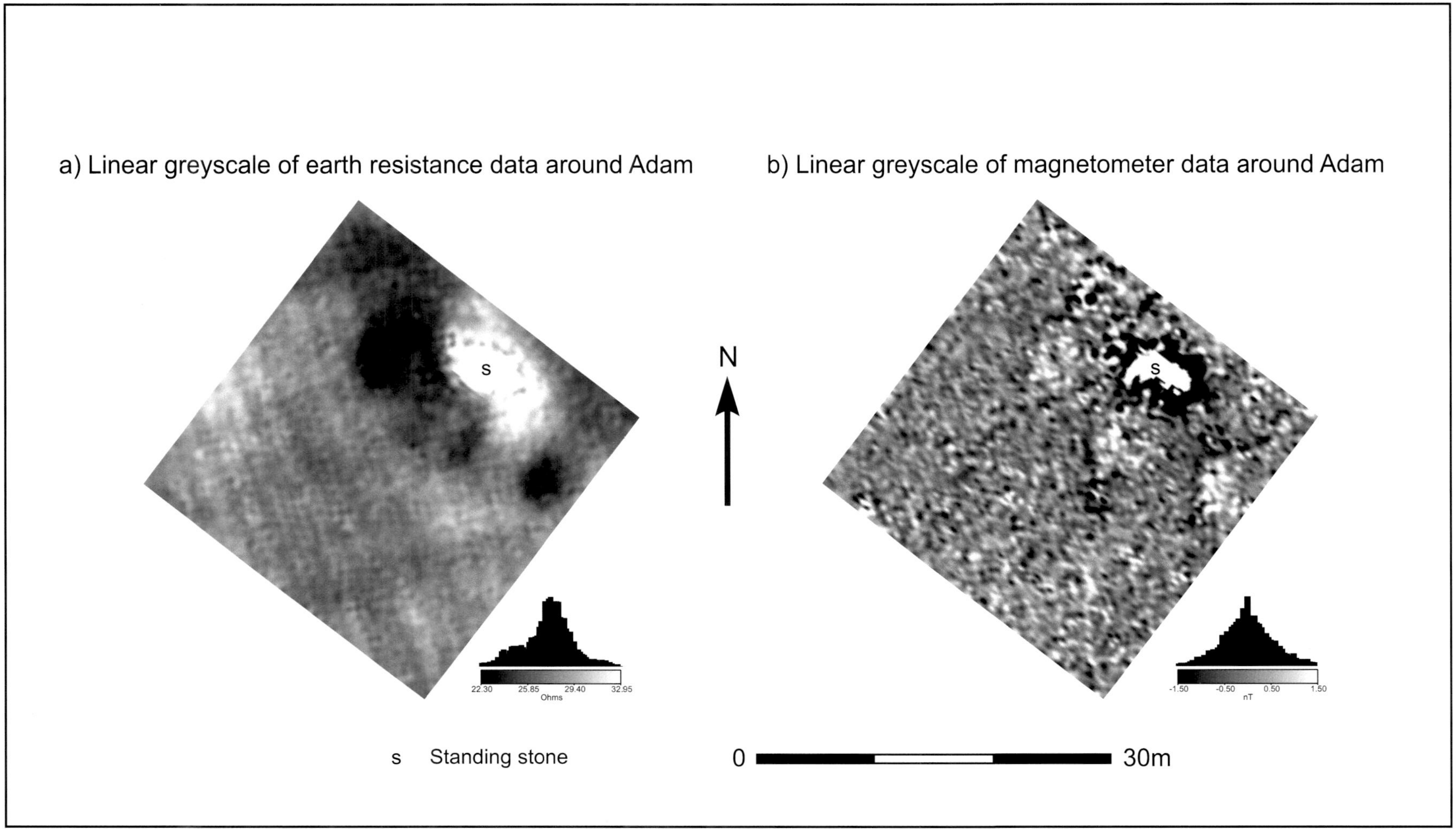

Figure 2.41. (a) greyscale plot of earth resistance data around the Longstones, and (b) magnetometer data from the same area

stone setting (Ucko *et al.* 1991, pl. 63B). Between the two was a third less compact area of lowered readings (perhaps itself composed of two parts). Together, these anomalies were each suggestive of underlying large and shallow pits – broadly comparable to the anomalies detected over the burning pits for L1, L3 and L4, although smaller.

The surroundings of Adam were also surveyed by magnetometry (FM36 fluxgate gradiometer; readings at 0.5 × 0.25m). The three main areas of lowered resistance were found to be characterised by slight but discernible concentrations of marginally raised magnetic activity (approx ±3 nT). A fourth area of magnetic disturbance seemed to be distinguishable to the north-west of Adam, but because it was less focused than the others and without any corresponding resistance anomaly was only very conjecturally interpreted as a possible pit. In the event, no feature was present here, and the magnetic activity may have been related to burnt material connected to the destruction of L15 in the topsoil.

Excavation later that year showed that the main anomalies were indeed the responses to three huge destruction pits (L11, L15 and L16: see below), their fillings retaining moisture as well as slightly magnetic burnt material (sarsen fragments). This was in contrast to the two outlying stone-holes (F.54 and F.83) of settings L12 and L13 which were not detected – being much smaller, filled mostly with chalky rubble, and unassociated with any burnt material.

In summary, the value of geophysical survey in the exploration for former stone settings and associated features is clear following this work. However, their elucidation by this means alone is by no means straightforward owing to the considerable variation in the nature of the features concerned and the constraints this imposes on their detection. Together with the ambiguities of the physical and documentary record, the geophysical re-location of former stone settings can be particularly difficult, and is often of itself unable to provide unequivocal solutions. Whilst the 1989 surveys were able to speculate on the presence of some stone settings, there was insufficient evidence to confirm the existence of the avenue, or to characterise the Cove settings; and whilst a part of the enclosure circuit was detected, its larger pattern was not.

Reviewing the earlier geophysical datasets in the light of excavation and more recent survey has been rewarding. Whilst geophysical survey and aerial photography have surely been indispensable, it is also apparent that resolving the problems posed by the remnants of the Longstones and the avenue lies in the use of complementary prospecting methodologies in tandem with selective excavation. Hopefully, the scope for applying further remote sensing technologies for the continuing elucidation of patterns in Longstones Field is not yet exhausted.

Excavation

Investigation Methodology

Avenue features were revealed in five trenches: four in the south-west corner of Longstones Field (Trenches 10, 22, 24 and 31); and in a single trench 320m to the north-east, close to the modern settlement of Avebury Trusloe (Figures 2.5 and 2.36). These have enabled the avenue course to be established over a distance of 500m, from its original start/end point immediately beyond the earlier enclosure to the area north of Trusloe Cottages. Trench 10 was originally intended to cover a regular 50 × 50m area centred over the four stone pits located on the 1999 geophysical survey. However, a decision was taken to extend the trench several metres to the south-west in order to investigate two further anomalies faintly visible on the 1989 geophysical survey. This extension to the trench, which with hindsight proved highly productive, combined with a lack of machining time to regularise its edges, resulted in its unintended erratic plan (Figure 2.42). Trench 22 was laid out to investigate the intervening pair of stones between those excavated during 1999 and the one remaining standing avenue stone, 'Eve'. Geophysical survey had failed to locate the positions of stones or stone destruction features here, suggesting, erroneously as it turned out, a gap in the avenue line. Trench 24 was positioned to explore features relating to the Longstones Cove recorded by Stukeley, and Trench 31 the pair to 'Eve'.

Although no stone settings were revealed to the south-west of the Cove in Trench 24 during the 2000 season, confirmation that the avenue did in fact terminate here was required. Therefore, in 2003 an area of 50 × 40m (Trench 30) was excavated immediately to the south-west of Trench 24. This was designed to expose features over a distance of 67m to the west of the Cove. Working on the basis of a longitudinal spacing between stones of 21–30m, as encountered on the excavated portions of the West Kennet and Beckhampton Avenues, the combined lengths of Trenches 24 and 30 were sufficient to expose two or three stone pairs if the avenue did indeed continue. Once the ploughsoil had been removed, the only features visible were a series of ploughmarks, the truncated bases of lengths of medieval furrow, and a linear feature identified in the 1989 geophysical survey that proved to be a ditch system of later prehistoric date. No stone-holes, stone destruction pits or stone burials were present, providing conclusive proof that the avenue did not continue in its known form beyond the Longstones Cove. The Trusloe excavation was intended to tie down the position of the avenue close to its mid-point.

Following ploughsoil stripping, the exposed surfaces were cleaned through a combination of shovel-scraping and trowelling of selected areas. A number of features were revealed cut into the chalk (Figures 2.43–2.45), prominent amongst which were sets of medieval ridge-and-furrow. That in Trench 10 ran north-south across the area, whilst in Trenches 22, 24 and 30 the system was aligned east-west. In neither instance did the alignment of the ridge-and-furrow seem to respect the position of the avenue or Cove, though individual furrows would occasionally terminate or be interrupted by the location of individual stones. In general, the former positions of stones were not difficult to locate. Often they were marked by oval patches of ploughsoil, charcoal and sarsen fragments filling the tops of post-medieval destruction pits, while stone-holes were sometimes identifiable by soil fills and protruding sarsen packing stones. The process of feature recognition was more difficult in four instances where the chalk backfill of medieval/post-medieval burial pits and that of deliberately infilled stone-holes did not show readily against the weathered chalk natural. A period of weathering, and any increase in ground moisture content through rain, dramatically increased the visibility of these features. In the eastern trench of Longstones south-west and at Avebury Trusloe the extent of any disturbance into the 'natural' could also be discerned by the disruption it caused in the regular pattern of involution hollows permeating the chalk and coombe rock.

Remarkably little prehistoric worked flint

Figure 2.42. (left) Aerial view of the 1999 excavations in Longstones Field, looking NE. Buried stones of the Beckhampton Avenue and post-Medieval stone burning pits are clearly visible

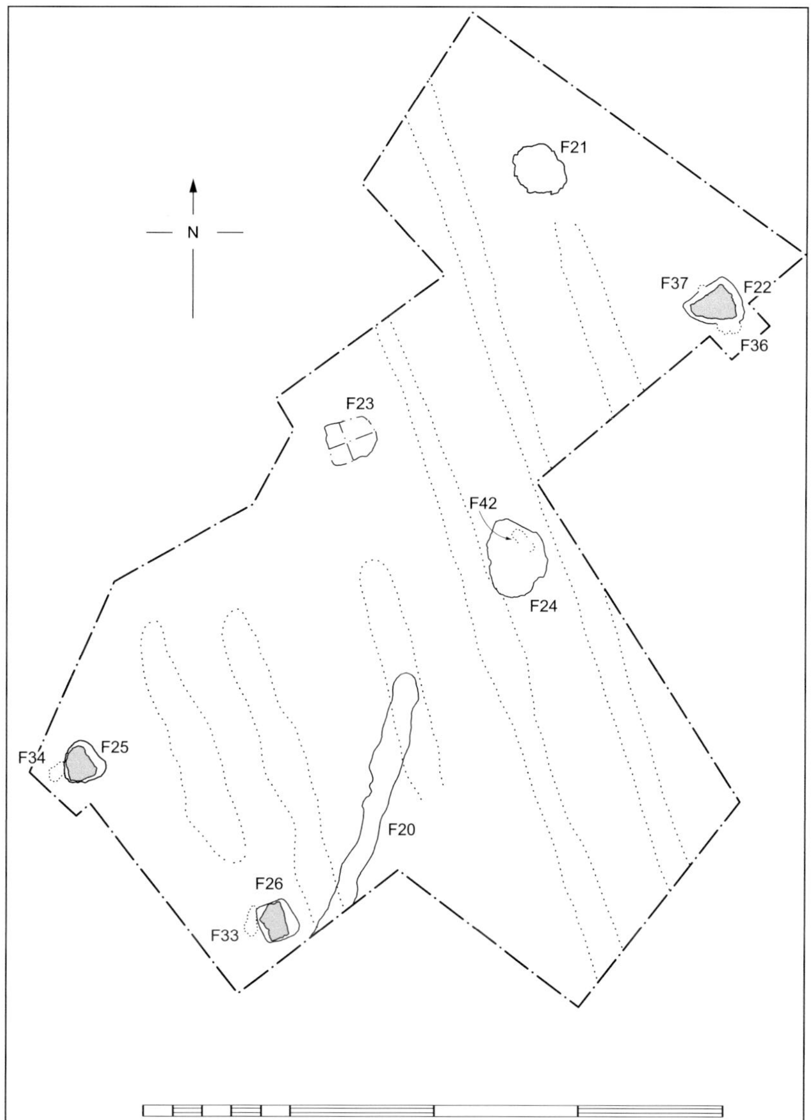

Figure 2.43. (below) Avenue features, enclosure ditch (F.20) and ridge-and-furrow (dotted outline) in Trench 10. Stones shaded

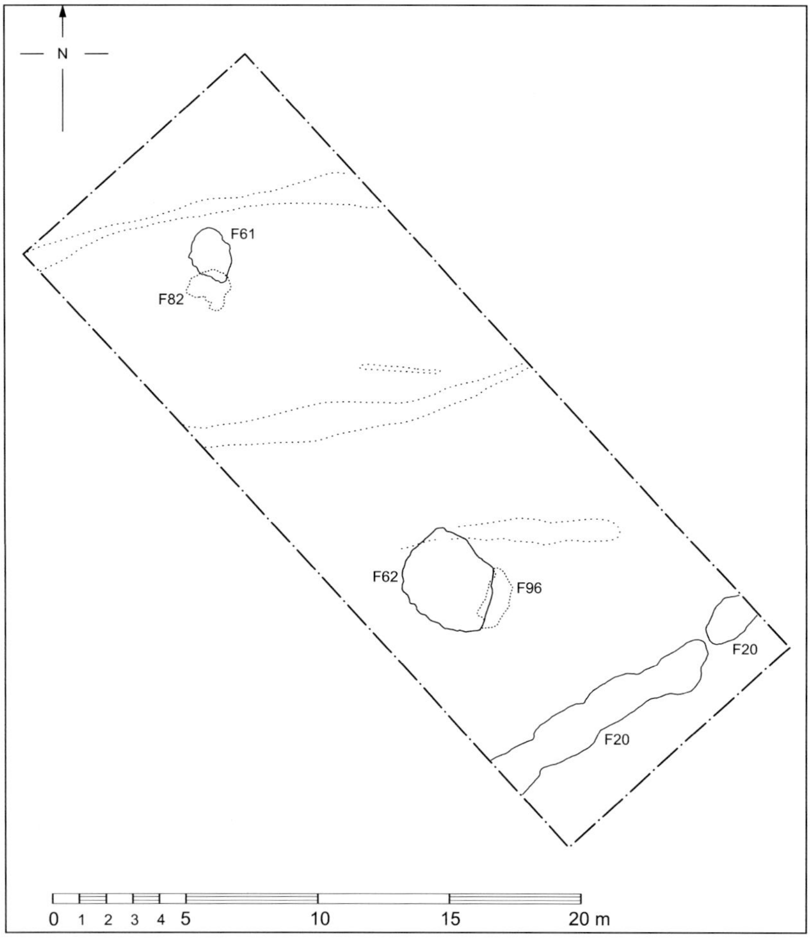

Transverse Intervals		Longitudinal Intervals	
L1-2	c.17	L1/2-L3/4	21-22
L3-4	c.15	L3/4-L5/6	30-32
L5-6	16.5	L5/6-L7/8	31-32
L7-8	15.5	L7/8-L9/10	c.28
L9-10	17	L9/10-L11*/12*/13*	c.34
L11-12*	20.5		
L11-13*	20.5		

Figure 2.44. (top) Avenue features, enclosure ditch (F.20) and ridge-and-furrow (dotted outline) in Trench 22

Table 2.18. (bottom) Transverse and longitudinal intervals (in metres) between stone settings of the Beckhampton Avenue. Where possible, measurements have been taken from the centre of stone-holes. Stones marked with an asterisk belong to the pre-Cove setting

was present in the ploughsoil over Longstones Field. An earlier campaign of surface collection by Holgate and Thomas showed the field to be more or less devoid of worked flint (Holgate 1987, fig. 1). During the 1999 season 36 one-metre square test pits were hand dug on a 10m grid over an area of 50 × 50m centred on Trench 10. Hand sorting of the spoil produced fragments of post-medieval pottery, tile and brick, along with a few pieces of sarsen. The only prehistoric finds were 13 pieces of worked flint, densities ranging between 0–2 pieces per test pit. Of those pieces, most were small flakes and chips. One scraper on a thermal flake was present. Two bladelets are possibly of Mesolithic date.

Stone numbers

It is not possible to provide a definitive numbering system for the stones of the Beckhampton Avenue in the way that has been attempted for those of the West Kennet Avenue or Avebury henge (Smith 1965). For the purpose of description, features associated with each stone – the stone-hole, and later burial and destruction pits – have been allocated an overall stone number with a letter prefix. Those in the western part of Longstones Field run from L1–16 (L=Longstones), beginning at the north-east of the investigated section and alternating between the northern and southern sides of the avenue (thus L1 and L2 relate to the first stone pair). Stone settings L1–10 belong to the avenue proper, L11–16 to the Cove and the original terminal (the 'pre-Cove setting'). For Trusloe, the single investigated stone setting is allocated the number T1 (T=Trusloe).

Longstones Field south-west

The 1999–2003 excavations demonstrated that the stretch of the Beckhampton Avenue running to the south-west corner of Longstones Field originally comprised two parallel lines of sarsen megaliths, very similar in format and construction to the restored northern third of the West Kennet Avenue (Smith 1965, 206–9). Along the avenue proper the stones were set in facing pairs, though this format changes at the original terminal (the 'pre-Cove setting') where there existed an arrangement of three stones set perpendicular to the avenue line. Transverse intervals between stones within individual pairs ranged from 15.0–17.0m and longitudinal intervals between pairs from 22.5–32.0m; the longitudinal spacing increasing to 34.0m between stone pair L9/10 and the pre-Cove setting (Table 2.18). These figures compare very closely with the ranges given for the spacing of stones on the West Kennet Avenue (Smith 1965, 206). Given that the distance between the stones within and between pairs does not increase or decrease uniformly along the exposed course of the avenue, such variation could be the result of imprecision in layout, or at least a sense that precise uniformity was not required, rather than conscious design. However, it might also reflect the particularities of avoiding setting stones too close to the backfilled enclosure ditch, though this was evidently not considered a structural problem in the case of stone L10 where the stone-hole nearly cuts the ditch.

Along its excavated length over this part of Longstones Field the avenue takes a straight course, running more or less due NE-SW towards the Longstones Cove (Figure 2.2). Here it is set on relatively level ground. The alignment is such that it runs through the erstwhile eastern entrance of the enclosure, following the flattened south-eastern length of the ditch circuit, though off-set to the south-east in such a manner that a substantial gap (*c.*20m) is left between the stones and the northern ditch terminal. That the enclosure was levelled prior to the construction of this length of the avenue is implied by the position of stones L6 and L10, which are sited on the line of the erstwhile enclosure bank. Other awkward spatial relationships support this sequence: the avenue continues across the south-western arc of the enclosure circuit; and the southern terminal of the main enclosure entrance is traversed by the avenue.

The avenue terminates immediately to the south-west of the earlier enclosure. Here the paired arrangement of stones gives way to a complex setting of six stones, at least three of which (L14–16) belong to the Cove itself, including the sole survivor 'Adam' (Figure 2.45). Using the size of the stone-holes and destruction pits as a proxy, the stones within this setting were more substantial than many of those belonging to the avenue proper (perhaps standing *c.*2.5–3.5m above ground). There is clear evidence of sequence and reworking within this setting. The Cove replaces a primary linear arrangement, 40m across, formed by stones L11–13 (the pre-Cove setting), set at right angles to the avenue with L11 on the line of the avenue's central axis. The stone-holes of L12 and L13 (F.54 and F.83) were deliberately backfilled with clean chalk rubble and, whilst their bases displayed signs of compression consistent with having held stones, it is unlikely that the megaliths within these stood for any length of time. The Cove was a subsequent elaboration, created on a slightly different alignment and utilising the existing and very substantial megalith L11 to form its south-eastern side. The two outlying stones L12 and L13 were most likely taken down at the time when the Cove was constructed and either re-set as part of the Cove, or removed. Although it cannot be demonstrated, it is not impossible that these are the megaliths shown on Stukeley's field plans lying recumbent near the Longstones long barrow.

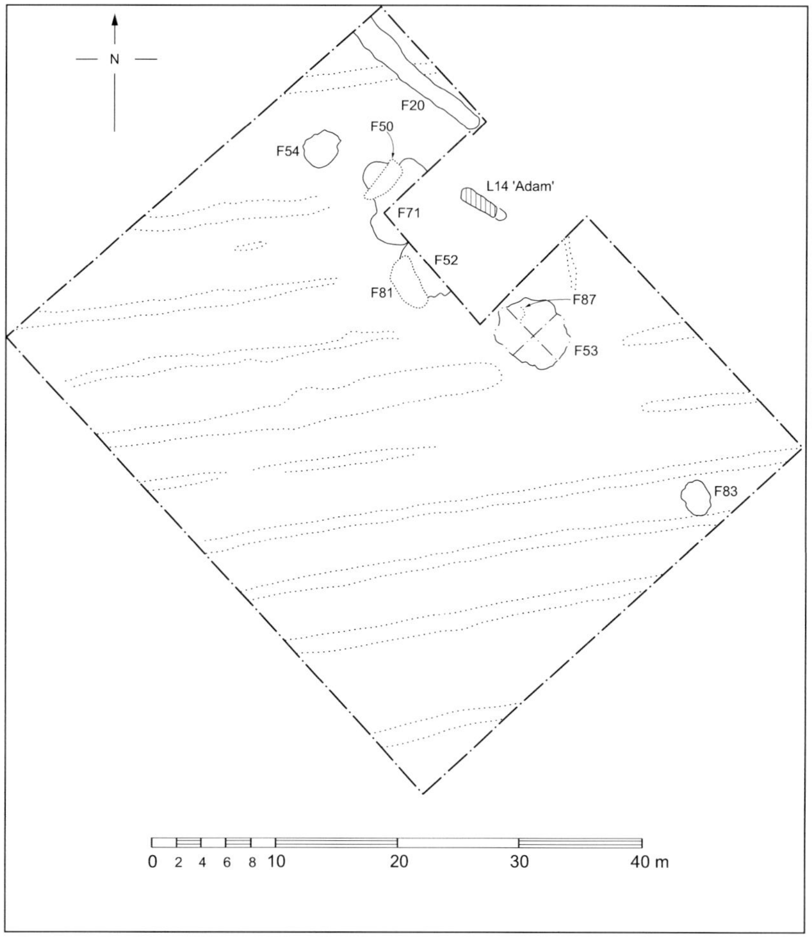

Figure 2.45. Avenue and Cove features, enclosure ditch (F.20) and ridge-and-furrow (dotted outline) in Trench 24

The positions of stones were determined by the presence of the original stone-holes, and later stone burials and destruction pits (Table 2.19). The later, medieval and post-medieval, features are described in detail elsewhere in this volume (Chapters 8–10). A careful search was made for the Neolithic stone-holes, and these were revealed in all but two instances (L1 and L3). Despite the full excavation of destruction pit F.21 (L1), no evidence of a stone-hole was located, although conditions were very dry at the time of excavation, making the recognition of chalky packing fills difficult. Alternatively, the stone-hole was removed during the destruction of the stone. The same may be true in the case of L3.

The stone-holes were mostly oval and relatively shallow, the majority cut only 0.2–0.5m into the chalk. Those of the pre-Cove setting were exceptional in terms of size, ranging between 0.6–0.8m deep, and must have

Table 2.19. Excavated and above-ground features associated with the Beckhampton Avenue and its destruction

Stone no.	Stone-hole	Burial Pit	Destruction Pit	Surviving Stone	Comment
L1	-	-	F.21	No	Stone-hole possibly not recognised
L2	F.35	F.22	-	Yes [407]	
L3	-	? F.23	-	No	Status of F.23 uncertain
L4	F.42	-	F.24	No	
L5	F.34	F.25	-	Yes [424]	
L6	F.33	F.26	-	Yes [435]	
L7	F.82	-	F.61	No	
L8	F.96	-	F.62	No	
L9	Unexc.	-	-	Yes ('Eve')	Surviving upright Avenue stone
L10	F.106	-	F.100	No	
L11	F.87	-	F.53	No	
L12	F.54	-	-	No	
L13	F.83	-	-	No	

held correspondingly larger stones. Beyond thin layers of compressed chalk rubble and occasional small sarsen boulders, little packing material was preserved within them. A setting of split sarsen packing stones remained *in situ* in F.42, single sarsens in F.96 and F.106, and displaced stones in the upper fills of F.33, F.26 and F.82. Most of the shallower stone-holes possessed very irregular sides and bases, pitted with numerous small hollows and undulations. This irregularity is not an original feature, being created in part by burrowing animals penetrating the soft fills of the stone-holes, and through the sides being torn away along with the compacted packing fill during the later toppling of the stones. Settings of post-holes were found cut into the bases of F.33, F.35, F.42, F.96 and F.106, though those in F.96 may relate to the toppling rather than erection of the stone. All were filled with mixtures of chalk rubble and clay loam, lacked any evidence of post-pipes, and clearly represented settings from which posts had been withdrawn. They are equivalent to Keiller's 'anti-friction stakes' (Smith 1965, plate XXXIX), noted during the 1930s excavations at Avebury and the West Kennet Avenue. There they were interpreted as the remains of wooden supports employed to steady the stones during erection and stop them from slipping out of line – in effect more 'friction' than 'anti-friction' devices; though Keiller's terminology has been retained here.

Having been 'decommissioned' in prehistory, the north-west and south-east stone holes of the pre-Cove setting, F.54 and F.83, survived more or less intact. Both features were distinctly different from the other excavated stone-holes by virtue of their pure chalk rubble fills; incidentally making them difficult to detect on the surface (F.83 only appearing after a period of weathering). Morphologically, both were remarkably similar. Deeper, sloping linear recesses on the south sides of both bases may be leverage points to facilitate the erection or removal of the stones, and hollows along the northern edge of F.54 could represent settings for anti-friction stakes. The bases of both were extremely compacted and smoothed, consistent with compression caused by the former presence of large stones. Given the size of the stone-holes the stones were probably of above average stature, perhaps standing as much as 3–3.5m above ground. The stones could not have stood long, being removed soon after erection and the stone-holes then backfilled with chalk rubble.

It is difficult to gauge how the stones were set from the evidence of the stone-holes alone. Whilst it is assumed that the faces of the stones were consistently set parallel with the line of the avenue, this need not always have been the case. The axis of the stone-holes provides the best indication, assuming that a relationship exists between stone-hole and stone morphology, and indeed most are roughly aligned along the avenue course. F.42 (L4) is more problematic, since here the stone-hole is set at right-angles to the avenue line. Either the stone within this (unfortunately now destroyed) was twisted along its length such that its upper surface was at an acute angle to its base, or it was originally set so that it faced onto the *line* of the avenue. The latter is a more likely explanation since tabular sarsen slabs rarely display twisted longitudinal profiles. Given that this stone was situated at the point where the avenue began to bisect the enclosure, a distinctive setting could well have been chosen to mark this significant locale.

Despite the ravages of later destruction,

four of the original megaliths survive along this stretch of the avenue, one still standing (L9), and three buried in later pits (L2, L5 and L6) (Figures 2.46–2.48). All are in their own way distinctive semi-geometrical blocks of sarsen, chosen for their shape and size, but also, we suspect, because of their distinctive features and biographies (cf. Gillings and Pollard 1999). One of the buried blocks, L5, possesses traces of axe polishing on one surface and later, perhaps even Neolithic, modification of that side through extensive pecking (Figure 2.47). Another, L6, is has a markedly 'folded' surface and natural perforations (Figure 2.48). All three buried blocks are between *c*.2.3–3.0m in maximum dimension, and would have stood c.2.0–2.5m high; being supported in stone-holes cut c.0.2–0.4m into the chalk. The greater depth of the stone-holes for L7 and L8 suggest the stones held in these were taller than those further east, and this is borne out by the surviving stone L9 ('Eve') that stands over 3m high. This might indicate that the stones increased in size as they approached the terminal of the avenue, but such a pattern is not consistent since the stone-hole for L4 is a relatively large feature, while that for L10 (the pair to 'Eve') quite diminutive. Working out how each of the buried stones was originally set is not an easy process – in this respect we have less confidence than did Alexander Keiller during his reconstruction work at Avebury. Deposits of soil in the perforations running through the southern end of stone L6 suggest that this end of the sarsen was originally set in the stone-hole, while either the northern or southern ends of L5 could have provided suitable bases for that stone. Given the size of the remaining stone-hole, L2 was most likely set on its western end, creating a very distinctive splayed profile when erected.

Figure 2.46. (top) The buried sarsen of setting L2
Figure 2.47. (middle) The buried sarsen of setting L5
Figure 2.48. (bottom) The buried sarsen of setting L6

Detailed stone and stone-hole descriptions

The Avenue

L1

No stone-hole was detected. Within the post-medieval destruction pit F.21 was 106.5kg of sarsen flakes and fragments, some displaying signs of burning.

L2

Stone-hole F.35, Stone [407]

Located on the south side of burial pit F.22 and partly truncated by it, the stone-hole [431] was of an irregular oval shape, 1.6 × 0.9m and 0.4m deep (Figure 2.49). It possessed moderate sloping sides merging with a dished base. In both plan and profile the pit was very irregular, and had clearly been subject to disturbance from root penetration and/or animal burrowing. The fill comprised a compact choc-

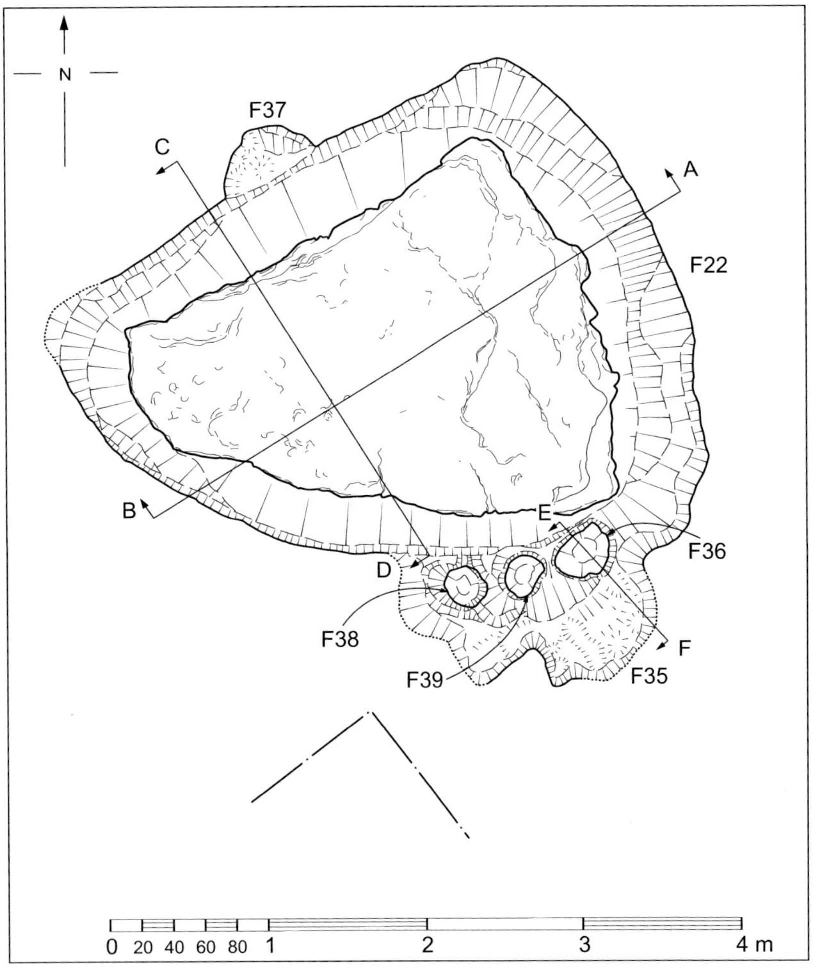

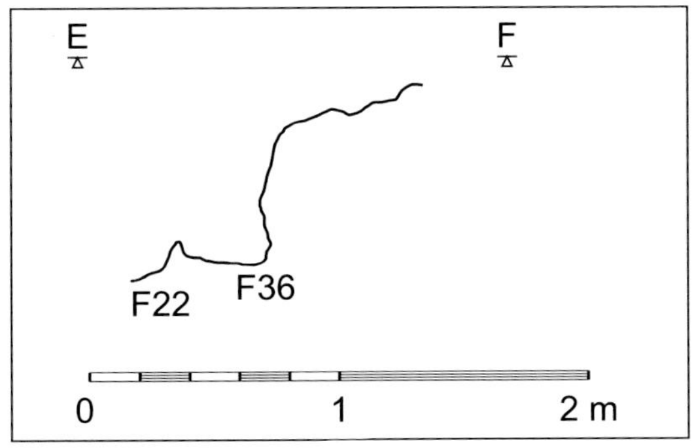

olate-brown clay loam [429], with occasional chalk pieces towards the sides and base.

A setting of three post-holes, F.36 [433], 38 [441] and 39 [443], was cut into the base of the stone-hole, forming an east-west alignment 1.2m across. Circular and oval, regularly cut, with dished bases, the post-holes were between 0.25–0.43m deep (taken from the base of the pit) and 0.25–0.32m in diameter (Figures 2.50 and 2.51). F.36 was slightly undercut towards its base. All were filled with loose chalk rubble and sparse brown silty clay ([432], [440] and [442] respectively); the rubble often lying horizontally within the fill. Given the absence of post-pipes, the posts must have been withdrawn rather than left to decay *in situ*.

Here the megalith survived through later burial in pit F.22. It comprised a large triangular

Figure 2.49. (above) Stone-hole F.35, buried sarsen [407], burial pit F.22 and pit F.37

Figure 2.50. (above far right) Profile of post-hole F.36 within stone-hole F.35

Figure 2.51. (right) Excavated stone-hole F.35, showing post-holes F.36, 38 and 39

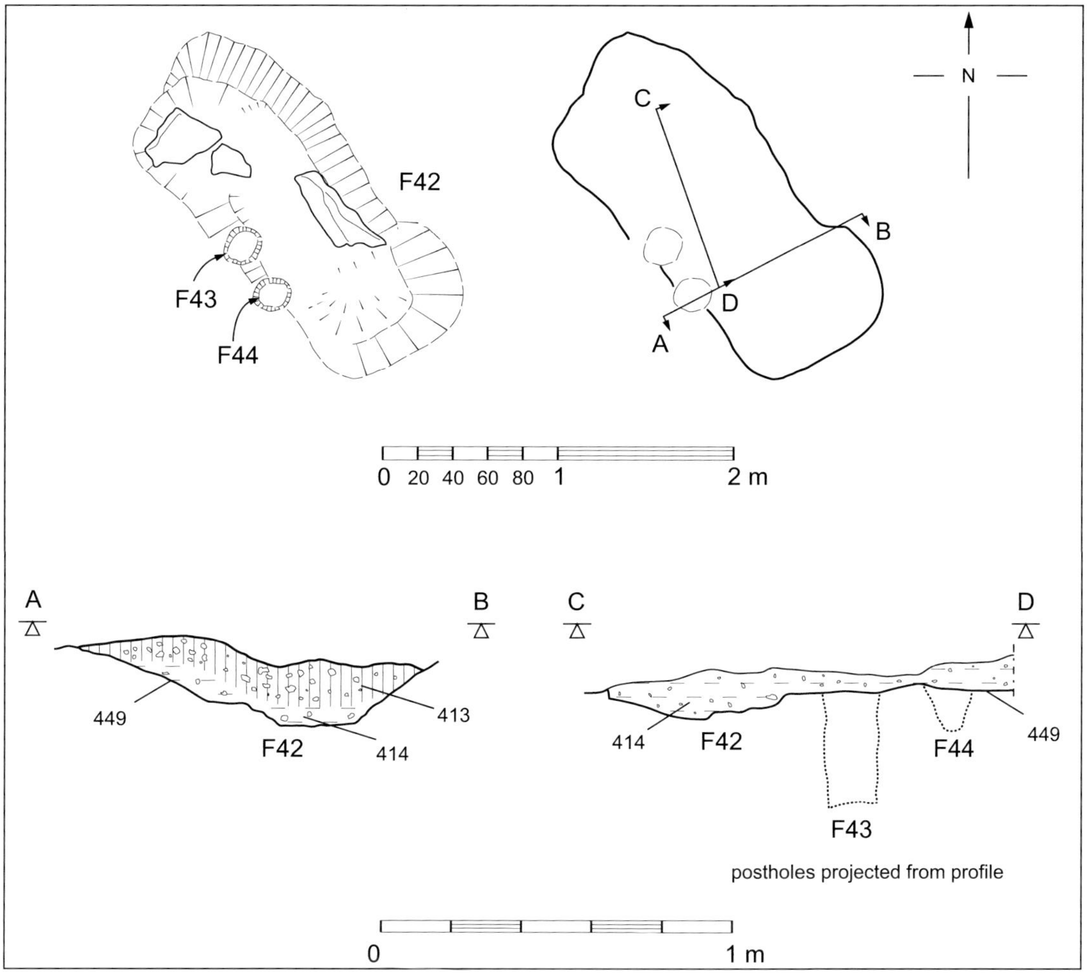

Figure 2.52. Stone-hole F.42 and post-holes F.43 and 44

block of unmodified sarsen [407], 3.00 × 2.46m and *c.*0.8m thick; the upper surface being covered in numerous small natural pock marks, and the thicker eastern end being notably stepped in profile (Figure 2.46).

A small pit, F.37, had been cut by the burial pit on its north-western side. Surviving as a semi-circular scoop [436], 0.68 × 0.35m across and 0.2m deep, the sides and base were irregular, and the feature was filled with an orange-brown clay loam containing some chalk and worked and unworked flint [437]. The status of the pit is uncertain, though it was located more or less diametrically opposite stone-hole F.35 and evidently pre-dated the burial pit.

L3

No trace of a stone-hole was found, but the position of a stone was marked by a burial pit, F.23, from which a stone was later removed. If the burial pit can be taken as a proxy for the size of the buried stone, the sarsen here was in the order of *c.*3.0 × 2.5m.

L4

Stone-hole F.42

The stone-hole [449] was revealed in the base of destruction pit F.24, the upper part of the feature being truncated by the latter. Forming an elongated oval, 2.0 × 0.8m and up to 0.5m deep, the stone-hole had moderate to steep sides and a slightly undulating base (Figures 2.52 and 2.53). The lower fill [414] consisted of a soft and fairly pure dark brown clay loam, above which was a chalky brown clay loam, [413]. The original stone packing included three large (up to 0.6m) blocks of split sarsen, embedded within the fill on the northern and eastern sides of the stone-hole. Opposite the largest block were two post-holes, F.43 and F.44, cut into the base of the stone-hole against its south-west side. Between 0.15–0.20m in diameter and 0.35–0.40m deep, both were filled

Figure 2.53. (above) Excavated stone-hole F.42 showing post-holes F.43 and 44 and sarsen packing

with loose chalk rubble ([450] and [452] respectively). From the burning pit F.24 came 136.5kg of sarsen flakes and fragments.

L5

Stone-hole F.34, Stone [424]

Located on the west side of burial pit F.25, and partly truncated by it, the stone-hole comprised an oval pit [439], 1.6 × 1.2m, and up to 0.2m deep. The sides were moderately steep, and merged with an uneven base (Figure 2.54). The north-eastern quadrant was over-cut during excavation where an area of what was subsequently recognised as heavily compacted chalk natural was initially taken to be packing. In the excavated south-western quadrant there

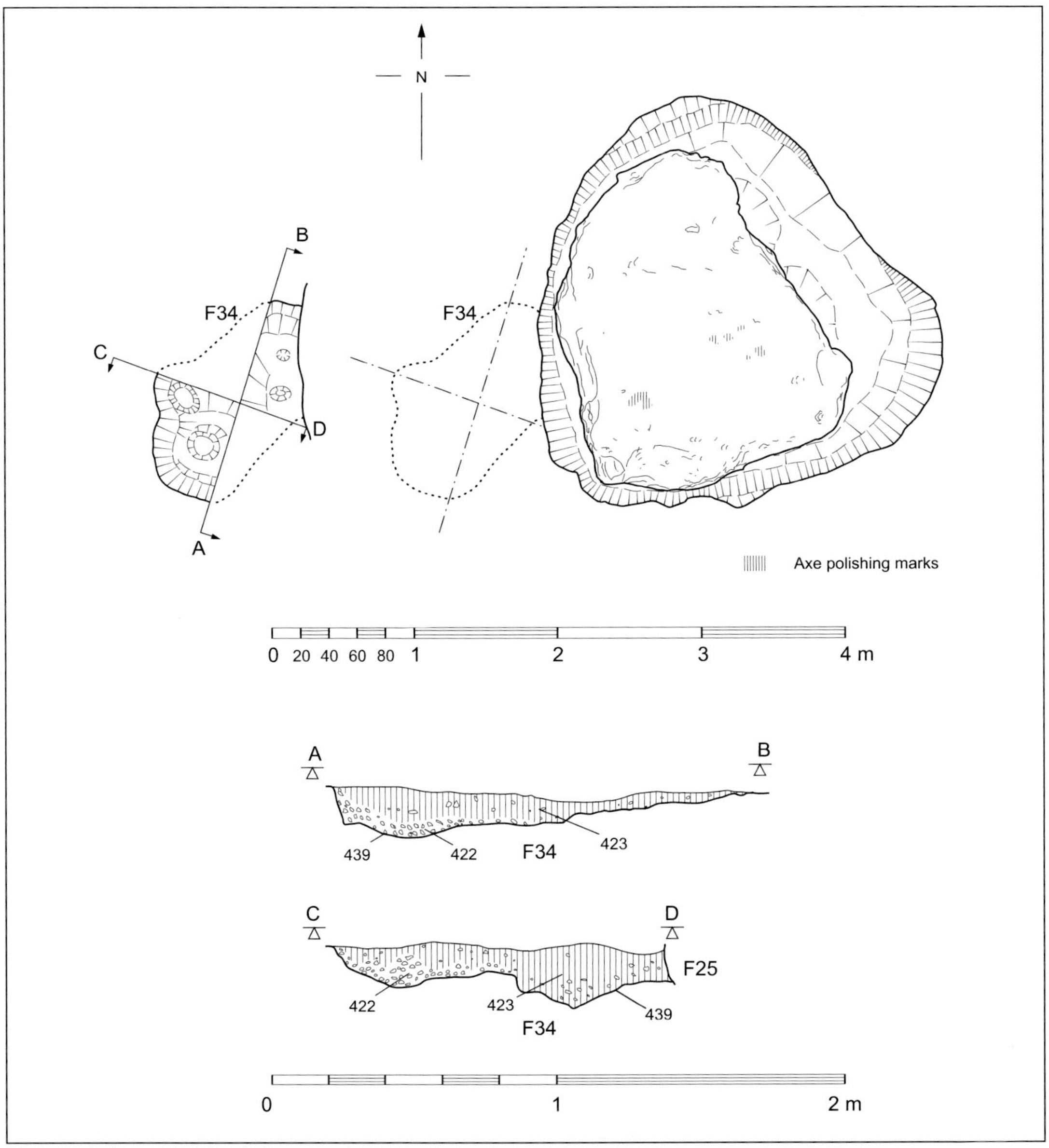

Figure 2.54. (right) Stone-hole F.34 and buried sarsen [424]

were two shallow circular depressions, *c*.0.2m across and 0.05m deep, cut into the base. The status of these is uncertain, though they might represent the remnants of shallow post-holes.

A very small amount of compact chalk rubble packing [422] was present on the base and sides of the feature, particularly on the south. Above this was a 'post-destruction' fill of chalky chocolate-brown clay loam [423], containing occasional pieces of flint.

Burial pit F.25 contained a sub-triangular sarsen block [424], 2.34 × 1.90m across, and between 0.6–0.7m thick. The upper surface of the stone was smooth and even, broken by only a few natural holes and depressions, whilst the underside was slightly concave. On the exposed upper surface were a number of artificial features, including a sub-rectangular wedge-hole towards its northern end, and a set of three stone axe-polishing marks on the southern (Figure 2.55). The wedge-hole, regularly cut, 0.08 × 0.06m across and 0.06m deep, presumably relates to an abortive attempt at breaking up the stone prior to its burial; the hole being filled with the same chalk rubble packing as the pit itself. The axe polishing marks were between 0.20–0.30m long and 0.10–0.29m wide, all roughly running east-west, and took the form of extremely smooth and slightly concave wear marks on the stone. Irregular in outline, though with sharply defined edges, these looked as though they may have been partially pecked away, which if correctly interpreted implies that some attempt had been made to 'dress' the surface of the stone.

L6

Stone-hole F.33, Stone [435]

The stone-hole [438] was situated against the western edge of burial pit F.26, and was partly truncated by it. It took the form of a sub-oval pit, aligned north-south, 1.83 × 0.90m across and 0.35m deep (Figure 2.56). The sides were irregular, though generally steep, either merging or forming a defined junction with an irregular base. Animal or root disturbance was noted in the sides of the pit in both excavated quadrants.

Across the base of the pit was a discontinuous layer of compact angular chalk rubble packing within a chocolate-brown clay loam [427]. Whilst very compact in the top and towards the centre, this became looser below. On the east side this had been disturbed by the kick-up of the stone when toppled. The upper fill [428] was a compact chocolate-brown clay loam containing some small chalk (particularly towards the edges), a few small and medium sized (0.05–0.25m) sarsen blocks, and very occasional flecks of charcoal.

Figure 2.55. (above) Detail of traces of polishing produced by the grinding of stone axes on the surface of stone [424]. Note areas of pecking that have removed much of the polished surface

Two post-holes, F.40 and 41, forming a north-south arrangement, were cut into the base of the stone-hole on the northern side. Set 0.1m apart, both were circular cuts ([445] and [447] respectively), steep or vertical sided with dished bases. F.40 was 0.22m in diameter and 0.28m deep (from the base of the stone-hole), and F.41 0.35m diameter and 0.19m deep. F.41 had been heavily truncated by the collapse of the sides of F.33 when the stone was toppled. Both were filled with a uniform loose chalk rubble mixed with a fine brown clay loam ([444] and [446] respectively). There were no signs of post-pipes and it is assumed the posts were withdrawn rather than left to rot *in situ*.

The original megalith survived within burial pit F.26. The stone [435] was a sub-rectangular block of sarsen, 2.50 × 1.70m, and up to 1.25m thick. Although quite regular in plan, the upper and lower faces were extremely 'featured'. The upper face was bisected by a series of large cracks and folds in the rock, and there were numerous natural depressions and perforations (Figure 2.57). Three large natural perforations, *c*.0.10–0.15m in diameter, ran through the southern end of the stone. The central of these was filled with a largely stone-free brown clay loam [448], which contained a curious assemblage of worked flint and a split cattle tibia. A

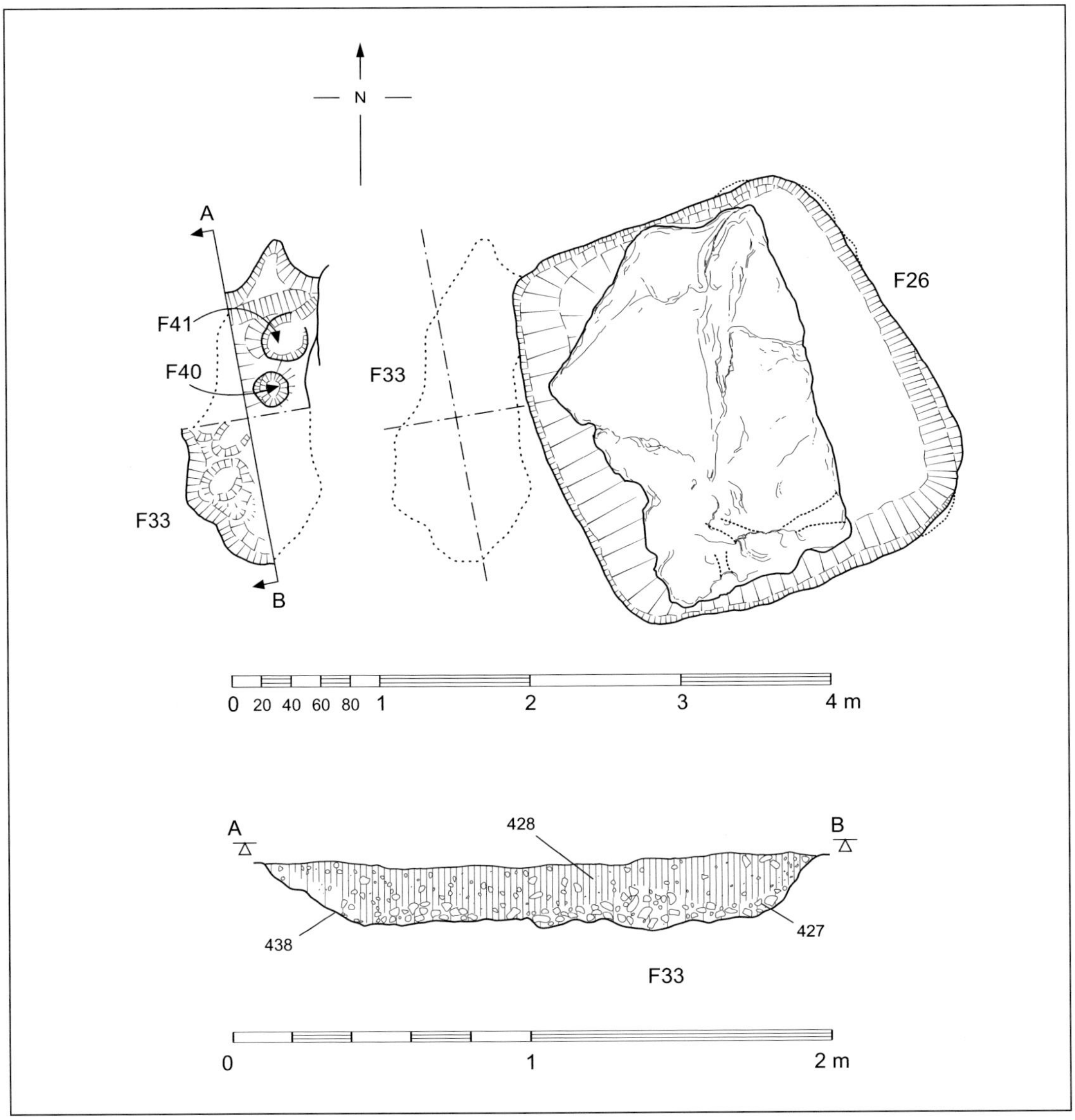

Figure 2.56. (right) Stone-hole F.33, associated post-holes F.40 and 41 and buried sarsen [435]

Figure 2.57. (below) Detail of the base of stone [435] showing natural perforation and heavily 'folded' form

radiocarbon determination of 1170–1280 cal AD (Beta-140991: 810±40 BP) was obtained from the bone. As with the sarsen in F.22, black staining was visible on the protected sides and undersurface of the stone.

L7
Stone-hole F.82

The stone-hole comprised a sub-rectangular cut [635], 1.6 × 0.9m and 0.55m deep, with a flat base and, with the exception of the north-east edge, steeply sloping sides (Figure 2.58). Cut into the centre of the north-west portion of the base was a small, irregular sub-rectangular depression, 0.04m deep. The south-east portion of the stone-hole edge had been heavily disturbed by the base of a large burrow.

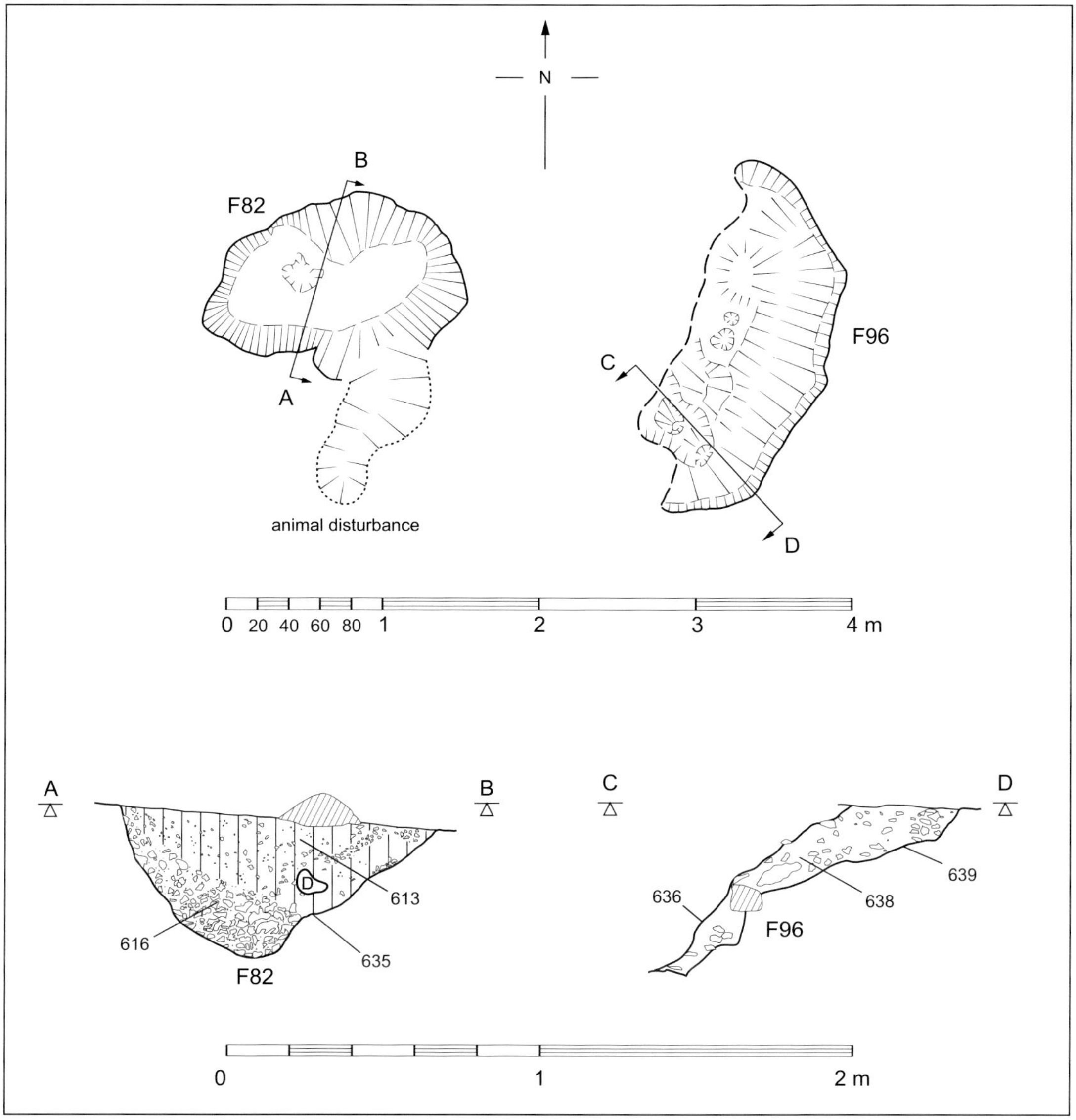

Figure 2.58. Stone-holes F.82 and 96

Filling the cut was a basal deposit of very loose pale beige silt and chalk rubble [616]. Embedded within this was an unburned sarsen packing stone (0.36m across) that had a flint core resting upon its upper surface. The sarsen and core were directly above the shallow scoop in the base of the stone-hole. Above this deposit was an upper fill of mid-brown chalky silt [613] with three large lumps of unburned sarsen (up to 0.46m across), two projecting onto the surface of the feature. The sarsen most probably represents re-deposited packing stones within a weathering deposit, itself showing evidence of animal burrowing.

With the exception of the burrow disturbance, the stone-hole is, unusually, largely intact. The destruction pit, whilst located directly adjacent to the feature, does not cut the edge of the stone-hole. Whilst a number of packing stones and a quantity of packing material remained *in situ*, there was no evidence of any 'anti-friction' stake-holes, though the small feature cut into the base of the stone-hole could represent the remnants of a post setting.

L8

Stone-hole F.96

Little survived of the stone-hole, and ambiguities surround the extent of the feature due to the familiar processes of compression to the natural caused by the stone, animal burrowing, and damage created through the digging of the destruction pit (Figure 2.58). The stone-hole [877] first became visible after

Figure 2.59. The one remaining standing stone of the Beckhampton Avenue, 'Eve', with the burning pit of setting L10 in the foreground

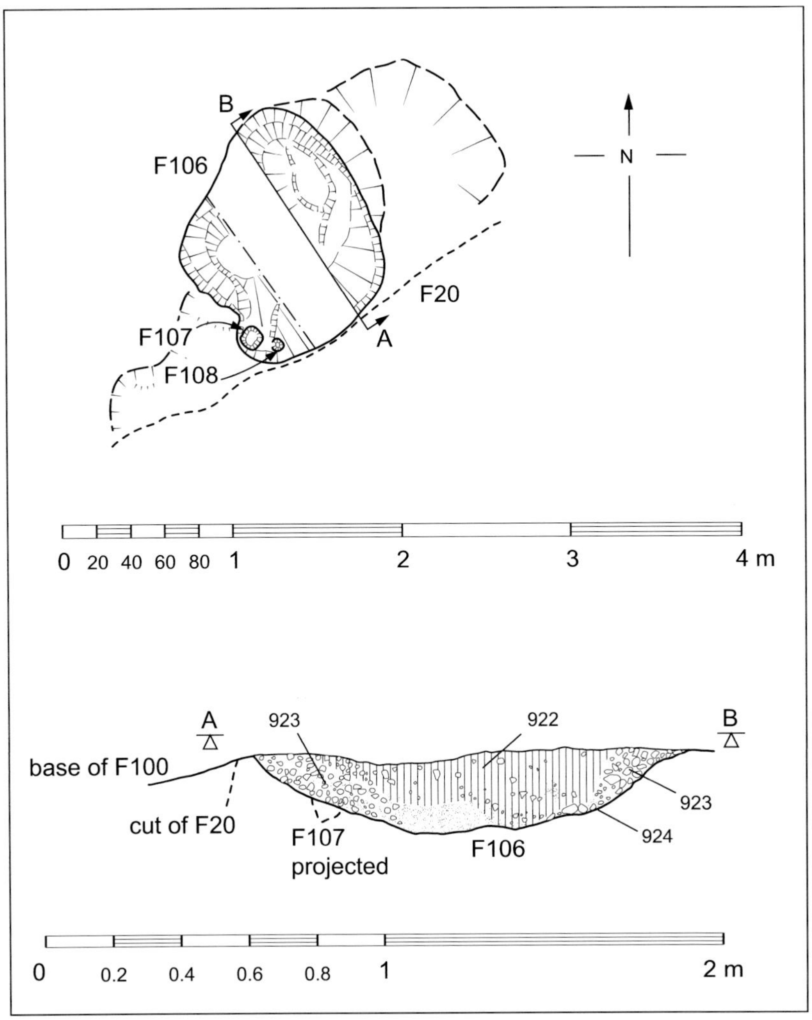

Figure 2.60. Stone-hole F.106 and associated post-holes F.107 and 108. Note the proximity of the enclosure ditch, F.20

the removal of burning debris from the southern end of the destruction pit. Here, a large (0.3m across) unburned sarsen stone was found resting upon an area of compacted natural. This compacted area formed a distinct step adjacent to the rear of the destruction pit, and had a gently rounded upper edge. A tentative reconstruction would see the stone-hole as oval, *c.*1.6 × 1.2m and up to 0.55m deep. No original fill remained within the feature.

L9

Colloquially known as 'Eve', this is the only stone of the avenue that remains standing (Figure 2.59). A fairly irregular block when viewed from the reverse and sides, the sarsen is carefully set so that when faced from the south-east (*i.e.* inside the avenue) it displays some degree of geometric regularity, with a flat face, straight sides and a 'gabled' top (equivalent to Keiller and Piggott's Type A: Smith 1965, 197). It stands 3.3m tall with a maximum width of *c.*2.3m. Animal burrows observed at the base on the north side of the stone in 2000 had exposed sarsen packing stones within the upper fill of the stone-hole.

L10

Stone-hole F.106

Stone-hole F.106 was separated from the ditch of the earlier Longstones enclosure by as little as 0.02m; nonetheless this was sufficient to deny any direct stratigraphic relationship between the two features. Sub-oval, the stone-hole [924] was 1.40 × 1.16m across and up to 0.3m deep (Figure 2.60). On south and east sides the upper profile was steep, gradually merging with the irregular base; while on the north it was moderate at the top, becoming steeper in the lower profile. Irregularity in the base was probably caused by the weight of the stone, the base being compacted to such a degree that it was often difficult to follow the interface between the chalk packing and stone-hole base. Two 'anti-friction' stake-holes, F.107 and 108, were present against the southern side of the pit; perhaps part of a line that could extend under the unexcavated central baulk. Situated 0.07m apart both [927] and [928] were oval in plan, 0.05–0.10m in maximum dimension, tapering, and 0.07 and 0.12m deep. They were filled with a firm pale brown silty clay, [925] and [926].

The remaining *in situ* stone-hole packing [923] was a moderate to highly compacted chalk rubble within a pale brown silty clay, thickest and most extensive towards the sides. In the centre of the feature and towards its northern edge this became a homogenised, off-white structure-less chalk, resulting from post-depositional compression created by the overlying stone. The upper fill [922] accumulated after the stone fell or was toppled. A compact brown silty clay with some chalk rubble and occasional patches of fine pale grey chalky silt mixed in, it contained one small displaced packing stone. A slight weathering hollow had formed around the stone-hole and there was evidence of some animal disturbance. Filling this was a chalk-rich brown silty clay [907].

Given the small size and shallowness of the stone-hole, along with the relative absence of packing stones and the few 'anti-friction' stake holes, it is unlikely to have held a substantial stone; certainly nothing as large as its pair, 'Eve'. This said, there is a possibility that F.106 represents the truncated base of a deeper stone-hole dug in part through the former bank of the enclosure. However, it seems unlikely that any sizeable remnant of bank remained when the stone-hole was dug since there are strong indications that the enclosure earthwork had by this stage been levelled.

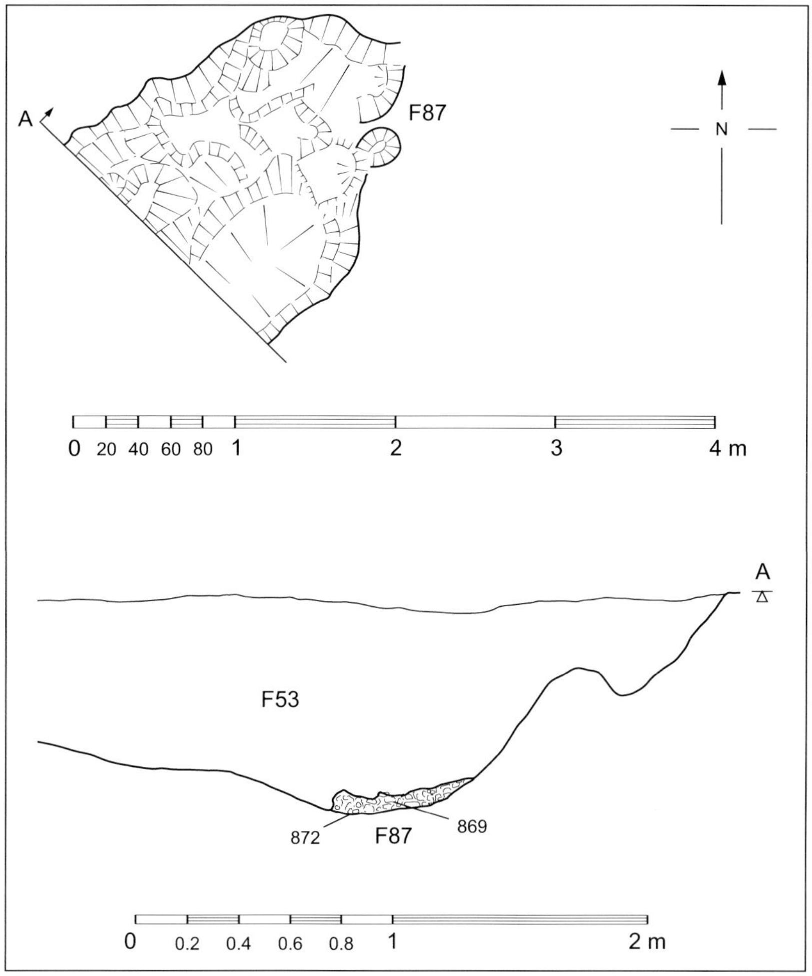

Figure 2.61. Stone-hole F.87 of the pre-Cove setting

The pre-Cove setting

L11

Stone-hole F.87

Both the stone-hole and destruction pit were subject to 50 per cent excavation. F.87 survived on the north-eastern edge of destruction pit F.53, much of it truncated by the latter. Form and dimensions are difficult to gauge, especially since only half of the feature was dug, but the stone-hole would appear to have been oval, set NE-SW, around 3.0m in length and 0.8m deep (Figure 2.61). The base was clearly compacted by the weight of the stone. The surviving northern edge was steep, but sloped more gently to the south. Forming the northern end of this feature was a vertically cut 'promontory' of solid chalk. On the base of the stone-hole was a thin layer of heavily compressed and degraded chalk [869].

The stone was set along the axis of the avenue. In destroying the stone, a destruction pit was cut from the south sloping down towards, and directly up to, the base of the stone-hole, effectively digging away its south-eastern edge.

L12

Stone-hole F.54

The stone-hole [808] was oval and slightly irregular in plan, 2.8 × 2.5m and up to 0.7m deep (Figure 2.62). The upper sides of the pit were moderate to steep, and on the north side became near vertical in the lower profile. There was a sharp junction between the sides and the base, except to the south. The base was generally flat, though cut into this was an undercut triangular depression close to the south edge, up to 0.3m deep with a sloping base, and a series of four shallow depressions (less than 0.3m and under 0.1m in depth) along the northern edge. The latter could represent denuded holes for 'anti-friction' stakes. The chalk natural forming the central base and west side of the pit was notably smoothed and

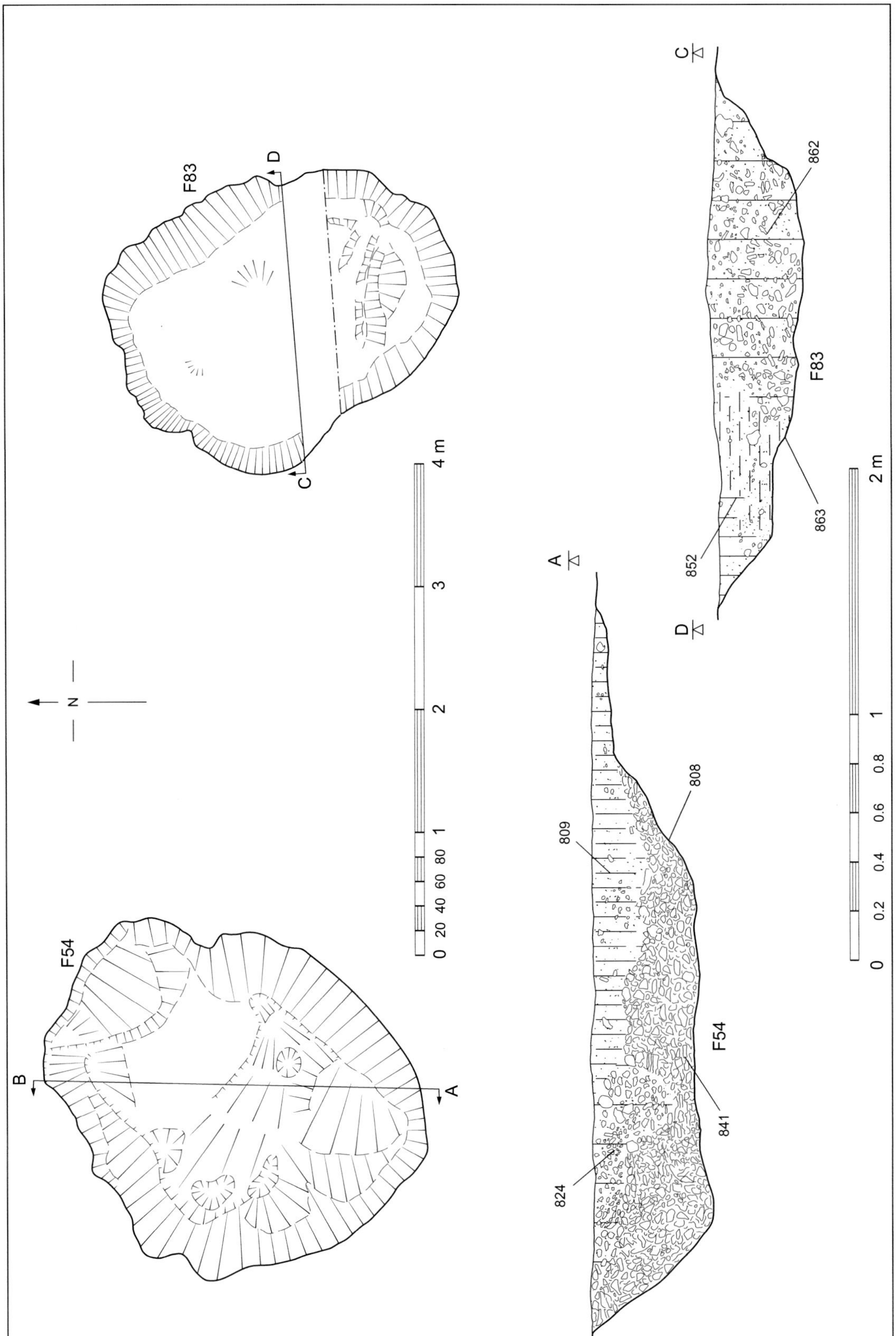

Figure 2.62. Stone-holes F54 and 83 of the pre-Cove setting

Figure 2.63. (left) The earliest depiction of the Longstones Cove? Aubrey's drawing of the 'Devil's Coits' as redrafted by Long (Long 1858, fig. 2)

Figure 2.64. (below) The Longstones Cove under excavation, August 2000, from the NE

compressed, consistent with the transformation caused by the weight of a large stone.

The main body of fill [824] was of chalk rubble within a sparse brown silty clay loam, containing occasional patches of creamy decayed chalk. The rubble became looser with depth. On the south side this was overlain by a thick layer of compact chalky brown clay loam [809]. A few pieces of worked flint, some perhaps intrusive, came from [809].

L13

Stone-hole F.83

Morphologically similar to F.54, this was an irregular oval stone-hole, 2.8 × 2.4m and up to 0.6m deep [863] (Figure 2.62). The sides were steep with a well-defined junction to a slightly dished base, except on the east where they were shallower and sides and base merged. As with F.54, in the south-eastern corner a narrow slot with near vertical sides had been cut close to the edge of the base. The base of the slot itself was defined by two parallel shallow grooves, and perhaps represents a setting for levers used in the erection or removal of the stone. A zone of compaction was again discernible in the centre of the base.

The bulk of the fill was of chalk rubble within a pale brown silty clay loam [862]; tip lines indicating that this material had entered the feature from the west. Over this, and confined to the east side, was a grey-brown silty clay with some chalk [852], becoming more humic towards the top.

The Cove

Situated at the end of the avenue immediately south-west of the enclosure, the Cove was recorded by the antiquary William Stukeley as a box-like arrangement of three massive sarsen stones open to the south-east. Of these, the back stone had fallen well before the time of Stukeley's visits in 1722–4, that making-up the south-western side was recently broken-up, and only one stone remained standing ('Adam': L14). The position of a fourth stone (now known to be L11) was depicted by Stukeley as lying some distance to the south-east, and this he believed belonged to the avenue proper. Aubrey had earlier depicted an arrangement of three standing stones (Figure 2.63), perhaps comprising settings L11, L14 and L16, and omitting the recumbent block of L15.

Three substantial stone destruction pits (F.71, 52 and 53) were revealed following stripping of the ploughsoil over the site of the Cove in Trench 24 (Figures 2.45 and 2.64), and were clearly visible on the pre-excavation geophysical survey. These marked the location of stones recorded as recently removed (L11 to the south-east and L16 to the south-west) and lying recumbent (L15 to the north-west) by Stukeley in 1722–4. L11 belongs to the pre-Cove setting described above, the remaining two, along with 'Adam', to the Cove proper. In its finished form the Cove incorporated the existing stone L11 to form its south-eastern side. The Cove therefore comprised a four-sided, rectilinear setting of massive sarsens, *c.*15 × 10m across, aligned NW-SE, with splayed sides 'opening' to the south-east. Rather than being located on the axis of the avenue, it was positioned so that its centre lay on the avenue's northern line. The long axis of the setting was more or less at right angles to that of the avenue. This alignment is just off-set to the west of the South Street long barrow; though the presence of L11 would have meant that for anyone standing in the centre of the setting a clear view was afforded of the barrow through the sizeable gap between L11 and L14. The size of the destruction pits and remaining portions of the original stone-holes (F.50 for the back stone L15, and F.81 for the western side stone L16) indicate that sarsen blocks equivalent in size to 'Adam' were employed, that is standing 3.5m or so above ground level.

The excavation of the Cove vindicates Stukeley's observations regarding the format of the setting, though it is clear that his southern-most stone (L11) was not, as he thought, part of the southern line of the avenue, but was in fact set within its centre. This shows that the Cove was not an open-box arrangement of three stones, as appears to be the case with the supposedly analogous setting within the Northern Inner Circle at Avebury (Smith 1965), but a 'closed' rectilinear setting.

The stone-holes had suffered considerable disturbance as a result of early 18th century stone destruction episodes, that of L15 (F.50) being largely obliterated. A sizeable section of the stone-hole for L16 (F.81) did survive, though was much disturbed on its eastern side by the destruction event, while the fill had been extensively penetrated by animal burrowing. Elements of the original packing of chalk rubble and small sarsen boulders remained *in situ*. Animal bone was present within the packing, apparently in a primary position, but when samples of this were radiocarbon dated the results gave ranges in the Roman and early post-Roman periods, indicating that this material was intrusive (see Chapter 7). While relatively few pieces of worked flint were found when excavating the enclosure ditch and features belonging to the avenue, nearly 4000 pieces of flintwork were recovered from the stone-holes and later destruction pits of the Cove.

Figure 2.65. (above) The sole survivor of the Longstones Cove, 'Adam', from the SW, with the partially excavated stone-hole and destruction pit of setting L16 in the foreground

L14

The stone known as 'Adam' is the sole survivor of the Cove (Figure 2.65). The stone fell to the south in December 1911 and was re-erected in July–August 1912 (Cunnington 1913). Excavations undertaken at the time revealed an oval or sub-rectangular stone-hole, 4.1 × 2.0m,

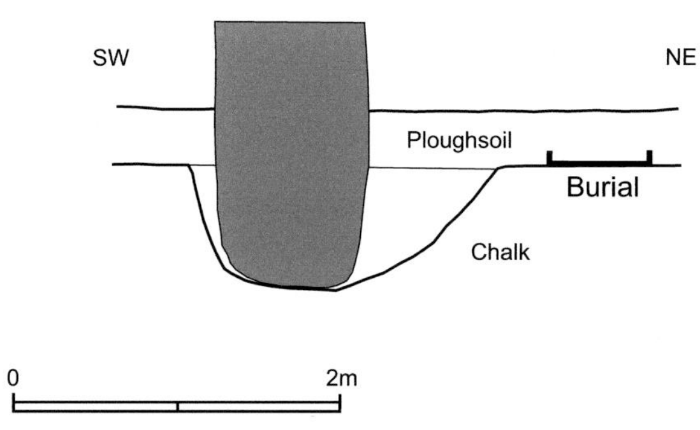

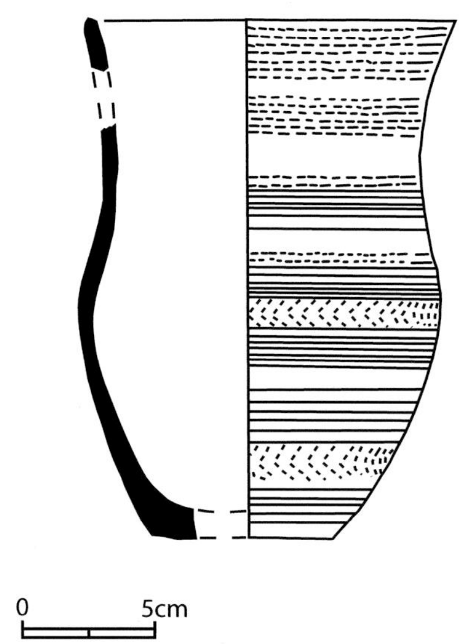

Figure 2.66. (right) Cunnington's profile of the stone-hole for 'Adam', and the N/MR Beaker recovered from the crouched inhumation adjacent to the stone (after Cunnington 1913 and Clarke 1970, fig. 233)

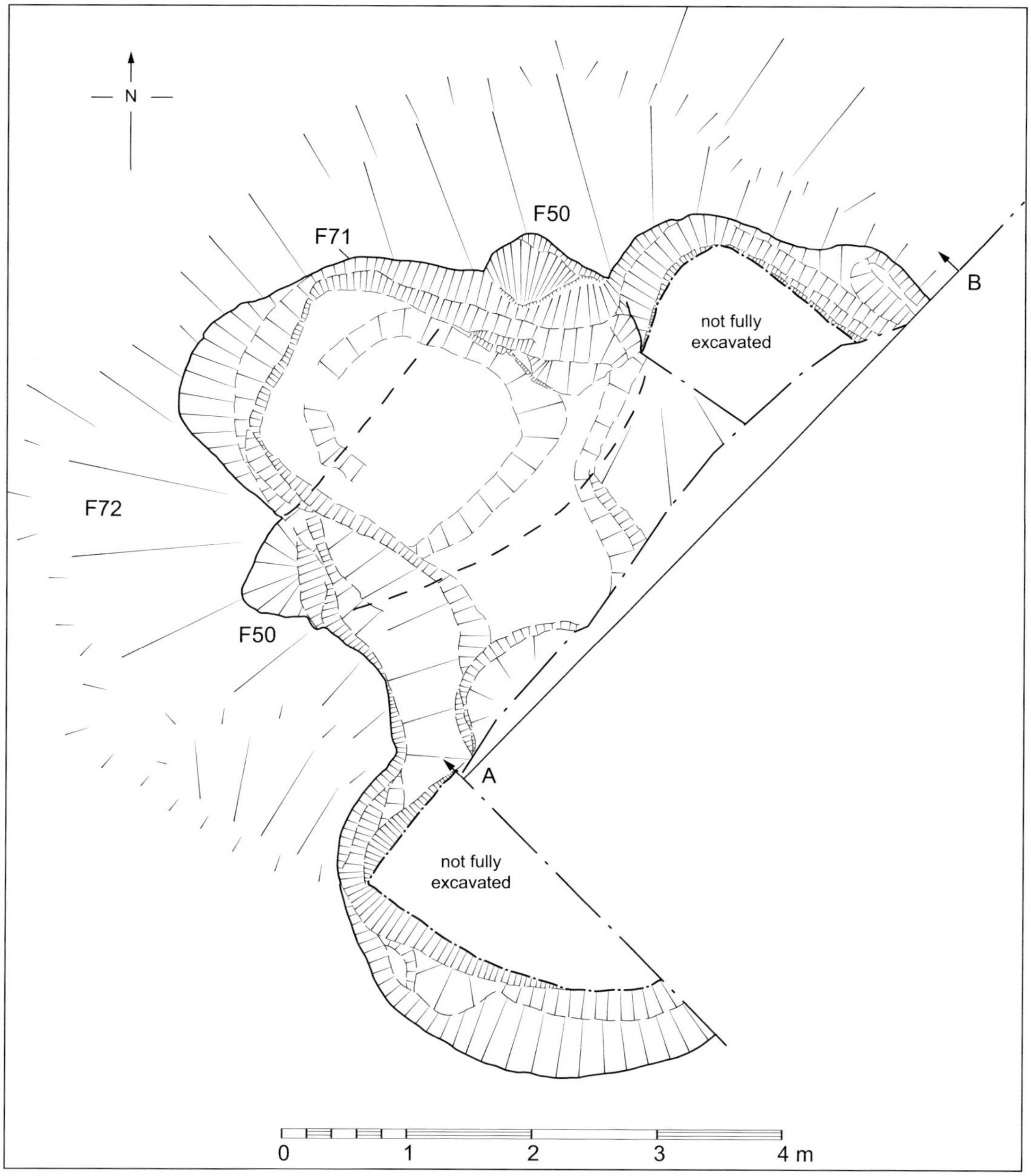

Figure 2.67. The remains of stone-hole F.50 cut by the massive post-medieval burning pit F.71

being widest at the eastern end. The stone-hole was cut 0.7m into the chalk; the north-eastern side sloping more gently than the south-western, presumably to create a ramp down which the stone was lowered and erected (Cunnington 1913, 3). Around 150 sarsen packing stones were discovered in the fill, most being found towards the eastern (front) end of the pit (see L16, F.81 for details of a similar arrangement). The excavation also revealed a poorly preserved inhumation burial placed in a shallow pit close to the centre of the stone on its northern side. Crouched, with head to the east, the burial was accompanied by a comb-decorated N/MR Beaker (Clarke 1970, no. 1051, fig. 233) (Figure 2.66). A fragment of another Beaker and animal bones were found in the stone-hole packing (Cunnington 1913, 5), though given the extent of animal disturbance noted elsewhere these may be intrusive.

The stone currently stands 3.4m tall with a maximum width of 4.0m. Sub-rectangular in shape, it has been set to create an asymmetric diamond profile (a good example of Keiller and Piggot's Type B: Smith 1965, 197). The process of re-erection led to the stone being tipped slightly too far to the south, so that the 'corner' on the south-east edge is set *c.*0.5m lower than originally placed (cf. Colt-Hoare 1821, plate 15, 2). At the time of excavation the weight of the sarsen was estimated at 62 tons (Cunnington 1913, 6).

L15

Stone-hole F.50

The north-western arm of the destruction pit F.71 cut through the remains of the original stone-hole, F.50, virtually obliterating it (Figure 2.67). All that survived were the very ends of the stone-hole on the north-east and south-west side, and here only the tops of the fill remained. From these scant traces, the stone-hole [802] would appear to have been oval or sub-rectangular, *c*.3.5 × 1.5m, aligned north-east – south-west. If the low shelf running between the north-west and south-west arms of the destruction pit followed the base of the stone-hole at this point, the latter can be assumed to have had a depth of between 0.6–0.7m. The remnants of the fill comprised two layers of chocolate brown silty clay, [859] then [858], the former mixed with much small sub-angular chalk. Bone, worked flint and sherds of Medieval pottery came from [858].

A substantial weathering-cone, F.72, had formed around stone-hole F.50 after the stone had fallen. Centred on F.50 and reflecting to some degree its plan, it took the form of an oval hollow [815], 8.0 × >4.5m, and up to 0.35m deep. It was filled with a basal layer of friable dark brown clay loam with varying amounts of chalk [864], over which was a similar but less chalky loam [800]/[814]. Large quantities of worked flint came from this, along with some bone and abraded sherds of Roman and Medieval pottery. Since the pottery may well be residual it helps little in dating the fall of the stone and the consequent formation of the weathering-cone around the void left in stone-hole F.50. However, a fair interval (perhaps of several centuries) between the stone fall and its destruction in the 1720s would be necessary for a weathering-cone of this size to form.

A shallow sub-rectangular scoop, F.88, was cut into the base of the weathering-cone on the east side, 0.2m from the edge of F.71. Over 0.6m × 0.4m, with a maximum depth of only 0.08m, it had shallow to steep sides and a flat base. It was filled with a compact pale brown chalky loam [874], containing some broken sarsen and flint flakes. The upper fill of F.71 sealed the scoop, though the presence of sarsen fragments in its fill might link it with the destruction event.

Four possible prehistoric sherds (weighing 17g) in flint-tempered fabrics were recovered from the base of the ploughsoil around L15.

L16

Stone-hole F.81

The stone-hole comprised an elongated oval pit [871], flattened along its eastern (inner) edge, 4.5 × 1.2m and up to 0.9m deep (Figures 2.68–2.70). Like so many of the stone-holes, this feature had not faired well. On the northern and western sides the upper profile had been extensively disturbed by animal burrowing, and on the east was effectively removed by the digging of the destruction pit F.52. Where surviving or reconstructable, the stone-hole sides were very steep to near vertical along the inner edge, and vertical to moderately sloping elsewhere. The base was very uneven, perhaps more a product of animal disturbance and differential compression caused by the weight of the stone it held, than original intent. In general, the western (outer) side of the stone-hole base was shallower than the eastern, suggesting that the stone had been hauled in from this side and set upright against the eastern edge (see L14). This would accord with a zone of very severe compression of the base in the centre of the eastern side, where two packing stones had been pushed into the solid chalk, and with the presence of a line of 'anti-friction' stake-holes along this inner edge. Seven such stake-holes were observed (F.89–95), each under 0.15m in diameter and 0.10m deep, regularly spaced, though in a discontinuous line, against the basal inner edge of the stone-hole.

The fill sequence would have begun with the erection of the stone. Sarsen packing stones were then placed around its base. Though disturbed during the stone destruction and through subsequent plough truncation, c.80 packing stones [867] remained in the stone-hole fill (Figure 2.69). These comprised unmodified medium-sized boulders (0.10–0.55m); smaller sarsens set towards the centre against the megalith, larger stones in the south of the stone-hole. They were concentrated in a band running from the north of the stone-hole along the centre to the south end, leaving a clear central zone off-set to the east, *c*.1.5 ×

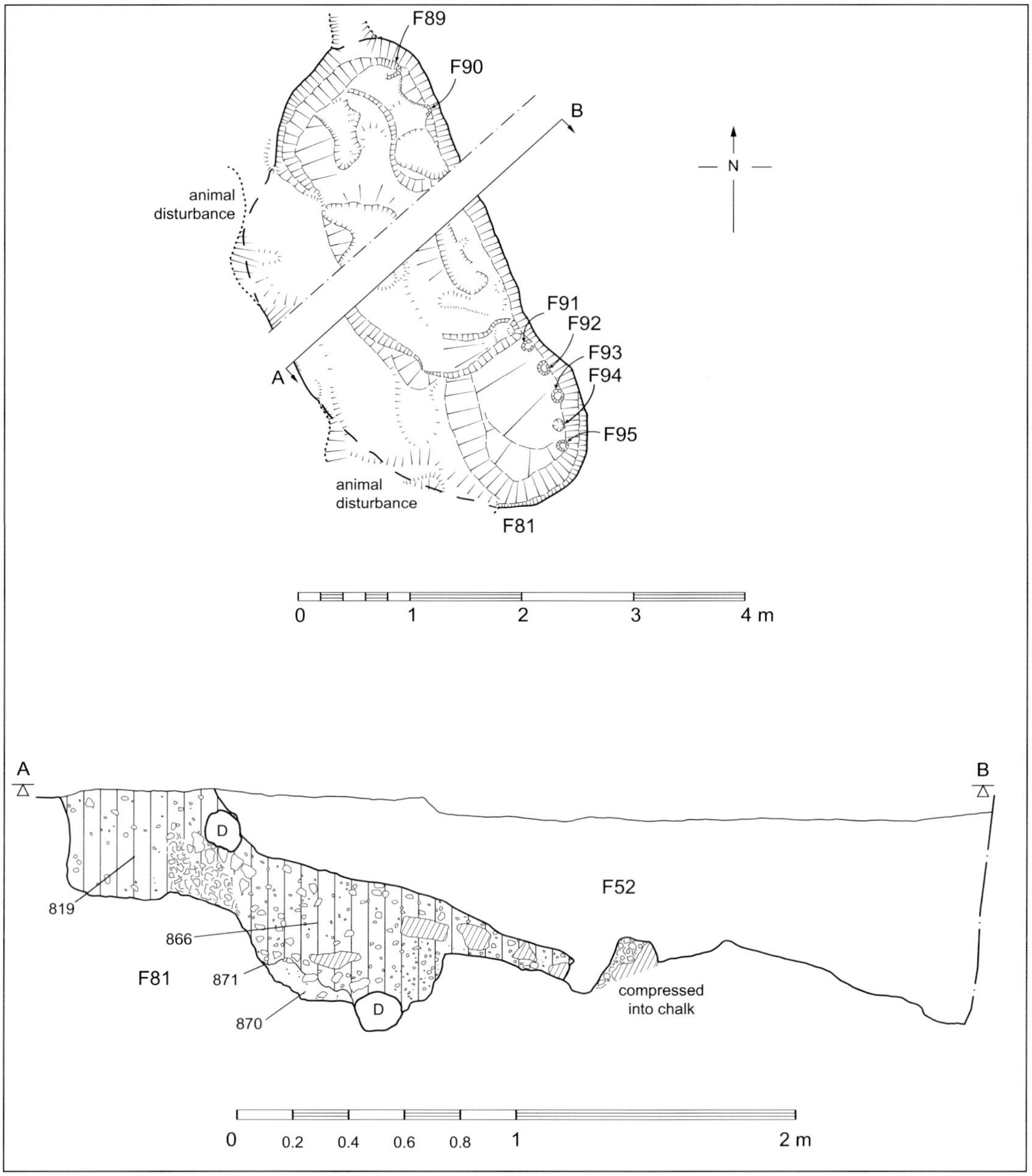

Figure 2.68. Stone-hole F.81 and associated stake-holes F.89–95 of the Longstones Cove. Note the irregularity of the base caused by compression induced by the weight of the stone

0.7m, where the stone had stood. In places the boulders were piled two to three deep, rising to the top of the fill on the south where a few had been removed by the plough (their positions being marked by voids in the fill). A few had split, either when dropped into the stone-hole or through pressure from the overlying megalith. Taken in conjunction with the zone of compression in the stone-hole base, the position of the packing boulders implies the stone was set as a 'diamond', with the southern lower stone edge supported by a ramp of sarsen packing rising from the centre of the stone-hole.

Filling the voids between the packing stones was a compact re-deposited chalk [870] within a pale brown silty clay and brown clay loam. Intermittently distributed, this was much disturbed in the upper 0.2m by animal burrowing. It contained numerous pieces of worked flint and a few fragments of bone, almost certainly introduced by animal burrowing since the latter yielded early 1st millennium AD radiocarbon dates. Above this was further chalk rubble packing [866] within varying quantities of pale orange-brown silty clay, being more humic towards the centre. Both [870] and [866] were compressed into a

Figure 2.69. (top) Stone-hole F.81 partially excavated with sarsen packing in situ

Figure 2.70. (bottom) Stone-hole F.81 on completion of excavation

particularly dense clay where the weight of the stone had exerted the greatest pressure upon them. The upper fill of chalky brown to orange-brown silty clay loam [819] had suffered extensive animal disturbance.

Artefactual material

Worked flint from the Longstones Cove and Beckhampton Avenue

Nick Snashall

The lithic assemblage associated with the Longstones Cove and pre-Cove setting comprises a total of 4026 items. The majority of these came from features associated with settings L15 and L16 of the Cove (Figure 2.71). 720 flints were recovered from F.53, the destruction pit of stone L11, and a further four from F.54, the stone-hole of stone L12, both of these stones having formed part of the pre-Cove setting. Given the disturbed nature of the majority of the contexts from which the lithic material was recovered, for the purposes of this analysis the assemblage from contexts associated with the pre-Cove setting and the Cove have been combined.

Raw materials

A substantial proportion of material within the assemblage is patinated, though there is considerable variation in the degree of patination. Where it is possible to visually characterise the raw material used (*i.e.* where items are unpatinated and/or retained diagnostic cortex), the majority of the debitage comprises chalk flint (or from clay-with-flints), with a smaller but consistently present minority possessing extremely thin rolled cortex suggesting a riverine source. In addition, a single trimming flake of very coarse grey chert was recovered from [800].

Much of the chalk flint present possesses a thin cortex and exhibits signs of frost fracturing. In many instances this material is poor quality, fossiliferous material with considerable colour variation. In some cases this appears to come from very small nodules. Such material would have been available close by from the Upper Chalk (or clay-with-flints). The selection of such poor quality raw material suggests a concern with immediacy over quality of product, which is also reflected in the core reduction techniques evidenced in the assemblage.

Analysis of raw material usage for the tool and core components within the assemblage echoes the pattern already described (Table 2.20). In both cases the predominant raw material is chalk flint, which comprises 40.7% of the tool assemblage and 37.1% of the core assemblage. A significant but smaller proportion of derived material forms 23.7% of the tool assemblage and 31.1% of the core assemblage.

Only a small number of primary flakes are present within the assemblage. However, a significant minority of secondary flakes are in evidence, suggesting that material was brought to the site in a semi-prepared state.

A concern with expediency is demonstrated by the presence of a considerable quantity of reworked material. Though some multi-phase patination is undoubtedly due to damage caused to lithic material during episodes of stone destruction, recycling of earlier materials can be seen on a number of tools where earlier debitage or implements have been reworked into new tools. A notable example of this is present within the material recovered from F.53 [807] where a significant minority of pieces have multi-phase patination. One core rejuvenation tablet, and a number of flakes that exhibit signs of careful trimming and platform preparation, have been subsequently reworked.

Core reduction techniques

The ratio of flakes to narrow flakes to blades present in the assemblage is heavily flake dominated at 22:5:1 (Table 2.21). The majority of flakes are thick and heavy, many with pronounced bulbs of percussion suggesting the use of hard hammers. This supposition is supported by the presence of four flint hammerstones (Table 2.22). The majority of flakes have previous multi-directional removals

Table 2.20. (left) Longstones Cove cores and tools: raw materials

	Patinated	**Chalk Flint**	**Derived Flint**	**Total**
Total Cores (incl. frags)	42	49	41	132
% cores	31.8%	37.1%	31.1%	
Total tools (incl. trimmed, worn, misc. retouched)	63	72	42	177
% tools	35.6%	40.7%	23.7%	

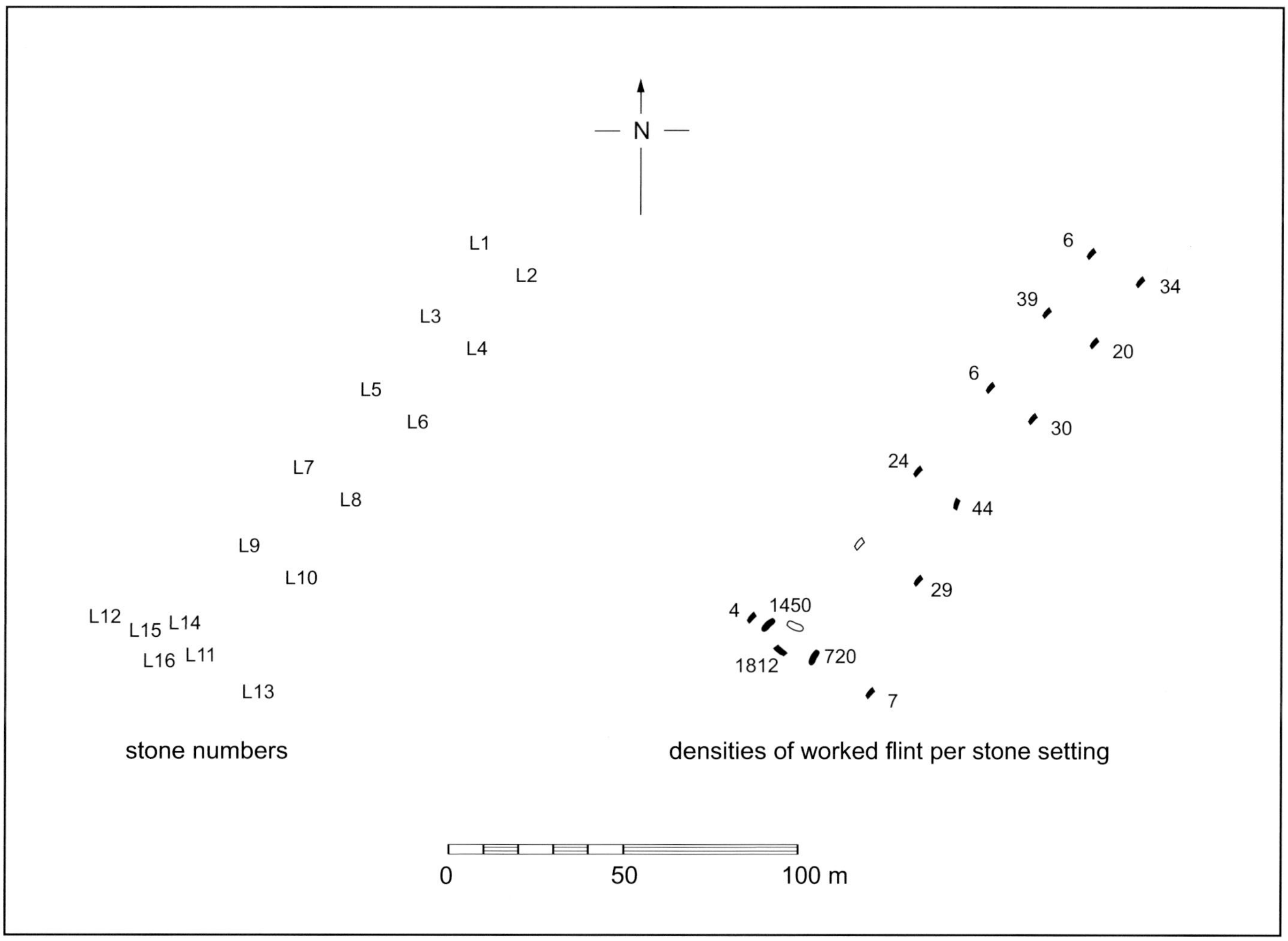

Figure 2.71. (below) Distribution of worked flint from excavated features of the Beckhampton Avenue and Longstones Cove

Feature	Context	Flake	Narrow Flake	Blade	Flake/narrow flake/blade	Chunk	Chip	Ridge Trimming Flake	Trimming Flake	Retouch Flake	Crested Blade	Core Rejuvenation Tablet	Plunging Core Rejuvenation Flake	Thermal piece	Unmodified flint nodule/lump	Unclassified burnt frags	Stone frag. (non-conchoidal fracturing)	Total
	[001]	7	3	-	5	-	1	10	2	-	-	-	2	4	-	-	-	**34**
F.50	[858]	2	-	-	2	-	1	-	-	-	-	-	-	-	-	-	-	**5**
	[859]	44	-	-	2	-	-	-	-	-	-	-	-	-	-	-	-	**46**
F.52	[805]	11	3	1	50	7	9	10	18	-	-	-	1	-	-	-	-	**110**
	[820]	56	88	-	67	26	11	63	22	-	-	4	6	5	-	-	-	**348**
	[821]	11	3	1	17	5	2	14	8	-	-	3	1	-	-	3	-	**68**
	[822]	1	-	-	-	-	-	-	-	-	-	-	-	-	-	-	-	**1**
	[844]	-	1	1	3	-	-	4	3	-	-	-	-	-	-	-	-	**12**
	[851]	-	-	-	1	-	-	-	-	-	-	-	-	-	-	-	-	**1**
	[853]	12	-	-	19	9	-	12	8	1	-	-	-	-	-	3	-	**64**
	[855]	-	-	1	7	1	-	6	2	-	-	-	-	-	-	1	-	**18**
	[856]	2	-	-	1	4	-	3	-	-	-	-	-	-	-	-	-	**10**
	[859]	2	-	-	1	1	-	-	-	-	-	-	-	-	-	-	-	**4**
	'Clean'	7	1	-	7	2	-	3	4	-	-	-	1	-	-	-	-	**25**
F.53	[807]	71	12	3	115	33	7	28	16	-	-	3	-	1	-	33	3	**325**
	[842]	39	2	2	64	15	5	7	6	-	-	-	1	-	-	4	-	**145**
	[846]	6	-	-	2	1	1	-	-	-	-	-	-	-	-	27	2	**39**
	[860]	8	2	-	12	3	-	-	-	-	-	-	1	-	-	-	-	**26**
	[861]	2	1	-	11	3	-	-	-	-	-	-	-	-	-	4	1	**22**
	[865]	5	2	-	6	2	-	-	-	-	-	-	-	-	-	1	-	**16**
	[868]	25	4	-	27	2	-	3	1	-	-	-	-	-	-	1	-	**63**
	'Clean'	24	2	1	12	2	-	2	-	-	-	-	-	-	-	2	3	**48**
F.54	[809]	1	-	-	-	-	-	-	-	-	-	-	-	-	-	-	-	**1**
	[824]	-	-	1	-	-	-	-	-	-	-	-	-	-	-	-	-	**1**
F.71	[801]/[829]/[838]/[839]	34	11	7	23	23	2	49	7	-	-	5	3	-	2	-	-	**166**
F.72	[800]	175	21	7	180	114	21	72	25	4	-	3	11	2	1	12	-	**648**
	[814]	90	11	5	117	38	4	38	6	-	-	-	2	2	1	10	-	**324**
	[864]	29	3	-	31	28	-	8	1	1	1	1	1	-	-	4	-	**108**
F.81	[819]	190	28	9	280	49	7	37	32	-	-	4	15	-	1	15	-	**667**
	[866]	93	16	2	117	42	1	26	19	-	-	2	3	-	-	10	-	**331**
	[870]	9	2	2	13	6	-	-	6	-	-	-	-	-	-	-	-	**38**
F.88	[874]	1	-	-	1	-	-	-	-	-	-	-	-	-	-	1	-	**3**
Total		**957**	**216**	**43**	**1193**	**416**	**72**	**395**	**186**	**6**	**1**	**25**	**48**	**14**	**5**	**131**	**9**	**3717**

Table 2.21. Longstones Cove lithics: debitage and unmodified

on their dorsal surface. A large proportion of facetted, and a smaller number of facetted and trimmed, flake platforms are in evidence. This is entirely consistent with the predominance of multi-platform cores (Table 2.23).

A notable number of hinge and, in slightly lower numbers, step fractures are visible in flake terminations. This to some degree reflects the use of poor quality raw materials, but also shows a concern with expediency exhibited in the bulk of the assemblage over and above the desire to follow carefully controlled traditions

	F.50	F.52	F.53	F.54	F.71	F.72	F.81	Total	% of Assemblage
Combination Tools	-	2	-	1	1	6	2	**12**	11.8
Scrapers	-	1	-	-	-	-	1	**2**	2.0
Sawing / Cutting / Engraving	-	6	7	-	2	30	16	**61**	59.8
Piercing	-	2	2	-	1	17	-	**22**	21.6
Knives & Retouched Blades	-	-	-	-	-	-	1	**1**	1.0
Hammerstones	1	-	-	-	-	-	3	**4**	3.9
Total	**1**	**11**	**9**	**1**	**4**	**53**	**23**	**102**	

Table 2.22. Longstones Cove lithics: breakdown of tools (classifiable)

Feature	Context	Core Fragment	A1	A2	B2	B3	C	D	E	Levallois	Flaked lump	Core on a flake	Total	% of All Cores
	[001]	1	-	-	-	-	1	-	1	-	-	1	**4**	3.0%
F.52	[805]	-	-	-	-	-	-	-	-	-	-	1	**1**	0.8%
	[820]	4	-	-	-	-	3	-	2	-	-	2	**11**	8.3%
	[821]	1	-	-	-	-	1	-	-	-	1	-	**3**	2.3%
	[853]	1	-	-	-	-	-	-	-	-	-	-	**1**	0.8%
	[855]	1	-	-	-	-	-	-	1	-	-	-	**2**	1.5%
	[859]	-	-	-	-	-	1	-	-	-	-	-	**1**	0.8%
	'Clean'	-	-	-	-	-	1	-	-	-	-	-	**1**	0.8%
F.53	[807]	-	-	-	-	-	2	2	-	-	-	2	**6**	4.6%
	[842]	2	-	-	-	-	-	-	-	-	1	1	**4**	3.0%
	[846]	1	-	-	-	-	-	-	-	-	-	-	**1**	0.8%
	[860]	3	-	-	-	-	1	-	-	-	-	-	**4**	3.0%
	[861]	1	-	1	-	-	-	-	-	-	-	-	**2**	1.5%
	[865]	-	-	-	-	-	-	-	-	-	-	-	**0**	0.0%
	[868]	-	-	1	-	-	1	-	-	-	-	-	**2**	1.5%
	[824]	-	-	-	-	-	-	-	-	1	-	-	**1**	0.8%
F.71	[801]/[829]/[838]/[839]	4	-	-	-	-	2	-	1	-	4	1	**12**	9.1%
F.72	[800]	13	-	3	-	3	9	2	3	-	-	-	**33**	25.0%
	[814]	3	-	1	1	-	3	-	4	-	2	1	**15**	11.4%
	[864]	3	1	-	-	1	3	2	2	-	-	-	**12**	9.1%
F.81	[819]	4	-	3	-	1	1	-	3	1	-	-	**13**	9.9%
	[866]	1	-	1	-	-	1	-	-	-	-	-	**3**	2.3%
Total		**43**	**1**	**10**	**1**	**5**	**30**	**6**	**17**	**2**	**8**	**9**	**132**	
% of Total Cores (incl. frags.)		32.6	0.8	7.6	0.8	3.8	22.7	4.6	12.9	1.5	6.1	6.8		

Table 2.23. Longstones Cove lithics: cores

of stone working. The presence of 48 plunging core rejuvenation flakes may indicate attempted recovery of errors in core working that had been created by the presence of hinge and step fractures, and in some instances may themselves be the result of poor core working control. The style of working and the presence of both keeled and Levallois cores are indicative of a later Neolithic date for the majority of the assemblage. The relatively diminutive size of the Levallois-style cores (Table 2.24) hints at the limited production of oblique arrowheads on the site, and are certainly an indicator of a more controlled approach to core reduction than is evident in the majority of the later Neolithic component within the assemblage.

The presence of 488 chunks and chips is probably due to the crudity of stone working techniques adopted together with the spontaneous fracturing of poor quality flint. In a number of cases it is also almost certainly the result of damage associated with later destruction activity.

Alongside the apparent crudity of the stone working present within the majority of the assemblage a more careful tradition of working is also evident. Some of the core rejuvenation tablets relate to the rejuvenation of multi-platform cores, but a number also bespeak of a more controlled (and possibly earlier) element that is further demonstrated by the presence of 11 single platform and six double platform cores (Table 2.23). A total of 70.6% of the single and double platform cores in the assemblage exhibit scars that include blade and/or narrow flake removals (Table 2.25). In contrast, flake removals predominate in all other core types. A1, A2 and B2 type cores are also on average smaller than all other core types present except the two Levallois cores (Table 2.24). This suggests a greater concern with husbanding of resources in the working of these cores than is otherwise evidenced. Taken together with the evidence for multi-phase patination that indicates recycling of earlier materials, this suggests an underlying element of probable earlier Neolithic date that pre-dates the bulk of the lithic material associated with the construction and use of the Cove. Echoes of this earlier assemblage can also be seen in the presence of a crested blade recovered from [864] (Table 2.21).

Core Weights & Dimensions	Average Weight (g)	Average Length (mm)	Average Width (mm)	Average Thickness (mm)
Core A1	42.0	60.0	35.7	22.5
Core A2	33.4	42.8	34.4	26.8
Core B1	-	-	-	-
Core B2	42.0	52.8	39.0	23.1
Core B3	63.2	49.8	39.7	30.8
Core C	71.6	53.1	40.8	31.7
Core D	57.7	55.0	39.5	24.8
Core E	80.4	54.4	40.9	26.2
Core Levallois	28.0	44.2	39.5	15.3
Flaked Lump	250.5	82.4	65.0	44.0
Pieces esquillee	-	-	-	-
Core on a flake	78.4	64.2	47.6	25.0
All cores (excluding frags.)	82.7	55.8	42.7	29.5

Table 2.24. Longstones Cove lithics: core weights and dimensions

Balance of assemblage

It is clear from the high proportion of debitage present (88.4%) that material was worked at the

	Blade	Flake	Narrow Flake	Blade / Narrow Flake	Blade / Flake	Narrow Flake / Flake	Narrow Flake / Flake / Blade	Total
A1	-	1	-	-	-	-	-	**1**
%	*0.0%*	*100.0%*	*0.0%*	*0.0%*	*0.0%*	*0.0%*	*0.0%*	
A2	-	3	-	1	2	4	-	**10**
%	*0.0%*	*30.0%*	*0.0%*	*10.0%*	*20.0%*	*40.0%*	*0.0%*	
B2	-	-	-	-	1	-	-	**1**
%	*0.0%*	*0.0%*	*0.0%*	*0.0%*	*100.0%*	*0.0%*	*0.0%*	
B3	-	1	-	-	-	4	-	**5**
%	*0.0%*	*20.0%*	*0.0%*	*0.0%*	*0.0%*	*80.0%*	*0.0%*	
C	-	18	-	-	-	11	1	**30**
%	*0.0%*	*60.0%*	*0.0%*	*0.0%*	*0.0%*	*36.7%*	*3.3%*	
D	-	3	-	-	-	3	-	**6**
%	*0.0%*	*50.0%*	*0.0%*	*0.0%*	*0.0%*	*50.0%*	*0.0%*	
E	-	12	-	-	-	4	1	**17**
%	*0.0%*	*70.6%*	*0.0%*	*0.0%*	*0.0%*	*23.5%*	*5.9%*	
Levallois	-	1	-	-	-	1	-	**2**
%	*0.0%*	*50.0%*	*0.0%*	*0.0%*	*0.0%*	*50.0%*	*0.0%*	
Flaked Lump	-	6	1	-	-	1	-	**8**
%	*0.0%*	*75.0%*	*12.5%*	*0.0%*	*0.0%*	*12.5%*	*0.0%*	
Core on a flake	-	5	-	1	-	3	-	**9**
%	*0.0%*	*55.6%*	*0.0%*	*11.1%*	*0.0%*	*33.3%*	*0.0%*	
Total (exc. frags)	**0**	**50**	**1**	**2**	**3**	**31**	**2**	**89**
%	*0.0%*	*56.2%*	*1.1%*	*2.3%*	*3.4%*	*34.8%*	*2.3%*	

Table 2.25. Longstones Cove lithics: core removal scars

Feature/context	[001]	F.50	F.52	F.53	F.54	F.71	F.72	F.81	F.88	Total	% of Assemblage
Debitage / Prep	30	51	649	602	2	164	1048	1010	2	**3558**	88.4%
Cores	4	-	20	20	-	12	60	16	-	**132**	3.3%
Unmodified	4	-	5	10	-	2	6	1	-	**28**	0.7%
Unclassifiable Burnt	-	-	7	72	-	-	26	25	1	**131**	3.3%
Trimmed / Worn	2	-	10	4	1	-	11	17	-	**45**	1.1%
Misc. Retouched	-	-	6	3	-	2	7	12	-	**30**	0.8%
Tools (classifiable)	-	1	11	9	1	4	53	23	-	**102**	2.5%
Total	**40**	**52**	**708**	**720**	**4**	**184**	**1211**	**1104**	**3**	**4026**	
% of Assemblage	1.0%	1.3%	17.6%	17.9%	0.1%	4.6%	30.1%	27.4%	0.1%		

Table 2.26. Longstones Cove lithics: overall composition of assemblage

site (Table 2.26). Formally classifiable tools comprise only 2.5% of the total assemblage. Even when miscellaneous retouched and trimmed and worn items are added, this figure still only accounts for 4.4% of the whole. This is remarkably low and might, in some instances, be taken to suggest that some tools made at the site were removed for use elsewhere. This remains a possibility, but it should be remembered that the poor quality of flint selected for use and the expedient approach taken to core reduction evidenced in the majority of the assemblage mean that it is likely that higher than normal quantities of waste would have been produced in the production of any given implement.

Destruction activity has clearly affected the nature of the recovered assemblage with 3.3% comprising unclassifiable burnt lumps. The high proportion of broken (and therefore unidentifiable) flakes/narrow flakes/blades, which account for 32.1% of the assemblage, is also almost certainly due to activity associated with stone destruction (Table 2.21). In addition to the four hammerstones present, a number of the 'unmodified' flint nodules show signs of abrasion. It is not, however, clear whether this has been caused as the result of post-depositional damage associated with destruction activity, or whether there has been some attempt to use them as *ad hoc* percussion instruments.

Tool assemblage

The tools represent a remarkably constrained range of activities. The formal tool assemblage is dominated by sawing and cutting tools which comprise 59.8% of the assemblage (Table 2.22). A further 21.6% of the assemblage is made up of piercing implements. In addition the overwhelming majority of the combination tools contain elements from one or other of these categories. Only two scrapers, plus an additional two combination tools incorporating a scraper element, are present. The overall balance of the tool assemblage shows remarkable similarities with that encountered in the Falkner's Circle excavations (Chapter 3, this volume).

A full summary of formal tools, utilised flakes and pieces with miscellaneous retouch can be found in Table 2.27. The following provides a more detailed account of a number of items of particular note.

Denticulates

F.72 [800]. Denticulate with a scraper-like edge. Made on deeply creamy-white patinated chalk flint.

F.72 [814]. Denticulated flake.

F.72 [864]. Denticulate exhibiting signs of extreme wear down the right-hand side.

F.81 [866]. Denticulate scraper made on an irregular flake with bulb removed; Carefully worked in comparison with much of the rest of the assemblage.

Combination tools

Saw + notch

F.71 [801]. Made on a broken hinged flake with the notch formed on the broken, proximal end. Saw extends the entire length of the right-hand side.

Saw + awl

F.72 [814]. Made on a flake and comprising two separately worked awls and a saw.

Table 2.27. Longstones Cove lithics: tools

Feature	Context	Edge trimmed flake	Edge trimmed narrow flake	Edge trimmed blade	Edge trimmed flake with edge gloss	Edge trimmed n. flake with edge gloss	Worn edge flake	Misc. unifacially retouched	Bifacially worked misc. tool	Saw & notch/es	Saw & awl	End scraper & notch	End scraper & awl	Saw & spurred projection	Saw & trimmed	Denticulate & saw	Notch & piercer	Side-end scraper	Scraper on a non-flake blank	Denticulate	Saw	Serrated Piece	Notch	Awl	Piercer	Spurred piece	Hammerstone	Total
	[001	2	-	-	-	-	-	-	-	-	-	-	-	-	-	-	-	-	-	-	-	-	-	-	-	-	-	2
F.50	[858	-	-	-	-	-	-	-	-	-	-	-	-	-	-	-	-	-	-	-	-	-	-	-	-	-	1	1
F.52	-	-	-	-	-	-	-	1	-	-	-	-	-	-	-	-	-	-	-	-	-	-	-	-	-	-	-	1
	[820]	6	3	-	-	-	-	4	-	-	-	-	-	-	-	-	-	-	1	-	-	-	2	-	-	-	-	16
	[821]	-	-	-	-	-	-	-	-	1	1	-	-	-	-	-	-	-	-	2	-	-	1	-	-	-	-	5
	[855]	1	-	-	-	-	-	-	-	-	-	-	-	-	-	-	-	-	-	-	-	-	1	1	1	-	-	4
	[859]	-	-	-	-	-	-	1	-	-	-	-	-	-	-	-	-	-	-	-	-	-	-	-	-	-	-	1
F.53	-	-	1	-	-	-	-	-	-	-	-	-	-	-	-	-	-	-	-	-	-	-	1	-	-	-	-	2
	[807]	3	-	-	-	-	-	2	1	-	-	-	-	-	-	-	-	-	-	1	3	1	1	-	2	-	-	14
	[842]	-	-	-	-	-	-	-	-	-	-	-	-	-	-	-	-	-	-	-	-	-	-	-	-	-	-	-
F.54	[824]	-	-	1	-	-	-	-	-	-	-	1	-	-	-	-	-	-	-	-	-	-	-	-	-	-	-	2
F.71	[801]	-	-	-	-	-	-	-	1	1	-	-	-	-	-	-	-	-	-	-	2	-	-	1	-	-	-	5
	[838]	-	-	-	-	-	-	1	-	-	-	-	-	-	-	-	-	-	-	-	1	-	-	-	-	-	-	2
F.72	[800]	3	2	1	-	-	-	4	2	-	-	-	1	-	-	-	-	-	-	2	7	1	2	6	5	3	-	39
	[814]	1	2	1	-	-	1	-	1	1	2	-	-	1	1	-	-	-	-	1	8	-	2	-	1	-	-	23
	[864]	-	-	-	-	-	-	-	-	-	-	-	-	-	-	-	-	-	-	3	1	-	3	2	-	-	-	9
F.81	[819]	2	-	-	-	-	-	3	-	-	-	-	-	-	-	-	-	-	-	-	5	1	1	-	-	-	2	14
	[854]	-	1	-	1	1	1	3	-	-	-	-	-	-	-	1	-	-	-	-	1	-	1	-	-	-	-	1-
	[866]	6	2	-	-	-	2	4	-	-	-	-	-	-	-	-	1	1	-	3	3	1	-	-	-	-	1	24
	[870]	-	-	-	-	-	1	2	-	-	-	-	-	-	-	-	-	-	-	-	-	-	-	-	-	-	-	3
Total		**24**	**11**	**3**	**1**	**1**	**5**	**25**	**5**	**3**	**3**	**1**	**1**	**1**	**1**	**1**	**1**	**1**	**1**	**12**	**31**	**4**	**15**	**1-**	**9**	**3**	**4**	**177**

End scraper + notch
F.54 [824]. Made on a partially cortical flake of chalk flint previously worked and showing multi-phase patination.

Saw + spurred projection
F.72 [814]. Made on a previously used flake. Shows multi-phase patination. Broken.

Saw + trimmed
F.72 [814]. Made on a previously broken flake.

Denticulate + saw
F.81 [854]. Denticulate on left hand side, saw extends down right hand side and across proximal end. Shows multi-phase patination.

Notch + piercer
F.81 [866]. Made on a thick secondary flake with facetted platform. Piercer worked at distal end. Notch worked down right-hand side with inverse retouch.

Serrates
F.53 [807]. Made on a bladelet. Very carefully worked.
F.72 [800]. Made on a blade.
F.81 [819]. Made on a narrow flake. Broken.
F.81 [866]. Broken.

Notches
Of the 15 notched pieces present, seven are made on flakes, three on narrow flakes and two on blades.

Awls
F.72 [800]. Shows multi-phase patination. Made on earlier piece with thick yellowy-brown patina.
F.72 [864]. Worked all the way round. Rotating type.

Piercers
F.72 [800]. Large, heavy and very expediently worked. Signs of wear towards 'point' down one side.
F.72 [800]. Made on a hinged flake. Extreme end of 'point' is broken.
F7.2 [800]. Heavy use damage to point.

Spurred pieces
F.72 [800]. Made on a thick, heavy flake. Double spurred piece formed by the removal of notches between the spurs. Signs of wear to both of the spurs and to the notches between the spurs.
F.72 [800]. Made on a thick, heavy flake. Spur formed on a scraper-like edge.

Edge retouched knife
F.81 [866]. Made on a narrow flake, with abrupt blunting retouch down one edge. Deep white patination.

Hammerstones
F.50 [858]. Cortex and thermal alteration suggests this piece is on surface flint. Weight 142g.
F.81 [819]. Weight 819g.
F.81 [819]. Broken (not weighed).
F.81 [866]. Irregular cortical nodule. Weight 660g.

Saws
F.53 [809]. Thick narrow flake with retouch on both faces in alternate patches. Retouch forms the second phase of patination.
F.72 [800]. Removals on distal edge of hinged flake. Retouch forms the second phase of patination.
F.72 [800]. Made on previously broken narrow flake or blade.
F.72 [814]. Small area of working on a previously broken flake. Indications of wear present.
F.72 [814]. Made on extensively flawed extremely poor chalk flint.
F.81 [819]. Saw formed by retouch on the right-hand side of flake. Significant indications of wear.
F.81 [819]. Significant signs of wear on saw edge.

Edge-trimmed and worn edge pieces
F.81 [854]. Broken edge-trimmed flake with edge gloss. Trimming and gloss located on left hand side of ventral surface.
F.81 [854]. Worn edge flake exhibiting indications of extremely heavy wear. May originally have been an edge-trimmed flake.
F.81 [854]. Worn edge flake made on a broken flake (*i.e.* broken before, not subsequent to, use).

Seven out of 24 edge-trimmed flakes are trimmed/utilised on more than one edge; four out of 11 edge-trimmed narrow flakes are trimmed/utilised on more than one edge; one example is made on a ridge trimming flake and one on a rejuvenation flake; one of the three edge-trimmed blades is trimmed/utilised on

	No.	% of Total Assemblage
Material unknown	125	51.2%
Chalk flint	92	37.7%
Derived flint	2	0.8%
Flint (unknown origin)	24	9.8%
Sarsen	1	0.4%
	244	

	No.	% of Total Assemblage
Unpatinated	16	6.6%
Single phase patination "blue"	77	31.6%
Single phase patination "white"	121	49.6%
Multi-phase patination	30	12.3%
	244	

% On Dorsal Surface	No.	% of Total Assemblage
0	101	41.4%
>0-25%	73	29.9%
>25-50%	24	9.8%
>50-75%	17	7.0%
>75-99%	17	7.0%
>100%	3	1.2%
Entirely cortical flake	-	0.0%
Cortex on platform only	9	3.7%
	244	

Table 2.28. (top) Beckhampton Avenue lithics: raw materials

Table 2.29. (middle) Beckhampton Avenue lithics: patination

Table 2.30. (bottom) Beckhampton Avenue lithics: percentage cortex

more than one edge; and three out of five worn edge flakes are worn on more than one edge.

Scrapers

F.81 [866]. Side and end scraper expediently made on a squat thick flake.

F.52 [820]. Scraper on a non-flake blank. Multi-phase patination shows three phases of working.

Miscellaneous retouched (unifacial)

F.52 [820]. Semi-abrupt retouch along distal edge of flake. Retouch forms second phase of patination.

F.52 [859]. Very worn area of retouch down right-hand side of flake. Possibly a saw.

F.53 [807]. Broken flake. Possibly a denticulate.

F.71 [838]. Possibly an awl with a broken point.

F.72 [800]. Possibly a scraper.

F.72 [800]. Possibly an awl with a broken point.

F.81 [866]. Very worn. Possibly a saw.

Miscellaneous retouched (bifacial)

F.71 [801]. Possibly uncompleted roughout for an arrowhead of uncertain type. Entirely unpatinated flint.

F.72 [800]. Small notch worked on the right-hand side of the dorsal surface and blunting retouch down the left-hand surface. Ventral and dorsal surfaces alternately worked to form a probable awl, the point of which is broken.

F.72 [800]. Several notches and a spur worked on the dorsal surface. A small area of invasive retouch along the left-hand side of the ventral surface and a denticulate formed at the distal end. Made on a thick squat flake with multi-phase patination.

Worked flint from Avenue contexts

The lithic assemblage from the excavated section of the Beckhampton Avenue adjacent to the Longstones Cove comprises a total of 244 items. Of these, 149 pieces (61.1% of the assemblage) were recovered from destruction or burial pits, 86 (35.3%) from the stone-holes, and four items from pit F.37 (of uncertain date). A further five flints were recovered from the topsoil.

Raw materials

Within those elements of the assemblage where characterisation of raw materials was possible, the largest proportion was chalk flint of local character (37.7% of the total assemblage) (Table 2.28). Like the chalk flint in the Cove assemblage, much of this material possesses a thin cortex and is poor quality and fossiliferous, suggesting a concern with immediacy of supply over quality of product. However, in contrast to the Cove assemblage, only two items of derived, riverine flint and none of chert were present. A single sarsen hammer stone was also present.

Multi-phase patination is evident on 12.3% of the assemblage (Table 2.29). This is consistent with the reworking of earlier materials. As with the recycling evident in the Cove assemblage, this may suggest an opportunistic approach to the gathering of raw materials or may signal a more deliberate choice of previously worked raw materials.

Primary flakes account for only 1.2% of the assemblage (Table 2.30), providing a very clear picture of preliminary preparation of raw materials having taken place away from the site. Just over half of the pieces (57.4%) are secondary flakes and tools that retain some cortex, suggesting that relatively small nodules of surface flint were utilised.

Feature	Context	Flake	Narrow Flake	Blade	Flake/narrow flake/blade	Chunk	Chip	Ridge Trimming Flake	Trimming Flake	Retouch Flake	Core Rejuvenation Tablet	Plunging Core Rejuvenation Flake	Thermal piece	Unclassified burnt frags	Total
	[001]	2	-	-	1	-	-	1	-	-	-	-	-	-	**4**
F.21	[400]	-	-	-	1	2	-	1	1	-	-	-	-	-	**5**
F.22	[401]	2	-	-	3	1	-	1	2	-	-	-	-	-	**9**
F.23	Backfill	2	-	1	-	-	-	-	-	-	-	-	-	-	**3**
	[405]	8	-	2	6	2	2	2	6	1	2	1	-	-	**32**
	[434]	-	-	-	-	-	-	1	-	-	1	-	-	-	**2**
F.24	[404]	1	-	-	1	-	-	3	3	-	1	-	-	-	**9**
	[409]	1	-	-	-	-	-	-	-	-	-	-	-	-	**1**
	[415]	-	-	-	-	-	-	1	-	-	-	-	-	-	**1**
F.25	[421]	-	-	-	-	-	-	4	-	-	-	-	-	-	**4**
	[429]	1	-	-	-	-	-	-	-	-	1	-	-	-	**2**
F.26	[426]	1	-	1	-	-	-	-	-	-	-	-	-	-	**2**
	[448]	1	-	-	-	-	-	1	-	-	-	-	-	-	**2**
F.33	[428]	2	-	-	4	6	1	1	6	-	1	-	1	-	**22**
F.35	[429]	1	-	-	2	-	-	-	13	-	-	1	-	1	**18**
F.37	[437]	1	-	-	-	-	-	2	1	-	-	-	-	-	**4**
F.42	[413]	-	-	-	-	-	-	-	-	-	-	1	-	-	**1**
	[414]	-	-	-	1	-	-	2	-	-	-	-	-	-	**3**
F.62	[610]	5	3	-	11	1	-	7	1	-	-	-	-	-	**28**
	[612]	4	1	-	2	-	1	3	1	-	-	-	-	-	**12**
F.82	[613]	4	1	1	2	1	2	2	-	-	-	-	-	-	**13**
	[616]	3	1	-	-	-	-	2	-	-	-	-	-	-	**6**
F.83	[852]	1	-	-	2	-	1	1	2	-	-	-	-	-	**7**
F.100	[901]	4	1	-	6	-	-	2	3	-	1	-	-	-	**17**
F.106	[907]	1	-	-	-	-	-	-	-	-	-	1	-	-	**2**
	[922]	1	-	-	-	-	-	2	-	-	-	-	-	-	**3**
Total		**46**	**7**	**5**	**42**	**13**	**7**	**39**	**39**	**1**	**7**	**4**	**1**	**1**	**212**

Table 2.31. Beckhampton Avenue lithics: debitage and unmodified (excluding cores)

CORE REDUCTION TECHNIQUES

The assemblage is flake-dominated with a ratio of flakes to narrow flakes to blades of 9.2:1.4:1 (Table 2.31). Analysis of previous removals on cores reinforces the predominance of flake production seen in the flake ratios (Table 2.32).

The pronounced bulbs of percussion and thick, heavy flakes present in the majority of the assemblage point to a predominance of hard-hammer working. This is supported by the presence of a single sarsen hammer stone recovered from stone-hole F.35 [429]. Expedient core working combined with poor quality raw materials accounts for the presence of a significant minority (18.45%) of hinged and step-fractured flake terminations, suggesting

	Blade	Flake	Narrow Flake	Blade & Narrow Flake	Blade & Flake	Narrow Flake & Flake	Narrow Flake & Flake & Blade	Total
Core C	-	2	-	-	1	4	-	**7**
%	0.0%	28.6%	0.0%	0.0%	14.3%	57.1%	0.0%	
Core D	-	2	-	-	-	1	-	**3**
%	0.0%	66.7%	0.0%	0.0%	0.0%	33.3%	0.0%	
Core E	-	1	-	-	-	-	-	**1**
%	0.0%	100.0%	0.0%	0.0%	0.0%	0.0%	0.0%	
Flaked Lump	-	3	-	-	-	-	-	**3**
%	0.0%	100.0%	0.0%	0.0%	0.0%	0.0%	0.0%	
Core on a flake	-	-	-	-	-	1	-	**1**
%	0.0%	0.0%	0.0%	0.0%	0.0%	100.0%	0.0%	
Total (exc. fragments)	**-**	**8**	**-**	**-**	**1**	**6**	**-**	**15**
%	0.0%	53.3%	0.0%	0.0%	6.7%	40.0%	0.0%	

	No.	% of Total Assemblage
Feathered	104	42.6%
Hinged	29	11.9%
Step fracture	16	6.6%
Plunging	1	0.4%
No visible termination	94	38.5%
	244	

Table 2.32. (top) Beckhampton Avenue lithics: core scars by core type

Table 2.33. (bottom) Beckhampton Avenue lithics: flake terminations

knapping errors were a regular occurrence (Table 2.33).

In contrast to the Cove lithic assemblage, no single or double platform cores were identifiable, with multi-platform and keeled cores predominating (Table 2.34). The expedient nature of the majority of the core working represented is emphasised by the presence of three amorphous, and extremely large, flaked lumps (Table 2.35), one core made on a flake, and in the lack of any platform preparation in over 40% of the assemblage (Table 2.36). However, it should be noted that despite the lack of type A and B cores, there are some indications of more careful methods of working. These include the presence of 78 trimming and ridge-trimming flakes and seven core rejuvenation tablets (Table 2.31). This echoes the pattern of working evidenced on a much larger scale in the Cove assemblage.

Balance of assemblage

Debitage forms 85.0% of the assemblage, with only 2.8% of the total being represented by formally classifiable tools (Table 2.37). When trimmed, worn and miscellaneous retouched pieces are added to this, all tools and utilised items account for only 4.4% of the assemblage. This is remarkably similar to the proportions represented in the Cove and Pre-Cove assemblage, and may, as suggested in the discussion of that material, be the result of expedient working methods and poor quality raw materials, although it is also possible that some tools were removed for use elsewhere.

Destruction activity seems to have had less of an impact on the Beckhampton Avenue assemblage than the Cove material, with consistently lower proportions of unclassifiable burnt lumps, broken flakes, narrow flakes, blades, chunks and chips occurring in the former.

Tool assemblage

The formal tool assemblage is dominated by sawing and cutting tools, which together make up 57.1% (Table 2.38). The single combination tool present is also a saw/notch. One hammerstone is also present. The predominance and proportion of sawing and cutting tools is remarkably similar to that within the Cove assemblage, though unlike the latter material, no piercing activities (beyond the use of projectiles) are represented in the implements present. A single fragment of a later Neolithic oblique arrowhead may go someway to confirming the suggestion that a small element of the core working represented in the Cove assemblage was connected with the production of transverse arrowheads.

Summary of tools

A summary of formal tools, utilised flakes and pieces with miscellaneous retouch can be found in Table 2.39. The following provides a more detailed account of a number of items of particular note.

Miscellaneous retouched

F.62 [612]. Small fragment of bifacially worked flint. Too thick in section to have been part of an arrowhead or laurel leaf.

Saws
F.24 [404]. Saw made on a previously broken flake.
F.24 [404]. Saw made on a core rejuvenation tablet that had itself been previously recycled from a very heavily patinated piece of poor quality dark grey mottled flint. Weight 294g.

Arrowhead
F.100 [901]. Small fragment of an oblique arrowhead.

Hammerstone
F.35 [429]. Sarsen hammerstone. Weight 120g.

Distribution and associations

The majority of material in the Cove assemblage is consistent with a later Neolithic date, but a smaller element of earlier Neolithic material is clearly represented, some of this having been drawn upon, alongside other locally available raw materials, in the later Neolithic. It is tempting to speculate that the earlier material is related to the construction or use of the South Street long barrow, situated only 75m to the east of the Cove site, but this cannot be certain. Serrated items are generally held to be earlier Neolithic in date. It is interesting to note in this connection that of the four serrated pieces present two are made on blades and a third on a narrow flake (the fourth is broken and not identifiable to flake type). Given the overwhelming dominance of flakes within the assemblage as a whole, the four serrated pieces may therefore relate to the identified earlier Neolithic component of the assemblage.

A total of 54.6% of all cores present were recovered from contexts associated with stone L15 with 45.5% of these coming from F.72. Six of the 10 awls within the assemblage come from F.72 [800] and a further two from F.72 [864]. The two remaining awls were recovered from F.81 [819] and [854]. Five of the nine piercers present come from F.72 [800] and one from F.72 [814]. All three of the spurred pieces were recovered from F.72 [800]. The concentration of debitage and tools found in this area suggests that it formed the focus for both knapping activity, and subsequently, tool use. The heavy use-damage evident on a number of the implements present around stone L15 and elsewhere suggests that substantial use was made of the tools on site.

Feature	Context	Core fragment	Core C	Core D	Core E	Flaked Lump	Core on a flake	Total
	[001]	-	1	-	-	-	-	**1**
F.21	[400]	1	-	-	-	-	-	**1**
F.23	Backfill	-	-	-	-	-	1	**1**
F.24	[404]	-	1	1	-	-	-	**2**
F.26	[426]	-	-	-	-	1	-	**1**
F.33	[428]	1	-	1	-	-	-	**2**
F.35	[429]	1	-	-	-	-	-	**1**
	[414]	-	-	-	-	1	-	**1**
F.62	[610]	-	1	-	-	-	-	**1**
	[612]	-	1	-	-	-	-	**1**
F.82	[613]	2	-	1	-	-	-	**3**
F.100	[901]	1	3	-	1	1	-	**6**
Total		**6**	**7**	**3**	**1**	**3**	**1**	**21**

	Av. Wt (g)	Av. Length (mm)	Av. Width (mm)	Av. Thickness (mm)
Core C	188.1	62.7	62.7	37.4
Core D	84.7	60.1	45.2	29.1
Core E	20.0	37.6	34.7	17.2
Flaked Lump	225.3	53.1	40.6	29.6
Core on a flake	50.0	56.6	46.8	20.5
All cores (excl. frags)	**154.5**	**58.2**	**48.2**	**31.7**

	No.	% of Total Assemblage
No visible platform	76	31.2%
No platform preparation	99	40.6%
Trimmed	31	12.7%
Facetted	25	10.3%
Facetted and trimmed	13	5.3%
	244	

	No.	% of Total Assemblage
Debitage / Prep.	210	85.0
Cores	21	8.5
Unmodified	1	0.4
Unclassifiable burnt	4	1.6
Trimmed / Worn	3	1.2
Misc. Retouched	1	0.4
Tools (classifiable)	7	2.8
Total	**247**	

Table 2.34. (top) Beckhampton Avenue lithics: core type by context

Table 2.35. (above) Beckhampton Avenue lithics: core weights and dimensions

Table 2.36. (above left) Beckhampton Avenue lithics: platform types

Table 2.37. (left) Beckhampton Avenue lithics: balance of assemblage

Table 2.38. (right) Beckhampton Avenue lithics: breakdown of tools

Table 2.39. (below) Beckhampton Avenue lithics: tools including utilised pieces

	No.	% of Total
Combination Tools	1	14.3%
Sawing / Cutting / Engraving	4	57.1%
Arrowheads	1	14.3%
Hammerstones	1	14.3%
Total	**7**	

Feature	Context	Edge trimmed flake	Bifacially worked miscellaneous tool	Saw & notch/es	Saw	Notch	Transverse arrowhead	Hammerstone	Total
F.23	[405]	-	-	1	-	-	-	-	**1**
F.24	[404]	1	-	-	2	-	-	-	**3**
F.33	[428]	-	-	-	1	-	-	-	**1**
F.35	[429]	-	-	-	-	-	-	1	**1**
F.62	[610]	-	-	-	-	1	-	-	**1**
	[612]	-	1	-	-	-	-	-	**1**
F.82	[613]	2	-	-	-	-	-	-	**2**
F.100	[901]	-	-	-	-	-	1	-	**1**
Total		**3**	**1**	**1**	**3**	**1**	**1**	**1**	**11**

With reference to features of the Beckhampton Avenue, notable concentrations of lithic material came from stone-holes F.33, F.35 and F.82. These features also contained the only four items from the tool assemblage that can be regarded as having been recovered from an entirely undisturbed context; a saw from F.33, a sarsen hammerstone from F.35 and two edge-trimmed flakes from F.82. Both the tool assemblage and the core working techniques are entirely consistent with a later Neolithic date. The most chronologically diagnostic item – the fragment of an oblique arrowhead – was recovered from destruction pit F.100 and must therefore be regarded as residual. A significant concentration of cores (six of the 21 cores and core fragments present) came from destruction pit F.100 [901]. Though this material, like the arrowhead, is residual, it represents twice the number of cores found in any other context; as such, this area may have formed a particular focus for core working or disposal. The proximity of F.100 to the concentration of core working associated with the Cove should also be noted.

Many elements within the Beckhampton Avenue assemblage echo the material recovered from the Cove and Pre-Cove settings. This includes the similarity in the balance of the assemblages and the predominance of sawing and cutting tools in both cases. However, there are also points of divergence. Derived material forms only a tiny proportion of the Avenue material, whilst it makes up almost a quarter of the Cove assemblage. The difference in the balance of raw materials may reflect a difference of association or purpose in the selection of appropriate raw materials in the two locations, or it may be the result of chronologically differing choices. What is most remarkable, however, is the way in which the Beckhampton Avenue and Cove assemblages, like those from the West Kennet Avenue and Falkner's Circle excavations described in Chapter 3, seem to have been the product of a constrained, possibly task-specific, set of activities, which in all cases emphasised the use of cutting and sawing activities and were the product of largely expedient working practices.

Worked chalk

A fragment of chalk with possible signs of working came from the rubble packing [866] of stone-hole F81. The piece is fragmentary, up to 35mm in length and 27mm in width, and displays two deep parallel grooves (the most complete being 5mm wide and 6mm deep), above which is a zone reduced by scoring. The U-shaped profile to the grooves would seem to rule out their being produced by animal scratching, although the extensive animal disturbance within this feature should be noted. The worked surfaces of the piece have a gentle convex profile, suggesting that in its original form the object may have been cylindrical. Analogies might be found with the carved chalk phalli, cylinders and discs from the henge at Mount Pleasant, Dorset (Wainwright 1979, 167–71, figs. 75–7).

Molluscan analysis

Rosina Mount and Andrew Mann

A spot sample was taken from the original fill of stone-hole F.81 (L16), which had held one of the sarsens forming the Longstones Cove. The assemblage was characterised by *Pomatias elegans*, *Pupilla muscorum* and *Cochlicopa* sp. Some shade-loving species were represented by single shells (*Discus*, *Oxychillus*). Some examples of *Pomatias* and *Vallonia excentrica* appeared to be recent rather than sub-fossil shells (Table 2.40).

This assemblage is obviously contaminated so its value is limited. The dominant species are typical of habitats where there is broken ground. *Pomatias elegans* requires shade and moisture and a loose soil into which it can burrow, and is often taken as an indicatory of clearance. *Pupilla muscorum* is characteristic of places where the earth is bare of vegetation, such as patches of broken ground on grazed chalk grassland.

Table 2.40. Mollusca from series LSE 00 73

Pomatias elegans	30 (3 modern)
Cochlicopa sp.	10
Vertigo pygmaea	1
Pupilla muscorum	32
Vallonia excentrica	5 (4 modern)
Discus rotundatus	1
Nesovitrea hammonis	1
Oxychilus sp.	1
Helicella itala	4
Trichia hispida	2
Cecilioides acicula	56

Avebury Trusloe

Through a combination of excavation, observation and documentary research it was possible to trace the course of the Beckhampton Avenue from the western entrance of the Avebury henge along the High Street and as far as Truslow Manor Farm. In addition, the excavations in Longstones Field south-west established its course over a 150m stretch as it approaches the Longstones Cove and avenue terminal. However, the precise line of the avenue between these two points – a distance of *c.*700m – remained unclear. The only guide comprised the field records and drawings of William Stukeley. As with his records of the other extant portions of Avebury (see Ucko *et al.* 1991), inconsistencies in scale and perspective made it difficult to translate his observations to a modern map base with any precision. Further, many of the sarsens in this portion of the avenue's length had already been removed prior to his period of fieldwork. As a result, we were left with a 'zone of likelihood' rather than a definitive pathway for the avenue over this stretch. Following work on the West Kennet Avenue in 2002, it was also apparent that any assumption that the entire course of the avenue comprised regular paired stone settings could represent an over-simplification of a more varied structural form.

In an attempt to confirm the course of the Beckhampton Avenue in this area excavation of a further stone pair was planned, focusing on the eastern end of Longstones Field adjacent to the hamlet of Avebury Trusloe (Figure 2.5). From a critical analyses of Stukeley's unpublished field notes and drawings it was clear that the likely route of the avenue passed close to the northern edge of the modern housing estate at Trusloe.

Geophysical survey

Prior to excavation, a geophysical survey was undertaken across the full extent of the Stukeley 'probability zone' in an attempt to optimise the location of excavation trenches. Previous experience had illustrated the difficulties faced in using geophysical techniques to identify the features marking stone settings, burials or burning pits (see above). Chalk and sarsen are effectively inert for the purposes of magnetic detection and, despite the burning associated with many stone destruction events, the resultant magnetic signature is difficult to distinguish from more general noise (Ucko *et al.* 1991, 160). Resistivity has proved more useful in detecting traces of avenue settings, but the shallow, ephemeral nature of stone destruction pits and relatively small stone-holes makes detection erratic. As the experiences of 1999 and 2000 had illustrated, the detection of even substantial buried stones can be highly dependant upon ground conditions.

The baseline of the survey grid was centred upon the north-east corner of the modern housing estate. The grid was designed to capture at least three stone pairs if they did indeed pass through this area. Within the grid readings were taken at 1m intervals using a 0.5m probe spacing; data was processed using Geoplot 3 software. The results of the survey are given in Figure 2.72, where a number of features can be identified (A–E).

Running NE-SW across the area is a sinuous low resistance anomaly corresponding to a wide, shallow depression in the surface topography of the field (Feature A). The undulating, irregular form suggests strongly that this is a geological feature. There are also a number of more diffuse, irregular high

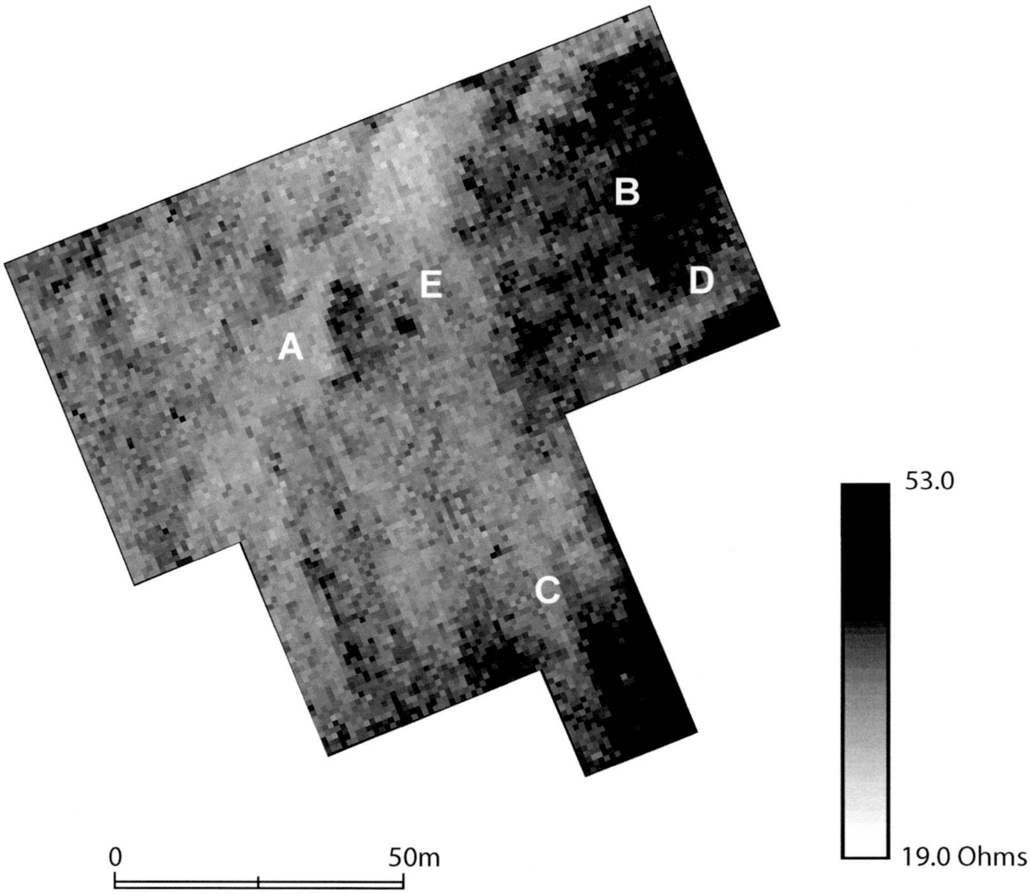

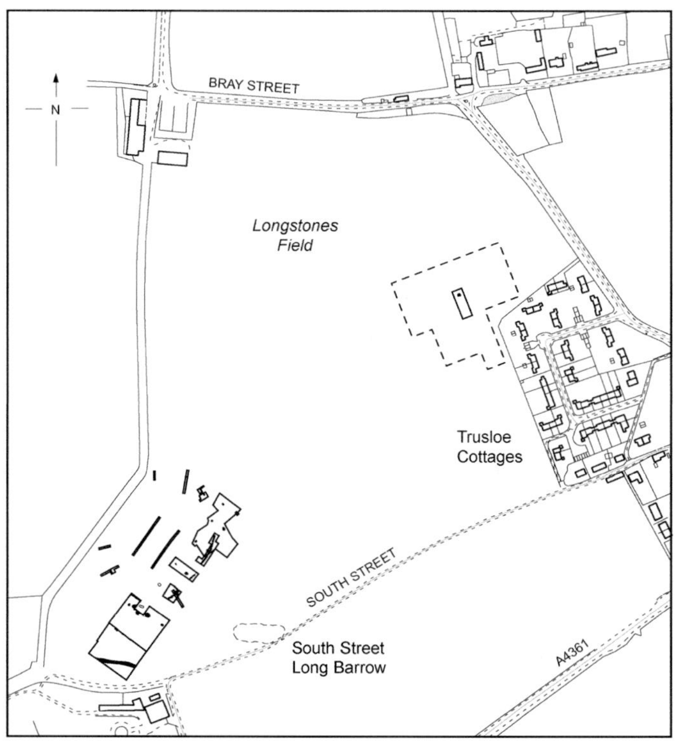

Figure 2.72. Avebury Trusloe: resistivity survey results and the location of the excavation trench. Incorporates data © Crown Copyright/ database right 2007. An Ordnance Survey/ (EDINA) supplied service

resistance anomalies at the eastern edge of the area (B) and adjacent to the boundary fence of the village (C). In each case the irregular form and trend direction paralleling feature A suggest a geological origin, however feature C does appear to echo a faint but regular linear banding that runs NW-SE across the area and may reflect previous ploughing regimes.

The final features (D and E) were the most promising with respect to the possible course of the Beckhampton Avenue. Within the general spread of anomaly B is a discrete high resistance anomaly (D). Feature E corresponded to a second well-defined high resistance anomaly. These responses resembled closely the stone burial anomalies detected in the area of the Longstones enclosure in 1999. Assuming anomalies D and E both correspond to stone burials their 44.5m spacing would suggest that there is a missing stone pair between them, given the range of longitudinal spacing for the West Kennet (Smith 1965, 206) and excavated section of the Beckhampton Avenue to the south-west.

On the basis of the geophysical survey the decision was taken to focus excavation upon anomaly E. In an effort to minimise disruption to the adjacent housing estate and the farm traffic accessing the field, excavation was limited to a single 30 × 10m trench. This led directly to a dilemma: if the anomaly did mark a buried stone on the line of the avenue, did it lie on the north or south side? The geophysical results were of little help here, failing to detect any further anomalies to either the north or south of D or E. After careful consideration, the decision was taken to extend the trench from anomaly E to the south. This was taken on two grounds: the linear relationship between anomalies D and E, and the alignment of the excavated portion of the avenue extending from Longstones Cove. Stukeley's records suggest a relatively smooth, gently curving course to the avenue. If these anomalies marked buried stones on the same side of the avenue the projected line would chart a course away from the alignment of settings L1–L10, and would accordingly require a marked change in direction further along its course. If, however, anomaly D was on the south side of the avenue and E on the north, a much gentler curve would be effected. Variation in the local topography also supported the latter interpretation. Although subtle, the ground does drop noticeably to the north of anomaly E. If this marked the northern edge of the avenue then the feature would sit atop this area of relatively high ground as it curves towards the Longstones Cove. On this basis, the trench was laid out over the anomaly and extending 25m to the south.

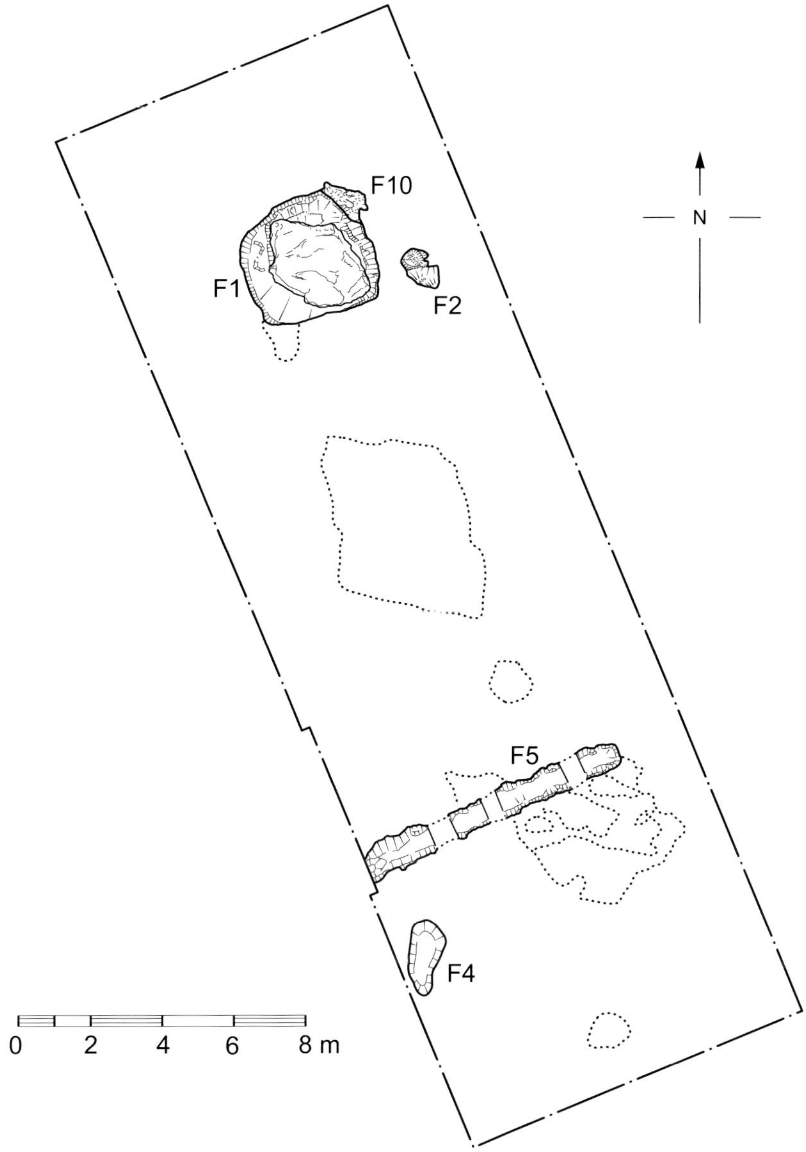

Figure 2.73. Avebury Trusloe: excavated features

Excavation results

The ploughsoil was removed by machine. This sat above a layer of lower ploughsoil, [002], thin and discontinuous in the northern end of the trench, becoming progressively deeper to the south. No features (*e.g.* shallow stone destruction pits) were recorded cutting into this lower ploughsoil, which was removed during a second stage of machining. The natural

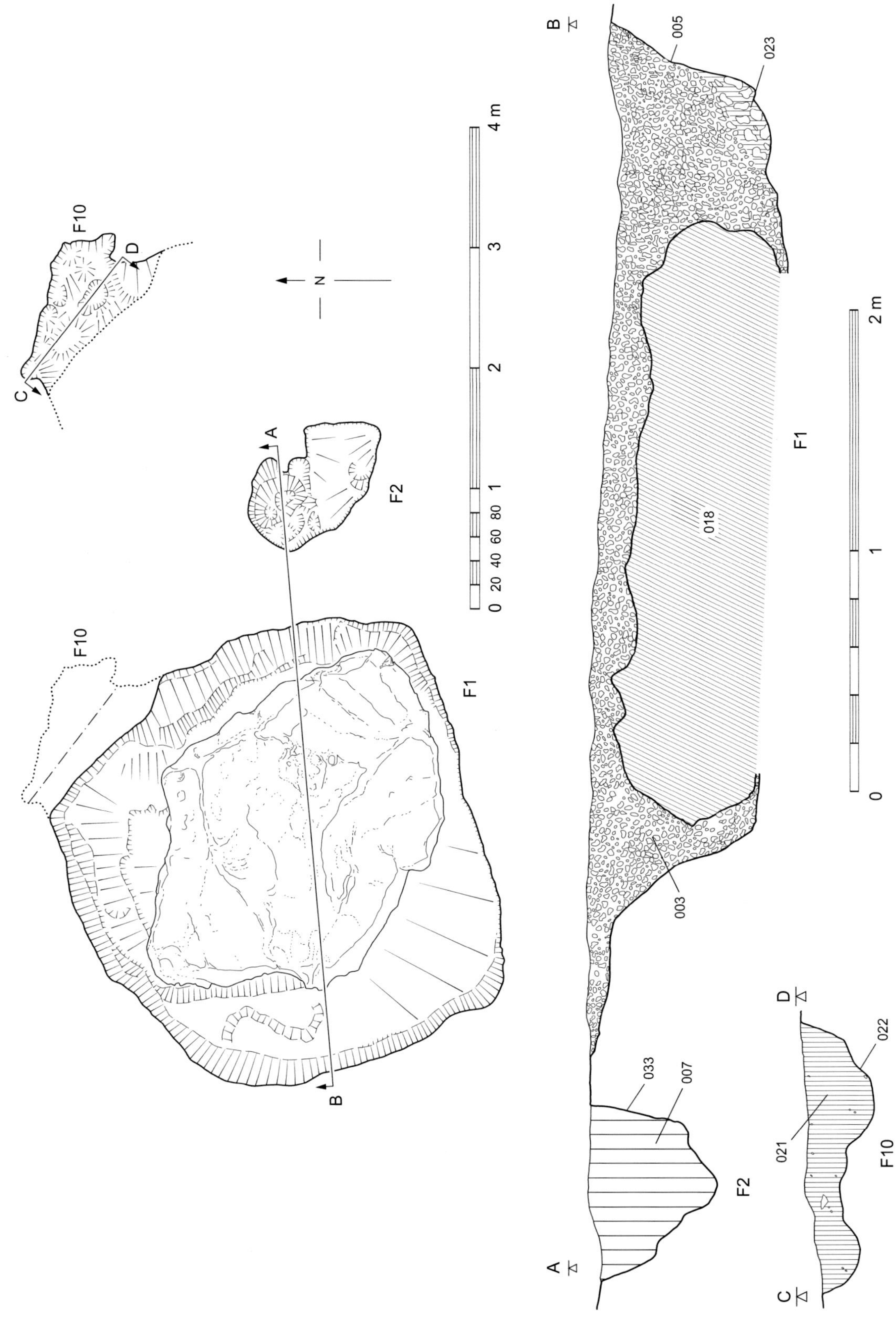

Figure 2.74. Avebury Trusloe: stone burial F.1, stone-hole F.10 and pit F.2

Context	Preparation flake	Rejuvenation flake	Flake	Chip	Core	Flaked piece	Shatter fragment	Retouched / utilised
[001] / [002]	-	-	1	-	-	-	-	1 (n)
F.1	1	3	17	7	-	1	1	-
F.2	-	6	18	12	1	3	3	4 (k, s, 2u)
F.4	-	1	1	-	-	-	-	-
F.5	-	1	2	3	-	-	-	1 (md)
F.6	-	-	2	1	-	-	-	-
F.7	-	1	1	-	-	-	-	-
F.8	-	1	1	-	-	-	-	1 (u)
F.9	-	-	1	-	-	-	-	-
F.10	2	-	4	3	-	-	-	2 (p)
Total	*3*	*13*	*48*	*26*	*1*	*4*	*4*	*9*

Table 2.41. (top) Worked flint from the Avebury Trusloe excavations (k = knife; s = scraper; u = utilised flake/blade; md = microdenticulate; p = piercer; n = notched)

comprised a distinctive deposit of banded coombe rock and silt. Several features were cut into the natural (Figure 2.73). Of these, six were of natural origin (F.3, 6, 7–9 and 11), comprising possible tree-throw pits and areas of animal disturbance.

T1

Stone-hole F.10, Stone [018]

Anomaly E was found to correspond to a medieval stone burial pit, F.1, located in the northern third of the trench. Lying on the base of the pit was a substantial, irregularly shaped sarsen, [018], 3.2 × 2.2m in maximum dimension and up to 0.6m thick (Figures 2.74 and 2.75). The upper surface of the stone was largely flat and smooth, with gently sloping facets towards the edges, and a small area of natural pocking. In contrast the lower surface was more faceted and markedly concave, resulting in a substantial void between the underside of the stone and the base of the burial pit. Details of the pit are given elsewhere (Chapter 9).

The original stone-hole, F.10, was located immediately north-east of the burial pit, a large part of its south-western side having been cut away by the later feature. The remnant stone-hole, cut [022], was irregular, *c.*1.3 × >0.7m in extent and up to 0.3m deep. Its base along the northern edge was smooth and compact, and merged into the side of the cut. By contrast, the remainder of the base of the burial pit was markedly irregular, showing no signs of compression and possessing a sharp junction with the pit sides. On the west was a noticeable step in the base of the pit. Forming a continuous feature with the stone-hole on its eastern side was a group of shallow hollows, filled with a relatively chalk-free reddish brown silty-clay [021]. These may correspond to stake and post settings related to the original erection of the sarsen. The remainder of the stone-hole was filled with a distinctive compacted, chocolate brown silty-clay, [031], sealed by a thin layer of weathered silty-chalk [028].

Figure 2.75. (above) Avebury Trusloe: buried sarsen [018] with pit F.2 in the foreground

Eleven pieces of worked flint were found in the stone-hole fill (Table 2.41). These include a homogenous collection of unpatinated and fresh flakes, most apparently from the same core. They are broad, hard-hammer struck, with no evidence of platform preparation, and therefore likely to be of late 3rd or early 2nd millennium BC date. Two piercers were also recovered from this feature, one a broken tip on a cortical flake, and the second on a large and irregular trimming flake with expedient and marginal retouch. All of this material could have been deposited at the point when the stone was erected, or around its base once standing. In contrast, the worked flint that found its way into the fill of the much later stone burial pit,

F.1, includes five carefully worked blades and no retouched or utilised pieces.

Other features

A metre to the east of the stone burial pit was a small pit, F.2 (Figure 2.74). The cut [033] was sub-circular, 0.7 × 0.5m and 0.5m deep, with moderate to steeply sloping sides and a stepped base. The primary fill comprised a thin lens of chalky brown clay loam [017] adhering to the eastern edge of the feature. This was in turn sealed by a very uniform, compact brown silty clay with very sparse chalk inclusions [007]. From the latter came a sarsen hammerstone and 47 pieces of flintwork: a mixed assemblage, with many small flakes and blades alongside larger pieces of debris that include shatter fragments, flaked pieces and an irregular flake core. In one instance a flaked piece makes use of a large and heavily patinated older core. The flakes and blades appear to derive from several cores. Among the retouched and utilised pieces are an end and side scraper on a small flake, two utilised blades and a cortically-backed knife on a narrow flake (Table 2.41). None of these pieces are particularly diagnostic, and the collection may even be a mix of earlier Neolithic and later pieces. The pit was considered to be prehistoric during excavation, however a radiocarbon date of 890–1020AD (at 95.4%: Wk17355) was obtained on charcoal from the fill.

In the southern third of the trench were two features, a length of shallow ditch, F.5, and adjacent to this a small pit, F.4. The ditch [011] was flat-bottomed, 0.2m deep and 0.7m wide, and ran SW-NE across the trench, terminating 1.5m from its eastern edge. Its fill [010] comprised a stiff reddish brown silty-clay with occasional small fragments of chalk and flint, and a small piece of sarsen. Finds included several pieces of worked flint and a small lump of coke. Although the coke suggests a relatively recent origin, the feature was sealed beneath the lower ploughsoil [002] and the material could be intrusive given the animal disturbance noted in the area. In the absence of more definitive dating evidence, a later prehistoric (later Bronze Age – Iron Age), Romano-British or early Medieval date for the feature is likely. In contrast to much of the worked flint from feature fills, that from the ditch is noticeably patinated and presumably derived.

Pit F.4 comprised an oval cut [006], 1.20 × 0.65m and 0.4m deep, with a rounded, gently stepped base and moderately sloping sides. It was filled with a very clean reddish brown silty-clay [004], from which two flint flakes were recovered.

In total 108 pieces of worked flint were recovered during the Trusloe excavation, all but one from feature fills (in part a consequence of the machine removal of topsoil and lower ploughsoil). Of these, the majority (88 or 81%) came from the key group of features in the northern third of the trench: the stone-hole F.10, burial pit F.1 and adjacent pit F.2. Such a concentration reflects more intense Neolithic depositional activity in this area, around the avenue stone setting (Table 2.41).

Taking the assemblage as a whole, there are notably few preparation flakes (amounting to only 2.8%), implying that most cores were brought on site in a partially worked state, while the large number of chips shows the later stages of knapping were taking place within this area. On technological grounds the assemblage looks to span the 4th to perhaps early 2nd millennium BC, with the earlier material – finely worked blades and narrow flakes – indicating activity of sorts, if perhaps quite transient, prior to the construction of the avenue. The background scatter represented by material from F.4–9 includes several pieces that look to be 4th millennium BC in character, with a good number of blades and narrow flakes, including one from F.5 with micro-denticulation and another, from F.8, with fine microflaking resulting from utilisation along one edge.

Discussion

Although the excavation succeeded in identifying one of the former avenue stones, and so tying down the position of the avenue at this point along its length, no sign was found of the presumed pair for stone setting T1. As a confirmatory exercise, a second resistance survey (employing a sampling interval of 0.5m) was undertaken on the surface of the natural following removal of the upper and lower ploughsoil. The results showed conclusively that there are no further buried stones (or any other features) in the area of the trench. There are several possible explanations for this absence. The most prosaic is that the trench was simply in the wrong place. The original assumption that T1 is a stone on the northern as opposed to the southern side of the avenue may have been incorrect, meaning that the other stone of the pair lies a further 15 or so metres to the north. An alternative and more likely scenario is that the long axis of the trench was not oriented perpendicular to the line of the avenue at this point, the second setting lying just outside the excavated area. However, as work on the West Kennet Avenue has illustrated (Chapter 3), the assumption of an unbroken line of stone pairs may not hold for the full length of both avenues. It may be that the two widely spaced stones suggested by the geophysical results accurately represent the form of the avenue at this point along its course. Given the limitations of the geophysical results discussed earlier, the only way to resolve this would be through extensive open area excavation between anomalies D and E (T1).

Observations and fieldwork on the area south-west of Longstones Field

Driven by a desire to see symmetry with the West Kennet Avenue, in terms of format, length and number of stones, William Stukeley placed the termination of the Beckhampton Avenue well beyond Longstones Cove, at a location *c.*1.5km to the south-west near Fox Covert. This he described evocatively as 'a most solemn and awful place' (Stukeley 1743, 36); a location perhaps selected because of the visibility of both Silbury Hill and the Sanctuary from this point, and because of the presence of a round barrow cemetery, mirroring that on Overton Hill. This final stretch we now know to be erroneous, as in fact both Piggott (1985, 95) and Ucko *et al.* (1991, 243) had earlier hinted. Nonetheless, there remains a major ambiguity relating to the status of various sarsen settings to the south-west of Longstones Field. In several of Stukeley's drawings a pair of recumbent stones is shown a short distance to the south-west of the Cove, close to the eastern end of the Longstones long barrow (*e.g.* Gough Maps 231. Fol. 7v, 217r, 223r) (Figures 2.32 and 2.33). Two or more stones are recorded as having been removed by Richard Fowler around 1700 at the crossroads formed by the Calne road (A4) and the 'Field Way' that ran past Longstones long barrow (Gough Maps 231. Fol. 7v). In 1968 the digging of a GPO cable trench alongside the A4 revealed a large sarsen buried within a pit cut at least 0.5m into the chalk (Vatcher 1969). Recorded by Faith Vatcher, this has the attributes of a medieval stone burial or a prehistoric sarsen-capped grave. It lay on the approximate line of Stukeley's avenue extension (*i.e.* to the east of the Field Way), and may indeed be one of the stones 'pulld down by Richd. Fowler' (Gough Maps 231. Fol. 7v) (Figure 2.76).

The status of these additional stones is uncertain. They could well be components of one or more separate monuments, either groups of standing stones, parts of a circle or some other configuration. While a highly speculative interpretation, the paired stones adjacent to the long barrow might be those taken from the original terminal setting of the avenue (L12 and 13) and moved south-west to form an outlying setting that marked the position of the avenue from the lower ground around the head of the valley running from Beckhampton. There are other possibilities. Stukeley shows these stones recumbent, and perhaps they were always so, being blocks abandoned *en route* as part of an unfinished megalithic construction. It is unfortunate that little information survives relating to these, or to the two stones by the Calne road removed by Richard Fowler. The position of the partially excavated 'Vatcher' stone is however precisely recorded, and it should prove possible at some future stage to investigate this fully. While one interpretation would see it as a medieval or early post-medieval stone burial, it is tempting to relate it to the sarsen-capped Beaker graves known from the region (Cleal 2005). In addition to the burial placed against 'Adam' (L14), two such graves are known within the vicinity of the Longstones: in Beckhampton Field (Cunnington 1926), associated with a Beaker of Clarke's type S4 (1970, fig. 982); and near The Grange, where a child inhumation was accompanied by a carved chalk object, flint flakes and an N2 Beaker (Young 1950; Clarke 1970, fig. 516). Both were chance discoveries, and many other flat graves could exist in the area. As to why megalithic settings and Beaker flat graves might be concentrated in this area, notice should be taken of their distinctive topographic position and relationship to elements of the later Neolithic complex. In addition to their proximity to the Longstones

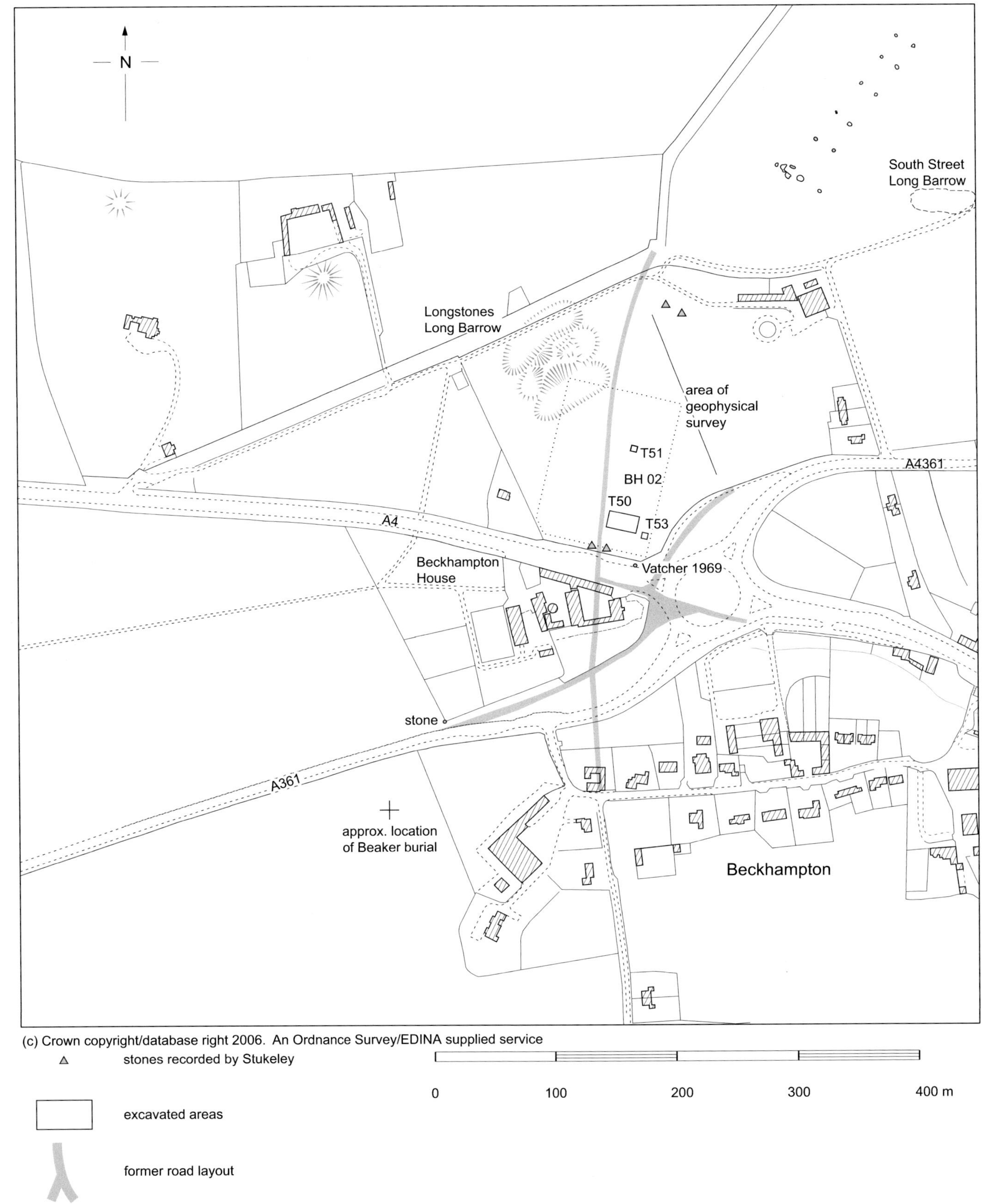

Figure 2.76. The area to the SW of Longstones Field, showing the position of other sarsen settings and the location of the 2002 excavations in Long Barrow Field

Cove and Beckhampton Avenue, these settings were clustered around the spring that feeds the Beckhampton stream, at the head of the dry valley along which the Devizes road (A361) now runs, and located with vistas east towards Silbury Hill and west down the broad valley. The Beckhampton stream connects to Silbury Hill, while seasonal rising ground water at the head of the valley to the west affords this location a changing, even liminal, character (Cleal 2005, 122).

Survey and excavation in Long Barrow Field, 2002

During autumn 2001 and spring 2002, before the Beckhampton Avenue was demonstrated conclusively to stop at the Longstones, geophysical survey and excavation was undertaken in fields to the south-west in order to test Stukeley's putative avenue continuation. Two areas were chosen for investigation: the southern part of Long Barrow Field (SU087 690), and the north-east corner of Beckhampton Field (SU 085 687).

Geophysical survey in Long Barrow Field *Andrew David*

The area of the geophysical survey is shown on Figure 2.76. The survey covered the available open ground, down to grass, between the long barrow and the road (A4) in the hope that any possible continuation of avenue features through this area might be detectable. Given the lack of convincing anomalies or features south-west of Adam and Eve in Longstones Field, the increasing distance from the known alignments, and the difficult geophysical issues (see above, and Ucko *et al.* 1991, 199), such hopes were not pitched very high. However, if the tail of Stukeley's 'snake' really did pass south of the barrow, then survey was a necessary precursor to exploratory excavation.

Both magnetometry and earth resistance surveys were undertaken. The magnetometer survey used FM36 fluxgate gradiometers, with readings taken at 1.0m × 0.25m. Two buried pipe alignments were identified, as well as a NNW-SSE trend of former cultivation; however, no anomalies of archaeological significance were apparent. The earth resistance survey used an RM15 meter, Twin Electrode configuration, mobile probe spacings of 0.5m and 1.0m, and reading intervals of 0.5m × 0.5m and 0.5m × 1.0m, respectively. The results of the 0.5m data are illustrated in Figure 2.77. There is little to suggest anything of obvious prehistoric significance. The trenches carrying the pipes seen in the magnetometer survey were detected as linear low resistance anomalies, and the cultivation trends are also clear, including an apparent furrow (or ditch, see discussion of F.100, below). An unexplained narrow linear high resistance anomaly, some 30m in length, enters the survey area from the west, and in the northern half of the survey area there are rectilinear patches of relatively high resistance defined by quite sharp linear boundaries within the lower resistance background. These and other patterns are unexplained, but perhaps relate to former land boundaries and associated variations in historic land use. A very faint linear band of lower resistance might possibly

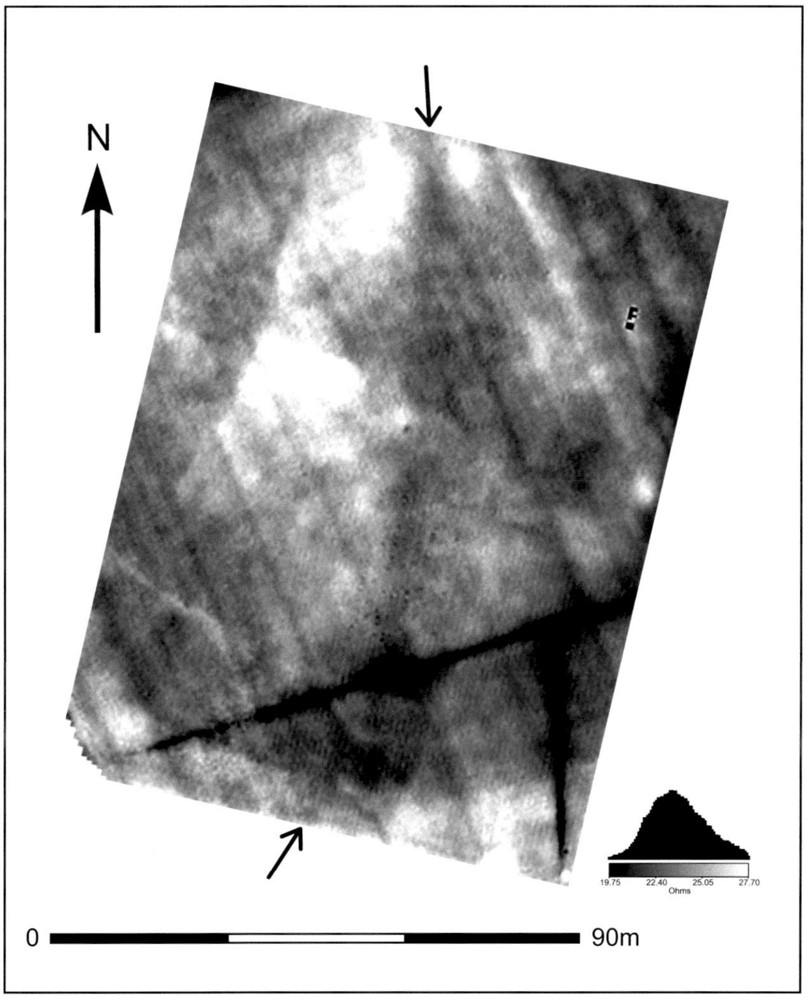

Figure 2.77. Results of the geophysical survey in Long Barrow Field. Arrows indicate the position of the former Field Way

indicate a survival of the former 'Field Way' although the exact alignment is unclear.

Excavation

Following the geophysical survey, three trenches were excavated in Long Barrow Field (full details of this work can be found in the archive report: Gillings *et al.* 2002a). A series of narrow ploughmarks and the broader furrows of medieval ridge-and-furrow cultivation were cut into the chalk natural in all three trenches (Figure 2.78). In Trench 50 it could be seen that the NE-SW aligned ploughmarks pre-dated the ridge-and-furrow. A length of shallow ditch or cultivation furrow, F.100, ran NW-SE across the western third of Trench 50. The complex profile of the feature suggested it had been re-cut on at least two occasions. Patches of darker soil within the fill, seen in plan but not section, could represent the position of stake settings. Finds were very few, though included an iron nail and clay pipe stem

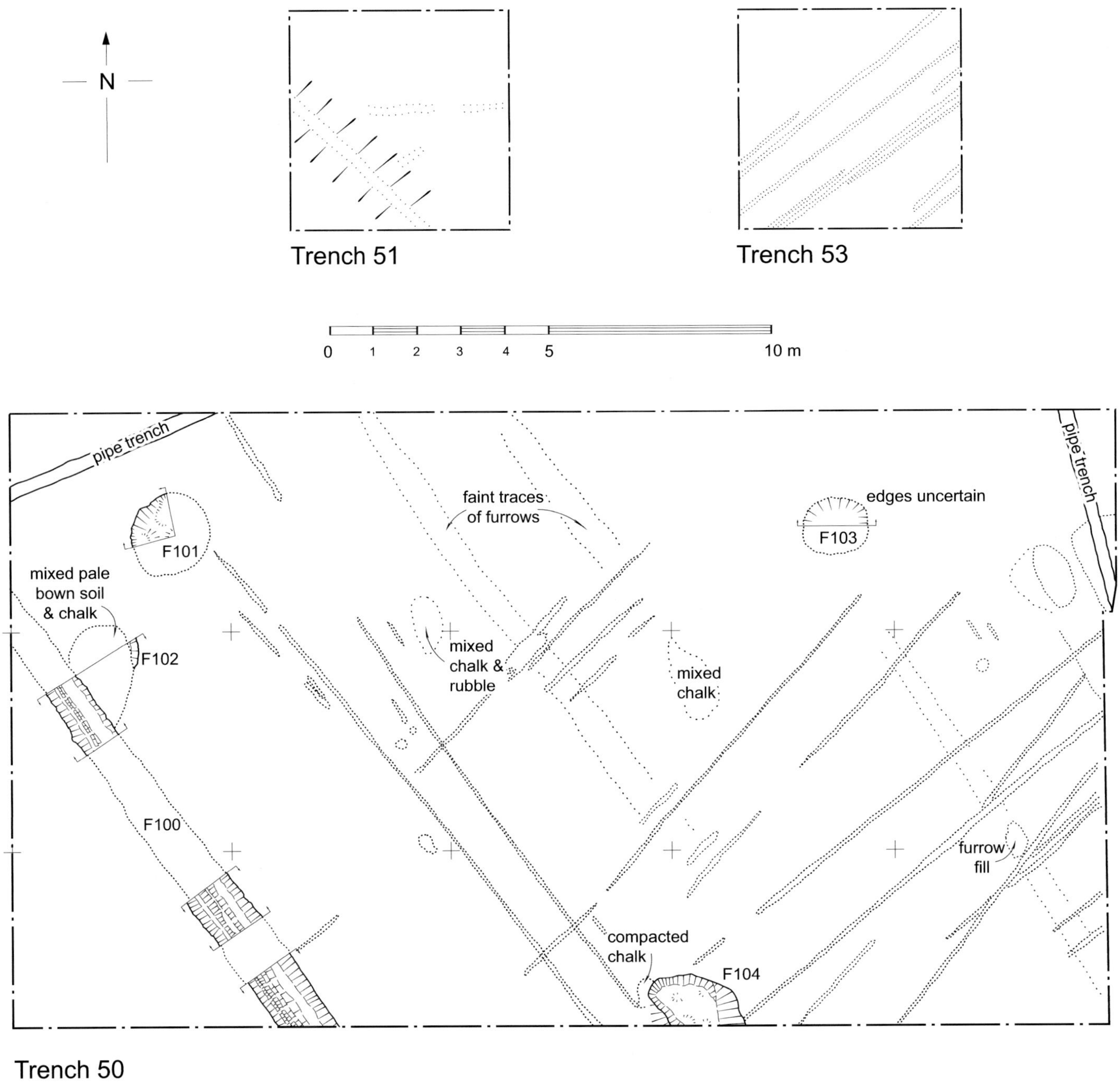

Figure 2.78. Excavated features in Long Barrow Field

from the top of the fill, both conceivably intrusive. Its course parallel to the ridge-and-furrow, and indeed it may even be part of it, suggests a late medieval or early post-medieval date.

A flat-based oval scoop, F.102, was situated close to the western edge of the trench, immediately east of F.100. Filled with a compact dark orange-brown clayey silt containing fragments of burnt chalk, its date and function are uncertain. On its western side it was partly sealed by a localised spread of chalky 'up-cast', which in turn was cut by linear F.100. Other investigated features within the trench proved to be natural. F.101 and 103 may represent root-disturbed patches of chalk, while F.104 is perhaps a tree-throw pit.

Topsoil artefact densities were examined prior to machine stripping by means of fifteen 1.0 × 0.5m test pits, dug to the top of the chalk. A large quantity of post-medieval artefactual material was recovered, including a range of ceramics, 17th–19th-century clay pipe, and several coins (those identifiable spanning George III to George V). This is almost certainly refuse from the former Catherine Wheel Inn (now Beckhampton House), situated immediately across the road from the excavation trenches (Parslew 2004, 38). Very few pieces of prehistoric worked flint were present.

Surface collection and geophysical survey in Beckhampton Field, 2001

Earlier and later Neolithic flint artefacts had been collected from Beckhampton Field by M.E. Cunnington and others in the early 20th century (English Heritage, NMR SU 06 NE 186; Holgate 1988, 237, 242). The extent and precise location of this scatter, which it was initially thought might relate in some way to the Beckhampton Avenue, were unknown, and further investigation was desirable. Working from Stukeley's published prospects and from ground observation, O.G.S. Crawford had in fact postulated that the south-western terminal of the avenue might lie in this area (Crawford 1923, 53). Following the results of excavations in Longstones Field in 2000 and 2003 we now know this to be erroneous.

A combination of gridded surface collection and targeted geophysical survey was employed to evaluate this area (Figure 2.79). Surface collection was restricted to an area of 210 × 90m in the north-eastern corner of the field. All artefactual material was collected, with the exception of obviously post-medieval brick and tile, from a series of 10 × 10m squares laid out on a 40m grid running parallel to the northern field edge. In total, 18 squares were intensively walked. Artefactual material was recovered from nine collection units. Prehistoric material (exclusively worked flint) came from six of these, the density of worked flint ranging from only 1–3 pieces per square. Most of the flint comprises irregular hard-hammer struck flakes, four of which have been modified by limited retouch. Two of these pieces are notched through marginal retouch, as is a large thermally fractured flake. A single irregular core displays several incipient cones of percussion, consistent with unskilled knapping. Although there is little that is chronologically diagnostic, the presence of irregular debitage and notched flakes might imply that much of the flintwork is of 2nd millennium BC date. Other finds were of Roman/medieval and post-medieval date, and included an undecorated copper alloy button and fragments of clay pipe stem.

Other finds were recovered outside the collection units during the course of the geophysical survey. These included a scraper, an invasively flaked knife and a sarsen flake with a concave area of retouch on the distal end. Both the scraper and knife are of forms likely to be of earlier 2nd millennium BC date. A rapid reconnaissance further into the field resulted in the discovery of a later Neolithic discoidal core from close to the line of the Roman road (SU 084 684).

The resistivity survey covered nine 20m-square grids in the north-eastern corner of the field, within the fieldwalking grid. A probe spacing of 0.5m was employed with readings taken on a 0.5m grid. The survey revealed a number of anomalies, although the overall picture was dominated by underlying geological trends. The visible anomalies correspond to two linear features, which most likely indicate field drains and/or pipe-trenches, and a series of low resistance areas reminiscent in terms of size and shape of stone destruction and extraction pits. Although its precise position is unknown, one of these anomalies most likely relates to the stone 'burial' and Beaker grave recorded by Cunnington (1926). These features may extend much further into the field, since aerial photographs show dark

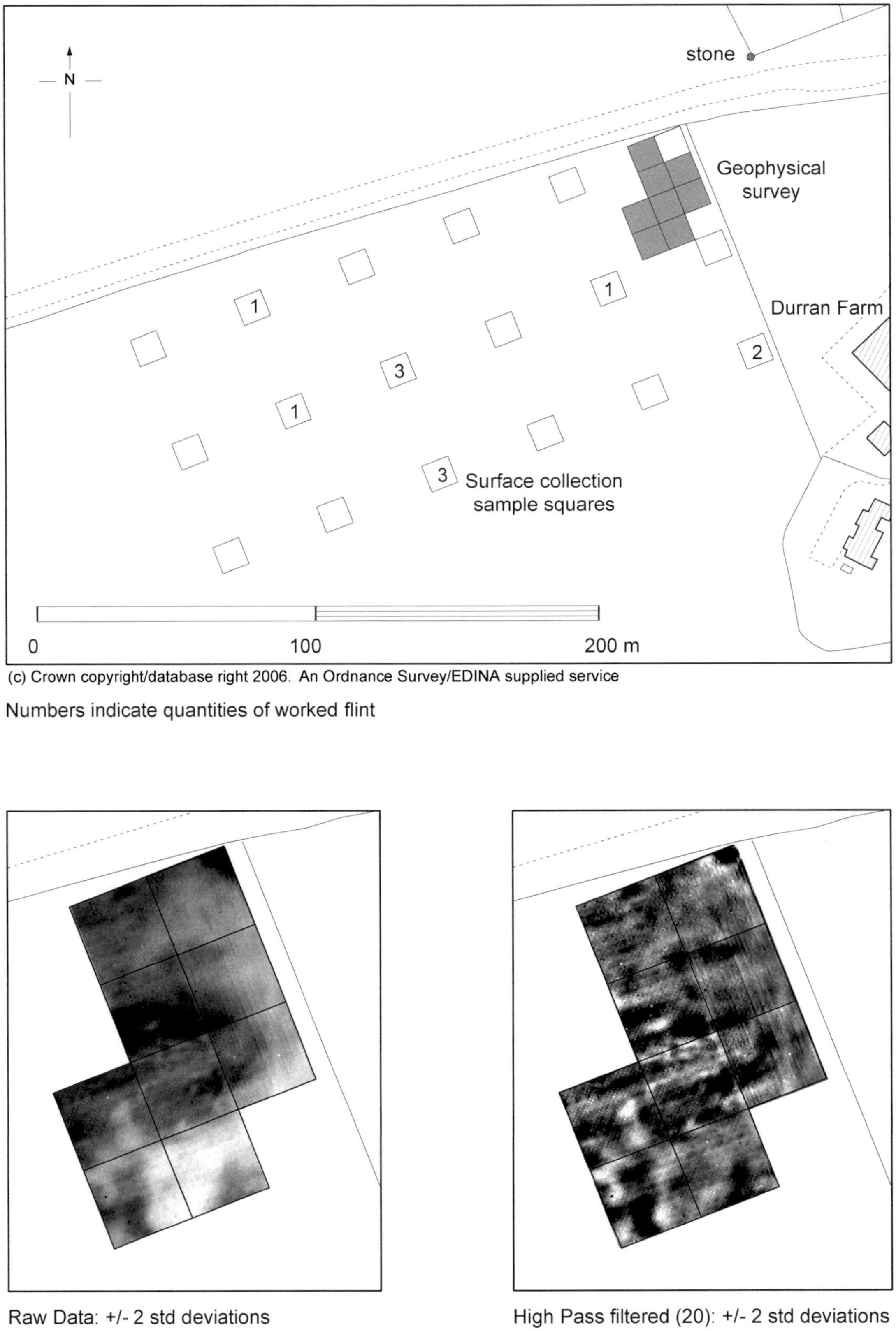

Figure 2.79. Beckhampton Field: surface collection and geophysical survey results

'blotches' indicative of other large pits stretching for at least 100m beyond the survey area.

The low resistance anomalies visible on the geophysical survey require testing by excavation before any firm conclusion can be made regarding their character. Nonetheless, the presence here of large naturally-occurring sarsens embedded within the drift geology, one of which has recently been dragged out and dumped in the north-east corner of the field, strongly suggests that the anomalies mark stone extraction pits. Some of these are certainly of recent date (there are records of 'stone digging' in the 19th century: Parslew 2004), but others could be prehistoric pits from which sarsens were taken for the construction of the Beckhampton Avenue and other megalithic settings. It is interesting to note that W.E.V. Young recorded several circular depressions on the higher ground to the north, close to The Grange, which he took to be later prehistoric pits or graves, similar to that containing the infant inhumation and Beaker, from which covering stones had been removed (Young 1950, 315).

Geophysical survey at Manor Farm, Avebury Trusloe, 2005

James Gunter and Vaughan Roberts

A geophysical survey was undertaken in June 2005 of part of the paddock to the west of Manor Farm, Avebury Trusloe (SU 095 697), on the projected route of the Beckhampton Avenue. The aim was to try and identify the course of the avenue at this point along its length and, if successful, to see whether its paired stone format continued.

The survey area comprised an 80 × 80m area made up of sixteen 20 × 20m survey blocks (Figure 2.80). The alignment of the grids was oriented along the predicted line of the avenue, which, coincidentally, followed that of the fence. There were no visible earthwork features in the paddock. Resistivity survey was undertaken using a Geoscan RMS15 twin probe array, employing a one metre zigzag traverse, with sampling at one metre intervals. Survey results were analysed using Geoplot software.

Results

A number of anomalies were detected. These include three linear features: one corresponding to the modern fence line; one a high resistance feature, probably a modern pipeline, running diagonally across the southern corner of the grids; and a low resistance feature, perhaps a narrow ditch, running on a similar course across the northern corner of the surveyed area.

Of greater interest are two discrete high resistance anomalies on the projected avenue line, and an arc of four low resistance anomalies, regularly and symmetrically disposed with two on the projected avenue line and 'outliers' to the north-west and south. The former are oval, between 3–5.5m in maximum dimension, and set 18m apart. They are likely to correspond to burials of avenue stones. Although the transverse spacing between these is slightly greater than the 16m recorded for excavated stone settings in Longstones Field south-west, the discrepancy may be explained by the burial process offsetting the stones from their original positions.

The low resistance anomalies look to mark large pits *c.*5m across. They could be chalk/marl pits, though their symmetrical arrangement in relation to the avenue line suggests they may be post-medieval stone destruction pits. If they mark the positions of erstwhile stones then they show a variation to the normal arrangement of paired settings. One interpretation would see them as part of a circle with a diameter of *c.*60m metres and made up of around eight stones, if the spacing remains consistent. More likely, the central features are part of the avenue, while the outliers (either stones or pits) define an elaboration at this point. This is obviously an area that would benefit from further exploration through excavation.

The eastern section of the Beckhampton Avenue: earlier observations and reconstruction

Since the late 1960s five features likely to be related to stone positions on the Beckhampton Avenue have been recorded during archaeological work between the western entrance into the Avebury henge and Manor Farm Avebury Trusloe. All of these features were discovered during the monitoring of pipe and cable laying work, and so often in far from ideal archaeological conditions. As a consequence, the level

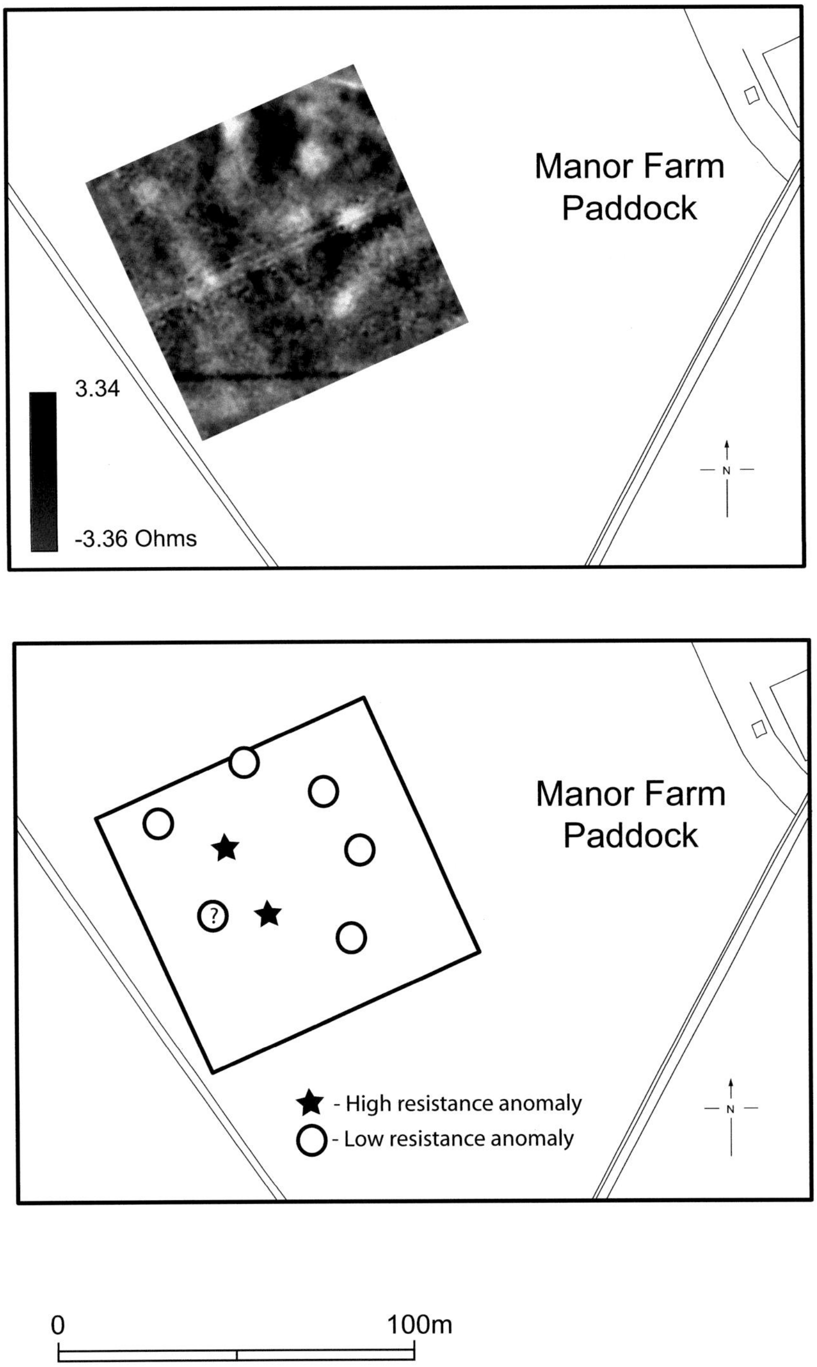

Figure 2.80. Manor Farm, Avebury Trusloe: geophysical survey results. Incorporates data © Crown Copyright/ database right 2007. An Ordnance Survey/ (EDINA) supplied service

of their recording is highly variable. They nonetheless provide invaluable information on the course and format of the avenue in its eastern section, much of which is now obscured by the buildings, gardens and paddocks of Avebury High Street (Figure 2.81).

During 1968 and 1971 Faith and Lance Vatcher recorded two stone burning pits, a stone burial and a pit from which a buried stone had apparently been removed (information held in Alexander Keiller Museum, Avebury). The latter (site code AV68), observed in a GPO cable trench, was situated on the High Street close to the Lych Gate to Avebury church. Where cut by the cable trench, the pit measured *c.*2.5m across. In 1971 an extensive system of pipe trenches was dug between Avebury Trusloe and Avebury as part of the Marlborough-Ramsbury drainage scheme (site code AV71). Three putative avenue features were observed to have been cut through by the trench, and were labelled by the Vatchers Sites A–C. Site A, comprising a burning pit, was situated immediately east of Trusloe Manor Farm barn. Site B is more difficult to locate precisely using existing records, but was situated very close to the eastern edge of Butler's Field at its junction with the northern property boundary of 'Ashcroft'. Here, a burning pit, c.2m across, and containing a sherd of early post-medieval pottery (listed as 16th century), was adjacent to a possible stone-hole. From the existing, rather schematic, sketch sections, both the Site A and B features look to be typical burning pits: that is shallow cuts, with sloping sides and basal deposits of burnt material (see Chapter 10). Site C, at 'Ashcroft' on the western end of the High Street, comprised a pit containing a large deliberately buried sarsen, *c.*1.5 × >1.3m across. It was considered by the Vatchers to be a stone from the southern side of the avenue that was toppled inwards.

A second buried stone was discovered more recently (October 1997–January 1998) during a watching brief undertaken as part of the refurbishment of an electricity cable running from the sub-station situated in the north of Butler's Field (Wessex Archaeology 1998). At a point 41m from the north end of the trench was a substantial pit >2m wide and >0.66m deep (feature 512), which contained a sarsen 1.8 × >1 × >1m across; the remainder of the feature being filled with a dark bluish-brown silty clay, perhaps of alluvial origin. There are, in addition, local reports of buried sarsens being discovered in the front gardens of properties along Avebury High Street. One such was until recently visible adjacent to the garage for Harper's Cottage at the western end of the High Street.

While arguments might be advanced for these *not* being avenue features, and instead

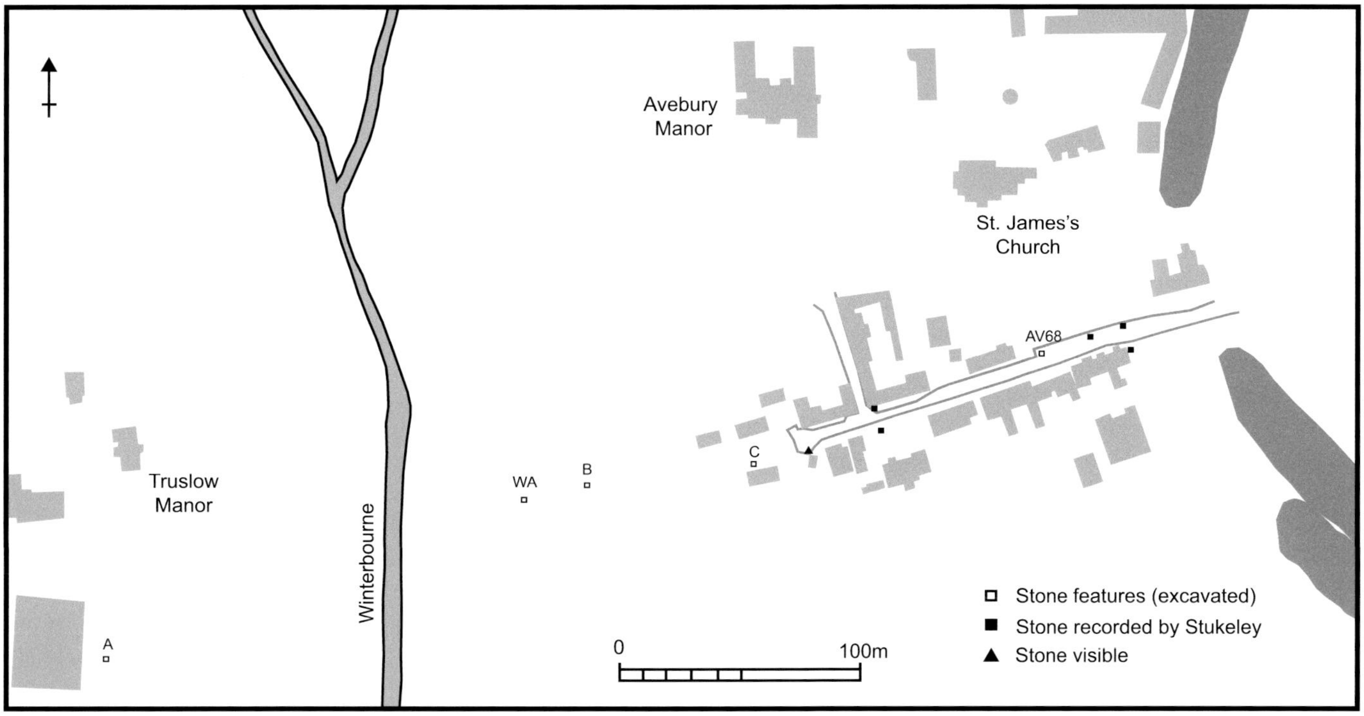

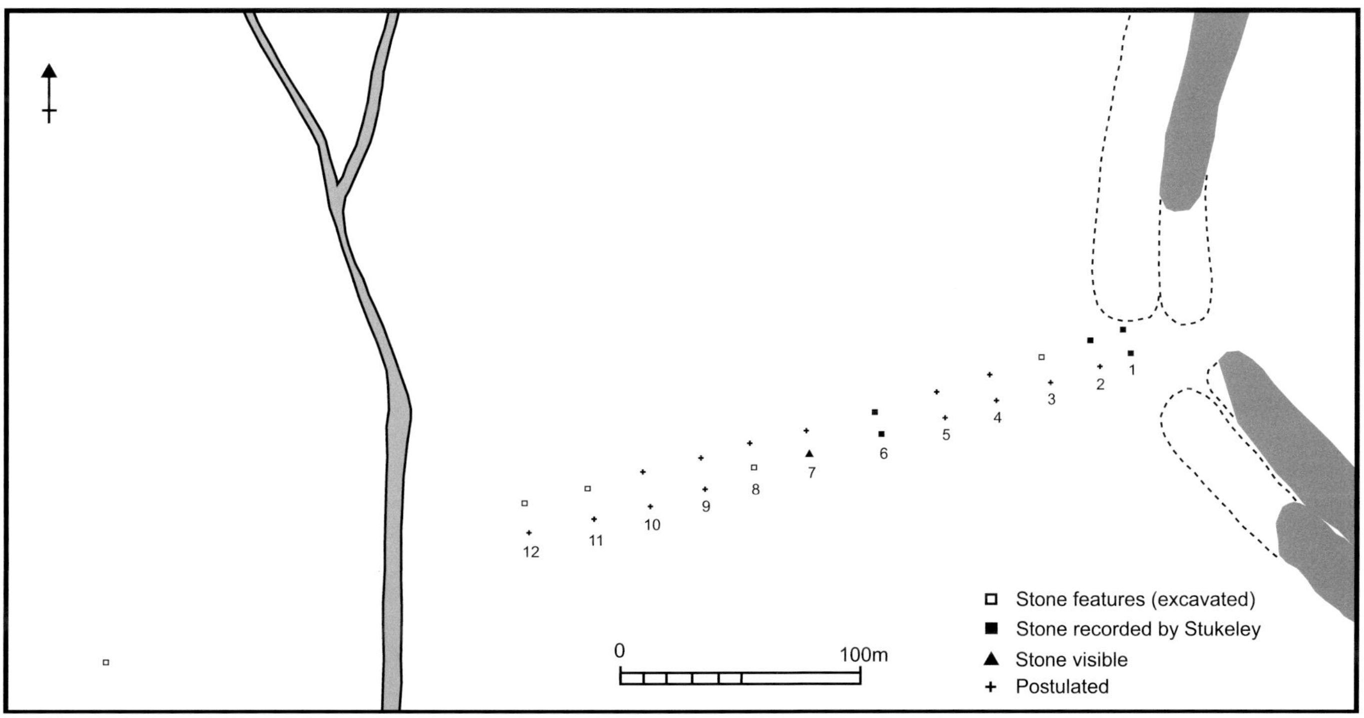

Figure 2.81. Antiquarian and archaeological observations of stone settings belonging to the Beckhampton Avenue as it approaches the western entrance of the Avebury henge (top); reconstruction of the Beckhampton Avenue as it approaches the western entrance of the Avebury henge (bottom). Incorporates data © Crown Copyright/database right 2007. An Ordnance Survey/(EDINA) supplied service

being burials and burning pits related to naturally occurring sarsens, the weight of evidence suggests otherwise. When plotted, all these features fall on the projected line of the avenue as determined by Stukeley's much earlier observations (Stukeley 1743; Ucko *et al.* 1991). Furthermore, their spacing replicates that of the avenue stones investigated in Longstones Field. Thus, the longitudinal distance between feature 512 and Site B is c.28m (*i.e.* one interval), that between Site B and Site C *c.*70m (three intervals), that between Site C and the Harper's Cottage stone *c.*25m (one interval), and that between Harper's Cottage and AV68 *c.*100m (four intervals). If Stukeley's records of fallen and removed stones along the High Street are included, it now becomes possible to reconstruct the 270m or so of the avenue as it approaches the western entrance of the henge (Figure 2.81). The two stones he records as being recumbent adjacent to the south-east corner of the churchyard would seem to represent the northern components of the first two pairs; the eastern-most being situated against the foot of the henge bank. AV68 would then mark the northern stone of pair 3, Stukeley's recumbent stones in front of the Rectory pair 6, the Harper's Cottage stone the southern of pair 7, Site C the southern of pair 8 (as correctly interpreted by the Vatchers), Site B one of pair 11, and feature 512 the northern stone of pair 12. Site A may be anomalous, in so much as it seems to lie around 10–20m south of the projected avenue line, but given the potential complexity of the avenue as revealed to the west of Manor Farm (see above), it should not be discounted as belonging to this monument. To the north of Site C, the flattening of the southern side of the enclosure surrounding Trusloe Manor Farm could well reflect the former presence of the avenue when this earthwork was created during the medieval or late Saxon period.

One major anomaly remains. It is evident that the avenue does not approach the centre of the western entrance into the henge, but is off-set by around 10m to the north, creating a distinctly untidy junction between the two monuments (Figure 2.81). This is still reflected in the course of the present day High Street, set-out during the mid-late Saxon period along the avenue line (Pollard and Reynolds 2002–10). Keiller's excavations located the southern terminal of the henge ditch 12m to the south of the High Street, while observations by the Vatchers showed the northern terminal to be partially backfilled and to extend under the present road (Vatcher 1969, 127). This episode of backfilling most likely occurred when the High Street was extended into the henge during the medieval period, and represents a rationalisation of what would otherwise have been an untidy kink in the road line. By making an off-centre approach to the western entrance, the Beckhampton Avenue reproduces the awkward arrangement seen with the West Kennet Avenue as it nears the southern entrance to the henge (Smith 1965, 209).

Discussion

The course of the Beckhampton Avenue

Confirming the termination of the Beckhampton Avenue at the Longstones Cove, and being able to tie-down part of its mid-section near Avebury Trusloe and its eastern-most length along Avebury High Street, allows much of its course to be delineated with some confidence and precision (Figure 2.2). Describing a gentle arc, it extends over a distance of 1.3km. It begins at the western entrance of the Avebury henge, though off-set slightly to the north, with the present-day High Street following its course for the first 150m. Observations by the Vatchers and Wessex Archaeology demonstrate its continuation across the northern end of Butler's Field, here bisecting a former late Mesolithic and early Neolithic occupation area (Evans *et al.* 1993, 151–3). It must then cross the Winterbourne *c.*40m south of the present bridge, providing at this point a clear prospect of Silbury Hill to the south, before climbing gently up-slope and running through the yard of Trusloe Manor Farm. The crest of the rise north-east of Trusloe Cottages, where geophysical survey suggests the paired format of the avenue gives way to a more elaborate setting, provides a panoptic location with views of the Avebury henge, Silbury Hill, Windmill Hill and the Longstones. From this point the avenue runs south-west, skirting the northern edge of Trusloe Cottages and another area of earlier Neolithic activity, then descends into an area of lower ground before ascending the slight rise on which the Longstones are situated.

To what extent the paired stone format is

maintained along much of the avenue's length is uncertain, especially in the light of the geophysical survey at Manor Farm, and must await future excavation. However, if a continuous setting of paired sarsens the avenue would have originally included around 100 stones, based on a projected figure of 50 pairs. The longer West Kennet Avenue was made up of an estimated 190+ sarsens (Smith 1965, 206–8); a figure which may now need to be revised down given the apparent break north of New Cottages (see Chapter 3).

Dating the Beckhampton Avenue

Despite the scale of 1999–2003 excavations, bone, antler and other organic material was not recovered from the excavated stone-holes of the avenue, and so radiocarbon determinations could not be obtained. In itself this may be telling, in that the absence of antler or bone in the packing suggests prohibitions existed on the deposition of such material at the time the stones were erected. In the case of the Cove, where bone from apparently primary contexts was submitted for radiocarbon dating, Roman and early post-Roman dates were unexpectedly obtained. The material here was clearly intrusive, having been introduced through later animal burrowing. Since the majority of the stone-holes were shallow and the fills badly disturbed by the toppling, burial and breaking of stones the chances of finding suitable dating material were always going to be slim. The extent of animal and other disturbance also ruled-out the application of Optically Stimulated Luminescence dating. In terms of diagnostic artefactual material, the only item is a later Neolithic oblique arrowhead from the destruction pit associated with stone L10.

Determining the chronology of the avenue is therefore dependent upon physical/structural relationships with other monuments and deposits or features. These include its relationship with the Avebury henge, the Longstones enclosure and the Beaker burial excavated by Cunnington against stone L14 of the Longstones Cove (Cunnington 1913). Since there is no evidence to suggest that the avenue continued beyond Avebury's western entrance into the henge interior, the former must be contemporary with or post-date the earthwork, which we know to be of two phases of construction (Pitts and Whittle 1992), the second (Avebury 2) dating to around the 26th century BC (Pollard and Cleal 2004). At its western end, we can be confident that the avenue is later than the Longstones enclosure. No direct stratigraphic relationship was present between the two, but the levelling of the enclosure circuit only makes sense as a prelude to the construction of the avenue, while the diminutive size of the stone setting closest to the erstwhile enclosure ditch (that of L10) in comparison to its partner (L9 'Eve') suggests an awareness on the part of the avenue builders of the potential instability of the ground at this point, being so close to the backfilled ditch. The extrapolated mid-3rd millennium BC date for the levelling of the enclosure should, therefore, date the construction of this stretch of the avenue.

Placed against an upright megalith, the burial with a N/MR Beaker at the foot of stone L14 ('Adam') has to provide a *terminus ante quem* for the Cove, which we know was a reworking of the original avenue terminal. Cleal (2005, 118) places this Beaker and the vessel associated with the burial at the foot of stone 29a of the West Kennet Avenue in the last quarter of the 3rd millennium BC. A similar date is implied according to Needham's 2005 scheme for British Beakers: the shape of the vessel placing it in his Tall Mid Carinated group, for which he provides a range of *c.*2250–1950BC (Needham 2005). The S-profile Low-bellied Beakers from graves at the feet of stones 18b and 25b on the West Kennet Avenue (Smith 1965, 209–10; Clarke 1970, nos. 1070 and 1071) have a similar currency within Needham's scheme.

The relationship to the Longstones enclosure and perhaps Avebury on the one hand, and to the Beaker burial at the foot of Cove stone L14 on the other, bracket the earlier and later ends of the likely date span. This leaves a probable range of *c.*2600–2000BC for the construction of the Beckhampton Avenue, within which we would favour a date in the third quarter of the 3rd millennium BC. This should not preclude the possibility of the monument being created in stages over a period of several generations – a project more punctuated and negotiated than executed according to a single scheme – but at present the only firm evidence of phased construction relates to the reworking of the western terminal and the creation of the Longstones Cove.

The creation of the Beckhampton Avenue

and structurally analogous West Kennet Avenue occurred during the latest Neolithic of the region. This 'horizon' witnessed a particularly intense phase of monument building within the wider landscape, which saw the creation of key elements of the complex such as the Outer Circle at Avebury, the stone phase at the Sanctuary, the primary mound at Silbury Hill and parts at least of the West Kennet enclosures (Pitts and Whittle 1992; Pollard 1992; Whittle 1997b; Pollard and Cleal 2004; Bayliss *et al.* 2007). The implications of this will be discussed in Chapter 6.

The format and construction of the avenue and associated activities

The format of the excavated section of the Beckhampton Avenue replicates so closely that of the investigated northern third of West Kennet Avenue that the two constructions must have been conceived at the time of their construction as similar entities, if not parts of one overall 'grand design'. The paired arrangement of sarsens, the same range of longitudinal and transverse stone spacing, and the same technologies of stone erection (seen with the 'anti-friction' stake supports) are repeated at both. This is not to argue that the two constructions were strictly contemporary, since there is latitude to think of these monuments as unfolding projects worked out over an extended period of time (Barrett 1994), but in their final incarnation they were evidently intended to resemble one another. As such, there is no reason to assume any 'functional' difference between the two avenues.

When excavating the West Kennet Avenue, Alexander Keiller envisaged the monument as a highly regularised arrangement of megaliths, with stones being set on a common axis and carefully paired to present contrasting lozenge and pillar settings (Keiller and Piggott 1936; Smith 1965, 206). In fact, such regularity is not present throughout, as will be demonstrated in the following chapter. The avenues were more than just stone-lined corridors, constructed using megaliths as though they were simple building blocks. The stones themselves held significance, in terms of their material and ontological qualities, biographies of previous usage and prior locations in the landscape (Gillings and Pollard 1999). Constructing the avenues therefore involved a complex process of negotiation, not just between those engaged in these projects, but also in terms of appropriate action towards the stones themselves and the places to which they would be dragged and set upright. It was a process of choosing suitable stones and deciding both how and where was most auspicious to erect them. Distinctive megaliths were deployed to mark points along the avenues significant because of the history that adhered to those locales or their position within the landscape. The working out of these 'negotiations' with stone and place can be seen in the detail of the settings excavated in Longstones Field south-west. Marking the point where the avenue entered the earlier enclosure, stone L4 was set at right-angles to the avenue line. The next pair along, L5 and L6, comprised stones of similar size, though both possessed unusual characteristics: L5/[424] retained traces of axe polishing on one surface, while L6/[435] was a notably 'featured' block with many natural folds and perforations. The last stones of the avenue proper included one particularly massive megalith (L9 or 'Eve') and, using the size of the stone-hole as a proxy, a pair to this (L10) that was comparatively diminutive. Any desire to create symmetry may have been compromised by the particularities of circumstance.

A recurrent feature of the excavated stone-holes was the absence within them of any antler, bone or pottery. This is striking when one considers how antler picks were most likely employed in digging the stone-holes and perhaps in levering the stones into position. So 'clean' were the remnants of undisturbed packing that care must have been taken to exclude such organic and ceramic material from the stone-holes. In stark contrast, massive quantities of worked flint were deposited around the Cove and smaller amounts in and around the stone-holes of the avenue. Snashall suggests this material was generated by a constrained, possibly task-specific, set of activities, which emphasised cutting and sawing, and was perhaps connected to the movement and erection of the stones. These acts of lithic deposition were both specific to the stones and frequently took place after the megaliths had been erected: worked flint was rare in undisturbed primary stone-hole fills. Surface collection undertaken in the 1980s (Holgate 1987) and test-pitting prior to the 1999 excavation revealed that lithic densities are incredibly very low across the field, and so the concentrations associated with the megalithic settings are genuinely localised and stone-specific. Such activity was part of a more widespread practice within the region of depositing lithics, especially debitage, around the bases of standing stones, seen also on the West Kennet Avenue, at the Falkner's Circle, the Sanctuary and within Avebury (Gillings and Pollard 2004, 75). Close by, a large quantity of later Neolithic-early Bronze Age flintwork was carefully buried in a pit cut into the proximal end of the South Street long barrow (Ashbee *et al.* 1979, 272); here perhaps associated with a phase of elaboration that saw the addition of sarsen boulders to the 'business end' of this monument (depicted in Stukeley 1743, pl. 24, but from excavation evidence clearly not primary). By contrast, bone and ceramics were formally deposited around posts at the Sanctuary and the West Kennet palisades (Pollard 1992; Whittle 1997b). It is difficult not to conclude that symbolic relations were being expressed between flint, or its transformation through knapping, and sarsen on the one hand, and between bone, ceramics and wood on the other. The connection may have between materials of perceived ancestral origin – stones of various kinds – as opposed to those substances more intimately associated with the productive technologies of the living (cf. Parker Pearson 2004). With links to 'life, spirits and the sacred' (Boivin 2004, 6), stone is commonly envisaged to be a potent, even animate, media that requires respectful treatment through prescribed and often gendered actions at the points of extraction, working and deposition (Taçon 1991; Boivin 2004). Depositing debitage around the bases of standing stones could have variously served to reaffirm a link between flint and sacred realms and origins, to have ascribed specific gender linkages to the megaliths themselves, or to have acted as offerings to personified/deified stones. Whatever the specific meaning or intended outcome of these practices, the fact that the flint had been transformed through working seems to have been of up-most significance.

The relationship between the Longstones Enclosure and Beckhampton Avenue

The relationship between the avenue and the earlier Longstones enclosure is a curious one. At its south-western end the avenue was laid out to run through the enclosure entrance, though off-set slightly to the south-east, and terminate immediately beyond the earlier ditch circuit. Its position therefore respected or referenced the enclosure. However, the levelling of the enclosure circuit was undertaken either as part of the process of constructing the avenue, or had occurred sometime earlier. So there exists the possibility that the avenue's creation simultaneously involved the surface eradication of the earlier monument while also 'commemorating' its former presence. Its prior existence was acknowledged through a new monumental creation.

Such a sequence of building, destruction/eradication, followed by further construction has been identified among later Neolithic timber constructions in the region, here perhaps conceived as unfolding ritual cycles. At the West Kennet enclosures sections of palisade were subject to deliberate burning, followed perhaps by replacement: as Alasdair Whittle eloquently expresses it, 'from the flames of one conflagration a successor arose' (Whittle 1997b, 158). A comparable but visually less dramatic process took place at the Sanctuary, where posts within specific rings were erected, removed and replaced on a frequent basis, certainly before the timbers had time to rot (Pitts 2001a). These 'repeating megadendric rituals' (Pitts 2001b, 246) could have operated over short timescales, being rites that materialised concepts of impermanence, renewal and cyclical regeneration within the domain of the living (Whittle 1997b, 158; Parker Pearson and Ramilisonina 1998). By contrast, the cycle of building, destruction and further building evidenced with the Longstones enclosure and Beckhampton Avenue is more a story of material transformation – from chalk to sarsen – than one of renewal, and operated over a timescale of many generations. It is not, of course, impossible that the enclosure's demise and its commemoration through stone were pre-determined from the outset, as one element in a greatly attenuated ritual cycle that also took in developments at Avebury, the West Kennet Avenue and the Sanctuary, but equally such transformations may have come about through the inventive play of symbolic resources and historical contingency.

The creation of the avenue can also be read as a 'lithicisation' of the Longstones enclosure, repeating a process seen at many other later

Neolithic monuments. The replacement of timber circles with ones of stone is attested locally at the Sanctuary (Cunnington 1931), and further afield at Balfarg, Fife (Mercer 1981), Machrie Moor 11, Arran (Haggarty 1991), Site IV, Mount Pleasant, Dorset (Wainwright 1979), and Stanton Drew, Somerset (David *et al.* 2004), among others (Gibson 2005, 53). Following both ethnographic analogy (*e.g.* Bloch 1995) and particular material associations, it seems clear that in a later Neolithic context wood and stone had quite specific metaphoric, ontological, even literal, associations with different states of being: wood as a transient material connected to the domain of the living, stone as an enduring medium associated with the dead and ancestors (Parker Pearson and Ramilisonina 1998; Parker Pearson *et al.* 2006). The process of timber decay and replacement by stone at monuments like the Sanctuary could be a potent metaphor for the human transition from life, through the liminal stage of recent death and decay, to a re-incorporation into the domain of ancestral spirits. With timber circles such processes were acted out sequentially, but in the mid-3rd millennium BC the differential deployment of wood and stone within specific constructions making up the monument complexes at Stonehenge and Avebury could be read as marking the position of different structures within extended funerary rites of passage (*ibid.*).

Was the process in operation at the Longstones of replacing a chalk monument (or at least a turfed earthwork) with one of stone fundamentally different to the conversion from wood to stone seen at certain timber circles? If we take a perspective based around issues of materiality, while earth, chalk and turf were surely regarded as generative, vitalising substances, it is easy to envisage how they might be thought of as ontologically distinct from wood. As a brilliant white, semi-durable medium that came from the ground itself, chalk like other forms of stone could even have embodied explicit ancestral qualities (Taçon 1991; Bender 1998). Furthermore, we have seen how the form and context of the enclosure may have made reference to earlier sacred traditions and an ancestral past – it was already closely associated with 'other-worldly' realms before its stony transformation. In this respect, the earthwork-to-stone metamorphosis *was* different to that of timber-to-stone at the Sanctuary and elsewhere. An alternative is to see the lithicisation of the enclosure variously as a process of commemoration, as a further stage of ancestralisation or 'hardening', and also (through its levelling) as a radical controlling or negation of the agency and associations of the earlier monument.

The sequence of replacement of an earthwork with stone settings is far from unique, and in fact seems to be a recurrent 'narrative' at many monuments of this date across the British Isles. It is seen, for example, at Long Meg and her Daughters, Cumbria, where the large stone circle is now recognised to replace an earlier oval earthwork enclosure of likely Neolithic date (Soffe and Clare 1988). That several of the stones project out of the levelled ditch at Long Meg might even imply deliberate backfilling of the ditch prior to the creation of the stone settings, as at the Longstones. For the Great and SSW Circles at Stanton Drew, Somerset, the sequence can be read as running from timber settings to earthwork enclosures, with stone circles contemporary with or later than enclosing ditches and banks (David *et al.* 2004). On the basis of their distinct lithologies, the short 'avenues' leading to the Great and NE Circles here could be later additions still (Burl 1993, 43). Curiously, the setting out of the avenues leading to both the latter circles involved a minor shift in axis, such that that leading to the Great Circle was set several degrees to the south of the previous northeast-southwest alignment given by the enclosure; while the avenue running into the NE Circle comes in at an oblique angle (David *et al.* 2004, fig. 7). This process of 'axial shift' is repeated at several monuments within the Wessex region, including Avebury. Axial re-orientation is seen between the timber and stone phases at the Sanctuary (Pollard 1992), at Stonehenge during phase 3 (Cleal *et al.* 1995, 170) and at the Longstones enclosure, where the line of the Beckhampton Avenue is off-set to the south of the earlier enclosure entrance (Figure 2.82). It is also repeated with both the West Kennet and Beckhampton Avenues as they approach the southern and western entrances into the Avebury henge, here creating distinctly awkward arrangements. In each case the architecturally-prescribed routes into these monuments was moved by a few degrees, creating minor but significant reorientations. That such axial shifting took place at the points in the lives of these sites when they converted into stone

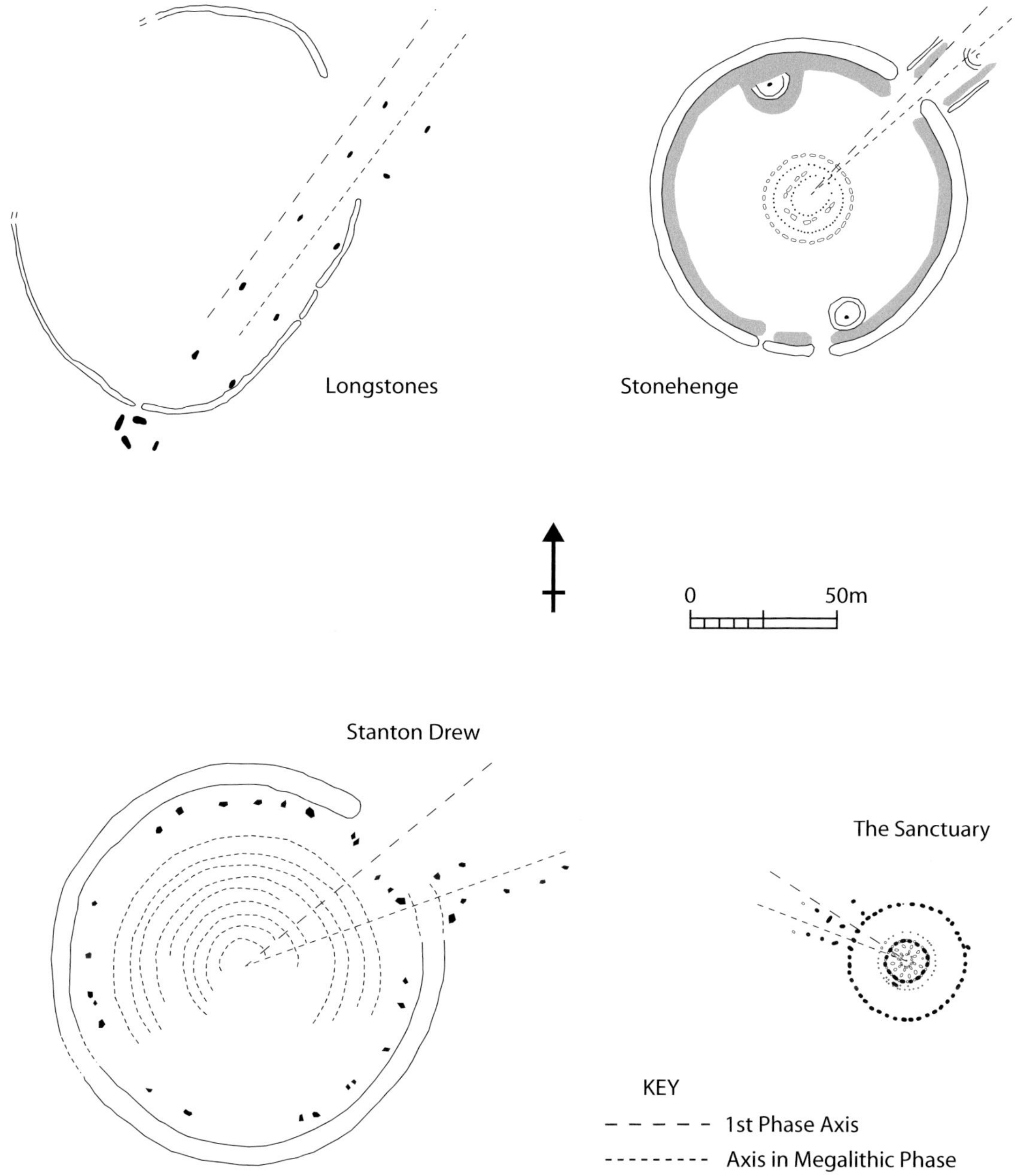

Figure 2.82. Lithicisation and 'axial shift' at selected later Neolithic monuments

monuments is telling. Following the arguments relating to later Neolithic materialities presented above, was the intention in each instance to create an 'ancestral' or commemorative route that flanked earlier 'unmarked' pathways into these monuments? Were routes for the living supplanted by routes for spirits, ancestors or participants in commemorative ceremonies? Whatever the precise motivation or meaning, these changes highlight the critical re-negotiation and transformation of these monuments, and the way they were to be encountered, at the time of lithicisation.

In other ways the Longstones sequence reflects broader trends in Neolithic monument construction that had a very long ancestry, structured around the twin themes of enclosure and linearity (Bradley 1998). The bisection of an earlier enclosure by a later linear monument (the Beckhampton Avenue) has parallels in the 4th millennium BC. Cursus monuments were laid out over enclosures at Fornham All Saints, Suffolk (Palmer 1976), and Etton, Cambridgeshire (Pryor 1998), while a bank barrow was constructed so as to overlap the enclosure at Maiden Castle, Dorset

(Sharples 1991). These were acts of incorporation and reinterpretation of earlier constructions (Bradley 1993, 101–3), which might also serve to legitimise later sacred traditions. Pryor sees the construction of the Etton and Maxey cursus monuments over the earlier enclosure as 'a symbolic means of transferring the ideological importance of the old site to its successors', the henge monuments and ring-ditches located on the higher ground of the Welland valley (Pryor 1998, 373). Much the same interpretation could be offered for the linking of the Longstones enclosure to the Avebury henge. However, these instances predate by many centuries the sequence seen with the Longstones enclosure and Beckhampton Avenue. In the mid-3rd millennium BC world it was more usual to enact an alternative sequence, and to construct circular monuments (henges and timber circles) over earlier linear constructions. The location of the Maxey and Thornborough henges over the silted ditches of cursus monuments are cases in point (Pryor *et al.* 1985; Harding 2003). What was happening in the Avebury landscape with the deliberate laying out avenues over earlier monuments and areas of previous activity was therefore unusual, if not a conscious replication of earlier practices. However, it was not without analogy. In terms of scale and format, and perhaps date, the setting out of the Carnac stone alignments so as to incorporate earlier long mounds, and their termination against megalithic enclosures or cromlechs, would seem to present a very similar set of events (Burl 1993, 131–46).

We do not know whether the decision to level the enclosure, transform its location through the erection of stones, and physically link it to the Avebury henge by means of the avenue was achieved through consensus or was contested. Whatever the circumstances, this was surely a very political act, inasmuch as it asserted a commonalty between the two monuments that may not have existed previously. If the Longstones enclosure stood for earlier sacred traditions and the Avebury henge for new beliefs and forms of socio-political authority (Harding 2003, 9), then here we are witnessing the appropriation of one regime of values by another – a re-writing of history even. But such a reading of events perhaps overstates the differences between the two enclosures, both of which may have begun at similar times and both of which incorporated references to an ancestral past through their landscape setting and architectural form. Avebury was as much worked out of the resources and fragments of the past as was the Longstones enclosure (Burl 1979, 13–20; Barclay 1999).

The Cove and avenue terminal

The original western terminal of the avenue comprised a linear setting of three stones set perpendicular to the avenue line. As we have seen, this was short-lived, the outer stones being taken down and either moved elsewhere (perhaps to a location near the Longstones long barrow) or re-set as part of the Cove (Figure 2.83). The interval of time involved is not known, though there is no reason to assume it was particularly long. The new arrangement, created by constructing the Cove, resulted in an asymmetric terminal, yet the Cove is so distinctive and so monumental that it can be seen as a monument in its own right, rather than a simple elaboration to the end of the avenue. Perhaps the intention existed to extend the avenue further to the south-west, with the Cove serving to mark its original termination, the project being abandoned early on. There may be more dynamism to the megalithic settings here than is first apparent.

By virtue of its archaeological categorisation, if not original conceptualisation, the Longstones Cove is related to similar box-like megalithic settings associated with henges at Avebury, Arbow Low, Site IV Mount Pleasant and Stanton Drew (Burl 1988). That at Cairnpapple now looks dubious (Barclay 1999, 39). As with the variation seen in henge monuments and timber circles, coves form a very loose and disparate category of constructions, with much architectural variability being evident, from the simple three stone arrangement at Stanton Drew to the complex multi-stone box with outliers at Site IV, Mount Pleasant (Wainwright 1979). Such variation is a reminder that 'late Neolithic monumental architecture was not composed of a series of ideal types' (Thomas 2004, 106), and that each construction resulted from particular circumstances, desired effects and histories of development.

Burl regards coves as a transitional form between burial chambers and stone circles; in effect serving as open-air versions of chambered tombs, and holding an attendant mortuary

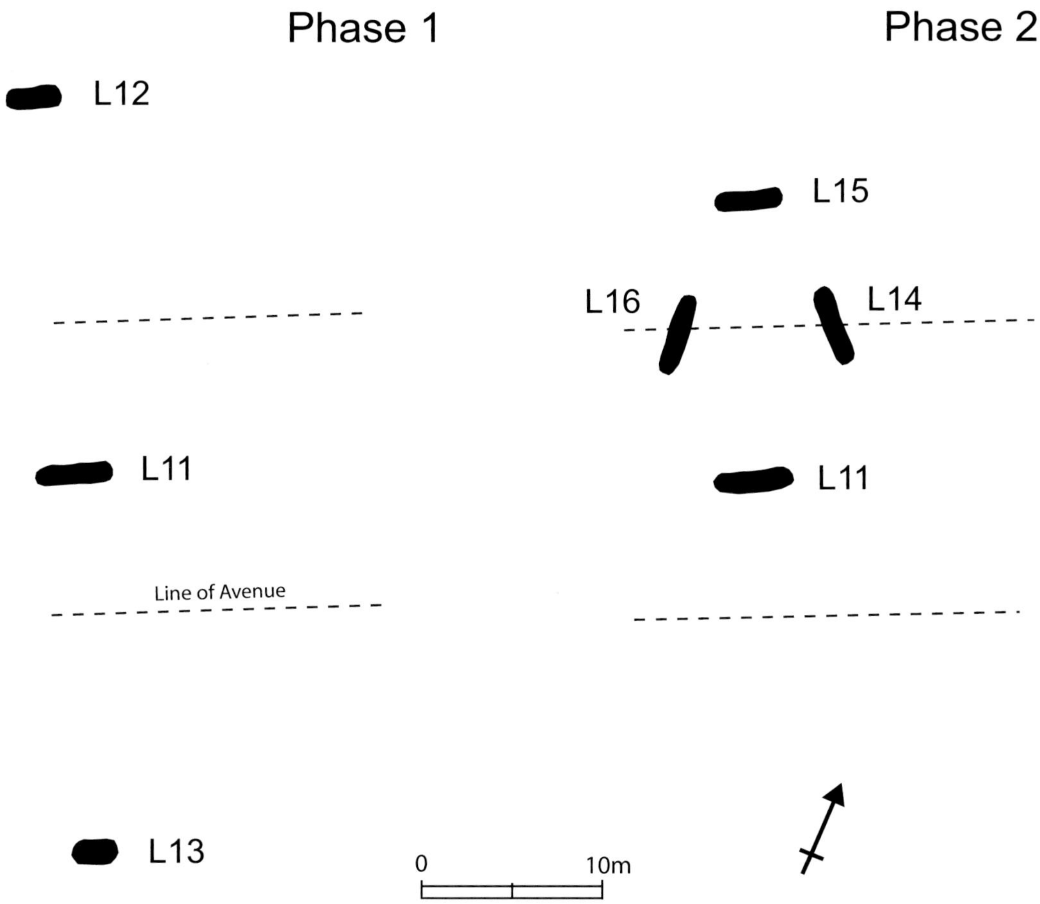

Figure 2.83. Reconstruction of the pre-Cove and Cove settings at the Longstones end of the Beckhampton Avenue

function (Burl 1988; 2002, 145). Such a position within schemes of architectural evolutionary development is becoming more difficult to sustain, especially since the Longstones and Site IV coves now look to belong to the very end of the Neolithic, and so are contemporary with, if not later than, early stone circles. However, the similarity between coves and the megalithic chambers of 4th millennium BC tombs is not in doubt, raising the possibility that some may well have been conceived as deliberate emulations of these earlier constructions. Their function is more difficult to determine. None of those excavated has produced evidence of a link with mortuary practices – as exposure areas or ossuaries – although bone deposits would not survive in an open environment. Taxonomy can create its own restrictions, and we should be wary of assuming that similarities in architectural form can be mapped on to commonalities in function (Thomas 2004).

We would see the Longstones Cove as essentially commemorative, or at least serving to explicitly reference what had gone before at this particular place – it was a lithic version of the earlier enclosure against which it was set. However, in an interplay between the symbolic demands of local circumstances and wider influences, inspiration for its creation and form may have come from contemporary, or near contemporary, constructions elsewhere. Potentially several centuries old by this stage, the Cove within the Northern Inner Circle at Avebury could have provided one precedent. Slightly further afield, though closer in time, is the phase 3ii Sarsen Trilithon setting at Stonehenge (Cleal *et al.* 1995). Of similar dimensions, the splayed arrangement of stones at the Longstones Cove creates a not dissimilar effect in providing an impressive enclosed space (Figure 2.84). In fact, taken as a whole the sequence at the Longstones is curiously reminiscent of that at Stonehenge: both begin with enclosures of unusual form, there is evidence for backfilling of the ditches (though on a lesser scale at Stonehenge), and around the middle of the 3rd millennium BC both

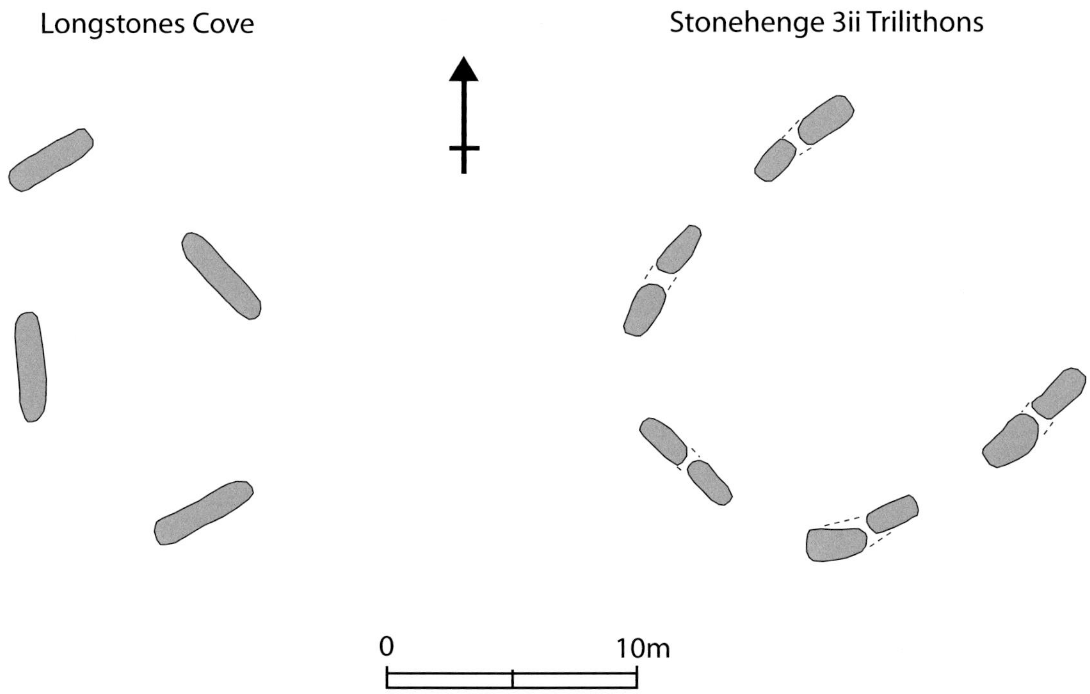

Figure 2.84. The Longstones Cove and Stonehenge phase 3ii trilithon setting compared

underwent a process of lithicisation. It seems unlikely that such parallel sequences are coincidental, especially given the proximity of the Avebury and Stonehenge landscapes and the degree of transmission of news and people (and stones) that must have occurred between them. Perhaps we are seeing the result of a process of competitive emulation, or the physical manifestation of similar cosmologies, mythical cycles or structures of ceremonial practice.

The Cove and the Sanctuary: architectural references

Away from Avebury, the Beckhampton Avenue terminates at the Longstones Cove, while the West Kennet Avenue ends with the timber and stone settings of the Sanctuary. Both 'terminal' monuments are at first sight very different constructions: one a large megalithic box, the other a series of concentric circles. However, both were created in locations with long histories of activity and share a similar geometric precision that is otherwise missing along the avenues. When examined from the point of view of the dimensions utilised in their layouts a number of commonalities emerge. Thus, the original terminal of the Beckhampton Avenue (the pre-Cove' setting) is *c.*40m across, while the overall diameter of the Sanctuary (as defined by the stone settings of Ring A) is 41m (Cunnington 1931) (Figure 2.85). Both monuments may have been laid out using standardised units of measurement approximating 2.5m. In order to achieve the arrangement of symmetrical splayed sides, the Longstones Cove was apparently laid out according to an isosceles triangle of dimensions *c.*22 × 15m, the apex situated just to the north-east of former stone L12. Its overall dimensions are *c.*17 × 10m (Figure 2.86). The distance from the notional apex to the 'front' edges of stones L14 and L16 is *c.*15m, while that between the latter points is *c.*10m. The geometric regularity and consistent occurrence of measurements divisible into units approximating 2.5m is too much to be coincidental. By contrast, the transverse and longitudinal intervals between the stones making up the avenue vary within a range of several metres, suggesting that their positions were paced out rather than measured.

The form of the Sanctuary embodies similar, if not greater, geometric order. The setting out of the primary post settings in particular involved the application of relatively sophisticated plane geometry (Case 2004). With diameters of 41m, 20m, *c.*10m and 4.6m, Rings A, B, D and F look to embody the same unit of measurement as was employed at the Longstones Cove. Bradley has observed further design relationships between elements of the

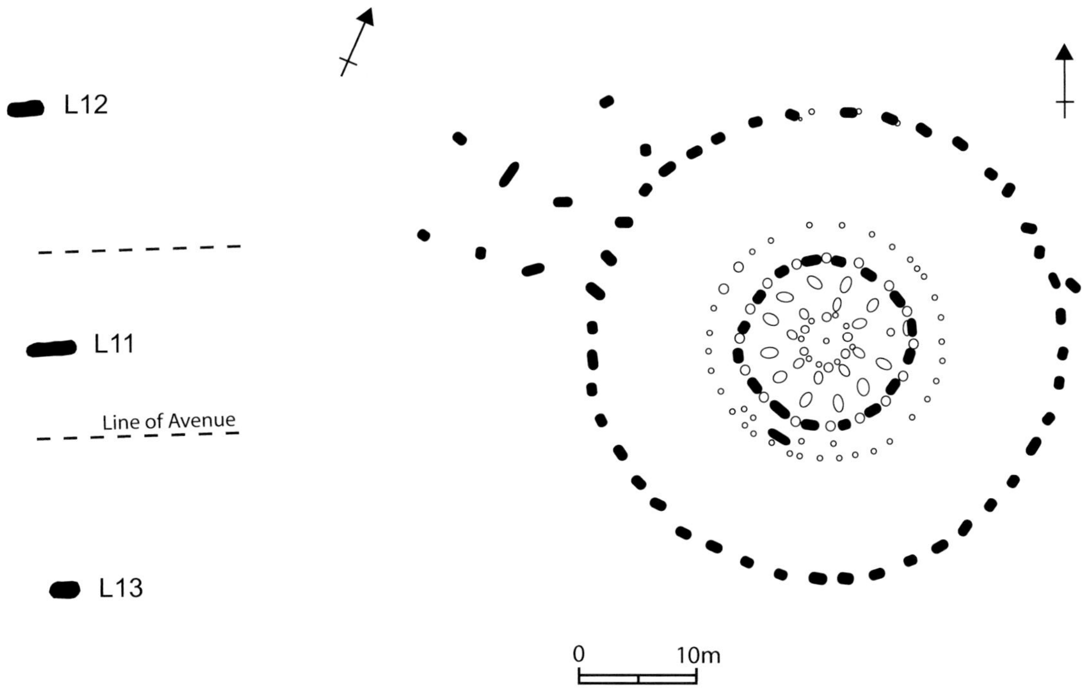

Figure 2.85. (left) The ends of both Avenues: the pre-Cove setting at the Longstones and the Sanctuary on Overton Hill

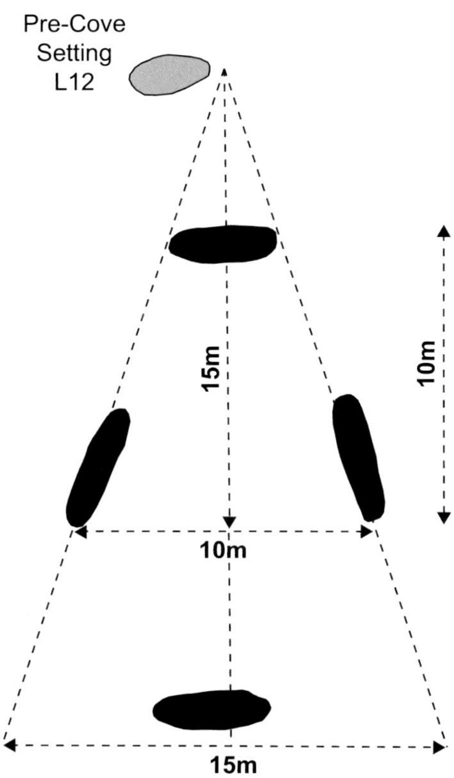

Figure 2.86. (below left) The geometry of the Longstones Cove

wider later Neolithic monument complex (Bradley 2000, 107, fig. 32). He points out that the ring of stakes that perhaps forms the first structure at Silbury Hill possesses the same diameter as the timber circle at the Sanctuary; while the platform created on the summit of Silbury during its final phase is both the same size as the primary mound and of a similar dimension to the stone settings at the Sanctuary. It is also potentially significant that the diameters of the phase I, II and III mounds at Silbury – at *c.*35m, *c.*73m and *c.*150m – show a doubling with each episode of construction (Whittle 1997b).

The application of common units of measurement, formal geometry in layout, and a process of modulation within key elements of the monument complex surely held a 'distinctive metaphysical significance' (Case 2004, 117). While using different units of measurement rather than a common 'megalithic yard', the same process of geometric and measured layout can be seen at other major later Neolithic public monuments, such as the passage grave at Newgrange, the phase 3 settings at Stonehenge and the Southern Circle at Durrington Walls (Powell 1994; Chamberlain and Parker Pearson pers. comm.). Such precise layout is nonetheless rare in a Neolithic context, suggesting that knowledge of such practices was restricted or reserved for structures of especial significance. Ethnographically, similar geometric principles are and were commonly applied in the construction of sacred buildings, from Buddhist temples to early Christian churches (Crump 1990, 135–

140). The integration of complex geometry served to replicate underlying principles of divine order, of cosmic harmony, and afford such constructions a symbolic potency. As points of entry into, and/or exit from, the Avebury complex – representing a passage from one domain to another – it is easy to understand why the Sanctuary and Longstones Cove and pre-Cove settings were subject to such elaborate procedures of construction, affording them with a potency generated through the agency of sacred geometry.

3

Monumentality in the third millennium BC – the West Kennet Avenue and Falkner's Circle

3.1. The West Kennet Avenue

As one of the more familiar components of the Avebury complex, the West Kennet Avenue needs little introduction. An analogous construction to the Beckhampton Avenue, its course runs from the southern entrance of the Avebury henge to the timber and stone settings of the Sanctuary on Overton Hill, 2.4km to the south-east (Smith 1965, 206–10). Alexander Keiller's excavation of the northern third of the avenue between 1934–5, and observations made between 1957–60 of toppled and broken stones in the area of West Kennet, have allowed much of its course to be mapped closely (Figure 3.1). As a result, there has existed a sense of the monument as being 'known' and familiar, although details of the antiquarian record and a programme of geophysical survey undertaken in 1989 suggest more structural complexity than is often acknowledged (Ucko *et al.* 1991, 186–94; Burl 2002, 150–2). In particular, Stukeley's claim of a West Kennet Cove, situated half-way down the length of the avenue at a point where it is crossed by the modern road, remains a matter of some contention (Ucko *et al.* 1991, 190–3; Burl 2002, 150–1).

Notwithstanding such ambiguities regarding its precise format, with archaeology's turn to social theory, cultural geography, phenomenology and embodiment in the 1990s, the West Kennet Avenue featured prominently within interpretive accounts of the British later Neolithic. As a defined route still extant within the landscape, it offered the possibility of 're-experiencing' one particular journey and set of encounters with the Avebury complex; while its architecture suggested restriction and gradation in terms of the numbers and order of participants processing along its course, and so its potential deployment in the enactment and negotiation of power relations. In effect, the West Kennet Avenue became a prime source of evidence for the choreography of social practice during the later Neolithic. Three studies in particular stand out: those by Thomas (1993), Barrett (1994) and Watson (2001).

Writing in 1993, Julian Thomas commented on how the creation of the avenue tied down and defined an approved way of moving through the landscape, 'insinuating rather than forcing a particular passage' (Thomas 1993, 41). The avenue served to produce a specific set of encounters with existing monuments that was as much about embodied experience as it was vision. Participation in processions reproduced acceptable practice, while the differential and graded positioning of participants enabled power relations to be played out – there were those that led, and others that followed. In interpreting the curious 'kink' in the avenue as it finally approaches the southern entrance into Avebury (Smith 1965, 208), Thomas suggested that this was a deliberately contrived architectural feature, rather than a product of phased re-working, designed to conceal views into the centre of the henge until the last moment of procession (Thomas 1993, 42). John Barrett's 1994 account followed a similar line of argument by emphasising how procession established an order, and facilitated exclusion of the uninitiated (Barrett 1994, 15). Through this, dominant forms of social discourse might be reproduced and the conditions created for the establishment of an elite (Barrett 1994, 28). Furthermore, by emphasising how people worked knowledge-

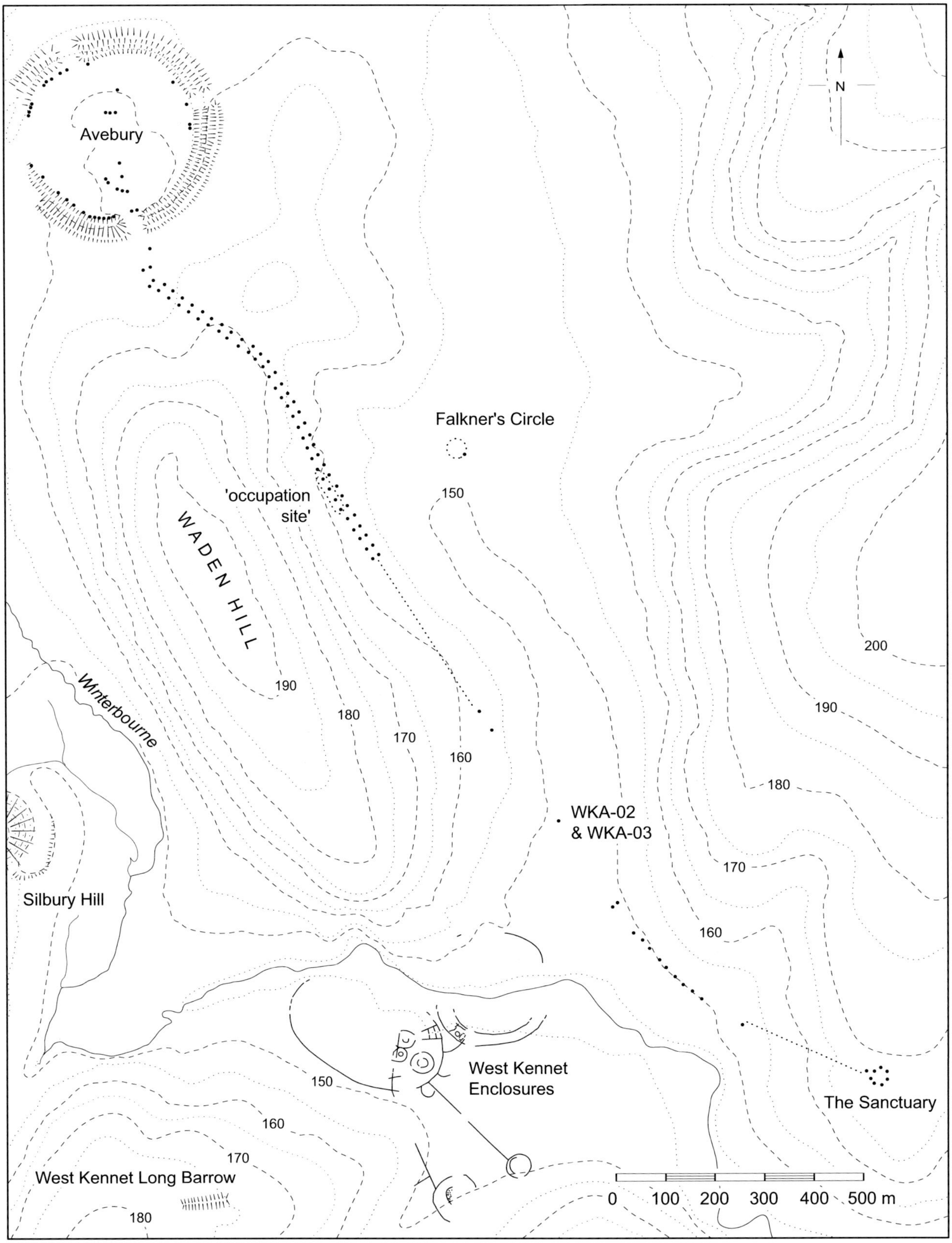

(c) Crown copyright/database right 2006. An Ordnance Survey/EDINA supplied service

Figure 3.1. The mapped course of the West Kennet Avenue, showing the location of the 2002 and 2003 excavations on the avenue and at the Falkner's Circle

ably within given physical conditions and received and accepted forms of practice, Barrett also stressed that 'processional activity did not begin with the construction of the stone rows of the Beckhampton and the Kennet Avenues... these rows are merely the physical manifestation of its existence' (Barrett 1994, 15). A novel insight into the conditions in which these avenues were constructed was therefore offered, namely that their creation formalised or monumentalised existing pathways rather than imposing a new 'planned' architecture upon the landscape.

Working within a phenomenological perspective, Aaron Watson's 2001 paper sought to explore the diverse sensory qualities of places within the later Neolithic Avebury landscape, and how those aesthetic qualities influenced human relationships. Power relations were less of an issue for Watson, instead the choreography of experience presented by the monuments was woven into a referencing of history and the physical landscape. The West Kennet Avenue featured within this. Watson noted that while moving along the northern third of the avenue as it approached Avebury, the earlier enclosure on Windmill Hill was framed by the monoliths of the avenue, thus creating a visual linkage between important places and serving to conflate a sense of past and present (Watson 2001, 300). He suggested that 'people were in some way physically playing out beliefs about their history during the act of moving along the Avenue' (Watson 2001, 300), an interpretation that we have also followed (Gillings and Pollard 2004, 82; Pollard 2005).

Post-processional perspectives

Two recurrent features of these approaches are, first, the assumption that people processed down the avenue, and second, that the order of that procession went from the Sanctuary and Overton Hill to Avebury. Curiously, the issue of whether people were ever intended to process along the avenue is not questioned, nor are similar studies produced for the three other routes into the henge. The focus on the southern henge entrance and the West Kennet Avenue is surely a legacy of survival and fieldwork, in that this monument is largely unobstructed by modern development and has seen extensive excavation and restoration along its northern third. In relation to the first point, far from being a given fact, the issue of whether people progressed down the avenue is becoming more contentious, especially in the light of claims that stone monuments were built not for the living, but for the ancestral dead (Parker Pearson and Ramilisonina 1998). This is an issue that we will return to later in this chapter.

When our project first began (at that time under the title 'Negotiating Avebury'), our interpretive direction was very much informed by the kind of phenomenological agenda promoted in the work of Chris Tilley, Julian Thomas and others (Pollard and Gillings 1998). Survey and stone recording along the West Kennet Avenue was a part of this, undertaken during 1997–8 in order to generate data for interactive Virtual Reality models that would facilitate ersatz digital encounters with the changing architecture of the monument complex (see Earl and Wheatley 2002). However, that work never progressed far. Recognising how illusory our understanding of the physical fabric of the monument complex was, the project took a new direction that focussed more heavily on excavation. Within this, work on the Beckhampton Avenue prompted a greater interest in the biography and construction of the avenues, as opposed to phenomenological analysis. The interpretive direction of studies of Neolithic monumentality were also shifting, with an increasing concern towards understanding materiality and the construction process itself (see Richards 1996; Parker Pearson and Ramilisonina 1998; Cummings and Fowler 2004; Cummings and Whittle 2004; Richards 2004a).

Excavations on the West Kennet Avenue, 2002 and 2003

During the summers of 2002 and 2003 the project undertook limited excavations on the line of the West Kennet Avenue. The aims were: to confirm the continued presence and course of the avenue in its middle section; to recover material that might aid its dating; to look for possible evidence of phased construction; and to explore further the pre- and post-construction history of the monument. The latter included investigation of any pre-avenue occupation, indications through subtle surface traces of procession, post-construction episodes of artefact deposition and burial, and the nature and chronology of stone destruction episodes.

At the time, firm knowledge of the exact course of the West Kennet Avenue was limited to two stretches and its points of origin (Avebury) and termination (the Sanctuary on Overton Hill). Of the reliably mapped stretches, the 800m length directly to the south-east of Avebury excavated and restored by Keiller in the 1930s (Smith 1965, fig. 71) is best understood (Figure 3.1). The known extent of this was extended by a further 120m as a result of geophysical surveys undertaken by the then Ancient Monuments Laboratory of English Heritage in the late 1980s (Ucko *et al.* 1991, pl. 62). The second stretch comprises a much more fragmentary 240m length running to the south-east of the area around New Cottages and West Kennet House. This is known from a combination of surviving stones and chance observations of avenue-related destruction features (Smith 1965, fig. 72). The mapped course of the avenue between these fixed stretches was largely conjecture, particularly in the area directly to the north of the farm buildings behind New Cottages (Ucko *et al.*'s Area C), where geophysical survey proved inconclusive and the only known stone was one marked on the 1883 Ordnance Survey map. Even Stukeley's records depicted only a single standing stone on this part of the avenue's length (Stukeley 1743, pl. XIX), which represents a key stretch of the monument as it nears the area of the West Kennet palisaded enclosures (Whittle 1997b).

In addition to the ambiguities surrounding the precise route and form of the mid section of the West Kennet Avenue, high-quality dating evidence for the stone settings was, and remains, somewhat meagre. There are no radiocarbon determinations from any of the stone-holes (Pitts and Whittle 1992, 206), and little diagnostic artefactual material was recovered in direct association during Keiller's excavations. That present in primary contexts included flint flakes and small fragments of earlier Neolithic bowl and Peterborough ware from stone-holes 25a and 30a (Smith 1965, 232), all of which is likely to be residual from earlier episodes of occupation. Burials with Beakers and an unusual carinated bowl had been interred in pits dug at the feet of stones 22b, 25b and 29a *after* they had been erected (Smith 1965, 209–10), and Beaker sherds were found above the packing in stone-holes 12a and 33b (Smith 1965, 232). A large sherd of Grooved Ware in good condition from the primary fills of stone-hole 15b (Smith 1965, fig. 79, P367) seemed to present the best artefactual association, especially since this fragile pottery must have been deposited soon after breakage. However, Keiller's unpublished description of stone-hole 15b (45 in his scheme) casts severe doubts on whether this was in fact a stone-hole. While containing a basal layer of compacted chalk, the feature is described as being 'completely circular' with an upper fill of 'soft dark earth with a slight admixture of small chalk rubble' (information from records in the Alexander Keiller Museum, Avebury). Both features would be highly unusual for a stone-hole. Furthermore, the finds from this feature, which included eight flakes, a quantity of animal bone (including a pig mandible, a cattle mandible, metapodial and horncore and ribs) and the sherd, sound more like the contents of a Grooved Ware pit than they do a stone-hole. It would appear that the true location of stone 15b, if it was ever present, now needs to be established.

Three hundred metres to the south of stone 15b, the avenue crossed an area of earlier occupation, taking the form of a midden spread, post-holes and pits (Smith 1965, 210–6). Much of the pottery associated with this is of Peterborough Ware, including Ebbsfleet, Mortlake and Fengate forms. Shell-tempered Grooved Ware was recovered from post-holes 1 and 9 and Pit 1 (Smith 1965, 233–4). Lithics from the surface scatter and post-holes include fragments of Group I and VII axes, flakes and scrapers with facetted platforms, discoidal cores, and leaf-shaped, chisel, oblique and barbed-and-tanged arrowheads (Smith 1965, 234–43). The bulk of the assemblage is of later 4th to mid 3rd millennium BC date. Temporally bracketed between episodes of middle-late Neolithic occupation and a series of Beaker burials, and physically linked to the Sanctuary and Avebury, the date of the avenue most likely lies in the second half of the 3rd millennium BC. As with the Beckhampton Avenue, we would favour a date in the third quarter of that millennium, but must await confirmation through further refinement of the chronology.

A possibility also exists that the avenue was constructed in a series of phases over a protracted period of time. The issue is highlighted by Burl (1993, 72), who sees the avenue as originally consisting of two sections that were subsequently linked, one running towards Avebury and the other to the Sanctuary. Furthermore, using the survey data of Thom, he points out that in its excavated northern third the avenue is composed of a series of relatively straight sections rather than a smooth curve, which could indicate separate episodes of construction (Burl 1993, 45–7). Whether these mark the construction work of individual years, or of longer intervals, remains uncertain.

Excavation Results

The avenue was investigated by means of a 25 × 40m area, sited immediately to the north of New Cottages farm buildings, West Kennet (Figure 3.2; SU 112686). This area encompassed the location of a putative avenue stone, reported by O G S Crawford as having been buried in the winter of 1921–2 in order to prevent it from being dragged away and broken up (Smith 1965, 207n). The excavation was designed to establish whether that stone had been part of the avenue as suggested by Crawford and Smith, and to search for other stone-holes and destruction evidence along the presumed course of the avenue. This area had previously been covered by a resistivity survey

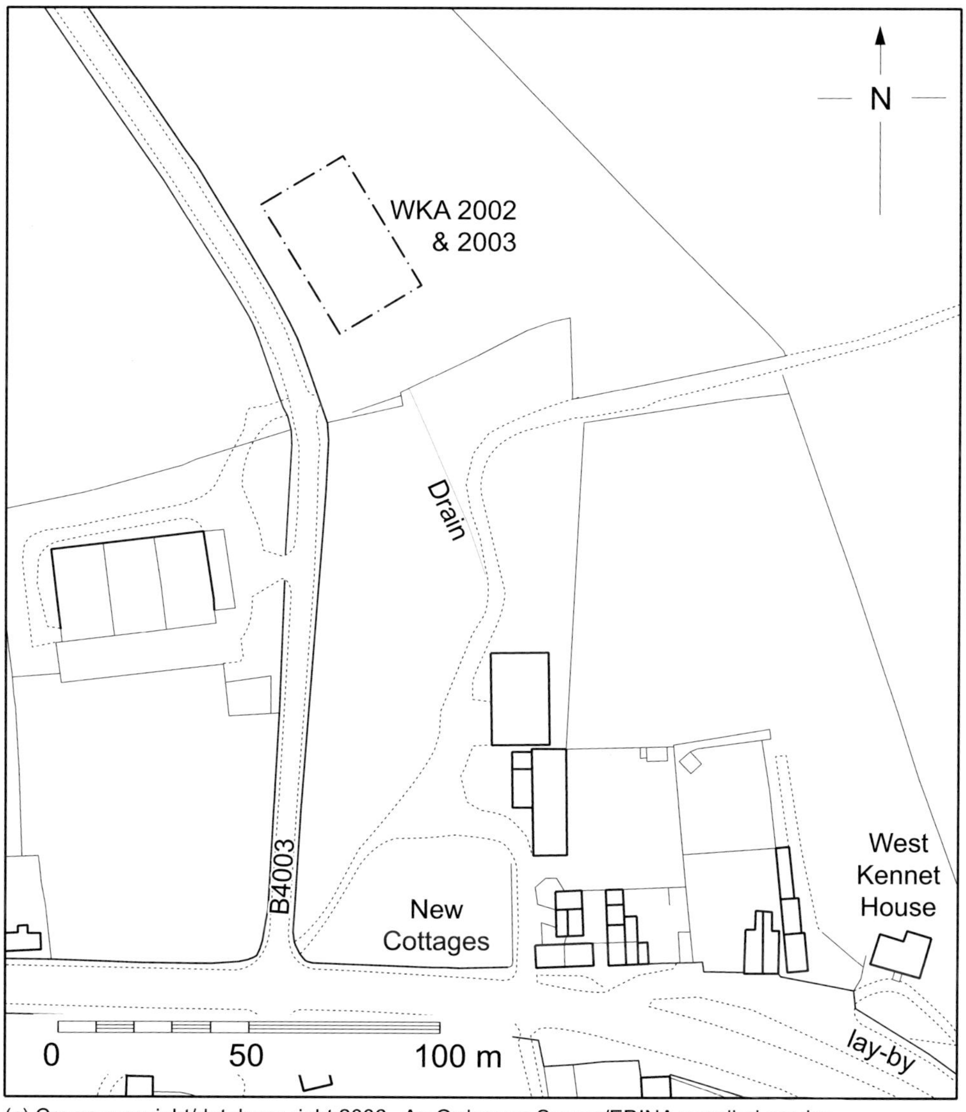

Figure 3.2. Detailed location of the 2002 and 2003 excavations on the West Kennet Avenue

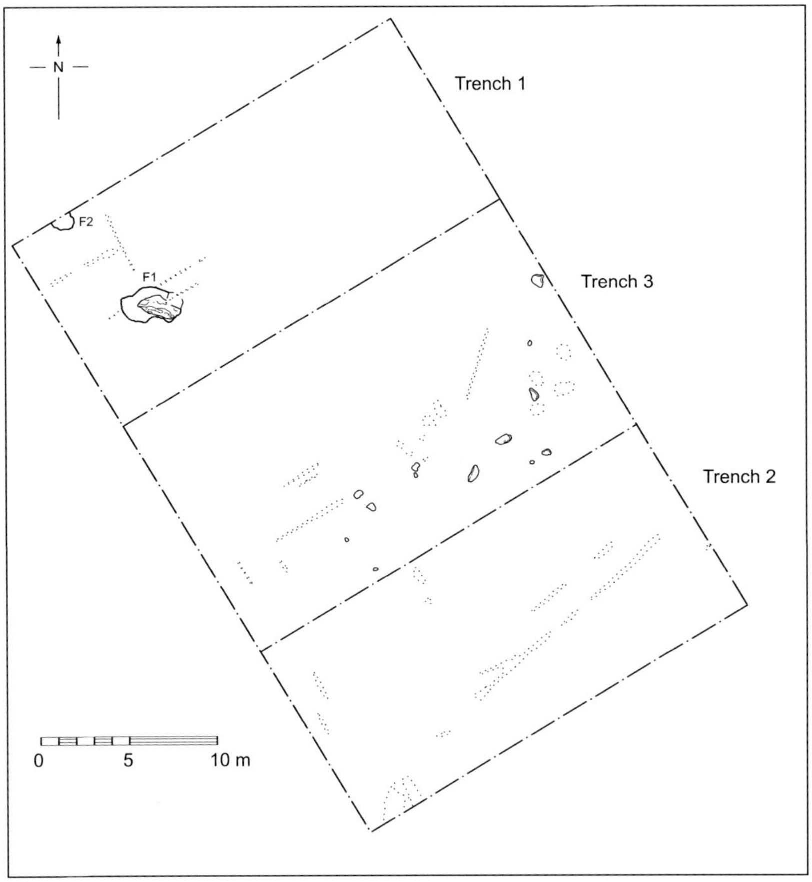

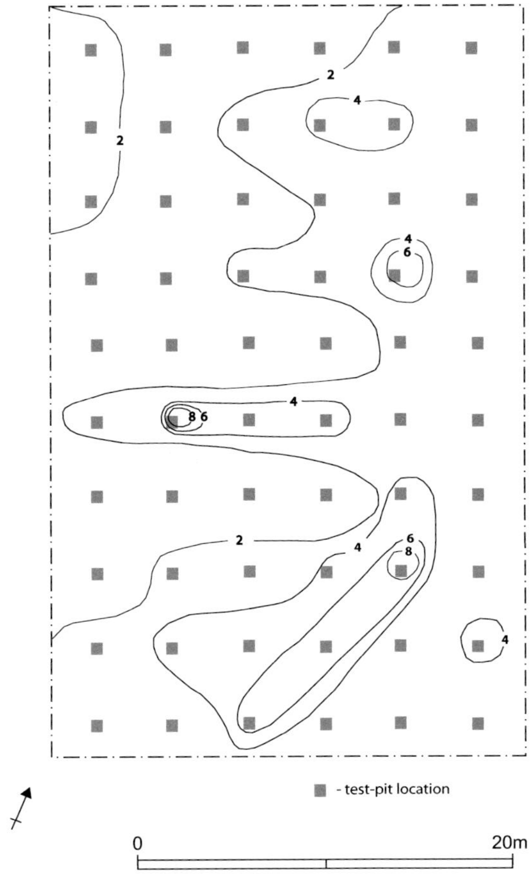

Figure 3.3. (above) West Kennet Avenue: features revealed during the 2002 and 2003 excavations

Figure 3.4. (right) West Kennet Avenue: densities of worked flint from topsoil test pits

conducted by the Ancient Monuments Laboratory in September 1989 (Ucko *et al.* 1991). Although no stone settings, burials or destruction pits were visible, the survey seemed to show a sub-circular anomaly around 25m in diameter lying across the line of the avenue at this point, which demanded further investigation.

It was hoped to excavate the whole area during one season (2002). However, restrictions placed on the Scheduled Monument Consent meant that the turf and topsoil (until recently a ploughsoil) was to be removed by hand. Comprising a deep and heavy, clay-rich loam, the topsoil proved time-consuming to remove, and so a decision was taken to confine the 2002 season to two 25 × 12m blocks within the zone for which Scheduled Monument Consent had been granted (Figure 3.3). The northern area, Trench 1, was sited to include a portion of the resistivity anomaly and the buried stone mentioned above. This stone was estimated by Smith to be on the west side of the avenue, in stone position 63b (Smith 1965, 207n). If this was the case then Trench 1 should have included evidence relating to stones 63a and 63b. Trench 2 was placed 15m to the south of this, to cover the area which, on the same assumption, would have contained features relating to stones 64a and 64b. In August 2003 the remaining 25 × 16m between Trenches 1 and 2 was fully excavated. This was designated Trench 3. Mercifully, on this occasion consent was given to remove the topsoil by machine.

Test pit sampling

As a first stage of excavation, artefact densities within the topsoil were examined across the whole of the 25 × 40m area by means of a grid of 1 × 0.5m test pits placed at 4m intervals. This constituted a 3.5% sample of the topsoil. The soil from the test pits was hand-sorted, while, to provide a control on the level of recovery, a single bucket of spoil from each pit was screened through a 13mm sieve. Forty-eight of the 60 test pits produced prehistoric worked flint, the density varying between 0–9 pieces per pit (average 2.6). In general, densities were lower in the western, up-slope part of the area, and greatest in the south-east, perhaps reflecting enhanced colluviation here (Figure 3.4). The worked flint comprises a mixed assemblage (Table 3.2), with many pieces likely to be of later Neolithic or Bronze Age date, though one heavily patinated blade is probably Mesolithic, and there are two earlier Neolithic edge-trimmed blades. A small number of sherds and fragments of prehistoric pottery were also recovered from the test pits. These include several earlier Neolithic sherds (vessel 2, see below) and a single sherd of Peterborough Ware (vessel 4).

Geology and buried soils

Colluvial deposits were revealed following the removal of the topsoil. In the south and east, where the ground dropped into the base of the dry valley, the clay and gravel natural was covered by a deposit of brown clay loam colluvium [012]/[050], which in turn sealed a thick buried soil [051], both deposits being up to 0.3m thick at the lowest point of the area. Both within and beneath this buried soil, and in some instances bedded into the top of the underlying natural, was a series of small and medium-sized sarsen boulders [052]. Comprising round blocks of reddish-brown sarsen between 0.2–1.0m in maximum dimension, they were distributed in an approximate east-west band across the middle of the area. Their distribution is probably due to a combination of natural (peri-glacial) deposition and limited early clearance. Quantities of worked flint and sherds of early Neolithic pottery were recovered from the top of the buried soil. Of note, a localised concentration of small sherds and fresh flint flakes was revealed over an area of 0.5 × 0.5m around two of the sarsens close to the eastern edge of Trench 3. Upon returning in 2003 it was evident that not all of the colluvium [012]/[050] had been removed from the eastern side of Trench 2, and so prehistoric features may have gone unrecognised. However, if megalith settings had been present here and subject to medieval or post-medieval toppling, burial or destruction, their presence would have been detected via features cut into the early colluvium.

The drift geology 'natural' here comprised very heterogeneous soliflucted deposits of clean yellow-buff silty sand, large areas of chalk gravel, and many involution hollows containing an orange-brown silty clay with flint and sarsen pebbles. An area of soliflucted chalk gravel in Trench 1 is of particular interest as this deposit is probably responsible for the geophysical signal detected by the Ancient Monuments Laboratory in 1989.

Features

A number of features cut into the mixed and complex sub-soil geology. These comprised several shallow plough scores, slumped topsoil patches that were tested by excavation, and two pits, F.1 and F.2. F.1 was found to correspond to the pit within which the 'Crawford sarsen' was buried in the winter of 1921–2 (Figure 3.5). The stone itself [031] rested within the base of the pit. It was sub-rectangular in shape, 2.6m long, 1.2m wide and considerably over 1m broad, this last dimension extending into the unexcavated portion of the pit fill (Figure

Table 3.1. (below) Prehistoric pottery from the West Kennet Avenue

Table 3.2. (bottom) Worked flint from the West Kennet Avenue (k = knife; s = scraper; u = utilised flake/blade; r = retouched flake/blade; p = piercer; n = notched; fr = fabricator; ax = axe; hs = hammerstone)

Vessel	Context	Sherd Nos.	Notes
1	[019]	3	Early Neolithic
1	[001]	11	Early Neolithic
2	[001]	8	Early Neolithic
3	[005]	1	
4	[001]	2	Peterborough Ware
4	[012]	4	
5	[001]	1	
6	[001]	1	
7	[001]	2	?Beaker
8	[001]	1	?Beaker
9	[050/051]	2	Early Neolithic
10	[051]	6	Early Neolithic

Context	Preparation flake	Rejuvenation flake	Flake	Chip	Core	Flaked piece	Shatter fragment	Retouched / utilised
Test Pits	8	14	41	57	5	1	6	23 (k, 4s, 16r, n, fr)
[001]	19	12	88	51	6	10	1	30 (2k, 8s, 2u, 13r, n, 4hs)
[012]/ [050]	5	4	25	12	3	-	1	9 (k, u, 4r, p, n, ax)
[051]	1	3	15	22	1	-	1	4 (2u, 2r)
F.1 [005]	-	-	1	-	-	-	-	-
F.2 [003]	1	-	5	1	-	-	-	-
F.2 [019]	2	1	11	2	-	-	-	-
Total	*36*	*34*	*186*	*145*	*15*	*11*	*9*	*66*

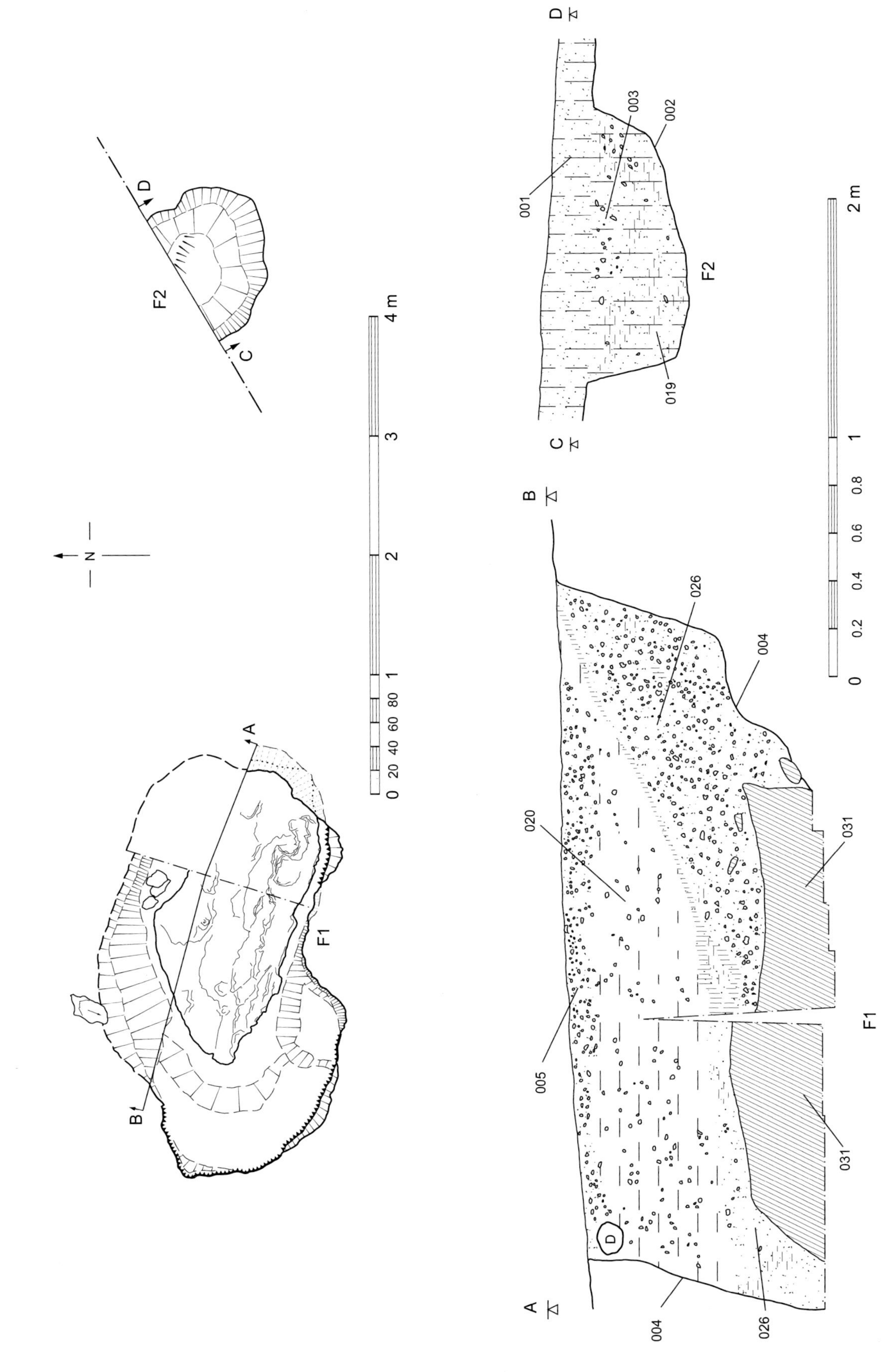

Figure 3.5. West Kennet Avenue: stone burial F.1 and pit F.2

Figure 3.6. (left) West Kennet Avenue: buried sarsen [031] in pit F.1 from the west

Figure 3.7. (right) West Kennet Avenue: pit F.2 from the SE

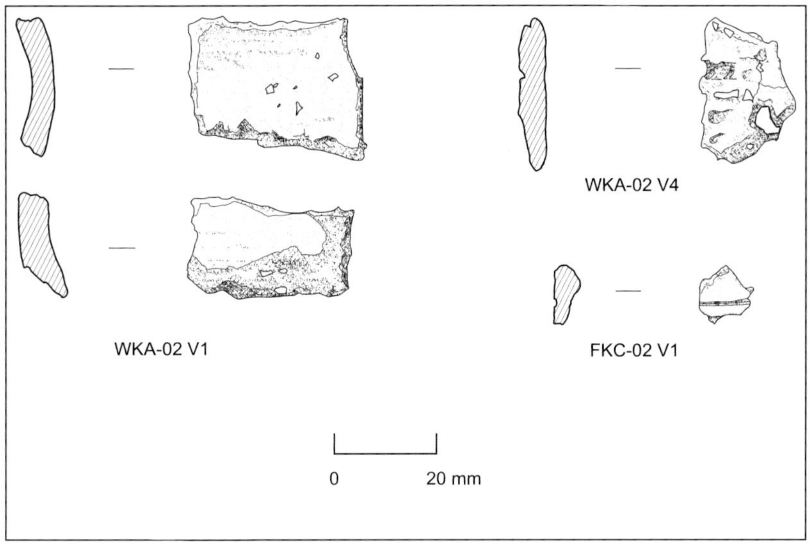

Figure 3.8. (above) Prehistoric pottery from the West Kennet Avenue (WKA-02 site code; V=vessel number) and Falkner's Circle (FKC-02 site code; V=vessel number).

3.6). There is considerable variation in the surface texture of the stone, with the north-east face being relatively smooth, while the south-west side was heavily marked by natural step fractures. The size of the stone is consistent with it being an avenue stone, although no trace of its attendant stone-hole was discovered.

Situated in the north-western corner of Trench 1, F2 first appeared as a very small area of loose dark brown loam (003). Once this was removed it was realised that it represented a small patch of soil filling a slumped hollow in the top of a much larger feature. This feature was a sub-circular pit [002], only a portion of which was within the area excavated (Figure 3.5). The excavated part of the pit was up to 0.4m deep and up to 1.2m in diameter, the edges being straight-sided and the base bowl-shaped (Figure 3.7). The main fill of this feature was a friable mid orange-brown silty clay loam [019] containing sparse charcoal fragments, worked flint and sherds of earlier Neolithic pottery.

Prehistoric pottery

Rick Peterson

A total of 42 sherds of hand-built prehistoric pottery were recovered from excavated areas on the West Kennet Avenue (Table 3.1). The pottery represents parts of eight vessels in six different fabrics. The majority of the pottery was recovered from the topsoil, both from the sample test pits and from the base of topsoil during cleaning. In most cases the pottery is highly abraded although, given the fact that the bulk of the assemblage came from the topsoil, sherd survival seems to have been surprisingly good. Two subsoil features produced Neolithic pottery: a single residual sherd came from the fill of the stone burial pit F.1; and three sherds of a single vessel from the fill of the Neolithic pit F.2.

Pottery from three different periods appears to be present. Vessels 1, 2, 3, 9 and 10 are probably earlier Neolithic in date. Vessel 4 is Peterborough Ware together, possibly, with vessel 5. Vessels 7 and 8 may be Beaker. Two vessels merit discussion in more detail.

Fourteen sherds of vessel 1 survived, three in the fill of pit F2 and the remainder in topsoil. Vessel 1 seems to have been a carinated or S-profiled bowl (Figure 3.8). It had been smoothed externally on the body. Vessel 1 was relatively thin-walled (between 5–6mm in the surviving portions), very dark grey in colour, except for the outer surface which was a dark greyish brown, and tempered using crushed flint. The fabric was hard with a slightly irregular fracture.

Five sherds of vessel 4 were recovered from topsoil contexts. It was not possible to reconstruct the form of this vessel, except that it appeared to be flat-based, but one sherd showed a whipped cord impression. Sherds of vessel 4 were between 6–10mm thick, dark grey in colour, except for extensive light brown patches on the outer surfaces, and tempered using crushed flint and grog. The fabric was moderately soft with a laminated fracture.

Vessel 1 is probably part of the class of fine carinated bowls identified by Herne (1988, 16) from the earliest part of the Neolithic. Pits containing Neolithic pottery and worked stone are also known from the nearby eastern side of Waden Hill (Thomas 1955; Ros Cleal pers. comm.). The good survival of earlier Neolithic pottery in the topsoil at West Kennet may point to the nearby presence of either a larger number of pits or a subsoil spread of midden material such as that noted by Keiller further to the north (Smith 1965, 210–3). The presence of sherds from vessel 1 in the topsoil indicates that the pit containing this vessel was until recently being truncated by ploughing.

Vessel 4 is Peterborough Ware, but is too fragmentary to be confidently placed in one of Smith's (1974) three sub-styles. Peterborough Ware sherds are known from Keiller's excavations on the West Kennet Avenue (Smith 1965, 232–3) but they are rare. Similarly, there was only a single Mortlake sherd from the nearby West Kennet enclosures (Hamilton, in Whittle 1997b, 93).

Worked flint

Of the 502 pieces of worked flint recovered during the 2002–3 excavations, 74% (372 pieces) came from the topsoil [001], here including finds from both test pits and casual collection during manual stripping and cleaning (Table 3.2). This material is clearly of mixed date, and includes regular blades that may be 4th millennium BC, along with numerous hard-hammer struck flakes, crude flake cores and irregular scrapers that would not be out of place in a Bronze Age assemblage. Hill-wash and cultivation has undoubtedly brought much of this material from a variety of locations into the bottom of the valley. As such, the topsoil assemblage perhaps tells little of the kinds of activities that took place in this locale.

In contrast to the heavily rolled condition of many of the worked flints from the topsoil, those pieces from the lower colluvium [012]/[050] and buried soil [051] in the eastern part of the trench are in much fresher condition. They cannot have moved far, or not at all in the case of those from [051], and therefore relate to activities within this location. The flint is generally unpatinated, allowing macroscopic examination of its colour and quality. It ranges from a dark brown to pale grey-brown, with varying amounts of inclusions. With a lightly weathered cortex, it was probably collected from nodules extracted from locally occurring Upper Chalk or clay-with-flints.

The flakes from the soil deposits are generally thinner, less squat and display signs of more controlled reduction than many of those from [001]. Overall, the character of working is more akin to that encountered in 4th millennium BC than later assemblages; and such a date would match the ceramic evidence. There are few preparation flakes (making up only 6% of this part of the assemblage), suggesting that prepared cores were brought on to site and further worked down. Of the cores, three were worked to produce flakes and one blades. Retouched and utilised pieces account for a fairly high 12.3% of the assemblage, and are dominated by tools used for cutting and light-duty tasks (*e.g.* utilised and miscellaneous retouched flakes), with scrapers being absent. In contrast, scrapers make up a high proportion of the tool assemblage from the nearby, and later, West Kennet Avenue occupation site (Smith 1965, 237). Of note is the broken blade of a polished axe in a mottled grey flint, from the colluvium [012]/[050]. A large flake has been struck from one side of the axe either subsequent to or following breakage. In its original form the sides of the axe look to have been facetted. The blade itself is highly polished and retains a very sharp edge (Figure 3.9.3).

The small collection of 23 pieces from the earlier Neolithic pit F.2 includes a relatively large number of blades, narrow flakes and thin flakes removed by soft-hammer percussion. With the exception of one flake, most of the debitage is small and derives from the working of at least two cores. No retouched or utilised pieces are present. The very fresh condition of all the material from F.2 implies only limited or protected surface exposure prior to deposition within the pit.

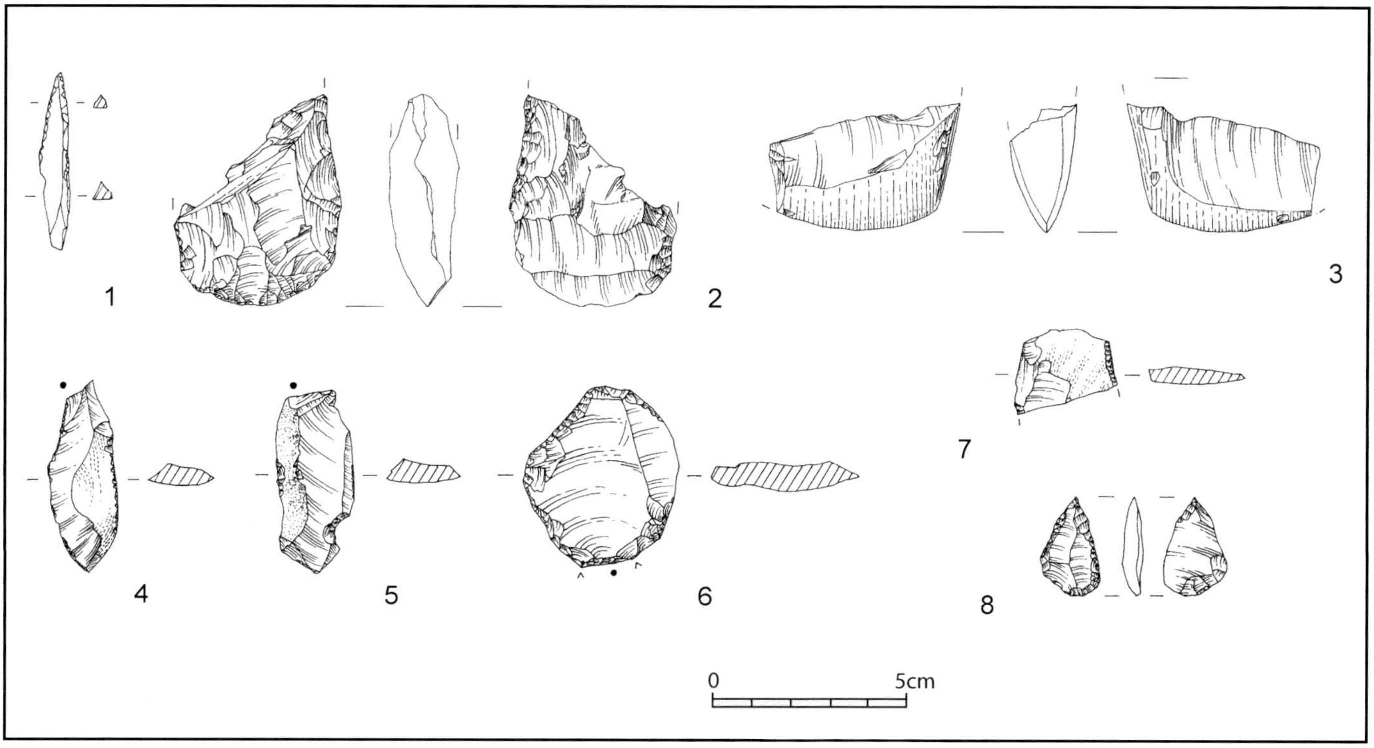

Figure 3.9. Worked flint from the West Kennet Avenue (3–5) and Falkner's Circle (1–2, 6–8). Scale of microlith (no. 1) is ×2

Discussion

There was a sense of irony at the completion of the West Kennet Avenue excavations. Having in previous seasons found an avenue presumed lost (the Beckhampton Avenue), we then appeared to have 'lost' one presumed found (the West Kennet Avenue). What the excavations along the suggested line of the West Kennet Avenue have served to stress is how our knowledge of the course and form of this seemingly well-understood monument is in fact partial.

Although a large buried sarsen was discovered (in F.1), this is almost certainly the stone recorded by Crawford as having been buried in the winter of 1921–2, its position according exactly with the measurements given by Smith (1965, 207n). Given the absence of an attendant stone-hole, it is still not clear whether this stone had even been standing, although Stukeley's drawings of the avenue (Stukeley 1743, pl. XIX) show a stone in this position as upright (Figure 3.10). It is entirely possible that any traces of an original stone-hole may have been destroyed during the digging of the burial pit F.1.

Smith's tentative identification of this as stone position 63b (Smith 1965, 207n) is slightly problematic in view of the absence of any evidence for other stone settings in the rest of the excavated area. There are three possibilities. First, the avenue may not be continuous in this area and the stone in F.1 may be a natural sarsen boulder. Second, the stone may indeed be part of the avenue, but the avenue itself is markedly different in this section of its length, taking the form of a single line of stones with a slightly different interval to those in the section excavated by Keiller. Unfortunately the 1989 earth resistance survey was inconclusive beyond about 900m from the henge (beyond stone pair 44: Ucko *et al.* 1991, 189–94). Whilst some stone placements were conjectured (*ibid.*, pl. 62) the resistance response was too unclear to identify even these with any certainty. Third, previous estimates of the line of the avenue in this area may simply have been wrong, and this stone may be part of the eastern side of the avenue, with the western side lying under the present B4003.

The lack of any stone settings in Trench 2 seems to discount the last of these options: if F.1 represented a stone on the eastern rather than western side of the avenue, then we would still have expected to find evidence for stone 64a. While providing more plausible explanations, the other alternatives are much more difficult to resolve. If the avenue line north of

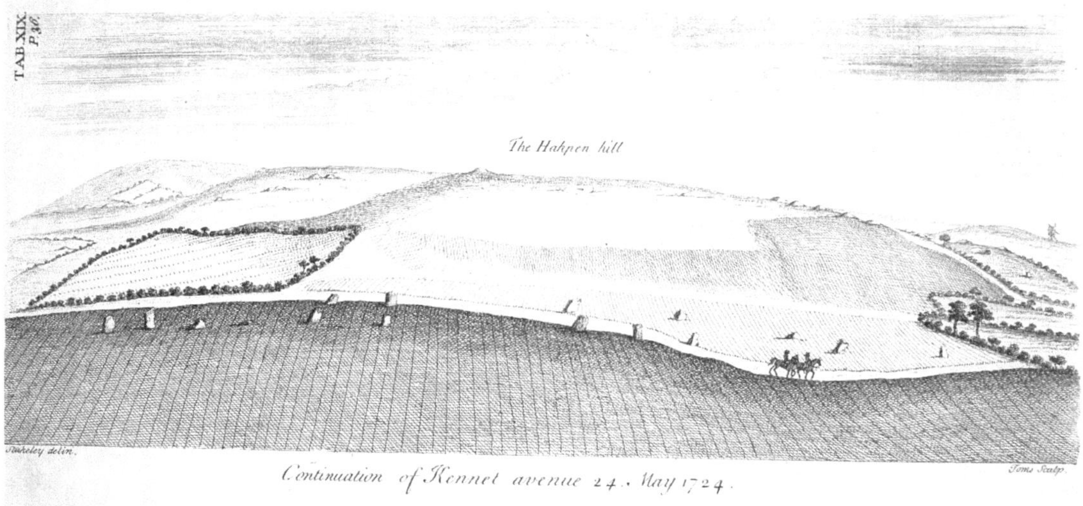

Figure 3.10. Stukeley's published prospect of the central section of the West Kennet Avenue (Stukeley 1743, pl. XIX). The stone recorded by Crawford and excavated in 2002 may be that isolated on the far right of the engraving

New Cottages does not correspond to the accepted pattern of paired standing stones, with horizontal and longitudinal spacing falling within the reasonably well-defined limits given by the excavated portions of the West Kennet and Beckhampton Avenues, the sampling strategy employed here is far from adequate. That we failed to find the expected with such strategies does not mitigate against the unexpected, and we may simply have missed stone settings because of an abnormally wide spacing along this part of the avenue's length.

Explanations have to be offered as to why the avenue is discontinuous in this area, or comprises an alternative arrangement to the paired stone settings seen in its northern and south-east thirds. Was it unfinished, or could its change in format here relate to the proximity of the West Kennet palisaded enclosures (Whittle 1997b)? Perhaps the 'gap' respects a route into enclosure 1 from the dry valley leading up to areas of contemporary occupation on Avebury Down, or reflects a perception that it would be inappropriate to construct stone settings so close to the timber enclosures (the argument of contrasting materialities: Parker Pearson and Ramilisonina 1998). An alternative is to see the bottom of the dry valley as sufficiently special or important in the minds of the avenue builders, because of the sarsens here, or the perceived nature of the earlier occupation, that no further monumentalisation was required, or was prohibited.

Pre-avenue activity

The only unambiguously prehistoric feature discovered during the excavations was the early Neolithic pit, F.2. It is similar in size and shape to other pits from the region, such as those excavated on Windmill Hill (Smith 1965, 22–33; Whittle *et al.* 2000, 141–4), the eastern side of Waden Hill (Thomas 1955), and, more recently, by Wessex Archaeology close to stone 15b of the West Kennet Avenue (Mike Allen pers. comm.). The fill included a 'token' selection of worked flint and sherds, the absence of animal bone being due perhaps to the acidity of the drift geology here. Both the pit and the scatter of early and middle Neolithic pottery and worked flint across this area relate to at least two episodes of occupation or some other form of short-lived activity. Clearly extending beyond the boundaries of the excavated area, the full extent of this artefact scatter remains to be mapped.

The discovery of this material adds to a growing body of evidence for occupation in this valley over the 4th and 3rd millennia BC (Holgate 1988, table 4; Thomas 1999b, 200–1). Mention has already been made of the West Kennet Avenue midden and pits on the eastern slope of Waden Hill. Early Neolithic pottery has also been discovered on at least two occasions from Hackpen, 400m to the north-east (Piggott 1939 and observations in 2006), and, to judge from the material recovered from buried soils under later round barrows, formerly extensive pottery scatters may have existed on adjacent areas of Overton Down (*e.g.* Smith and Simpson 1966). Much of this evidence has so far derived from the valley sides, but with the recognition of buried soils containing *in situ* artefact scatters sealed under later colluviation, further investigation of the valley floor offers considerable potential to enhance our knowledge of the character and scale of Neolithic occupation in the region.

The logic of avenue construction

Thomas sees the construction of the Avebury avenues as a means of drawing together disparate places of existing significance and creating a unified monumental complex (Thomas 1999b, 220). Thus, the Beckhampton Avenue incorporated within its course the earlier Longstones enclosure and an area of later Mesolithic and early Neolithic occupation in Butler's Field (Evans *et al.* 1993, 151–3). In the same fashion, the West Kennet Avenue took in the midden site at the foot of Waden Hill, the area of early and middle Neolithic occupation north of New Cottages, and terminated at a monument (the Sanctuary) built on a site with a lengthy history of activity (Cunnington 1931; Pollard 1992).

Following Barrett's argument, it is entirely reasonable to suppose that the avenues monumentalised existing pathways between these places (Barrett 1994, 15), providing formalised routeways for procession across the landscape that took in along their way places of historical significance. Elsewhere (Gillings and Pollard 2004, 81–2; Pollard 2005), we have suggested that myths and stories relating to particular places were perhaps retold as part of the orchestrated movement of participants along the avenues during major ceremonies, serving to perpetuate collective memory of important events and their placing in the landscape. Such processes of 'bodily remembrance' are particularly potent. As Connerton describes, ceremonies are highly effective mechanisms for preserving *versions* of the past, and it is through prescribed bodily behaviour during such (for example, gesture and formalised patterns of movement) that collective memory is sedimented (Connerton 1989). Connerton also shows how re-enactments of prior, prototypical actions, relating to prototypical events or people of either an historical or mythological nature, are a frequent component of commemorative ceremonies. This is seen with the widespread celebration of New Year and the Christian sacrament as repeated creations of the cosmogonic act. Commemorative ceremonies serve to remind a community of its 'identity as represented by and told in a master narrative', providing a form of 'collective autobiography' (Connerton 1989, 70). Did the avenues recreate mythical trails, and was procession along them a re-enactment of prototypical journeys into the area by the region's first inhabitants?

It may well be the case that the avenues marked out mythical or ancestral routeways, but can we assume that living people as opposed to non-corporeal beings walked in ceremony along them? The notion that the West Kennet Avenue was used for processions has a long pedigree, going back to the time of John Aubrey (Burl 1993, 72), and is now taken as unquestioned fact. Alex Gibson reiterates a commonly held view when he describes the West Kennet Avenue as 'the most concrete of evidence for processions in British prehistory... [being] wide enough to accommodate people, animals and the trappings of ceremony' (Gibson 2005, 107). There is undoubtedly a contemporary logic to the idea of avenues as processional routes because we associate architecture with functional employment, viewing constructed spaces as entities created in order to be used. However, an alternative is provided by the 'construction perspective' championed by Colin Richards and others, which views building work as an outcome in itself (Evans 1988; Richards 2004a). In this respect, creating the avenues may have been the prime objective, not their utilisation as ceremonial pathways. Perhaps, as a monumental record of earlier routeways, their creation actually marked the end of formal procession, as Johnston has argued for the much earlier Dorset Cursus (Johnston 1999, 46).

In support of an interpretation of the avenues as 'empty', memorialised pathways, some of their physical features might be seen to mitigate against their use for procession. The awkward angles at which both the West Kennet and Beckhampton Avenues join the southern and western entrances into the Avebury henge would create an untidy and chaotic end to any ordered movement, though perhaps this was intended. Highly significant, but not previously noted, is the occurrence along parts of the West Kennet Avenue of numerous sarsen boulders, demonstrating that its interior surface was not the smooth, levelled sward that marks its northern third today. In his unpublished 'cuttings' reports, Alexander Keiller noted the

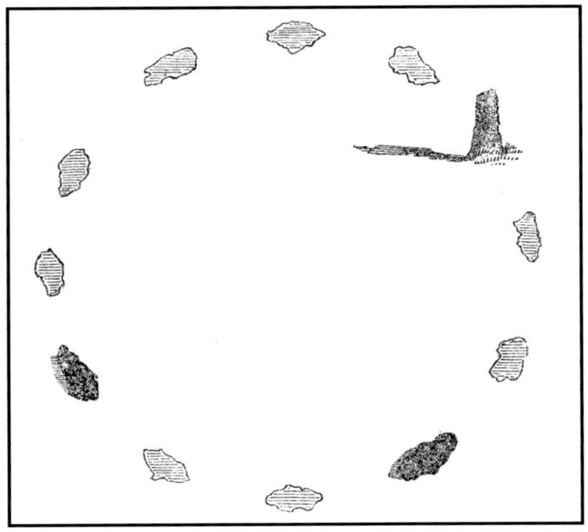

Figure 3.11. Long's depiction of the Falkner's Circle as observed by Falkner in 1840 (after Long 1858)

frequent occurrence of natural sarsens in the area of his avenue excavations, particularly along that stretch running from the southern limit of the restored section up to the rise where the road now crosses the avenue line (Keiller n.d.). Keiller's interest in these related to how they might be mistaken for packing stones. The sarsens ranged from tiny boulders up to substantial blocks over a metre in length, and were often found in clusters and natural linear arrangements. Keiller thought a number had been removed by farmers at a relatively recent date, leaving tell-tale extraction pits that could be over 2m in length. Embedded within the Coombe Rock, in many instances they projected into an overlying buried soil within which artefact scatters occurred. Some, for example a stone in cutting II3R (around stone 36a), projected sufficiently high into the overlying colluvium and topsoil to have been hit by modern ploughing. The implication is that in the Neolithic their tops were proud of the surface. The blurring of constructed monument and natural sarsen spread becomes all too evident, as does the difficulty of processing along a route littered with projecting stones over which participants might trip. In the light of this evidence the West Kennet Avenue takes on a much more 'hybrid' quality, as a lithicised version of an earlier route that combined artificially set stones with natural spreads of sarsen boulders and traces of earlier occupation. These features could have afforded the avenue with tremendous agency. As an amalgamation of all these elements, its status, and that of the Beckhampton Avenue, may have been regarded as potent, perhaps otherworldly. Turning the arguments for procession on their head, could the spaces enclosed within these lines of stone have even been taboo?

3.2. The Falkner's Circle

Antiquarian records allude to the former existence of several small stone circles both within the region and further afield to the south of Swindon (Pollard and Reynolds 2002, 110–12; David *et al.* 2003; Burl 2004). Their significance has been eclipsed to some extent by the scale and fame of the core monuments of the Avebury complex, and as a result of the varying degrees of clearance and destruction they have suffered, yet their presence is telling of the varied monumental repertoire and of different scales of construction and community engagement. Of five small stone circles documented by antiquaries within the immediate region, the Sanctuary was relocated and excavated by the Cunningtons in 1930 (Cunnington 1931), while that at Winterbourne Bassett has recently been relocated and tested by excavation (Jim Gunter pers. comm.). Despite educated guesses, the precise location of the eight-stone circle at Clatford in the Kennet valley to the east remains uncertain (Piggott 1948; Meyrick 1955), and the claimed circle at Langdean Bottom, to the south of the Sanctuary, has been reinterpreted as a later prehistoric hut circle or medieval feature (Burl 2004, 207–8). This leaves the Falkner's Circle, the closest of the group to the Avebury henge, and the circle with the poorest level of antiquarian documentation (Long 1858a, 345–6).

The site of the Falkner's Circle is located 750m to the south-east of Avebury, in the bottom of the broad dry valley defined by Waden Hill and Avebury Down/Overton Hill that runs from Avebury to West Kennet (SU 1097 6932). The first record of its existence came from the observations of a local antiquary, Mr. (Richard?) Falkner, in 1840. While out riding he claimed to observe the partial remains of a circle of 12 stones (Figure 3.11). His account was published in 1858 by William Long:

> 'In the dip of the hill between the Kennet avenue and a slight oblong earthwork on the slope of Hackpen Hill, a solitary stone is standing. Mr. Falkner of Devizes, has favored [sic] me with the following account of his observations in connection with it. "The stone which

you saw in a field on the left, when you went along the avenue towards Kennet, was seen by me in 1840. I went to it, and found it was one of a circle that had existed at some former period. There were two other stones lying on the ground, and nine hollow places, from which stones had been removed, making twelve altogether. I made a note of it at the time, and the person with whom I was riding observed it also. The circle was then in a meadow, which was broken up a few years afterwards, and two of the stones removed. The circle was 282½ yards from the nearest part of the avenue. I could not have been mistaken as to the fact of a circle being there, and considered the discovery of sufficient importance to write to the Rev. E. Duke on the subject, who was not aware of what I told him, nor could he explain the matter at all, – only suggesting that the stones might have been set round a large tumulus, – but the ground was quite flat within the circle, which was about 120 feet in diameter." (Long 1858a, 345–6)

Today a single large sarsen set within a hedgerow is all that remains to mark the location of this monument (Figure 3.12). Given the absence of any orientation or topographical landmarks on the published plan, its precise setting always remained unclear. Hints of its position were, however, provided by an archaeological map of the area published by A C Smith in 1884, which shows the circle extending to the north of the remaining stone (Smith 1884).

The monument is unusual in that no earlier antiquarian account exists. The area of the circle is represented in a very sketchy fashion in one of Stukeley's panoramas of the Avebury complex (Bodleian MS Eng. Misc. b65 fo 109). Here the site appears to lie at the southern end of a natural sarsen trail marked as 'grey wethers'. In a field immediately to the north he appears to depict a single recumbent stone and a rather cryptic label 'This within the stone(?)', while on the western slope of Hackpen Hill he shows a circle of ten stones, perhaps intended to be the kerb of a barrow. That Aubrey, Stukeley and Colt Hoare did not recognise the site of the Falkner's Circle need occasion no great surprise. By the 18th century only one stone remained upright, and this was obscured from view by its position within the hedgerow that formed the tithing boundary between Avebury and West Kennet.

The remaining stone is a large tabular block of grey sarsen standing 1.28m high, with a maximum basal width of 2.10m, its long axis set east-west (Figure 3.12). The top of the stone is pitted by several natural depressions and its surface is covered by extensive lichen growth.

Figure 3.12. The remaining, and half-buried, stone of the Falkner's Circle

In the area of the excavation closest to the stone there is a considerable accumulation of topsoil and sub-soil suggesting that the level at which the stone is set is some 0.5m below the present ground surface. As such, the overall length of the stone must be in excess of 2.0m, and when originally erected it would have stood *c.*1.8m high. The stone is of the same distinctive grey sarsen that was extensively employed in the megalithic settings at Avebury and in the two avenues (Smith 1965). It is markedly different to the reddish-brown sarsen with a smooth cortex that occurs in the immediate valley bottom environs of Falkner's Circle. As such, it may have been brought to this location from sarsen spreads not far to the north-east.

The 2002 Excavations

The site was investigated over a four-week period during August and September 2002. Both prior to and following excavation, the site was subject to a geophysical survey undertaken by the Centre for Archaeology, English Heritage. Earth resistence and magnetometer survey covered ground both to the south and north of the hedge-line, revealing a number of anomalies to the north of the remaining stone. Several of these appeared to lie in an arc radiating out to the north-west from the position of the extant stone. A decision was therefore taken to excavate the area adjacent to the stone north of the hedge-line.

Geophysical survey

Louise Martin

As the orientation of the possible stone circle

relative to the single remaining standing stone could not be determined, an initial survey-grid 60m × 60m in size, divided into four squares, was centred on the stone and extended into the two fields to either side of the field boundary. Excavation results following the surveys of 2002 prompted a return visit in 2003 to extend the grid a further 30m to the north.

Both magnetic and earth resistance data were collected. As the magnetic signature from burning pits or buried stones is slight, as seen elsewhere during the Longstones Project, a sample interval of 0.25 × 0.5m was used to increase the chances of characterising small or weak anomalies. The first four grid-squares were surveyed using Geoscan FM36 fluxgate gradiometers, the final northernmost two with Bartington *Grad601* fluxgate gradiometers.

The earth resistance survey was once again conducted with a Geoscan RM15 resistance meter, MPX15 multiplexer and an adjustable PA5 electrode frame in the Twin-Electrode configuration using mobile probe spacings of 0.5 and 1.0m, taking readings at 0.5m along each traverse. Only the field to the north of the boundary was surveyed.

Changes in cultivation regime between the visits resulted in different background responses being recorded by both techniques. However, this had most implication for the earth resistance survey where there were additional variations in soil moisture and contact resistance between May 2002 and 2003; the initial data set has therefore been subject to a low pass gaussian filter to improve the appearance of the combined data plot.

Neither set of data provided unequivocal evidence of former stone settings (Figure 3.13). The earth resistance data revealed broad areas of contrasting resistance, mostly too large to equate with individual stone positions or destruction pits. The magnetic data identified a spread of smaller and perhaps more suggestive positive anomalies. Some correlations between earth resistance and magnetic anomalies were suggestive of significant features lying on an arc approximately 44m in diameter and intersecting with the standing stone – a tempting alignment which became the focus for excavation. Feature F.6, a stone destruction pit, had been clearly detected in both geophysical datasets, as had F.7 and F.9, and the possible stone-hole F.3. However, several other equally suggestive anomalies are spread about within and beyond the arc that tentatively joins these latter features, and these remain uninvestigated. Whilst the excavated features might therefore correspond with Falkner's observations, the geophysical data unfortunately does not yet confirm the presence of a former circle. (The survey is fully reported in Martin 2004).

Excavation methodology

There is often an inherent difficulty in detecting the presence and format of destroyed megalithic settings. Stone-holes and associated features such as destruction pits are generally small and widely-spaced, meaning any search for patterning (*e.g.* with an avenue or a circle) necessitates the stripping of a reasonably large area, rather than targeted 'key-hole' excavation or trenching. Recognising this problem, the excavation initially comprised a 40 × 10m area set against the hedgerow and orientated NE-SW (Trench 1), with an additional 5 × 5m area (Trench 2) laid-out to investigate a geophysical anomaly 25m to the north of the surviving standing stone. Prior to machine stripping, the ploughsoil was sampled by means of a grid of twenty-seven 1.0 × 0.5m test pits dug at four metre intervals across the original 10 × 40m area. These yielded a low density scatter of worked flint (between 0–5 pieces per test pit if debitage chips <15mm are excluded), sarsen fragments and post-medieval pottery. Following the first stage of ploughsoil stripping and cleaning, no coherent pattern could be discerned in the distribution of features or deposits. Trench 1 was therefore extended, eventually to cover an area of *c.*710 sq. metres (Figure 3.14). Initially this involved the opening of two additional 5 × 5m areas to the south-west and north-west on projected arcs encompassing the remaining standing stone and feature F.1, which was at first thought to be a stone-hole. Once the status of this feature was re-evaluated and other features (F.3, F.6 and F.8) recognised to mark stone positions, it was possible to predict the true arc of the circle. A 10 × 29m extension to the trench was then made to the north-west in order to investigate more of the interior of the circle and locate another stone-hole (F.9).

Results

Some difficulty was initially encountered in detecting features, or at least the edges of such, because of the varied nature of the subsoil and

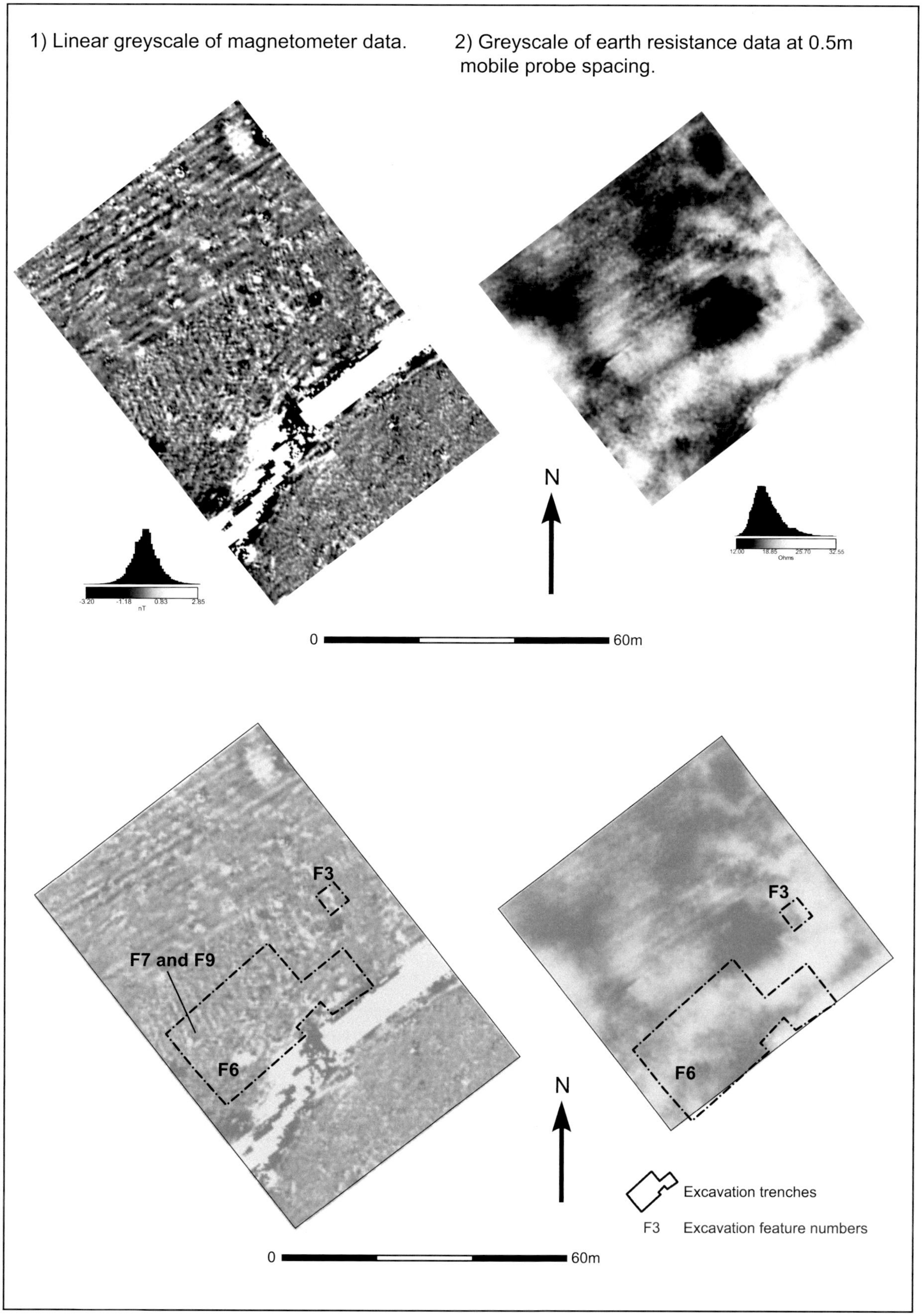

Figure 3.13. Falkner's Circle: geophysical survey results and interpretation

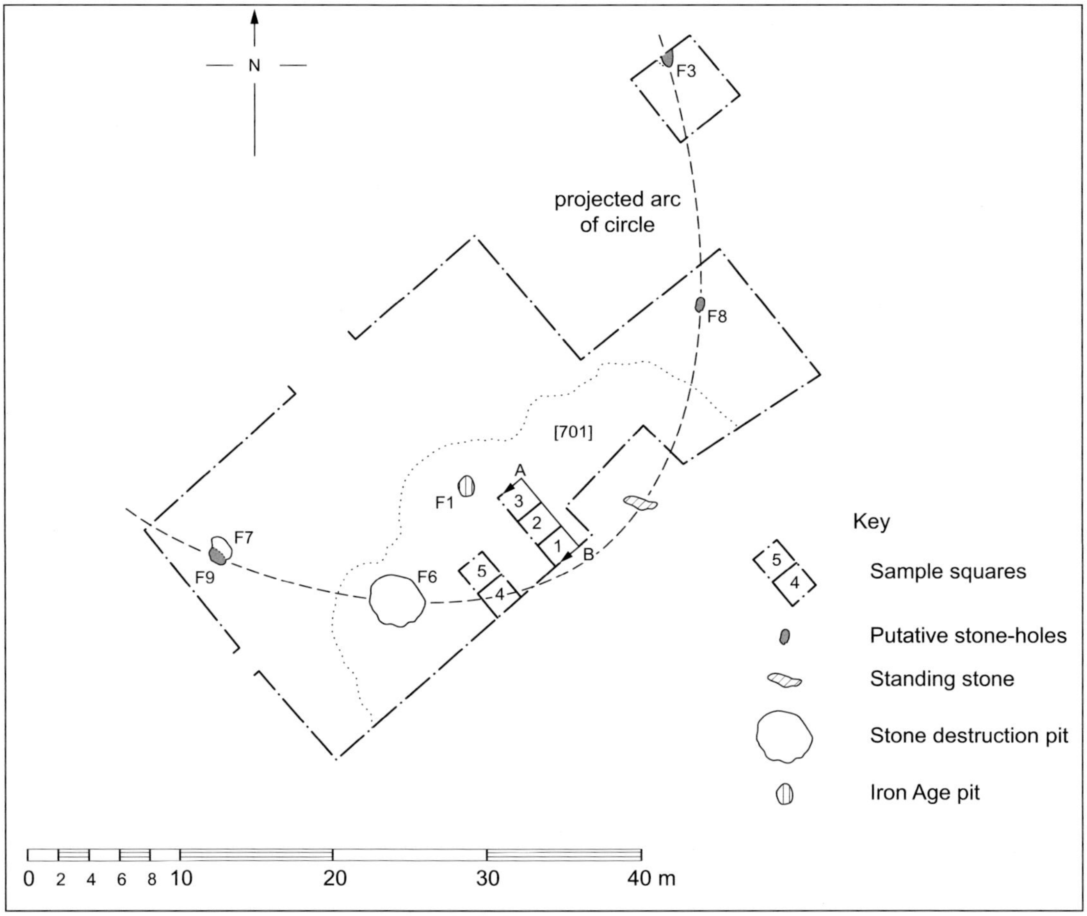

Figure 3.14. Falkner's Circle: excavated features and deposits

Figure 3.15. (left) Aerial view of the Falkner's Circle excavations from the NW. Photo B F C Taylor

Figure 3.16. (right) Falkner's Circle: general view of the excavations with the remaining stone in the left middle ground and burning pit F.6 under excavation in the foreground

natural. The geology here comprised a chalky gravel extensively pock-marked by clay-filled solution holes overlying Middle Chalk. In the eastern part of the area numerous small and medium-sized (0.1–0.8m) sarsen boulders were embedded within this matrix (Figures 3.15 and 3.16).

A thick orange-brown sandy clay buried soil [701] extended across the eastern and southern part of trench. This was noticeably paler over a 2m wide strip against the hedgerow, here marking the area outside cultivation. It soon became apparent that the soil filled a large natural hollow, *c.*30 × >11m in extent, on the south-eastern side of the excavated area. Most likely a large solution feature, this was at least 0.4m deep towards its centre (Figure 3.17). Large quantities of worked flint were present within the buried soil, particularly close to the remaining standing stone and a large pit F.6. In order to gain a better sense of the density of lithics within the buried soil, five 2 × 2m test-pits were dug through [701] at points where the concentration of worked flint seemed

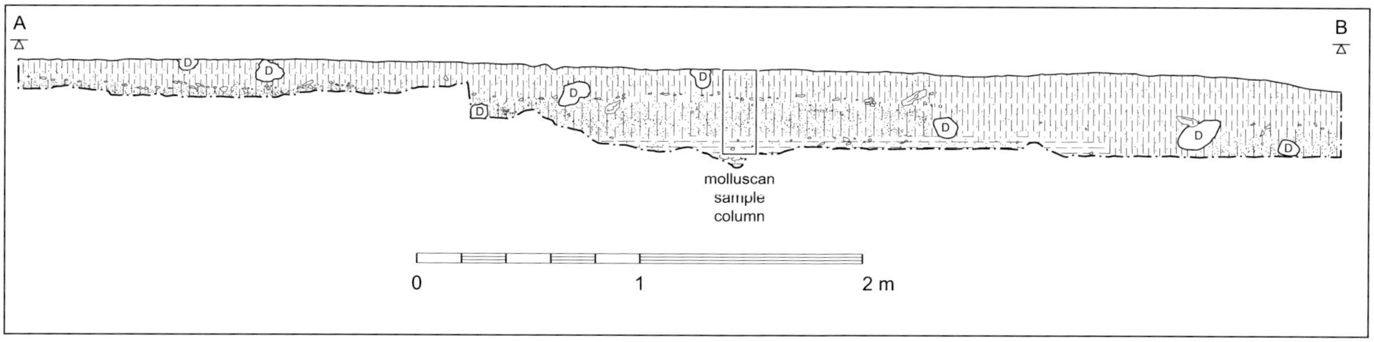

Figure 3.17. Falkner's Circle: section through buried soil [701]

greatest. Densities of worked flint where found to be high, averaging 91 pieces per 2 × 2m square, and ranging from 33 pieces in Square 3 to 143 in Square 2. Much of the flintwork is in a very fresh condition, and is dominated by flake debitage of a later Neolithic-early Bronze Age character. Debitage chips are well represented and a number of pieces re-fit, suggesting that the flint represents *in situ* knapping. In addition, several pieces of Mesolithic flintwork were recovered, including a microlith and a broken tranchet axe. Samples were taken from the deepest part of the buried soil for molluscan analysis, but these did not produce any shells.

An intermittent spread of fire-reddened clay and charcoal flecking [707] was traced over an area of *c.*10 × 4m within the centre of the buried soil. Restricted to the upper part of the soil, this most likely relates to episodes of post-medieval stone destruction otherwise attested by stone destruction pits. Cutting into the top of the soil was a network of animal burrows extending over an area of several metres between pit F.6 and the standing stone. One burrow contained a mass of bones from at least two chickens (identified by Ruth Young).

Several pits were observed to be cut into the chalky gravel and buried soil. Five of these (F.3, F.8, F.6, F.7 and F.9), along with the surviving standing stone, lay on an arc with a diameter of *c.*44m, and correspond to anomalies detected during the geophysical survey (Figure 3.18). They are spaced with a reasonable degree of regularity between 13–17m apart. F.3, F.8 and F.9 have been interpreted as possible stone-holes, while F.6 and F.7 are stone destruction pits (these are described in Chapter 10). All the features were associated with quantities of burnt and fragmented sarsen. The first of these, F.3, was cut into the top of a natural solution feature, and extended beyond the confines of the trench to the north-west. It comprised an oval pit [712], >0.8 × 0.6m in extent and up to 0.2m deep. The sides were shallow to moderate on the east and steep to near vertical on the south and west, the base being undulating and deepest on the south. It was filled with a dark brown sandy clay [711] containing a large amount of burnt and fractured sarsen and charcoal flecks, along with 14 pieces of worked flint. Around this, and perhaps set within remnant packing that was difficult to distinguish from the orange-brown clay fill of the solution feature, were several small (<0.3m) sarsen blocks. These may represent surviving *in situ* packing stones.

F.8 comprised a roughly oval pit [731], *c.*1.0 × 0.6m and only 0.1m deep. The sides of the feature were again shallow to moderate, being steepest on the west, merging with an uneven base deepening towards the centre. In places the base was very compact. The pit was filled with a compact dark orange-brown silty clay [730] containing abundant fragments of burnt and fractured sarsen. The sarsen fragments, which looked to derive from more than one stone, were set at angles within the fill, being concentrated towards the centre of the feature. A geophysical anomaly corresponding to the area of this feature, which also appeared to detect burnt material within the ploughsoil, suggests this could be the remnant of a much more extensive erstwhile spread of stone destruction debris.

The large pit F.6 was the most substantial feature encountered, and is considered to mark the former position of a large standing or recumbent stone. No trace of a stone-hole was encountered, though it could easily have been cut away by the digging of the destruction pit. The depth of the pit and its dished base suggest that it was cut *around* rather than *against* a stone. Around 8.5kg of burnt and fractured sarsen came from the pit fill. All of this appeared to derive from the breaking of a single and

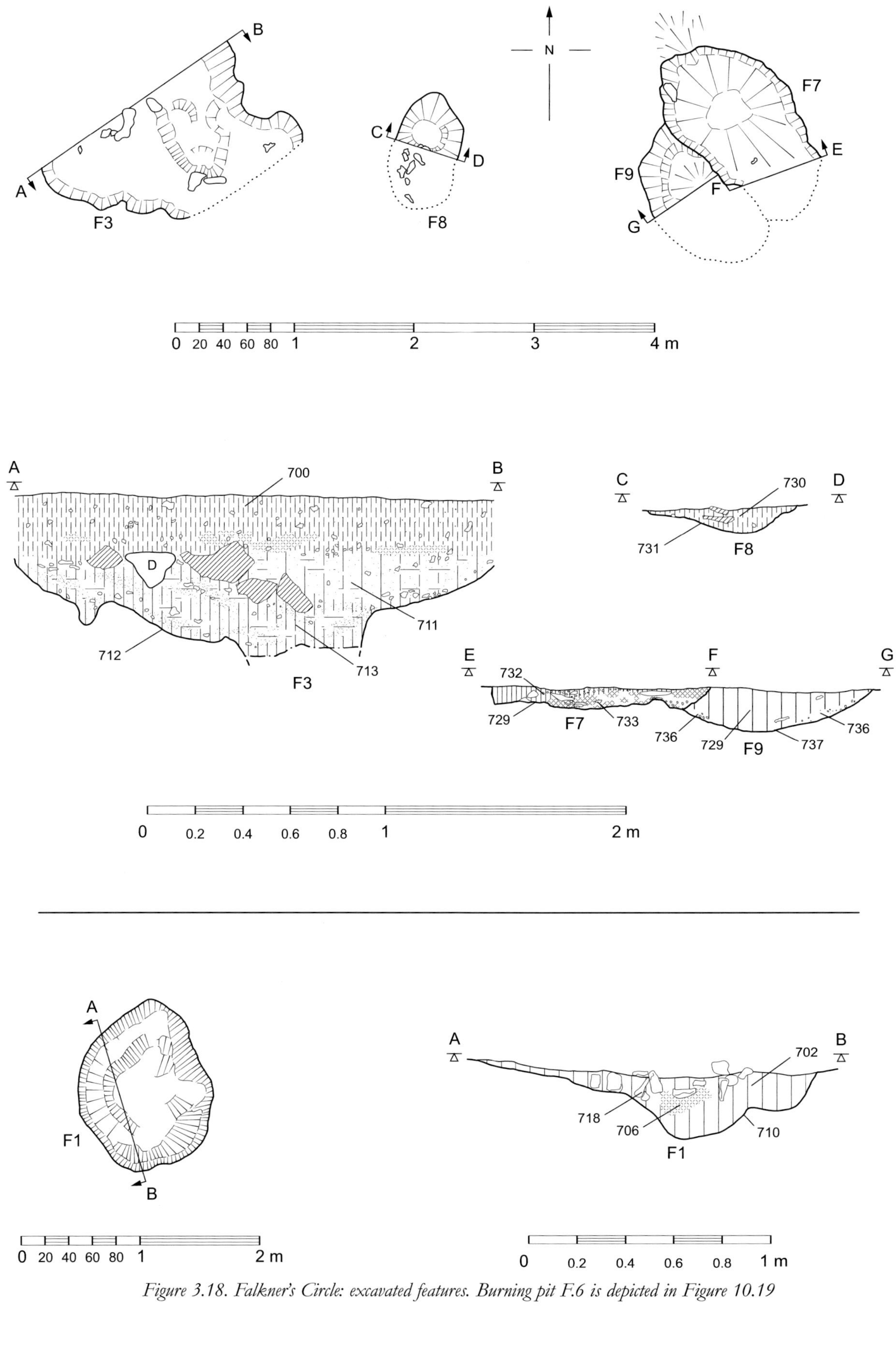

Figure 3.18. Falkner's Circle: excavated features. Burning pit F.6 is depicted in Figure 10.19

presumably very substantial stone. In addition, two small sherds of Grooved Ware were recovered along with quantities of flint debitage. The latter were clearly in a derived context, having been disturbed during the digging of the pit and re-deposited when the feature was backfilled.

In only one instance was a stone-hole associated with a separate burning pit. The stone-hole, F.9 [737], was oval, 1.3 × 08m and up to 0.18m deep, with shallow sloping sides, slightly deeper in its lower profile, merging with a dished base. The basal fill [736] was a brown silty clay mixed with fine chalk rubble, most likely a remnant of original packing. This formed a thin lens on the base and sides, being thicker on the sides. In the base of the feature the fill was noticeably compact, with small pieces of sarsen compressed into its top. Over this, and forming the bulk of the fill, was an orange grey-brown silty clay [729] containing frequent charcoal flecks and some fractured sarsen. F.9 was cut through by destruction pit F.7 on its north side.

A sixth feature, F.1, was sited 10m to the west of the standing stone. Although containing burnt sarsen, the character of this feature was somewhat different to the others. Much of the sarsen consisted of broken small blocks rather than fragments of larger stones, and charcoal was noticeably less abundant. The pit [710] was sub-circular, 1.4 × 1.1m in plan, and 0.4m deep. It possessed a stepped profile, with steep sides to the top, becoming shallow in the lower profile, and merging with a dished base. During excavation the feature cut was often difficult to follow. It was filled with a very dark brown sandy clay [706] containing fine charcoal flecks and some burnt sarsen. Above this was a firm dark orange-brown sandy clay [702] with fragments of burnt sarsen and some flecks of burnt soil, and a tightly defined concentration of small and medium-sized sarsen blocks [718]. The latter, 1.0 × 0.7m in extent and up to 0.2m deep, appeared to fill a localised re-cut [719] within the centre of the pit. The sarsen included both rounded and angular fragments, many displaying evidence of heat fracture. At least one stone appears to have fractured *in situ*. A radiocarbon date calibrating to 410–340BC and 310–200BC at 95.4% probability (2283±35BP: Wk-17356), obtained on carbonised weed seeds, places the feature firmly within the middle Iron Age. Unlike a stone-hole, this feature may instead be an elaborate hearth base or special-purpose pit.

Prehistoric pottery

Rick Peterson

Three sherds of prehistoric pottery came from the Falkner's Circle excavations, parts of two different vessels in the same fabric (Table 3.3). All the pottery is probably Grooved Ware. Vessel 1 comprises a plain sherd and a decorated fragment from the fill of stone destruction pit F.6. Vessel 2 is a single sherd from the buried soil layer [701].

The surviving portion of vessel 1 is between 5–6mm thick, dark orange-brown or grey-brown in colour except for the inner surface and margin which is very dark grey. The fabric is soft with a hackly fracture. The decorated fragment (Figure 3.8) is very small but preserves a single fine groove made with a worked stone point after the clay had dried to a leather-hard state.

Vessel 1 is certainly Grooved Ware and may derive from a context associated with the use of the stone circle. The fragmentary nature of the sherds makes it difficult to discuss this vessel further except to note that the clear, well-executed groove may contrast with the pottery from the nearest substantial Grooved Ware assemblage, that from the West Kennet enclosures (Whittle 1997b). At that site the bulk of the pottery was decorated without the use of grooving (Hamilton in Whittle 1997b).

Worked flint

The majority of the 1074 pieces of worked flint from the Falkner's Circle excavations were recovered from the topsoil [700] and buried soil [701], with smaller quantities coming from stone-hole F.3 and destruction pit F.6 (Table 3.4; Figure 3.9). Varied kinds of debitage (preparation and rejuvenation flakes, chips, cores and so forth) and a limited range of implements are present. Although there are compositional variations between contexts, the different ratios of unretouched flakes to chips (defined as pieces under 15mm) between the feature fills on the one hand, and the topsoil [700] and buried soil [701] on the other, can be

Table 3.3. Prehistoric pottery from the Falkner's Circle

Vessel	Context	Sherd Nos.	Notes
1	[728]	1	Grooved Ware
1	[728]	1	Grooved Ware
2	[701]	1	?Grooved Ware

Context	Preparation flake	Rejuvenation flake	Flake	Chip	Core	Flaked piece	Shatter fragment	Retouched / utilised
[700]	3	5	43	92	1	5	2	7 (2k, ah, m, n, r, u)
[701]	52	19	273	386	9	6	26	12 (6r, 3u, ax, k, n)
F.3								
[711]	-	-	3	9	-	-	2	-
F.6								
[717]	2	-	8	23	1	-	1	-
[720]	3	2	17	2	2	-	2	-
[721]	-	1	1	-	-	-	-	-
[722]	2	1	18	15	3	2	6	1 (h)
[725]	1	-	4	1	-	-	-	-
Total	*63*	*28*	*367*	*528*	*16*	*13*	*39*	*20*

Table 3.4. Worked flint from the Falkner's Circle (ah = arrowhead; ax = axe; h = hammerstone; k = knife; m = microlith; n = notched; r = retouched flake/blade; p = piercer; u = utilised flake/blade)

explained as a consequence of different levels of recovery.

Much of the worked flint is unpatinated and in very fresh condition, especially that from the buried soil [701]. The raw material is comparable to that utilised on the nearby West Kennet Avenue occupation site (Smith 1965, 236), being a dark flint with internal spots and streaks, a weathered cortex and frequently exhibiting thermally fractured surfaces. Nodules of this rock could be readily obtained from locally occurring Upper Chalk or clay-with-flints deposits.

The assemblage includes both late Mesolithic and later Neolithic/early Bronze Age components. At least eight Mesolithic pieces can be identified from [700] and [701] on typological and technological grounds, and by virtue of their distinctive heavy patination in an assemblage of otherwise unpatinated pieces. These include several regular blades/bladelets, a rod microlith and the cutting edge of a tranchet axe (Figure 3.9.1 and 3.9.2); the latter being recovered from the area immediately north-east of the remaining standing stone. Unless marking the edge of a larger scatter, their presence testifies to fleeting visits to this locale during the period, perhaps taking the form of hunting forays or temporary encampments while moving through the area.

A high percentage of the material from the topsoil and buried soil is probably contemporary with the circle (*i.e.* of later 3rd or early 2nd millennium BC date); and it is surely not coincidental that the greatest concentration of flint from [701] occurred within the environs of the remaining megalith and the stone setting represented by F.6. Debitage is well represented and implements are few (only 2.1% of the total). The flakes are hard-hammer struck and quite irregular, tending to broad rather than narrow, although a number of finer narrow flakes and blades are present. Core rejuvenation was quite informal and mostly confined to the removal of step-fractured areas and protruding ridges; there are likewise few obvious signs of platform preparation. The informal approach to the reduction strategy implied by these features is also reflected in the occurrence of irregular multi-platform flake cores. As such, there is no indication of specialised production for knives, arrowheads or other complex tools. Since there are comparatively few cortical flakes, and certainly a dearth of large preparation flakes from the initial stages of nodule testing and core preparation, it may be inferred that cores were brought onto the site partially prepared. Knapping seems to have occurred *in situ* around the area of the stones, as evidenced by the ubiquity of chips and several instances where it has been possible to refit sequences of flakes.

The limited assemblage of post-Mesolithic implements is largely composed of miscellaneous retouched and utilised pieces. From [700] is a small implement that may either be an oblique arrowhead or an elaborately retouched piercer (Figure 3.9.8), the style of working being consistent with the former, though it is thicker than would normally be expected for an arrowhead. Of the knives from [700] one is fragmentary with marginal retouch (Figure 3.9.7), the other oval with semi-invasive working (Figure 3.9.6). The absence of scrapers is notable and may, along with the infrequency of implements, indicate that a restricted or specialised range of activities lay behind the generation of this assemblage (*i.e.* it was not occupation in the conventional sense).

Discussion

We can be reasonably confident that we have found the features observed by Falkner in 1840, and that they correspond closely to his observations. His hollows must relate to stone destruction pits, the truncated remains of which were found during the excavation. As further corroboration, the surviving stone along with F.3, F.8 and F.9 all fall on the projected arc of a circle *c.*44m in diameter, a dimension close to his 120 feet. Nonetheless, some ambiguities remain: the results of the magnetometer survey present a rather messy picture, with some anomalies lying on the projected arc of the circle, others to the inside and outside of this; on the basis of the spacing of the stone-holes and destruction pits a circle of only 10 as opposed to his 12 stones can be reconstructed; and with their gently sloping sides and shallow depth F.8 and F.9 might be seen to make rather unconvincing stone-holes. The last two observations are perhaps easiest to address. First, there is no need to demand a truly regular arrangement of megaliths, especially since some variability is seen to exist in the spacing between the excavated features; and it has to be acknowledged that as a 'class' of monument, stone circles do not always comprise geometrically perfect settings with stones set at precise intervals (Burl 2000). There is no doubt that the setting of the one remaining stone appears rather awkward in relation to the projected circle, with its long axis being perpendicular to the arc. Again, there are precedents for this, at Cerrig Arthur, Gwynedd, and Castlerigg, Cumbria, for example, where such 'misaligned' stones are also set on the south-east (Burl 2000), presumably reflecting the particular cosmological significance of this direction. With regard to F.8 and F.9, the presence of debris from episodes of stone breaking within these features strongly implies that they held stones, whether these were artificially set or not. It should also be stressed that the anomalies observed on the magnetometer survey most likely relate to the breaking of stones, and can only provide a general indication of where they were originally set.

We would argue that the features revealed during the 2002 excavation are those of a stone circle as originally claimed by Falkner, but recognise that alternative readings of the evidence are possible. A counter argument could, for example, see the putative stone-holes at Falkner's as depressions left from the removal of naturally occurring sarsens, and the destruction pits likewise related to agricultural clearance of larger stones within a sarsen 'trail'. The absence of a stone-hole associated with destruction pit F.6 might support this, but the pit is sufficiently large to have destroyed any former stone-hole. Besides, the presence of large quantities of worked flint and sherds of Grooved Ware show this particular stone and the one surviving upright were the focus for activity during the later Neolithic. The presence of the remaining standing stone, which has evidently been brought to the site and deliberately erected, shows that in one form or another this location was 'monumentalised'.

The circle as a hybrid construction

If not a wholly constructed monument, but one created from a combination of fortuitously sited sarsens and erected stones, then the Falkner's Circle becomes all the more interesting. Its 'hybridity' would emphasise once again the cultural significance ascribed to natural sarsens, both singular and as spreads. A blurring of 'nature' and 'culture', it would tell of the identity, subjectivity and even animate qualities stone was regarded to hold during the Neolithic and earlier Bronze Age (cf. Tilley *et al.* 2000; Tilley 2004). The circle's creation would be less of a social project, since it required only limited modification and addition, and more an elaboration of a 'given' feature created through other, perhaps ancestral, agencies. The location of the monument is perhaps telling. It is set very much within a bowl-like landscape, a location characteristic of many later Neolithic monuments (Bradley 1998). Views of the Avebury henge are blocked by gently rising ground to the north, but the site is inter-visible with a long stretch of the West Kennet Avenue. However, more significant than the visual field of the monument may be its position in relation to the natural sarsen trail within this valley documented by Stukeley (Bodleian MS Eng. Misc. b65 fo 109) but removed by later clearance. The circle lies at the southern end of this trail, seemingly at the point where the large 'grey wethers' – similar to those employed in the Avebury settings and the two avenues – diminish in number and smaller blocks of reddish-brown sarsen become more prevalent. Perhaps it is this 'liminal' setting on the edge of one of the great stone fields that made this a location significant enough to monumentalise. The same may also be true at Clatford, where that circle was created close to the junction of the Kennet and the sarsen-strewn valley leading up to the Devil's Den. If we acknowledge the considerable mythological and ancestral significance of stone, and follow the lead of ethnographic analogy in seeing how stones can be considered to hold varying degrees of agency (*e.g.* Theodoratus and LaPena 1994; Roe and Taki 1999), then at the Falkner's Circle we may have a monument *to* stones as opposed to one *for* people.

The circle as a 'conventional' monument

If we accept the features as those of a conventional, artificially constructed stone circle then how does it relate to comparable megalithic settings in the region? First, the absence of any post-holes at the Falkner's Circle shows that the sequence of timber-to-stone represented at the Sanctuary (Cunnington 1931; Pollard 1992) does not hold true for all the region's smaller stone circles. In this respect, the creation of a stone monument without a timber predecessor at the Falkner's Circle is analogous to the construction of the massive outer and two inner circles within the Avebury henge. However, any comparison with Avebury immediately highlights how diminutive a monument the Falkner's Circle is in relation to many of the region's massive late Neolithic constructions. It pales besides Avebury, Silbury Hill and the West Kennet palisades. This is hardly a project that drew upon large numbers of people and resources to enable its construction, the labour requirements probably being equivalent to those of a medium-sized Bronze Age round barrow. In terms of its dimensions and demands upon labour, it might be regarded as the stone equivalent of the small timber circles discovered within the West Kennet enclosures (Whittle 1997b).

The Falkner's Circle may have served as a shrine for a single family or kin-group, marked a holy place within the landscape, or simply memorialised an important, even mythological, event that was deemed to have taken place here. Could, for instance, the presence of later Mesolithic worked flints, which are otherwise uncommon within the region, indicate an enduring historical/mythological significance to this locale? Was it one of those 'ancestral places' whose marking through the creation of monuments became so important during the later 3rd millennium BC (Pollard 2005)? In terms of the practices that took place here before, during or following construction, the excavated evidence tells of the setting up of stones, the working and deposition of large amounts of flint, and the use or deposition of a small number of pottery vessels. This was not routine occupation, nor probably feasting (though the buried soil was too acidic to preserve ancient bone). It is tempting to read the rather unusual lithic and ceramic assemblages as indicative of restricted participation in activities here, maybe visits by initiates or elders only. That it sits slightly out on a limb, unconnected to other monuments and 'ignored' by the course of the West Kennet Avenue, could tell of either its fleeting significance or its difference to other later Neolithic constructions on the valley floor.

4

Monumentality in the third millennium BC – the Avebury Cove

> 'We cannot conceive any thing bolder, than the idea of those people... setting up these stones.' (Stukeley 1743, 24)

Situated in the centre of the Northern Inner Circle at Avebury, the Cove represents one of the most enigmatic and visually engaging components of the henge (Smith 1965, 201–2). With this truly monumental setting megalithic construction at Avebury reached its apogee. In its original form the Cove was a box-like setting of at least three massive sarsen slabs, probably open to the north-east (Figures 4.1 and 4.2). Only two stones survive today, the southern Stone I, and western Stone II, standing 4.9 and 4.4m above ground respectively (stone numbers refer to those given in Smith 1965). A third, northern, stone (III) is recorded by early antiquaries such as Aubrey, Charleton and Stukeley. Described by Stukeley as being 'full seven yards long, of the same shape as its opposite, tall and narrow' (Stukeley 1743, 24), it fell in 1713 and was broken up. From the evidence of early antiquarian plans, there are hints that a fourth stone may have existed, either forming the eastern side of a 'closed' box, or as a recumbent within the centre of the setting (Ucko *et al.* 1991, 227–32). Ten metres to the east is a group of three small stones lying half-buried (Smith 1965, fig. 68, E). A 1975 geophysical survey hints at the presence of others to the north (Ucko *et al.* 1991, 224–6), perhaps components of a façade of smaller sarsens similar in format to that fronting the Obelisk in the Southern Inner Circle (Smith 1965, 199). Further stones probably existed to the north-east, south-east, south-west and north-west of the Cove (Pollard and Gillings 1998, 153). A full account of the recent history of the setting and of earlier investigations here has been compiled by Gingell and Montague (1996).

Avebury's north-eastern quadrant, within which the Cove lies, has seen little excavation. With the exception of Piggott's work designed to test the validity of claims for a third, northern, 'inner' circle (Piggott 1964), the only recorded excavations are those undertaken by antiquaries at the Cove. There is little detail relating to the first of these, by Henry Brown and others in the early 19th century (Long 1858a, 325–6). Brown seems to have found a hollow in the centre of the setting – almost certainly the post-medieval burning pit for Stone III – where he believed an altar stone had been set on which sacrifices were burnt (Long 1858a, 325–6). More systematic work followed in 1865, directed by William Cunnington III, A. C. Smith and Bryan King (Smith 1867). This work is remarkable for its clearly defined research agenda, which sought to refute the suggestions made previously by Fergusson that Avebury was of post-Roman date and comprised a vast cemetery (Gillings and Pollard 2004, 166). Cunnington, Smith and King dug four trenches at the Cove: one on either side of the western stone (II); one against Stone I (although there is no indication as to which side); and the final on the eastern side of the setting to assess the presence or otherwise of a fourth stone. Unfortunately, no plan exists of these trenches. The work did reveal evidence of sarsen boulder packing in the stone-holes of both, and within the interior of the Cove deposits of burnt sarsen and straw in two distinct locations. The latter must be post-medieval destruction deposits, though it is not clear if these were contained within a burning pit or formed part of a surface spread. A

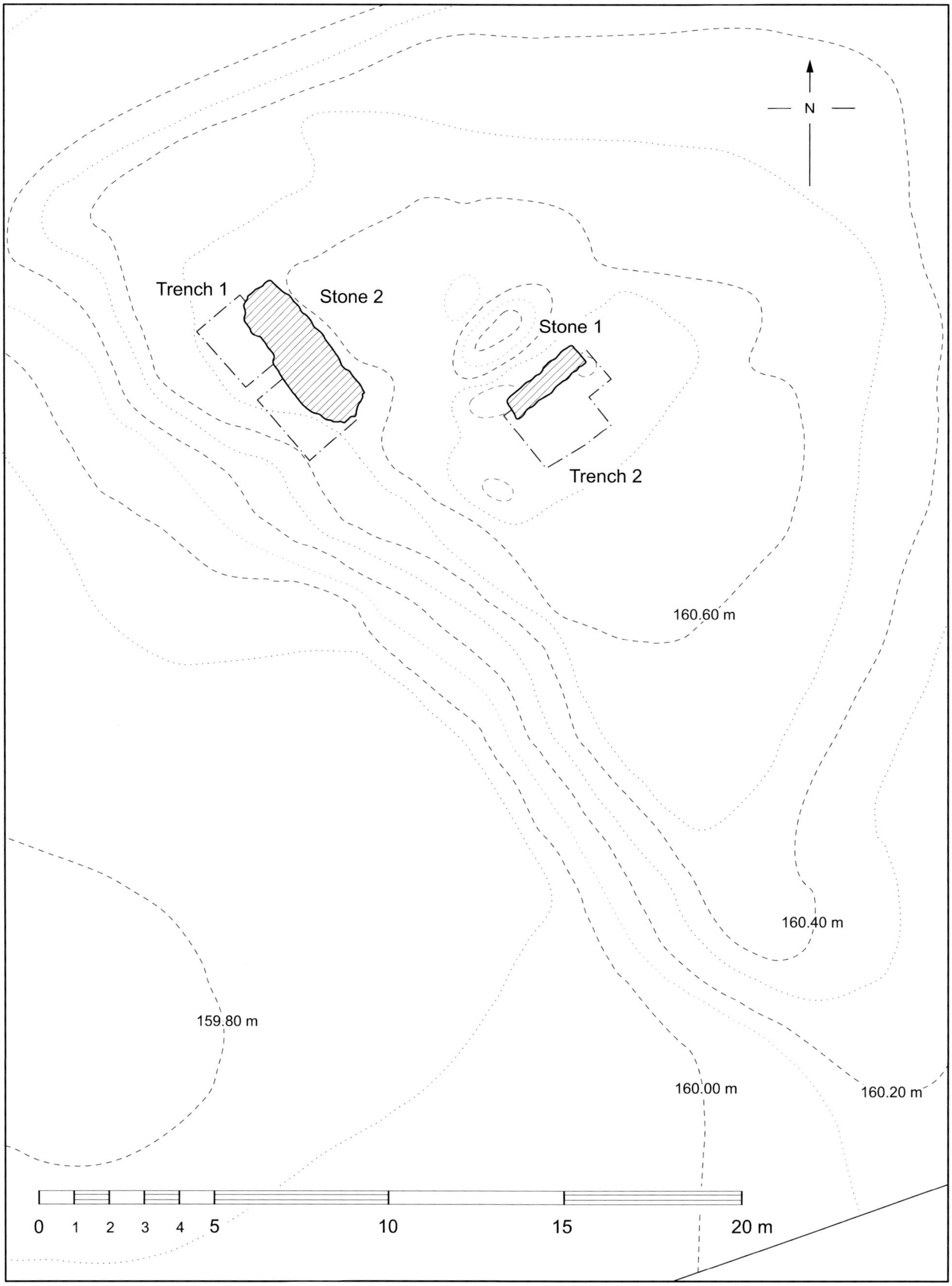

Figure 4.1. Avebury Cove: location of the 2003 excavation trenches

Figure 4.2. Stukeley's view of the Avebury Cove stones from the NE (Stukeley 1743, pl. XV)

geophysical survey undertaken in 1975 does show a large anomaly to the north of Stone II which can be correlated with some confidence to a Stone III destruction pit (Ucko *et al.* 1991, pl. 68). Depending on one's reading of the 1867 account, this looks to lie well beyond the area of the 1865 excavations and is therefore unlikely to be the feature encountered by Cunnington, Smith and King.

The excavations described here were undertaken in advance of major engineering work to stabilise the two remaining megaliths. They were funded by English Heritage and the National Trust, and covered by Class Consent. The decision to stabilise the stones followed the production of a desk-based assessment that presented evidence for a steady increase in the angle of lean to both of the stones (Gingell and Montague 1996). There was good reason to believe that one or both might fall without warning, and that re-setting them in a vertical position was the most realistic course of action to take. The engineering solution demanded that trenches be dug alongside the outer faces of both stones in order to enable them both to be pushed to the vertical and to provide space for concrete footings. Disturbance of *in situ* archaeological deposits was inevitable, and a programme of excavation was therefore written into the project design.

Although undertaken in a 'restoration' context, the excavation was also backed by a series of three academic aims. The first was to attempt to establish the date of the Cove and seek evidence relating to phasing or reworking of the setting. Excavation at the Cove was seen to provide a rare opportunity to gain much-needed and important information relating to the chronology of the megalithic settings within Avebury (Cleal and Montague 2001), which despite best efforts remains inadequate (Pitts and Whittle 1992; Pollard and Cleal 2004). The second, involved an assessment of the technology of stone erection (*e.g.* the use of ramps, packing materials, anti-friction stakes, *etc*) practised here; while the third was to establish, as much as possible given the limited area of excavation, something of the history of the setting. These were accompanied by a wider series of questions relating to the chronology, structure, activities, meanings and materialities of the Avebury monument, and an understanding of cove structures in general (Burl 1988).

The work was undertaken in advance of stone stabilisation over nine days in early April 2003. Two trenches were hand excavated: Trench 1 on the west side of Stone II and Trench 2 on the east side of Stone I. In both instances the trenches were located on the outside of the Cove. The size of the trenches was constrained both by the brief given and by the positioning of scaffolding, which often made excavation an uncomfortable (though safer) process.

Excavation results

Trench 1 (Stone II)

Trench 1 was laid out against the western side of Stone II, the 'back stone' of the Cove. Its 4.9m length was dictated by the need to excavate across the full width of the stone, while the presence of the scaffold meant that it could be no more than 1.8m wide, narrowing in the centre to 0.9m due to the outward bulge of the face of the stone. In order to provide a transverse section of the stone-hole a 0.5m wide central baulk was left in place throughout the course of excavation and still remains. A ground penetrating radar survey commissioned by the engineers prior to the excavation suggested the buried portion of the stone only extended to a maximum depth of 1.2m below the present ground surface. However, as the excavation progressed, it became clear both that the stone was much more deeply set than anticipated and that a considerable depth of 'made ground' existed against its western face. The recognition that the base of the stone is in excess of 2.5m below current ground level led to a re-evaluation of its stability and ultimately a decision not to attempt to move and re-set it. By this late stage in the work it was also becoming clear that the excavation could not proceed safely without a re-design of the scaffold and a lateral extension to the trench. Consequently, the excavation stopped at a maximum depth of *c.*2.4m without reaching the base of the stone-hole or removing all of the archaeological deposits.

Figure 4.3. Avebury Cove: deeply stratified deposits of 19th and 20th century dumped material against the SW face of Stone II, Trench 1. Note inverted frying pan behind scale

The deposits encountered were much deeper and more complex than anticipated, giving a very 'urban' feel to the whole excavation (Figure 4.3). In addition to the stone-hole itself, there were successive dumps of soil and refuse against the stone, dated by abundant artefactual material to the late 19th and early 20th centuries, a series of pits, including at least one earlier excavation trench, and a post-hole. These are described in sequential order, beginning with the earliest.

Prehistoric features

There were two features of prehistoric date, the stone-hole F.6 and a small pit, F.8, in the north-west corner of the trench (Figure 4.4). The stone-hole F.6 [041] was a substantial feature that extended across and beyond the full length of the trench. Although it was originally planned to excavate fully the stone-hole, the unanticipated depth of deposits, the physical difficulties encountered in working within a narrow and deep trench, and the decision not to re-set the stone, meant that this feature was only partially explored. Its overall extent is therefore difficult to gauge, though a clear return was visible at the northern end, and, taking into account the width and thickness of the stone, the overall length of the cut is likely to be in the order of *c.*5m, and width *c.*2.5–3.0m. In plan, it appears oval with rounded ends and is slightly bayed, particularly in its southern half where the sides were noticeably 'pushed out' at one point. In profile, the cut was regular, very steep to near vertical, though slightly ramped at the very top where this had escaped later disturbance. A more gentle slope to the sides at the northern end of the stone-hole appears to conform to the tapering shape of the base of the stone at this point, implying that the stone-hole was

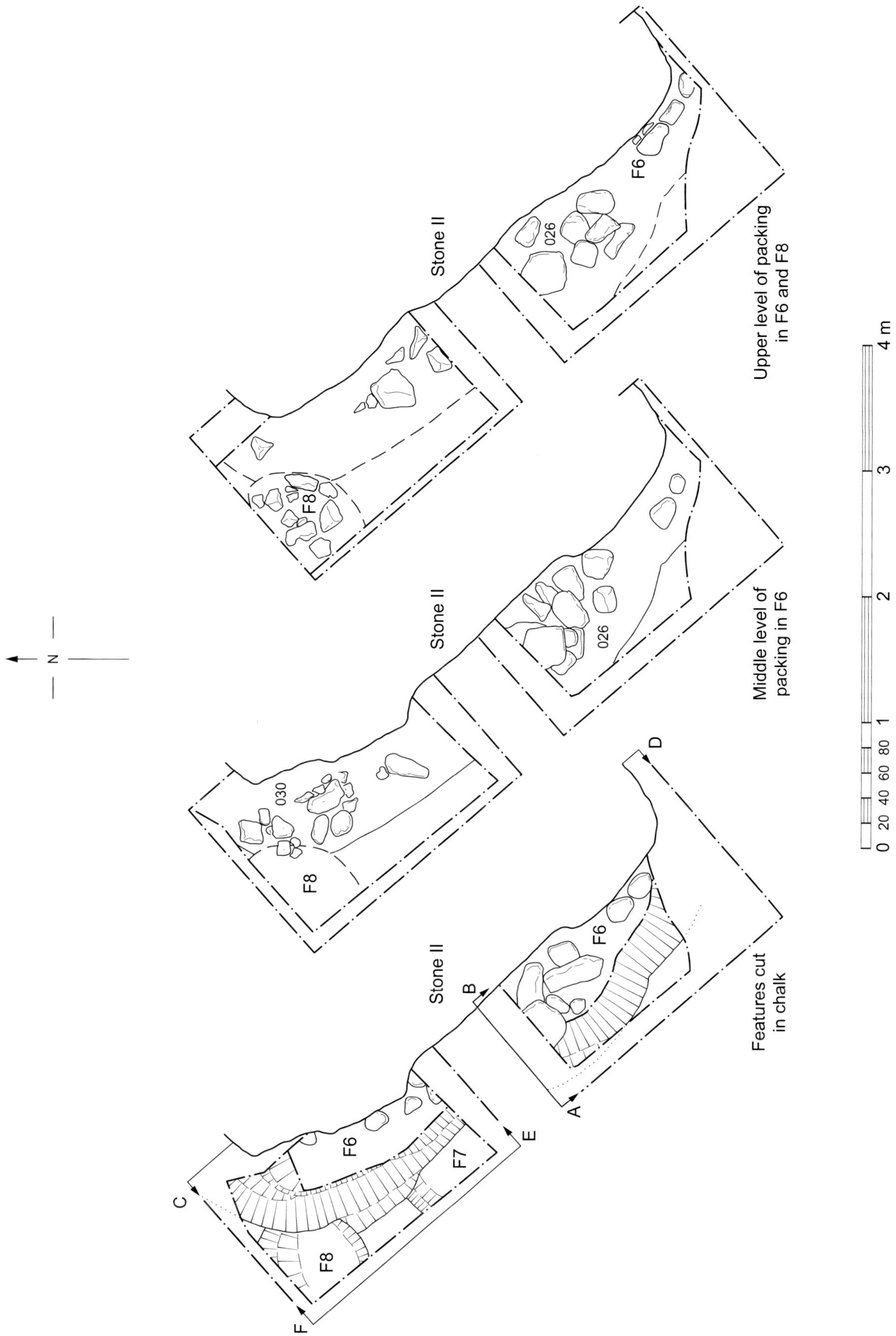

Figure 4.4. Avebury Cove: excavated features and deposits in Trench 1

Figure 4.5. Avebury Cove: the northern end of Trench 1 at the end of the excavation, showing the cut of stone-hole F.6

carefully cut to reflect the form of the megalith it was intended to receive (Figure 4.5). The stone-hole was cut, in its upper profile at least, into Middle Chalk.

In the southern half of the trench the stone-hole fills were removed to a maximum depth of 1.1m below the top of the chalk natural, and in the northern to *c.*0.7m. The presence of the tops of further substantial packing boulders and voids at the base of the excavated deposits indicates that its full depth is likely to be in the order of 1.5m, if not more (Figure 4.6). This will make it the deepest stone-hole excavated so far at Avebury (Smith 1965, 218).

The stone-hole was filled with deposits of chalk rubble, clay and sarsen. Against the edge of the stone-hole, and largely confined to its northern end, was a highly compacted lens of chalk rubble [037]. Though lacking the blocky structure of natural chalk (presumably due to compression), this may represent the *in situ* remnants of a crushed edge to the pit rather than a true fill. Its presence might imply that the stone was pushed into the stone-hole from the western, outer, side. Overlying this, and commonly, though not exclusively, confined to the edge of the pit and its lower fills, was a deposit of sub-angular chalk rubble within a mid-brown silty clay [021]. Much of this had the appearance of being pushed into the stone-hole from its western side, and presumably comprises re-deposited chalk rubble originally dug from the stone-hole (Figure 4.7).

However, the most extensive non-stone component of the fill was a tenacious orange-brown clay [022]. Perhaps of alluvial origin from a brown earth parent material, this is remarkably clean, containing only very fine sand particles. It filled much of the stone-hole, particularly up against the stone and around the sarsen packing boulders. Clay of a similar or identical nature was routinely encountered during the Keiller excavations at Avebury and along the West Kennet Avenue, having been used as a packing material in stone-holes (Smith 1965, 221). In contemplating its function, Smith suggests that:

> '… it would have served to indicate whether or not the stone was properly balanced before the supporting timbers were removed. If the stone began to lean to one side a gap would appear between its base and the clay on the other.' (Smith 1965, 221)

The main support for the stone, particularly in the early stages of its setting, was provided by a packing of sarsen boulders [026]. This comprised several courses (a minimum of seven in the deepest part of the excavation) of small to medium-sized sarsens, each between 0.1–0.6m across. From limited exposure of the lowest levels of the stone-hole, it looked as though a continuous course of packing boulders was set across its base, wedged between the side of the stone-hole and the megalith itself. There was some sense of size grading, with larger blocks being used in the lower part of the packing and smaller in the upper, though this was not invariable. Above the lower courses the distribution of packing stones was uneven. There were localised concentrations, notably in the southern section of the stone-hole where a very tightly defined block of boulders was present, *c.*1.0 by 0.8m across and three to four courses thick. The southern extent of this group also corresponded to a vertical interface between the clay [022] and chalk rubble [021] fills. While it was initially thought that this distinction could correspond to a re-cut, it is more plausible to see it as evidence for vertical shuttering and compartmentalised filling of the stone-hole. It is difficult to envisage what functional advantage this could have had, unless staged filling allowed the stone to be temporarily supported while still capable of being manipulated into its correct position (*i.e.* pivoting around a central block of fill). Alternatively, it could reflect the kind of compartmentalised construction common in earlier structures such as long mounds (cf. local examples at South Street and Beckhampton Road: Ashbee *et al.*

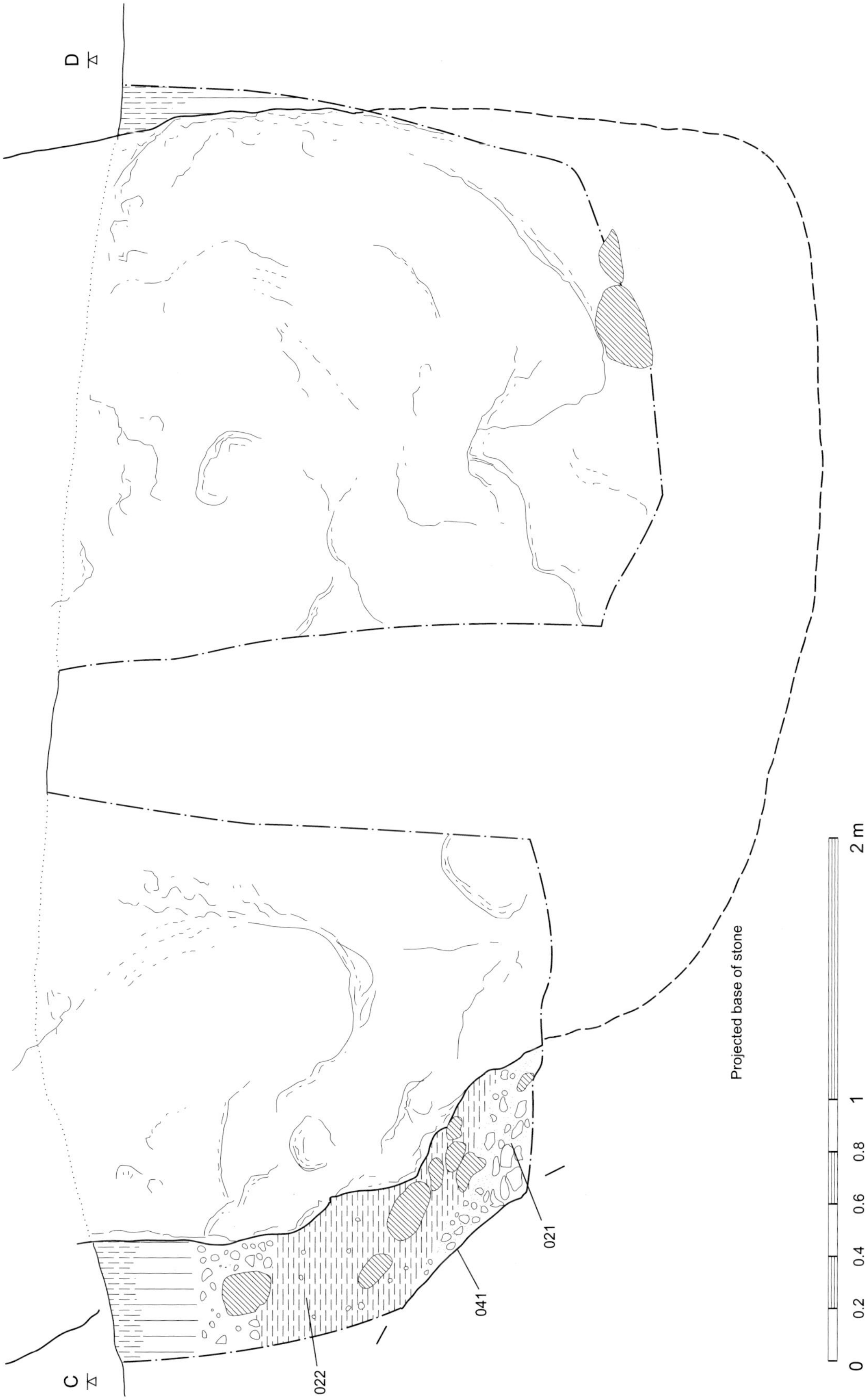

Figure 4.6. Avebury Cove: longitudinal profile of Trench 1, stone-hole F.6 and Stone II

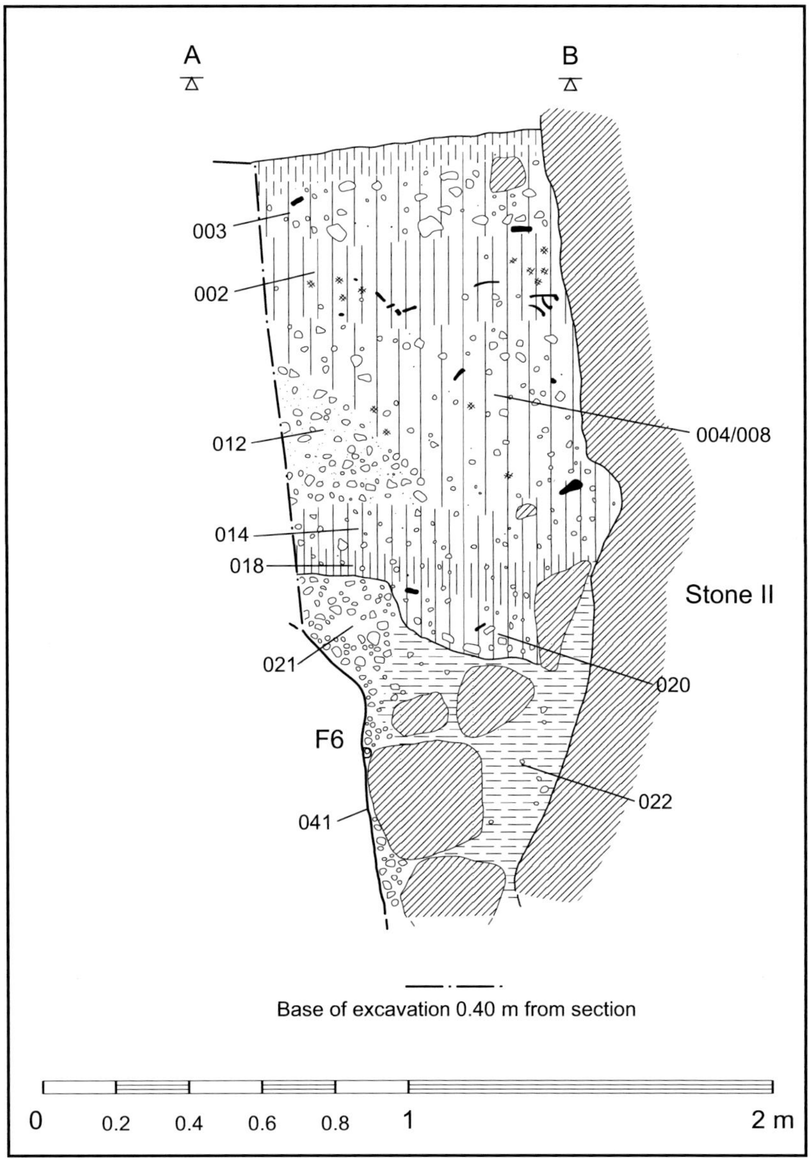

Figure 4.7. (above left) Avebury Cove: SE-facing section of baulk in the centre of Trench 1, showing the fills of stone-hole F.6 and later (post-medieval) deposits

Figure 4.8. (above right) Avebury Cove: upper sarsen fill of pit F.8

1979). In the northern half, packing stones were confined to the clay with a surface-like spread of small sarsens [030] sealing the main part of the packing at the northern end of the stone-hole. Up to two stones thick, it extended over about a square metre at a point where the stone began to overhang the stone-hole. This material may have been used to provide additional support.

One other feature is regarded as early (*i.e.* prehistoric), though its purpose remains unclear. Pit F.8 was situated in the north-west corner of trench, its north and west edges extending just beyond the excavated area (Figures 4.4 and 4.8). It comprised an oval scoop [034] around 0.7m across and up to 0.2m deep. The pit sides were shallow, slightly steeper on the south, merging with a dished base. The bulk of the fill [029] was a grey-brown silty clay with abundant small to medium sized chalk lumps (Figure 4.9). In the top of this, and ringing the edge of the feature, were around 10 small sarsen blocks. These looked to form an extension to deposit [030] sealing stone-hole F.6. Stratigraphically, F.8 appeared to post-date F.6, though if overlaid by [030] this implies the chronological gap between pit and stone-hole is not great. The pit is too shallow to have acted as a post-hole, and the character of fills would not support such an interpretation. Amongst a range of alternative interpretations, it could represent a stone-hole or the base of a support used during the erection of the Cove stone. No finds were present within the fill.

Later features and deposits

The remaining deposits within the trench are dated by associated material culture to the post-medieval period, the earliest perhaps of the late 17th century. First in the sequence is a sub-rectangular pit, F.5, situated in the southern half of the trench and extending into the central baulk (Figure 4.10). At least 1.0m long and 0.6m wide, narrowing towards the south end, it was up to 0.2m deep, though perhaps slightly truncated in the upper profile by later activity. The sides of the cut [020] were moderate to shallow and the base highly irregular where it came down onto the top of the sarsen packing in F.6. It was filled with a sticky chocolate-brown clay [019] much darker against the stone where it became quite 'humic' and contained some small chalk. Quantities of late 17th- –early 18th-century glass came from this. Given its morphology and position it might, tentatively, be suggested that the pit results from an early and unrecorded antiquarian exploration.

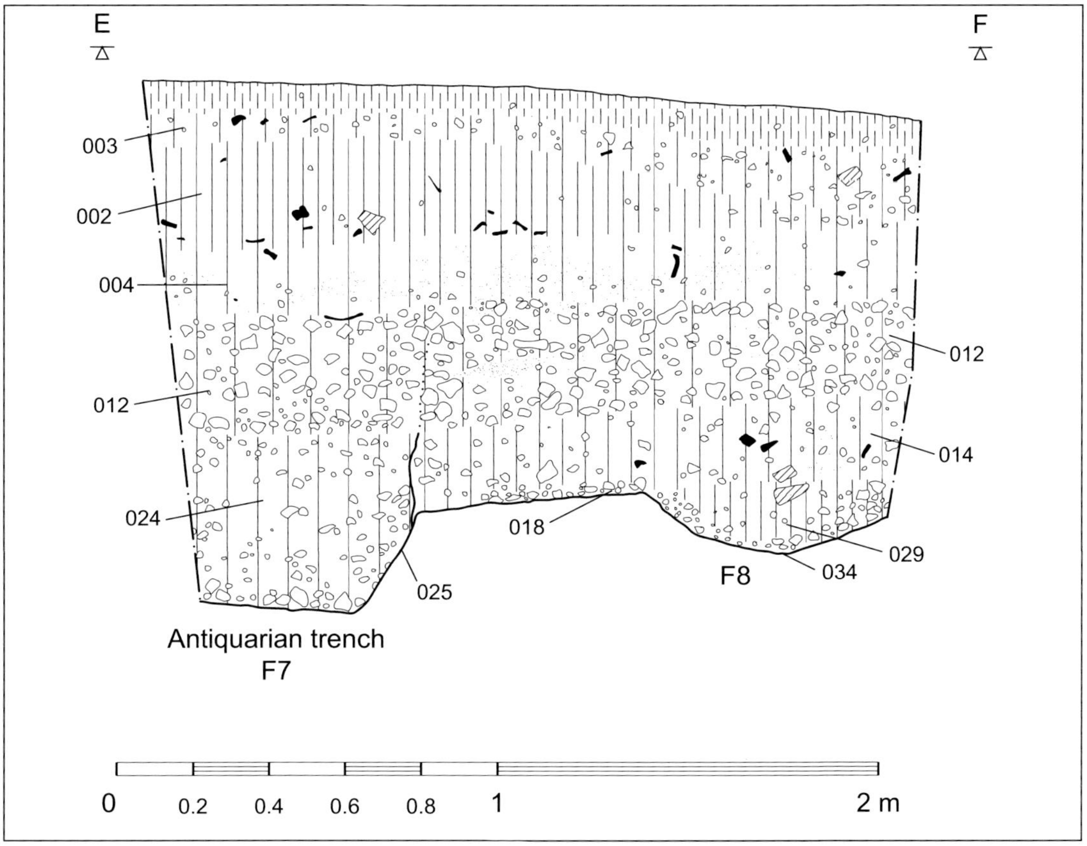

Figure 4.9. Avebury Cove: NE-facing section of the northern half of Trench 1 with pit F.8 and the antiquarian excavation trench F.7

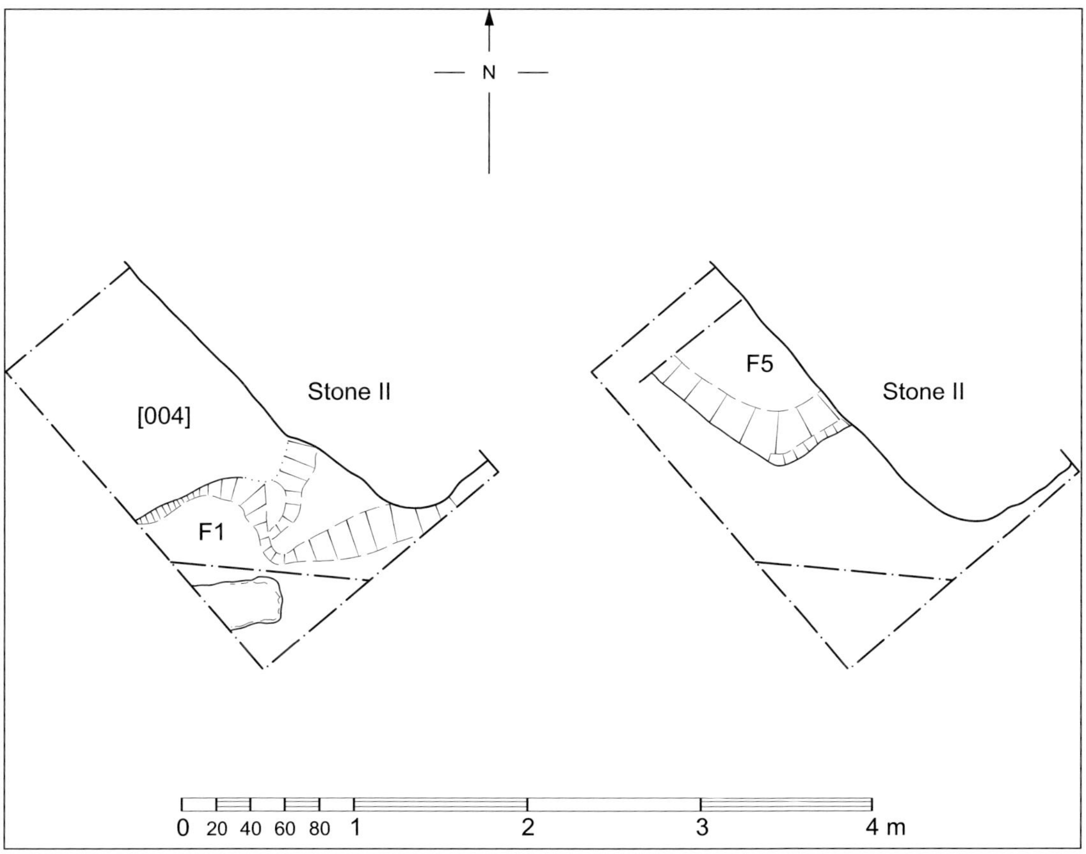

Figure 4.10. Avebury Cove: post-medieval features in the southern end of Trench 1

Figure 4.11. An early 20th-century view of the Avebury Cove from the north. Note the proximity of Rawlins' Cottages and the boundary wall against Stone I (left), © Lilywhite Ltd. Triangle, Halifax

Figure 4.12. An early 20th-century view of the Avebury Cove from the NE, reproduced with kind permission of J. Ovens

F.5 was sealed by a layer of quite loose chalk rubble in a pale grey-brown silty clay [018] and over this a firm light grey-brown silty clay containing small chalk pieces [014]. The latter is probably a buried soil. Finds included 17th- and 18th-century pottery, bottle glass, clay pipe and brick, and a single rim sherd of 12th- to 14th-century Kennet Valley ware (identified by Lorraine Mepham). These in turn were cut through by a regular east-west trench, F.7, that could relate to the 1865 excavation directed by William Cunnington III and A. C. Smith (Smith 1867). Situated just to the north of the baulk and extending beyond the excavated area to the west, this was a regular cut that ran to 0.4m from the face of the stone. As exposed, the cut [025] was rectangular, 0.6 × 0.65m in extent and up to 0.46m deep, with steep sides and a flat base (Figure 4.9). The fill [024] was a mixture of small to medium chalk rubble in a friable beige silty clay, containing occasional pieces of brick and 19th-century pottery and glass. It also contained two substantial sarsen blocks (each up to 0.3m in maximum dimension), which appear to be displaced packing stones from the stone-hole. The narrowness of the trench corresponds closely to those of the Cunnington and Smith excavations discovered by Keiller in the centre of the Southern Inner Circle (Smith 1965, fig. 69).

Above this was a substantial layer of compact re-deposited chalk rubble [012] within a pale grey-brown silty clay. Against the western side of the trench this was found to be up to 0.35m thick. North of the baulk [012] was overlain by a thin layer of firm dull orange-brown silty sand [013]. Further layers of dumped material ([004], [002], [007] and [003]) and three cut features (F.2, F.3 and F.1) followed, all dated by pottery and other household refuse to the late 19th and early 20th centuries. The overall effect of these was to considerably raise the level of the ground surface against the back of the stone.

Figure 4.13. (top opposite page) Avebury Cove: prehistoric (F.9) and post-medieval features in Trench 2

Figure 4.14. (bottom opposite page) Avebury Cove: SW-facing section of Trench 2

Trench 2 (Stone I)

Set against the southern face of Stone I, Trench 2 was initially 3.0m long and up to 1.1m wide (Figure 4.1). Following the discovery of unstable rubble and backfill deposits from the demolition during the 1950s of adjacent outhouses, and in consultation with English Heritage, the National Trust and contracting engineers, a decision was taken to extend the western two-thirds of the trench by a further 2.2 × 1.0m. This was necessitated not on archaeological grounds, but because of the need to bond the cement to be used in stabilising the stone against solid deposits. Although layers of 20th century soil, building debris and refuse were not as deep as those in Trench 1, the surface of the natural chalk was still 0.75m below the present ground surface. Only one feature was pre-modern, the stone-hole itself. Medieval activity is perhaps attested by two sherds of Kennet Valley ware (identified by Lorraine Mepham) from a late context. Other features and deposits were of 19th- to mid-20th-century date, and included a wall and concrete floor belonging to an outbuilding at the rear of Rawlins' Cottages, demolished in 1956 (a detailed account of these is held in the archive) (Figures 4.11 and 4.12). The outbuilding is visible on a number of early postcards and photographs held in the Alexander Keiller Museum. These show a single-storey structure of sarsen and brick with a pantile roof.

Prehistoric features

Only a small portion of the stone-hole, F.9, was exposed and excavated (Figure 4.13). The cut [045] was traced over a length of 2.0m, and reached a maximum width of 0.3m. It extended beyond the excavated area to the east, and was severely truncated over a length of 0.7m in the western half of the trench by the foundation of the later outbuilding wall. A return to the feature is indicated by a slight curve to the pit in its exposed eastern end. Cut 0.6m deep into the Middle Chalk, the sides of the stone-hole were vertical to moderate (at the east), curving into a flattish base (Figures 4.14 and 4.15). The straight southern edge of the stone-hole looks to have been carefully cut to reflect the flat face of the stone; the latter apparently being erected from the inside of the Cove and set against the exposed edge of the pit.

A thin lens of chalk rubble [046] covered the side and base of the stone-hole. Much of the fill was a firm reddish brown clay with little chalk [044]. Although this might be interpreted as material that steadily filled the void created as the stone began to lean, it is not dissimilar in appearance to clay fill [022] noted in stone-hole F.6 (see above). This may of course be original packing material from the top of the feature that has slowly slipped into the lower portion of the stone-hole as the stone moved. Some animal disturbance was recognised at eastern end of the feature. No packing stones were encountered.

Worked flint

Compared with the considerable quantity of lithic material recovered from the excavation of the Longstones Cove, very little worked flint was present here. In total, only 19 pieces were recovered, the majority from Trench 1 (Table 4.1). However, despite the small size of the assemblage, it does possess distinctive characteristics. Most of the material is in very fresh

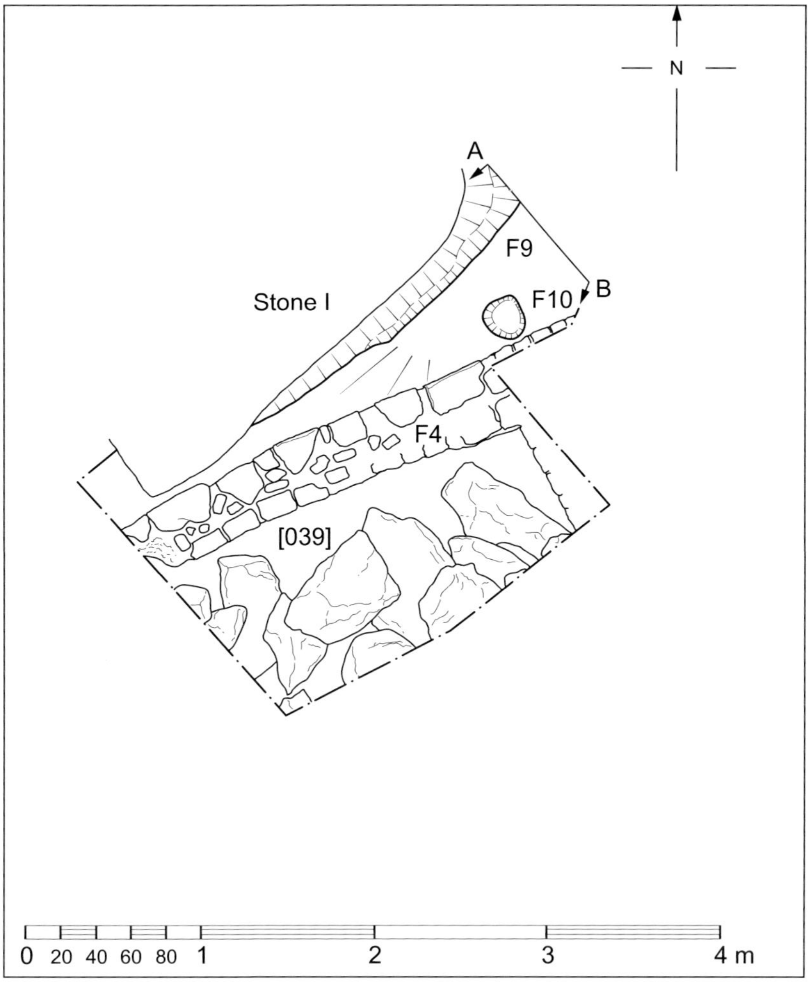

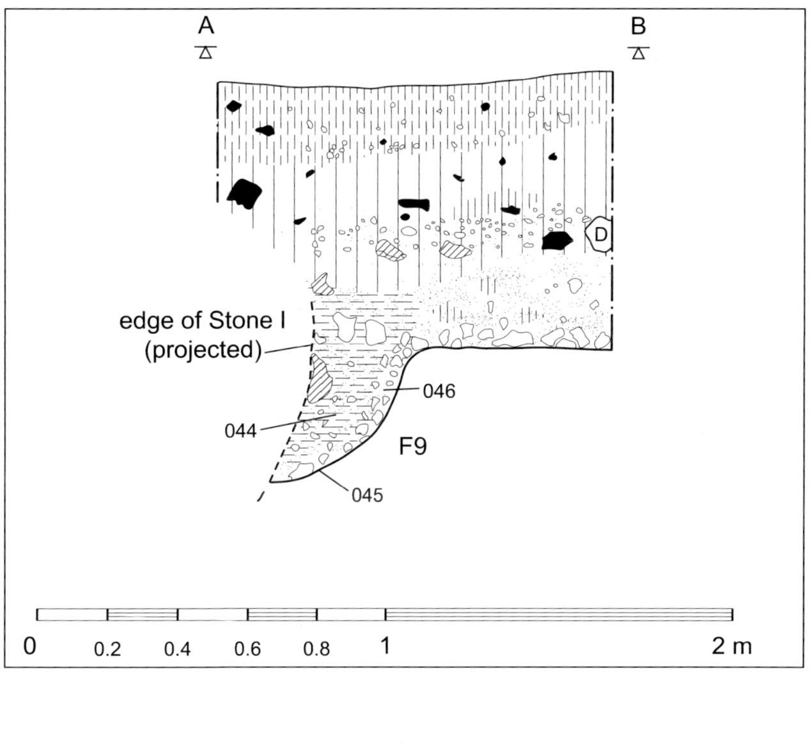

Table 4.1. Worked flint from the Cove

Trench	Context	Rejuvenation flakes	Flakes	Chips	Flaked pieces	Retouched
1	[002]	-	-	-	-	1
1	[003]	-	1	-	-	1 (piercer)
1	[018]	-	-	-	1	-
1	[021]/[022]	1	5	1	4	1 (knife)
1	[024]	-	-	-	-	1
2	[001]	-	-	-	1	-
2	[044]	1	-	-	-	-
Total		*2*	*6*	*1*	*6*	*4*

Figure 4.15. Avebury Cove: Trench 2 close to the end of the excavation, showing stone-hole F.9 within which Stone I is set, telegraph post-hole F.10, and the post-medieval wall F.4 emerging beneath sarsen make-up [039]. See also Figure 4.11

condition and largely unpatinated. There is an absence of primary preparation flakes and retouched pieces are well represented. Of the debitage, all the flakes show signs of hard-hammer working. They derive from several nodules, including one (from [021]/[022]) of river or glacial gravel flint, the natural surface being extensively worn and slightly ochre-stained. Of the retouched pieces from Trench 1, flakes from [002] and [024] display areas of limited marginal retouch; the piercer from [003] is on a thick trimming flake with marginal bifacial retouch defining a blunt point at the distal end; while the knife from [021]/[022] is on a lightly patinated trimming flake worked with limited, expedient retouch along one edge.

The most unusual components of this assemblage are the six 'flaked pieces' from [018] and [021]/[022], and [001] in Trench 2. The four examples from [021]/[022] are cuboid to spherical in shape, and display extensive flaking, giving them a 'core-like' character. However, all display varying degrees of crushing on one or more edges. In one instance this is very extensive and accompanied by localised polishing. At <50mm across, all are probably too small to be hammerstones. The two other examples are also marked by similar localised crushing on their edges, that from [001] being a small nodule with expedient bifacial flaking. Such wear or edge-damage may have been created by repeated pressing, grinding or scraping against hard materials. Given their context, it is tempting to relate this activity to processes surrounding the erection of the Cove stones, though quite what this might be remains unclear.

Optically stimulated luminescence dating

Ed Rhodes and Jean-Luc Schwenninger

Two OSL samples were collected from deposits within the stone-hole of Stone II. On the basis of the stratigraphic integrity of these deposits, only the lower sample (from [022]) was prepared for dating, as a possibility existed of later contamination in the upper one. *In situ* gamma measurements were made around the site and for the upper sample, but for the lower sample, no *in situ* measurement was possible. However, based on the geometry and appearance of the different units, and using measured values, a gamma dose rate has been estimated for the OSL age calculation. Beta dose rate components were calculated from K, U and Th contents, which were determined using NAA. The measured water content value of 30 ± 5 % was used in the calculations, and the measured overburden thickness of 1.1 m.

Single grain OSL measurements were made on sand-sized quartz extracted from the lower sample, field code AV03-02, laboratory code X1559, using a Risø automated system based on a green laser. It was expected that incomplete zeroing might be encountered, as deposition into a pit can be rapid and chaotic. A single aliquot regenerative-dose (SAR) protocol was used (Murray and Wintle 2000) with preheating of 220°C for 10s before natural and regenerated OSL measurement, and heating at 200°C for 10s following each test dose. The single grain dose distribution

	Context	Sample type	Result	Calibrated range (Cal AD) at 95.4% confidence
OxA-12897	[021]	*Hordeum Vulgare*	296±27 BP	1490-1660
OxA-12898	[021]	*Hordeum Vulgare*	312±27 BP	1480-1650
OxA-12935	[021]	*Hordeum Vulgare*	306±27 BP	1480-1650
OxA-12936	[022]	*Hordeum Vulgare*	330±27 BP	1480-1650
OxA-12937	[022]	*Hordeum Vulgare*	339±26 BP	1470-1640

Table 4.2. Radiocarbon dates from the Cove

displayed a relatively wide distribution of insensitive grains, but four much brighter grains formed peaks at 3.3 and 5.9 Gy. In order to assess the meaningfulness of this small data set, 48 small aliquots of around 50 to 80 grains were measured, using a similar SAR protocol. A main peak at 6.0 Gy, and subsidiary peaks at 1.4 and 9.0 Gy were observed.

Using the parameters described above, an OSL age estimate of 3120 ± 350 BC is derived, using the small aliquot equivalent dose value of 6.0 ± 0.2 Gy. Age calculation was as described by Rhodes *et al.* (2003). Some caution should be exercised in the interpretation of this age estimate. Firstly, the single grain and small aliquot data appear broadly to agree, with a peak at around 5.9 to 6.0 Gy, and subsidiary peaks or data points on either side, presumably representing non-zeroed grains (for greater equivalent dose values) and intrusive grains (for lower dose values). However, in the case of a complex mixed dose population, the identification of the appropriate dose value is not always straightforward. Secondly, the dose rate estimate required a projected gamma dose rate value and includes a high water content. Both a lower water content value, and a gamma dose rate based solely on the NAA-derived K, U and Th contents have the effect of lowering the age estimate, which should perhaps be considered a maximum age estimate.

We have demonstrated the suitability of material present in these archaeological contexts to provide quartz grains with bright OSL signals suitable for dating. It is possible that the measured high OSL sensitivities of some grains and consistent signal zeroing were caused by burning at the site, rather than the method being reliant on daylight to rest the signal at the time of deposition. A significant number of small aliquots, in which the signal is dominated by only a few grains, give a strikingly consistent result, providing some confidence in this dose estimate. Clearly, there is significant scope for further OSL dating of similar contexts, and good potential to derive more robust age estimates for this and other megalithic monuments.

Radiocarbon dating

Five radiocarbon dates were obtained on charred grains of six-row barley (*Hordeum Vulgare*) identified by Ruth Young. The grain was recovered from the flotation of soil samples from the packing material [021]/[022] of F.6 in Trench 1. It was assumed at the time that these provided secure prehistoric samples that might date the erection of Stone II. However, all the dates fall within a tight calibrated range spanning 1480–1660AD at 95.4% probability (Table 4.2). The grain is evidently intrusive and does not provide a date range for the construction of the setting.

Discussion

Given an initial assumption that post-medieval activity and landscaping in the area would have had a detrimental effect on the prehistoric archaeology, the excavations produced surprising results. As anticipated, later building activity had created much disturbance around Stone I, but prehistoric deposits were still present. In the case of Stone II, the stone-hole was found to be substantially intact despite antiquarian exploration and later pit digging. Of a 'key-hole' nature and being restricted to the outside of the two remaining stones, the excavations did not provide information on any features or activities inside the Cove, nor did they resolve the issue of whether the setting originally included a fourth or even fifth stone. They did, on the other hand, produce valuable information relating to the date of the Cove and activities surrounding its construction.

Very little prehistoric artefactual material came from the fills of the stone-holes, being restricted to worked flint and comprising just one flake from F.9 and 12 pieces including a knife from F.6. No antler picks or fragments of such were present in F.6. While this may appear surprising given the scale of this feature and the number of picks presumably required for its excavation, the absence of antler repeats a pattern seen with other megalithic settings in the region where bone, antler and pottery was seemingly excluded from deposition in stone-holes. Overall, the setting looks remarkably 'clean', and therefore conforms to a picture common across much of the henge (Smith 1965, 226–8).

It was hoped that charred grain recovered from the packing of F.6 might provide radiocarbon determinations to date the erection of Stone II, but this material proved to be intrusive and considerably later. Optically Stimulated Luminescence (OSL) dating met with more success. The result might suggest the stone was set up around the end of the 4th or the beginning of the 3rd millennium BC, making this setting a particularly early component of the monument, although at two sigma the full range spans the early 4th to mid 3rd millennia BC. If an early date is accepted it is perhaps contemporary with the first phase earthwork of the henge, and pre-dates by several centuries the construction of the Outer Circle and avenues (Pollard and Cleal 2004). It could be one of the first components of the monument, as argued by Burl (2002, 145), providing a focus for the construction of the Northern Inner Circle, the earthwork enclosure and other features. If such a scheme is accepted, it would imply that some of the largest megalithic settings making up the monument are also its earliest, confounding any vision of a progressive increase in the scale of lithic monumentalisation.

It should be acknowledged that the OSL result provides a date for the setting up of Stone II and not a chronology for the Cove as a whole. It may be that the Cove was of a single construction, though the possibility of sequence remains, with the massive western stone as a primary element to which were added the flanking southern (I) and northern (III) megaliths. In favour of their belonging to a single constructional event are details relating to the stone-holes themselves. Taking the observations of Stukeley (Ucko *et al.* 1991, 228–9), the 1865 explorations and the 2003 excavations, the stone-holes of all three megaliths (I–III) included sarsen boulder packing. A similar deposit of brown clay packing was also found in both F.6 and 9. Once created the Cove may have undergone elaboration or modification. Of considerable interest in this respect is the small oval pit, F.8, adjacent to stone-hole F.6. The stratigraphic evidence is slightly ambiguous, but this feature appeared to post-date by a limited margin the erection of Stone II. The presence within this shallow pit of small sarsen blocks might favour its interpretation as a small stone-hole, large enough to support a sarsen of the scale of those making up the putative façade running to the east and north of the Cove. Any future investigation of this area should seek to determine whether F.8 is a single feature or part of a more extensive setting running off the Cove.

Constructing the Cove

The 'weathering' lip to the edge of the stone-hole and the deposit of compacted chalk against its side suggest Stone II was erected from the west (outside). Set against a near-vertical edge, Stone I may have been levered into its stone-hole from the north (inside). Entirely unexpected, and apparently unrecorded in any of the other stone-holes excavated at Avebury, was a compartmentalisation of the packing deposits within F.6. It may be that the enormous scale of Stone II necessitated a complex process of propping and support during its erection, the differential packing reflecting this. But we should be wary of viewing the construction of these settings in purely pragmatic engineering terms. There could be considerable symbolism in the deployment of different materials as packing, while their separation might bespeak of the intention to mark diverse participation in the process, much as has been claimed for the segmented form of causewayed enclosure ditches (Startin and Bradley 1981).

The most surprising result of the excavation was the recognition of the sheer size of Stone II. Partially buried under thick post-medieval deposits, the base of this stone is now known to lie around 3m below the present ground surface. Perhaps tapering towards its base, this makes the stone a massive block *c.*7 × 4.5 × 1.5m in extent (around 47 cubic metres), weighing in the region of 100 tonnes. It is and was the largest stone within the henge, even more substantial than the Obelisk that formerly stood in the centre of the Southern Inner Circle (Smith 1965, 198). It even ranks amongst the largest megaliths in Britain. The Rudston monolith is taller, at 7.9m, as is the largest of the Devil's Arrows at Boroughbridge (at 6.8m above ground), both in North Yorkshire, but these are thinner, more pillar-like stones estimated to weigh around 40 tonnes. The movement and erection of Stone II represented a colossal act of communal labour, especially if accompanied by the setting up of the two other Cove stones, which are substantial blocks in their own right. Labour estimates for moving and erecting megaliths vary enormously (Richards and Whitby 1997, 233), and are clearly dependent upon the techniques chosen and the nature of the terrain. Given the experimentally derived estimates of around 200 people required to haul a 40 tonne block (Richards and Whitby 1997, 237), the movement of Stone II was evidently a task that involved several hundred people. Efficiency may not have been an issue, and it is easy to imagine that many more people than was functionally necessary might have been drawn to take part in such a highly memorable project. The numbers involved strongly suggest that a workforce was assembled which included people from outside the immediate region, people persuaded to participate because of obligations and debts, or tempted by the prospect of feasting and celebration.

This was a project embodying a high degree of risk, since a stone of this size had never before been moved and erected in southern Britain. It was a project in which personal and group reputations could be shattered and the sacred qualities of the site brought into question if the work met failure (Richards 2004b). At other times and in other places the ambitions of erecting vast megaliths resulted in disastrous consequences, as the stones toppled and broke. Such was the case with the Grand Menhir Brisé at Locmariaquer, originally 20m long and weighing around 250 tonnes (Hornsey 1987). The same fate met the colossal 'great stela' of Aksum in Ethiopia. Over 33m long and weighing some 517 tonnes, it is now clear that this fell and shattered while being erected (Phillipson 1994). Such disasters might even signal the end of megalithic traditions, driven to more and more unsustainable extremes by the competition involved in setting up ever larger stones. In the case of the Cove, the project was successful and could have provided stimulus for further episodes of stone raising. We can imagine that considerable celebration must have ensued, after which people returned to the places from where they came, eager to recount the memorable story of the 'great stones'. This was history.

The stones chosen for the Cove may not have been brought far, conceivably from the sarsen spreads at the foot of Avebury Down only a few hundred metres from Avebury, or even closer still. Our understanding of the original extent of the sarsen spreads in this landscape remains very poor. This said, the stones were chosen for their size, shape, biographies and associations (Gillings and Pollard 1999), rather than the ease by which they could be obtained. Stone I is highly distinctive, being a thin and unusually smooth block with an angled top. The choice is presumably deliberate and draws upon a wider architectural feature, since similar tilts and angled tops are seen on a number of portal dolmens around the Irish Sea, and at the Stones of Stenness in Orkney, which Whittle suggests may relate to 'a general sense of propitiousness based on body side... or horizon orientation' (Whittle 1997a, 154). Presumably Stone I was chosen for these formal qualities, while Stone II was singled out because it comprised one of the largest and therefore most notable blocks available.

While much emphasis has been placed on labour demands, we should not neglect the physical impact of moving stones. Freeing these sarsens from the ground by digging around and under them, and hauling such massive blocks across the landscape would have left its own legacy of physical traces. Pits and hollows were created during the removal of these sarsens, and were perhaps left open as a reminder of where stones once where. In this respect, it is worth noting that rather than being flint extraction pits as originally proposed by Passmore (Thomas 1991, 163), large hollows visible on nearby Hackpen/Avebury Down could equally represent sarsen extraction pits. Once the stones were freed, swathes would have to cleared across the sarsen fields in order to create routes along which the stones could be dragged. These wide routeways of cleared ground would remain visible as features connecting the Cove with near and distant stonefields, acting as reminders of the points of origin of these stones and of their journeys. In their own way these traces were as monumental as the finished megalithic projects themselves.

The structure and symbolism of the Cove

Much remains uncertain about the function and symbolism of the Cove, especially since ambiguities continue to surround the precise format of this setting. However, if not to begin with, it became one of two zones of 'deepest space' within the henge, the other area being that between the Obelisk and façade at the centre of the Southern Inner Circle. That, along with the central space within the Southern Inner Circle, it constituted the most secluded component of the monument in its developed form implies that it may have come to be regarded as the most sacred part of the henge. Its position as 'deepest space' has led some prehistorians to suggest that here a selected few will have gathered in special ceremonies, the architecture of the setting creating a kind of screen or closed stage that amplified their presence and emphasised the distinction between those allowed inside and those that would watch and listen from a distance (Barrett 1994, 17–18). The particular acoustic qualities of such a box-like arrangement of stones, variously distorting, muffling and projecting sounds, might have added to the effect (Watson and Keating 1999). However, if the setting was in fact four-sided, as the antiquarian evidence and analogy with the Longstones Cove might imply, then the Cove's position within the choreography of ceremonial practice may need rethinking. A four-sided setting could indicate exclusion, an *absence of people* and perhaps space so sacred that the living were not allowed to enter. There is certainly little evidence at present for deposition, burial or other post-construction Neolithic activity within the setting. In interpreting the role of the Cove much depends on whether one might wish to see this and other settings like it as fundamentally implicated in social strategies, as spaces built to be used as opposed to structures in which it was the act of construction that mattered, or as monuments in which it was a symbolic imperative and dealings with ancestral or other non-corporeal agencies (*e.g.* spirits or deities) that took centre stage.

One aspect that is clear is that coves form a very loose and rather unsatisfactory category of structure – effectively a lumping together of square and rectangular stone settings of presumed Neolithic and early Bronze Age date that may or may not have direct associations with henges. The difference in scale, format and setting of those at Avebury, the Longstones, Mount Pleasant, and Stanton Drew is quite considerable, though all are united by their box-like arrangement of stones and their status as 'structural enigmas' (Burl 1988). While not considered a cove, the inner arrangement of five sarsen trilithons created at Stonehenge during phase 3 may in fact provide a closer architectural analogy for the Avebury Cove than any other setting. Not dissimilar in scale, both are set on a SW-NE axis, their largest stones are at the 'back' or south-west, and both are surrounded by further rings of stone (Cleal *et al.* 1995). They also form the 'centres' of two of the most complex stone circles in Britain. Although no solar or lunar alignments can be reliably provided for the Avebury Cove, the dominant SW-NE axis bespeaks of the common cosmological significance of these directions, linked to that of the midwinter sunset and midsummer sunrise, with the attendant timing of ceremonies for these points of the year (Parker Pearson *et al.* 2006).

The potential link between the Cove and megalithic settings at Stonehenge can be taken as a stepping-stone to other interpretations. Stonehenge 3 is a stone version of a later Neolithic multiple timber circle (*e.g.* Durrington Southern Circle: Wainwright and Longworth 1971), which in turn may be seen as highly symbolised versions of smaller timber structures that lie on an architectural continuum with houses and temporary shelters (*e.g.* Trelystan, Powys: Britnell 1982) at the bottom end of the spectrum. Recognising this, and accepting some degree of formal comparison between the Cove and inner trilithons at Stonehenge, opens another analogy. The Cove and Northern Inner Circle could be seen to replicate in stone, and on a truly massive scale, the format of contemporary dwellings, with a central four-stone setting (Cove/hearth) and an outer ring (stone circle/wall). The notion of the Northern Inner Circle and Cove as a highly symbolised version of a late Neolithic dwelling, or at least drawing heavily upon the spatial format of such, would have parallels elsewhere. In general, it is not uncommon for sacred architecture to draw upon the quotidian (*e.g.* Waterson 1990, 48–53). Specifically relating to the British Neolithic, both Hodder (1982, 224–6) and Richards (2005, 218–25) have drawn attention to the way in which the megalithic settings of the Stones of Stenness henge monument replicate features of later Neolithic Orcadian houses. This is more than mere representation, since the central four-stone setting within the Stenness henge replaces a hearth, and the monument may even have begun as a house (Richards 2005, 218–25). There is no reason why a similar integration of routine ('domestic') and sacred domains, woven together by common cosmological principles, may not have structured the evolving architecture of the Avebury megaliths; and so it remains a tantalising possibility that the symbolic significance of the Northern Inner Circle/Cove resided in its allusion to other forms of architecture, including that of dwellings.

One final issue to consider is the relationship between the settings that make up the Northern and Southern Inner Circles at Avebury. Both are highly unusual stone circles in that they enclose complex central arrangements of megaliths, but then this should occasion no surprise since Avebury is hardly a 'typical' later Neolithic monument. Of similar dimensions, and perhaps comprising contemporary constructions, the circles are nonetheless distinct from each other in terms of the format of the central settings: those in the Northern Inner Circle including the Cove and outlying stones; while the Southern Inner Circle encloses the Obelisk, façade and outlying stone D (Gillings and Pollard 2004, 11–15). The arrangement within the Southern Inner Circle is difficult to parallel, although Pitts and Whittle present the intriguing possibility that the Obelisk may be related to early traditions of menhir construction (1992, 210), while the façade may allude to the format of linear monuments of the earlier Neolithic, or to the stone kerbs surrounding megalithic long mounds (Smith 1965, 65). Whatever the architectural inspiration, an intention existed to make the settings enclosed by the two Inner Circles different. As such, constructing the Inner Circles was not simply about creating a nested hierarchy of space – that is deeper and deeper spatial zones as one moved into the monument – since this could have been achieved through a series of concentric rings. The obvious implication is that the two circles represented different domains, were constructed and used by separate moieties, or were linked to different sets of practices. Stukeley had recognised this during the early 18th century, originally envisaging the Southern and Northern Inner Circles as 'Solar' and 'Lunar' temples respectively (Ucko *et al.* 1991, 86). The notion that they might be dedicated to different celestial deities is no longer accepted, though this is certainly not the most outlandish interpretation that could be offered. The recent focus on movement within monuments, the orchestration of ceremonial practice, and the employment of graded space to define social distinctions could be brought in to play. Perhaps the circles were visited in succession, or at different times of the year, with distinct ceremonies undertaken at each? Perhaps access to a particular circle was determined by group affiliation, gender or level of initiation? Or perhaps they were simply commemorative, being constructs that stood for key domains: the notion of the 'house' and community in the case of the Northern Inner Circle/Cove; past achievements, earlier sacred traditions and myths of origin in the case of the Southern Inner Circle/Obelisk/ façade? Once again, much depends on whether we envisage Avebury as a monument where people would amass to take part in large-scale ceremonies, much in the model of a medieval cathedral, or whether it was a place set aside for ancestors and spirits, visited only on occasion, reverently, in order to erect further stones and undertake propitiatory rituals.

5
Landscape, environment and monumentality

The aim of this chapter is to place the work discussed in Chapters 2–4 into the context of the wider landscape, to better understand how the various monumental activities within the Avebury area developed through time, and in spatial relation to each other. As such it serves as an essential prelude to Chapter 6, which examines the significance of the excavation results and explores how the various monuments and activities relate to the archaeology of other regions. The present synthesis was prompted in part by the new environmental data generated by the project, but more significantly by the need to see how the various monuments may have related to earlier developments in the Avebury area, and how they may have influenced the emergence of the later prehistoric landscape of the region. To do this, a full review of the environmental data from the region was undertaken and an attempt then made to place the monument complex within its regional spatial and chronological context.

Emphasis is given equally to the natural environment and the evolving monumental landscape, and in so doing, it is hoped to try to avoid a simplistic separation of natural environment from cultural landscape. Given the scale of the monumental enterprise represented at Avebury, it is perhaps more useful to try and write an account of the developing landscape that avoids the conventional view of a natural world as Cartesian 'canvas' for human activity (Thomas 1996, 84). Instead, we might begin from an acceptance of the extent to which the Avebury landscape is both cultural and natural at the same time, with monument construction both influenced by and influencing the distribution of plant communities. Both philosophically and practically, the entire landscape through this period is to some extent an artificial creation and the distinction between 'natural' and 'cultural' (Bradley 2000) may be more meaningful to contemporary readers than it ever was to the prehistoric communities of the Avebury region. For this reason, no separate structure is provided for discussing the distribution of monuments to the distribution of different plant communities: these are interwoven and interconnected within the text as they must have been within both the social and physical world of Avebury's prehistory.

Despite this, the discussion tends to progress from the general to the more specific with respect to the evidence for the character of the Avebury landscape and, because evidence for the environment tends to be less spatially and chronologically specific, the chapter starts with a consideration of the kinds of plant communities that may have existed within the Wessex chalklands at this time. It then goes on to work chronologically through the evidence, considering within each time period the more specific environmental evidence alongside discussion of the developing monument complex, the spatial relationships between monuments, and between monuments and landscape. The first section of this chapter deals mainly with more general evidence for the character of the palaeoenvironment and the geological, soil and topographic characteristics of the Avebury landscape which, together with the activities of human communities, have guided the development of plants and influenced the choices made by the prehistoric communities of the region.

Each phase of environmental and monumental development is then discussed with a view to summarising these in an accessible way and placing them within a chronological framework. The main outcome of this exercise is a series of spatial representations showing the different plant communities in the Avebury landscape as they developed through time. This is, in part, an attempt to update the influential work undertaken by Bob Smith (Smith 1984; 1985), which will be discussed below, and it draws heavily on the work of John G Evans and collaborators (Evans 1970; 1971b; Dimbleby and Evans 1974; Dimbleby 1976; Ashbee *et al.* 1979; Evans and Smith 1983; Evans 1990; Evans *et al.* 1993) and Alasdair Whittle (Whittle 1990; 1993; 1997b; Whittle *et al.* 1999), and also on more recent environmental interpretations of the Avebury region and other areas of the Wessex chalklands (French 1988; Allen 1997; 2000a; b; 2001; French and Lewis 2005).

Each phase of environmental reconstruction is linked, as far as possible, to the data from which it derives and although these are inevitably highly speculative, it is hoped the chosen form of presentation will make the reader aware of those aspects of the reconstruction that are most closely linked to the physical evidence and those which are more fanciful.

Wider context and chronology

In geological and pollen terms, the period of interest falls entirely within the Flandrian (current) interglacial, encompassing Subboreal to Subatlantic phases (see Table 5.1). Pollen diagrams are the most useful source of primary evidence for the vegetational changes that took place but are less relevant at the smaller scale we are interested in here and are also less directly applicable to the chalklands than to most other regions of Britain (and Europe), although several have been argued to be partly or wholly representative of the environment of the chalklands. Instead, our understanding of the palaeoecology of the Avebury landscape owes much to the work of John G Evans who established the utility of preserved snail shells as environmental indicators and, through the analysis of snail fauna recovered from archaeological contexts, established the general sequence of environmental events on the Wessex chalklands from the late glacial onwards (Evans 1971b; a; Evans 1972; 1975; Evans and Jones 1979; Evans *et al.* 1985; Evans *et al.* 1993).

While the chronology of the later Neolithic is reviewed in Chapter 6, an influential scheme for the Avebury landscape has been the five phase sequence proposed by Whittle (1993). Although Whittle's model is not adopted here, there should be little problem in associating the chronological framework used below with Whittle's scheme. Unfortutately, the chronological resolution with which it is now possible to discuss the period of major monument construction during the third millennium BC

Climatic Phase (Blytt-Sernander)	**Pollen Zone** Godwin/West	**Period**	**Climate and Vegetation**	**approx. date** cal. BC (uncal bc)
		Roman	*Deterioration*	
Subatlantic	VIII	Iron Age	Cold and wet, general deterioration. High rainfall.	
		Late BA	Decline of lime, increase of ash, birch and beech	
			Fl. III	1100BC (950bc)
		Middle BA	*Stable*	
		Early BA	Warm and dry, low rainfall, wind-blown deposits.	
		Final Neolithic	Woodland regeneration in southern England	
Subboreal	VIIb		2500BC (2000bc)	
		Late Neolithic	Declining warmth. Landnam and first agriculture. Elm decline:- 3350BC (2300bc)	
		Middle Neolithic		
		Early Neolithic		
				4000BC (3200bc)
			Optimum	
Atlantic	Fl. II	Later Mesolithic	Climatic optimum, warm and wet. Increase of 2°C, poly-climax forest. Increase of alter, some clearances	
	VIIa			
				6000BC (5500bc)

Table 5.1. Subset of Allen's (2000b, 38) table of climatic zonation to show the general context of this work in both archaeological and palaeoecological terms

is not yet matched for the other periods considered. As such, the chronology of the region is divided into periods of around 300 years for the Neolithic, with divisions of the Bronze Age remaining more conventional at about twice that length. This is a pragmatic division that emerged as the work progressed mainly from the dating of the environmental sequences. It would certainly be possible to discuss the later Neolithic with a finer chronological resolution and possibly also the earlier Bronze Age which Cleal (2005) subdivides into three separate phases, but a broader chronology was adopted, firstly because the number of environmental sequences in smaller phases would itself have become very small, and secondly to maintain roughly equal time periods through the whole period under consideration. Rather than adopt a numeric or letter-based sequence, the closest 'conventional' periods (early, middle and late Neolithic and early, middle, late Bronze Age) have been used, with additional timespans being given names that fit with these – namely a 'transitional' phase between the Mesolithic and Neolithic, and a 'final Neolithic' phase in addition to the more conventional 'later Neolithic'. While far from perfect, these phases seem to work with the available evidence, but are certainly not proposed as having wider applications.

Schematic representations

As Allen (2000a) and others have pointed out, the first serious attempt to represent the changing environment of the Avebury area at a regional scale, and in explicitly spatial terms, was the work of Bob Smith (Smith 1984; 1985). His 'schematic representations' of the environment in the early, mid and later Neolithic (Figure 5.1), have been highly influential in popular, artistic and academic understandings of the environmental changes that took place through the Neolithic. Smith's approach was to systematically examine a range of sources of evidence for environment including snail sequences, pollen diagrams, faunal remains, charcoals and soils. He also considered the impact of human activity, both occupation and monument construction. Of the methodology and purpose of the drawings, he wrote that they:

> '... represent visual concepts of how the Avebury landscape might have appeared at the end of the early, mid and late Neolithic. Encircled areas are those for which palaeoenvironmental evidence is available, the remainder of the picture is partly conjectural, and partly based on fieldwalking (Wiltshire SMR) and observed regularities in the way land was used within the reference areas.' (Smith 1984, 113; 1985, 149)

The strength of these drawings is the clarity with which their part-icon, part-map style manages to convey the mixture of conjecture and inference that seems to have guided their creation. There remain great strengths in the overall approach taken by Smith, linking, for the first time, an explicit spatial model of the environment with the data from which it is

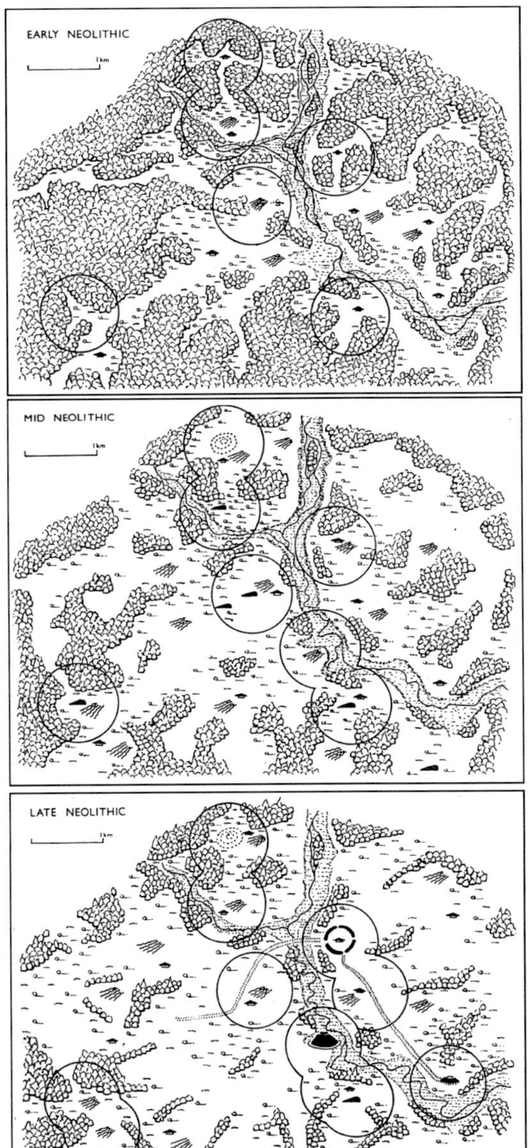

Figure 5.1. Schematic reconstructions of the landscape of the Avebury region for the early (top), middle (centre) and later (bottom) Neolithic. Reproduced from Smith 1984 (figs 8, 9 and 10)

derived, and it provides to this day an exemplar of integrating archaeological evidence with palaeoenvironmental data. Unsurprisingly after 20 years a few aspects of the work may now be regarded as problematic. The use of faunal remains to support environmental inferences is questionable. It is admitted that 'there are a bewildering number of taphonomic factors to consider' (1984, 103; 1985, 135), and the interpretative weight given to relative proportions of cervid/ovicaprid and the incidence of wild fauna as evidence of available grassland seem optimistic. Faunal assemblages from the Avebury region, as elsewhere in southern England, tend to show a predominance of cattle in the earlier Neolithic, far more pigs than cattle in the later Neolithic, with sheep growing in importance from the earlier Bronze Age. While the increasing importance of sheep must reflect significantly greater availability of pasture from the early Bronze Age onwards, it is far harder to explain other patterns in similarly simple terms. The assemblages are not from small domestic sites, but mainly from ceremonial monuments and the possibility that parts of the assemblage derive from feasting events involving significant movement of stock and/or meat, perhaps from outside the region, or the deliberate raising of selected animals must be high. Faunal data such as this may indeed be deeply meaningful, but probably reflect more of social and cultural trends rather than the environment immediately around the sites from which the assemblages derive (Richards and Thomas 1984; Albarella and Serjeantson 2002). The calculations of estimated labour inputs for the major monuments have also largely been overtaken by revisions to the chronologies which suggest that some monuments (including Avebury) may span a far longer time period than previously thought. Few would now argue there is much to gain from knowing the total number of person-hours it would take to construct, for example, Silbury, if we cannot also know whether a figure represents, say, 100 people for five weeks or five people for 100 weeks. At the same time, one of the constructional activities that may tell us most about environmental change – the felling of trees for the West Kennet palisade enclosures (Whittle 1997b) – was entirely unknown at the time Smith was writing.

The goal of this chapter is therefore to revisit Smith's aims and also to contribute to Allen's call for the production of 'high resolution interpretative maps of landscapes which: can be challenged and interrogated by further work; provide a basis for understanding settlement and society and provide the opportunity of critically examining our artefactual and site databases in relation to topography and physiographic zones' (1998, 15). Allen (1997) has attempted a similar task for the Stonehenge landscape, although this differs in approach mainly because of the differences in the quality and type of evidence for the two regions. With the exception of Holgate's work (1987), there is far less detailed surface survey data available for Avebury than for nearby Salisbury Plain, and certainly nothing close to the coverage and detail which the Stonehenge Environs Project provides (Richards 1990).

Perhaps less obviously Smith's work also has affinities with the artistic reconstructions undertaken by Jane Brayne for the Alexander Keiller Museum (unpublished, but see Allen 2005, 82–3). Both of these involved a thorough and detailed consideration of the environmental evidence, although it might be argued that Brayne's paintings – despite their 'artistic' nature – offer a more explicit connection to the evidence used to generate them than some GIS-based maps. Certainly the marginal pencil notes beside the paintings show not only the contour-map origins of the perspective, but also indicate quite specifically the ways that archaeological evidence was interpreted.

Various formal statistical or simulation methodologies were explored for extrapolating from the specific conditions at individual sites to the more general pattern across the landscape but, ultimately, none proved applicable in this context. The dataset is too taphonomically complex and simply does not provide sufficient information for reliable simulations of the woodland ecology to be run at this time, although future work may draw on, for example, fire or natural clearing models for improvements. The reconstructions, therefore, are essentially manual interpretations, guided by the environmental sequences by iteratively drawing and re-drawing the various clearances, cultivation plots and regeneration of woodland so that it seems to 'fit' what is known about the region as it develops. As well as the environmental sequences, this allowed account to be taken of the distributions of monuments across the landscape as these must be intimately bound up in the changes to the natural vegetation.

To build up a picture of the whole landscape, this chapter has employed the obvious technology in use today which was not available to Smith, Geographic Information Systems (GIS), although this has both advantages and disadvantages. The advantage of GIS is that it provides a framework within which all the environmental evidence may be presented, visualised and manipulated in a relatively intuitive spatial framework. The main disadvantage is that the formality of GIS provides no obvious method for speculating or developing imaginative reconstructions to the extent that is necessary with such an ambiguous and complex data set. Outputs from GIS are more 'precise' in the sense that they require data to be accurately georeferenced and highly structured, but may also appear sterile in comparison to the liberal, graphical style of Smith's originals or Brayne's watercolours. The reconstructions developed below therefore try to emulate some of the strengths of Smith's drawings by adopting a relatively intuitive graphical presentation of different environments, although are still more map-based than Smith or Brayne. Importantly, however, they attempt to maintain the explicit link with the sites from which the evidence derived in a similar way to Smith's drawings and Brayne's marginal notes. Circles are shown around the source sites themselves at a radius of 200m to indicate the immediate zone for which the (usually molluscan) evidence might give some confidence and also at a radius of 1500m to suggest the zone within which other environmental indicators (pollen, charcoal) might be regarded as more relevant. Of course these are both gross simplifications, but are shown both to allow summaries of the environmental sequences to be included in the period reconstructions and also to give a general indication of the increasing level of speculation that is involved in reconstructions of different parts of the landscape. It remains a fact of life that we have most specific environmental information from those places (archaeological sites) that most palaeoecologists would regard as being least useful in understanding natural processes.

The environmental sequences reviewed for this exercise are shown in Table 5.2 which also serves to avoid repeating references in the text below. Dates discussed in the text in relation to these sites refer to specific archaeological horizons, and are given as ranges to two standard deviations.

Table 5.2. (on opposite page) Sites with environmental evidence that are mentioned in the text. The abbreviation UKVP is used to refer to the Upper Kennet Valley Project.

The Avebury landscape

For the sake of this chapter, the 'Avebury area' has been defined as a rectangle with the upper left corner truncated. This gives a semi-regularised study region which includes all the long mounds south as far as the southern chalk scarp, but excluding the Vale of Pewsey. It roughly follows the edge of the Lower Chalk to the north-west and extends far enough to the north and east to include all of the Marlborough Downs, and far enough to the west to include the long mounds on Kings Play Down and the Mesolithic/Neolithic site at Cherhill.

Geology, topography, hydrology and soil

Lower Chalk forms the north-western and southern parts of the study region, often capped with chalk fractured by periglacial action, solifluxion deposits and cryoturbation structures such as the involution pockets of calcareous Aeolian silt (Evans 1968) encountered during excavations at Beckhampton. Harder, Upper and Middle chalk forms the high downs to the north and south of the Kennet valley to the east of the region. These are capped by a series of discrete clay-with-flints deposits, whose origins are complex (Fisher 1991) and which usually consist of non-calcareous reddish clay containing numerous flints. Despite the nomenclature, however, it is not always clay, sometimes being more like sand. Clay-with-flint occurs in patches above the chalk, mainly on interfluves but is more widespread in the south-east of the region, where today it underlies West Woods and Savernake Forest.

The area is divided by the Kennet valley which, in its upper reaches, is a winterbourne. The river is particularly important within the Avebury landscape because the porosity of the chalk means that there is little surface water to form smaller streams and gulleys. Instead, sources of fresh water in the region are restricted to springs and the river itself. In fact, the Kennet can only really be regarded as a reliable watercourse below Swallowhead Springs (between West Kennet Long Barrow

Site name	Grid ref	Reference	Dating	Source of evidence
Avebury G55	SU102679	(Smith 1965)	Final Neolithic, Early Bronze Age, Romano-British	Pre-barrow pits and ditch fill of bell barrow
Avebury (school)	SU102698	(Evans 1972)	Early Boreal – later Neolithic	Tree hole and buried soil beneath bank
Avebury (barn)	SU101700	(Evans *et al.* 1985)	Early Boreal – later Neolithic	Tree hole,and buried soil beneath bank
Avebury (UKVP)	SU098697	(Evans *et al.* 1988, Evans et al. 1993, Mount 1991)	Mesolithic to IronAge	Tree throw pit and valley sediments: 'Avebury soil' and 'West Overton' formation.
Beckhampton Barrow 4	SU091690	(Powell et al. 1996)	?Early/middle BA to ?Roman	Primary and secondary fills of round barrow ditch
Beckhampton Road	SU066677	(Ashbee *et al.* 1979, Dimbleby & Evans 1974)	Transition to Early Neolithic, Early Bronze Age	Buried soil beneath long barrow. Ditch of round barrow (at eastern end of Long Mound)
Burderop Down	SU169764	(Gingell 1992)	Neolithic, early Bronze Age to early Iron Age	Subsoil hollow and buried soil beneath disc barrow and fills from barrow ditch
Cherhill	SU031701	(Evans & Smith 1983)	Later Mesolithic, Neolithic to middle Bronze Age	Tufa and Mesolithic soil, Neolithic ditches
Dean Bottom	SU147742	(Gingell 1992)	Final Neolithic, middle to late Bronze Age	Fills of a storage pit containing Beaker pottery; infill of BA hut platform
Easton Down	SU064661	(Whittle *et al.* 1993)	Transition, Early Neolithic to later Bronze Age	Tree throw pit, Old ground surface beneath mound, ditch fills, buried soil in ditch
Fyfield Down I Lynchet	SU141710	(Bowen & Fowler 1962, Evans 1972, Fowler & Evans 1967)	Transition to ?Roman	Tree hole beneath the lynchet, pre-lynchet buried soil, lynchet accumulation
Hemp Knoll	SU069673	(Robertson-Mackay 1980)	Early Neolithic to later Bronze Age	Buried soil beneath round barrow and round barrow ditch
Horslip	SU086705	(Ashbee *et al.* 1979)	Transition, Final Neolithic/ early Bronze Age	Buried soil beneath mound, ditch fills (assoc. with Beaker pottery)
Knap Hill	SU121636	(Connah 1964)	Early Neolithic to Final Neolithic	Buried soil beneath the bank, ditch fill
Longstones Enclosure	SU089694	(This volume)	Later Neolithic	Fills of Neolithic enclosure ditch
Marden	SU091584	(Evans 1972)	Early/mid Neolithic, later Neolithic	Pre-henge soil, fills of henge ditch
Millbarrow	SU094372 20	(Whittle 1994)	Early Neolithic to Final Neolithic	Pre-barrow post-holes and pits, fill of outer ditch
Piggledene	SU142687	(Fowler 2000)	Final Neolithic	Auger samples from colluvial deposits
Pound Field	SU135682	(Powell *et al.* 1996)	Bronze Age? – dating is not secure	Horizon initially interpreted as pre-barrow soil, later regarded as unstratified
Roughridge Hill	SU060660	(Evans 1972, Proudfoot 1965)	Early/middle Neolithic, early to middle Bronze Age	Buried soil beneath Bishops Cannings 62, ditch fill of Bishops Cannings 61
Silbury Hill	SU100685	(Whittle 1997)	Later Neolithic	Old ground surface beneath mound. Turves from the mound
South Street Long Mound	SU091693	(Ashbee *et al.* 1979)	Pre-transition, Early Neolithic to early Bronze Age	Tree throw hollow, Pre-barrow features, buried soil beneath mound, fills of long barrow ditches
Stukeley Barrow	SU107684	(Powell *et al.* 1996)	?Early or middle Bronze Age to post-Roman	Primary and secondary ditch fills of round barrow
West Kennet Pal. Enclosure	SU109681	(Whittle 1997)	Final Neolithic	Postpipes in ditch of palisade enclosure 2
West Kennet Long Barrow	SU105677	(Evans 1972, Gowlett *et al.* 1986)	Early Neolithic	Snail series from buried soil beneath the mound
West Overton G6B	SU120684	(Smith & Simpson 1966)	Presumably Bronze Age	Grey clay under the central area of the barrow (provenance unknown)
West Overton (UKVP)	SU135685	(Evans *et al.* 1988, Evans et al. 1993, Mount 1991)	Mesolithic to Iron Age	Valley sediments: 'North Farm Formation', 'Avebury Soil' and 'West Overton Formation'.
Windmill Hill	SU087715	(Dimbleby & Evans 1974, Whittle *et al.* 1999)	Transition, Early Neolithic to, early Bronze Age	Subsoil hollow and preserved soil beneath bank and fills of ditches

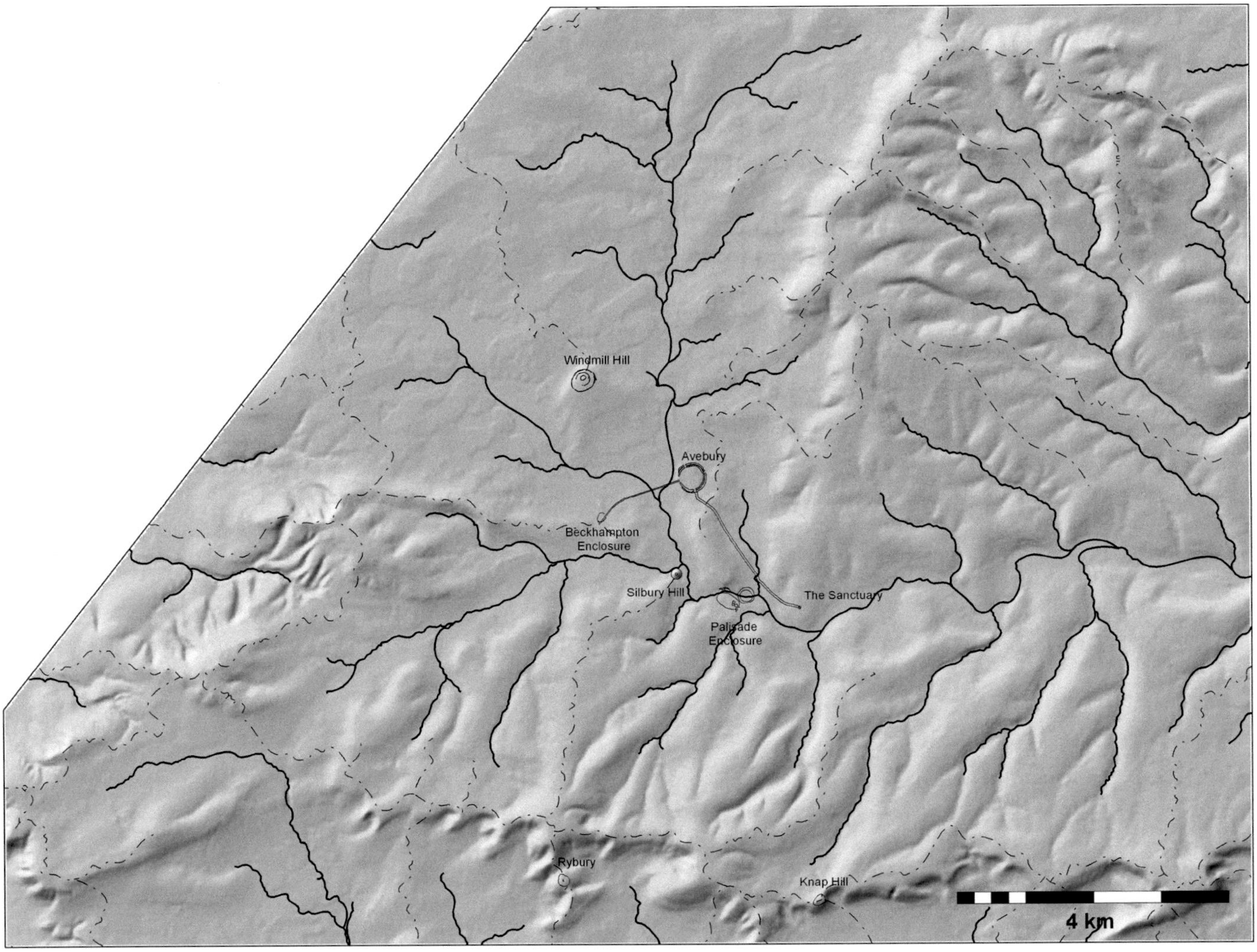

Figure 5.2. Relief and drainage of the Avebury area, showing the main prehistoric monuments

and Silbury Hill) after which it flows eastwards, effectively bisecting the downs to the north and south (Figure 5.2). The hydrology of the region is very relevant to the establishment of permanent settlement, and for keeping animals in areas away from springs (as at Cherhill) or the more permanent stretches of the river. Southern England has rarely been short of rain, however, and the collection and management of rainwater (Fowler and Blackwell 1998, 42) and, at least as early as the Medieval period, the practice of creating clay-lined ponds are obvious adaptations to this. It is probable that there were similar practices during earlier periods. Although there is no evidence for management of water in this way, features such as 'dew ponds' have not often been excavated, though at least one example appears to have late Bronze Age origins (Gingell 1992). More recently, boreholes supply water to many farms and prior to the industrial scale extraction of water from the chalk for drinking water and canals, the water-table must have been far higher and wells may have been feasible even on the high downs.

To the south of the area, the scarp of the chalk forms a natural barrier between the Avebury region and the Vale of Pewsey, while chalk download continues to the east eventually merging with the Berkshire Downs. The distribution of archaeological sites, particularly long mounds suggest that, archaeologically, the eastern edge of the region might be considered to be the river Og. A series of dry valleys radiate from the Kennet Valley itself forming obvious routes that can be used to pass between the more exposed higher downs and the floodplain. Many of these formerly contained quantities of superficial sarsen stones whose size probably varied from small boulders to stone slabs several metres across. These are another relic deposit formed into 'streams' in valley bottoms under periglacial conditions from highly denuded earlier deposits that once capped the chalk. Now largely cleared, these sarsen fields must have formed one of the most distinctive features of the Avebury landscape and been highly significant to human communities visiting or living in the region long before the incorporation of such stones into circles, coves and avenues at Avebury and Stonehenge.

Following Limbrey (1975; 1978), it has long been accepted that the original soils in the region were far more uniform than today. The current range of soils extends from highly impoverished grey rendzinas to argyllic brownearths, but it has been generally accepted that prior to the Neolithic the landscape was dominated by argillic brownearths, formed under the acidifying conditions of closed woodland, which became gradually more calcareous through the effects of clearance and anthropogenic interference (Fisher 1991). This is obviously a simplification because there are sequences where the development of soil was affected in different ways: at Avebury, for example, the area became long grassland which formed a dense vegetational mat eventually leading to decalcification of the soil profile (Evans 1972; Evans *et al.* 1985). More interestingly, recent work in the Allen valley (French and Lewis 2005) has concluded that in this area there was originally a mix of deep, argyllic brownearths on clay-rich areas and more calcareous brownearths elsewhere that were 'predisposed' to becoming grassland. While it is dangerous to simply transfer these results to the Upper Kennet Valley, it does now seem reasonable to assume that, while argillic brownearths may have been widespread in those areas of closed-canopy woodland, quite different and more calcareous brownearths may have existed under areas of less dense woodland, while the parts of the Avebury landscape underlain by clay-with-flints as opposed to those areas on calcareous deposits must always have supported different, perhaps deeper and more acidic, soils and therefore different plant communities before significant intervention by human communities.

Palaeoenvironmental data sources

The two major sources of direct evidence for environmental change for the chalklands, and Avebury in particular, are pollen and molluscs. To a lesser extent insect remains can be used where they are preserved, and charred macroscopic plant remains (charcoals and seeds) may give information about presence of individual species, although movement of crops, cut wood and other plants by people in prehistory make these less suitable for inferences related to their recovery points. As was stated above, pollen diagrams are far less relevant to the chalklands than to many other areas of Britain due to the poor preservation of pollen in calcareous substrates, and the absence of glacial lake basins in which stratified deposits of peat may have accumulated. With very few exceptions (*e.g.* Allen and Scaife in Cleal *et al.* 2004), pollen analyses within the chalklands have either been derived from soils and ditch-fills of archaeological sites, or from small peat deposits a short distance from the chalklands. In this latter case, it is extremely difficult to argue that the environmental sequences precisely reflect those of the chalklands.

Waton (1982; 1983) describes a core from Winnal Moors, north of Winchester, an area surrounded by chalk, and claims that this may be broadly representative of the vegetation history of the chalklands in this area (about 80 to 90% of the recorded dry land pollen may have been derived from the surrounding downlands). This sequence suggests later Mesolithic (6000–4500BC) woodland dominated by alder, lime, elm and oak with some indications of raised herb pollen from the preceding Boreal period. A major decline in tree pollen (including hazel) occurs around 4500BC while most herb pollens, especially grasses, increase in the period 4500 to 3200BC, which also sees the first occurrence of cereal pollen. From the mid Neolithic (3200BC) to the early Bronze Age (1700BC) the series shows first a fall in tree, shrub and hazel pollen, which then rises again before falling at the end of the zone. No cereal pollen is present here, but there are higher levels of grasses (50–75%). From 1700 to 800BC there is a transitory fall in birch, oak and hazel with a corresponding rise in grass pollen, followed by an increase in oak and hazel and reduction in grass. In the later part of this zone (later Bronze Age) cereal pollen occurs again.

Another sequence was obtained by Waton (1983) from Snellsmore Common, north of Newbury although here the small size of the deposit led him to conclude that the majority of the pollen (77%) derived from within 20m of the deposit, and only 10% could have come from the chalk. During the early Neolithic (*c.*3750–3200BC) it suggests birch and hazel woodland, with birch declining through time while oak, lime, alder and ash all increase and grass and bracken pollen also decline. The later Neolithic/early Bronze Age (*c.*3200–1800BC) continues to show a woodland flora, with further decline in birch and a large rise in alder. The middle Bronze Age zone (1800–1100BC) shows mostly oak with alder and hazel and some lime, but it is not until the later Bronze Age (perhaps 1100BC) that any real decline in woodland is observed, notably oak, alder and hazel, accompanied by increasing grass pollen, birch and herbs. Even here, woodland continues and herb pollens never exceed 3% of tree pollen. Waton (1983) also analysed an exceptionally deep polleniferous sediment (almost 18m) at Rimsmoor, 4km south west of Bere Regis on the southern edge of the Dorset Downs. Six radiocarbon dates, projected into a time-depth curve revealed an astonishingly high rate of accumulation of the peat (1983, 156), but he again concluded that most of the pollen was unlikely to have come from the chalk downland less than 1km away. The series shows a later Mesolithic/earliest Neolithic phase (*c.*5800–3750BC) of oak, hazel and alder woodland with a little lime and ash although grasses are present in significant numbers, and two cereal grains are recorded. There is a pronounced elm decline around 3750BC, and the period 3750–2250BC (early to mid Neolithic) shows a decline of grass pollen and a major decline of alder, with smaller temporary reductions of lime, oak and ash. Hazel increases during this period with a peak of *plantago lanceolata* and bracken. However, tree, shrub and hazel pollen is consistently high indicating woodland throughout the early and middle Neolithic. From around 2250 to 1250BC (mid/later Neolithic to mid Bronze Age) there is a significant fall in lime pollen, and temporary reductions of oak, elm, birch, alder and hazel. *Plantago lanceolata* is present throughout this period and – as at Snellsmore – it is not until the middle Bronze Age (*c.*1250BC) that a major clearance is apparent, with all tree pollen reducing and grass and herb pollens increasing. Other pollen sequences show similar patterns but, given Waton's conclusions with regard to the origins of pollen, none can really be argued to show either the extent or type of woodland on the downs. They may indicate the range of species that were present around the chalklands at this time (birch, hazel, oak, lime, alder and ash), without providing information on their proportions or dates of clearances and perhaps support the idea that clay areas neighbouring the chalklands were more densely wooded and less subject to clearance than the chalklands themselves.

Pollen from the fills of monument ditches and/or buried soils is far more likely to represent the environment of the chalklands, but presents entirely different interpretative problems. It is rarely well preserved due to the generally calcareous sediments and is usually recovered from a single deposit and so does not provide a sequence for a pollen diagram. Nonetheless, at least seven dated archaeological deposits in the area provide pollen evidence and these confirm the presence of the tree species expected from pollen sequences from further afield (notably oak, hazel, birch and lime) in the immediate surroundings of these sites prior to construction, while hawthorn and yew are attested from charcoals from Windmill Hill. From the pollen evidence, the majority of the seven sites appear to have been constructed in substantial clearings (Horslip, Windmill Hill, Beckhampton Road, Silbury) with woodland or scrub not far away, or within a mosaic of different environments that includes both open vegetation and scrub woodland (South Street, Easton Down). Only Knap Hill, south of the region, appears to have been wooded before construction activity began, and there the woodland appears to have been of a very open or patchy character (see below).

Snail shells survive best within calcareous or non-acidic sediments and are therefore far more significant within the Wessex region as a source of environmental indicators, but interpretation of molluscan sequences is not without problems. Just as for pollen, there are complex taphonomic considerations regarding the relationship between fauna and death assemblage, and between the death assemblage and the sub-fossil assemblage (Evans 1972; 1978). Biological activity within archaeological sediments, particularly soils, can also lead to a mixing of the assemblage and a blurring of the chronological resolution of the sequence. Selective movement of shells through a soil profile, or biopeturbation, can even lead to a patterning of shells within a non-accumulating sediment which is derived not from chronological change in the life-assemblage but from entirely taphonomic factors. Lastly, snails from ditch sediments must be treated with caution because ditches commonly support a microhabitat which is quite different from the rest of the local environment, normally wetter and with taller herbs than the surroundings. Even allowing for these uncertainties, however, it is clear that evidence of snail fauna from archaeological monuments presents the most direct evidence for the prehistoric environment of the Avebury region for the time in question.

Plant communities and their habitats

Pollen, charcoal and plant remains provide us with the range of species present in the chalklands, although the interpretative problems discussed above with relation to both stratified and archaeological pollen make it difficult to model the proportions of different species present. In order to model the distribution of different plant communities at the end of the Mesolithic, it is therefore necessary to understand the habitat preferences of the main tree species that are assumed to be represented by these charcoals and pollens.

The principle trees assumed to represent the climax vegetation in the region are summarised in Table 5.3, together with some indication of their range of size and ecological preferences (Birks *et al.* 1975; Godwin 1975a; b). The two

Table 5.3. The main tree species and their habitat preferences, mostly from Godwin (1975a) and Rackham (1980)

Species	Variants	Preferences	Approx Height (max)	Approx Height (ave)	Habitats
Alder	*Alnus glutinosa*	Wet conditions	25	12	Valley bottoms, around water sources (springs), gently sloping flat clay soils although does not necessarily indicate wet ground. Also a strong coloniser and pioneer species of secondary woodland.
Ash	*Fraxinus excelsior*	Moist conditions	40	18	Shade intolerant, seral species, similar to alter. Expansion after elm decline may represent the spread of ash as a transient coloniser before giving way to oak, elm and lime.
Beech	*Fagus sylvatica*	Alkaline soils	45	20	Chalk and oolitic limestone. Arrived in British Isles just before 3000BP (Birks 1989). In Sub-Atlantic invaded areas of former oak forest cleared by people (Godwin 1975b).
Birch	*Betula pubescens (B. verriculosa)*	Strongly light-demanding	22	10	Majority of pollen is tree birch. Quick growing and short-lived. Tolerates a variety of soil conditions, is an excellent coloniser of disforested habitats before shade-tolerant species become established. Also forms climax vegetation in some impoverished situations.
	Betula pendula				
Elm	*Ulmus glabra*	Similar to lime	30	20	Probably occupied a similar ecological position to lime on the chalklands. With oak, forms a major component of climax vegetation on upper and middle chalk succeeding faster-growing colonisers such as hazel.
	Ulmus procera				
	Ulmus carpinifolia				
Hazel	*Corylus avellana*	Basic soils, but also tolerates damper neutral or mildly acid soils.	15	3 (shrub) 8 (tree)	Occurs commonly as a shrub but also grows to form medium-sized trees. Is a coloniser species forming secondary woodland/scrub, can occur as scrub at the edge of woodland, as under-shrub beneath oak or ash woodlands, or in hazel copses as fairly pure stands.
Lime	*Tilia platyphyllis*	Tolerant of poor soils	30	20	A minority component of oak woodland in a wide range of habitats. Thorley (1981) claims Lewes diagram represents selective exploitation of separate elm/lime community on moist, base-rich soils of valley sides which attracted early agriculturalists. Waton (1983) however argues that this pollen may represent the basin and not surrounding chalklands.
	Tilia cordata				
Oak	*Quercus robur*	Wide variety of soils	43	25	Diagrams for zones VIIa and VIIb show that oak dominated the forest in Britain particularly in the South west. In east and southeast, oak is rather less dominant possibly because of competition from lime and alder.
	Quercus pertaea				
Pine	*Pinus sylvestris*	Lower temperatures	35	25	Not present in great numbers, prefers acid soils and does not compete with broad-leafed trees unless temperature is lower than Atlantic/sub-boreal periods. Only present in small percentages during stage VIIa (probably in e.g. dryer areas of raised bogs) and even less in stage VIIb.
Willow	*Salix spp*	Wet environments	20	4	Quick growing, and prefer an abundance of water.

native species of oak are quite similar, but it may be the English oak (*Quercus robur*) that is represented in the south of Britain where it formed a substantial proportion of the climax woodland with elm (*Ulmus glabra*). Lime (*Tilia platyphyllis* and *T. cordata*) was also an important component of forests in southern Britain, and, as it prefers less acidic soils, may have been more widespread on the chalk rather than the clay-with-flints. In areas less likely to reach full closed canopy woodland, such as steeper slopes, hazel (*Corylus avellana*), birch (*Betula pubescens, B. Pendula*) and ash (*Fraxinus excelsior*) would have been a more significant component. Hazel in particular seems to have been very common and can occur as stands of hazel copses and in scrub at the edge of woodland, as well as occurring as an understorey shrub and being a coloniser species. Although it is a prolific producer of pollen, and hence over-represented in pollen diagrams, alder (*Alnus*) was clearly a component of woodlands in lowland Britain, presumably occurring in wetter areas such as floodplains, which must also have included willow (*Salix* sp.). Pine (*Pinus sylvestris*) appears to have been present (for example, at Beckhampton Road long barrow), but only in small numbers, probably failing to compete with the broad-leafed trees except in the coldest microclimates. Other minor components of the oak and elm woodland, occurring either as understorey shrubs or colonising species, may have included food-providing species such as cherry, crab apple and elder, as well as hornbeam, holly, hawthorn, rowan, whitebeam and yew. Where natural clearings regenerated to woodland, it is likely that birch, hazel and ash may have formed initial secondary woodland, gradually giving way to less shade-tolerant and larger species such as elm and oak.

From this we might suggest that the more acidic soils of the clay-with-flints, which are generally not steeply sloping, may have supported a community principally of oak, elm and lime with some alder on the more clay-rich soils while patches of secondary woodland consisted perhaps of ash, hazel, birch and other minor species. The more alkaline soils of the chalk, particularly where the woodland canopy was less complete or more frequently interrupted, may have been rather less dominated by oak and elm. There may have been more lime present, a significant amount of hazel in the understorey and ash, hazel and birch colonising clearings. On steeper slopes, a far less dense woodland, possibly even scrub in places, may have formed the climax vegetation with hazel forming the majority species accompanied by some of the 'coloniser' species while in wetter situations such as floodplains, alder may have dominated.

Before the Neolithic (before *c.*4200BC)

There is no evidence for permanent or large-scale human activity within the Avebury region during the later Mesolithic, and Whittle (1993) summarises the current consensus that Mesolithic activity may have been 'slight and episodic, with occasional hunting forays into what would have been a wooded, but rather uniform and dry environment' (1993, 31). The conventional interpretation of the pollen evidence for environmental conditions at the

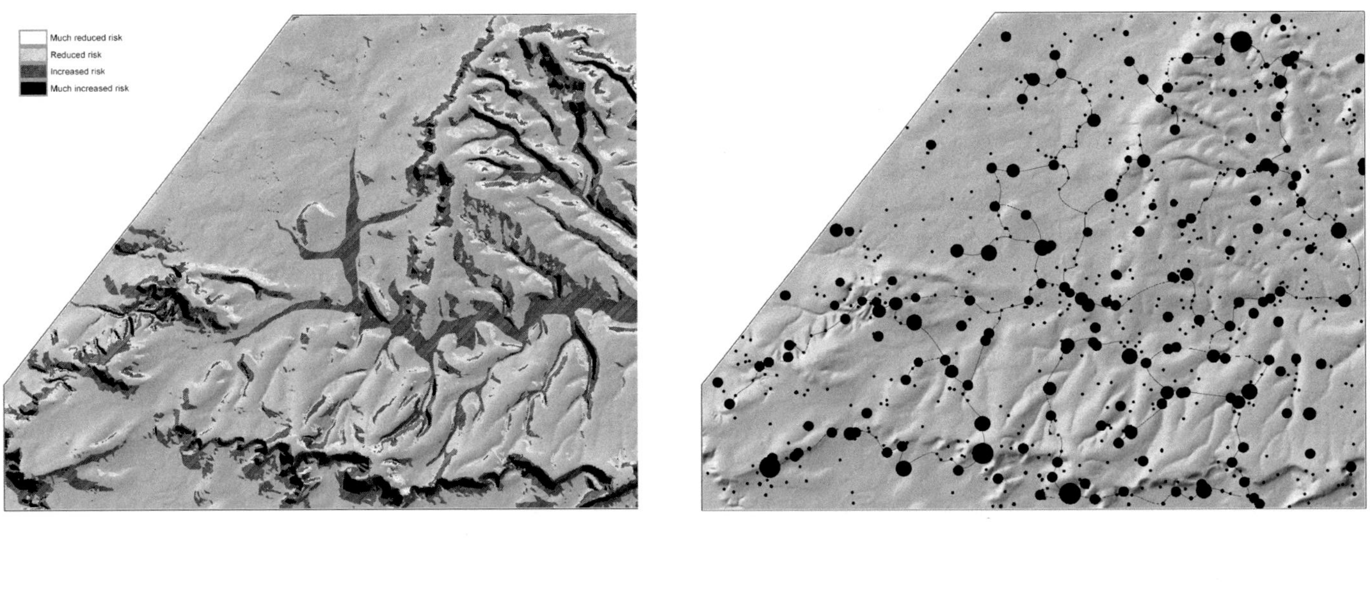

Figure 5.3. Formal speculation: patterns of pre-Neolithic clearings and pathways

start of the Neolithic would suggest fairly uniform deciduous woodland, principally oak and elm, with other species such as hazel, birch and lime present in smaller numbers (Figure 5.4). This view of uniform, closed, climax woodland was not seriously challenged until Vera (2000) argued that the pre-Neolithic landscape of the whole of Europe should be better understood as parkland than woodland. This view has not gained widespread acceptance, but there is now a growing acknowledgement within the ecological literature that the climax vegetation may not have been as complete as had been previously thought. Allen now considers that there are 'areas of the chalklands of southern England where the Neolithic woodland may not have existed as a complete blanket' (2005, 83), while recent work in the upper Allen valley (French and Lewis 2005), with which the Avebury area has several morphological and archaeological similarities, has shown that this part of the chalklands may not have become completely wooded during the Mesolithic period, with parts of the area appearing 'never to have been as uniformly wooded as conventional ecological models have previously maintained' (2005, 130). With this in mind, it is worth considering whether the evidence for the Avebury area fits this kind of interpretation, and the later Mesolithic environment might have more closely resembled that of the Allen valley, where it is now argued that 'patches of the downland may have been preadapted to supporting stable open grassland with associated rendzina soils from the very beginning of the Holocene' (2005, 130).

There are various sites in the Avebury area where molluscan evidence attests the presence of pre-Neolithic woodland. A subsoil hollow at South Street long barrow (Ashbee *et al.* 1979) contained a late Boreal woodland molluscan fauna, with pollen indicating the presence of hazel, elm, birch and oak, while mollusca from subsoil hollows beneath the bank at Avebury (Evans 1972; Evans *et al.* 1985) show the

Figure 5.4 The pre-Neolithic landscape

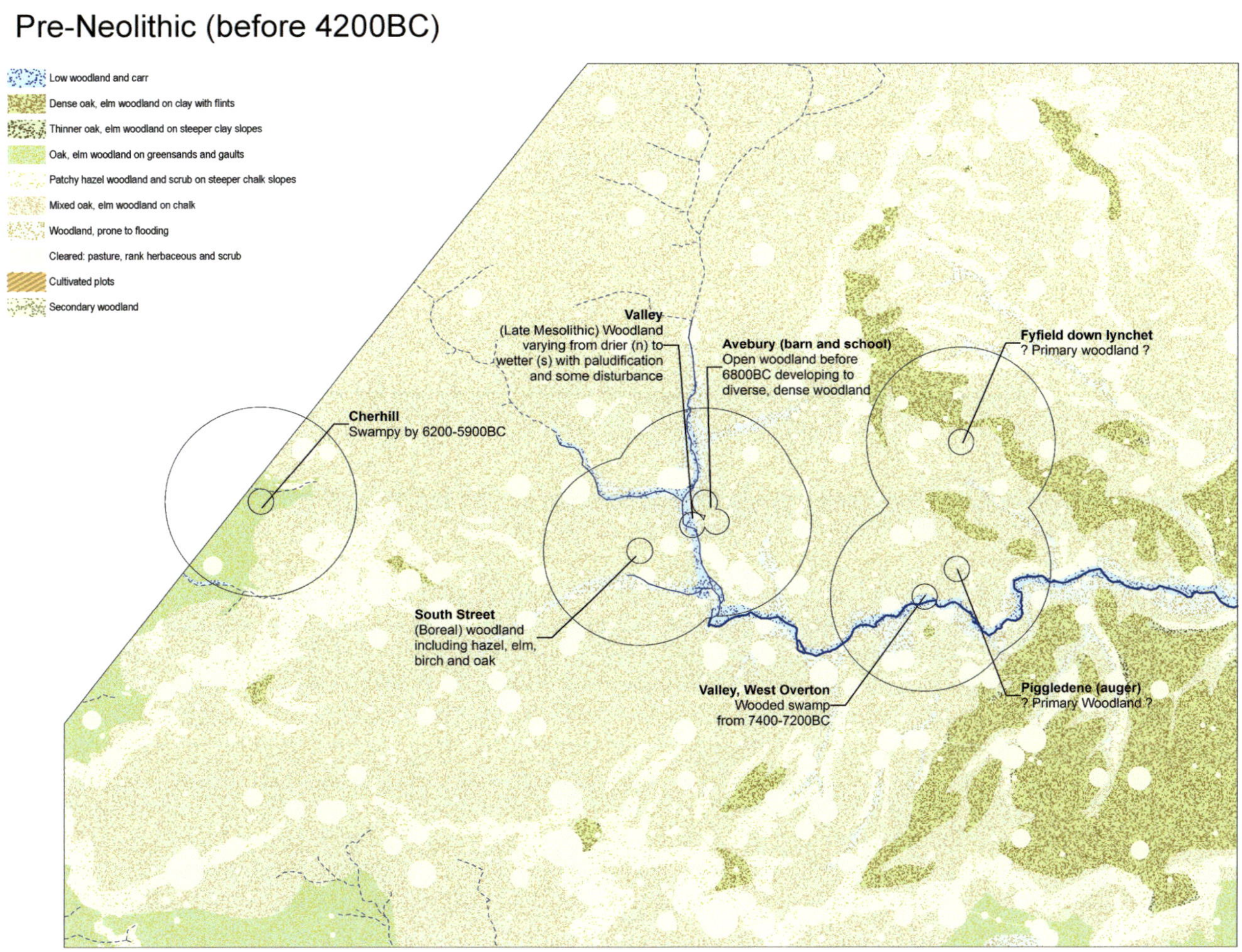

presence of open woodland before *c.*6800BC developing to diverse, dense Atlantic woodland. Nearby, in the Kennet valley at Avebury (Evans *et al.* 1993), Atlantic woodland faunas were also recovered from subsoil hollows that indicated variation over space from drier to damper conditions and there is also some evidence for disturbance of woodland and paludification associated with, but not necessarily dated by, late Mesolithic flints.

Further east, the later Mesolithic soil at Cherhill (Evans and Smith 1983) contained a late Mesolithic flint industry, and showed woodland conditions becoming progressively more swampy by about 6200–5900BC (not interpreted as due to human influence) and to the west in the Kennet Valley at West Overton (Evans *et al.* 1993) there is evidence of wooded swamp from around 7400–7200BC onwards, also contemporary with Mesolithic activity evidenced by finds of flint and chert. A little further down the valley the basal deposits in Piggledene (Fowler 2000), revealed by augering, contained evidence of woodland which, although not dated, may indicate the presence of primary woodland whose existence on the Downs could be suggested by the Fyfield Down lynchet (Bowen and Fowler 1962; Fowler and Evans 1967; Evans 1972), where a subsoil hollow beneath the pre-lynchet soil also contained a woodland molluscan fauna. Neither Piggledene nor the lynchet on Fyfield Down can be considered to be well dated horizons, however, and either, or both, could relate to much more recent deposition.

Despite evidence for the presence of closed woodland in both Boreal and Atlantic periods, the uniformity of the pre-Neolithic woodland may have been overstated. It is hard to interpret the pollen evidence as indicating anything other than that the majority of the surface area was covered by closed-canopy woodland, but an open proportion of the area (maybe 10–20%) may not be detectable from the regional pattern. The presence of red deer (*Cervus elaphus*) at several sites and aurochs (*Bos primigenius*) at, for example, Windmill Hill may suggest precisely this. Although red deer can flourish in both open and closed environments, the presence of auroch hints that clearings and/or swampy areas were also present. The habitat preferences of aurochs are difficult to assert with any surety: Vera (2000) argues they were open parkland animals, although historical accounts and the work of researchers such as van Vuure (2005) suggest that aurochs natural habitat may have resembled that of the forest buffalo (*Syncerus caffer nanus*), with a mixture of closed forest, more open areas and swamps. Regardless of this, it is likely that aurochs moved in herds and would therefore have created and maintained pathways within the woodlands.

As Brown (1997, 141) has observed, the spatial pattern of clearings caused by windfall are complex, but we should expect a preponderance of clearances of less than 2ha with a few much larger clearings (tens of hectares) with areas with higher exposure to prevailing wind or on the floodplain expected to have a higher numbers of clearings. Other causes of natural clearings would have included river erosion and beaver activity where there was running water (Coles 1992; Brown 2000), although neither of these need have been very significant given the small scale of the upper Kennet river. During periods of drought, there would also have been a risk of forest fire, ignited by lightning strike, which could have cleared substantial areas of closed woodland and taken generations to regenerate. It is obviously impossible to accurately estimate the positions of natural clearings, which would have formed a shifting mosaic as some regenerated to woodland, and newer areas were subject to windfall or other natural processes. On the downs in the north-east of the region one of the effects of the substantial, now vanished, sarsen deposits must have been to hinder full climax woodland where stones were densest, perhaps creating a number of clearings with a high density of often quite large sarsens within them.

Woodland is therefore likely to have been regularly interrupted, particularly on the floodplain and exposed areas, by natural clearings interlaced with pathways. The mixture of vegetation is also likely to have been very different in the wettest areas – tending towards alder and hazel carr in places directly adjacent to the river itself. It is probable that there was variation between the soils and vegetation on chalk parent materials, which would have been better drained and more alkaline, and those on clay-with-flints. Here it has been assumed that the clay-with-flints supported a denser, oak/elm woodland than the chalkland where a less complete canopy of oak, elm and lime may have been more typical.

Woodland is also likely to have been much less dense on the steepest slopes, where the climax vegetation may even have stopped short of woodland in the strict sense. The evidence relating to the pre-enclosure environment at Knap Hill is interesting in this regard because of its situatation close to the steep slopes of the southern chalk scarp, and the snails and pollen evidence may therefore be indicating something of the character of these parts of the landscape. The original analysis of the molluscan evidence interpreted the data as representing 'open scrub'(Connah 1964, 19), while Evans (1972) refers to pollen data representing 'hazel woodland' (citing 'Dimbleby *pers comm*'). The difference between these, and the openness of the pre-enclosure environment can be overstated, however. A review of the molluscan data shows that of the 15% open country species, about half are *Vallonia costata* which can also occur in woodlands, while the shade-loving species contain rupestral species such as *Clausilia bidentata* and *Acanthinula aculeata* in significant numbers. Despite this, there is no doubt that the pre-enclosure environment at Knap Hill (from the molluscs) and its surroundings (from the pollen reported by Evans) was very far from closed-canopy woodland, perhaps being better interpreted as a mixture of very patchy woodland and scrub with a high proportion of hazel. It is, of course, possible that the openness of the environment prior to the enclosure is because the woodland here is secondary following earlier clearance episodes, but there is no doubt that Evans sees this as uncleared land as he refers to the situation of Knap Hill as 'in some way special' (1972, 246) and contrasts it with the forest clearance that had occurred at the sites of long barrows, such as Horslip and South Street prior to their construction. If this is accepted, then our conclusion must be that the exposed situation of Knap Hill and its proximity to the steeper slopes of the scarp significantly restricted the development of full closed-canopy woodland and that this is likely to have applied to other similar topographic settings.

Some impression of the vegetational mosaic at an arbitrary point in time can be obtained by a using a simple model to represent the generation of natural clearings. This can be generated by combining those aspects facing the prevailing winds (south-westerly) with those areas on the river floodplain and areas with the steepest slopes. Using these, a 'windfall risk' map can be generated and in turn used to generate appropriate densities of random points according to risk of windfall. These can then be joined together by pathways to give a crude impression of the general aspect of the landscape. Figure 5.3 shows the outcome, the results of which clearly should not be taken too literally as this method is effectively a formal method of speculation. Although the clearings are rather too regular and no account is made of, for example, forest fires or animal activity, it does give an impression of how such a shifting mosaic of clearings and connecting paths may have looked. Clearings would have shifted through time as new windfalls, fires or other circumstances created new ones, and former ones regenerated. At any given time, therefore, the clearings would have been in various stages of regeneration and contain a mixture of pasture, tall herbs, shrubs and scrub vegetation. It is possible that some of them may have been maintained in a more-or-less cleared state by animal grazing or trampling, perhaps around watering points on the floodplain or even by Mesolithic visitors keen to promote browse for animals or to manage forest resources for their benefit, as has been suggested as an interpretation of the area of paludification within the Avebury valley (Evans *et al.* 1993).

Mesolithic/Neolithic transition (*c.*4200–3700BC)

With the possible exception of the valley west of Avebury (Evans *et al.* 1993), there is little convincing evidence of human influence on the Avebury environment before *c.*3700BC. There are, however, a few sites that could indicate anthropogenic change in this timespan, which may either suggest early, perhaps rather transient occupation of the area by farming communities, or the impact of hunter-gatherer groups whose lifeways had been influenced by contact with farming. Both of these could take place simultaneously or in close succession, and in the absence of clear settlement evidence it is hard to know how these would be distinguishable archaeologically without the presence of ceramics or the building of characteristically Neolithic monuments.

One example is from Horslip long barrow (Ashbee *et al.* 1979). The buried soil beneath the mound contained a dry grassland molluscan fauna while pollen evidence suggested that the site had been cleared, and possibly cultivated, before being maintained as grassland, while the surrounding area began to regenerate to hazel scrub and woodland. If the date of 4350–3650BC is accepted (and suitable caution needs to be observed with respect to any single radiocarbon date, more so with less recent determinations) then this sequence of events took place before around 3650BC at the latest, and is the earliest evidence for clearance in the region. Perhaps also relating to this phase is the subsoil hollow beneath the pre-bank soil at Windmill Hill, from which charcoals of oak, hazel, hawthorn, birch and yew were recovered. Analysis of the poorly-preserved pollen from this level (Dimbleby 1965; Dimbleby and Evans 1974) as indicating 'grassland with sparse woodland' has now been discounted by Walker (Whittle *et al.* 1999, 162) on the grounds of differential preservation, and the molluscan sequence from the pre-bank soil more reliably indicates woodland, followed by clearance and occupation (with woodland remaining nearby). This sequence is earlier than the pits, post-holes and a grave which are dated to 3940–3520BC and Whittle *et al.* (1999) suggest a long period of utilisation of the site, with evidence of cultivation, presence of cereal remains, animal parts and deposition of hearth material. The mound of West Kennet long barrow (Evans 1972; Gowlett *et al.* 1986) overlay a buried soil with a mixed woodland/open-country molluscan fauna, progressing to an open country fauna some time before the 3800–3300BC date obtained from skeletal material within the mound. Some woodland therefore existed on or close to the site prior to clearance, although the original woodland fauna was not preserved.

Further from the core of the region, a subsoil hollow in the old ground surface below Easton Down long barrow (Whittle *et al.* 1993) provides evidence of diverse woodland on the higher downs to the south-east prior to 3630–3440BC. To the north-west, a similar subsoil hollow was stratified beneath a Neolithic ploughsoil, itself preserved under the disc barrow adjacent to the Burderop Down settlement. This contained evidence of long herbaceous vegetation: an immature open environment colonised by weed species. The interpretation suggests small-scale clearance of the landscape with some secondary scrub regrowth, although there is no faunal evidence for primary closed-canopy woodland at this site. This is chronologically less secure, although is stratified below a Neolithic ploughsoil that contained pottery of early and later Neolithic date.

It must be accepted that calibrated dates for Neolithic sites that could pre-date 3700BC cover wide ranges and that, on current dating evidence, it is quite possible to argue that Neolithic activity in the area is entirely absent prior to *c.*3700BC. Any changes that did take place during this timespan may not have been extensive. With the possible exception of Roughridge Hill, there is no real evidence for cereal cultivation, although small scale cultivation of cereals or even horticultural activity should not be ruled out. It is possible that the period represents a transitional phase during which hunter-gatherer groups adopted aspects of Neolithic lifestyles, perhaps animal husbandry, and/or pioneer agriculturalists made transient forays into the area, and it therefore seems likely that the landscape remained broadly as it had been in the later Mesolithic, with perhaps some dispersed small-scale clearances adding to the existing natural mosaic of closed canopy, clearings and wetter areas interspersed with tracks.

Figure 5.5 speculates that the clearance for early settlement around Windmill Hill and Horslip could be related to an early episode of activity north of Swallowhead springs and around the river. This area may have been attractive more for the availability of water than for its agricultural suitability, and we may envisage similar pioneer ventures or Mesolithic adaptations being responsible for the mixed fauna recovered from West Kennet long barrow. On the Marlborough Downs, early visitors would have encountered the trails of sarsen stones, some of which were highly distinctive, within clearings and woodland. These must have formed cogent cultural landmarks, which could have acted as meeting places and locations for gatherings and rituals. Few of these are now *in situ* on the downs, but of those that are at least one, on Lockeridge Down, still has the furrows of repeated use for polishing stone axes (Fowler 2000, 66–8). The early, open environment suggested for Burderop Down may therefore partly reflect clearance around some of these sites, perhaps by extending or joining together natural clearings and the thinner forest cover that may have existed where high densities of sarsens prevented full forestation.

Earlier Neolithic (*c.*3700–3400BC)

This period may be defined by the first sustained and reliably dated construction of monuments by human communities and represents a new phase in the use of the Avebury area. Domestic animals, particularly cattle, but also ovicaprid and to a lesser extent pigs, seem to have been both economically and symbolically central to the early Neolithic landscape. There is also clear evidence for the use of agriculture, although there is little evidence that this was economically more important than the continued exploitation of wild animals and plants in the region. Most of the dated construction activity for long mounds and chambered tombs (long barrows) occurs in this phase, and evidence for the environment during this time comes largely from these contexts and from buried soils preserved beneath later monuments (Figure 5.6).

At South Street long barrow, marks that probably indicate use of a rip-ard were sealed under a buried soil (dated *c.*3660–3370BC). Here, it appears that cultivation was followed by a short period – perhaps only a decade or two – of grassland which was probably maintained by grazing. Pollen evidence is interpreted as indicating a mosaic of clearings in scrub woodland, becoming more open through time. Dates for the construction of the barrow range from 3660–3020BC although the most reliable date is perhaps that from an antler embedded in the coombe rock of the mound, dated to 3490–3020BC. Prior to that, it appears that the area was subject to local clearance with areas of scrub woodland remaining around the site. Four molluscan samples were taken from the pre-barrow soil beneath Beckhampton Road long barrow (Ashbee *et al.* 1979), which dates to before

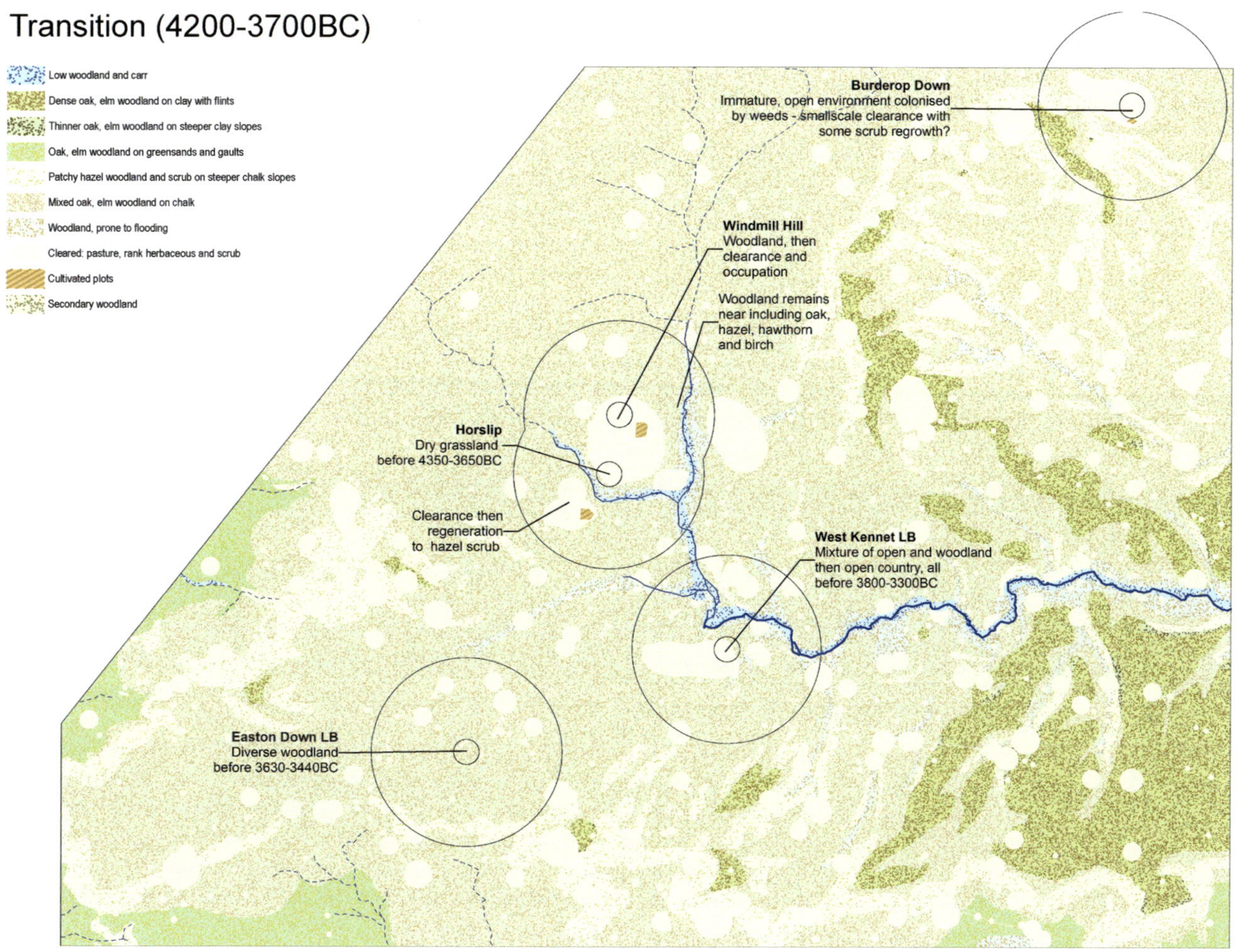

Figure 5.5. Landscape of the Mesolithic/Neolithic transition

3370–2910BC. Three of the samples (their stratigraphic relationship, if any, is not recorded) indicate woodland, while the fourth indicates long-lived (grazed) grassland. Pollen from this horizon suggests on-site open conditions with nearby scrub/woodland margin (predominantly hazel, then lime, some pine and oak) while both oak and hazel charcoal were also present.

One of the best dated sequences is that from Easton Down long barrow (Whittle *et al.* 1993) where the old land surface beneath the barrow contained a turfline dated to 3630–3440BC and construction of the barrow took place perhaps around 3500BC (although dates span 3650 to 3100BC). Molluscan evidence suggests that clearance of the existing woodland occurred not long before the monument's construction, culminating in grassland with a vegetation boundary or nearby woodland. Pollen indicates that the wider environment consisted of a mosaic of grassland, wasteground, bracken and scrub surrounding the site, while plant remains show some evidence of cereals in the area. At Millbarrow, pre-barrow post-holes and pits, dated to between 3910 and 3380BC (Whittle 1994) provide soil evidence for disturbance, possibly cultivation, while the primary fill of the outer ditches contain a molluscan fauna indicative of short grassland. From this, the excavators suggest that the barrow was constructed in an open environment, a sequence that is similar to the situation at West Kennet long barrow which seems to have been constructed in an environment of dry open grassland sometime between 3800–3300BC (Gowlett *et al.* 1986).

This is also the main phase of activity at causewayed enclosures in the region. The early occupation at Windmill Hill continued during

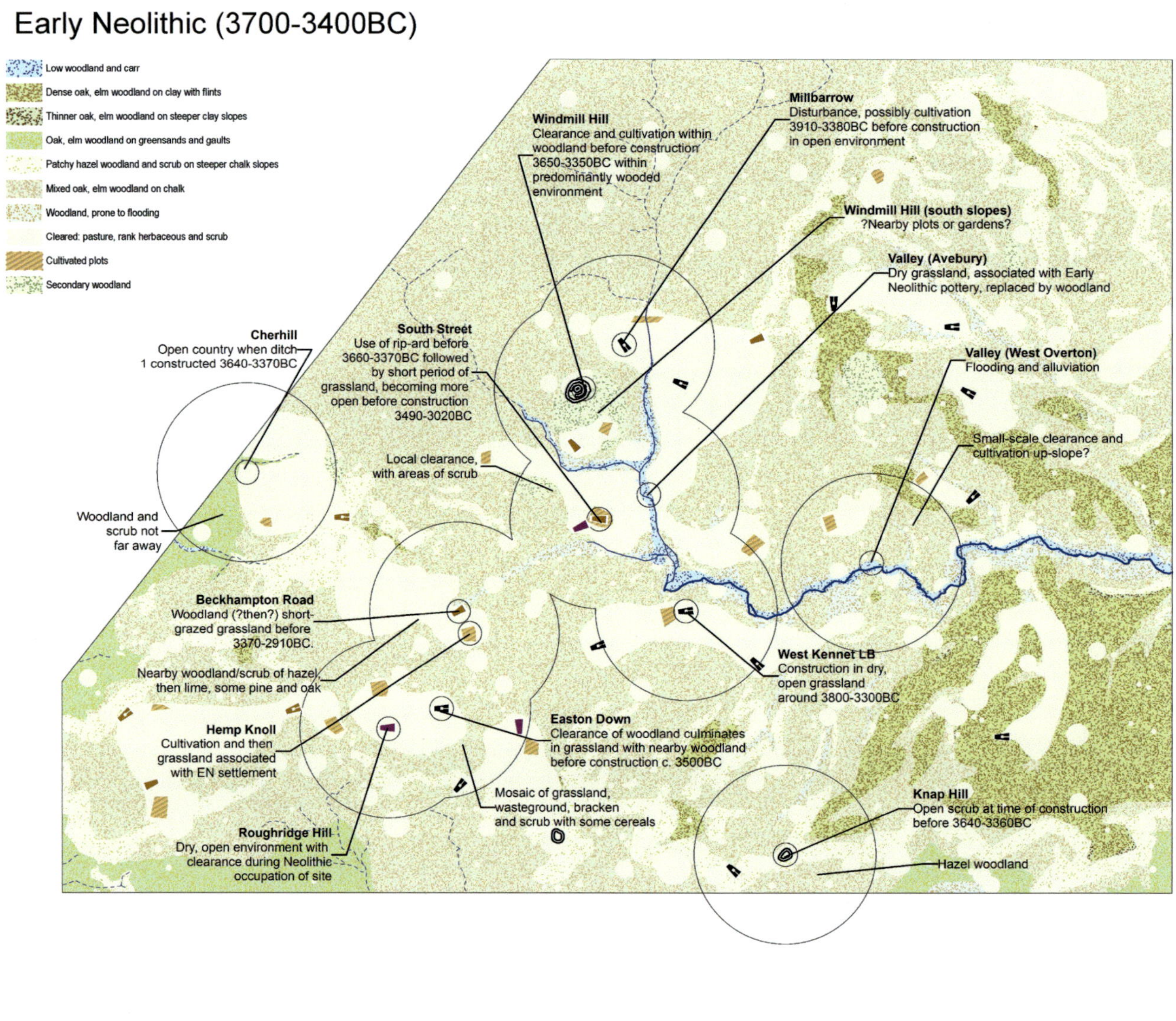

Figure 5.6. Landscape of the early Neolithic

this phase, with clearance and cultivation amongst woodland. There is also evidence from the south slope of Windmill Hill, outside the enclosure, for further earlier Neolithic activity with deposition of worked flint, and pits containing cereals, wild seeds, fruits, nuts and remains of vegetable tubers all of which could imply the existence somewhere nearby of plots or gardens. The construction of the three circuits of enclosure ditch *c.*3650–3350BC as either one or several events, appears to have taken place in a predominantly woodland environment. The primary ditch fills at Knap Hill (Connah 1964) have almost exactly the same date as Windmill Hill of 3640–3360BC, before which the buried soil beneath the enclosure bank (associated with Windmill Hill pottery) must date. As discussed above, the best interpretation of the pre-enclosure environment at Knap Hill may be of a patchy woodland, with the steep slopes nearby perhaps dominated by a mixture of hazel scrub and woodland.

A possible settlement site with early Neolithic bowl pottery is associated with the buried soil beneath Hemp Knoll round barrow (Robertson-Mackay 1980), dated to *c.*3500–3100BC, suggesting that a grassland environment may have already been cultivated at some time in the past. At Roughridge Hill, pre-barrow pits associated with early Neolithic pottery also contained a molluscan fauna indicating a dry, open environment. Here, the excavators state that clearance of former woodland was accomplished during Neolithic occupation of the site. At Cherhill, the digging and primary fill of ditch 1 is associated with plain Neolithic pottery and dated to before 3640–3370BC. It contained an open country molluscan fauna, indicating clearance of

Figure 5.7. Landscape of the middle Neolithic

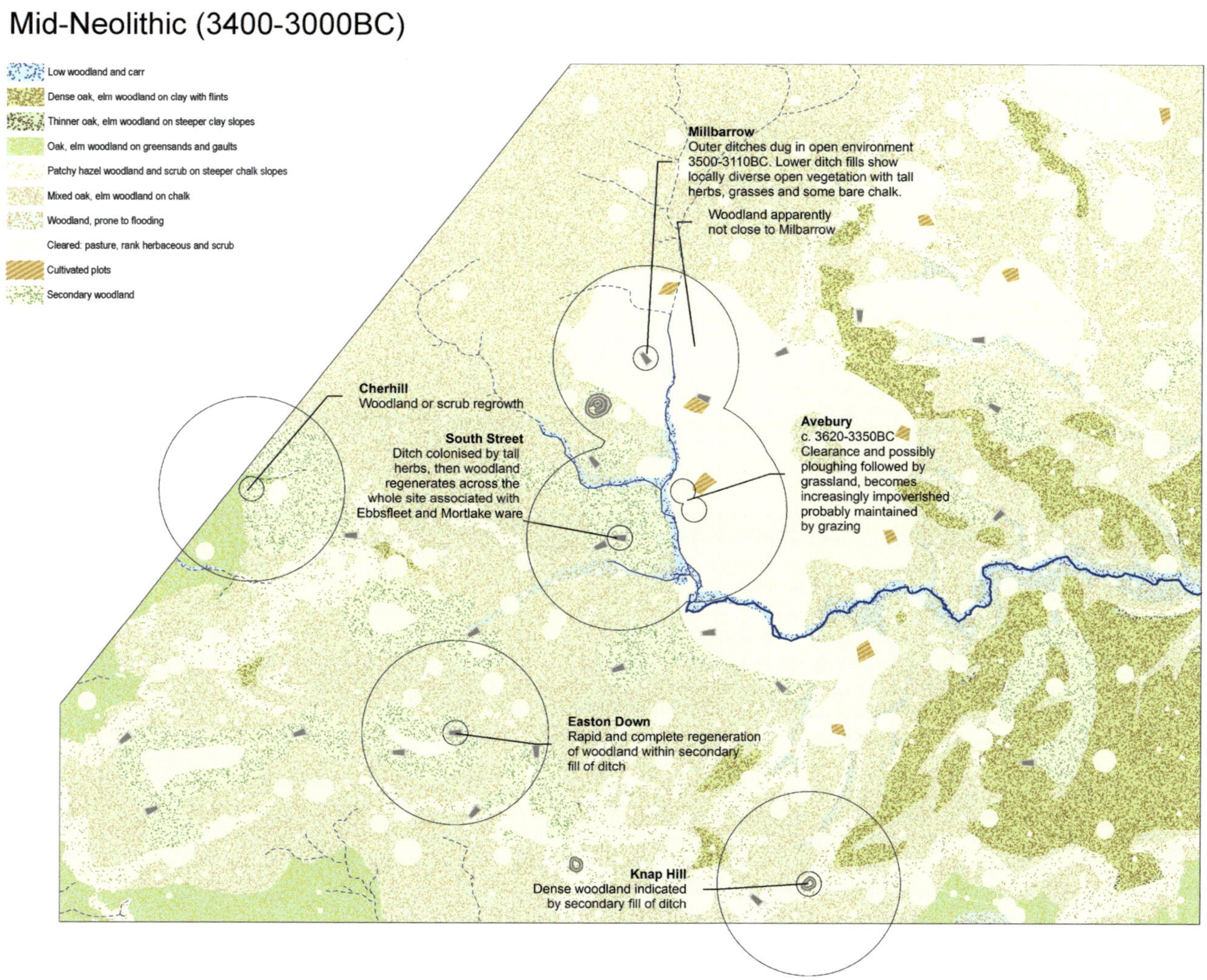

(presumably primary) Mesolithic woodland at this time, although woodland and/or scrub were never very far away.

Changes in the Kennet valley itself are shown by molluscan faunas from valley deposits at Avebury, where dry grassland (similar to that of chalk downland) replaced earlier woodland in layers associated with early Neolithic pottery. Lower down the valley at West Overton deposits showing flooding and alluviation, with upslope cultivation and woodland clearance, are associated with early Neolithic flint and pottery, although it is suggested that the response to clearance in terms of sedimentation is weak, and therefore probably indicates rather small-scale events. The dispersal of long mounds across the region suggests that areas of clearance and cultivation extended at least as far south and west as Roughridge Hill and Cherhill, and activity may also have continued to intensify on the Marlborough Downs.

Middle Neolithic (*c.*3400–3000BC)

This phase corresponds broadly with Whittle's phase D (1993, 35) for which he argues that there is a trend to more scrub or woodland in the Avebury area, and that little monument building takes place. Regeneration of woodland at this time is suggested from at least four sites. The secondary filling of the South Street ditch indicates that, at first, the long barrow's flanking ditches became colonised by tall herbs, but that by the time of the deposition of the top of the secondary fill (associated with Ebbsfleet and Mortlake pottery) woodland had regenerated across the whole site. Further to the east, at Cherhill, there is also evidence for woodland/scrub regrowth over the site that probably relates to this period and to the south-east at Easton Down long barrow there is evidence for rapid and complete regeneration of woodland within the secondary fill of the ditch. At Knap Hill too, the secondary fill of the ditch indicated a dense woodland environment.

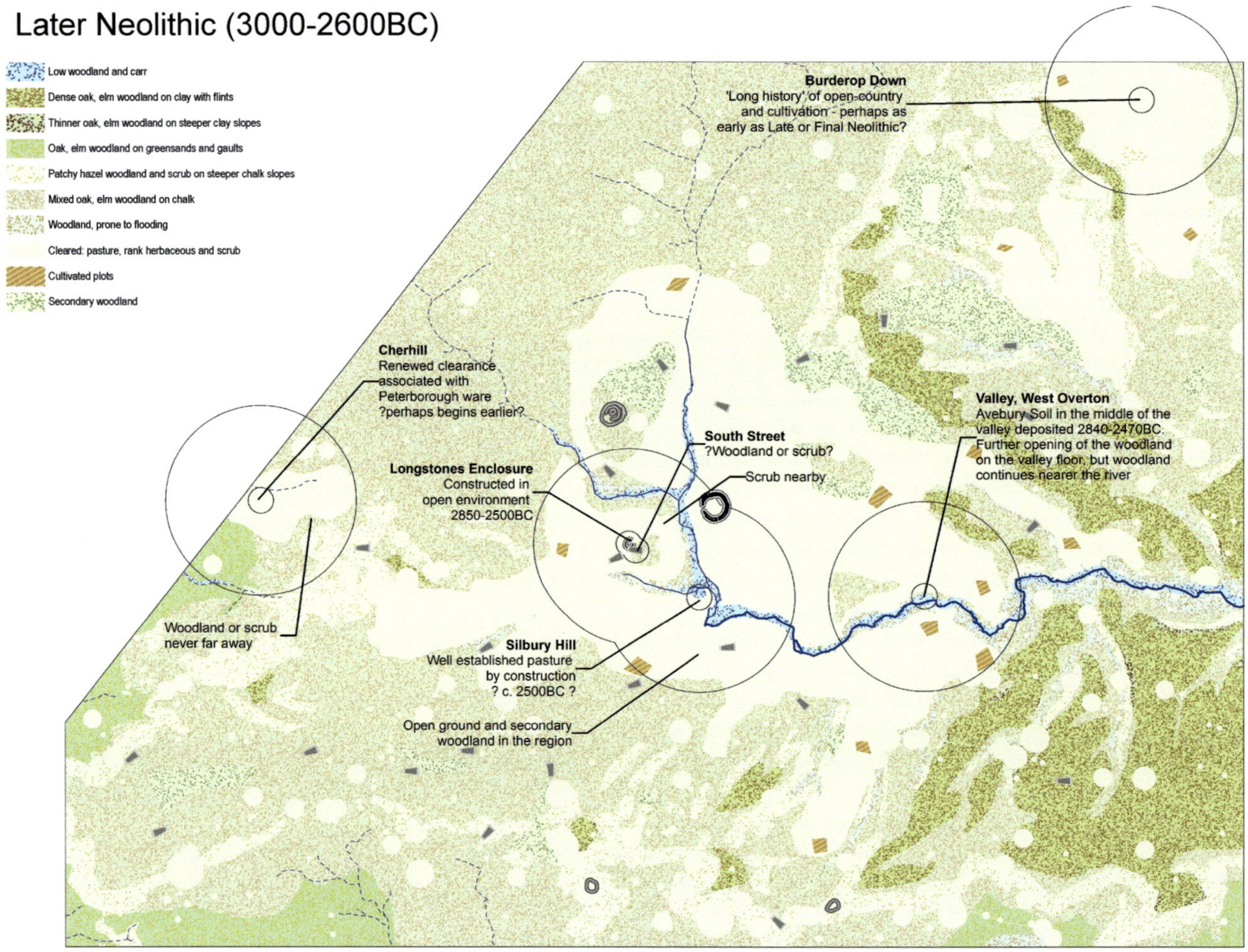

Figure 5.8. Landscape of the later Neolithic

The situation at Millbarrow is less clear cut. The outer ditches appear to have been dug around 3500–3110BC in an open environment, probably of short-turfed grassland. The secondary fill then accumulated with a locally diverse open vegetation in the ditch, with tall herbs, grasses and some bare chalk. It is suggested that there is a lack of human disturbance. Woodland is not very close although the upper secondary fill in the outer ditch does show eventual establishment of woodland on the site (although this may date to a little later). At Avebury itself there is no sign of woodland or scrub regeneration around this time. The turf-line of the pre-bank soil has a date of 3620–3350BC from the barn excavations, and the molluscan sequence suggests clearance, possibly ploughing, followed by grassland which became increasingly impoverished over time, and was ultimately ungrazed or lightly grazed. This is confirmed by the Avebury School excavations, where the same pre-bank soil similarly indicated clearance, possibly ploughing, followed by short-turfed grassland probably of long duration, most likely maintained by grazing.

The number of relevant horizons with environmental indicators that can be reliably attributed to this phase is actually rather small and evidence for woodland regeneration mainly derives from the ditches of long barrows. This evidence certainly could support the assertion of an economic and/or social hiatus through the whole area, although it appears that woodland regeneration was not taking place at Avebury at the time, and woodland was apparently not very close to Millbarrow either.

An alternative interpretation of these sequences might be that long barrows became isolated copses of woodland within a landscape that actually continued to be cleared, albeit we have no evidence for that continued clearance as it did not involve building new monuments

Figure 5.9. Landscape of the final Neolithic

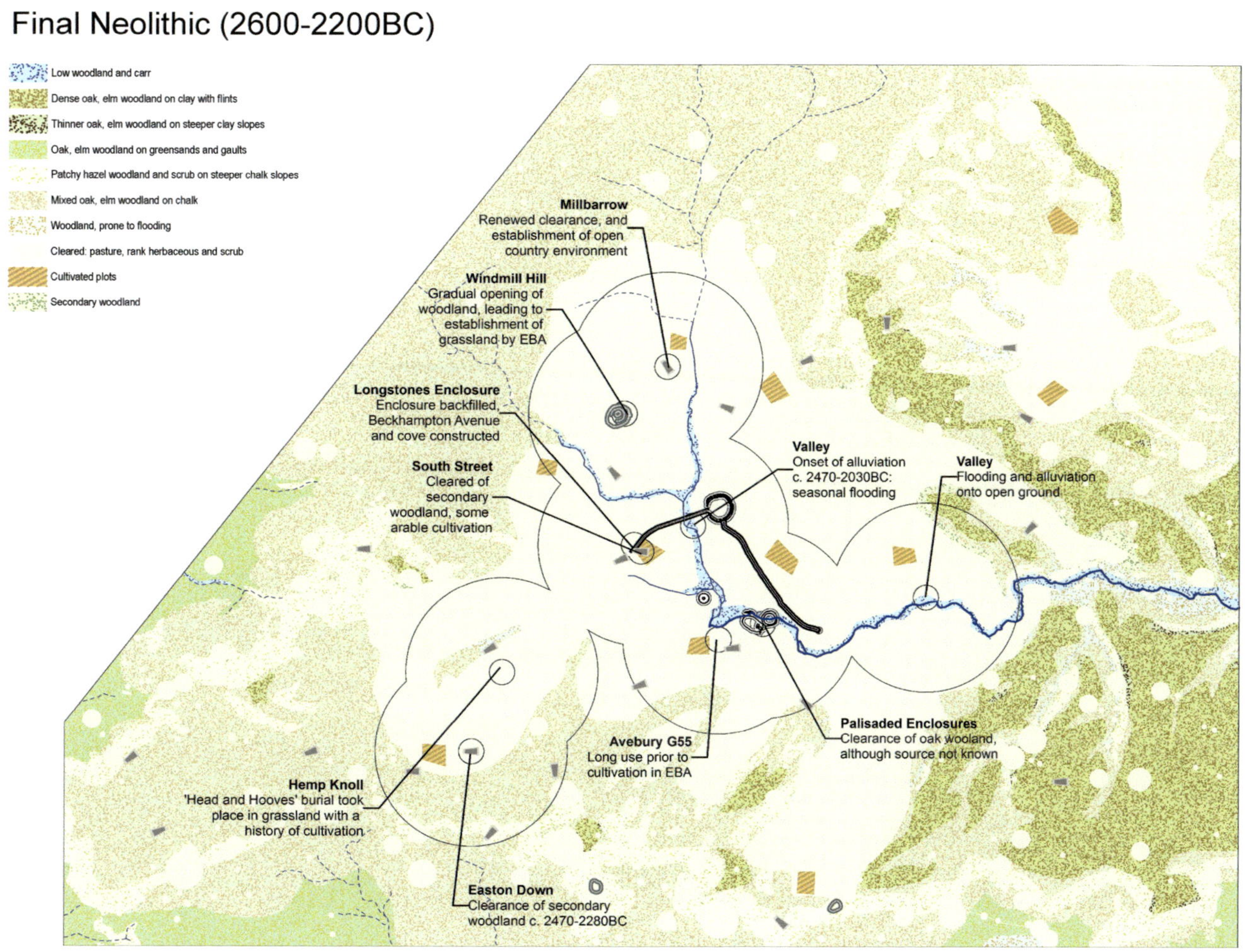

whose deposits date to this period. If the end of the earlier Neolithic is seen as more of a social and cultural re-orientation than an economic hiatus, then the avoidance of earlier monuments, or perhaps a continued use that involved allowing them to revert to woodland, could be envisaged. This, however, does not so easily explain the woodland regeneration at Cherhill or Knap Hill, and until more evidence is available we may do better to think of the changes to the landscape as a re-focusing of activity onto the core area around the Kennet rather than a global contraction of opened areas. This would also provide a plausible landscape context for the later and final Neolithic sequence of monuments which differs so markedly from the earlier Neolithic in its concentration of monument-construction activity around the upper reaches of the Kennet valley itself.

Figure 5.7 suggests how the landscape may have developed in this way, with the opening of the landscape to the east of the valley around what was to become the Avebury monument complex continuing, while cleared areas to the west of the region from South Street westwards may have been abandoned and allowed to regenerate to secondary woodland. There is no firm evidence for the situation on the Marlborough Downs to the north east of the region, although the reconstruction speculates that clearances and settlement may have continued here through this timespan.

Later Neolithic (*c.*3000–2600BC)

In the west of the region, although there is clearly evidence for woodland regeneration in the earlier part of the middle Neolithic, Cherhill provides evidence for renewed clearance in a buried soil associated with Peterborough

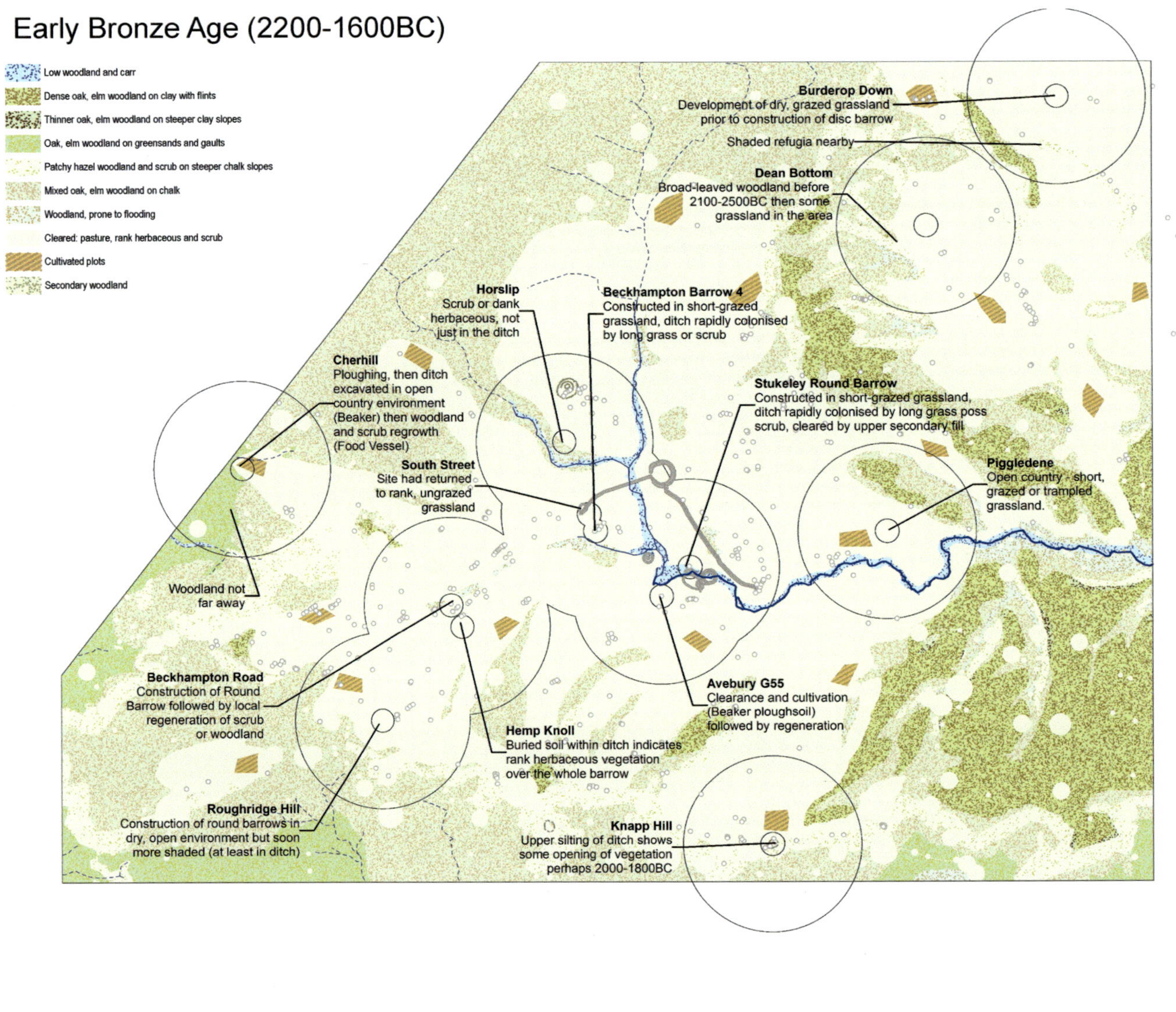

Figure 5.10. Landscape of the early Bronze Age

pottery which could represent activity late in the middle Neolithic phase (*c.*3200BC onwards), or early in the later Neolithic. Either way, woodland or scrub appears to never have been very far away.

On the higher downland to the north-east, the disc barrow next to Burderop Down sealed a Neolithic ploughsoil that revealed a long history of open country and cultivation, while – as described above – the subsoil hollow beneath it suggested that primary woodland had long since been cleared from the vicinity.

It is within this open grazed grassland that the Longstones enclosure was constructed around 2820–2660BC, then backfilled perhaps two or three centuries later, and through which the Beckhampton Avenue was constructed. Although no analysis of the pre-construction environment was possible, soil micromorphology (Lewis, Chapter 2) suggests that an argillic brownearth once present at the site had already developed into a rendzina by the time of construction so that, while woodland must have once been present, clearance must have taken place some considerable time before construction. The molluscan analysis (Mount *et al.*, Chapter 2) of ditch fills suggests a dry, open environment which persisted throughout the life of the enclosure. This was probably short grassland maintained, presumably, by animal grazing. The possibility of nearby scrub is also suggested by the presence of a few shade-loving mollusca in the ditch and charcoals of blackthorn, hazel, birch, hawthorn and gorse may hint at the general species mix of this. Although there was some woodland nearby, then, no trees were allowed to grow on or around the enclosure between its excavation and deliberate backfilling.

This needs to be set alongside evidence from

Figure 5.11. Landscape of the middle Bronze Age

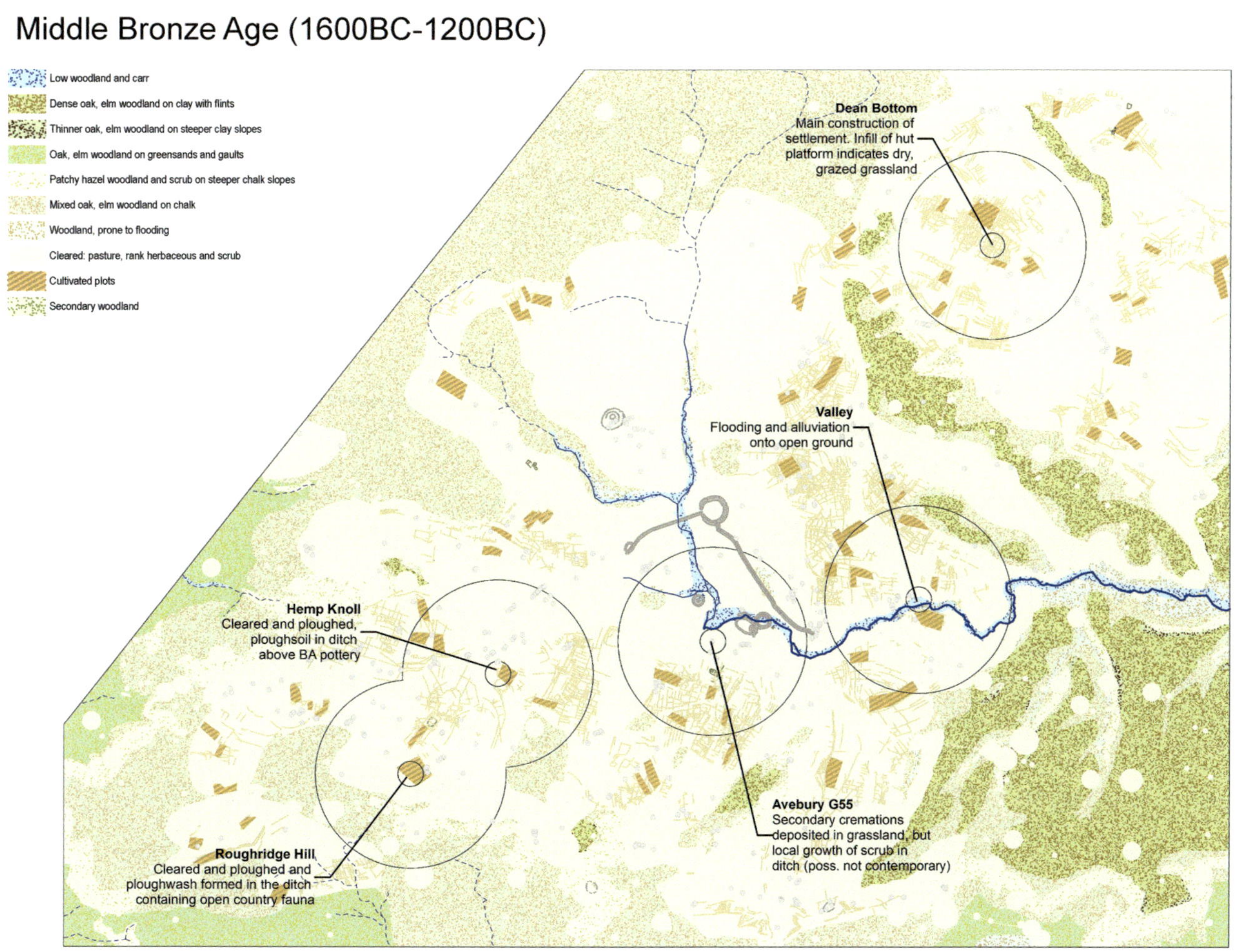

South Street, less than 100m east of the Longstones enclosure. The cultivation episode shown by the ard marks cut into the buried soil beneath South Street (3490–3020BC) correlates well with the suggestion from the soil analysis of the Longstones enclosure that a rendzina had developed by the time of the latter's construction. Grassland must therefore have existed in the vicinity for far longer than the 10–20 years after cultivation suggested by Evans for South Street itself (Ashbee *et al.* 1979). Perhaps more interestingly, South Street provides evidence for woodland regeneration during the middle Neolithic, perhaps a few hundred years earlier than construction of the Longstones enclosure (3361–2782BC).

It is tempting to see these two sites as complementary, with the Longstones fauna demonstrating renewed clearance in the whole area after a mid-Neolithic woodland regeneration shown by the South Street sequence. However, the presence of shade-loving species in the Longstones molluscan fauna also suggests the existence of shaded refugia around 1600m from the site which easily includes South Street itself, and may allow greater credence to be given to the alternative suggestion (Mount *et al.*, Chapter 2) that South Street could have become a wooded refugia by the later Neolithic while the area around continued to become increasingly, if patchily, more open.

The reconstruction in Figure 5.8 envisages that the extraordinary range of monument building that took place during this time did so within an already fairly open landscape around the site of Avebury, within which a mosaic of secondary and surviving primary woodland would have been found. Traces of earlier human activity at, for example, South Street and Windmill Hill may have been encountered or visited within wooded copses, from which social prohibition prevented the significant cutting of trees or opening of the landscape.

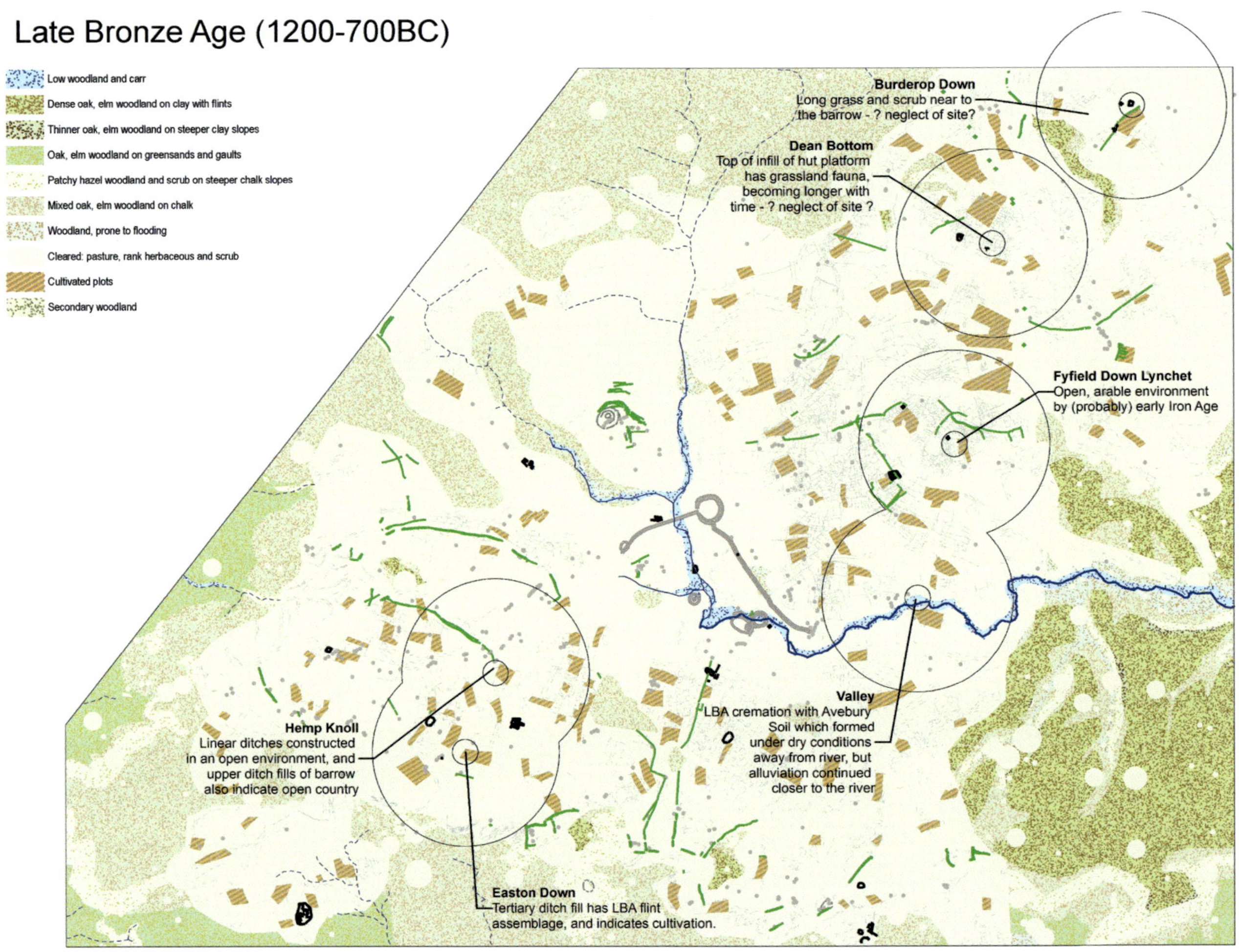

Figure 5.12. Landscape of the later Bronze Age

Some of the early structures at Avebury seem to have been constructed early in this phase, perhaps around 3000BC, in far more open countryside. The first bank (and inferred ditch) at Avebury must have been constructed around this time, as could the Cove.

Within the by now largely open Upper Kennet Valley the impact of even the first earthwork at Avebury must have been immense. Although the scale of the first earthwork, and even its architectural style, may not have differed hugely from the causewayed enclosure at Windmill Hill, its position is rather less obviously prominent: it is, in fact, located on a small rise that is barely visible from the south and south-west. The earthwork itself – particularly when new – may have been intended partly as a very public statement. Its centrality of position and the openness of the landscape around it ensured that it was visible not from the approaches to the region, as sites such as Windmill Hill may have been, but from much of the occupied landscape of it – the space within which the community went about its habitual activities. Rather than a marginal place of meeting, encountered at special times of the year, Avebury would have been experienced by the community in its daily round, passing through and/or past the enclosure in order to move around the area. As the various enhancements and additions to the monument developed, including the second, immense bank and ditch and other architectural elements of the henge, the visual impact of this monument must have – as researchers such as Barrett (1994) and Thomas (1993) have argued – not only reflected but also generated social change.

Elsewhere the landscape must have continued to be opened and transformed. The population expansion that must be evidenced by the sheer scale of monument construction, must suggest an acceleration of the opening of tracts of landscape for animal grazing and perhaps cultivation. The Marlborough Downs may have become substantially cleared during this and the succeeding time span, leaving sarsen stones that had marked clearings and pathways for generations now exposed to a visual appropriation that was to be followed in the final Neolithic and early Bronze Age by a physical one.

Final Neolithic (*c.*2600–2200BC)

The character of the valley floor seems also to have changed significantly towards the end of the Neolithic: at Avebury, the onset of alluviation dates to perhaps 2470–2030BC indicating seasonal flooding of grassland, while lower down the valley at West Overton the 'Avebury soil' towards the middle of the valley floor produced a date of 2840–2470BC and contained later Neolithic flint and pottery, including Beaker which suggests the latter end of that range. Molluscan evidence suggests further opening up of woodland on the valley floor itself, with relatively dry grassland away from the river but continuation of woodland nearer to the river. This is followed by deposition of the 'West Overton Formation', with flooding and alluviation onto open ground perhaps after *c.*2400BC (Figure 5.9). The onset of significant levels of alluvial deposition in the valley does suggest an increase in the surface area that was unprotected by vegetation, most likely in arable cultivation in the upper reaches of the river catchment. At the same time, this phase seems to represent a significant acceleration of monument construction activities in the region with the creation of the Outer Circle at Avebury, the Avenues, the Sanctuary and Silbury Hill, closely associated with Grooved Ware pottery which appears in the record from around *c.*2800BC. Although it seems likely that the main megalithic settings at Avebury were erected at this time, it is also probable that the erection and/or replacement of stones could have continued well into the early Bronze Age. Of equal relevance to the landscape is the major shift towards the keeping and consuming of pigs that is evident from faunal remains from, for example, the West Kennet palisade enclosures.

Around Windmill Hill this phase probably saw a gradual opening up of the woodland, leading to the eventual establishment of grassland by the early Bronze Age. There was limited use of the enclosure ditches and also further occupation evidence from the south slope of the hill, outside the enclosure. Nearby at Millbarrow, the top of the secondary fill in the outer ditch shows renewed clearance of the site, with the establishment of an open country environment, probably grassland. This may also be broadly contemporary with the final backfilling event at Longstones enclosure prior to the erection of the Beckhampton Avenue, which also appears to have taken place in an open environment.

Construction of Silbury Hill took place during this phase (Bayliss *et al.* 2007). The primary mound was created in a well-established pasture/non-arable clearing, although the wider environment included both open ground and secondary woodland. The turf stack preserved a pollen sequence that indicated grassland, while insect remains suggest herb-rich, lightly grazed grassland and a radius of open ground of several hundred metres. The primary woodland (oak and lime) in the neighbourhood gradually retreated and was replaced by secondary woodland dominated by hazel and alder. This was followed by regeneration of hazel scrub on the site itself, in perhaps a mosaic of woodland and open ground, while seeds and mosses indicated mature grassland. Evans (1972, 266) concluded that the snail profile from the mound indicated an ancient plough soil, which had formed a thin turf line before burial, supporting dry, open grassland.

Close to Silbury, the West Kennet palisaded enclosures were being built using timber that appears to derive from managed secondary oak woodland (although dates range from *c.*2800–2000BC and the relative chronology of these monuments is not entirely clear). Whittle (1997b) speculates this timber may have derived from the clay-with-flints around 4km away although, interestingly, Easton Down long barrow is also about 4km from West Kennet and there the upper secondary ditch fill of the long barrow (dated to between 2470 and 2280BC) appears to show clearance of secondary woodland. It would be easy to read too much into that, but it does suggest that the timber for the palisades could have come from extended or renewed clearances on the chalk downs as from encroachments into clay-with-flints. Regardless of the source of materials, the building of Silbury and the construction of the palisade enclosures must both have been intimately bound up with substantial alteration of the environment. The stripping of turf for the mound at Silbury has already been mentioned, indicating the conversion of a substantial area of pasture to bare ground (at least temporarily), but the construction of the palisaded enclosures are equally important, providing direct evidence for the felling of about 2000 individual, mature trees (Whittle 1997b), which of itself represents the clearance of several hectares of woodland.

The later and final Neolithic acceleration in monument construction and the level of intervention in the landscape also coincides with a shift from raising cattle to keeping pigs, the implications of which have been commented on by, for example, Grigson (1982) and Smith (1984; 1985). It was noted above how the relative proportions of domestic animal remains cannot be easily interpreted as indicators of the environment close to the site of excavation because the taphonomy and social context of animal rearing, exchange and consumption are too complex. This point was reinforced by analysis of material from Durrington Walls (Richards and Thomas 1984), where deposition of faunal remains was argued to be highly 'structured' and which has subsequently also raised the possibility of 'ritual hunting' with bow and arrow (Albarella and Serjeantson 2002). Domestic pigs are highly flexible animals that are capable of consuming an extraordinary range of food including meat, vegetables, fruit, dairy products, carrion and even human excreta. Keeping them requires food, shade and water: the regular flooding of the valley floor would have suited them far more than cattle. Grigson considers it most likely that pigs were overwintered in captivity, with sows and young kept in until June or July and fed on whatever was available during that time, perhaps surplus cereals, stored fruits, nuts and various types of waste (1982, 305). Their dominance suggests the development of pannage, the tradition of turning out domestic pig into woodland to feed on acorns (and more recently beechmast) in the autumn, and they could also have been turned out onto cultivated land in the spring and after harvest where they would have eaten various kinds of vegetation, rooted for insects and worms or fed on carrion. Pigs eat various bulbs and rhizomes which may be beneficial in preventing cultivated plots becoming infested with bracken and weeds, and their rooting may also have softened the ground making cultivation easier. Within woodland, they would have significantly suppressed ground cover, reduced the diversity of the understorey, and promoted regeneration of some tree species over others – probably birch over oak (Grigson 1982, 300).

As a straightforward indicator of the range of environments present in the region at this time, therefore, the shift towards pig keeping –

or away from cattle (Thomas 1999b, 26) – does little more than suggest the continued presence of woodland for shelter and pannage, some of which may have had significantly less understorey shrubs and plants than previously. There are other implications, however. With a short gestation period, average litters of around six in the spring and rapid growth rates, pig rearing can produce prolific amounts of meat in shorter periods of time than other domesticated animals. This may have made it possible to 'gear up' meat production at particular times for feasting or ceremonial consumption associated with monument construction (Richards and Thomas 1984). If pannage was practiced at this time, then this may also hint at a change in how some parts of the woodland were conceived: it is possible that some woodland may have now come to be regarded less as 'wildwood' and more as a tenured resource.

It is worth briefly comparing the environmental evidence for character of the Avebury landscape during the construction of the major monuments with nearby chalkland landscapes with contemporary monument complexes. Allen (1997; 2000a) has reviewed the environmental evidence for Salisbury Plain, and described how that landscape may have developed over a similar time span to that used here and although there are many similarities with the Avebury region, there may also be interesting differences. Scaife (in Cleal *et al.* 2004) has recently reported a polleniferous sediment from the Avon valley near Durrington Walls which is argued to represent the environmental conditions during the Neolithic. The deposit analysed (Durrington 2) overlay a Devensian/early Flandrian deposit (which produced a date of around 7200BC) and was separated from it by a marked hiatus in deposition. Above, it was sealed by a much later deposit containing Roman pottery. While the possibility that the deposit may be Bronze Age is acknowledged by the author, he argues that it is likely to date to the Neolithic from the presence of cereals and by comparison with nearby molluscan evidence from Durrington Walls (Evans 1971a) and Woodhenge (Evans and Jones 1979). If a Neolithic date is accepted then the earlier-middle Neolithic landscape of the Avon valley prior to the development of the Durrington complex shows 'substantial evidence for anthropogenic activity in the local area and specifically for arable activity' (Cleal *et al.* 2004, 231) and raises the 'interesting possibility that such clearance and land use was responsible for the re-initiation of sedimentation in the Allen valley after a hiatus of possibly thousands of years' (Cleal *et al.* 2004, 232), attributable to clearance of interfluvial ridges during the earlier or middle Neolithic. There may also be similarities between the upper Avon valley and the upper Allen valley where recent findings point to vegetation and landscape change taking place earlier than previously thought and where a 'stable soil, slope and valley system was established well before the 3rd millennium BC' (French and Lewis 2005).

In the case of both Avon and Allen valleys, therefore, current interpretations suggest significant clearance during the 4th millennium BC which contrasts with the Avebury landscape where, although there is some indication of flooding and alluviation associated with early Neolithic pottery at West Overton (Mount 1991; Evans *et al.* 1993), evidence suggests that rather little alluviation and sediment deposition took place in the river valley until around 2500–2400BC. These difference may reflect the different times at which the intensity of clearance and agriculture on ridges reached a sufficient density to initiate significant levels of loss from soils, although it must be recognised that the source of the sediment (and hence the postulated location of agricultural clearance) is unknown beyond the obvious statement that it derived from hillsides further up the river. Nevertheless, both the beginnings of the construction activity at Durrington, and the earlier (*c.*3200BC) development of the Dorset Cursus may have taken place in significantly more open environments than previously believed, while construction activity around Avebury may have been initiated in a far less generally open landscape.

It is also worth focussing briefly on two aspects of the change that this final Neolithic phase seems to bring in the Avebury landscape: first the appropriation of sarsens from the dry valleys and the Marlborough Downs for use in the monument complex, and second the connecting together of significant places with the Avenues. The use of sarsens in monuments does not start at this time. Many of the early Neolithic long mounds are megalithic structures with chambers of sarsen, for example

West Kennet, and sarsens also occur beneath both Beckhampton Road and South Street long barrows. In addition, some other megalithic structures may also be early (such as the Avebury Cove, discussed in Chapter 4). However, the scale of movement and the size of the stones involved does seem to increase at this time. Many of these stones must have been transported from the Marlborough Downs, where the continued opening of the landscape may have so radically changed their setting that they came to be thought of as moveable objects for the first time. Instead of places, some of the stones now became artefacts that could be appropriated into new projects complete with their associations, stories and histories.

Accounts of this process have inevitably tended to focus on changes that took place in areas the sarsens were *moved into*, rather than *removed from*. The importance of the emergence of a large-scale sarsen architecture, however, is as much to do with changes taking place on the higher downland as the architecture of Avebury and as such it would have transformed both. On the high downs, the removal of significant numbers of sarsen stones for incorporation within the monument would have created space. This would perhaps have been less physical (although the actual area of the stones involved may be non-trivial) as symbolic, in that the high downs must previously have been richly populated with stones, each potentially with deep associations. The steady removal of these must have changed the cognitive landscape of the high downs beyond recognition, leaving them far less redolent with the kind of cosmological significance that was now attached to the monument complex itself. Released from some of these meanings, perhaps even becoming a landscape of absence or even loss, the high downs may from this point onwards have been ripe for the kind of agrarian reorganisation and settlement that we see come to full fruition in later prehistory.

The flip side of this process is the increased formality and symbolic architecture of the Avebury complex itself. The architecture of the Avenues has been discussed in Chapter 3, and the results of this project have to some extent undermined the conventional notion that they formed monumentalised routes of procession. It now seems possible that they may have been laid out next to, rather than along existing paths, and there must now be significant doubt that they formed continuous pairs of stones in the way previously imagined. Whether or not the Avenues were intended for actual processions, however, they do reflect some concern with movement through the landscape, and with connecting up existing places of importance.

Early Bronze Age (*c.*2200–1600BC)

One of the features of a number of sites from this period is the presence of 'Beaker plough-soils': cultivation horizons with sometimes quite numerous sherds of Beaker pottery incorporated within them (as, for example, at Cherhill and Avebury G55). These have been interpreted as evidence for the spreading of domestic rubbish, animal and plant refuse on cultivated plots to increase fertility. More recently, it has been suggested that the breaking and scattering of Beaker pottery within soil may be more intentional. Evans (2003) suggests that this is part of a process of 'entexturing' that helped people understand the land: 'It may even be that Beaker pottery was made with this specific intention in mind, to break it up into small yet still quite recognizable fragments and scatter in on the soil', further that Beaker pottery occurs in soils which formed across the ditches of earlier monuments suggests 'that the ploughing and the pottery were symbols of opposition or cancellation, ways of eradicating the past' (2003, 81). What may be happening is therefore partly a change in treatment of earlier monuments. While many of these appear to have been allowed to regenerate to woodland, from the middle Neolithic onwards, or perhaps found other non-agricultural uses (pannage, for example) the focus for cultivation in the final Neolithic and early Bronze Age may now have been explicitly centred on opening up areas of woodland formerly not cleared *because* they contained earlier monuments and the 'entexturing' of these places with pottery may perhaps be intimately related to the need to re-admit these places to the productive landscape (Figure 5.10). In the east of the region, at Cherhill, the area over ditch 1 was ploughed at this time and ditch 2 was excavated, also associated with Beaker pottery. Molluscan evidence demonstrates an open country environment, with some arable cultivation, but with woodland or scrub never very far away.

If so, then the pattern was not repeated

everywhere in the region. At Horslip long barrow, the lower buried soil within the ditch (associated with Beaker pottery) shows an environment of scrub or dank herbaceous vegetation which is probably not just confined to within the ditch. The ploughsoil at Avebury G55, which contained early Neolithic, Peterborough and Beaker pottery, produced a molluscan fauna indicative of a long history of use, ending with a period of cultivation which the fauna in pre-barrow pits (associated with long-necked Beaker) suggest was then followed by regeneration of woodland. Molluscan evidence from the pre-barrow soil and turf stack at Hemp Knoll, suggests that construction of the round barrow (with 'head and hooves' burial and Beaker) took place in grassland with a history of cultivation.

Further from the centre of the region, to the south the upper silting of the ditch at Knap Hill is dated to 2600–1800BC, associated with long-necked Beakers, and shows some opening up of the vegetation on this site. To the north, the evidence from the disc barrow next to Burderop Down shows development of dry, grazed grassland on the site prior to construction of the disc barrow, while the barrow ditch itself contained longer vegetation and indicated the nearby presence of shaded refugia, suggesting that the clearance was fairly localised. The pre-settlement Beaker activity at Dean Bottom, consisting of three features and a storage pit, produced a molluscan fauna indicating broad-leaved woodland prior to 2500–2100BC, at which time midden material was deliberately dumped at the site. It is claimed by Allen (in Gingell 1992) that the fauna from this material provides evidence of long grassland/scrub indicating poorly managed downland, but given the taphonomic considerations that relate to midden deposition it is hard to sustain the view that this deposit is a simple reflection of the local environment. The auger survey of Piggledene produced a buried soil, overlain by colluvial deposits. This soil contained Beaker sherds and also an open country molluscan fauna suggesting dry, short, grazed or trampled grassland. Whatever the date of the woodland indicated by lower deposits, it is clear that it had been cleared by this date.

Where environmental indicators can be assigned to this phase, they often show local conditions of scrub or ungrazed grassland prevailing soon after construction activities. Construction of the round barrow (associated with Collared Urn) at the site of Beckhampton Road long barrow is one example. Although the immediate site was presumably clear at the time of construction, molluscs from the primary ditch fill and turf line indicate local regeneration of scrub or woodland soon after. The turfline of the buried soil complex at South Street also contained Bronze Age pottery, including a Food Vessel, and molluscan analysis indicates that the site had returned to rank, ungrazed grassland at this time. At Cherhill the lower buried soil in ditch 2 is associated with Food Vessel, and molluscs appear to show woodland or scrub regrowth. Similarly at Hemp Knoll, molluscan analysis of the buried soil within the round barrow ditch indicates rank herbaceous vegetation (or perhaps scrub) over the whole area of the barrow. A similar sequence from Roughridge Hill indicates construction of round barrows within a dry, open environment, but by the time that the ditch filling had stabilised and a buried soil had formed a more shaded environment existed, at least within the ditch. Woodland and scrub was probably never very far away throughout this sequence. Presumably the Stukeley and Beckhampton 4 round barrows (Powell *et al.* 1996) also relate to the early Bronze Age. Molluscan analysis shows that the first of these was constructed in short-grazed grassland (primary ditch fill), but the ditch fairly rapidly became colonised with long grass, possibly scrub (secondary fill), which had been cleared by the time of the upper secondary fill that contained a fauna indicative of short grazed grassland again. Similarly, Beckhampton round barrow 4 also appears to have been constructed in short-grazed grassland (molluscan fauna from primary ditch fill) and its ditch too become fairly rapidly colonised with long grass or scrub (secondary fill). There is at least one exception to this pattern however: the early Bronze Age soil in the ditch at Easton Down long barrow developed in open country conditions, possibly with light cultivation.

If it were not for the Beaker ploughsoils, therefore, these might actually be argued to provide clearer evidence for an episode of land abandonment in the early Bronze Age than that claimed for the mid Neolithic, perhaps associated with the end of major monument construction in the region. As for the ditches of earlier Neolithic monuments, however, these sequences might rather indicate the treatment of their immediate surroundings after construction. Any significant level of woodland regeneration across the landscape would also be expected to reduce the level of sediment run-off from the valley sides, which is clearly not supported either by the presence of Beaker ploughsoils or by the evidence from West Overton, where deposition of the 'West Overton Formation' continued to show flooding and alluviation onto open ground.

It is also the case that the vast majority of the round barrows must belong to this period (Cleal 2005, 117), and their distribution and sheer number also argue cogently against any significant or widespread woodland regeneration at this time. There are several interpretations of the distribution of round barrows ranging from Fowler and Blackwell's (1998) notion that they were located around the edges of cultivated land to avoid using the best farmland, to Cleal's detailed analysis that identified three typical situations of 'barrows and cemeteries overlooking rivers', 'barrows overlooking monuments' and 'barrows associated with winterbournes' with the second of these being 'by far the most common location for cemeteries' (2005b, 121). These may also be regarded as complementary to, rather than contradictory of, the more established notion that round barrows may have been constructed along tracks or pathways within the landscape. Whatever the detailed rationale behind the choice of location for round barrows, the environmental evidence does suggest that they may have generally been constructed in more marginal areas, and that their immediate environs were usually removed from grazing or cultivation after construction. With plenty of colonising species close by, their immediate environment would have quickly become overgrown and, in extreme cases, may have been absorbed back into the shifting edge of woodland. By contrast, other parts of the landscape continued to see a pattern of more formal cultivation and animal grazing. The scale of construction in the valley may have reduced considerably, but the stones and earthworks within it attracted continued attention: further stones may have been erected or replaced at this time, while burials with Beaker grave goods were inserted at the base of some stones at least in the earlier part of this phase. By the end of it, however, it seems clear that the emphasis for ceremonial activity was far more dispersed than it had been previously. Despite the possibility that barrow locations may have overlooked the monument complex, the monumental landscape no longer had a clear focus on the Upper Kennet Valley. Pasture, agriculture and scrub must have extended far away to the south-east and become well established on the Marlborough Downs.

Middle and later Bronze Age (*c.*1600–600BC)

Although only six environmental horizons in the area can be reliably assigned to the middle Bronze Age, there is little doubt from regional pollen diagrams that the environment became significantly more open during the mid to late 2nd millennium BC, resulting in the development of a landscape with a far more recognisably agrarian aspect (Figure 5.11). There seems to be a steady shift of emphasis away from the Neolithic and Early Bronze Age 'centre' of the region around the headwaters of the Kennet towards settlement and agricultural activity on the high downs to the east and south. It is unsurprising, therefore, that of the available sequences only Avebury G55 does not clearly indicate clearance or open conditions, and then the evidence is equivocal. A grassland molluscan fauna is associated with secondary cremations, deposited a few centuries after barrow construction but the possibly contemporary buried soil within the ditch, above the primary fill, contained a mollusc fauna indicating local growth of scrub. This difference could indicate that the two are not, in fact, contemporary although there also remains the clear possibility that it reflects the micro-environment of the ditch.

All other environmental indicators that can be placed in the middle Bronze Age indicate open landscape. Roughridge Hill was finally cleared and ploughed, and a ploughwash horizon (probably at this phase, although not precisely dated) formed in the ditch containing a restricted open country fauna. Hemp Knoll was also cleared and ploughed, with a ploughsoil within the ditch above a layer containing a Bronze Age flint industry. At Cherhill, there was clearance and establishment of grassland, probably over the entire site, during the infilling of ditch 2. Again, there is no precise dating evidence but the excavators believe this relates to the early or middle Bronze Age. The main occupation of the settlement site at Dean Bottom spans the middle to late Bronze Age, and the infill of a hut platform associated with Deverel-Rimbury and post-Deverel-Rimbury pottery produced a molluscan fauna indicating open, dry grazed grassland. In the valley at West Overton, alluvial deposition of the 'West Overton Formation' onto open ground around the river continued.

There is little doubt that the middle Bronze Age sees a significant shift in the ways that human communities existed within the landscape. The conventional view may be that this represents a series of economic and social changes that include greater craft specialisation, and certainly more permanent settlements. Evidence from those settlements – of which perhaps open settlements may be generally earlier than enclosed ones (McOmish 2005) – suggests far greater focus on intensive agriculture, evidenced by finds of quernstones and sarsen rubbers, while the field systems clearly imply a far more structured and intensive approach to cultivation that probably including systems of crop rotation. However, it may be misleading to view this as simply representing the end of monument construction and the beginning of functional agrarian activity. The economic trend away from shifting patterns of cultivation to a more fixed system of production and settlement certainly ensured that the new activities were more bound to the production of cereals and animals, but we might equally view these changes as a shift of emphasis away from a monument complex in the valley to a new monument complex composed, as before, of a range of familiar components such as earthworks, sarsen alignments and ditches.

The paucity of well dated later prehistoric sites in the core of the region makes it difficult to make specific references to environmental changes during the later Bronze Age there, but regional pollen diagrams leave little doubt that in general the landscape once again became more open at this time (Figures 5.11 and 5.12). From around 1000BC onwards these show the expansion of beech into Britain, which may have made a marked difference to the mixture of tree species on the chalklands as the soil became notably more calcareous as a result of the continued expansion of ploughing and clearance. At the edge of the valley at West Overton a middle or later Bronze Age cremation within the 'Avebury soil' indicates that the floodplain may now have consisted of more dry ground, although alluviation appears to have continued closer to the river. Higher up on the downs, many of the field systems and settlements (such as Burderop Down and Dean Bottom) were established or enlarged at this time and this phase may see the onset of significant colluviation. The top of the disc barrow ditch next to the late Bronze Age settlement at Burderop Down contained a fill that appears to have been deliberately dumped from the adjacent settlement. This contained a diverse, mixed molluscan assemblage claimed to indicate long grass and scrub near the barrow (interpreted as neglect of the site) within a setting of more managed, grazed or tilled landscape. The main occupation of the settlement at Dean Bottom continued into this period, and the top of the infill of a hut platform produced a grassland molluscan fauna, with the grass becoming longer as the site was neglected.

Although the Avebury complex may not have been the focus for the same scale of ceremonial activity in later prehistory, there is no real evidence that the area was abandoned or allowed to regenerate to woodland, and activity – of which the linear earthwork excavated to the west of the Longstones Cove (see Chapter 7) is an example – may have been widespread. At Hemp Knoll, for example, linear ditches were constructed in open environment at this time, and the upper fill of the barrow ditch also contains open country fauna. The distribution of field systems and, later, linear ditch systems may give some clue to the limits of the cleared landscape by the later Bronze Age. They do not currently seem to extend into the areas of clay-with-flints in the south-east of the region, hinting at the survival of woodland in this part of the region well into later prehistory (Kirkham 2005). The excavation (this volume) of a later prehistoric linear ditch adjacent to the Longstones suggests that their absence in the 'core' of the later Neolithic monument complex may have more to do with visibility and survival, however.

Monuments in their landscape

This chapter has strayed far beyond the immediate interpretation of the results of fieldwork in the Avebury region in order to try and place the new archaeological and environmental findings discussed in Chapters 2–4 into a wider context. Within this, we can see how the evolving monuments at Beckhampton, Avebury and West Kennet cannot be understood as isolated from the wider developments in the Avebury landscape. The construction of Longstones enclosure, perhaps around the time of the first bank and ditch at Avebury, was undertaken in the substantially open, grazed landscape that coalesced around the Upper Kennet Valley after the changes of the middle Neolithic that are perhaps best interpreted as a shift in activity eastwards. Once set in motion, the monumental focus remained firmly on this part of the landscape for the whole of the 3rd millennium BC as the monumental enterprise of Avebury itself evolved and was augmented by the two Avenues.

The activities at the Longstones enclosure and Cove, the Avenues and Avebury itself have to be understood as taking place within a world composed of monuments, paths, fields and woods each of which, in their own way, was a product of the way in which the landscape was created and modified by human agency. Giving greater attention to the wider landscape allows us to consider how the monumental activities in the core of the area may have impacted on the wider Avebury region. Attention is drawn to the impact of removing sarsens from the downs for stone circles and avenues, and this may be part of what Evans (2003) saw as the 'entexturing' of the landscape that took place at this time and which the site-specific focus of excavation may not bring to the fore. If the movement of sarsens created a new texture to some parts of the wider landscape, then we may also focus on the wider impact of other activities related to 3rd millennium BC construction in the region, for example the clear-cutting of trees to construct the timber enclosures at West Kennet and the stripping of turf for the mound at Silbury. In all of these cases we have tended to focus on the destination of the 'materials' in question – stone, timber, turf – rather than the possible impact of their removal from somewhere else. It is relatively easy to understand how the monuments themselves provided an enduring and permanent feature of the landscape, but perhaps the source areas too were indelibly altered by their new textures.

6

Monumentality in the 3rd millennium BC – Avebury and beyond

The project's principal aim was to enhance our understanding of the context and chronology of monumentality in the later Neolithic of the Avebury region. In this we met with both success and some frustration. In terms of the key results, excavations confirmed once and for all the existence of the Beckhampton Avenue; they demonstrated that a ditched enclosure in Longstones Field belongs to the later Neolithic; that an anomalous gap exists in the middle section of the West Kennet Avenue; that the claimed Falkner's Circle is indeed a Neolithic stone monument; and that the Avebury Cove incorporates one of the largest megaliths in Britain. The known diversity of monument forms within the region is further highlighted by the addition of the Longstones enclosure and cove, and by the simple circle at Falkner's; while the presence of the Beckhampton Avenue illustrates the sheer scale of the megalithic settings created in and around Avebury during the later Neolithic. From the Sanctuary on Overton Hill to the Longstones Cove at Beckhampton, via the Avebury henge, the megalithic settings of this complex can know be seen to stretch for a distance of 4km, effectively forming a single monument by the later stages of the 3rd millennium BC. Further, there are strong suggestions that natural spreads of sarsen within the landscape were respected and worked into the monumental fabric.

Perhaps the most dramatic result of the project's work was the confirmation of the existence of the Beckhampton Avenue. Excavations in Longstones Field and near Avebury Trusloe helped to establish its morphology, its course leading from the western entrance of the Avebury henge and its termination near Beckhampton. The arrangement of paired sarsens making up the excavated portion of the avenue is remarkably similar to that found along the northern third of the West Kennet Avenue, and the two may indeed be contemporary constructions. That they are comparable in design and intended function is further enforced by a curious feature of their relationship to the monuments that they connect. It is notable that the final stretches of both avenues are off-set in relation to the respective entrances of the Avebury henge to which they lead, and indeed to the earlier entrances into the Sanctuary and Longstones enclosure, implying that they were never intended for formal procession, but may have been set out *alongside* pre-existing routes of movement. This would certainly explain the curious flattening of the southern side of the earlier Longstones enclosure, which may respect a pre-existing pathway. Whether a reflection of the way in which such existing routes or pathways connected places of contemporary and historical/mythical significance, or a product of the intentional targeting of significant locales during the laying out the avenues, the latter took in along their lengths areas of earlier occupation and other activity. These included the midden spread at the foot of Waden Hill – the so-called West Kennet Avenue occupation site (Smith 1965) – further traces in the area excavated north of New Cottages; and the sites of earlier Neolithic occupation between Avebury and the Winterbourne, and north-west of Avebury Trusloe.

This incorporation of traditionally-significant places, which may be read as a deliberate referencing or citation of the past, seems to have been an important structuring principle in the creation of the avenues. The evidence for this is most striking in the case of the Beckhampton Avenue, which traversed and terminated immediately beyond the circuit of the earlier Longstones enclosure. The latter was created in the first half of the 3rd millennium BC, and was of unusual form, perhaps having affinities with much earlier traditions of causewayed enclosure construction. The enclosure occupied a part of the Avebury landscape that had been the focus for monument building during the earlier Neolithic, seen with the South Street and Longstones long mounds and possible mortuary enclosures, including the sub-triangular example that pre-dated the Longstones enclosure. Paradoxically, given the desire to commemorate its presence, the enclosure was deliberately levelled prior to the construction of the Beckhampton Avenue.

Turning to the West Kennet Avenue, our excavation of part of its mid-section north of New Cottages yielded a surprising result, in that here the avenue was shown to be either discontinuous or of a very different format. The apparent 'gap' in its course here may reflect its proximity to the West Kennet palisaded enclosures and routes from the Kennet up to areas of contemporary occupation on Avebury and Overton Downs. It may also have reflected the merging of the avenue line at this point with the natural sarsen spread following the base of the dry valley. Taken together with the results of the geophysical survey on the middle section of the Beckhampton Avenue near Trusloe Manor Farm, the work highlights how the format of both avenues may vary from the normal paired stone arrangements at certain points along their lengths. Re-evaluation of the records from the 1934–5 excavations on the northern third of the West Kennet Avenue has also shown how that monument incorporated natural sarsens along its length. The same 'hybrid' mix of artificially-set and naturally occurring stones might also be a feature of the Falkner's Circle, which was seemingly set at the edge of an extensive sarsen field. Unlike the double concentric circles of the Sanctuary on Overton Hill (Cunnington 1931), the Falkner's Circle was not preceded by a timber monument.

The sequence and chronology of monuments in the later Neolithic of the Avebury region

While the project was highly successful in revealing new details relating to the extent and character of the later Neolithic monument complex, refining the chronology of developments within the region during this period has proved more difficult. A good series of radiocarbon dates was obtained on animal bone and antler from the ditch of the Longstones enclosure, placing its construction in the period 2820–2660BC; while an Optically Stimulated Luminescence date from the stone-hole of Stone II of the Cove within the Northern Inner Circle of the Avebury henge suggests that this was set up around the end of the 4th or the beginning of the 3rd millennium BC (though the standard deviation for this date is very wide). However, because of the absence of securely-stratified organic material from the stone-holes of the Beckhampton and West Kennet Avenues, the Longstones Cove and the Falkner's Circle, we have not been able to obtain absolute dates for these constructions. This may not be a product of 'bad luck' on our part in finding suitable material, but rather a reflection of restrictions on the deposition of antler and other organics within these features at the time of stone erection. As a consequence, any reconstruction of the chronology of these settings is largely dependent upon structural and artefactual sequences. In this respect there is a marked contrast to the situation relating to the earlier Neolithic sequence, where recent programmes of radiocarbon dating on material from Windmill Hill and the region's long mounds by Alasdair Whittle, Frances Healy and Alex Bayliss are producing a highly refined absolute chronology (Bayliss *et al.* 2007; Alasdair Whittle and Frances Healy pers. comm.).

While acknowledging the difficulties faced in producing refined chronologies for the later Neolithic complex, the extent and quality of the dating evidence for this area still remains better than that for many other regions (see below), and sequences can be elucidated with varying degrees of precision and latitude. In 1993 Alasdair Whittle proposed a detailed and innovative six-phase sequence for the region's Neolithic (Whittle 1993, table 2). Three of those phases (D–F) spanned developments in the 3rd millennium BC: beginning in phase D (3361/3109-2916/2782BC) with, tentatively, simple stone circles and the earliest components of the West Kennet Avenue; then during E (2916/2782-2564/2457BC) the development of Avebury, the Sanctuary and the beginnings of Silbury Hill; followed in phase F (2564/2457-2133/1959BC) by the West Kennet palisaded enclosures and early Beaker burials (*ibid.*). Whittle's scheme built upon dates then recently obtained from the Avebury henge (Pitts and Whittle 1992) and resulting from his extensive fieldwork on the region's monuments, including the West Kennet palisades (Whittle 1997b). Since then, further radiocarbon dates have been obtained on material from the ditch and Outer Circle of the Avebury henge (Pollard and Cleal 2004), to which must be added the data obtained during the project reported here. Taken together, a review of the later Neolithic sequence is now timely.

Beginning with the Avebury henge, there now exists a possibility that the Cove and other stone settings within the centre of the monument, such as the Obelisk, could have been erected around 3000BC. The first phase of the earthwork (Avebury 1), represented by a smaller bank seen in section in the south-east and south-west quadrants (Pitts and Whittle 1992, 210), might also be placed close to the beginning of the 3rd millennium BC. The Avebury 2 earthwork is now firmly dated to *c.*2840–2460 cal BC, with the probability weighted towards the 26th century BC (Pollard and Cleal 2004). The stones of the Outer Circle are perhaps best dated by HAR-10327 at 2600–2000 cal BC (Pitts and Whittle 1992); though we know from artefactual and radiocarbon evidence that megaliths were being erected and re-set within the henge well into the early 2nd millennium BC (*e.g.* stone-holes D and 41: Smith 1965, 248; Pollard and Cleal 2004).

Belonging to the end of the first or beginning of the second quarter of the 3rd millennium BC, the Longstones enclosure may not be far removed in time from the Avebury 1 earthwork. Avebury 2 was perhaps followed by the creation of a new complex of palisaded enclosures in the valley bottom at West Kennet (Whittle 1997b). Available radiocarbon dates for these place their construction and use in the period *c.*2500–2000 cal BC; although an alternative reading, taking the full two sigma range, could produce a long chronology that would span *c.*2900–1800 cal BC, and so parallel the constructional sequence at Avebury (*ibid.*, table 1). Favouring a short chronology, Whittle argued that 'the succession of constructions, if such it was, must be presumed to have been swift' (1997b, 156). In terms of their individual elements, with one outlying date (BM-2602), the calibrated range for the inner and outer 'ditches' of Enclosure 1 covers 2500–2200 cal BC at 95.4% confidence. The dates for enclosure 2 are more problematic since the two results from the palisade circuit in Trench M do not overlap at two sigma (the overall span is *c.*2900–1800 cal BC). Dates from one of the outer radial palisade lines (Trench S), which abuts the circuit of Enclosure 2, give a range of 2580–2030, weighted towards 2580–2120 cal BC (*ibid.*, table 1). Activity could have gone on into the early part of the 2nd millennium BC, taking the dates for bone deposit 215 between the outer and inner circuits of Enclosure 1, this being associated with Grooved Ware (Hamilton in Whittle 1997b). However the radiocarbon dates are interpreted, it is clear that the complex is of more than a single phase. One possible sequence is a development from smaller circular timber settings, as seen within Enclosure 2, followed by partial enclosure and linkage through the construction of radial lines, and then the creation of the main enclosures, perhaps in succession (Pollard and Reynolds 2002, 115–6), but this remains largely hypothetical. The adjacent monumental mound of Silbury Hill has been the subject of a new programme of dating (Bayliss *et al.* 2007). Evidently of more than one 'phase' of construction (Whittle 1997b), new dates and re-evaluation of old ones suggest the primary mound was constructed in the third quarter of the 3rd millennium BC (the 24th or 23rd centuries), with completion either relatively swift or taking until the end of that millennium (Bayliss *et al.* 2007).

Placing other components of the complex within a refined chronology is more difficult at present because of the absence of absolute dates. However, on the basis of analogy, associated artefactual evidence and structural relationships, the timber settings of the Sanctuary can be placed in the middle of the 3rd millennium BC (Pollard 1992); and, as has been argued in detail earlier (Chapter 2), the Beckhampton and West Kennet Avenues to *c.*2600–2000BC, with a range in the third quarter of the 3rd millennium BC being favoured. While associated with Grooved Ware and later Neolithic worked flint, the chronology of the Falkner's Circle remains poorly understood.

In summary, the available evidence suggests that monument construction in the region spanned the 3rd millennium BC, though such activity could well have been punctuated rather than continuous. Within this pattern there is a sense that the scale and intensity of constructional activity increased at the end of the second and into the third quarter of that millennium. The four centuries between 2600–2200BC look to have been particularly busy, witnessing the creation of the Avebury 2 earthwork, the Outer Circle of that monument, the two avenues, the Sanctuary, the West Kennet palisades, the early stages at least of Silbury Hill, and other important events such as the levelling of the Longstones enclosure and final blocking of the West Kennet long barrow (Bayliss *et al.* 2007). Although large stones had been used previously in the creation of chambered long mounds and potentially 'early' megalithic settings such as the Cove, they were now employed on a much greater scale. Certain monuments – the Sanctuary and the Longstones enclosure, as well as Avebury to some extent – were subject to a process of 'lithicisation', being transformed from essentially timber or earthwork constructions to ones of stone or a hybrid mixture of materials. The avenues too might be seen as a product of this lithicisation process, marking the transformation to stone of existing pathways. This critical period between 2600–2200BC was also a time when the earliest Beakers appeared in the region (note the European beaker from the West Kennet long barrow: Piggott 1962, 45), and perhaps metalwork too. The rarity of stone axes from the West Kennet palisades is perhaps telling in this respect (Whittle 1997b, 93) since it might imply that copper versions were already in circulation and routinely used for the felling of large trees. With these novel material items came new inter-regional connections, and an enhanced awareness of distant places and practices that could have generated the inspiration for constructions such as Silbury Hill (Whittle 1997b, 150).

The creation of megalithic and perhaps timber settings (*e.g.* at West Kennet) did not cease as the 3rd millennium BC drew to a close, but continued, albeit on a limited scale, into the early part of 2nd millennium BC, contemporary with the establishment of round barrow cemeteries within the wider region (Cleal 2005). Repeatedly re-worked over a millennium or more, the Avebury henge is the one monument that we know spans the duration of this constructional activity. In culture-historical terms, there is no neat late Neolithic – early Bronze Age split. The dates from the West Kennet palisades demonstrate that, for a time, Grooved Ware and Beaker ceramics must have been in circulation simultaneously, though were employed in very different spheres of practice (a situation that also holds true for the Stonehenge region: Parker Pearson *et al.* 2006). Early Beakers accompanied burials placed at the feet of stones along the West Kennet Avenue, at the Sanctuary and Longstones Cove (Cleal 2005, 118–9). Grooved Ware by contrast has an association with timber and earlier earthwork monuments (*e.g.* Windmill Hill), and a usage as part of feasting or other formalised consumption events, as at the West Kennet palisades (Hamilton and Whittle 1999; Longworth and Cleal 1999). The 'old' and the 'new' worlds were co-mingled as practices influenced by traditions elsewhere were woven into an existing fabric of beliefs and ways of proceeding in the world. During the same period that an individual inhumation rite was being adopted, and the first round barrow cemeteries constructed, more long-lived and established traditions based around ancestral veneration were signalled by the deposition of disarticulated human bone in the ditch at Avebury (Pollard and Reynolds 2002, 125–8).

Avebury in context

Events in the Avebury landscape did not happen in isolation. Many other areas of Britain and Ireland developed as 'monumental landscapes' during the later 4th and 3rd millennia BC. We have tended to treat these complexes as similar phenomena, even though they vary greatly in scale, sequence and detail. There is, therefore, a need to account for parallel developments as well as diversity and difference; for the apparent 'success' of some regions (*e.g.* the Avebury and Stonehenge landscapes) in relation to others; and to explore both local contexts and trajectories, in addition to the playing-out of inter-regional social and ideological changes (Harding 2003). Behind these themes lie the key questions of why these complexes came into being when and where they did, and why they took their particular forms?

In order to explore these themes this chapter will review in brief the evidence from a number of later Neolithic monument complexes in southern Britain that have been the subject of a reasonable level of archaeological investigation, beginning with Wessex (Wiltshire and Dorset) and then moving outwards. The aim is to provide a context for the events and developments in the 3rd millennium BC landscape of Avebury described earlier. Behind this is a desire to understand how events in this particular landscape related to regional histories of monument development elsewhere, and to wider social and material worlds.

Wessex and its hinterland

It has long been recognised that there exists a concentration of remarkable monument complexes on the chalklands of Wessex, principally around Avebury, Stonehenge (in the southern part of Salisbury Plain) and Dorchester (Dorset) (Renfrew 1973). In addition there are smaller, though nonetheless significant, clusters of henges and allied monuments at Marden in the Vale of Pewsey, and around Knowlton and Wyke Down on Cranborne Chase (Barrett *et al.* 1991; Green 2000) (Figure 6.1). Only the large henge enclosure at Marden has witnessed excavation, and then on a limited scale (Wainwright 1971). Likewise the complex of four henges, a large mound and several ring-ditches/barrows adjacent to the River Allen at Knowlton remains relatively uninvestigated (Green 2000, 88–90). Discussion will therefore focus on the later Neolithic landscapes around Stonehenge and Mount Pleasant. Although lying outside the chalklands, the complex of stone circles at Stanton Drew in Somerset will also be discussed, because of its potential connection to developments in Wessex.

The Stonehenge Region

By the middle of the 3rd millennium BC the southern part of Salisbury Plain, close to the point where the Nine Mile River joins the River Avon, had developed as a major ceremonial centre equal to, if not exceeding, the stature of Avebury (Figure 6.2). During the course of the 3rd millennium BC both occupation and monument building focussed increasingly on an area of *c.*8 × 5km defined on its eastern side by the Avon; the latter river taking on an especial significance as the major landscape feature connecting the monuments at and around Durrington Walls to Stonehenge (RCHME) 1979; Richards 1990; Cleal *et al.* 1995; Darvill 1997; Parker Pearson and Ramilisonina 1998; Darvill 2005; Parker Pearson *et al.* 2006).

As with the Avebury landscape, initial Neolithic settlement here may have comprised a process of infill, since there is little indication of a sustained later Mesolithic presence. This

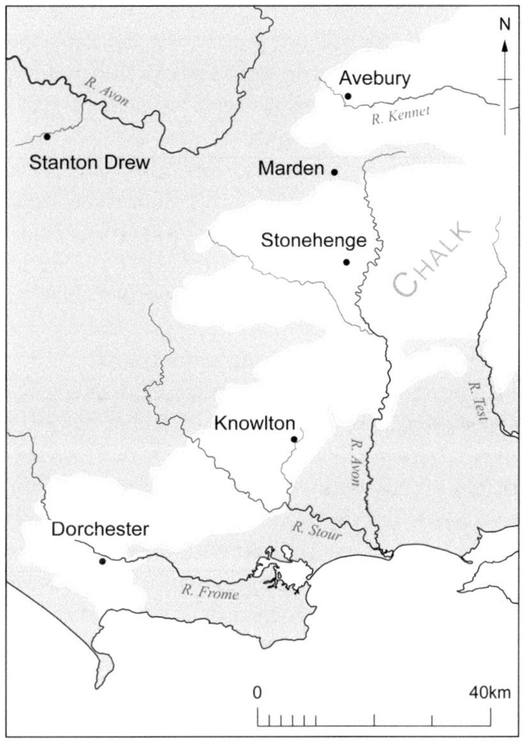

Figure 6.1. (left) Distribution of major late Neolithic monument complexes on the Wessex chalklands

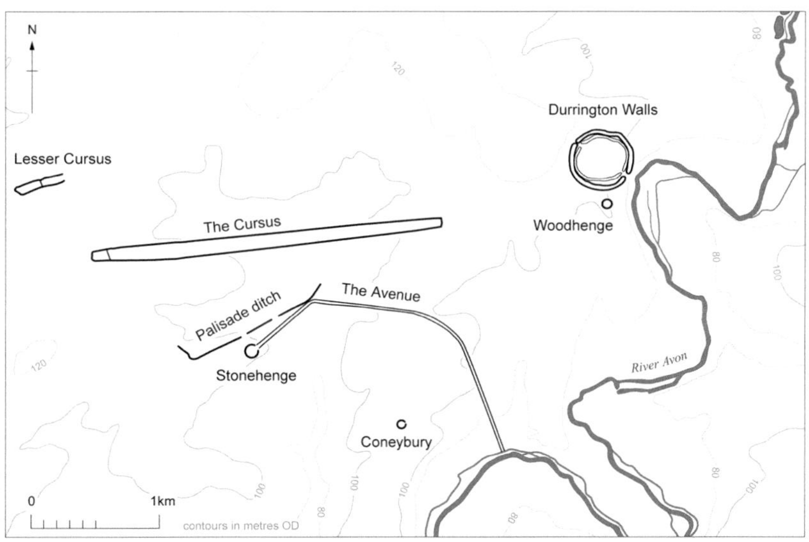

Figure 6.2. (below) The later Neolithic monuments of the Stonehenge region (after Cleal et al. *1995)*

is not, however, to state that the area was without significance to Mesolithic communities, as indicated by the line of massive post-holes dating to the late 9th – early 8th millennia BC, excavated in the Stonehenge car park (Cleal *et al.* 1995, 43–56) – an extraordinary and very early monumental expression. No direct connection can be drawn between these and the special status of this landscape during the Neolithic, unless their survival as slight hollows and a tacit acknowledgement of their significance via stories and myth provided a cue to the later siting of Stonehenge.

The early-mid 4th millennium BC saw the construction of a number of long mounds and an enclosure at Robin Hood's Ball, followed by a north-south division of the landscape through the creation of the Lesser and Stonehenge Cursus monuments. The one available radiocarbon date for the Stonehenge Cursus (OxA-1403: 2890–2460 cal BC) comes from an antler placed in a pit that is almost certainly secondary, and so does not date its construction, which most likely occurred in the second half of the 4th millennium BC.

The first century of the 3rd millennium BC saw a change of emphasis with the creation of the earthwork and Aubrey Holes of Stonehenge 1 within the centre of the region, to the south of the Stonehenge Cursus. Available dates from an internal pit and the ditch of the Coneybury henge, sited to the south-east of Stonehenge on high ground overlooking the Avon, indicate that this monument might also belong to the early part of the 3rd millennium BC (*c.*3100–2600 cal BC), and is perhaps the first indication of a shift in ceremonial focus towards the River Avon.

Very much paralleling developments in the Avebury landscape, ceremonial activity and monument building intensified markedly in the later part of the second and the third quarters of the 3rd millennium BC. This period saw the introduction of the sarsens and Preseli bluestones to Stonehenge – one of the most remarkable instances of long-distance movement of megaliths in European prehistory – and their setting and re-setting in various configurations between the late 27th and 20th centuries BC. Additionally, through the construction of an earthwork avenue, Stonehenge was connected to the River Avon. Contemporary with the early part of the Stonehenge 3 sequence is the creation of the massive Durringon Walls/Woodhenge complex on the bank of the Avon (Wainwright and Longworth 1971), and associated occupation and other more 'staged' activities marked by flint scatters and pit deposits along an arc from Coneybury via King Barrow Ridge to Durrington. A number of the pit deposits include structured deposits linked explicitly with ceremonial practices (*e.g.* Woodlands and the Chalk Plaque Pit: Stone and Young 1948; Harding 1988).

Dates for the large henge enclosure at Durrington Walls place its construction and use in the period *c.*2600–2300BC, and therefore contemporary with the introduction of the bluestones and sarsens at Stonehenge. There is clear evidence for re-working of the timber and earthwork components at Durrington, including modification of the Southern Circle and perhaps other internal ditched and wooden settings. The beginnings of large-scale feasting and midden deposition preceded the creation of the earthwork, the circuit of which may have been marked initially by post settings. To the south, and probably linked to Durrington via a southern entrance into the latter monument, are the earthwork and multiple timber circle of Woodhenge (Cunnington 1929; Pollard 1995b). The henge itself dates to the second half of the 3rd millennium BC, and was most probably created after the timber settings had been standing for some time, or had rotted. Excavations in 2006 revealed that two phases of stone setting had replaced posts in the southern part of the monument. Other, smaller, timber structures existed to the south of Woodhenge (Pollard 1995a). Both the Southern Circle and Woodhenge post rings share close architectural similarities with the phase 3 stone settings at Stonehenge. While employing very different materials in their construction, they must be considered as closely connected and conceptually integrated structures.

Stonehenge continued to be the focus for activity well into the first half of the 2nd millennium BC, as evidenced by the deposition of early and middle Bronze Age ceramics and the digging of the Y and probably Z holes at *c.*1650–1520 BC. The region had by this time become the focus for the creation of a large number of round barrow cemeteries, the distribution of which can be seen to ring Stonehenge and the courses of the Avon and

Nine Mile River (Woodward and Woodward 1996).

There can be little question that by the mid to late 3rd millennium BC activity within the Stonehenge landscape had taken on a distinct spatial structure. Much of the later Neolithic (Grooved Ware associated) occupation occurred in the east of the region, on high ground close to the Avon, and it is in this same area that those monuments most closely connected to periodic gathering and feasting – namely Durrington Walls and Woodhenge – were created. Stonehenge seems somewhat isolated to the west, until the establishment of round barrow cemeteries in the latest 3rd and early 2nd millennia BC, although it was connected to the Avon by its earthwork avenue. The much earlier Stonehenge Cursus continued to hold significance in the structuring of landscape-wide activity, effectively providing a northern boundary to the later Neolithic ceremonial complex and much of the contemporary occupation.

Such evident spatial organisation, and recognition that, via their connections to the Avon, Stonehenge, Durrington Walls and Woodhenge came to function as an integrated monument complex, has led to two innovative interpretations of the cosmological structuring of later Neolithic activity. The first was provided by Darvill (1997) who proposed that throughout the 3rd millennium BC the changing format of Stonehenge acted as a symbolic representation of the wider landscape. In its first phase the earthwork bank and posts held in the Aubrey Holes stood as images of the surrounding hills and woodland, with the course of the River Avon entering and leaving this landscape 'in exactly the same relative position as the north-east and south gaps occur in the earthwork at Stonehenge' (*ibid.*, 179). In phases 2 and 3 Darvill envisages a reworking of the single axial ordering of the monument and landscape (a 'linear binary' division) to one that involved their conceptual quartering (a 'linear quadruple' arrangement) (*ibid.*, 182–9). This involved the creation of two axes, both of which referenced sunrise and sunset at the opposite solstices. This four-fold partitioning of space was extended out of the monument, providing a conceptual quartering of the surrounding landscape that structured the placement of occupation, burial and other practices.

The second scheme was outlined by Parker Pearson and Ramilisonina (1998; see also Parker Pearson *et al.* 2006). This was based on a specific reading of the different materialities of stone and wood as employed in the construction of the later Neolithic monuments. Here, stone, because of its hardness and permanence, is seen as a medium connected metaphorically and ontologically with ancestral realms, and wood with the living. Thus, Stonehenge (which became a major late Neolithic cremation cemetery) was conceived during phase 3 as an ancestral monument, while Durrington Walls and Woodhenge (associated with large quantities of feasting debris) were connected to the ceremonial activities of the living community. Both timber and stone monuments were linked in one ritual cycle that extended across the landscape and saw the transition of the newly-dead into ancestors via their corporeal or non-corporeal journey from Durrington Walls/Woodhenge, along the River Avon, to Stonehenge. This interpretation of the complex was greatly reinforced by the recent discovery of an avenue linking Durrington to the river, and recognition that the Southern Circle at Durrington Walls and phase 3 sarsen and bluestone settings at Stonehenge are essentially the same kind of structure, just in different materials. Alignments of both groups of monuments on the midwinter and midsummer solstices provide a timing for the ceremonies undertaken here.

Dorchester, Dorset

The most southerly of the Wessex later Neolithic ceremonial centres developed on a 'spur' or ridge of chalk created by the confluence of the River Frome and River South Winterbourne at Dorchester, Dorset (Wainwright 1979; Thomas 1996; Healy 1997) (Figure 6.3). Although lacking a major stone monument on the scale of Avebury or Stonehenge, the complex here is comparable in a number of respects, including as it does a range of major earthwork and timber enclosures that together map out a similar structural history to that represented in the more northerly of the Wessex centres.

A sustained earlier Neolithic presence in this landscape is again indicated by traces of occupation, along with the presence of long mounds and the causewayed enclosure at Maiden Castle (Sharples 1991). During the

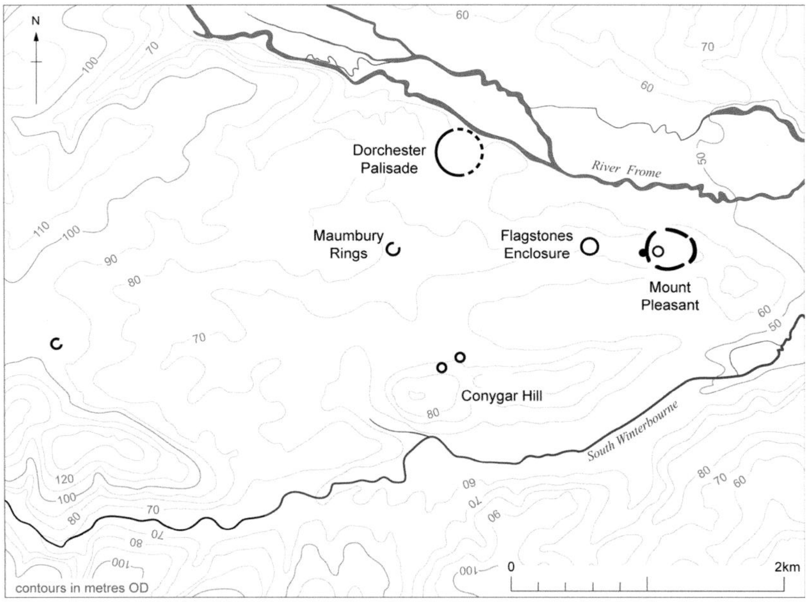

Figure 6.3. Later Neolithic monuments around Dorchester, Dorset (after Harding 2003, with additions)

latest 4th – early 3rd millennia BC the focus of activity shifted north from Maiden Castle and the South Dorset Ridgeway to the shallow basin formed by the confluence of the two rivers. Over the course of a millennium a linear complex of enclosures developed along the chalk ridge, with the henge of Maumbury Rings at the western end and that of Mount Pleasant at the eastern. The earliest of these is situated mid-way along the ridge at Flagstones. Constructed *c.* 3300–3000BC next to the contemporary Allington Avenue long mound, the enclosure may have replaced a sarsen stone circle or other setting. With a shallow, segmented ditch marking out a circuit *c.*100m in diameter, and very limited primary deposition of artefacts, the Flagstones enclosure is not dissimilar to those at the Longstones and Stonehenge 1. Child inhumations and an adult cremation were placed in the ditch at Flagstones while the primary fills were forming. In three instances these were associated with sarsen and calcareous sandstone slabs. The link between the human dead and stones recalls the earlier use of stone in the construction of nearby chambered tombs such as the Grey Mare and her Colts, leading Thomas to suggest that the creation of Flagstones marked 'the emergence of new practices within the context of traditional activities' (Thomas 1996, 193).

Other enclosures followed. The henge at Maumbury Rings (Bradley 1975) is imprecisely dated, with radiocarbon determinations on antler spanning *c.*2900–2000 cal BC. Defined by a ring of shafts 10m or so deep, this is a highly unusual monument associated with an equally unusual set of depositional practices. The shafts were rapidly refilled with chalk rubble and a range of materials that included pottery (Grooved Ware), carved chalk, red deer skulls and human remains, occurring predominantly in that order from the bases to the tops of the shafts. Bradley has recently suggested that this prescribed sequence of deposition may hold a narrative quality, perhaps the playing out in material form of myths of origin; and that a similar logic may lie behind the complex spatial patterning of deposits at Woodhenge (Bradley 2000, 123–4).

Several hundred metres to the north-east of Maumbury a substantial palisaded enclosure was revealed during excavations at Greyhound Yard (Woodward *et al.* 1993). Dates for this are again imprecise, with a range *c.*2900–2300 cal BC. So little exploration of the interior of this monument has been undertaken, because of the presence of the modern town of Dorchester, that it is impossible at present to know of the range of activities that may have taken place here. That a different set of practices may have been linked to this monument is perhaps indicated by its setting. In contrast to the ridge-top location of the other later Neolithic monuments, the Greyhound Yard palisade is located off-slope, close to the Frome, its circuit perhaps even intersecting the river. Analogy can be drawn with the river-side setting of the West Kennet palisades and Durrington Walls.

In terms of its scale, lengthy structural history and complexity, the henge enclosure of Mount Pleasant stands out as the pre-eminent monument within this complex. Available radiocarbon dates place the construction of the enclosure at the end of the first or in the second quarter of the 3rd millennium BC. The Silbury-like monumental mound of the Conquer Barrow on its western circuit may be broadly contemporary. The earthwork enclosure was thought to be broken by four entrances, however recent analysis of aerial photographs show the existence of a blocked fifth entrance on the south, along with previously unnoticed lengths of external ditch on the southern and western sides, and a hollow-way of possible prehistoric date leading from the eastern entrance towards the Frome

(Barber 2004). A circular henge with a single northern entrance (Site IV) occupies the centre of Mount Pleasant. Published sections suggest this began as a pit circle, later re-cut to form a penannular ditch (Wainwright 1979, figs. 8–12). This enclosed a multiple timber circle that was replaced by an elaborate stone setting or 'cove'. Wainwright considered spreads of sarsen flakes and charcoal in the surrounding ditch (dated to *c.*2150–1900 cal BC) to represent debris from the dressing of the stones; a treatment otherwise attested with sarsen megalithic structures only at Stonehenge. An alternative reading of the evidence sees the sarsen flakes as relating to the breaking-up of the stone settings (Pollard 1992, 218–9).

During the last two centuries of the 3rd and the first century of the 2nd millennia BC Mount Pleasant underwent a dramatic transformation. The western entrance was much reduced in size and a palisade constructed around the inside of the ditch circuit with restricted entrances at the north and east. These events are linked to an increased scale of deposition (especially of Beaker and early Bronze Age ceramics and lithics) at Site IV and around the northern entrance. Whether as a result of conflict or the culmination of a prescribed ritual cycle, the palisade was then partially destroyed through a combination of fire and the removal of posts.

The discovery during road-works of two small pit-rings associated with Grooved Ware pottery, on Conygar Hill to the south-west of Mount Pleasant, is a reminder that more diminutive and short-lived later Neolithic monuments exist within this landscape. Many more may lie concealed under modern-day development within Dorchester.

By the early Bronze Age the alignment of enclosures along the Mount Pleasant-Maumbury ridge was converted into one of barrows. Major round barrow cemeteries developed along the South Dorset Ridgeway and, to the west, surrounding and apparently respecting the presence of the late Neolithic monument complex (Woodward and Woodward 1996).

Stanton Drew

The group of three stones circles and a cove at Stanton Drew, Somerset, may have a very real connection to the Avebury and Stonehenge landscapes in that it lies on a route into Wessex from the west and the Bristol Channel (Burl 2000) (Figure 6.4). This is one of the routes along which the Stonehenge bluestones may have been brought from their place of geological origin in south-west Wales. The monument complex at Stanton Drew, which includes the second biggest stone circle in Britain after Avebury, is located in a bowl-like landscape setting, close to the junction of the rivers Chew and Avon. Composed of blocks of silicious breccia and oolitic limestone, the Great Circle is set on a terrace overlooking the Chew. To the north-east and south-south-west are two smaller circles (at *c.*30m and 40m across respectively); the latter set on a slight rise. Short avenues lead from the Great and NE Circles towards the River Chew. The Cove, comprising a setting of three stones, originally open to the south, is located 120m to the west of the SSW circle; and there exists an outlier (Hauteville's Quoit) 450m north-north-east of the Great Circle. The complex possesses an unusual spatial integrity in that the Cove, Great Circle and NE Circle are set on a precise NE-SW alignment, and the SSW Circle, Great Circle and Hauteville's Quoit on another that runs SSW-NNE (Burl 2000; David *et al.* 2004; Lewis 2005).

The complex is unusual in terms of its

Figure 6.4. The later Neolithic monument complex at Stanton Drew, Somerset (after David et al. *2004, with additions)*

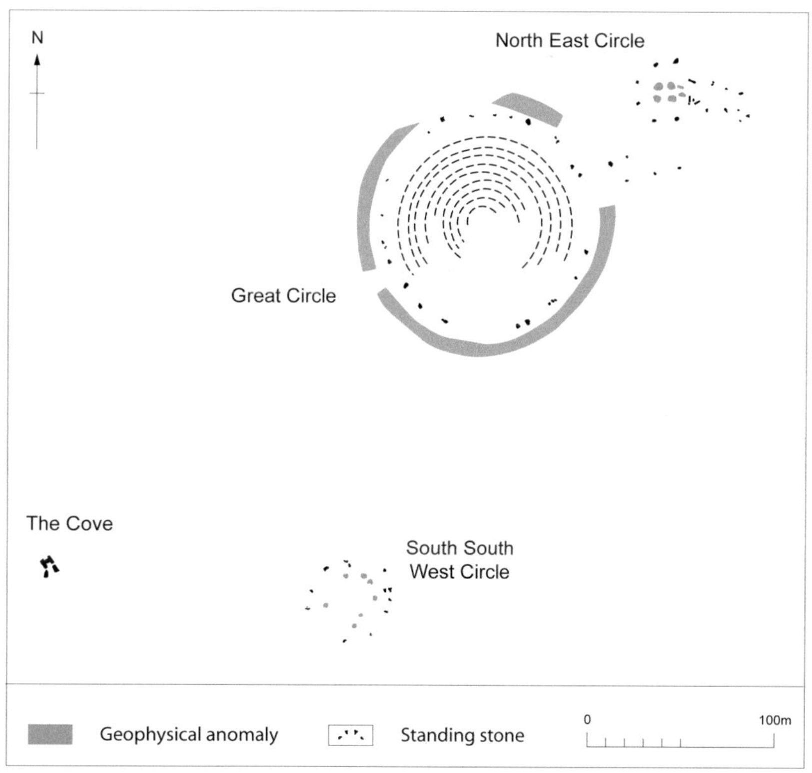

limited architectural repertoire, its spatially discrete nature, and in having no obvious 4th millennium BC precedent: it may have developed as a monument complex *de novo* during the 3rd millennium BC. The relative absence of Bronze Age round barrows within the area also suggests that its significance was short-lived. In these respects it differs greatly from the key Wessex ceremonial centres.

While no modern excavation has taken place at Stanton Drew, geophysical survey during 1997 and 2000 (David *et al.* 2004) revealed important structural details that imply each circle was of more than one phase of construction. The Great Circle is now known to have been enclosed by a ditch with a 50m wide entrance gap on the north-east side, while the interior contains a massive arrangement of nine concentric rings of anomalies, most likely post-holes. The SSW Circle is also enclosed by a bank or ditch, and central anomalies within both this and the NE Circle could be further post settings. The latter anomalies are not dissimilar in plan to a number of small later Neolithic timber circles enclosing central arrangements of four posts (*e.g.* the Durrington Walls Northern Circle and Durrington 68: Wainwright and Longworth 1971; Pollard 1995a).

The features revealed by the geophysical survey raise the possibility that the stone circles were preceded by wooden settings, which, on analogy with timber circles elsewhere (Gibson 2005), may initially have been unenclosed. Without any evidence for a surrounding earthwork, a simple timber-to-stone sequence can be postulated for the NE Circle: the axis provided by the stone avenue is off-set to that of the putative timber settings. In the case of the Great and SSW Circles the sequence could run from unenclosed timber settings to enclosed, followed by replacement in stone, or timber-to-stone with the henge earthworks belonging to the 'lithicised' phase.

That the megalithic avenue leading to the Great Circle (which may either be contemporary with the stone circle or a later addition: Burl 1993, 43) is off-set to the south of the entrance through the henge enclosure, suggests that the axis of this monument was later altered, perhaps at the time of lithicisation. As mentioned earlier in the volume (Chapter 2), exactly the same process of 'axial shift' occurred at Stonehenge during phase 3, at the Sanctuary, and with the Longstones enclosure/ Beckhampton Avenue when they were converted from timber or earthwork monuments into ones of stone. This raises the intriguing possibility of parallel sequences of development at Stanton Drew, Stonehenge and with the Avebury monuments. However, at present this remains speculative, and must await the results of any future programme of excavation at Stanton Drew.

Discussion

While superficially distinctive and drawing upon a varied architectural repertoire in imaginative ways that reflected local conditions of development (cf. Thomas 2004), the later Neolithic monument complexes around Avebury, Stonehenge, Dorchester and Stanton Drew share many points in common. With the Avebury and Stonehenge landscapes especially, but also to a lesser extent with that at Dorchester, it is possible to see parallel sequences of monument development. In all three regions new traditions of enclosure construction begin around the end of the 4th and beginning of the 3rd millennia BC (*i.e.* Avebury 1, Longstones, Stonehenge and Flagstones). By the middle of the 3rd millennium BC there existed a range of enclosure forms, key monuments were undergoing a process of conversion into stone, and attempts were made to produce integrated complexes that might facilitate single narratives of ceremonial practice through the construction of earthwork and stone avenues that linked together formerly separate constructions. As pre-eminent monuments within each of their respective regions, Avebury, Stonehenge and Mount Pleasant all show a particular intensity of reworking and modification that continued well into the earlier Bronze Age, challenging any notion of marked ideological change at the end of the 3rd millennium BC.

In terms of their chronology, format and material associations, a degree of equivalence might be identified between individual monuments in each of these regions. The similarities between the Longstones enclosure, Flagstones and Stonehenge 1 have already been alluded to. Structural developments at Avebury and Stonehenge also seem to map each other closely, and both monuments look, over time, to have acquired explicit associations with the ancestral dead (Parker Pearson and Ramilisonina 1998; Gillings and Pollard 2004). In terms of the narrative quality of deposition at both sites (Bradley 2000, 123–7), Maumbury Rings and Woodhenge can be conceived as analogous monuments that commemorated mythic events; while Durrington Walls and the West Kennet palisades are linked by their materiality and connections with feasting. Perhaps the enclosure at Greyhound Yard was the setting for similar practices?

Why each of these regions should develop along broadly similar lines is another matter. They obviously possess geographical proximity, and we must envisage that contacts of various kinds, via exchange, inter-marriage, journeying and so forth, existed between the communities attached to those places. Mobility among those populations – not everyone need have been resident in these areas all the time – also facilitated the transfer of news, knowledge and even labour for monument construction. It is not unlikely that some groups or individuals were involved in construction projects in more than one region, especially since knowledge acquired of ditch digging, the movement and erection of stones and more esoteric aspects of monument layout, for example, could have become an important and sought-after commodity. An alternative model would see strict affiliation between particular communities and an individual monument complex. In this scenario, separate groups, tied by historical association or networks of kinship and obligation, would be brought together (perhaps by charismatic leadership: Whittle 1997b, 148–9) to generate the necessary resources and engage in the construction of monuments within each region, while still possessing an awareness of events elsewhere. With identities and social standing bound to particular places, inter-regional competition and emulation could develop rapidly – each area claiming pre-eminent status as the key sacred locale and constructing massive and elaborate monuments that reinforced those claims. Perhaps this explains why we see the paradoxical situation of both analogous sequences *and* architectural diversity: a desire to maintain a distinct identity through the creation of architectures that reflected the contingencies of local circumstances was being worked out in relation to bigger political events.

This leads to the question of whether the Wessex monument complexes as a whole were the materialisation of a shared set of beliefs and practices, or whether religious values, cosmologies and concepts of the sacred differed markedly from one region to the next. For Harding the appearance of henges and allied constructions during the 3rd millennium BC was part of a 'religious revolution' that saw the up-take of an 'overarching set of religious beliefs and principles' across the British Isles (2003, 83). Given the extent of regional diversity in ceremonial practices across Britain during the later Neolithic (see below), this might be questioned, but for the Wessex region a case can be made for increasing symbolic and ceremonial unity. Parker Pearson has argued that the same metaphoric links between timber constructions and the living and stone monuments and the dead existed at both Stonehenge and Avebury, with each landscape being structured into separate ancestral and quotidian domains (Parker Pearson and Ramilisonina 1998). Mortuary rites that involved physical or spiritual passage between timber and stone monuments facilitated the transition between these domains. Since that paper was written the Beckhampton Avenue and Longstones enclosure have been added to the map of the Avebury landscape, but their inclusion need not alter the validity of the scheme. In fact, the termination of the Beckhampton Avenue in an area of the Avebury landscape that had a concentration of earlier monuments (*e.g.* South Street and the Longstones long mounds) and was largely devoid of later Neolithic occupation would fit with a conceptualisation of this as an ancestral space. The 'journey of the dead' would begin at the Sanctuary on Overton Hill, move along the West Kennet Avenue, through Avebury, then, leaving the western entrance, along the Beckhampton Avenue, across the Winterbourne and on to the Longstones Cove. Curiously, such a totalising model has resonance with Stukeley's pre-serpent interpretation of Avebury: the 'earth' temple of the Sanctuary being linked by avenues and the Avebury henge to the 'underworld' that lurked at the termination of the Beckhampton Avenue (Gillings and Pollard 2004, 156).

The same scheme can readily be applied to the Dorchester monuments. As the principal late Neolithic timber construction (preceding the palisade at Mount Pleasant), the enclosure at Greyhound Yard could mark the beginning of any funerary and ancestral-veneration ceremonies. The position of this monument and that of Mount Pleasant close to the Frome is significant, suggesting the river provided a connection between the two; now further enhanced by the discovery of a possible hollow-way leading from the eastern entrance of Mount Pleasant towards the Frome (Barber 2004). Passage down the river towards Mount Pleasant could have marked a liminal stage in this transitional journey, with reincorporation of the dead into the domain of the ancestors taking place following entry into Mount Pleasant and the megalithic 'cove' at Site IV, within the heart of the monument. In each complex – at Avebury, Stonehenge and Dorchester – the 'journeys' ended in enclosed stone settings: the 'houses of the dead'.

The timber-to-stone materiality interpretation works well for the middle and first quarter of the 3rd millennium BC, when these complexes were at their most 'developed', when individual monuments were integrated into single ceremonial centres through the construction of avenues, and when large stone was employed on a meaningful scale. It is not so easy to demonstrate earlier when quite different structures of practice may have operated. There may, for example, have been a time in the early 3rd millennium BC when Avebury 1 and the Longstones enclosure were the only 'active' monuments within that landscape; and Stonehenge 1–2 and Coneybury likewise within the southern part of Salisbury Plain. If coherence and conformity to a single ideal came to characterise the latter half of the 3rd millennium BC it could have developed gradually, fuelled by an increasing desire to emulate what was happening in adjacent regions.

Figure 6.5. Location of the monument complexes at Etton/Maxey, Dorchester-on-Thames, the Walton Basin, Thornborough and Ferrybridge

Beyond Wessex

By virtue of their scale and coherence alone, the Wessex ceremonial centres must be regarded as exceptional. Groups of later Neolithic monuments are known in many other regions of Britain, though they vary greatly in terms of their format, extent and histories of construction and use: the single henge and small cluster of ring-ditches at Arminghall in Norfolk, for instance, being a far cry from Avebury or Stonehenge. In order to highlight this diversity, and so illustrate the different trajectories of development that could exist within specific later Neolithic ceremonial landscapes, the archaeology of five distinctive monument complexes will be reviewed here. They comprise Etton/Maxey, Dorchester-on-Thames, the Walton Basin, Thornborough and Ferrybridge (Figure 6.5). These have been chosen because of the extent of recent investigation and the availability of published reports.

Although each of these complexes has witnessed detailed excavation and fieldwork, it will become apparent that our knowledge of their chronology and sequences of development remains far from perfect. There are several reasons for this. Good (*i.e.* well stratified, short-life and 'fresh' at the point of deposition) bone and charcoal samples suitable for radiocarbon dating are often not present; in some areas acidic geologies have resulted in the loss of bone and antler; sites that were not the focus for sustained depositional practices are 'clean' of dateable material; or excavation that has taken place has been on too small a scale to recover suitable dating evidence. The problem is widespread and not just confined to the regions considered here. Summary lists of available reliable radiocarbon dates for later Neolithic monuments provided by Pitts (2001b, appendix 2), Harding (2003, table 1) and Gibson (2005, figs. 42–3) are sobering in their brevity. Harding lists only 34 reliable dates for primary henge contexts, and Gibson 34 reliable and 24 'less reliable' dates for timber circles. Many of these relate to the Wessex monuments described above. Such chronological uncertainties make any understanding of possible parallel sequences, large-scale trends, or local trajectories extremely difficult to elucidate.

Etton/Maxey

The fen-edge setting of the Etton/Maxey complex in the Welland Valley of Cambridgeshire could not be more different to that of the Wessex chalklands (Figure 6.6). A considerable number of ring-ditches and hengiform monuments, probably constructed from the late 4th to the early 2nd millennia BC, are here distributed in a rather haphazard fashion across an area of slightly raised ground covering *c.*5 × 1 km – the so-called Maxey island (Simpson 1981; Pryor *et al.* 1985; Pryor 1998; French and Pryor 2005). Bounded by a migrating river system, this was a seasonally wet landscape that may, from early on, have been ascribed a liminal status. During the 4th millennium BC the area was given significance by the construction on its southern edge of the Etton causewayed enclosure, which acted as the focus for contemporary occupation, perhaps of a seasonal nature. A cursus was later created over the enclosure, and a second (the Maxey Cursus) set out on a similar NW-SE alignment to the north-west of Etton. Between them, the Etton and Maxey cursus monuments ran for a distance of over 2km diagonally across Maxey island, linking the braded networks of rivers to the north and south, and perhaps providing a dominant axis for movement. Rather than existing as a formal monument created in a single act, Pryor suggests the Maxey Cursus was constructed in stages over a protracted period of time as a series of 'events or episodes' (Pryor *et al.* 1985, 301).

These earlier 'public' monuments formed the focus for a steadily developing ceremonial landscape of smaller circular and oval ring-ditches and hengiforms. Some of these were very small and short-lived, such as the two contiguous henges with northerly entrances excavated in Field OS 124 (Simpson 1981). Both contained within their ditches deposits

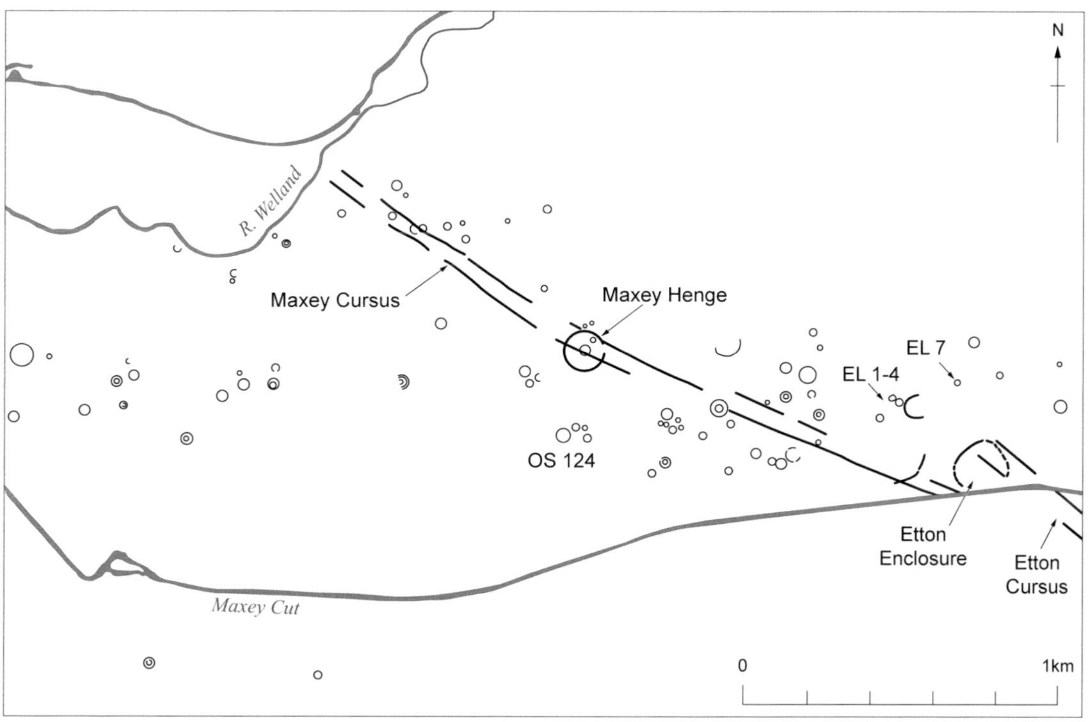

Figure 6.6. The Neolithic and early Bronze Age landscape at Etton/Maxey, Cambridgeshire (after French and Pryor 2005)

of cattle bone along with a decorated rib and two decorated antlers. A possible sherd of Grooved Ware and a chisel arrowhead hint at a later Neolithic date. Equally diminutive (with diameters of 7m and 5m) are two pit circles that supersede the Maxey cursus; limited re-cutting of the pits suggesting these were of more than transitory status.

A small cluster of monuments north of the Etton enclosure shows further diversity (French and Pryor 2005). These include a later Neolithic multi-phase hengiform (EL2) that began as a post setting within a ring-ditch, was then re-modelled as a sub-circular arrangement of pits, and finally as a horseshoe-shaped arrangement of pits surrounded by a ring-ditch. The active life of this monument must have been greater than many. Adjacent to this was another hengiform (EL4), consisting of a penannular ditch surrounding an off-centre sub-circle of pits; and to the south-east a large undated, but probably Neolithic, C-shaped enclosure. To the east, EL7 comprised a small (18m diameter) opposed-entrance henge, the ditch of which had been partially backfilled then re-cut on several occasions. Cremations were later inserted in EL2, 4 and 7. It is tempting to envisage each of these smaller monuments as being related to a specific kin group. As such, histories of construction, reworking, or rapid abandonment, could provide a record of lineage 'presence', subsequent success, failure or movement from the region.

The principal later Neolithic monument was constructed over the Maxey cursus. The Maxey henge was a large and complex construction different in detail to the smaller hengiforms and pit circles. Within an outer penannular ditch was a central ring-ditch enclosing a mound of turf and topsoil, while an oval barrow was set within the henge entrance. According to Pryor, the constructional sequence begins with the oval barrow being raised over a deliberately burnt timber mortuary structure. This was then followed by the outer ditch and external bank, the inner ditch with its internal bank and a two-phased mound. Pryor considers all of this to be 'strictly contemporary' and later Neolithic (Pryor *et al.* 1985, 303). The contracted sequence implies a highly staged unfolding of ceremonies that could have been directly linked to funerary rites of the individual buried under the oval mound.

There is within the Etton/Maxey landscape sequence a hint of a cycle from aggregation and large public constructions during the 4th millennium BC (the enclosure and Etton and Maxey cursus monuments), to smaller more kin-specific monuments and short-lived ceremony thereafter (*e.g.* EL2, 4 and 7), and finally back to the creation of a major monument with the events surrounding the Maxey henge. The creation of the latter may deliberately have referenced a by then distant past, since the builders of the Maxey henge chose to mimic or emulate the much earlier Etton enclosure in two important ways. Both monuments are of a similar scale (125 × 115m and 180 × 150m respectively) and have their longest axes set east-west. Later Neolithic interest in the Etton enclosure is certainly indicated by the deposition of large quantities of Grooved Ware and contemporary flintwork in the ditch of that monument and in interior pits.

Dorchester-on-Thames

The complex at Dorchester-on-Thames has excited interest since it was first discovered from the air between the Wars. As with the Etton/Maxey landscape, the monuments that make up this group define a very long history of activity, beginning with the creation of two long mortuary enclosures and a cursus (one of several on the gravel terraces of the Upper Thames Valley: Barclay *et al.* 2003) in the 4th millennium BC (Figure 6.7). Numerous small circular ditch-, pit- and post-defined monuments are clustered around the cursus, and to the immediate south-west is a large double-entrance henge, the 'Big Rings' (Atkinson *et al.* 1951; Bradley and Chambers 1988; Whittle *et al.* 1992; Thomas 1999b, 192–5).

Unlike many comparable ceremonial complexes, at Dorchester-on-Thames there appears not to have been a hiatus between the construction of nominally 'early' (linear) and 'later' (circular) Neolithic monuments. While there is an agreement that the linear monuments (VIII, 1) come early, that the cursus is a development from these, and that the Big Rings henge monument (site XIII) comes late in the sequence (there were sherds of Beaker in the primary ditch fill), the chronological position of many of the smaller circular monuments is open to debate (Table 6.1). Structural relationships and artefactual associations place some constructions (*e.g.* I, II and XI) early, even predating the cursus (site III), but most must postdate the latter. The matter of sequence is further complicated by the repeated reworking and modification of many of the circular monuments, hence the position of some in several of Thomas' phases. Sites I and II possess at least three phases, and site XI four. In contrast, sites IV, V and VI are of a single phase. Associated radiocarbon dates give ranges of 2920–2660 cal BC for site 2, 2950–2300 cal BC for site 3, and 3100–2870 cal BC for the first phase of site XI. Some components, including the large (*c.*60m diameter) circular monuments towards the south-eastern end of the cursus, are unexcavated and hence undated.

Perhaps telling of the playing out of similar ritual cycles, the sequence of events at sites IV, V and VI is strikingly similar. All begin as timber circles from which posts were removed (Gibson 1992), the ditches/pits then being backfilled or allowed to silt up before cremations were inserted into the top of them. At Site 3 the posts had been burnt out to their bases, and cremated bone then worked into the post-pipes, perhaps from surface deposits. The presence of large numbers of putative later Neolithic cremations (over 150 in total) from cemeteries in sites I, II, IV, V, VI, XI, 2 and 3 makes the Dorchester-on-Thames complex highly unusual in a southern British context (matched only by Stonehenge and Duggleby Howe in Yorkshire: Kinnes 1979). Their presence may speak of very real ancestral connections and the contemporary conceptualisation of the complex as a place of origins. Curiously, given the close association with mortuary rites, middle Neolithic inhumations and early Bronze Age burials are relatively

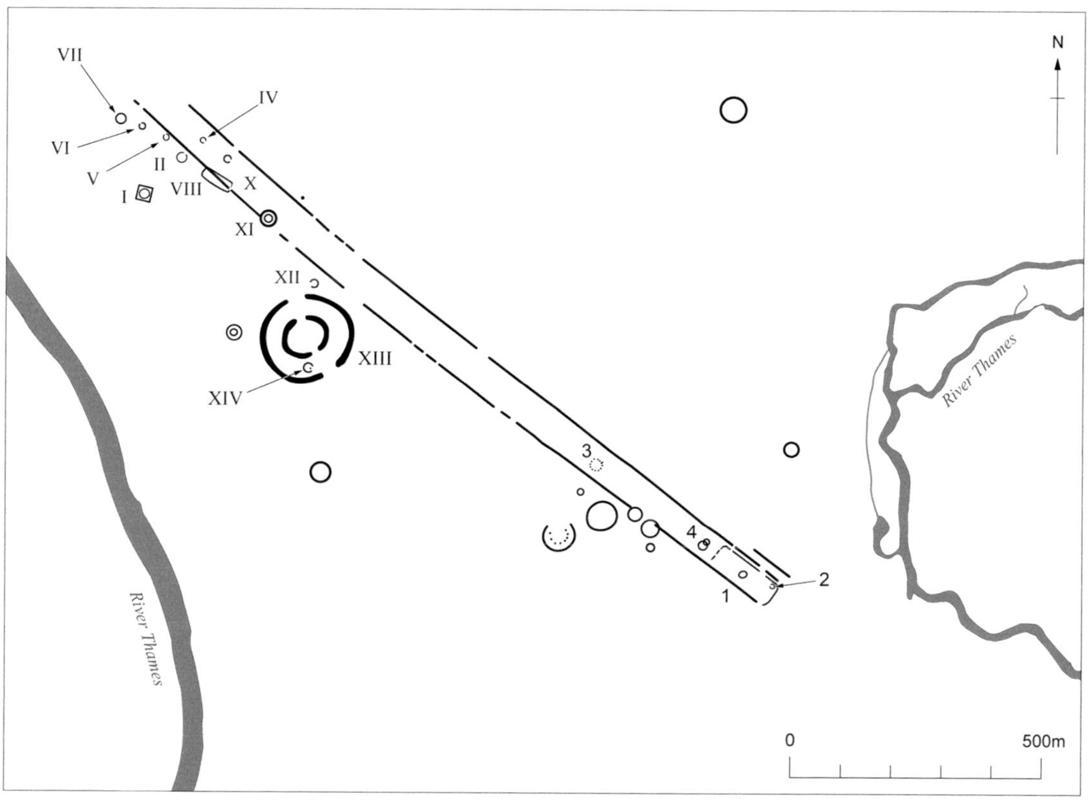

Figure 6.7. (left) The Neolithic monument complex at Dorchester-on-Thames, Oxfordshire (after Whittle et al. *1992 and Barclay* et al. *2003)*

Table 6.1. (below) Reconstructed sequences for the monuments at Dorchester-on-Thames

Bradley and Chambers 1988		Whittle *et al.* 1992			Thomas 1999	
Phase	*Site*	*Phase*	*Site*	*Character*	*Phase*	*Site*
A	II, VIII, XI, 1	1	VIII, 1	Beginnings	1	I, II, VIII, XI, 1
B	III	2	III (with II and XI?)	Formalisation and enhancement	2	II, XI
C	IV, V, VI, 3, 2, I, XIV	3	II, XI, IV, V, VI, 3, 2, I, XIV	Diversity and gradual change of tradition	3	I, III, XI
D	XII, XIII, VII, 4	4	XII, XIII, VII, 4	Dislocation	4	I, IV, V, VI, XI
E	IX	5	IX	Abandonment		

scarce here, a situation which contrasts with other foci in the Upper Thames Valley such as Barrow Hills and Stanton Harcourt (Thomas 1999b, 195).

Monument construction at Dorchester-on-Thames looks to span much of the 4th and 3rd millennia BC, with the pace perhaps decreasing by the middle of the latter millennium. Coming in at some point around 2000BC, the Big Rings is the final 'grand' statement. For Whittle it represents a radical novelty in terms of size and layout – an introduction of the exotic and a dislocation with the past (Whittle *et al.* 1992, 198) – but its form refers back to earlier circular monuments and the scale of its work recalls that of the cursus that provided such a long-term focus for activity here.

Walton Basin

The Walton basin on the Powys/Herefordshire border is the former bed of a post-glacial lake, from which the Knobley and Summergil Brooks now drain. Extensive flint scatters and a group of monuments occur on the basin floor close to the confluence of these rivers (Gibson 1999). The significance of this landscape during the earlier Neolithic is indicated by the presence of two cursus monuments (Figure 6.8). Later, 3rd millennium BC, constructions include stone monuments such as the Four Stones 'four-poster' circle close to the Hindwell cursus, a possible henge and monumental mound, and two massive palisaded enclosures (Walton and Hindwell II). It is the presence of the latter that marks out the special status of this landscape during the later Neolithic. The Walton enclosure is defined by individual post-pits and may have been constructed during the early part of the 3rd millennium BC. Like West Kennet enclosure 1 and perhaps Greyhound Yard, the river was utilised to form parts of its perimeter. With posts set in a continuous bedding trench the Hindwell II palisade presented a more solid barrier. Dated to 2800–2500 cal BC, it is the largest of the later Neolithic palisades known to date, enclosing an area of 25ha (800 × 400m). The configuration of massive enclosures, a possible henge

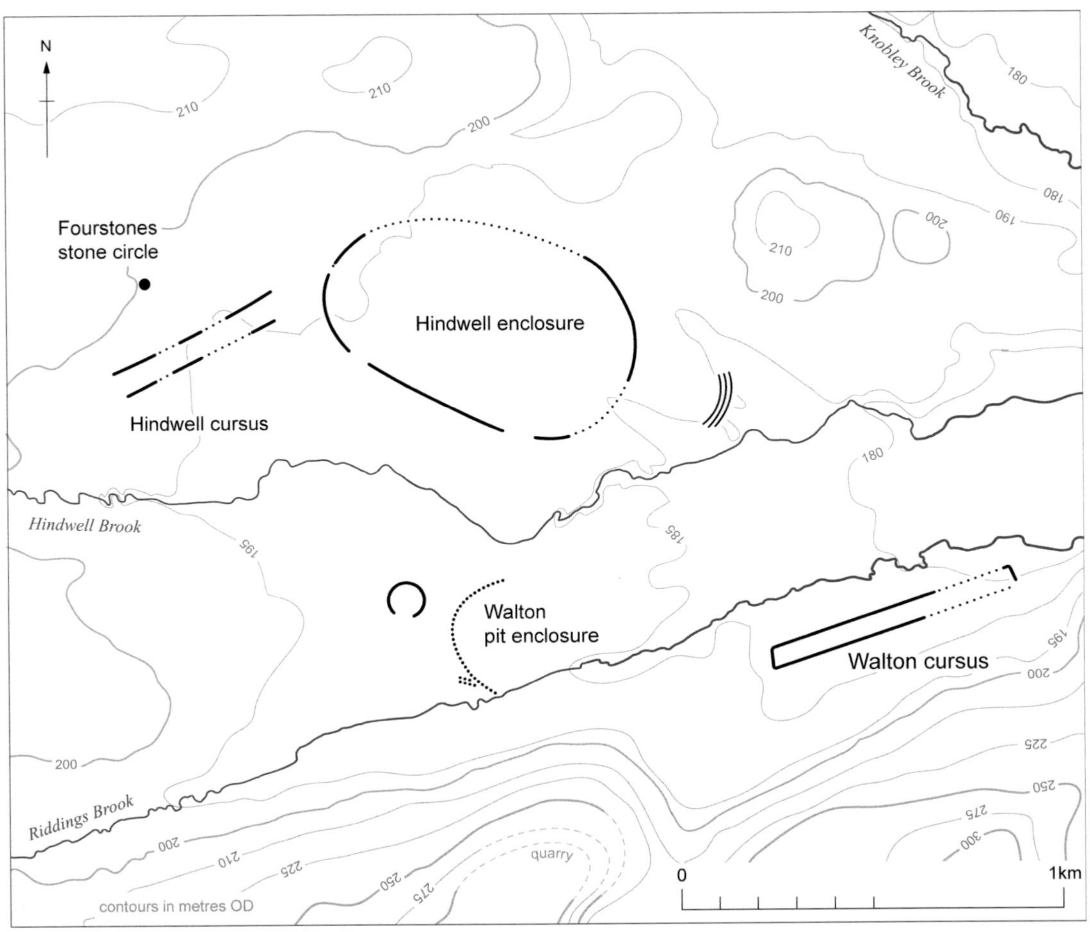

Figure 6.8. The Neolithic monument complex in the Walton Basin, Powys (after Gibson 1999)

and a large mound of putative later Neolithic date at Walton suggests parallels with the major Wessex monument complexes.

Thornborough

A series of six large, double-entrance henge monuments occupy a 12km stretch alongside the River Ure, north of Ripon in North Yorkshire (Harding 2000; 2003) (Figure 6.9). Three of these are arranged in a regularly-spaced linear group on low ground at Thornborough, in an area that also witnessed earlier Neolithic occupation and monument construction. The central henge is superimposed on an earlier cursus monument running perpendicular to the river, while the terminal of a second cursus has been identified adjacent to the northern henge. Early Bronze Age post alignments and a small number of ring-ditches cluster around the henge monuments. The

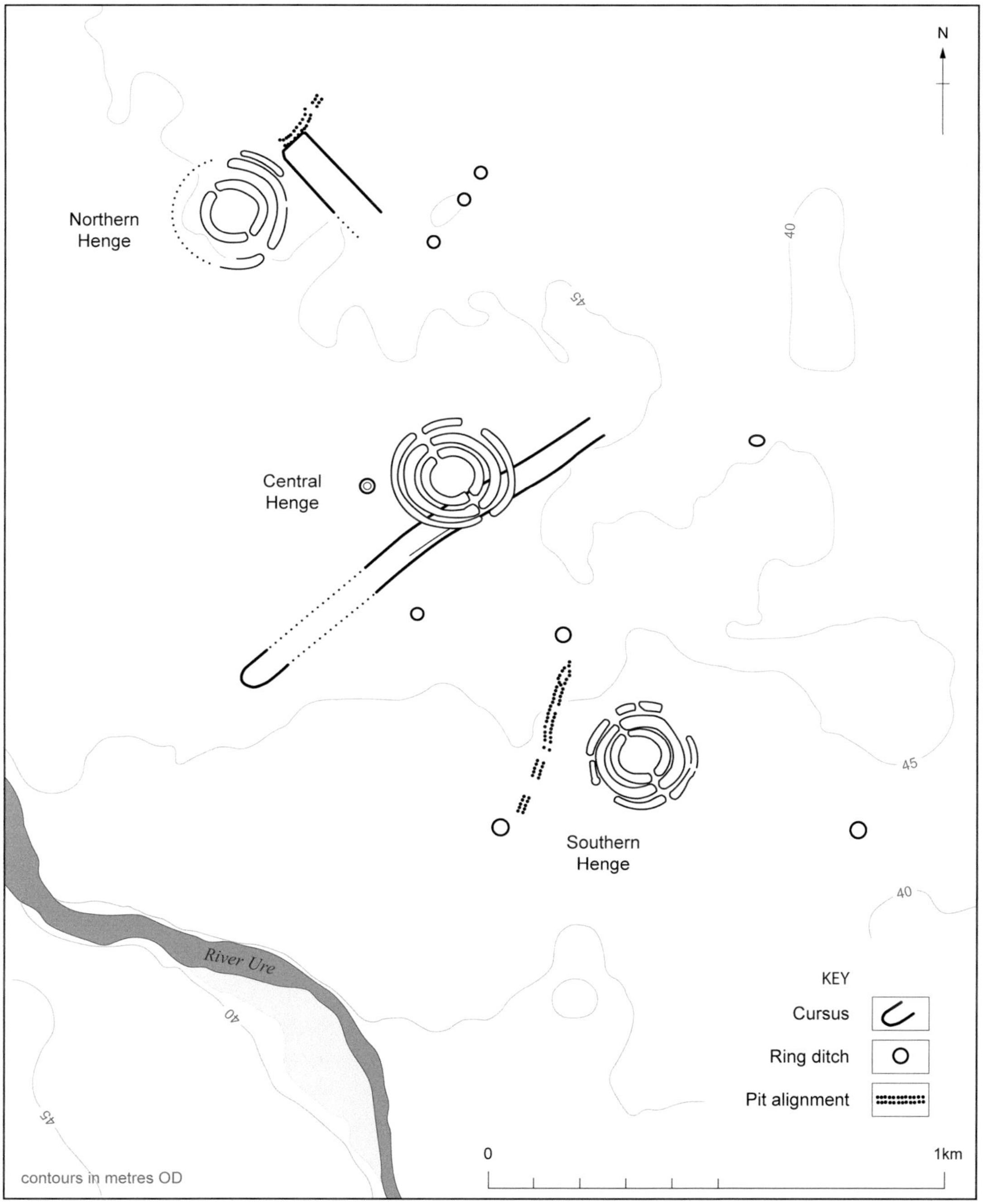

Figure 6.9. The Neolithic monument complex at Thornborough, Yorkshire (after Harding 2003)

entrances of all three henges are aligned NW-SE, though skewed slightly so that the interior of the northern henge cannot be seen from within the central henge. This axis follows the major trend of the River Ure, an important routeway from Wensleydale and the north-west of England into the Vale of Mowbray.

A striking feature of the Thornborough henges is their architectural similarity: all are of identical format and scale, with regular inner ditches and surrounding banks enclosed by segmented outer ditches. The results of recent excavations suggest the development of each of these monuments was synchronous, rather than being chronologically successive. As such, all three henges can perhaps be conceived as a *single* monument. Construction looks to begin with the creation of the outer ditches, to which the massive inner earthworks were then added. A date of 1750–1510 cal BC from a primary context in the southern henge (Harding 2003, table 1) could suggest this henge complex, or components of it, came very late. Contemporary occupation is attested by dense flint scatters on Chapel Hill, *c.*1km to the east of the central henge, and also to the west and north-west of the complex.

Harding has stressed the importance of the River Ure as a major routeway during the later Neolithic, perhaps tied to the movement of Cumbrian Group VI axes into Yorkshire, and envisages the Thornborough complex as a centre for pilgrimage along this route. In this scheme other very similar henge monuments to the south at Nunwick, Hutton Moor and Cana Barn map out a continuation of this 'spiritual journey' as it approaches the confluence of the Rivers Ure and Swale and the nearby alignment of massive megaliths at the Devil's Arrows. Perhaps a similar comprehension of materiality and cosmological order was in operation here to that evident in the mid-3rd millennium BC Stonehenge landscape, in that the journey down-river was also a movement, albeit greatly attenuated, from monuments of earth to ones of stones.

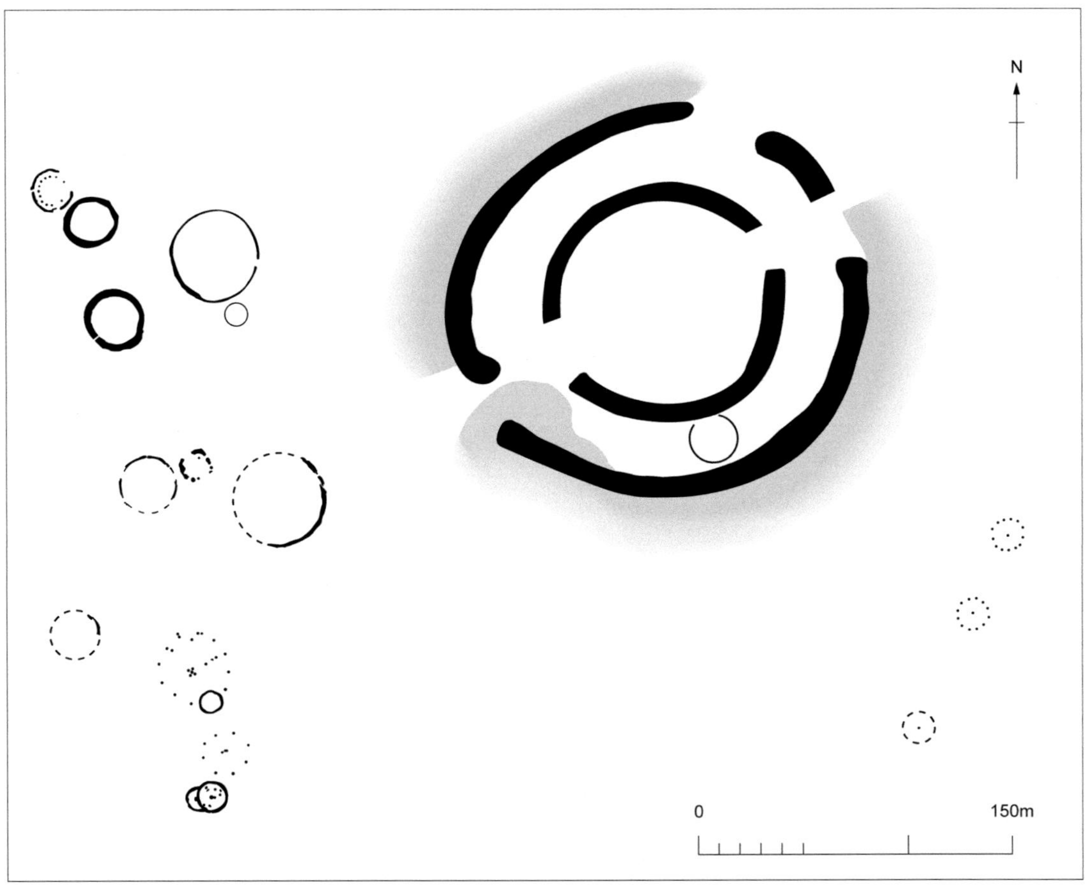

Figure 6.10. The Neolithic monument complex at Ferrybridge, Yorkshire (after Roberts 2005)

Ferrybridge

The large henge monument at Ferrybridge, 60km to the south of the Thornborough complex, bears a striking resemblance to the north Yorkshire monuments (Figure 6.10). This and a number of smaller circular ditched monuments and timber circles are sited on an area of ground between the Fryston Beck and Wash Dike close to the point where they join the River Aire, on the western edge of the Aire valley, West Yorkshire (Roberts 2005). A broad, low limestone ridge running NW-SE formed a notable topographical feature that was important in the structuring of the monument complex. This was modified, probably in the Neolithic, to give it a more linear structure, by cutting a wide channel that served to remove a short spur of limestone. Providing a largely conceptual boundary, the earthwork and timber monuments of the complex were set along and to the east of this. A number of monuments within this complex have been subject to excavation, principally during work in advance of the diversion of the A1 in 2001–2.

The principal monument is the Ferrybridge henge, a 250m-diameter enclosure, defined by double ditches broken by two opposed-entrances. It is aligned SW-NE, parallel with the Fryston Beck and Wash Dike. The monument incorporates several phases of construction, and appears to post-date a ring-ditch enclosed between the bank and inner ditch. There are potentially six episodes of construction related to the bank, the first corresponding to the digging of the inner ditch, the second to the outer (a reverse sequence to that claimed for Thornborough). Unfortunately, its chronology is not well understood, since three radiocarbon dates on charcoal (potentially residual) from the bank span the period *c.*3350–2140 cal BC. In addition, an Iron Age scabbard came from the primary fill of the inner ditch and Roman material from levels just above this, implying much later re-cutting.

There are 22 known Neolithic and Bronze Age monuments within 500m of the henge, mostly to the immediate west along the ridge, and to the south-east. The range of monument forms is very varied, including post-circles, hengiforms and round barrows. After the henge, the largest are hengiform 176 at *c.*42m and hengiform 178 at 45m, the ditches of these, however, being small and shallow. Others include a segmented ring-ditch enclosing a post ring and a linear timber 'screen' (hengiform 155); a sub-circular pit circle redefined by a segmented ditch (hengiform 162); four timber circles; a number of ring-ditches and a round barrow containing two Beaker burials dated to the last quarter of the 3rd millennium BC. Three of these constructions – hengiform 162, and timber circles 140 and 165 – were the focus for the deposition of cremations during an early stage. There exists a limited degree of spatial order, in that the four timber circles occupy a zone to the south of the hengiforms.

Phasing the developments at Ferrybridge is made difficult by the dearth of associated material culture (itself indicative of the limited scale of deposition and perhaps associated occupation), and the absence of radiocarbon dates from a number of the monuments. Of the smaller monuments, timber circle 165 probably belongs to the second half of the 4th millennium BC, and 'barrow' 114 and hengiform 162 to the early 3rd millennium BC. The early phases of the Ferrybridge henge may also come in at this horizon. Radiocarbon dates place timber circle 140 in the second half of 3rd millennium BC. Although undated, structural similarity between the North and South timber circles suggest they were constructed simultaneously or in rapid succession.

In contrast to the episodic reworking of the henge, none of the smaller monuments display much evidence for substantial alteration or reinstatement. This need not, however, indicate that their presence was transitory, as indicated by the insertion of much later (earlier Bronze Age) cremations in hengiform 162, and timber circles 140 and 165. Curiously, these three monuments had acted as foci for the deposition of cremations during the late 4th and 3rd millennia BC. That they should be selected as suitable places for much later mortuary activity implies the activation of a process of long-term memory that was not manifest in the periodic reinstatement of these monuments.

Theme and diversity in later Neolithic ceremonial centres

Regional variations in the format of later Neolithic monument types and material sequences and practices are increasingly recognised across the British Isles (Thomas 1996; Harding 2003; Noble 2006), and have been highlighted further here. The case studies presented above illustrate theme and diversity: a picture of common concerns surrounding the marking of the special, sacred qualities of certain landscapes, while doing so in relation to local social conditions, beliefs and histories of place. The challenge remains to understand how the manifestation of broader historical processes was played out on a local scale through the creation of monuments, and what the particularities of practice might tell us of regional identities and engagements with both the material world and that of supernatural agencies.

There existed a shared architectural repertoire across the later Neolithic of the British Isles, seen with the construction of versions of henge monuments, timber and stone circles, palisades and occasionally avenues and large mounds. However, a focus on these monument 'categories' has often resulted in an homogenised image of later Neolithic monumentality, and has taken our attention away from the very varied sequences and formats of the complexes these discrete monuments make up. An image of uniformity has also developed through the assumption that the major Wessex monument complexes – which, as was shown earlier in this chapter, share points in common in terms of sequences of development, meaning and even 'operation' – can be regarded as 'typical' for Britain as a whole. By considering the evidence from other regions we have sought to highlight the variation that exists. The 'chaotic' and fluid construction of the later 4th and 3rd millennium BC landscapes at Maxey/Etton and Ferrybridge provide a very real contrast with the coherent, even 'planned', structure of the Thornborough and Stanton Drew complexes. The presence of numerous small constructions (hengiforms and timber circles) at the former, and in other groups such as at Dorchester-on-Thames, could be telling of the absence of any dominant social control, of social fission, of the desire to maintain kin-group or lineage identity within more unstable larger communities. Equally they could represent responses to specific, short-lived social needs – 'a means of appealing to the supernatural' at times of crisis (Harding 2003, 88). In contrast, communities with greater long-term stability and an enhanced sense of corporate identity could have been responsible for the creation of the 'great' ceremonial centres of Mainland Orkney, the Boyne Valley and Wessex. But, we must be wary of viewing the character and scale of monumentality as a simple expression, index or outcome of the existence of particular forms of social structure. It may, after all, have been the demands of monument construction itself and sacred imperatives that created and maintained community cohesion or fission.

The case studies have also illustrated how varied local sequences can be. While once again recognising that the closely interlinked events in Wessex are the exception rather than the norm, there do not appear to be any distinct chronological horizons across the British Isles that mark the coming into being of these monument complexes, nor a general scaling-up of constructional activity, or a common end. The great henges, stone circles and passage graves of the Stenness/Brodgar complex on Mainland Orkney, for example, look to have been created over a tight period of three or four hundred years centring on *c.*3000BC (Ashmore 2000; Richards 2005). Contrast this with the seemingly continuous activity of monument building and reworking over a millennium-and-a-half at Dorchester-on-Thames, or the equally attenuated sequences represented by the Avebury and Stonehenge landscapes. Maxey/Etton and Dorchester-on-Thames share a similar 'end', marked by the creation of single major monuments – the Maxey and Big Rings henges. It is still difficult to determine how widespread this culmination in the making of 'great monuments' was. In these instances at least, the creation of large henges could signal moments of closure, dislocation (Whittle *et al.* 1992, 198), or even an end to ceremonial activity.

One recurrent, although by no means universal, feature is the development of these ceremonial centres in relation to earlier Neolithic constructions, and even traces of early 4th millennium BC occupation (*e.g.* Llandegai: Lynch and Musson 2004). There seems to be an especial relationship with cursus monuments, which are variously built over (*e.g.* Thornborough and Maxey), or next to (*e.g.* Walton Basin and Dorchester-on-Thames), with a common axis frequently being shared by both cursus and henge monument. This may represent a process of appropriating or negating the past (Bradley 1993, 100–7), or could reflect the intimate link that existed between both kinds of monument and important routes of movement through landscapes (Loveday 1998).

When considering regional trajectories of development, absences are almost as interesting as presences. Any assumption that all later Neolithic communities participated in the construction and ceremonial use of monuments is countered by the recognition of the relative or even total absence of henges and allied constructions from a number of regions of southern Britain. There are no great late Neolithic ceremonial complexes on the eastern edge of the East Anglian fens, in large parts of East Anglia, in the middle and lower Thames valley, Sussex and Kent, or on the chalk of the Lincolnshire or Yorkshire Wolds. Single henge monuments are known in these areas, but their presence is exceptional and they do not form parts of larger complexes. The absence of major monument complexes cannot be a product of low population densities or a lack of organisational ability preventing labour and resources being gathered to create major monuments. A sustained late Neolithic presence is well attested by dense flint scatters and pit clusters on the Yorkshire Wolds (Manby 1974; Harding 2006) and the Norfolk fen-edge (Healy 1996), for instance; while the ability to undertake large 'public works' is ably demonstrated by the scale of 3rd millennium BC flint mining at Grimes Graves in Norfolk (Barber *et al.* 1999). Why large monument complexes should be present in some areas and absent from others remains a matter for detailed consideration. One interpretation could posit marked regional differences in belief systems: those populations living across large tracts of the east and south-east of England being engaged in ceremonial and mortuary practices that appropriated natural landscape features (note, for example, the scale of stone axe deposition in the middle Thames: Adkins and Jackson 1976), or which did not require any kind of architectural or topographic foci. An alternative is to consider how certain regions and landscapes might have lent themselves to the enhancement afforded by the creation of monument complexes. Here, issues of cosmology, materiality and non-human agency become significant.

Monuments, cosmology, materiality and non-human agency

Our accounts of later Neolithic monumentality have tended to focus on monument construction as responding to, or being implicated in, the formation of social strategies, tensions or goals (Renfrew 1973; Bradley 1984; Barrett 1994). There is no question that such a sociological perspective has been highly productive and illuminating, and has produced some stimulating interpretive accounts of the British Neolithic. However, it is based upon an understanding of power and agency as residing solely in the domain of human practice, and has perhaps ignored the extent to which the creation of monuments and sacred landscapes was a response to the perceived agency of other things, especially that of supernatural beings, the legacy of mythic association and the 'spirits' of place (Carmichael *et al.* 1994). The challenge is to find ways of comprehending the conditions under which monuments were created that works together the interplay between such human and non-human agency.

A lead is provided by a recent body of literature that has sought to demonstrate how people and non-human components of the world are embroiled in heterogeneous networks that constitute each other. Various writers in the social sciences have highlighted how non-human things in their broadest sense – including material culture, architecture, fauna, flora and landscape features – are, like people, delegated identities, responsibilities and roles, and become points around which action is constrained and structured (Latour 1993; Boast 1997; Gell 1998; Latour 1999; Law and Hassard 1999; Graves-Brown 2000; Jones and Cloke 2002).This affords them a degree of agency – an ability to 'act back' and elicit responses. There is of course the question of where the limits of non-human agency might lie (Jones and Cloke 2002, chapter 3). For Gell things remain as 'secondary agents', lacking any intentionality of their own, and therefore only capable of operating with human associates (1998, 17). For Gosden, things are 'active in the manner of objects not in the manner of people' (2001, 164). They can elicit particular sensory responses or 'effects' which channel social action, sometimes in ways unanticipated, but that does not involve any intentionality on the part of the thing itself. So while people and object worlds are mutually constituted, and agency may be seen as variously distributed, there may be problems with objects being considered *de facto* as agents, 'having lives of their own outside of human constitution' (Meskell 2004, 4).

Within this argument 'context is everything' (*ibid.*, 6). Different kinds or degrees of agency may be seen to operate in varied circumstances, some being of more immediate significance than others. At a very basic level, the physical presence of a stone will force people to move around rather than attempt to walk through it; likewise the presence of a dangerous animal will guide people to take evasive action. Both are instances of non-human agency, but of a largely anecdotal kind. Of more interest are those situations where the emotive or sensory qualities of things have the capacity to elicit responses that significantly shape or alter human projects in unanticipated ways. These are objects that, like Trobriand canoe-prows, enchant in a spell-like fashion (Gell 1992), or 'raise hopes, generate fears, evoke losses, and delight' (Spyer 1988, 5). Emotive power is strongest in those things which hold such an 'excess' of association as to become threatening or destabilising, such as the effects of a deceased individual, which stand as an extension of the dead person, and so serve to 'presence' the deceased (Hallam and Hockey 2001). However, it is with those objects that are regarded as possessing purposive agency, that are seen to 'have life', or be the material form of spirits or deities, that any ontological distinction between human and non-human agency completely dissolves. As an example, the Erromangan of Vanuatu believe that certain stones bring harm or assistance to people depending on their treatment, but also act independently of human involvement, moving, procreating and even speaking (Roe and Taki 1999). Such perceptions of animate forces residing within objects, shrines and landscape features are not uncommon among small-scale societies (or indeed among modern neo-pagan groups) and would surely have coloured Neolithic world-views.

The creation of monuments involved an engagement and negotiation with various non-human agencies, including auspicious places, animate substances, spirits and other supernatural entities. It can be seen most clearly in the context of the landscape setting of many later Neolithic complexes, which do not occur in random locations nor, strictly, in all those areas that witnessed occupation. When all factors are considered, it is apparent that aspects of local topography were extremely important in determining where monuments might be built. Richards (1996) has drawn attention to the recurrent siting of henges in relation to water, and Bradley (Bradley 1998, 121–4) to the location of many later Neolithic monuments in bowl-shaped landscapes. They argue that the format of individual monuments can be read as an homology of the surrounding topography of those landscapes. Thus, for Richards, the banks and ditches of henges were a symbolic representation of enclosing hills and adjacent river channels, while a metaphoric association existed between the flow of water and human movement through henges.

Perhaps this line of interpretation can be taken further. Rather than simply replicating aspects of local topography, could the creation of these monument complexes have been a *response* to the perceived affordances and agencies that were seen to reside in certain landscapes? The relationship to rivers is particularly significant in this respect. Not only are so many of the ceremonial centres described here (and others, such as those in the Milfield Basin in Northumberland and Penrith in Cumbria) set adjacent to the confluence of rivers, but those rivers possess an easterly or southerly flow. Because of the direction of flow, those rivers were perhaps considered cosmologically auspicious, and afforded both potency and protection to the activities that took place within and around monumental constructions. The direction of flow might be linked to transformatory and regenerative power – assisting in the transition of the newly-dead into ancestors in the case of the Avon at Stonehenge. In other instances certain landscapes were perceived to embody 'inherent' cosmological qualities, making them the focus for special practices including monument building: the details of topography could determine the auspiciousness of a locale. This is best illustrated by the position of the major late Neolithic complexes on the northern and western isles of Scotland, at Machrie Moor on Arran, Calanais on Lewis, and Stenness-Brodgar on Orkney. It is surely far from coincidental that all were created on the western sides of their respective islands and within landscapes that, because of the topography created by rivers, lochs and surrounding hills, had a clear axial directionality to them. What is more, the Machrie Water, the East Loch Roag and the Stenness peninsula share a broadly NW-SE axis, an axis that, because of its relationship to midwinter sunrise and midsummer sunset, was recurrently referenced in the construction of later Neolithic monuments. In Wessex different landscape qualities may have mattered. Here, Neolithic communities responded to a potency seen to reside in the very geology of this region. As a pure white rock, chalk was perhaps regarded as a regenerative medium; hence its employment in the making of fertility symbols (phalli, balls and cups), and the desire to dig far into it, as seen with the excessively deep ditch at Avebury and the shafts at Maumbury Rings and Monkton Up Wimborne (Green 2000, 77–84). Such engagements with chalk can be viewed as being bound up with 'a set of relations of reciprocity with the earth itself' (Thomas 1999a, 76), relations that mediated the flow of generative substances and energies.

Earth, trees and stones were important agents within these landscapes, and should not be thought of simply as neutral building materials for the creation of monuments. Dealings with these substances acknowledged and negotiated their perceived ontological and agental statuses. As a case in point, the actions involved in the inversion of a large tree stump and its enclosure within a wooden palisade at the late 3rd millennium BC site of Holme-next-the-Sea, Norfolk (Brennand and Taylor 2003), surely bespeaks of an intent to control or negate something of the tree's 'power', however that was understood. The placing of deposits of human and animal bone around another inverted stump in the ditch of a long barrow at Eynesbury, Cambridgeshire (Ellis 2004), implies a connection between certain trees and the recent or ancestral dead that echoes connections otherwise emphasised by the placement of human remains within split trunk mortuary chambers (*e.g.* Haddenham: Evans and Hodder 2006). It is possible to conceptualise the Avebury sarsens in similar terms. The ubiquitous presence of sarsen within the landscape must have engendered mythical explanations for its presence, which might explain the developing association between stones and sacred realms during the course of the region's Neolithic; culminating in the employment of massive quantities of sarsen to construct the stone circles and avenues. In the mid 4th millennium BC sarsens had been woven into the fabric of long mounds in complex and highly conscious ways. At the Beckhampton Road long barrow, the edge of the mound was deliberately laid out to take in a small boulder, implying a pre-existing significance attached to this one particular stone; while at the analogous site of South Street a 'cairn' of nine large sarsen blocks occupied a proximal position under the mound that was normally reserved for mortuary deposits (Ashbee *et al.* 1979). At the latter site, sarsens were being acknowledged through their gathering and marking, and were subjected to an analogous process to that afforded to human remains – here a degree of 'care' and respect was being offered to stones. Elsewhere we have talked of the complex histories and identities of sarsens in the Neolithic (Gillings and Pollard 1999), and how such biographies conditioned the way in which certain blocks were appropriated for construction projects. Implied within this study was a sense that the individual stones making up the great late Neolithic monuments of the Avebury region always had an identity of their own, whether one that linked them to certain people, or an identity borne of their 'stoniness' and places of origin (Gillings and Pollard 1999; 2004). This biography constituted another form of agency – a legacy of association – that also had to be negotiated.

Coda: a return to the Avebury landscape

There may be no easy answer to the question of why the landscape of the Upper Kennet Valley was chosen for the creation of one of the greatest ceremonial centres in 3rd millennium BC Europe. As we have seen, it was most likely a combination of factors: the response to a lengthy Neolithic history of occupation and monument building; the agency and physical qualities of the landscape, there in the source of the River Kennet, in the chalk and the remarkable spreads of sarsen stone; the unfolding of inter-regional competition and emulation; and the contingency of history. Events here did not happen in isolation, but followed in their own way transformations that occurred across the British Isles and north-western Europe during the 3rd millennium BC. As with the histories of so many things, there existed a complex interplay of the large-scale and the local, and this is why the archaeology of the later Neolithic complex can be read at so many scales, and never satisfactorily encompassed by a single narrative.

Towards the end of the Neolithic a number of key monuments (and, in the case of the avenues, existing pathways) were transformed through their rebuilding in stone. This process of lithicisation marked a reconfiguration of the ontological domains within which these places and constructions operated: they seem no longer to have been part of the world of lived routine, but became special places set outside or alongside daily engagements. This is seen in the way that individual stones and the earthwork at Avebury now became the focus for the deposition of human remains, in the form of both inhumations and disarticulated bone. The transformation to stone of Avebury, the Sanctuary, the Longstones enclosure and the avenues marked a distancing, or at the very least a memorialisation, of certain monuments; it may even have turned them into 'dead spaces' rather than the locations for active ceremony as commonly believed. Such a reconfiguration of status was to have a legacy. Occupation was to continue around the immediate environs of these monuments into the early 2nd millennium BC, but then shifted onto the high downs around the valley, as if keeping a respectful distance that acknowledged the potency of these old places.

7

Later Prehistoric, Roman and early Post-Roman activity in Longstones Field

As highly visible and enduring components of the Avebury landscape, the megalithic settings of the Beckhampton Avenue and Longstones Cove continued to attract the attention of later communities living within the region. There is no evidence from Avebury or the avenue settings that standing stones had been deliberately buried or destroyed prior to the 14th century, although a number may have fallen, such as stone 40 of the Avebury Outer Circle which appears to have toppled during the Anglo-Saxon period (Chapter 9). We are therefore left with an image of a relatively intact series of megalithic structures surviving into the early 2nd millennium AD. Each later encounter with these invited interpretation (perhaps their framing through conjectural histories or myths), negotiation and accommodation that would have varied over time and according to context.

Many of those later encounters have left no obvious archaeological trace, but the excavations in Longstones Field did revealed a range of features and deposits that shed important light upon the nature of certain accommodations and understandings that were afforded to these settings during the later prehistoric, Roman and early post-Roman periods. Belonging to the early part of the sequence is an unusual and potentially long-lived ditch system that was created at the end of the Beckhampton Avenue, seemingly in response to the presence of the megalithic settings; while between the 1st and 7th centuries AD the Longstones Cove was the focus for the deposition of metalwork, animal bone and ceramics.

The later prehistoric ditch system

Located 60m to the south-west of the Longstones Cove, the later prehistoric ditch system is clearly visible on aerial photographs as well as the geophysical surveys undertaken by English Heritage (see Chapter 2 and Ucko *et al.* 1991, pl. 63). All show the feature crossing the corner of Longstones Field in an approximate NW-SE direction and taking a slightly erratic course, being straight over *c.*50m in its middle length, but turning suddenly to the north-west along its westerly third and more to the south-east in its easterly. A westerly offshoot may run towards the Beckhampton long barrow, although this feature could equally represent a slightly deeper length of medieval furrow, respecting as it does the line of later cultivation.

The course of the ditch system cannot currently be traced beyond Longstones Field. If it does continue, its easterly end may join another length of ditch visible as a cropmark *c.*150m to the south-east, running SW-NE along the side of Folly Hill. However, the latter is undated, and may in fact represent a medieval or post-medieval field boundary (Soffe 1993, 145). Of course, it is entirely possible that the ditch system is limited in its extent to the flat ground within Longstones Field. Additional geophysical survey may be required to successfully define its length and full course.

A 35m length of ditch F.102 was exposed and excavated in the south-western third of Trench 30 during 2003. It was sampled by means of five 2m wide sections: from south to north S.1, S.5, S.2, S.3 and S.4 (Figures 7.1–7.3). The overall width of the feature ranged between 3.8–5.4m; but upon excavation of the first section it became obvious that the ditch was made up of a series of separate cuts, reflecting a succession of redefinition events. At least six separate cutting/re-cutting episodes could be identified, though it is suspected that many other cuts could have been obliterated by later episodes of digging. The homogeneity of the fills often made the identification of individual cuts a very difficult process, except where there were marked variations in the compactness of the chalk rubble fills, or discrete steps in the ditch profile (Figure 7.2). For the same reason, it was a far from straightforward task to elucidate the absolute sequence of cuts, though 'early' and 'late' components could be identified.

The sequence may begin with a short length of pit alignment extending for a distance of at least 8m through S.2 and S.5. Four individual pits were revealed: cuts [978] and [986] in S.2, and [980] and [982] in S.5; each being circular or oval, 1.4–1.7m in diameter, and 0.61–0.70m deep. Well-cut, their sides were steep, in places vertical, merging with slightly dished bases. All were filled with chalk rubble mixed with pale brown silty clay ([979] and [987]; [981] and [983] respectively). In the upper part of pit [986], context [913] represented a lens of very compact chalk rubble and clay loam, coming in from the eastern side. Not all need be contemporary. In S.2 the northern-most pit [978] was observed to cut the edge of [986].

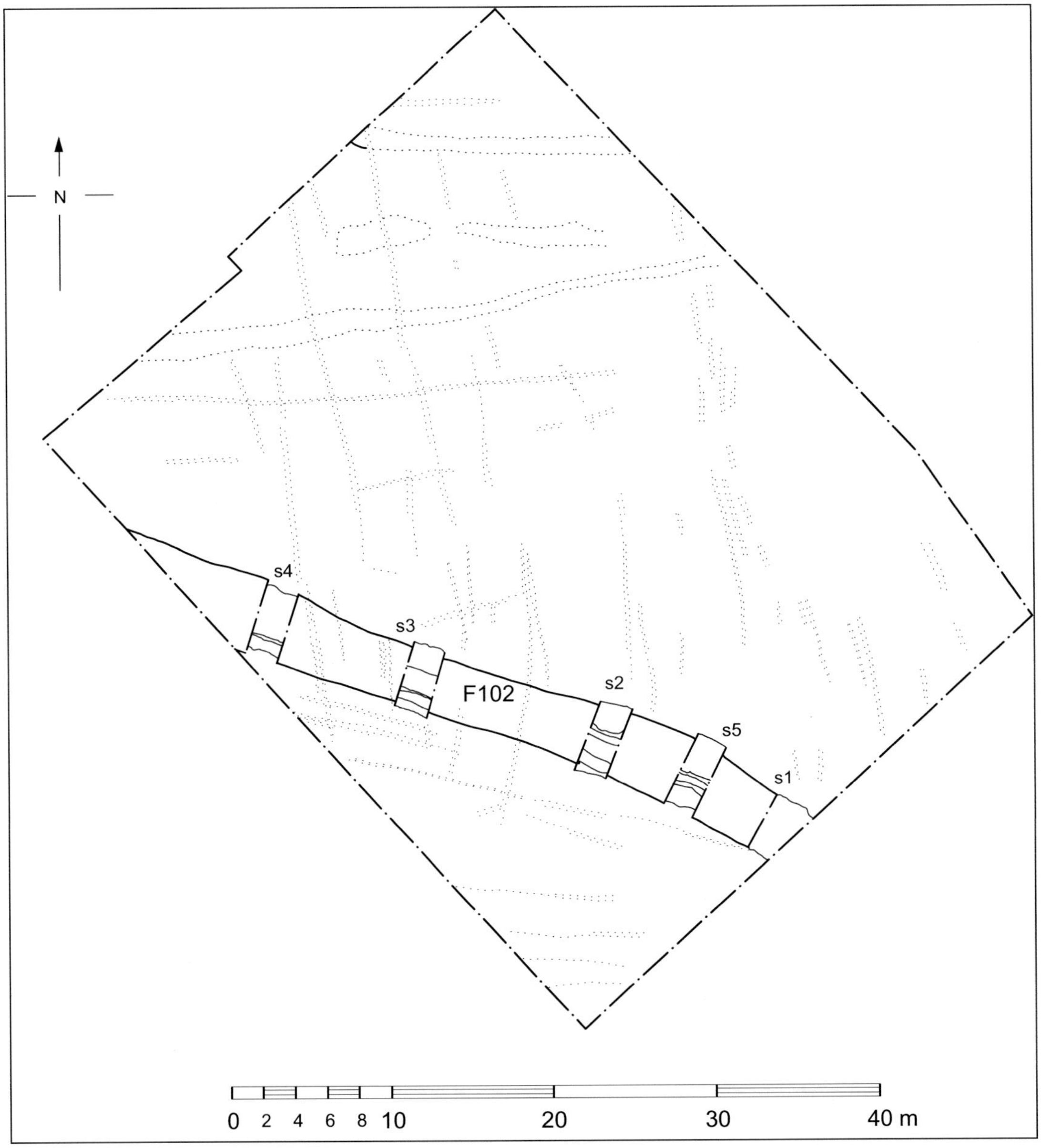

Figure 7.1. Exposed and excavated features in Trench 30 of Longstones Field. F.102 is the later prehistoric ditch system. Dotted lines mark plough furrows

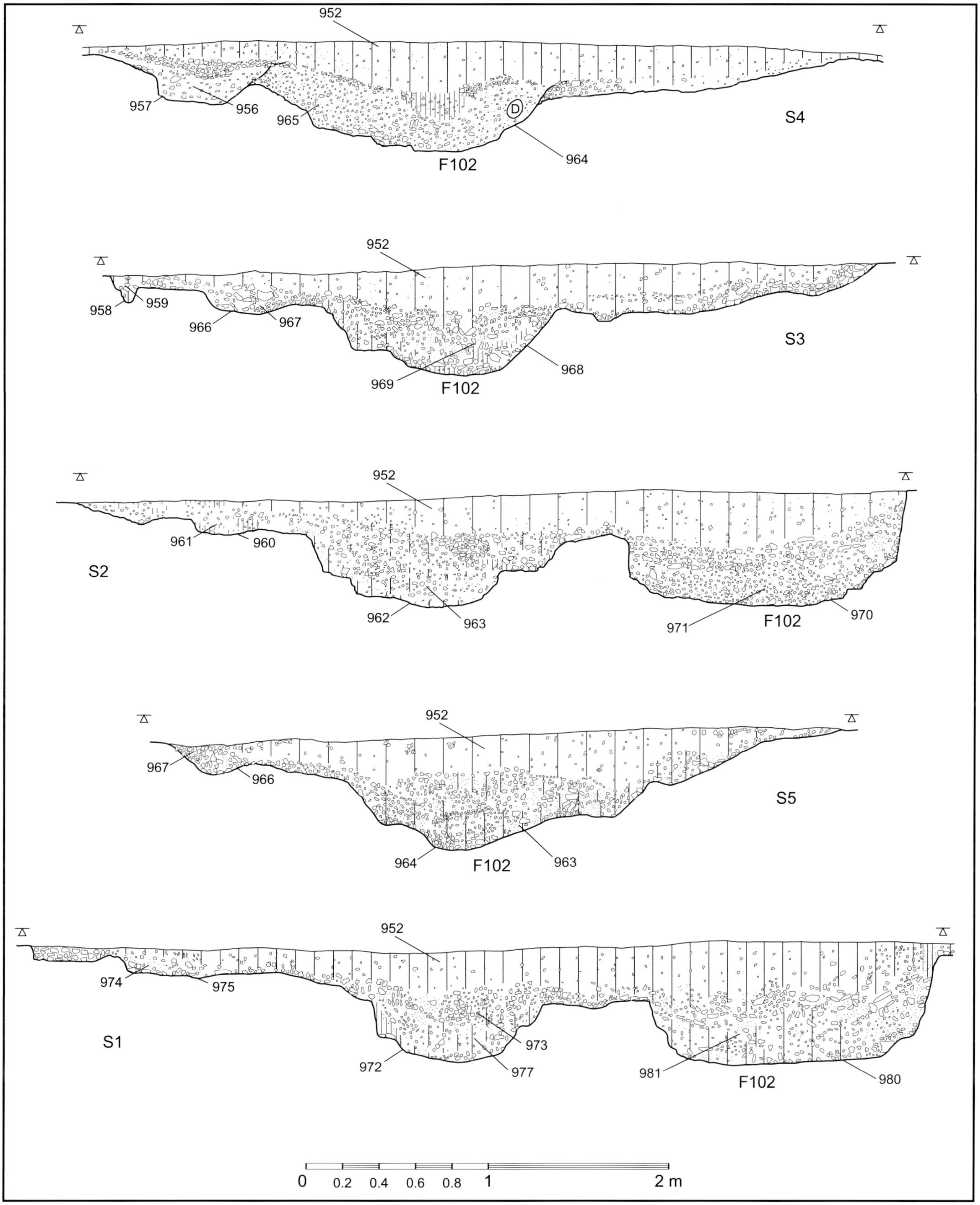

Figure 7.2. Sections of the later prehistoric ditch system F.102

Figure 7.3. Ditch system F.102 under excavation, from the SE

Apparently post-dating the pits was a broad, shallow ditch on the eastern side of F.102, [968]. Where still surviving, this was at least 1.1–1.7m wide and 0.2–0.3m deep, with a dished base. The fill [905]/[969] comprised a compact pale-brown clay loam with equal quantities of small chalk rubble, with occasional thin lenses of rubble against the eastern side and base.

Throughout its investigated length, the western half of [968] was cut through by a succession of later ditches that describe the centre of F.102. The two primary cuts of this central ditch were both similar in format, though it must be admitted that they were much truncated and in no instance is a full profile preserved. On the eastern side, cut [970] was up to 0.35–0.45m deep, with steep sides and a flat base. Ditch [906]/[989] to the west was similar in profile and dimensions, if slightly deeper in places. In some instances (*e.g.* S.2 and S.5) additional steps in the profile of these features hint at further cuts. The fills of the eastern and western ditches, [911]/[971] and [965]/[990] respectively, were of chalk rubble, occasionally very compact, interspersed with lenses of pale brown silty clay.

These in turn were replaced by a more substantial central ditch [962]/[964]/[966]/[972]/[988] late in the sequence. Between 0.60–0.70m deep and 1.1–1.5m wide, this possessed moderate sloping sides and a broad slightly dished base. It was filled up to half its depth with compact deposits of chalk rubble in a light brown clay loam, [912]/[954]/[963]/[967]/[977]. A primary lens of more loamy material, [966], perhaps a localised fall of topsoil, occurred on the base of the ditch in S.3. Sealing the main body of fill in S.1, S.5 and S.2 was a layer (up to 0.3m thick) of extremely compact, 'rammed' chalk, [910]/[973]/[976]/[953], which was initially mistaken for the base of the feature.

A small, shallow ditch defining the western side of F.102, [956]/[958]/[960]/[974], also looks to come late in the sequence. Flat-based with moderate sloping sides, 0.45–0.70m wide, and cut only 0.10–0.30m into the chalk, it was filled with a reasonably loose, fine chalk rubble in a brown silty loam, [957]/[959]/[961]/[975]. In S.4 this was overlain by a lens of purer chalk backfill, [955].

Sufficient of a hollow was left after these ditches had been cut and filled to collect a deposit of ploughsoil up to 0.35m deep: [902]/[904]/[950]/[951]/[952], a pale brown clay loam with some small chalk pieces. A single hand-made iron nail (identified by Graham Morgan) was recovered from this deposit along with a large rim sherd from a Roman New Forest colour-coat beaker (identified by Lorraine Mepham).

The feature was notable both for the extent of re-cutting and the very chalky fills. Under normal circumstances repeated re-cutting would lead to a decrease in chalk content, as the rock breaks down through mechanical and chemical weathering induced by re-exposure. Here, deposits of rubble, some extremely compact, filled the pits and ditches to a much greater depth than would have occurred under conditions of natural silting (Bell *et al.* 1996). The obvious conclusion is that the fills include an element of deliberate backfill, taking place soon after individual ditches were dug.

Finds from the ditch were very few, though included a small sherd of possible earlier Neolithic pottery from [902] (identified by Rick Peterson) and 32 pieces of worked flint. All of the worked flint is likely to be residual (Table 7.1). The assemblage comprises largely debit-

Context	Preparation flakes	Rejuvenation flakes	Flakes	Chips	Cores	Flaked pieces	Shatter fragments	Retouched
Section 1								
[902]	-	-	-	3	-	-	-	-
[910]	-	-	-	1	-	-	-	-
[912]	-	-	1	-	-	-	-	-
Section 2								
[904]	-	-	-	3	1	-	-	1 scraper
[979]	-	-	1	1	-	-	-	-
Section 3								
[950]	1	-	-	-	-	-	-	1 retouched flake
[959]	-	-	1	1	-	1	-	-
[967]	-	-	-	-	-	-	1	-
[969]	-	-	1	2	-	-	-	-
Section 4								
[951]	1	-	1	-	-	-	-	-
[955]	-	-	1	-	-	-	-	-
[957]	-	-	-	1	-	-	-	-
[965]	-	1	2	-	-	-	-	-
Section 5								
[952]	1	-	-	-	-	-	-	-
[973]	-	-	-	1	-	-	-	-
[981]	-	-	1	1	-	-	-	-

Table 7.1. Worked flint from F.102

age chips and small flakes, the majority of which are hard-hammer struck and of probable 3rd- or 2nd-millennia BC date. The single core from [904] in S.2 is multi-platform from which flakes have been removed. Of the two retouched pieces, that from [904] is an irregular scraper with steep, marginal retouch along one edge of the distal end; the other, from [950] in S.3, a small flake with limited marginal retouch.

The finds help little in dating the feature, although the absence of medieval and later ceramics, which were present in the overlying ploughsoil, and the morphology of the 'pit alignment' and ditches suggest strongly a later Bronze Age or Iron Age date (*i.e.* 1st millennium BC). The possibility of a Neolithic date was entertained, particularly given the feature's proximity to the Beckhampton Avenue, Longstones Cove and other Neolithic monuments in the locality. It does not, however, have the constructional 'style' of a Neolithic feature; the regular sides of the ditches giving the appearance of having been spade-dug.

Successively re-cut and backfilled, there is no doubt that the ditch is a rather curious feature, and one that does not conform to the conventional logic of a functional ditch. For most of its life it must have acted as a nominal and largely symbolic boundary, repeatedly reinstated through re-cutting, but instantly negated through backfilling. In this respect, the act of its creation/re-creation was likely to have been more important than any physical presence it held as an effective boundary. It is tempting to think that the ditch system served to cognitively divide two areas of the later prehistoric landscape: that to the east where the main megalithic settings of the Avebury complex lay; and the (by this stage) much more intensively used landscape of settlement and field-systems to the south and west. Both in this region and around Stonehenge, earlier megalithic settings seem to have been treated in a very circumspect manner during the later 2nd and 1st millennia BC, potentially even becoming 'taboo' space (Cleal *et al.* 1995, 491; Gillings and Pollard 2004, 86–8). Such is indicated in the Avebury region by the notable absence of early and middle Iron Age material culture, agriculture and settlement from the core area of the Neolithic monument complex (Bowden 2005). Here we may have a boundary whose principal role was to define and periodically reinstate a division between different ontological domains.

Other evidence for 1st millennium BC activity in and around the Avebury monuments is very ephemeral, and as a consequence more difficult to interpret. At Avebury itself, charcoal from stake-holes on the edge of stone 8 of the Outer Circle has been dated to 770–390 cal BC (Pitts and Whittle 1992, table 1). Unless deriving from natural fires, the suggestion is that at the very least people were visiting the stone settings and lighting fires there. Perhaps analogous in terms of the character of activity is the small pit F.1 excavated at the Falkner's Circle, for which a similar radiocarbon date was obtained (Chapter 3). Both could be regarded as evidence that megaliths acted as foci for the creation of hearths and the lighting of fires, though for what reason remains uncertain – was this veneration, or the product of fleeting visits by shepherds or others? It is important to stress the small-scale character of this activity, which should not be confused with the much later practice of fire-setting aimed at breaking-up the sarsens (Chapter 10).

Roman and early post-Roman activity at the Longstones Cove

The Roman period was one of relatively intensive occupation and dynamic change in the Avebury landscape. This was characterised by the construction of a major road (Margary 53) that cut directly across the region and the well-established routeways and megalithic settings (such as the West Kennet Avenue) that lay within it. It was also marked by a large-scale re-organisation of the agricultural landscape and restructuring of settlement patterns through the creation of new field systems, small farms and the emergence of villa sites that can be interpreted tentatively as estate centres (Pollard and Reynolds 2002, 149–82; Gillings and Pollard 2004, chapter 5).

This 'busyness' is evident if we look at the avenues and Longstones Cove. The path of the West Kennet Avenue was cut through by the road line as it made its way east-west across the landscape. At its closest point, the Beckhampton Avenue line passed as little as 500m to the north of the small town that developed to the north-east of Silbury Hill. At the terminus of the avenue the Longstones Cove settings sat within an area rich in Roman archaeology (Figure 7.4). Evidence from the tertiary ditch fills of the South Street long mound, located some 120m to the east of the Cove, suggests that cultivation was taking place in this area during the 1st – late 2nd century AD (Ashbee *et al.* 1979, 274, 289). In addition, some 850m to the south lay the line of the Roman road; whilst a villa site with tessellated pavements lay an equivalent distance to the north-west, at the foot of Windmill Hill. Closer still are the remains of possible Roman field boundaries 300m to the south-east of the settings.

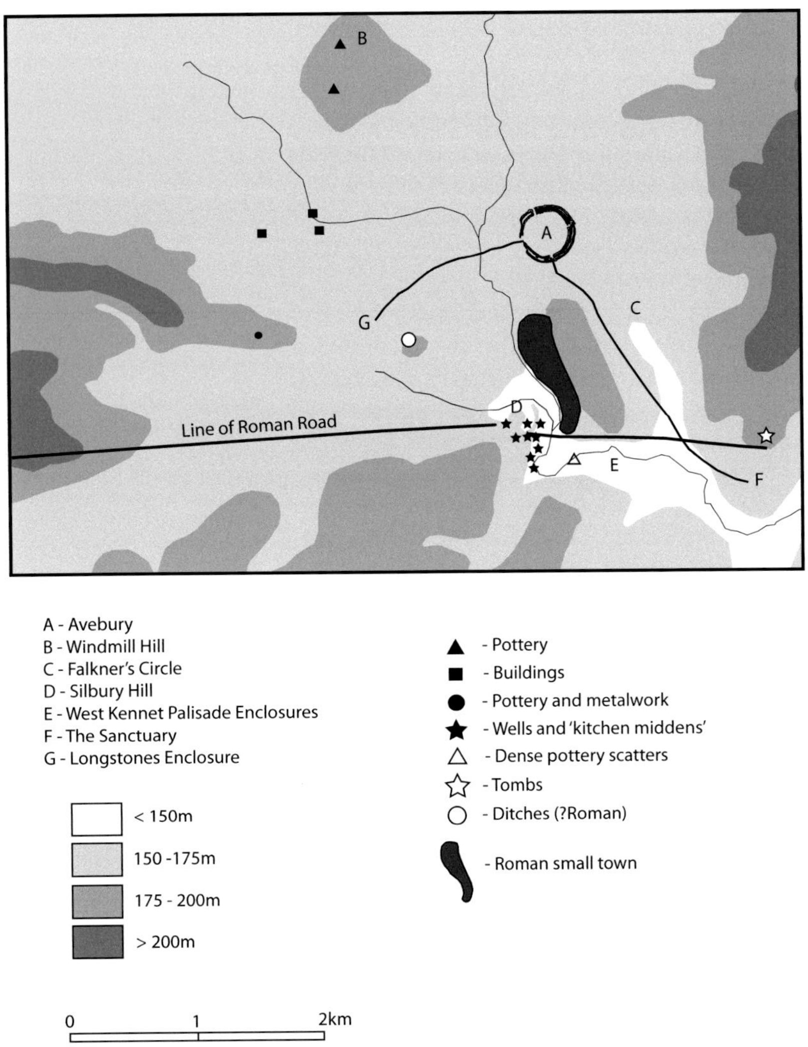

Figure 7.4. Roman sites and findspots in the environs of Avebury

Rather than marginalised, it is difficult to see the megalithic settings as anything other than physically embedded in a developing landscape of settlement and cultivation. However, whilst they may well have enjoyed a physical presence, it has recently been argued that with Avebury at least, its ideological potency in the contemporary Roman landscape was muted, the restructuring effected by the construction of the road and new field systems resulting in the henge and megalithic settings being effectively bypassed. This said, the stone settings may still have been places rich in mythical and folkloric associations ((Gillings and Pollard 2004, 94–100). An important question concerns the status afforded to the avenues and other settings. Unlike the Avebury sarsens, the standing stones making up the Beckhampton Avenue and Longstones Cove were not contained and focused within an earthwork. Instead these megaliths reached out, into and across a landscape that was in a state of dynamic reconfiguration, renegotiation and flux.

Within this context we have to place one of the more unexpected results of the excavation of the Longstones Cove. This was the occurrence within the disturbed fills of the stone-holes and the later destruction pits of Roman pottery, large quantities of animal bone, and a group of distinctive iron objects. Roman pottery was otherwise scarce within the areas excavated, and so its presence here was notable. The same was also true of the metalwork which came from the re-deposited fill of F.52 (the burning pit of setting L16), specifically from contexts [820], [821] and [851]. Although nails and other small fragments of iron were not unusual finds from stone destruction pits (*e.g.* from L3), spearheads and irregular plate fragments certainly were. The artefacts were concentrated in the area of a shallow sub-rectangular depression (>0.5 × >0.3m and 0.15m deep) in the south-eastern part of the base of F.52. The depression was set slightly back from the sides of the pit and filled with layers of chalky dark grey-brown loam, [855] and [856]. The evidence suggests that this is an earlier feature cut through by the digging of the destruction pit, and that the metalwork finds were originally contained within this, but disturbed during the creation of the burning pit during the early 18th century. Provisionally interpreted as a disturbed Anglo-Saxon burial (Gillings *et al.* 2002b, 257), the metalwork is more likely to be of Roman date (see below) and indicative of an unusual pattern of deposition taking place at the Cove during this period.

Much if not all of the animal bone from the disturbed stone-hole fills of the Cove is also likely to be of Roman or early post-Roman date. That contained within fills [870] and [866] of stone-hole F.81 was initially thought, because of its stratigraphic position, to be prehistoric and contemporary with the erection of the stone. However, radiocarbon dates on samples of this bone show that it relates to much later episodes of deposition, and had been introduced into the filling of the stone-hole by the action of burrowing animals (Table 7.2). OxA-10950 and 10951 are weighted towards the early 2nd–late 4th centuries AD whilst OxA-11112 and 11602 span the early 5th–late 7th centuries AD.

The animal bone is from a range of domesticates, including cattle, sheep/goat, pig and horse (see Coward below). Its original depositional context is unclear: it could have formed surface deposits placed against the stones of the Cove, or was buried in shallow pits that were destroyed by a combination of animal burrowing and the later process of stone destruction. The radiocarbon dates on the bone can be read as indicating either a long-lived process of deposition, spanning up to 600 years, or two or more discrete episodes.

As for the pottery, the range of vessel forms and fabrics give a similar chronological span that runs from the 1st to 4th centuries (see Cooper below). The distribution of Romano-British ceramic material is highly restricted, largely deriving from the fills of features associated with settings L15 and L16. In addition, during the excavation and re-erection of 'Adam' (L14) in 1912 a sherd of samian ware was recovered from the stone-hole fill along with 'several fragments' of Romano-British pottery (Cunnington 1913, 5–6). One possibility is that the material represents a surviving 'island' in an otherwise dispersed manuring scatter, the difficulties encountered in later periods of cultivating around the stones serving to preserve this material. Cunnington noted how the soil in the immediate vicinity of Adam had been dug over by hand instead of ploughed (Cunnington 1913, 4). As mentioned earlier, manuring was certainly taking place some 120m to the east of the Cove settings at South Street during the 1st–late 2nd century AD (Ashbee *et al.* 1979, 274, 289).

However, whilst the immediate area of South Street appears to have been cultivated, if the zone traversed by the avenue had been manured we might expect features related to other standing stones to have accumulated quantities of material in a similar way. In fact

	Context	Sample type	Result (BP)	Calibrated range (Cal AD) at 95.4% confidence
OxA-10950	[870]	Bone (*capra/ovis*)	1828±31	80–260
OxA-10951	[870]	Bone (*capra/ovis*)	1764±36	130–390
OxA-11112	[866]	Bone (*capra/ovis*)	1491±38	430–490, 530–650
OxA-11602	[866]	Bone (*capra/ovis*)	1405±33	580–670

Table 7.2. Radiocarbon dates from animal bone in F.52

the only avenue settings associated with Roman ceramics were L8 (two sherds) and T1 (one sherd). Roman pottery was also conspicuously absent from the ploughsoil during fieldwalking and test-pitting. The material from the Cove may well prove to result from manuring activity, and this could explain the small size and weathered condition of the sherds, but in light of the otherwise low frequency of finds and restricted distribution such an interpretation is difficult to maintain. Post-depositional processes such as weathering and subsequent agricultural activity will have transformed the assemblage, breaking down the sherds and even resulting in the complete destruction of some. The implication is that this material was originally deposited around the stones of the Cove, but the assemblage has undergone considerable attrition. As a result, we do not know the condition of the pottery when originally deposited, whether it arrived at the Cove as complete vessels or sherds, nor whether it formed a surface spread or had been incorporated in specially-dug pits that were disturbed by later activity.

Metalwork

Philip Macdonald and Philip Parkes

The excavators provisionally interpreted the ironwork recovered from F.52 as the grave goods from a disturbed early Anglo-Saxon inhumation (Gillings *et al.* 2002b, 254); however, the failure to recover any human skeletal material, combined with the Roman pottery and radiocarbon-dated animal bone associated with this feature, suggests that the ironwork could alternatively be of Roman date. Study of the ironwork does not provide a definite resolution to the problem of its date; however, given that none of the plate fragments (Nos 4–14) can plausibly be identified as shield fittings, that on typological grounds the spearhead (No. 1) could be either Roman or Anglo-Saxon in date, and that one of the plate fragments (No. 15) is a possible piece of *lorica squamata*, it is perhaps not unreasonable to suggest that the assemblage is at least as likely to be Roman as early Anglo-Saxon.

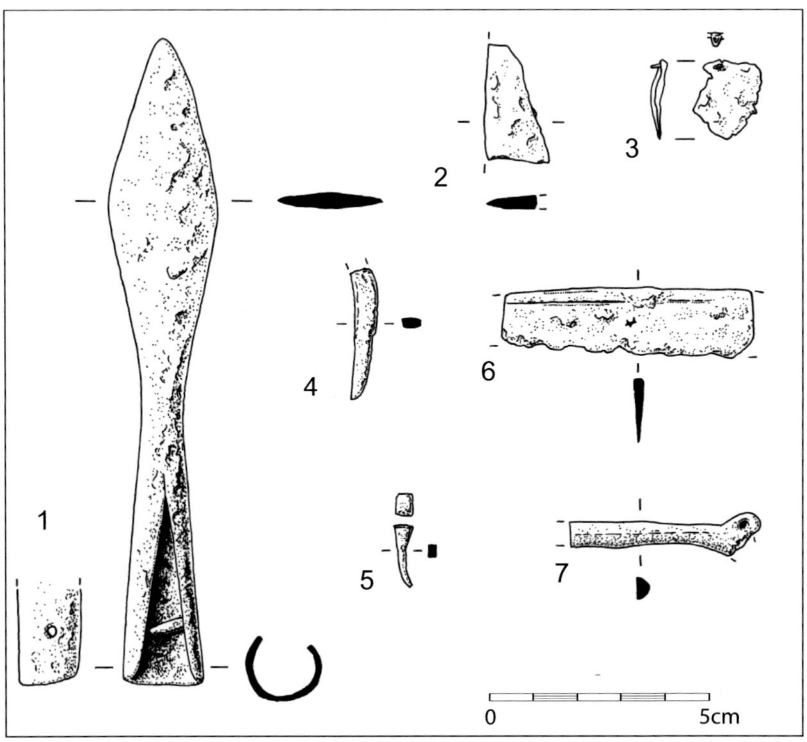

Figure 7.5. Roman and later ironwork from the Longstones Cove. Items 6 and 7 are described in Chapter 10

1. Spearhead, [820]

Small, well made, slightly asymmetrical, narrow leaf-shaped blade with gently curving shoulders, slightly rounded point and a lenticular cross-section (Figure 7.5.1). The thin conical socket is open with two opposing rivet holes set near the mouth of the socket, one of which retains part of an iron rivet. No traces of mineralised wood survive in the socket. Overall length 147mm, length of blade 81mm, maximum width of blade 25mm.

Spearheads are utilitarian objects whose form alters little through time. Consequently, their dating on typological grounds is problematic and the Beckhampton example could be of either Roman or early Anglo-Saxon date. Typologically, it can be identified as both an example of Manning's Type IA form of Roman spearhead (Manning 1985, 162–4) and Swanton's Type C1 form of Anglo-Saxon spearhead. Although Manning's spearhead typology is based on the collection from the Claudian fort at Hod Hill, Dorset, spearheads with leaf-shaped blades comparable to his Type IA were used throughout the Roman period in Britain. If the Beckhampton spearhead were of Roman date then it could plausibly be either a piece of military equipment or an example of a civilian hunting spear. Swanton's Type C1 spearheads are widely distributed across England and although their main *floruit* only extended to the end of the 6th century some later examples are known (Swanton 1973, 49, 51). Other examples of Type C1 spearheads from Wiltshire include those from Bassett Down (Goddard 1894–96, 105; Swanton 1973, 155, fig. 60b), Bulford (Shortt 1937–39, 352), Little Hinton (Swanton 1974, 61) and West Overton (Eagles 1986, 109, fig. 14.114).

2. Blade fragment, [820]
Blade fragment with a straight cutting edge (Figure 7.5.2). Possibly part of a knife, pair of shears or even a second spearhead. Surviving length 27mm, surviving width 15mm, surviving maximum thickness 4mm.

3. Nail or tack, [820]
Small headless nail or tack with a tapering rectangular-sectioned stem (Figure 7.5.5). The tip is missing and the end of the surviving part of the stem is slightly bent. Length 14.5mm, maximum thickness 4.5mm.

4. Strip fragment, [820]
Irregular-shaped strip fragment, triangular in cross-section. Possibly part of a fitting or binding. Length 37mm, width 14mm, thickness 6mm.

5. Plate fragment, [820]
Irregular shaped plate fragment. Dimensions 18.5 × 9 × 6mm.

6. Plate fragment, [820]
Irregular-shaped plate fragment with an angled curve towards one edge. Possibly several smaller fragments corroded together. Dimensions 41 × 21 × 1–6mm.

7. Plate fragment, [820]
Irregular-shaped plate fragment. Possibly several smaller fragments corroded together. Dimensions 47 × 21 × 1–7mm.

8. Plate fragment, [820]
Irregular-shaped plate fragment with an angled curve towards one edge. Dimensions 22.5 × 18 × 1–7mm.

9. Plate fragment, [820]
Sub-rectangular plate fragment. The possible remains of two iron stubs are set at one end; it is uncertain whether these are corrosion blisters or genuine features. Length 29.5mm, maximum width 18mm, thickness 1–3.5mm.

10. Plate fragment, [820]
Irregular-shaped plate fragment. Dimensions 23.5 × 21.5mm × 1–2mm.

11. Plate fragment, [820]
Irregular-shaped plate fragment. Dimensions 39 × 31.5mm × 1–3mm.

12. Plate fragment, [820]
Irregular-shaped plate fragment. Dimensions 18.5 × 13.5mm × 1–2mm.

13. Plate fragment, [820]
Irregular-shaped plate fragment. Dimensions 24 × 18.5mm × 1–2mm.

14. Strip fragment, [821]
Slightly curved tapering strip fragment. Length 30mm, width 6mm, thickness 2–2.5mm (Figure 7.5.4).

The excavators provisionally suggested that several pieces of shield fittings were recovered from F.52; however, study of the plate and strip fragments indicates that this identification can no longer be maintained (Gillings *et al.* 2002b, 254). The various irregular plate fragments recovered from the feature are too corroded and incomplete to identify their original shape and form with any confidence. Although some of the fragments could be derived from an early Anglo-Saxon shield boss there is no reason, based on the study of their form alone, why this particular interpretation should be favoured over any other.

15. Plate fragment, [851]
Irregular-shaped plate fragment. X-radiography and investigative cleaning has revealed a short length of iron wire which perforates the fragment in one corner and forms a small loop which protrudes from one side. Dimensions 19 × 15mm, thickness 2mm (Figure 7.5.3).

Although the identification is far from certain, the size of the fragment and its wire loop are consistent with it being part of a scale of *lorica squamata*. This is a form of Roman armour which is made up of rows of overlapping metal scales that were joined to each other by small wire links that passed through perforations on the edges of the scales (cf. Robinson 1975, 153–61). Recognising isolated examples of corroded iron scales is particularly difficult (Manning 1995, 14) hence the uncertainty over the identification of this fragment; however, given the possible Roman date of the spearhead and the definite Roman date of the associated pottery and radiocarbon dated animal bone, the identification of this piece as possibly being *lorica squamata* is not unreasonable.

Context	Fabric	Form	No. sherds	Weight	Date
F.52 [819]	Oxidised		1	1	
F.52 [819]	BB1		1	1	120+
F.52 [805]	CG Samian		1	1	
F.53 [842]	Oxidised		2	1	
F.53 [868]	BB1		1	9	120+
F.62 [612]	Sandy Oxidised		1	1	
F.62 [612]	Sandy E ware	Jar	1	2	1st cent
F.71 [800]	Wilts White slip	Flagon	1	2	
F.71 [800]	CG Samian	Dish	2	6	
F.71 [800]	BB1		3	13	120+
F.71 [800]	Wilts Oxidised		1	2	
F.71 [801]	Savernake	Jar	2	22	1st cent
F.71 [801]	Wilts Oxidised		1	2	
F.71 [839]	Sandy Reduced		1	7	
F.71 [801]-[829]	Wilts White slip		1	2	2nd–3rd cent
F.72 [814]	BB1	Jar	2	3	120+
F.72 [814]	Sandy Reduced		1	1	
F.72 [838]	Sandy E ware		1	12	1st cent
F.81 [819]	Sandy E ware		1	20	1st cent
F.81 [819]	Sandy Reduced		1	2	
F.81 [819]	SG Samian		1	1	
F.81 [819]	Oxidised		1	2	
Tr.24 chalk surface	Oxidised		1	2	
Total			*29*	*115*	

Table 7.3. (below left) Roman pottery according to context, form and fabric

Table 7.4. (below right) Summary of Roman fabrics in the assemblage by sherd count

Fabric	No. of sherds
Samian	4
BB1	7
Early wares	3
White slip	2
Greyware	3
Oxidised	8
Reduced	3
Savernake	2
Total	*32*

Romano-British pottery

Nicholas Cooper

In total 32 sherds of Romano-British pottery (weighing 120g) were recovered during the excavation of the Beckhampton Avenue and Longstones Cove. Pottery was recorded by specific fabric name when possible (cf. Tomber and Dore 1998) and by broad fabric category otherwise, and was quantified by number of sherds and weight. The material was generally in very poor condition (average sherd weight 4g) with highly abraded surfaces and a lack of diagnostic sherds hampering identification. However, imports, regional imports and distinctive Wiltshire fabrics were recognised. The assemblage is recorded by context (Table 7.3) and summarised by fabric (Table 7.4).

The sole imported fabric, samian ware, comprises one south gaulish sherd from a footring base of a cup, two joining central gaulish sherds probably from a dish and one other central gaulish scrap.

Black burnished ware 1 from South-East Dorset, represents the only regional import. The occurrence of seven sherds, in an admittedly small sample, is encouraging given that Avebury appears to fall in to something of a 'black hole' in the distribution of this ware as established by Allen and Fulford (1996, fig. 1), with levels falling below 5% in this area, whereas further to the north, the fabric makes up 40% of assemblages in Cirencester (cf. Cooper 1998, 335, Ceramic Phases 6 and 7, *c.*AD250–350). Only one rim is represented, appearing to come from one of the more unusual barrel-shaped bead-rim jars (Holbrook and Bidwell 1991, 100, type 3.1b). Five of the six remaining body sherds come from cooking pots, the other coming from a bowl

Other diagnostic fabrics include joining rim sherds from a jar in grog-tempered fabric of Savernake ware type of 1st century date (Tomber and Dore 1998, 191) and a sherd of a white slipped flagon probably from North Wiltshire of 2nd or 3rd century date (Cooper 1998, 325, fabric 95). The remaining material falls into more general oxidised (orange) or reduced (grey) ware categories varying in the sandiness of the fabrics and not precisely dated within the Roman period. However, three sherds belong broadly to the group of transitional fabrics identified as 'E' wares or early wares in the Oxfordshire region (Booth 1996) dating to the mid-later 1st century and occurring in a variety of fabrics containing a mixture of fine grog and more occasionally calcareous inclusions and predating the emergence of Romanised sandy fabrics towards the end of the 1st century.

Faunal remains

Fiona Coward

A total of 620 bones were counted from possible Romano-British and/or early post-Roman contexts, of which 203 (33%) were identifiable (Table 7.5). Species identified in the assemblage include cattle, sheep, pig and horse. Large carnivore remains, lagomorph, unidentified small mammal, amphibian and possibly bird bones were also recorded but are probably mostly intrusive to judge from their significantly better state of preservation.

The most common domestic animal was sheep/goat, comprising 18% of the assemblage. This material represented a wide spread of elements from most parts of the skeleton including teeth and skull fragments and phalanges as well as the meat-bearing long bones and vertebrae. On-site slaughter of animals (or even a single animal, given an MNI of 1) could thus be indicated, although no butchery evidence and very little burning was noted.

Cattle remains make up 10% of the material and these are mainly loose teeth, with two radii and a metatarsal also identified. Again, no butchery evidence was noted. Pig is represented by a single proximal radius, and horse only by two teeth. The limited evidence for these species thus precludes any significant conclusions

Table 7.5. Roman species representation

Species	Romano-British
Cattle	10
Sheep/goat	18
Pig	<1
Horse	2
Dog	1
Large carnivore	9
Lagomorph	2
Mole	15
Unid. Small mammal	23
Frog	16
Bird	3
Total identifiable	**203**
Unidentifiable	**417**
% identifiable	**33**
Total	**620**

Discussion

Cultivation was clearly taking place in the vicinity of the South Street long mound during the Roman period, but the degree to which this can be extended to the areas traversed by the Beckhampton Avenue and that of the Longstones Cove is uncertain. Whilst the avenue settings were remarkably 'clean' of Roman material a small, yet notable assemblage of metalwork, pottery and animal bone was recovered from features associated with the Longstones Cove. Taken together this material hints at some form of deliberate depositional practice taking place preferentially at the Cove, most likely (on the basis of the feature cut by the destruction pit of L16) within the area demarcated by the standing stones.

In light of the re-deposited nature of this material, ambiguities regarding the metalwork (Roman or Anglo-Saxon) and the broad chronological range indicated by the radiocarbon dates, unravelling the detail of this evidence is fraught with difficulty. Nonetheless, the specific distributions of this material and the fact that only animal bone was found in the lower fill of F.81 suggests that different depositional strategies may have been adopted for separate classes of material: the metalwork was perhaps placed in a large pit, pottery on the surface (to be subsequently reworked by cultivation), and bone most likely inserted into small pits or in some way 'dug in'. One possibility that has to be discussed is that we are seeing the remains of a heavily disturbed burial. In this regard it is worth noting that while no human bone was recovered from the current excavations, in 1722 William Stukeley made the following comment regarding the destruction of the stone, presumably recounted to him by the stone breakers:

> 'the Cove south side one of the Long Stones was fell down ~~a corpse~~ bones was found ~~under~~ it when the Landlord of the Hare and Hounds took it away (burning it) it containd 15 load a. the stone b. fallen c. standing Rd. Fowler.' (Bodl. MS Gough Maps 231 f244v).

However, accepting the caveat that perhaps as much as two-thirds of the destruction pit remains unexcavated, if these were the remains of a burial it is unlikely that no trace of human bone would have been recovered during the current excavations. More significant are the finds of pottery, animal bone and metalwork. All of the pottery is abraded and has clearly been circulating in the topsoil prior to the disturbance of any possible grave in the early 18th century. Further, though deposition of entire animal carcasses is a feature of 3rd–4th century AD rural inhumations in southern England (Philpott 1991, 200–6) they are rare in Wiltshire (Foster 2001, 169). As for spearheads and armour, such grave goods would not only be unique to Wiltshire, but the province as a whole (Philpott 1991). The final nail in this proverbial coffin is provided by the radiocarbon determinations on the animal bone, which highlight the prolonged rather than single-episode nature of the deposition.

Roman activity elsewhere in the region

It is useful to contrast these deposits with those recovered from other earlier monuments in the Avebury landscape. At the henge itself Stukeley spoke of 'several' Roman coins from in and around the earthwork (1743, 26) and in Gray's cuttings through the ditch *c.*10–20 sherds of fine and coarse pottery were found in the upper 2.5m of silting (Gray 1935, 112, 115, 118–9, 125–6). Also present in the upper ditch fills were a number of bronze objects, including two rings and a twisted wire bracelet found in the eastern ditch terminal of the southern entrance, and a 1st century AD bronze 'Aucissa' fibula some 90m to the west of the southern entrance (Gray 1935, 119, 125–6, 156–7). Keiller's campaigns of excavation within the interior of the henge recovered less than 50 sherds of Romano-British pottery along with fewer than 12 coins from the henge and West Kennet Avenue combined (Smith 1965, 243). Unfortunately there have been no detailed analyses of the pottery assemblages from either excavation, nor of the coins recovered by Keiller. As a result we cannot say when this activity took place, or even state with any confidence whether the low density of pottery was associated specifically with stone settings as opposed to representing a more general distribution across the interior. In all cases densities of material are low. As to the character of this activity, the one conclusion that can be drawn is that metalwork was being selectively deposited within the perimeter ditch. The fibula is of particular interest as the deposition of brooches appears to have been an Iron Age practice that continued into the Roman period, with such objects frequently found at pre- and post-conquest shrine and temple sites (Haselgrove 1997, 65; Jundi and Hill 1998).

Unlike the Beckhampton Avenue, the excavated portion of the West Kennet Avenue yielded much more evidence for Roman activity, with a total of *c.*50 sherds of Roman-British pottery along with a scattering of coins (Smith 1965, 243). This may well be a reflection of its more 'physical' presence within the contemporary Roman landscape – the line of the Roman road cutting directly across that of the stone settings, and the latter attracting the attention of anyone traversing the landscape along the roadway. That existing monuments did engage interest in this way is suggested by the presence of Roman burial mounds inserted amongst pre-existing Bronze Age round barrows where the road passes Seven Barrows Hill, to the north of the Sanctuary (Smith and Simpson 1966).

While many were perhaps ignored or simply accommodated into the routine inhabitation and working of the landscape, certain of the megalithic settings and prehistoric earthworks may have been regarded in entirely superstitious terms as places of efficacious good luck or supernatural potency. Precisely this kind of association is suggested by coin finds at sites such as the West Kennet long barrow (Piggott 1962, 55–6), and the metalwork deposited in the Avebury ditch. The deposits found at the Longstones Cove could also be read in this way. The small assemblages from these sites could just as well reflect the results of idiosyncratic or *ad hoc* events, limited in scale, rather than wholesale reincorporation of such monuments as shrines or active points in the contemporary religious landscape. The same interpretation might be applied to the Roman-period finds from Stonehenge, which include 20 coins, a range of brooches, pins and toilet instruments, and 1857 sherds of pottery (Cleal *et al.* 1995, 431–5). Rather than representing the debris from casual visits, this material was perhaps generated through a succession of personal acts of votive deposition, designed to exploit the perceived supernatural potency of the megalithic settings.

At Silbury Hill something very different was taking place (for a detailed discussion see Gillings and Pollard 2004, 98–100). Here we see the development of a possible small town, centred upon Silbury and extending northwards along the Winterbourne. Covering around 22ha, the site was associated with a group of what the original excavators termed 'wells' and 'kitchen-middens' extending to the south of Silbury Hill to the springhead at Swallowhead. These features were substantial and contained a variety of carefully placed deposits incorporating coins, jewellery, pottery, animal bone, iron tools, building material, sarsen and in one instance human bone. One need only contrast the material recovered from the ditch at Silbury Hill with that from the Avebury settings to gain an appreciation of the different practices taking place here. Excavation of the former revealed a deposit described as the 'Roman midden' that yielded substantial amounts of pottery, a bronze bracelet and over 100 coins (Whittle 1997b, 24). If the Avebury settings and earthworks had slipped into the background, becoming little more than places of superstitious efficacy, a new set of negotiations were taking place at Silbury as a large and thriving complex developed.

8 Bounding the Avebury landscape

One of the most striking aspects of the campaigns of excavation carried out between 1999 and 2003 was the quantity of medieval and post-medieval archaeology that was encountered. In many cases the presence of later historical features alerted us to the existence of former stone settings, and in the most extreme cases such features served as the only surviving proxies for former standing stones. This wealth of later historical evidence took the form of the vestiges of a number of distinct, and formerly widespread, practices centred upon the standing stones. The first of these was deliberate stone burial, the second destruction of the stone through direct fracture or fire-setting.

In the chapters that follow this evidence is discussed in detail, exploring the practices employed, the scales of activity involved and the motivations that lay behind the individual acts of burial and destruction. As well as detailed structural reports on the features encountered during the current project, this has also entailed a careful re-appraisal of the archive relating to the Keiller excavations of the 1930s, synthesising and bringing to publication a previously unexamined corpus of information relating to Avebury's medieval and later history.

It is not our intention here to offer a detailed discussion of Avebury during the medieval and post-medieval periods, instead readers are referred to recent syntheses of the site and its landscape (Pollard and Reynolds 2002, chapter 7; Gillings and Pollard 2004, chapters 7 and 8). A brief sketch is, however, useful. By the early 14th century Avebury had a manor house and a major church, with what Jope has described as an ordinary village of some 30 families (*c.*100 people) extending to the west of the henge along the axis of the Beckhampton Avenue (Jope 1999). Within the henge itself were a number of linear earthworks most likely associated with a small number of crofts and tofts laid out along the axis of the main east-west road (Figure 8.1). In the early 18th century the records of Stukeley, in particular his perspectival frontispiece to the *Abury* volume (1743), show how the village had extended into the henge proper, with a number of buildings surrounded by pastures, gardens and orchards (Figure 8.2).

In each case the landscape is very much a dynamic and lived one: a place not of silent earthworks and standing stones but instead one of grazing, cultivation and settlement. In examining the archaeological evidence from these periods it rapidly became clear that a detailed understanding of the way in which the landscape of Avebury was configured (in terms of landuse, boundaries and partitions) was an essential precursor to developing any understanding of processes such as stone burial and breaking. In the current chapter an attempt has been made to do precisely this, identifying possible boundary features and attempting to establish a relative chronology for them.

In the case of Avebury, given that the broad patterns identified are reconstructed largely on the basis of surviving earthworks, cropmarks and geophysical survey anomalies, precise morphology and dating remain unclear. Further, where excavation has taken place it has revealed an extremely complex and dynamic picture that makes generalisation extremely difficult. Similar problems arise in the case of the avenues. The work carried out by the current project has brought into question accepted ideas regarding the precise routes taken by these settings and assumptions regarding a standardised format (Chapters 2 and 3). To compound this, the fact that the areas traversed are not bounded in the same way as the interior of Avebury has resulted in a tendency for researchers to concentrate on avenue corridors or individual stone settings rather than broader landscape context. This tendency reached its zenith with the excavations of Keiller on the West Kennet Avenue who abandoned continuous trenching in favour of targeted squares predicted on the basis of expected spacing (Gillings and Pollard 2004, 179), but is still evident within more recent geophysical investigations.

The interior of Avebury

Our most detailed information regarding the partitioning of the space within the earthwork of the henge comes from the excavations carried out by Alexander Keiller between 1937 and 1939. To structure his investigations Keiller broke the henge interior down into four

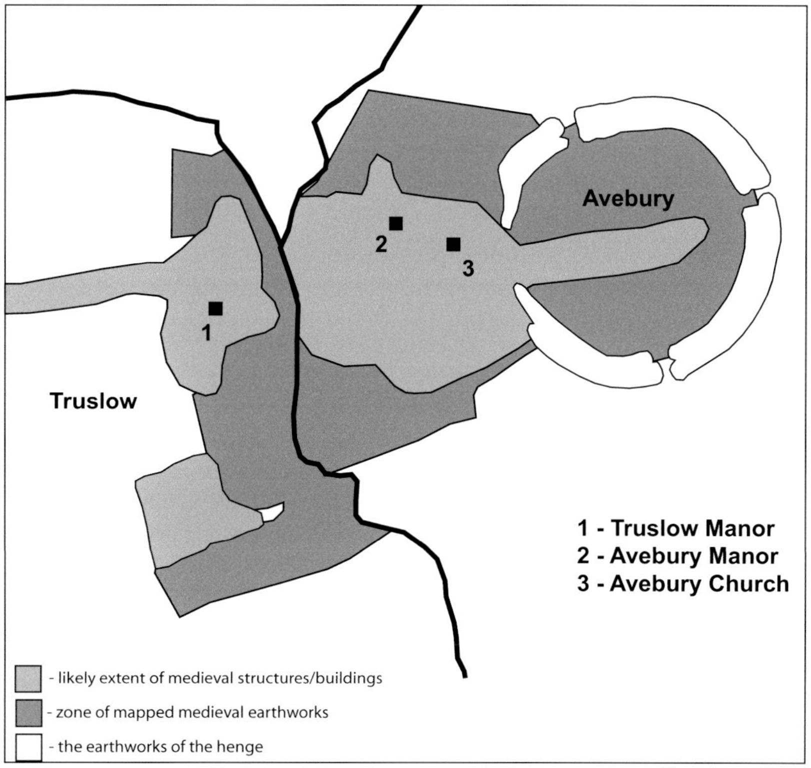

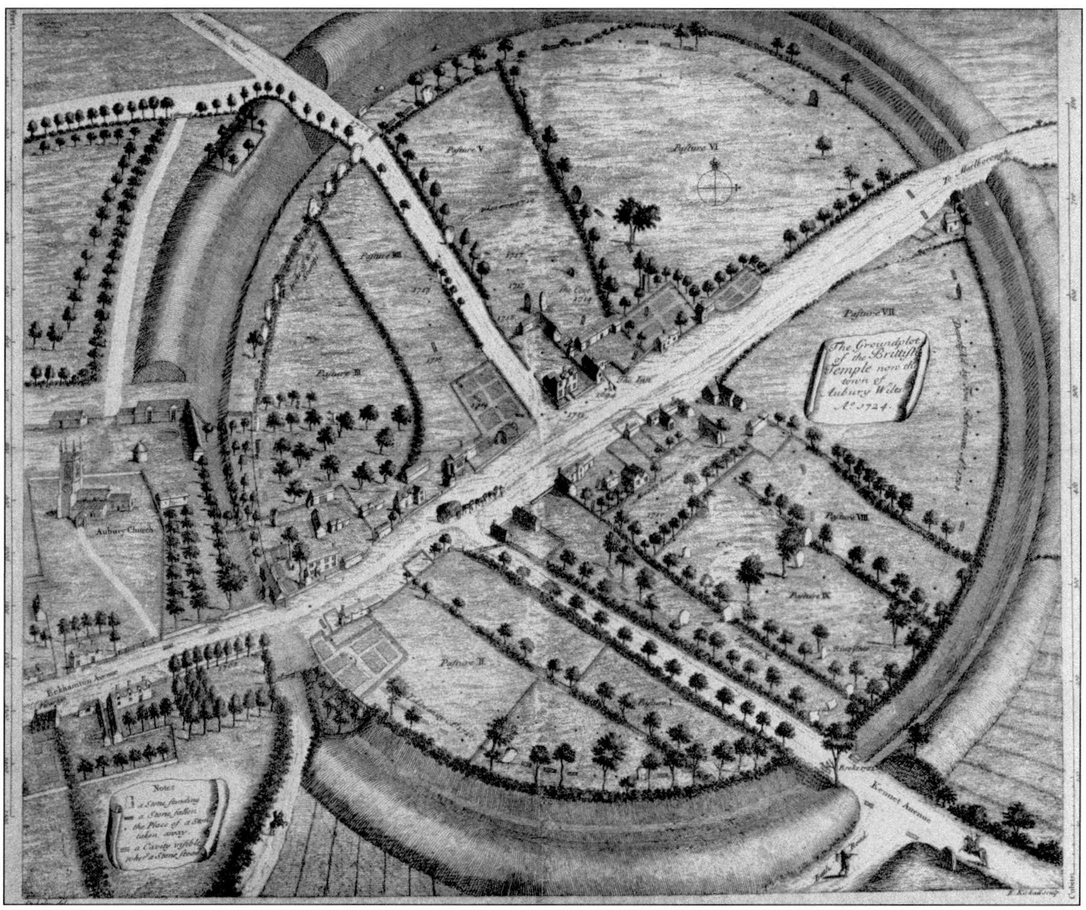

Figure 8.1. (above) Medieval settlement at Avebury (after McOmish et al. *2005, fig. 2.3)*

Figure 8.2. (left) Stukeley's depiction of Avebury in the early 18th century (1743 TAB.1 frontispiece)

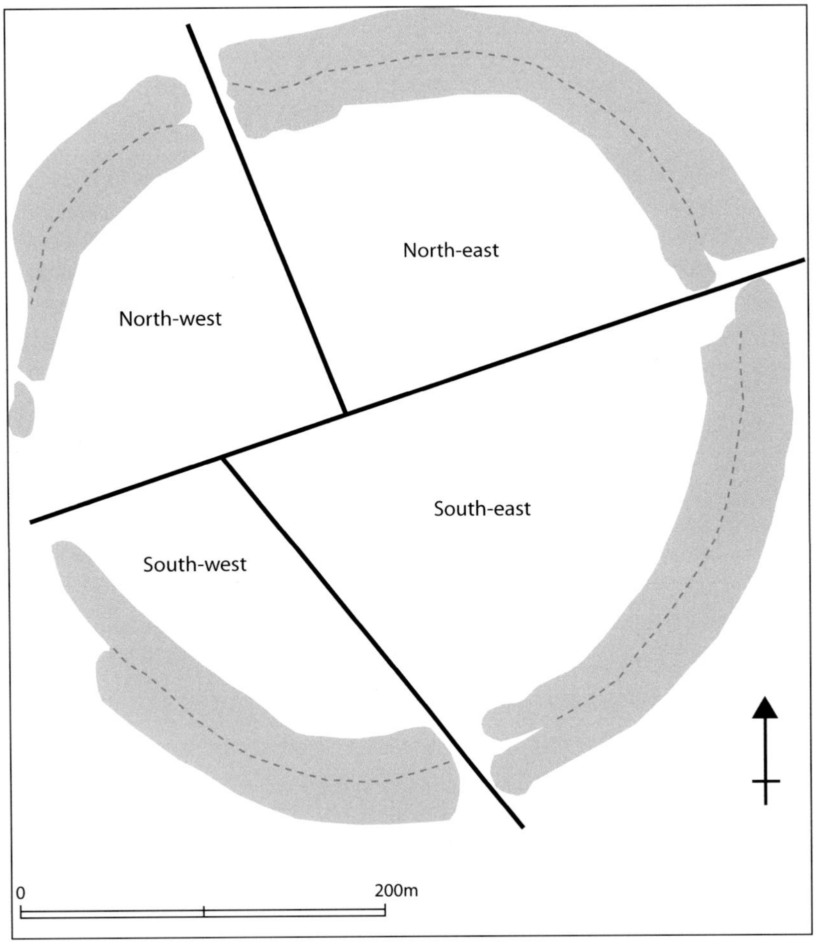

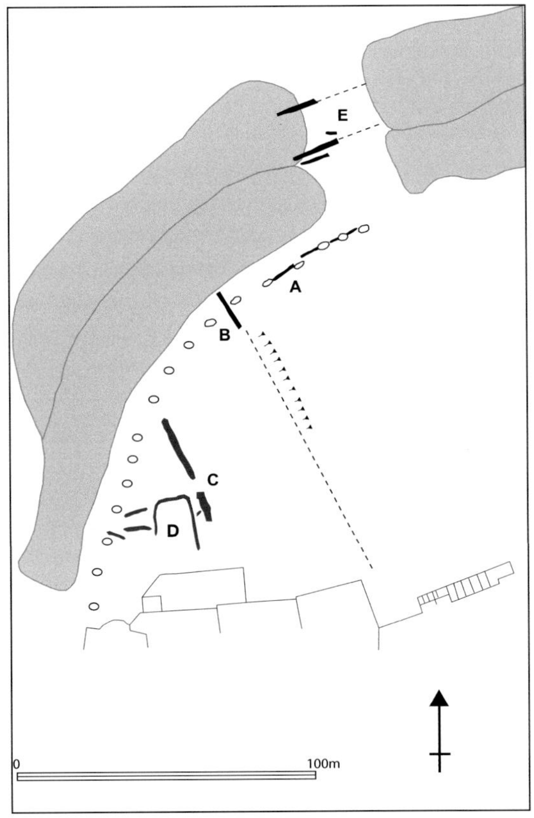

Figure 8.3. (above left) The partitioning of the interior of the Avebury henge into notional quadrants

Figure 8.4. (above right) Avebury: Earliest boundary features in the NW quadrant (reconstructed from unpublished Keiller excavation plans). Incorporates data © Crown Copyright/ database right 2007. An Ordnance Survey/ (EDINA) supplied service

quadrants (albeit of unequal area) structured around the axis of the north-south and east-west roads that passed through the interior, a schema that has been followed in the current discussion (Figure 8.3). In the North-West and South-West Quadrants excavation followed the arc of the Outer Circle, whilst investigations in the south-east were carried out using a notional 50 foot grid, with each individual grid square numbered and further subdivided into four 25 foot sectors. In each case numerous boundary features were encountered, excavated and recorded, the details residing in the unpublished archive held at the Alexander Keiller Museum in Avebury. The discussion below draws from the unpublished site notebooks, excavation diaries and surviving plan and section drawings.

The North-West Quadrant

Keiller's trenches followed a strip around the perimeter of the earthwork, centred upon the arc of the outer stone circle. These were supplemented by the excavation of an additional block in the area of the northern causeway and a small trench in the interior intended to ground-truth an apparently anomalous stone recorded in this position by Stukeley (for discussion see Smith 1965; Ucko *et al.* 1991, 203–6). Although focus was upon the prehistoric features, the excavations revealed evidence of a complex network of boundary banks, ditches and building foundations derived from a number of episodes of enclosure and remodelling, and it is to the credit of Keiller that these were carefully excavated and recorded.

The earliest boundaries take the form of a series of ditches. The first comprised a small, shallow feature (0.2–0.5m wide reaching a depth of 0.2m below the surface of the chalk) running between settings 42–46 and clearly lined up upon them, serving to link the upright sarsens together like beads on a string (Figure 8.4, A). It is curious that this ditch did not appear to continue beyond setting 42; it may have been that the arc of stones itself was deemed sufficient, if a boundary marker was felt necessary at all. Equally, a less substantial fence or hedgeline may have been in existence.

Further around the arc of the circle a stretch of V-shaped ditch was encountered, aligned

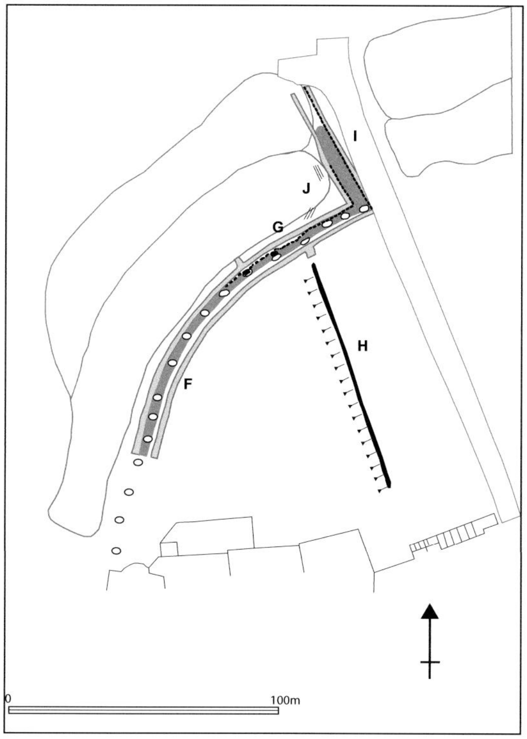

Figure 8.5. (left) Avebury: Later boundary phases in the NW quadrant (reconstructed from unpublished Keiller excavation plans). Incorporates data © Crown Copyright/ database right 2007. An Ordnance Survey/ (EDINA) supplied service

(though slightly to the east of) setting 41 and extending to the south into the interior of the henge (B). Although only a short section was excavated, the orientation and position of this ditch correlate closely with the line of a stepped boundary feature visible today as an earthwork, the ditch following its down-slope edge. The fill of the ditch contained four sherds of 12th–13th-century pottery. Another medieval boundary ditch was identified in the small cutting carried out within the interior of the sector, following the line of a shallow lynchet caused by a change in the underlying geology from Lower to Middle Chalk (C). The ditch contained 12th–14th-century pottery and followed an earlier, narrower ditch line. A fenceline appeared to run up against this boundary on the west and at the northern end of the excavated section there were post-holes and the suggestion of a possible building (D). The latter corresponds to a series of rectilinear parchmarks identified in this area in 1996 (Bewley *et al.* 1996). The final set of earlier ditches were encountered in the area of the northern entrance, and served to cut directly across the causeway closing off this former means of access. Referred to by Keiller as 'Transverse Ditches' four of these features were excavated (E).

At some point the small ditch linking settings 42–46 was sealed by a substantial perimeter bank (surviving to a height of 1.12m in 1937) that closely followed the arc of the Outer Circle, incorporating a number of fallen stones directly into its fabric (Figure 8.5, F). The material for the construction of the bank was provided by two ditches, one located inside the ring of stones (inner ditch) and one outside (outer ditch). These varied in depth and breadth along their lengths; where a section drawing survives (relating to the area around setting 34) the inner of these ditches was the more substantial, reaching a maximum width of 1.87m and depth of 0.38m, with sloping sides and a roughly flattened base. The outer ditch at this point appears to have been little more than a shallow scrape.

By the time this perimeter bank was constructed the V-shaped ditch adjacent to setting 41 had silted up and the inner and outer ditches clearly cut through it. Along the outer face of the perimeter bank from its junction with 'Longitudinal Ditch 2' (see below) as far as 3.58m beyond setting 41, a rough stone wall had been constructed making use of sarsen lumps liberated by the breaking through direct fracture of the latter and stone 42 (G). At setting 43, this perimeter bank was joined by another that corresponded to the boundary recorded by Stukeley as separating his pastures III and IIII (sic) (H). Whilst the perimeter bank was the result of a single construction episode, it is not clear from the records whether construction of this latter bank was contemporary with it.

In the area of the causeway the inner and outer ditches turned sharply to form a pair of what Keiller described as 'Longitudinal Ditches' (LD1 and LD2). These ran directly along the axis of the northern entrance, cutting across the earlier ditches that had effectively served to close it off (I). The material from these Longitudinal Ditches had been mounded between them to create a bank flanked by stone walls constructed using natural sarsen boulders and fractured lumps. This feature served to define the western edge of a roadway through the northern entrance. Although largely hidden beneath the modern road, excavation revealed evidence of rutting, horseshoes and deliberate maintenance suggesting that it was of sufficient breadth to accommodate carts and wagons.

Taken as a whole, the construction of these

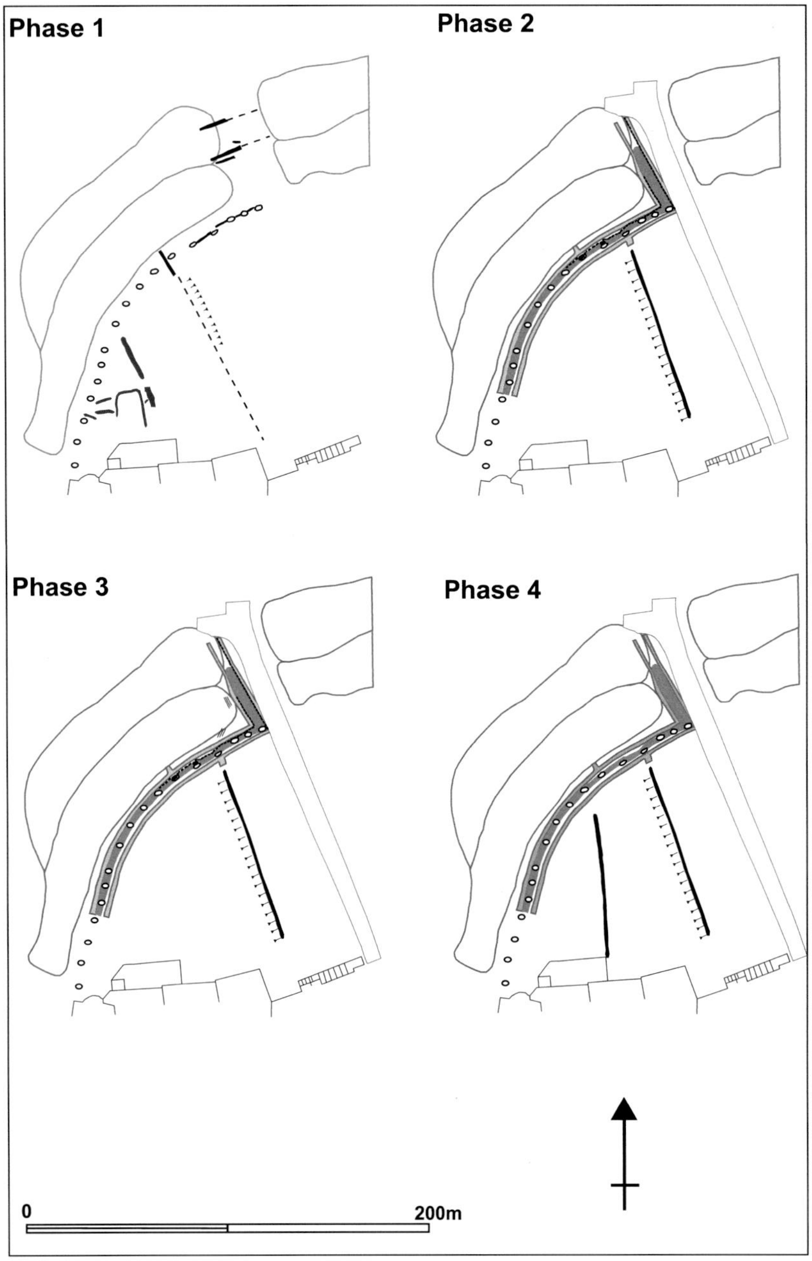

Figure 8.6. Avebury: Phasing of ditches and linear boundaries in NW quadrant. Incorporates data © Crown Copyright/database right 2007. An Ordnance Survey/(EDINA) supplied service

banks and ditches appears to have marked a period of dramatic re-organisation of the henge interior, with the abandonment of a number of internal boundaries and establishment (or perhaps reinforcement) of other lines through the construction of substantial banks. At some point following the construction of the perimeter bank, a second routeway into the henge was established, crossing the eastern end of the bank and silted edge of the main ditch to the west of LD2, before running along the strip of ground between the perimeter bank and the edge of the ditch as far as settings 33 and 34. The creation of this trackway appears to have been accompanied by the 'trimming' of protruding lumps of the fallen stones embedded in the perimeter bank, presumably to ease passage. The presence of rutting in the area of 43 and 44 suggests that this track was of sufficient size to accommodate wheeled traffic (J).

By the time Stukeley recorded this area of the site in 1724, no trace remained of the second trackway, and the bank appears to have been subsumed within a hedge. Some time after this date the destruction of a number of stones embedded in this boundary resulted in damage to the bank, its facing wall and the outer ditch. The fact that only the bank appears to have been reinstated suggests that by this stage the ditch and wall were no longer deemed significant.

To summarise these developments, assuming that the perimeter ditch linking settings 42–46, transverse ditches and linear boundaries running across the interior were broadly contemporary, the first phase of enclosure involved a series of boundaries that were closely aligned upon the standing stones (Figure 8.6, Phase 1). The ditches served to partition the interior into a series of strips that included the area of the northern causeway, suggesting that no thoroughfare existed at this time. That this is most likely medieval is suggested by the pottery finds from the ditch fills, though the issue of residuality must be firmly borne in mind (Jope 1999, 69).

This was subsequently revised during a period of major remodelling that saw the original strips redefined and a major thoroughfare opened up through the northern causeway of the henge. The ditches of the medieval system were replaced by banks, faced with sections of dry-stone walling (Phase 2). Like the medieval ditches, these banks also appear to have been aligned on stones. There is little to date this episode beyond the fact that it post-dated at least one silted up ditch that had been dated on the basis of pottery to the 12th–14th centuries. This was followed by a further remodelling that saw the creation of a second thoroughfare to the immediate west of the northern causeway, running along the perimeter of the main ditch (Phase 3).

By the 1720s and Stukeley's visits, this latter thoroughfare had completely disappeared. The northern causeway remained open and the banked boundary system persisted, being recorded by Stukeley as a set of hedges. Sometime after 1724, the flanking ditches and facing walls of the perimeter bank appear to have been allowed to fall into disrepair – subsequent damage inflicted during episodes of stone burning not being repaired. The final phase of re-organisation involved the establishment of a new boundary line, recorded on the 1794 Inclosure map, running due south from setting 40 (Phase 4).

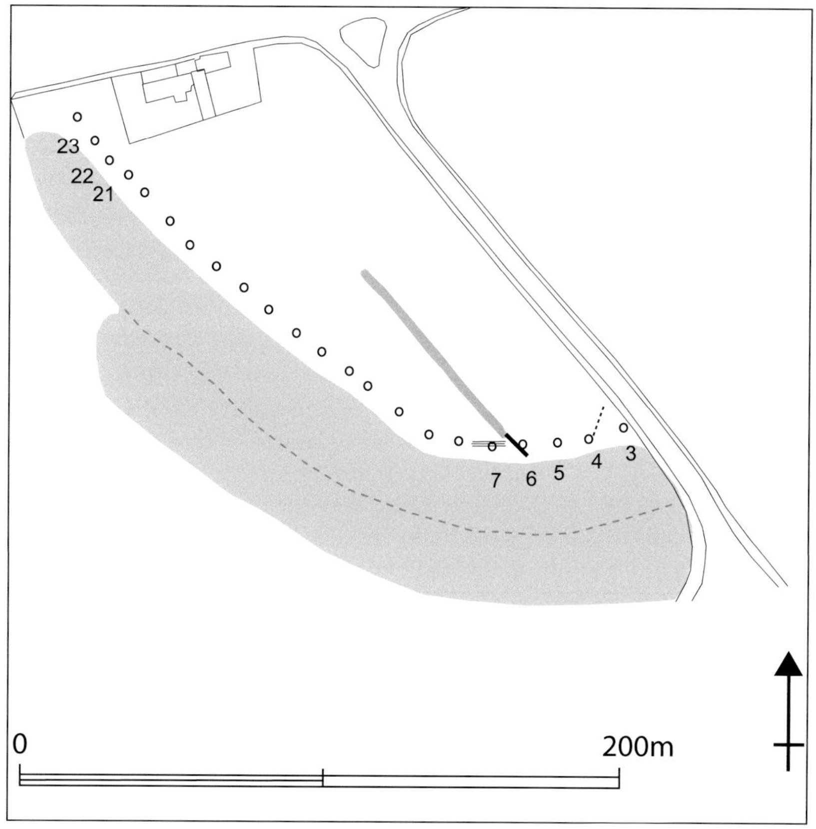

Figure 8.7. Avebury: Boundary features in the SW quadrant (reconstructed from unpublished Keiller excavation plans). Incorporates data © Crown Copyright/ database right 2007. An Ordnance Survey/ (EDINA) supplied service

The South-West Quadrant

As in the North-West, excavation was carried out on the basis of a series of cuttings that followed closely the arc of the Outer Circle (Figure 8.7). Although a number of boundary features were revealed, there was neither the complexity or sense of sequence evident in the North-West Quadrant. Immediately adjacent to the stone-hole of setting 4 and presumably aligned upon its standing position, was a lynchet. To the west of this feature Keiller noted a lowering of the level of the natural chalk (and commensurate increase in the depth of topsoil) which he argued reflected the impact of plough cultivation. There is some confusion regarding the precise orientation of this lynchet; it is described as running in a NW-SE direction in the notebooks yet drawn oriented NE-SW on the plan; nothing is visible today. In terms of dating, all that can be said with any confidence is that the ploughing and formation of the lynchet clearly predated the burial of stone 4.

Further around the arc of the circle a second boundary ditch was encountered cutting across the burial pit holding stone 6. This was typically 1.00m wide, reaching a depth of 0.76m below the turf and aligned on the linear earthwork that marks the former location of the boundary separating Stukeley's pastures I and II.

Perhaps the most intriguing evidence for landuse and partition is also the most ephemeral, taking the form of scoring and staining on the surface of the shallowly buried stone 7. On the basis of the staining Keiller argued that this was caused by iron ploughshares. What was unusual was the orientation of these marks, which suggested that at some stage cultivation had taken place aligned parallel to the edge of the ditch rather than along the NW-SE aligned strips, most likely following Parliamentary enclosure (1794) when the internal boundaries fossilising the early strip fields were finally removed.

As in the case of the North-West Quadrant, as the Outer Circle approached the western causeway, a series of structural features were encountered, with settings 21–23 falling within a garden associated with a cottage, stables and disused forge. These buildings were demolished during the course of the excavations revealing a complex sequence of activity in this area of the henge interior. That a medieval structure had stood in this area was suggested by the recovery of medieval masonry from the earlier phases of the cottage along with the discovery of two cess-pits close to settings 21 and 23. Morphologically very similar, 12th-century pottery was recovered from the base of the former, along with the complete skeleton of a dog in its upper fills. Other early features included the remains of a circular pit containing a sunken barrel.

At a later date a pond was dug to the immediate west of the cottage and over the area of the sunken barrel. Finds of late 17th- and early 18th-century coins in the basal silts of this feature provide a date for its construction; that it had been allowed to dry out by the time of Stukeley's visits is clear from his frontispiece where the site of the former pond is shown as a fenced area. An interesting parallel in terms of scale and positioning relative to the road, is the pond recorded by Gray in 1912 in the farm-yard to the south of the Cove.

At some point after 1724 stone 24 was buried in a pit at the base of the pond. This was followed by the deliberate in-filling of this feature and two phases of building. The first (construction of the forge) made use of well-made sarsen walling that was carefully aligned so as to avoid the bulk of the buried sarsen. Rather than avoid the buried stone a second wall, to the west, was built up to it and utilised in part blocks smashed from the buried megalith. A series of later constructional phases (using fragments of sarsen and brick) resulted in smaller buildings being added to the north and west of the forge.

Figure 8.8. Avebury: Boundary features in the SE quadrant (reconstructed from unpublished Keiller excavation plans)

The South-East Quadrant

In the South-East Quadrant a different excavation strategy was followed. Although the original intention appears to have been to excavate the area in its entirety, by the time the excavations had ceased in 1939 only a handful of full and partial grid squares had been excavated. The grid and excavated areas are shown in Figure 8.8, itself derived from a plan by W. E. V. Young and detailed a base-plan of excavated features produced by Denis Grant King (both unpublished, Alexander Keiller Museum).

As well as revealing detail of the Southern Inner Circle and its stone settings, a total of eight linear features were excavated (Figure 8.8, features 1 to 7). Feature 1 comprised a narrow ditch, some 0.4m deep below the surface of the chalk and containing sherds of 14th-century pottery. The ditch appears to have been aligned on settings 102 and 109 of the Southern Inner Circle, passing close to the base of the former stone when upright. Feature 2 was a wider, shallower ditch cut into, and closely following, the line of Feature 1. It is interesting to note that the line of this later ditch respected the position of stone 102 after it had fallen. Although originally thought to be Iron Age in date on the grounds of morphology, Feature 3 was subsequently dated to the 14th century on the basis of pottery finds and similarity to another excavated section of medieval ditch. This was a substantial feature, reaching a depth of 1.10m below the present turf-line and narrowing in width from 1.82m at the top to 0.29m at the flat base. On the basis of the fills Keiller argued that this ditch had been in use for a considerable period of time before its abandonment, showing evidence for a gradual sequence of silting and stabilisation. At some point in time it had been deliberately levelled, with bank material that had originally been piled up above the steeper edge being shovelled back in. He associated this deliberate levelling with a re-organisation of the boundaries at the time of Stukeley. Feature 4 comprised a U-shaped ditch some 0.43m wide and reaching a depth of 0.61m below the turfline. Upon excavation this was shown to contain sherds of 13th-century pottery. Feature 5 was described as a narrow, shallow ditch 0.97m wide at the top narrowing to 0.15m at the base, 1.0m below the turfline. On the basis of its fills and ephemeral nature Keiller argued that this ditch had not been left open for any appreciable period of time and most likely represented a hedgerow. That this was early was suggested by a 12th-century rim sherd on the base. Feature 6 appears to be a continuation of Feature 5 that is closely followed by a wider ditch whose upcast bank served to seal this earlier boundary line. The latter, Feature 7, contained pottery no later than the 13th century suggesting not only that Feature 6 is earlier still, but that this re-modelling of the boundary took place in the medieval period. Interestingly, in the base of Feature 7 were a series of five postholes that Keiller interpreted as marking the fenceline depicted in this position by Stukeley in the 1720s (1743 frontispiece, pls 14 and 15). This suggests that the line marked out by these earlier boundaries had persisted in some form until the early 18th century.

Accepting the caveat that some of the dated pottery finds from the ditches may have been residual, as with the North-West Quadrant the suggestion is of a complex sequence of medieval ditches and boundary lines. Some appear to have been repeatedly redefined during the medieval period, only to be deliberately levelled at some later date. The lines of others persisted, though the boundary itself appears to have taken many different forms over time. Looking to morphology, if we follow Keiller's interpretation of the excavated evidence it would appear that these early divisions were marked by ditches and, in one instance, a possible hedgeline. In later periods banks became more important, often sealing the earlier ditch line beneath them. These in turn were followed by the fences and hedgelines depicted by Stukeley in his panoramas and frontispiece.

Avebury Summary

Figure 8.9 brings together evidence from surviving earthworks, geophysical anomalies, parchmarks and excavation to present all of the data currently available for boundary features within the interior of the henge. Within the complex web, two distinct geometries can be discerned. The first is a grid-like arrangement aligned upon a NNE-SSW axis and the road network. This appears to be structured in the main around a regular series of rectangular strips. In addition to this rough grid are a series of more fragmentary lines that appear to have been laid out according to a wholly different alignment and structuring principle. In Figure 8.10 an attempt has been made to tease these patterns apart to offer specific snapshots of the henge interior at three different points in time. Figure 8.10a summarises the boundaries dated to the medieval period on the basis of Keiller's excavations. Figure 8.10b presents those boundaries recorded in the 1720s by Stukeley, whilst 8.10c depicts those recorded on the Inclosure map of 1794. Comparison of these individual plans and the overall patterns depicted in Figure 8.9 is informative.

Given the close correspondence between Keiller's medieval boundaries and this apparent grid, it can be suggested that the latter represents an intensive pattern of medieval enclosure within the earthwork of the henge. This appears to have comprised a series of tofts and crofts aligned NW-SE and oriented with respect to the roadways that crossed the interior of the henge (though clearly blocking the northern entrance). Evidence for agricultural practice in the medieval period can be

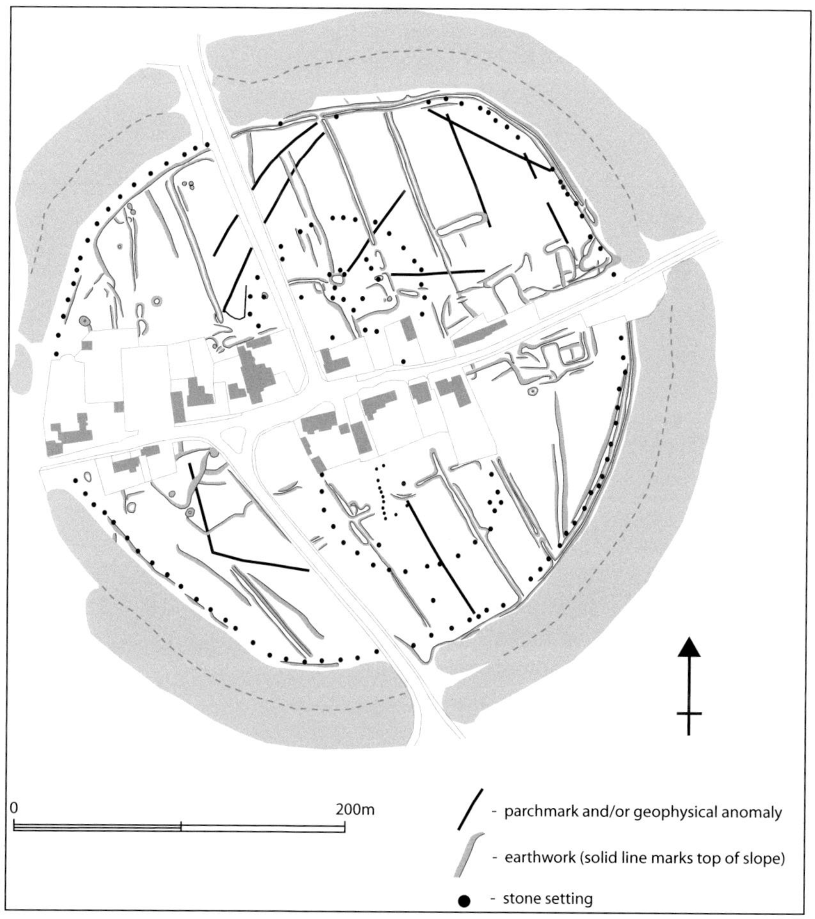

Figure 8.9. Avebury: Boundary features within the interior of the henge (reconstructed on the basis of surviving earthworks, geophysical anomalies, parchmarks and excavation evidence). Incorporates data © Crown Copyright/ database right 2007. An Ordnance Survey/ (EDINA) supplied service

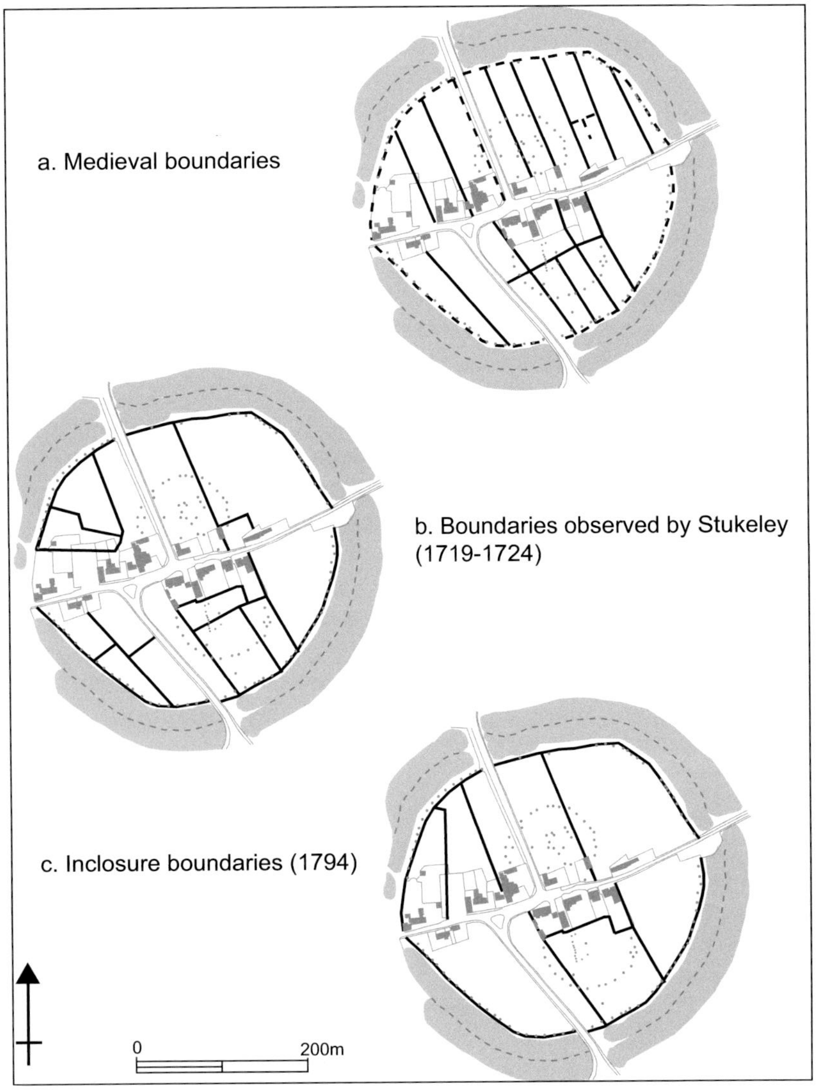

Figure 8.10. Avebury: Medieval, early 18th-century and late 18th-century patterns of partition and enclosure. Incorporates data © Crown Copyright/ database right 2007. An Ordnance Survey/ (EDINA) supplied service

seen from the ubiquity of pottery within the topsoil of the henge interior. Its presence was noted in Gray's excavations across the ditch and around one of the prostrate stones of the Southern Inner Circle (Gray 1935, 131–2). Keiller in turn found large quantities of medieval pottery spread across the areas he excavated, spanning the 11th to early 14th centuries (Gillings and Pollard 2004, 116–19). The presence of conjoining sherds at dispersed locations across the interior of the site suggests that the pottery was entering the topsoil as a result of manuring practices, which in turn suggests the presence of fields and garden plots (Jope 1999, 68–9). In a photograph taken of the ditch and bank in 1914, there also appear to be earthworks in the NE quadrant suggestive of ridge and furrow (Gray 1935, fig. 1; McOmish *et al.* 2005, 31).

Although common, the distribution of pottery is far from uniform across the interior of the monument. Limited excavation in the North-East Quadrant of the henge failed to recover any pottery (Piggott 1964) and that excavated by Keiller contained some large, fresh sherds which suggest that repeated episodes of ploughing or intensive cultivation were rare. In contrast, excavations undertaken some 40m east of the south-west entrance recovered abraded and worn medieval sherds, which suggest that more intensive activity was taking place in this area of the henge (Harrington and Denham 1986, 221).

What we can conclude from this is that the interior of the monument was subject to a planned intake sometime during the 11th to 14th centuries. This had served to parcel it up into a series of narrow rectangular units, separated by a network of major and minor ditches, supplemented by hedges. Manuring took place and the area may even have been in part ploughed, comprising perhaps a patchwork of market-gardens and small cultivated plots, interspersed with areas of pasture. The pottery evidence suggests that this episode of cultivation and manuring ended in the later 14th century (Jope 1999, 69), with the system presumably abandoned in its original form at this point. Some ditches were retained, though the boundary line was marked by a bank, whilst others were deliberately levelled. This alteration may have involved a single remodelling or, more likely, reflected a gradual and piecemeal process of rationalisation and change. If we compare this with the plan of 1724, it is immediately clear that the latter reflects a simplification of the earlier system. Some boundaries have been weeded out and others subdivided, yet the original system is preserved in its overall form and axis of orientation. By the time of Inclosure the pattern appears to have been further simplified though once again the medieval axis has persisted.

Although reliable evidence is sorely lacking for the interior, the pattern through time is one of simplification following an episode of planned partition that probably took place in the earlier part of the period between the 11th and 14th centuries. So far discussion has focused upon this grid system at the expense of the group of linear features that do not conform to this medieval grid pattern. Some of these result from relatively modern structures and boundaries cleared from the henge interior as part of Keiller and the National Trust's campaigns of heritage cleansing, whilst others reflect more recent footpaths and desire-lines. However, a number of anomalies remain that cannot be explained away in such a fashion, and these raise the tantalising possibility of a set of much earlier boundary features. In the absence of any excavation, the question of how much earlier is impossible to answer, though the apparent cross-cutting of lines to the immediate west of the Northern Inner Circle suggests that this pattern may represents a palimpsest of features, and thus may have been long-lived.

The Beckhampton Avenue

As discussed in Chapter 2, the line of the Beckhampton Avenue between Avebury High Street and the western entrance of the henge has been reconstructed on the basis of excavation and geophysical data, supplemented by documentary sources. With respect to the landscape traversed by the avenue and questions of land-use and organisation, our best information relates to two discrete areas, Butler's Field and Longstones Field (Figure 8.11). Butler's Field is divided into two halves by the course of the Winterbourne. The western portion is dominated by the earthworks of property boundaries, closes and other traces of settlement. To the east, earthwork surveys undertaken by the former RCHME revealed a complex of gullies and drains relating to a post-medieval water-meadow system (McOmish *et al.* 2005, 30–31, figs. 2.3, 2.7a and 2.7b). A series of excavations carried out in 1985 across the eastern half of the field have shed important light upon medieval and post-medieval practices in this area of the

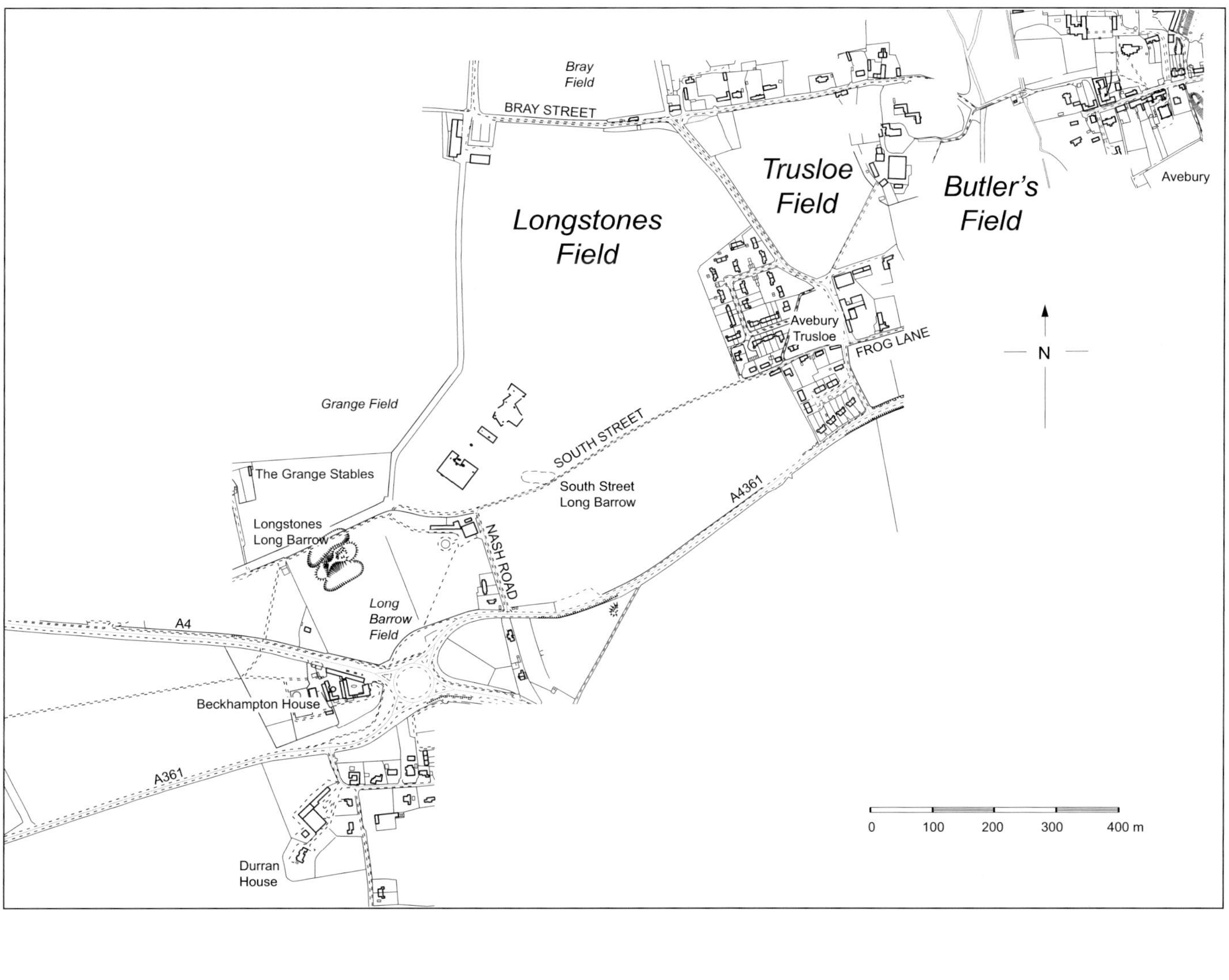

Figure 8.11. The location of Butler's and Longstones Fields. Incorporates data © Crown Copyright/ database right 2007. An Ordnance Survey/ (EDINA) supplied service

landscape. Excavation of an area of 3 × 15m in the northern part of the field, close to the line of the avenue, revealed a ditch terminal with associated gullies and pits cut into earlier alluvium and aligned on an approximate north-south axis. Over 2000 sherds of medieval pottery were recovered from these features suggesting a date somewhere between the mid 12th to late 13th century. The presence of medieval structures was confirmed in 1993 during excavations carried out by Wessex Archaeology on the line of the Kennet Valley Foul Sewer Pipe (Powell *et al.* 1996). These revealed further evidence of wall foundations, pits and several ditches of 13th to 14th century date. The animal bone assemblage recovered in 1985 was dominated by sheep, and taken together with the results of soil and molluscan analysis, suggests that this area may have been utilised for pasture in the early medieval period. That a change in land-use took place is evident from the medieval ploughsoil that seals the excavated features (Mount's Layer 4). Pottery finds suggest that this episode of ploughing continued until the 17th century, at which point the ploughsoil is sealed by a uniform layer of clay associated with the water-meadow system (Mount 1991, 99–111, 228). A cable-trench dug across the field during 1997–8 bisected seven linear features aligned east-west, that were interpreted as channels associated with this water meadow system. Interestingly, a process of deliberate back-filling appears to have been initiated some time in the 17th century, suggesting that the water-meadow experiment was not a long one (Wessex Archaeology 1998).

The evidence from the eastern half of Butler's Field suggests that in the early medieval period the landscape bordering the Winterbourne was a stable grassland used primarily for grazing. At some point, possibly in the later 12th century, this area of grassland was cultivated, and remained under the plough until some point in the 17th century when a water meadow was established.

Moving further to the west, whilst geophysical survey carried out in 2005 in Manor Farm Paddock, to the immediate east of Longstones Field, was successful in locating the course of the avenue, no anomalies consistent with boundary or cultivation features were detected (Gunter and Roberts 2005, 29–35). In contrast, the two campaigns of geophysical survey carried out in the west end of Longstones Field by the Ancient Monuments Laboratory revealed evidence of medieval cultivation in the form of distinct plough furrows (Ucko *et al.* 1991, pl. 63). Two clear alignments were evident; at the far western end the ridge-and-furrow was aligned east-west. At a point some 180m into the field, a substantial ditch running approximately north-south marked the junction with a second zone of ridge-and-furrow aligned on this boundary. The open area excavations carried out between 1999 and 2003 confirmed these patterns, the east-west block extending as far west as settings L7 and L8, with the area of settings L1–L6 bisected by north-south furrows (Figure 8.12).

At the eastern end of the field geophysical survey once again suggested the presence of plough furrows aligned approximately north-south. The excavation of setting T1 failed to reveal any plough furrows but this is perhaps not surprising given the appreciable deposit of lower ploughsoil in this area, no doubt a result of the proximity of the trench to an earlier headland (see below). Sealed beneath the lower ploughsoil was a length of ditch (see Chapter 2) running on an approximate east-west alignment. The presence of coke in the fill suggests a late date for this feature, although this could be intrusive given the presence of extensive animal disturbance in the vicinity.

Looking to the post-medieval period, very little documentary evidence survives with respect to Longstones Field. Plans drawn by Stukeley of the area of Longstones Field (Bodl. MS Gough Maps 231 f223; Bodl. MS Eng. Misc. b65 f63) whilst schematic, suggest that both Longstones Field and Manor Farm paddock were under cultivation at the time of his records. The field is not indicated at all on the Tithe map of the parish of Avebury and is depicted merely as a block of land owned by one William Norris Esquire on the 1794 Enclosure map. Detail does, however, survive in the form of a map of the estate of William Norris surveyed and drawn up in 1702, along with a detailed explanatory account of the individual fields recorded (WCRO 473/274) (Figure 8.13). With reference to the map, of particular interest are Short Seas Lane and Long Seas Lane which cross the field from approximately east to west. In a number of Stukeley's drawings (most clearly Bodl. MS Eng. Misc. b

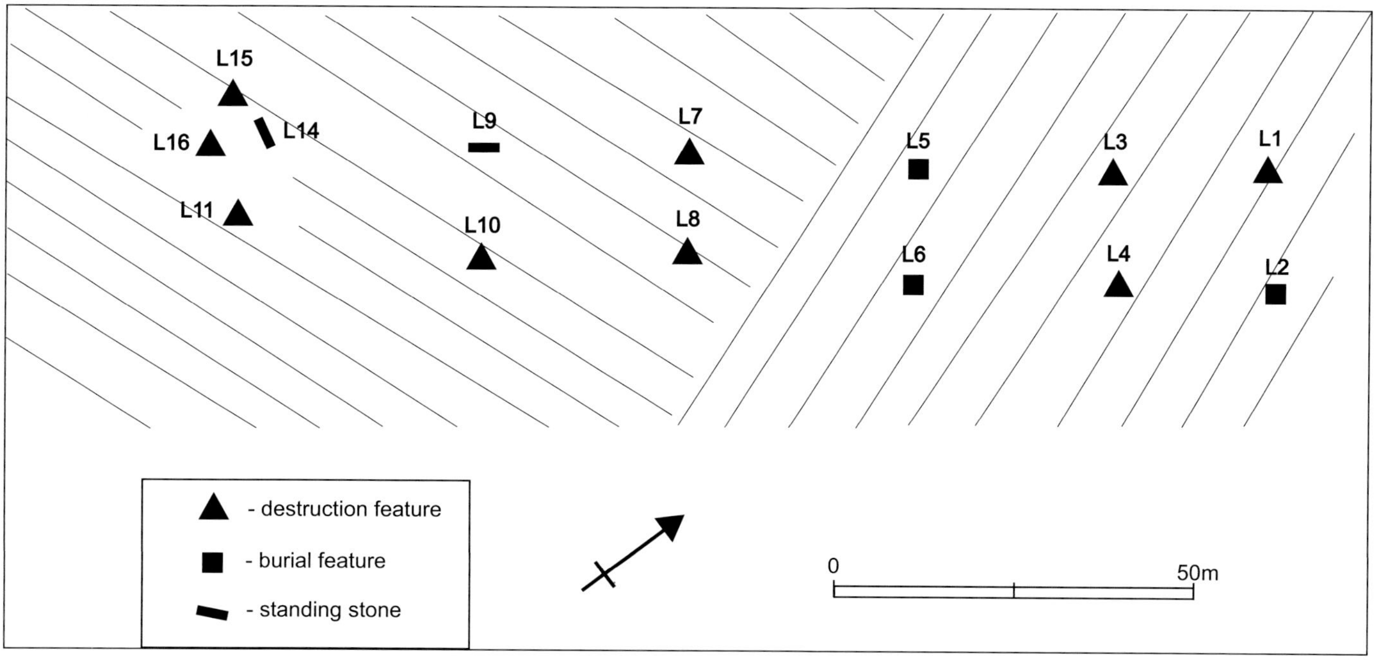

Figure 8.12. (above) Cultivation patterns in area of Longstones Cove (reconstructed on the basis of excavation data)

Figure 8.13. (left) Schematic representation of relevant features from the William Norris plan of Longstones Field (WCRO 473/274)

65 f63) the course of the Beckhampton Avenue is clearly shown entering the field to the north of this lane and crossing it to follow a gently curving NE-SW course to link up with the Longstones Cove. The location of the lanes today can be seen in the form of a large ploughed-out earthwork (Figure 8.14) suggesting that they sat upon a headland (Astill 1988, 71).

To the south of the lane the map clearly shows that the alignment of the medieval strip fields was preserved in this later partition. This is most evident in the westernmost block where individual strips are visible. The lack of any similar pattern in the area to the immediate north of the lanes suggests that this was not so intensively cultivated in the medieval period, though in the absence of any geophysical survey in this area this suggestion must remain speculative.

We can deduce from this that in the medieval period, the majority of land traversed by the avenue was under reasonably intensive cultivation. In the case of Longstones Field the area

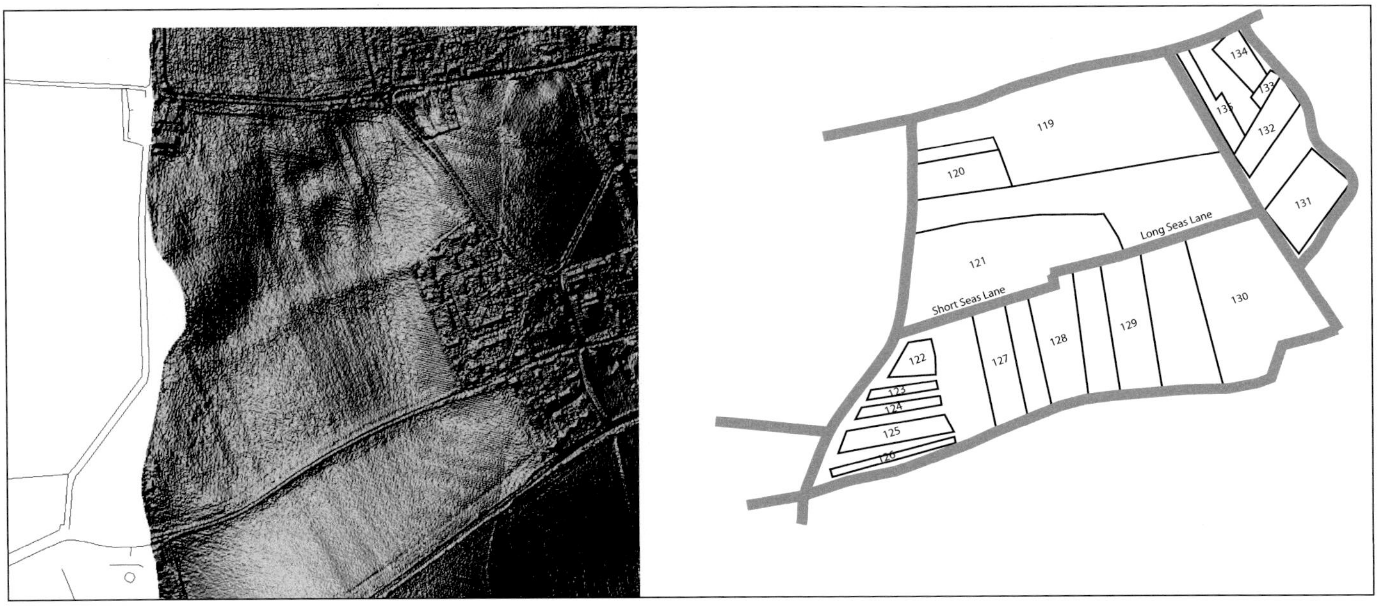

Figure 8.14. Ploughed out headland following Short and Long Seas lanes (LIDAR data copyright Environment Agency). Incorporates data © Crown Copyright/ database right 2007. An Ordnance Survey/ (EDINA) supplied service

to the south of the headland appears to have been ploughed intensively and it may not be a coincidence that Stukeley's records (*e.g.* Bodl. MS Eng. Misc. b.65 f63) suggest that whilst stones remained to the north of the headland and in the vicinity of the Cove, they were largely absent from the ploughed area of the field. The landscape continued to be intensively used into the early modern period, albeit following a period of reorganisation in or around the 17th century, with water meadow channels being deliberately filled and strip fields incorporated into larger parcels.

The West Kennet Avenue

Our knowledge of the landscape traversed by the West Kennet Avenue derives almost exclusively from geophysical survey which revealed evidence of ridge-and-furrow cutting across both the contour and avenue line (Ucko *et al.* 1991, 193); the excavations by Keiller; and detailed earthwork survey by the former RCHME (*e.g.* McOmish *et al.* 2005, fig. 2.3).

Both Keiller and Smith noted the presence of allotment gardens and fowl-runs covering the area of the avenue adjacent to the henge (Keiller and Piggott 1936, 426; Smith 1965, 209). These are visible today as a regular pattern of ditches and banks that appear to have been oriented with reference to the present day roads. Stukeley's drawn panoramas of the avenue line are also consistent in depicting the avenue as crossing cultivated fields (Stukeley 1743, pls XVIII, XIX, XXII).

Further detail can be fund in Keiller's unpublished notebooks which record three examples of a stone being used in the alignment of a boundary feature. Stone 23B had, at some time, fallen over a lynchet that ran adjacent to it. The position of the fallen sarsen was subsequently respected by a later boundary ditch that ran up to the stone. In the case of stone 20A, this had stood in the corner of a field defined by boundary ditches that had presumably been aligned upon it. A ditch had also been cut directly up against the base of setting 19A removing one half of the stonehole causing the stone to subsequently fall. An unpublished plan of the avenue line, annotated by Isobel Smith, recorded (albeit schematically) additional stretches of lynchet and ditch encountered during the excavations. Taken as a whole, the suggestion is once again of a series of settings embedded within a landscape of long-lived and intensive cultivation.

Ownership

In the main we can say little more than that by the medieval period the avenues became embedded within a landscape of cultivation that has persisted to the present day. In the case of Longstones Field however we can go a little further, as the Norris map of 1702 provides us with unique information regarding ownership of each of the designated blocks of land. Shaded in grey in Figure 8.12, are those parcels that were owned by the stone-breaker John Griffin (Griffon) (see Chapter 10). If we attempt to relate these bounded plots to the stones of the Beckhampton Avenue interesting patterns emerge. Although vagaries in the original survey make any direct overlay impossible, on the basis of its orientation and position adjacent to the east-west aligned strips, the large area of land owned by Griffin covers at least stone settings L1–L6. A further feature of note is the angled plot of land owned by John Griffon (Griffin) to the immediate east of the junction between Long Seas Lane and the drove way marking the eastern boundary of the field. Following Stukeley's drawings this slot of land appears to respect the angle of the avenue as it enters Longstones Field which raises the strong possibility that the land owned by John Griffin at this point was defined in large part by the course of the avenue. Stukeley certainly recorded stones being used by Griffin in the yard of Manor Farm and attributed the destruction of 20 stones in and around Longstones Field to him (1743, 34–5). It may well have been the case that Griffin was selectively acquiring land with extant stones, and it is interesting to speculate as to whether the northernmost of his individual east-west strips was that containing the Cove.

Stones and boundaries

Having examined the evidence for how the interior space of the Avebury earthwork was configured and partitioned, attention must now turn to the relationship between the boundaries and standing stones. Although Keiller's excavations in the South-East Quadrant revealed evidence of boundaries being aligned upon specific standing stones, close examination of Figure 8.9 fails to suggest any general relationship beyond the tendency for perimeter banks to follow closely the stones of the Outer Circle.

In the case of the Avenues, it appears that rather than respecting the line of an avenue or orientating with respect to the stones, the medieval ridge-and-furrow passed through it, with individual strips either skirting the sarsens or, in the case of the enormous Cove stones in Longstones Field, interrupting to accommodate them. The same seems to be true in the later period although in the case of Manor Farm paddock there is the tantalising possibility that at least one of Farmer Griffin's fields respected its line.

If there is little to suggest an active relationship between stones and boundaries, might there be a relationship instead between the boundaries and the pattern of stones that were selected for burial, burning, direct fracture, or respect? These themes are discussed in Chapters 9 and 10.

9
Stone burial

'Most of the stones thus pitched on end are taken away: only here and there doe still remain some curvilineous segments: but by these one may boldly conclude, that heretofore they stood quite round about, like a crown' (Aubrey, cited in Long 1858b, 7).

'Just before I visited this place, to endeavour at preserving the memory of it, the inhabitants were fallen into the custom of demolishing the stones... First they dug great pits in the earth and buried them. The expense of digging the grave, was more than 30 years purchase of the spot they possessed when standing' (Stukeley 1743, 15).

That a number of the standing stones making up the Avebury settings had disappeared prior to his survey of 1663 had been alluded to by Aubrey in his description of the monument. That they may have been deliberately buried was first mooted some 60 years later by the antiquary William Stukeley, based on the verbal testimony of the Avebury villagers: he did not observe any stones being buried or record any such events taking place during his visits to the site (1719–24). In the late 19th century the veracity of Stukeley's claim was put to the test by the Reverends A. C. Smith and W. C. Lukis who located 18 buried stones within the earthwork of the Avebury henge. It was not until the 1930s that any further archaeological investigation of such features took place, the campaigns of Alexander Keiller revealing a total of 41 stones that had been either completely or partially buried in pits close to their original standing locations. It was during the course of excavating a stone-burial of the Outer Circle that one of Avebury's most famous and evocative discoveries was made, the body of a man argued to be a barber-surgeon, crushed in the very act of burying a stone. Putting aside for one moment the human tragedy, the most striking aspect of the discovery was its date. On the basis of a pouch of coins found alongside the body the burial was dated to the period 1320–1350AD (Ucko *et al.* 1991, 178), much earlier than the later 17th-century date given by Stukeley for stone burial. This discovery pointed to either a very long-lived practice or an activity that had taken place exclusively in the medieval period, surviving into the early 18th century as a residual folk-memory, perhaps encouraged by the occasional discovery of buried stones during ploughing or the digging of garden plots.

Of these possibilities, the idea of a discrete episode of medieval stone-burial has been by far the most beguiling, quickly becoming sedimented within published histories of Avebury (cf. Ucko *et al.* 1991, 249; Gillings and Pollard 2004, 129). It is invariably associated with a desire by the Church to rid the site of potential (or actual) foci of pagan worship and ends with either the death of the barber-surgeon (becoming a cautionary tale) or the Black Death (swept away by the inexorable forces of history) (*e.g.* Burl 2000, 318).

During the course of the excavations carried out between 1999 and 2003 a total of four intact stone burials, along with a further two features that may originally have been burials, were encountered along the line of the Beckhampton Avenue. These were accompanied by a well-dated 20th-century burial on the notional line of the West Kennet Avenue. This fieldwork was accompanied by a detailed analysis and re-appraisal of the unpublished archival material relating to the excavation of stone burials by Keiller (1934–39). Together these provided a unique opportunity to revisit and examine critically the phenomenon of stone burial in the Avebury landscape.

Early encounters with buried sarsens

In contrast to stone-breaking (see Chapter 10), there are no 18th-century, or earlier, descriptions or depictions of the practice, nor any record of the impact stone-burial had upon the fabric of the monument. Following Stukeley, all we know for sure is how expensive it was.

Even in the case of burials that took place from the later 18th century, the information we have is brief and circumspect, taking the form of short notes relating specifically to *ad hoc* or unusual events (*e.g.* Long 1878, 330–1; Smith 1965, 207 footnote 2). For example, a stone thought to be part of the West Kennet Avenue was buried in a garden in the early 19th century in the village of West Kennet. More recently a stone suspected to be setting 63B was buried as part of a campaign of stone breaking carried out in the valley bottom during the winter of 1921–2 (see below).

The first archaeological encounter with deliberately buried stones took place in 1881 when W. C. Lukis and A. C. Smith hired a group of labourers with iron probes in an attempt to ground-truth the plan records of Stukeley. They succeeded in locating a total of 18 buried stones; 16 on the arc of the Outer Circle and two on that of the Northern Inner Circle. These were frequently very deeply buried, making detection difficult. In all cases the stones discovered were exposed and measured before the burial pits were back-filled and turfed over. To ensure that the locations were not lost they were carefully surveyed and labelled wooden pegs were hammered into the ground close to them[1] (Smith 1884, 139–143, pl. V).

The success of this probing exercise prompted other archaeologists to do likewise. For example, during the very dry summer of 1921, A D Passmore walked the presumed line of the West Kennet Avenue looking for evidence of parchmarks indicative of buried stones. Using a steel probe he located a buried stone to the east of West Kennet village which he duly excavated (Passmore 1926).[2]

The excavations of Keiller

In his excavation on the line of the West Kennet Avenue Keiller excavated 15 stone burials, with a further 15 encountered on the arc of the Outer Circle and 11 within the Southern Inner Circle (Figures 9.1 and 9.2). In the published interim reports only cursory mention is made of the burials. The final monograph offers little more, limiting discussion to the following statement:

> 'As a rule the burial-pits were dug to conform to the shapes of the stones they were to receive and were deep enough to sink the stones below the level of the undisturbed sub-soil. Clean chalk rubble was rammed into the hollow above the stone and the whole levelled so that no trace remained of the operation.' (Smith 1965, 177)

The implication is one of remarkable *consistency*, with all of the stone burials executed according to a single methodology. This in turn adds tacit support to the assumption that they were all buried in a single episode. A wealth of additional information survives in the form of excavation drawings, draft synthetic discussions and original site notebooks.[3] Although not as well documented as the features relating to stone destruction (see Chapter 10), careful study of these documents has enabled a fuller picture of the process of stone burial to be constructed. As will be seen from the discus-

Figure 9.1. Stone burials at Avebury excavated by Keiller. Incorporates data © Crown Copyright/ database right 2007. An Ordnance Survey/ (EDINA) supplied service

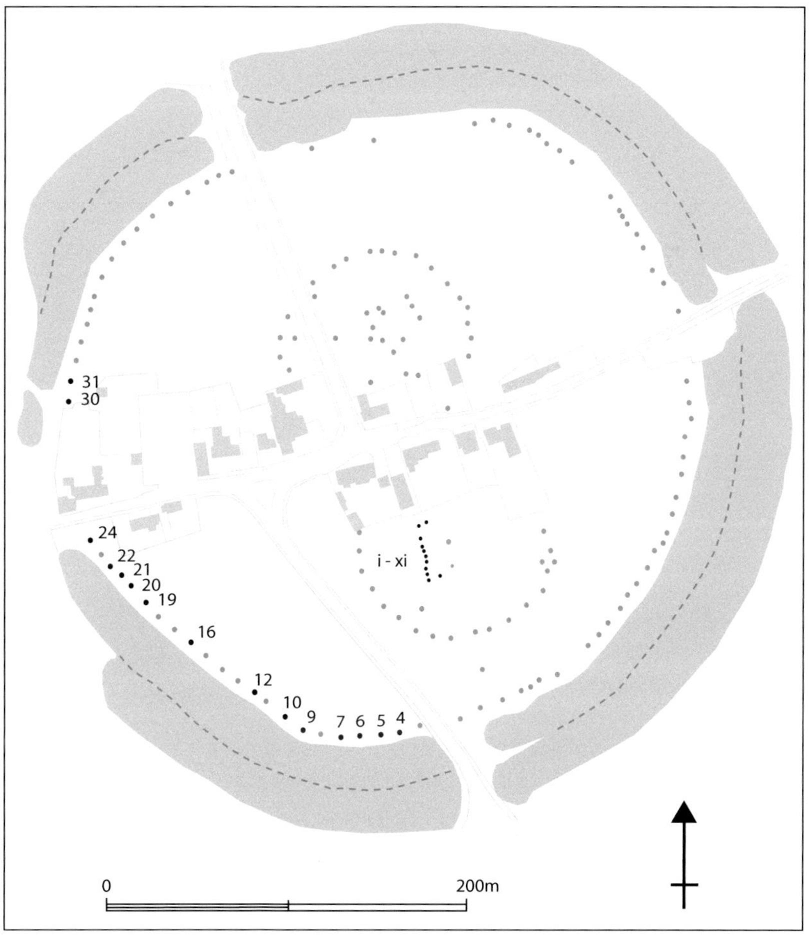

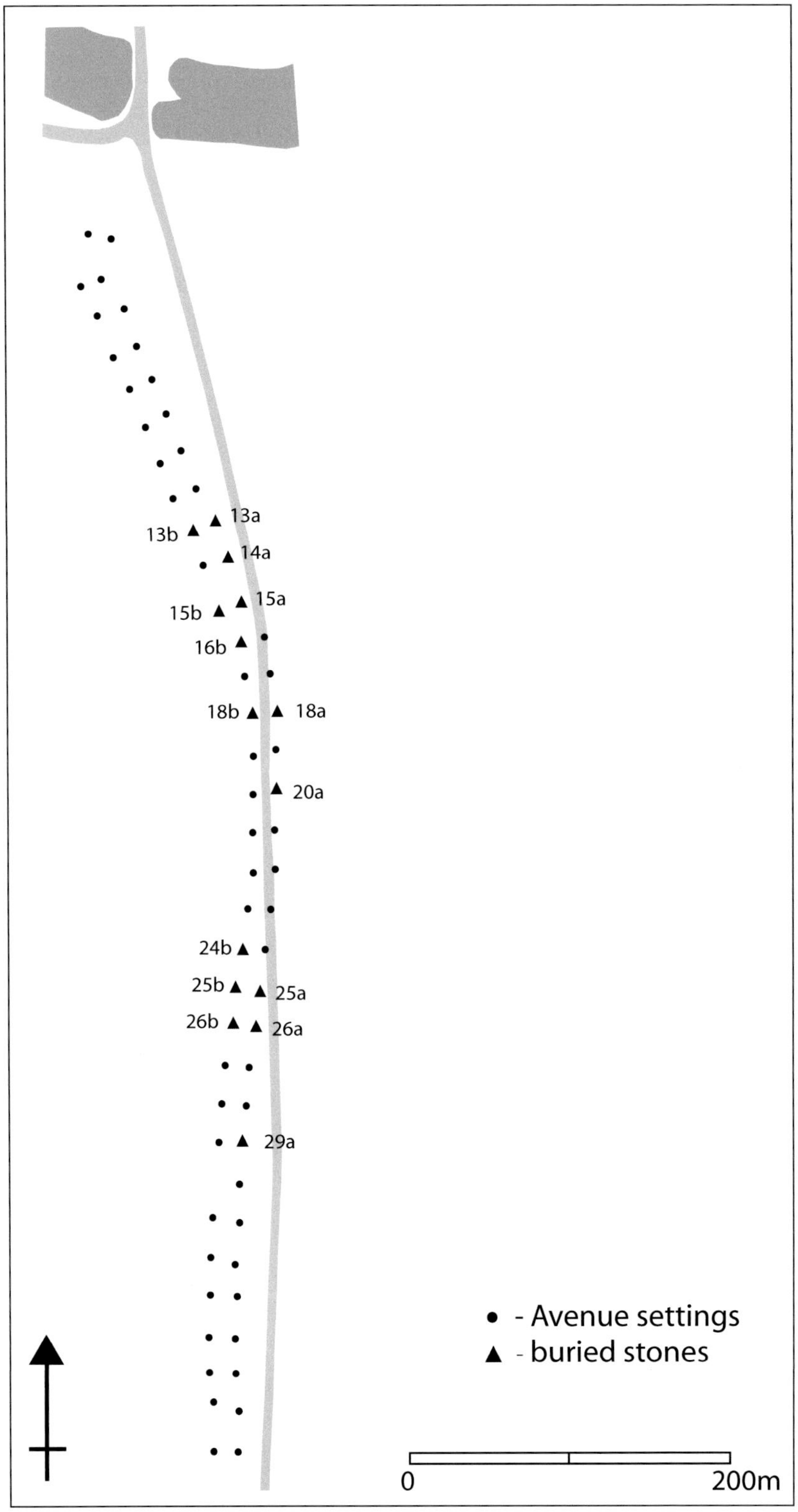

Figure 9.2. Stone burials on the line of the West Kennet Avenue excavated by Keiller.

sion below, when considered together the 41 burials excavated by Keiller paint a picture not of regularity in practice, but *inconsistency*, variation and pragmatism.

To ensure compatibility with the original excavation monograph (Smith 1965) the stone burials are grouped according to excavation campaign (*i.e.* West Kennet Avenue; North-West Quadrant, South-West Quadrant and South-East Quadrant). The numbering of stones also follows Smith's 1965 schema (clockwise from the southern entrance) rather than Keiller's working scheme (anti-clockwise from the northern entrance).[4] All recorded dimensions (either quoted in notebooks or measured from plans and sections) have been converted from imperial to metric and summarised in Table 9.1.

West Kennet Avenue (Figure 9.3)

Setting 13A

The digging of the burial pit totally destroyed the original stone-hole. The pit was deep and closely followed the shape of the stone.

Setting 13B

This pit did not mirror the shape of the stone and Keiller claimed that an irregularity on the NW side marked the point where the excavators realised they had over-dug and corrected. The pit cut through the stone-hole and was relatively shallow, the base sloping.

Setting 14A

The digging of this burial pit had partly cut into the stone-hole, the pit itself mirroring the shape of the stone.

Setting 15A

As with setting 16B, the burial pit was dug at a distance from the stone-hole (0.52m) and was described by Keiller merely as 'a very large pit'. Of interest is the fact that the shape of the stone and pit appear to be reversed (in much the same way as setting 5 of Avebury's Outer Circle) which implies that the procedure of manoeuvring the stone into the pit did not progress smoothly.

Setting 15B

The cut of this burial pit was largely vertical with a distinct ledge running halfway round the pit at a depth of 0.40m below the level of the chalk subsoil. This platform was substantial, projecting up to 0.70m into the pit. The base itself sloped down to the position of the stone.

Setting 16B

Although Keiller noted that no concession was made to the shape of the stone in digging this pit, the plan reveals a close correspondence. When the stone was levered into the pit it appears to have fallen at an angle, leaving one part to project above the level of the chalk (*i.e.* into the topsoil). This pit was separated from the stone-hole by 0.49m.

Setting 18A

The burial pit was cut very closely to conform to the shape of the stone, with very neatly cut vertical sides. The base of the pit was distinctive, sloping from one side to the other, leaving the narrow stone tilting along its long axis.

Setting 18B

This had been buried in a pit, however a pipe-trench and subsequent excavation carried out in 1913 made it difficult to reconstruct any details of this feature.

Setting 20A

This relatively shallow burial pit was dug in the corner of a former field in order to bury an already fallen sarsen. Further details of the pit were obscured by a later destruction pit dug to enable the stone to be broken up.

Setting 24B

The burial pit had been dug to the south of the fallen/toppled stone and originally seems to have been shaped closely to match the stone, even going as far as to shape the base to accommodate the folds and projections on the lower side of the sarsen. When this failed to lower the stone to a sufficient depth the pit was enlarged and deepened to the north and the stone dragged into this area. The digging of the pit had destroyed one half of the original stone-hole.

Setting 25A

This corresponded to a burial pit that had suffered damage from subsequent fox burrowing and the activities of stone breakers.

Setting 25B

According to Keiller the shape of this 3.80 by 3.05m burial pit approximated that of the stone albeit oversized. Although the stone is described as having been dragged down a ramp into the pit this is not evident in the surviving plan or section of the feature. The original stone-hole had been largely destroyed by the digging of the pit, which had also dug through an early Bronze Age grave (Smith 1965, 209–10).

Setting	Length	Breadth	Depth below surface	Depth below chalk
Outer Circle (northwest quadrant)				
31	4.30m	3.45m	2.44m	1.52m
30	4.19m	4.38m	2.35m	1.04 - 0.66m
Outer Circle (southwest quadrant)				
4	4.75m	4.00m	1.58m	1.10m
5	5.11m	3.57m	1.55m	
6	5.23m	3.69m	1.22m	0.82m
7	4.98m	4.06m	1.07-1.37m	
9	5.97m	4.73m	1.61m	1.13m
10	6.40m *	6.77m	1.83m	1.40m
12	4.80m	3.75m	-	-
16	4.00m *	4.43m	1.19m	0.58m
19	4.88m	3.75m	0.79m	0.52m
20	4.68m	4.12m	-	-
21	4.42m	3.06m	1.52m	1.22m
22	4.00m	2.40m	1.52m	1.22m
24	2.52m	2.03m	-	-
Southern Inner Circle				
i	2.80m	1.37m	-	-
ii	-	-	-	-
iii	2.65m	1.73m	-	-
iv	3.06m	2.24m	-	-
v, vi & vii	5.71m	2.65m	-	-
viii	2.04m	1.43m	-	-
ix	3.06m	1.22m	-	-
x	2.65m	1.63m	-	-
xi	-	-	-	-
West Kennet Avenue				
29A	-	2.44m	1.07m	0.40m
26B	3.70m	2.50m	-	-
26A	4.13m	3.40m	1.27m	0.83m
25B	3.81m	3.05m	1.07m	0.84m
25A	3.80m	2.83m	1.10m	0.67m
24B	3.50m	2.10m	-	-
20A	-	-	0.68m	-
18B	3.23m	1.80m	1.27m	0.73m
18A	2.37m	0.90m	0.91m	0.61m
16B	2.86m	1.52m	-	0.55m
15B	4.57m	3.89m	1.13m	0.88m
15A	3.17m	2.57m	1.14m	0.62m
14A	2.37m	1.67m	0.87m	0.72m
13B	3.73m	3.10m	0.93m	0.67m
13A	4.20m	2.20m	1.03m	0.70m
Crawford	3.40m	2.10m	1.74m	1.54m
Beckhampton Avenue				
L2	4.00m	3.16m	1.10m	0.90m
L3	3.40m	2.80m	0.76m	0.56m
L5	2.85m	2.90m	1.00m	0.80m
L6	2.70m	2.50m	1.62m	1.42m
L8	3.00m	2.30m	0.80m	0.60m
T1	3.30m	3.20m	1.03m	0.60m

- indicates that a measurement was not recorded
* records instances where the feature was not fully excavated
Where a range is quoted for depth measurements it indicates a sloping base

Table 9.1. Burial pit dimensions

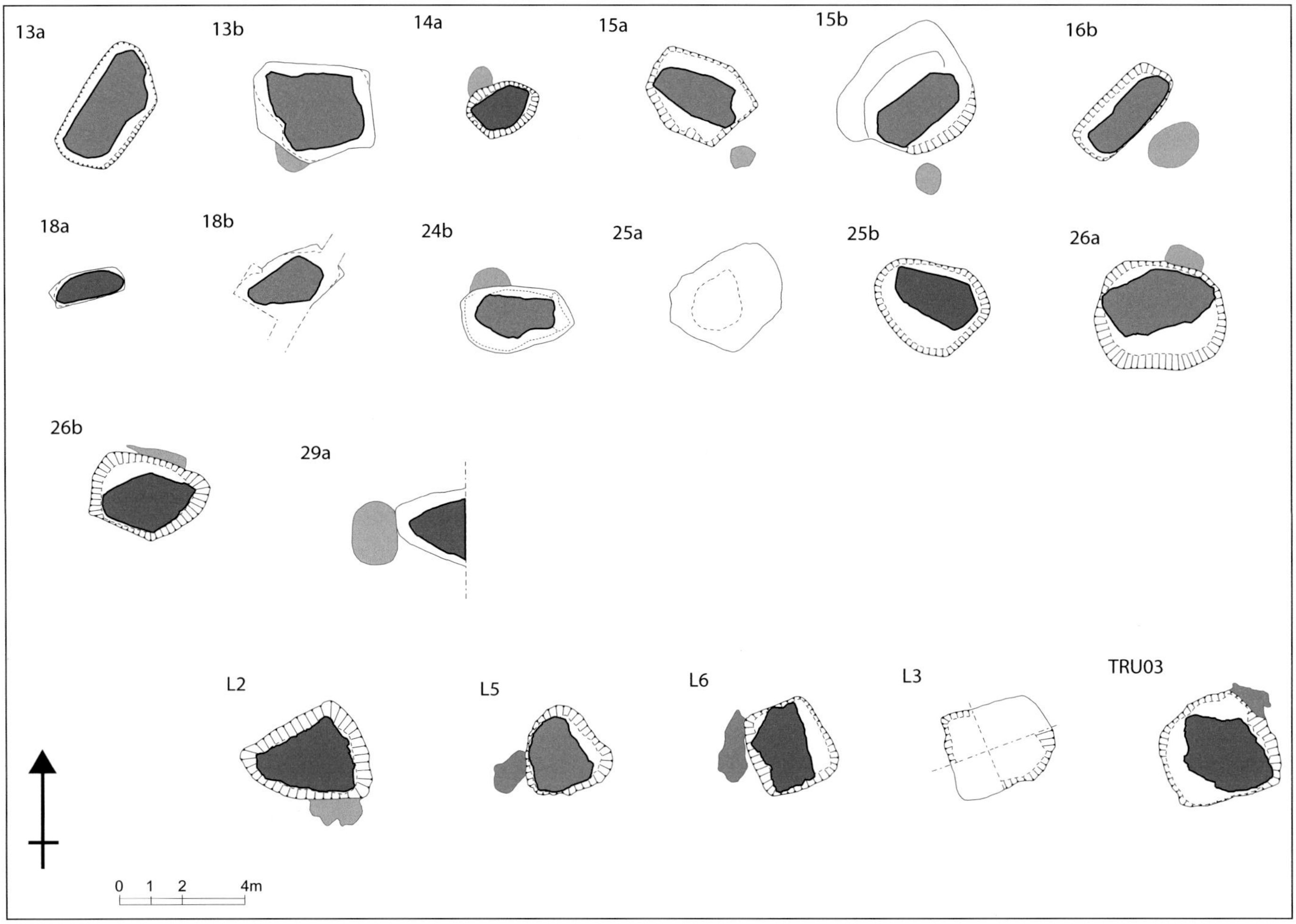

Figure 9.3. Burial pit morphology (West Kennet Avenue and Beckhampton Avenue)

Setting 26A
The burial pit here was much larger than the stone held within it. It had been dug downslope from the setting taking the form of a ramp. Once the stone had been slid into the pit the upper portion of the ramp was dug away to create a counter-slope to enable the stone to be lowered deeper into the ground.

Setting 26B
The burial pit had completely destroyed the original stone-hole. Whilst it mirrored closely the shape of the stone at the north end, the southern was enlarged, presumably to provide sufficient working space for the excavators.

Setting 29A
We have little information regarding this burial other than Keiller's note that it was 'cut closely to mirror the shape of the stone buried within it'. The plan is more informative indicating that a small un-dug ridge of chalk was left between the sarsen and the pit implying the former was standing when the pit was dug.

North-West Quadrant (Figure 9.4)
Setting 31
This carefully-shaped burial pit was found beneath the foundations of a later structure and appears to have taken the form of a ramp down which the toppled stone had been slid. Once the stone was in place the pit was deliberately backfilled. The efficacy of this approach was evident insofar as Keiller's workmen simply dragged the stone back up the ramp to remove it from its place of burial. The burial pit had been dug into one edge of the original stone-hole.

Setting 30
Rather than a single undifferentiated hole, the profile of this burial pit revealed a clear step, or platform, along one edge. It appears that the first stage was to dig a shallow pit next to the

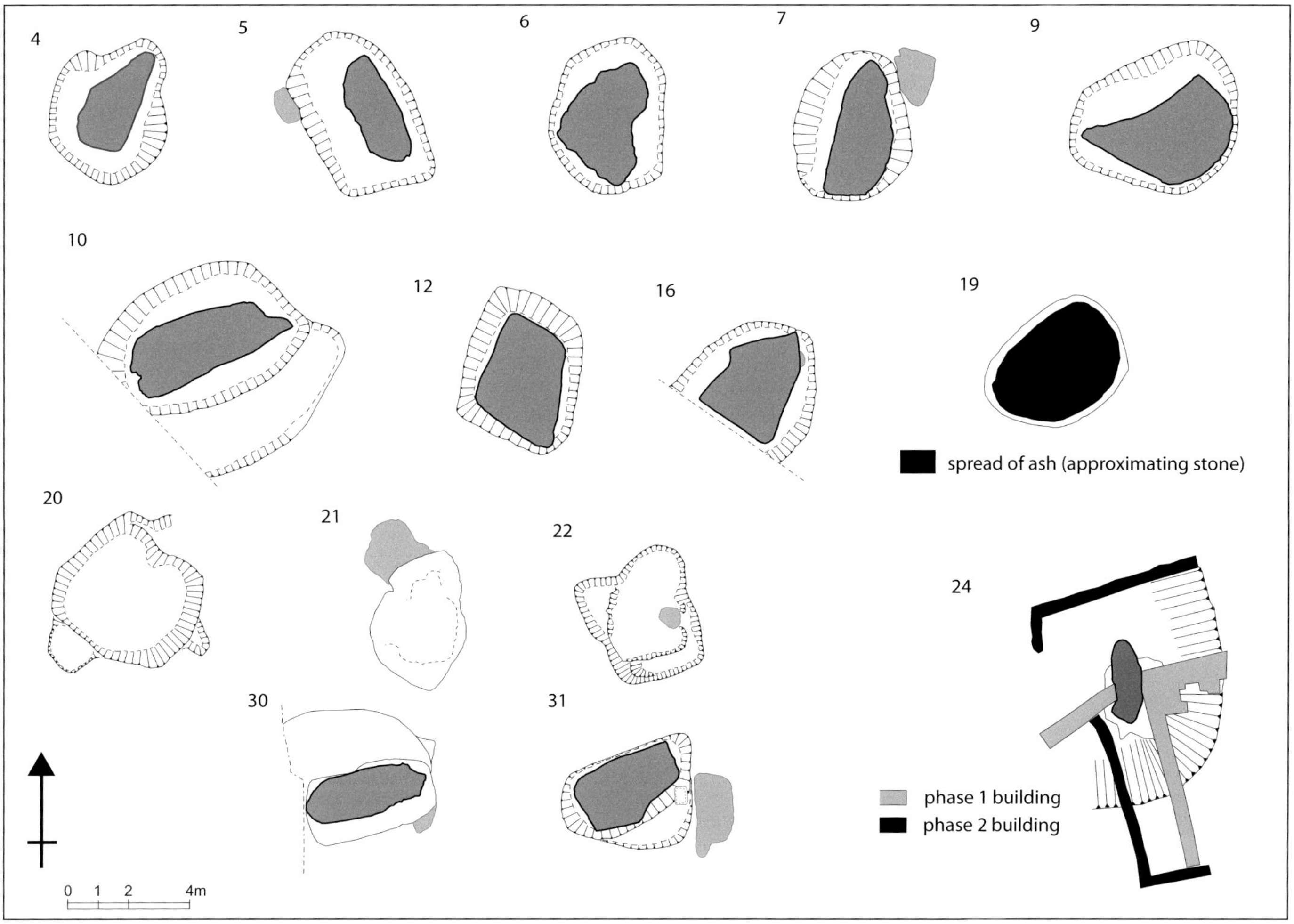

Figure 9.4. Burial pit morphology (Avebury)

fallen (or toppled) stone, into which the sarsen was rolled or levered. A much deeper pit shaped to receive the stone was then dug directly adjacent to this, markedly undercutting the base of the original pit. The stone was then rolled into this deeper pit landing not quite centrally within it. The whole structure, with its distinctive ledged profile, was then deliberately back-filled. Unlike the ramped pit of setting 31, Keiller's workmen had a much harder job removing this stone from its burial pit.

South-West Quadrant (Figure 9.4)

Setting 4

This burial pit was cut to deliberately echo the shape of the stone it was destined to hold, though enlarged by approximately 1.0m in all directions. On the basis of plan and photographic evidence the base of the pit appears to have been flat and even. To the east the pit cut through one half of the stone-hole, the only surviving remnant taking the form of a distinctive sloping side to the burial pit at this point and a shallow platform slightly above the level of the base.

Setting 5

In plan this oblong pit reproduces the shape of the stone only in reverse. As with setting 4 the pit was also oversized. This odd correspondence suggest that the stone either rolled unexpectedly (or conversely failed to roll *as* expected) when levered into the pit thus ending up back-to-front. The original stone-hole of the stone was cut through by the digging of the pit, a remnant surviving in one corner. Keiller was careful to note that the depth of the pit was not sufficient to keep all of the stone below the level of the chalk (*i.e.* out of the topsoil and potential reach of any ploughshare).

Setting 6

This pit was again cut generously but reflecting

the shape of the stone it was destined to receive. The digging of the pit completely removed all traces of the original stone-hole leading Keiller to conclude that it had been dug around (and beneath) the stone as it lay prone though no mention was made of how this might have been achieved. As with setting 5 the depth of the pit was not sufficient to ensure that all of the stone was out of the topsoil.

Setting 7
In terms of plan, whilst the shape of the pit very closely mirrored that of the stone at its base, the sides flanking the long axis of the sarsen were sloping, giving it a sub-circular appearance. The base was also sloping. Two things are of note. The first is that the digging of the pit had not interfered with the original stone-hole, as was the case with a number of the preceding burials investigated. The second was that the resultant pit was much too shallow to fully bury the stone, even beneath the topsoil, as one corner protruded above the turfline.

Setting 9
In plan this burial pit approximated the shape of the stone, though was once again oversized. The finished edges were smoothly cut and regular and the digging of the pit had completely destroyed the original stone-hole, only some displaced packing stones marking its approximate location. During the burial of the stone the sarsen appears to have slipped, pinning and crushing one of the excavators against one of the unfinished edges. At this point the stone burial was abandoned with no further slots dug or attempt made to alter the position of the stone; the corpse was covered over with soil and the pit back-filled.

Setting 10
Oblong in plan, this pit conformed to the familiar pattern of oversized pit approximating the shape of the stone it was intended to hold. The morphology of the pit was unusual insofar as the base was excavated to two distinct levels, with a marked ledge existing to the south of the stone. As in the case of setting 30, the ledge marked the base of the first phase of burial. This was then partially undercut as a second, deeper pit, was cut alongside. The digging of the burial pit completely destroyed all traces of the original stone-hole.

Setting 12
Little in the way of detail survives for this burial pit apart from a plan depiction. It seems to have been shaped to mirror the stone but was not deliberately over-dug, with the result that the stone fits unusually tightly within it. The sloping base of the pit resulted in only a partial burial, a portion of the stone's base projecting above the turfline.

Setting 16
On the basis of the surviving plan this pit conforms to the familiar pattern of being cut generously to approximate the shape of the stone. The original stone-hole was largely cut away during the digging of the pit, however the shallow depth of the latter meant that the base of the stone-hole remained intact.

Settings 19–22
These were all stones that having been buried, had subsequently been discovered and burned. As a result it was difficult to determine the relationship between the pit and the stone (now destroyed) it once held. In saying this, the burial pits of settings19 and 20 both appeared to have been shallow, with straight, neatly cut sides. In contrast, those relating to settings 21 and 22 were both very deep and incorporated the original stone-hole in the cut.

Setting 24
That an unsuccessful attempt had been made to break up this stone using direct fracture was evident from the discovery of a broken iron wedge embedded in it close to the base. Having failed to break the stone it had been rolled and manoeuvred downslope from its original stone-hole into a shallow, rectangular pit that had been cut into the base of a largely dried up pond. The pit was dug in two stages and left to accumulate silt prior to the stone being buried in it. The pond was subsequently levelled and built over, the latter foundations resulting in disturbance and damage to the stone.

South-East Quadrant (Figure 9.5)
Stone burials were limited here to the small stones making up the rectangular setting adjacent to the Obelisk (stones *i–xii*). As for settings 19–22 of the Outer Circle, the burial pits marking settings *i*, *ii*, *ix*, *x* and *xi* had subsequently been dug into and badly disturbed.

Although damaged by later digging, the pit

originally holding stone *i* was regularly cut and substantial, separated by a distance of 0.60m from the stone-hole. The burial pit for setting ii was completely destroyed by later destruction digging, though appears to have been dug directly adjacent to the stone-hole.

Better preserved were the pits associated with the burial of settings *iii–viii*. The burial pit for stone iii was dug 0.70m away from the stone-hole, the sarsen then toppled and manoeuvred into it using levers and bars, causing damage to one edge of the pit in the process. In terms of morphology, some concession was given to the shape of the stone in digging the pit, the former sitting tightly within the latter. In contrast, the pit for stone iv appears to have been dug up to the base of the stone and is remarkably rectangular and large in relation to the stone held within it, showing little evidence that stone shape was considered in its preparation. The lack of information regarding the profile of the pit makes it difficult to ascertain whether it had been dug around a toppled/fallen stone or against a standing one.

The same approach was adopted in dealing with stones *vi* and *vii*, the digging of the burial pits (and subsequent modifications – see below) removing much of the stone-hole in each case. The burial of stone vi was particularly interesting as it appears that the stone had fallen awkwardly into the pit scoring (and presumably wedging against) one of the sides. To correct this, and complete the process of burial, further digging was carried out.

One of the most peculiar burials was that of stone *v*. Rather than placed in its own carefully prepared burial pit, an area between the burial pits of settings *vi* and *vii* was enlarged and this small stone placed within it. The stone was clearly buried 'out-of-sequence' and the *ad hoc* nature of this act is evident in the very rough sides and base of this pit that contrast with the apparent care taken over the other burial features.

In the case of setting *viii* the burial pit was cut through an earlier ditch and separated from the original stone-hole by an un-dug ridge of chalk 0.33m wide, suggesting the stone had been standing when the pit had been dug. Unlike setting *iv*, the shape of the pit closely mirrored that of the stone, the latter fitting tightly within it. The final stone burials (settings *ix*, *x* and *xi*) had been too badly damaged by later digging to reconstruct the burial episodes, beyond noting that the surviving fragments of the pit for the burial of setting *ix* were deep and well-formed.

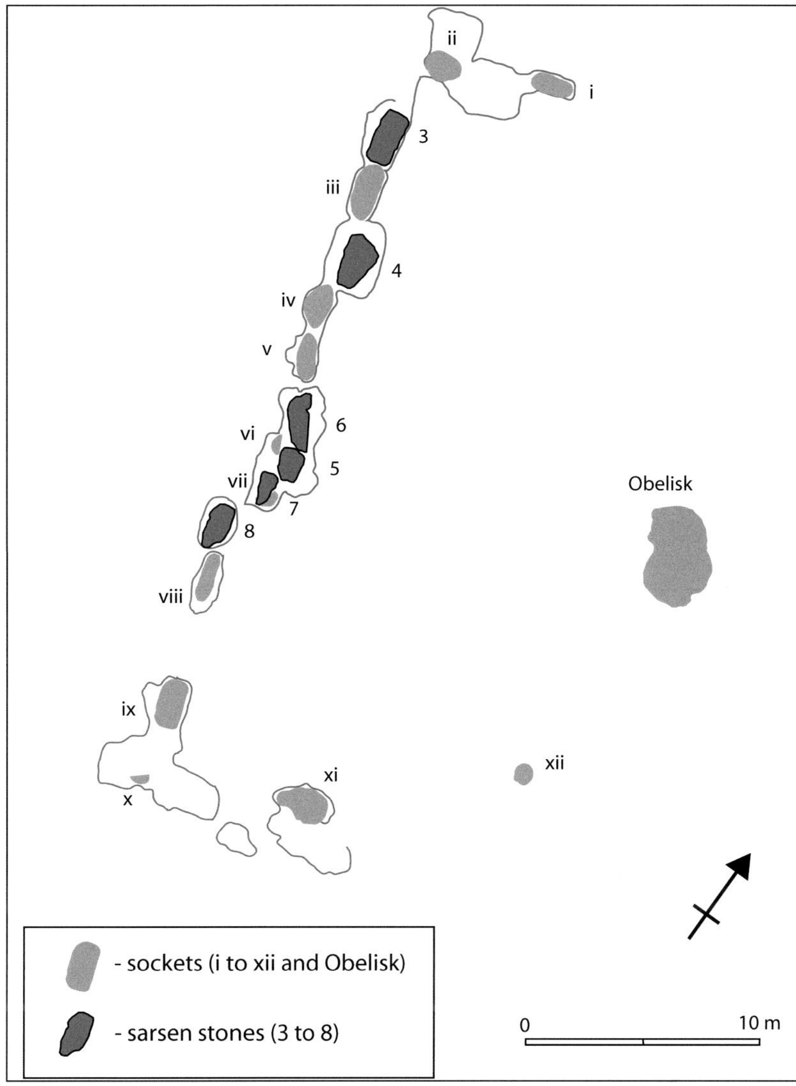

Figure 9.5. Detail of burials within Southern Inner Circle (after an unpublished plan of the Keiller excavations by Denis Grant King)

Excavations on the Beckhampton Avenue

During the excavations carried out between 1999 and 2003, four burial pits containing former standing stones were excavated, along with two features that can be interpreted as shallow burial pits from which the stone was subsequently removed (Figures 2.36 and 9.3).

Setting L2 (F.22)

The burial pit [412] was 4.00 × 3.16m across and up to 0.90m deep, cut to carefully mirror the shape of the stone contained within it

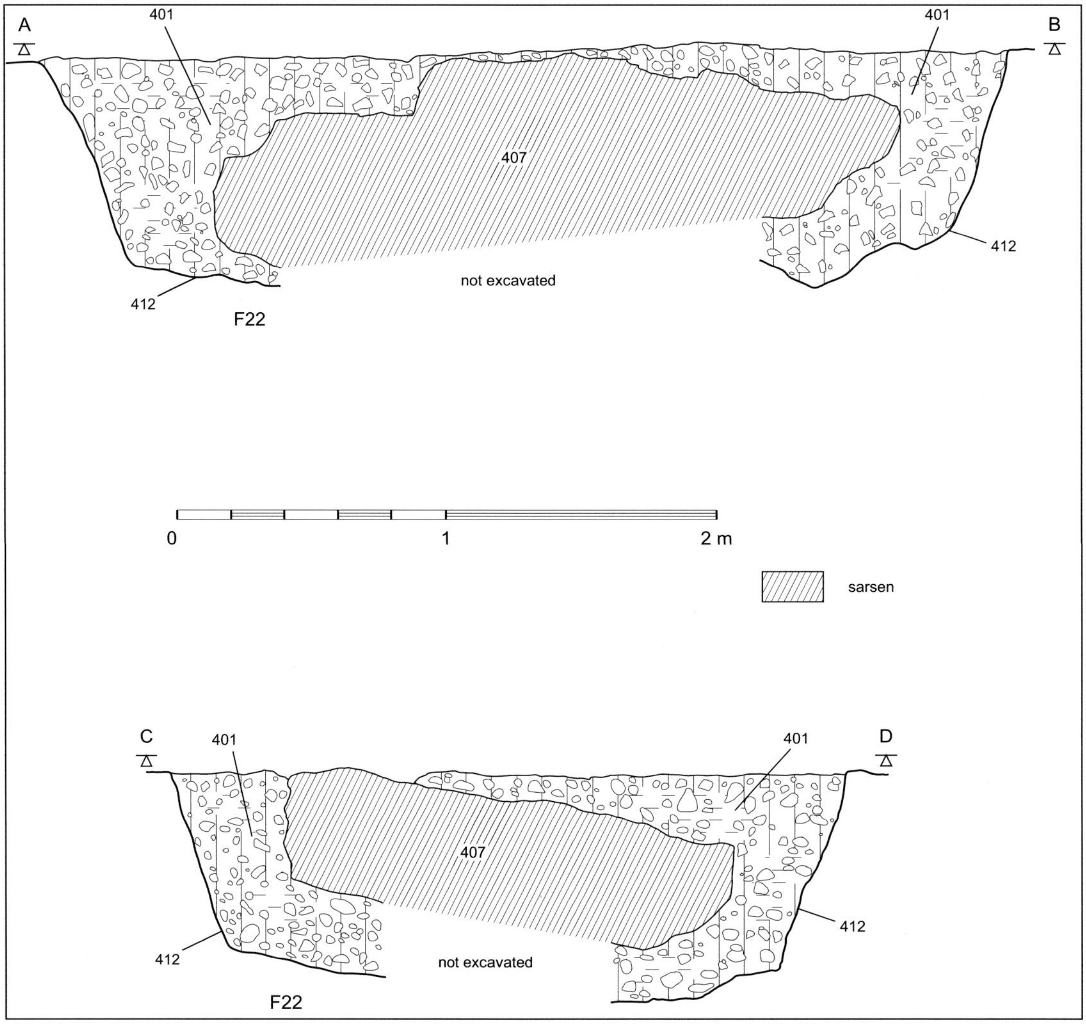

Figure 9.6. Sections of stone burial pit F.22 (setting L2). For section locations see Figure 2.49

(Figures 2.49 and 9.6). The pit appears to have been very carefully dug, with steep to near vertical sides and a slightly dished base. The junction between sides and base was gently rounded. A large block of sarsen [407] lay centrally within the pit, the western tip of the stone projecting just above the level of the chalk. It rested on the base of the pit at one or more points of contact rather than lying flush. Patches of black staining were visible on the protected sides and undersurface of the stone which may reflect the decayed remains of former areas of lichen growth.

Following incorporation of the stone, the pit was filled with a mixed chalk rubble within a creamy brown clay loam [401], becoming progressively looser with depth. As the stone rested on a concave face there were a number of large voids beneath it where the chalk backfill had not penetrated; it is interesting to note that no effort had been made to deliberately pack these voids with material.

The digging of the pit had served to cut away the majority of the stone-hole, the truncated remains of which survived on the southern side of the main burial pit. A second feature (F.37), had been cut by the burial pit on its north-western side (see Chapter 2).

Setting L3 (F.23)

F.23 was unusual in that it no longer contained a buried stone. Subjected to 50% excavation, it comprised a sub-rectangular pit [411], 3.40 × 2.80m, and up to 0.56m deep, with a marked depression in the base corresponding to the former position of a buried stone (Figures 9.7 and 9.8). The sides were moderate to steep and the base dished. The lower fill [434] comprised a compact chalk rubble within a brown clay loam, appearing as a distinct slump against the

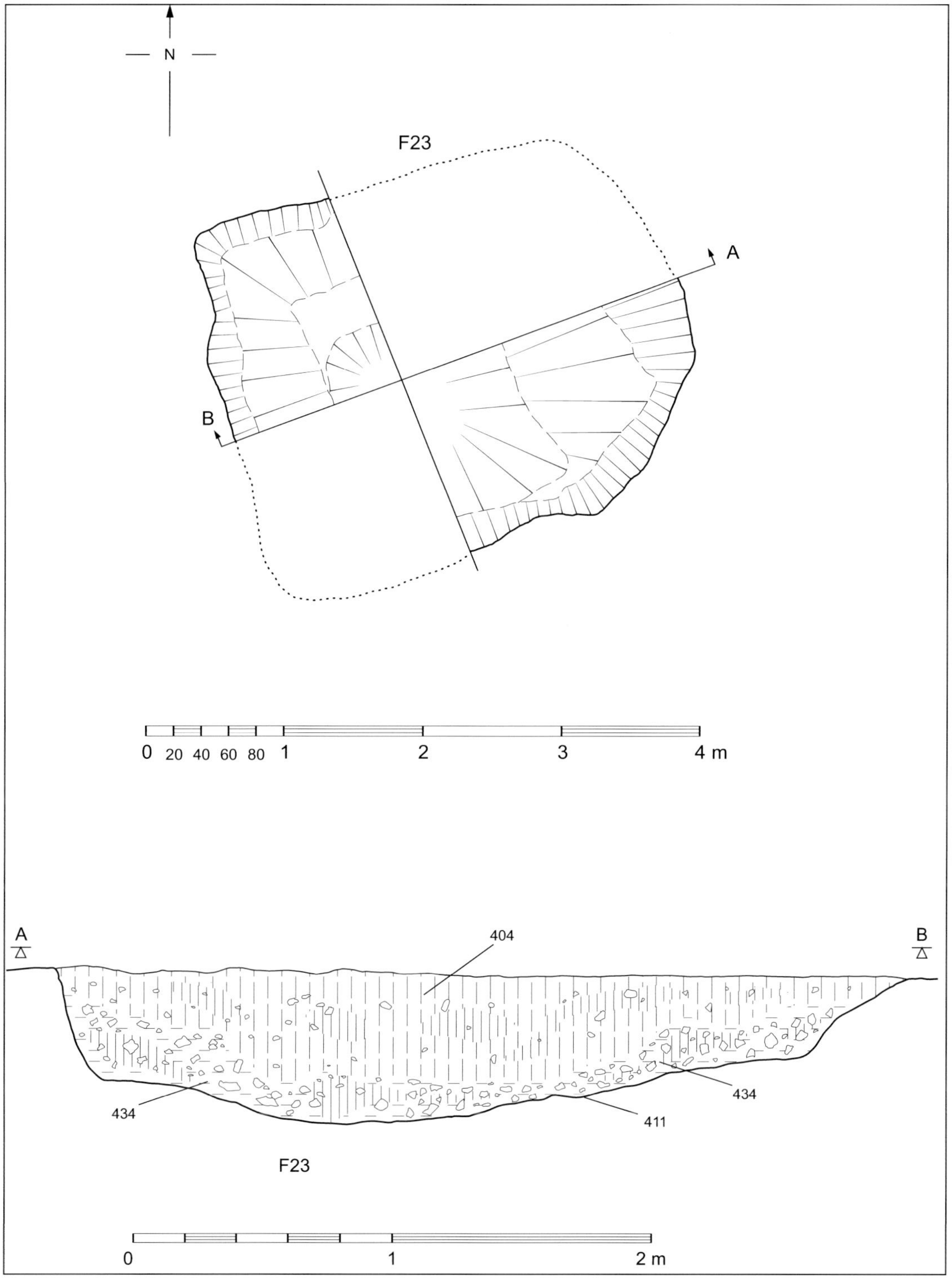

Figure 9.7. Probable stone burial pit F.23 (setting L3)

southern pit edge. This deposit presumably entered the pit as the stone was removed. The upper fill [405] was of a homogenous brown clay loam ploughwash with occasional small pieces of chalk and rare flecks of charcoal. Fragments of clay pipe, pieces of iron fitting, a small amount of animal bone, and sherds of medieval and post-medieval pottery were recovered from this context.

This appears to mark a burial pit from which the stone had subsequently been removed. Taking the size of the pit as a proxy, it would have contained a sarsen in the order of *c*.3.00 × 2.50m, consistent with the dimensions of

other buried stones along this stretch of the avenue. However, this burial pit is unusual insofar as it lacks the depth and regularity of cutting associated with the burial pits of L2, L5 and L6 and there was no evidence of a truncated stone-hole (although it must be remembered that only 50% was excavated). The stone-hole may have been particularly shallow and removed by ploughing, or (as is more likely) may lie in the unexcavated portion. This feature is discussed further in Chapter 10.

Setting L5 (F.25)

The north-westernmost of two burial pits exposed at the west end of Trench 10, this burial pit [420] was regularly cut, attaining a

Figure 9.8. (above) F.23 on completion of excavation

Figure 9.9. (right) Stone burial pit F.25 (setting L5)

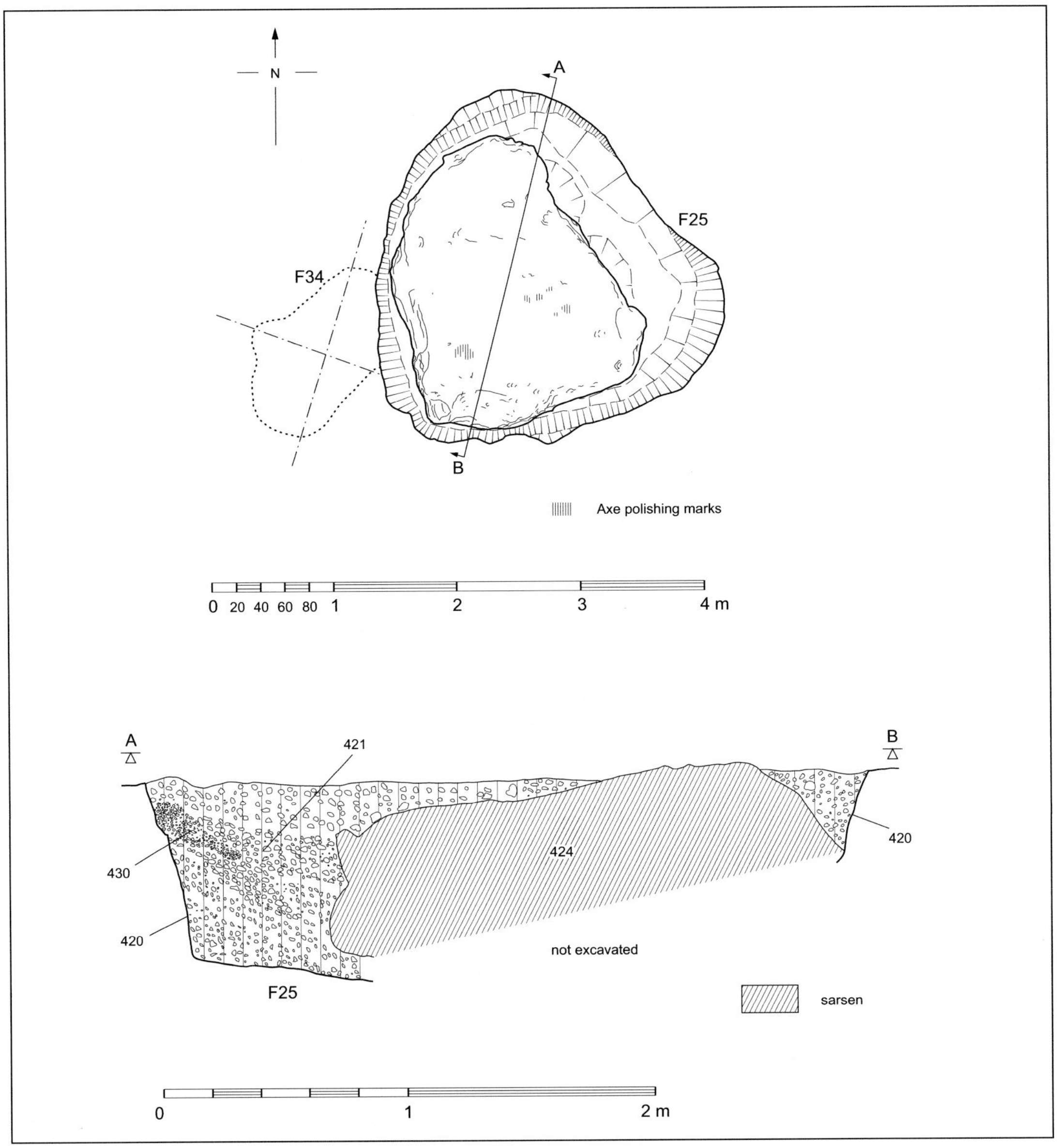

depth of 0.80m (Figure 9.9). It was cut to reflect the shape of the stone, being sub-triangular with rounded corners, 2.85 × 2.90m. The sides were very steep to vertical, although undercut to the north-east, with a sharp junction to a slightly dished base. It contained a sarsen block [424] of similar shape. This did not lie centrally within the pit, but more to the south-west, adjacent to the stone-hole F.34, leaving a sizable gap to the north-east. The stone was slightly raised to the south, a small portion of the upper surface projecting into the ploughsoil. The upper surface of the stone was marked by a sub-rectangular wedge-hole, regularly cut, 0.08 × 0.06m across and 0.06m deep. This presumably relates to an abortive attempt to break up the stone prior to its burial; the hole being filled with the same chalk rubble packing as the pit itself.

Following the incorporation of the stone, the pit was rapidly filled with chalk rubble [421]. This was highly compacted in its upper 0.10m, and included a thin lens of 'puddled' greyish chalk [430] on the northern edge of the fill. Below, the angular chalk rubble became progressively looser, and was mixed with small quantities of brown loam. Tip lines were clearly visible in section. The rapidity of the filling was indicated by the presence of numerous voids around and especially under the stone. There were no finds from the fill. Located on the west side of the burial pit, and partly truncated by it, were the remains of the original stone-hole.

Setting L6 (F. 26)

This took the form of a regularly cut, sub-rectangular pit [425] with rounded corners, 2.70 × 2.50m, and up to 1.42m deep (Figure 9.10). The north, east and south sides were steep to vertical, in places slightly undercut. Adjacent to the original stone-hole on the west, the sides sloped in at a moderately steep angle below 0.35m; perhaps 'battered back' to avoid destabilizing the stone whilst the burial pit was being dug. The sides terminated abruptly against a flat base. Clear scrape marks were visible on the north side where the stone had brushed against the edge of pit. Curiously, the pit appeared much deeper than was necessary to contain the sarsen. Although the stone itself was sub-rectangular, the pit does not appear to have been deliberately cut to mirror the shape of the stone (as was the case with setting L5).

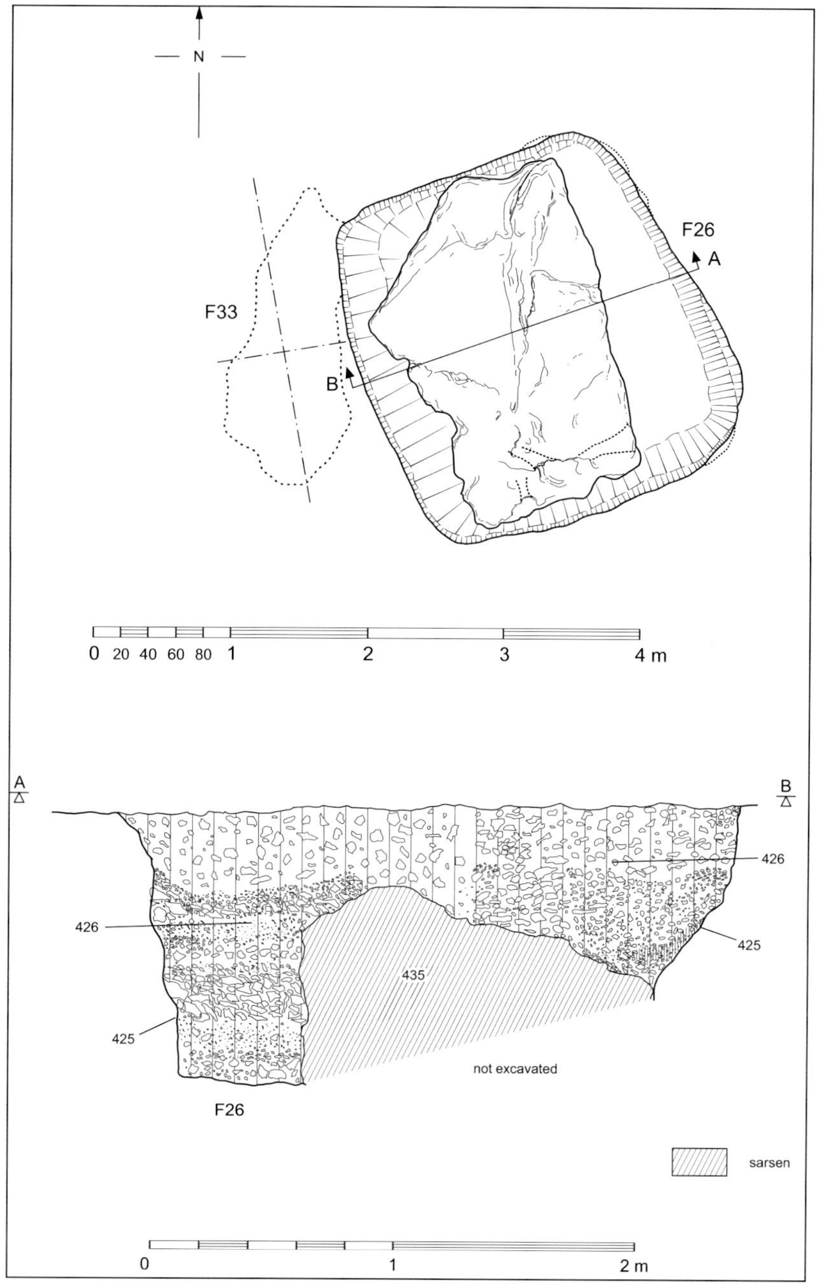

Figure 9.10. Stone burial pit F.26 (setting L6)

As with the sarsen in F.22, black staining was visible on the protected sides and undersurface of the stone.

The pit was filled with angular chalk rubble with some fine brown clay loam [426], the upper 0.10m being very compact. This became progressively looser with depth, and there were voids below the stone where it had not penetrated. Clear tip lines were visible in section. A few medium-sized (0.20–0.30m) lumps of unmodified sarsen occurred within the fill, perhaps deriving originally from packing deposits in the adjacent stone-hole. Finds from the fill consisted of a small amount of worked flint and a chopped cattle rib. The stone-hole [438] was situated against the western edge of burial pit F.26, and was partly truncated by it.

Setting L8 (F.62)

A complex stone destruction feature, there is the possibility (though by no means certain) that this *may* represent a shallow stone burial that had subsequently been dug into and the stone destroyed at a later date (Figure 9.11). The feature is discussed in detail in Chapter 10.

T1 (F.1)

This took the form of an approximately square, straight-sided pit, 3.30m × 3.20m, reaching a depth of 0.60m below the surface of the natural [005] (Figure 9.12). With the exception of the stone-hole the sides were straight and the bottom flat, the latter pecked into solid chalk. That this was difficult work is suggested by the tip of an iron knife that had broken off after becoming embedded in the base. Lying on the base of the pit was a substantial, irregularly-shaped sarsen stone [018]. The concave lower face of the stone resulted in a void between the sarsen and the pit base. Lying directly on the base of the pit in this void was an iron nail. Although the pit itself was regular in shape, the stone was not lying centrally within it, the south-eastern projection pushed tightly against one corner. Restricted access and safety considerations precluded the removal of the final deposits of pit fill from beneath the stone at this point but it appears that the stone was at least partly wedged against the edge of the pit. This would explain the size of the void

Figure 9.11. Stone burial and burning pit F.62 (setting L8)

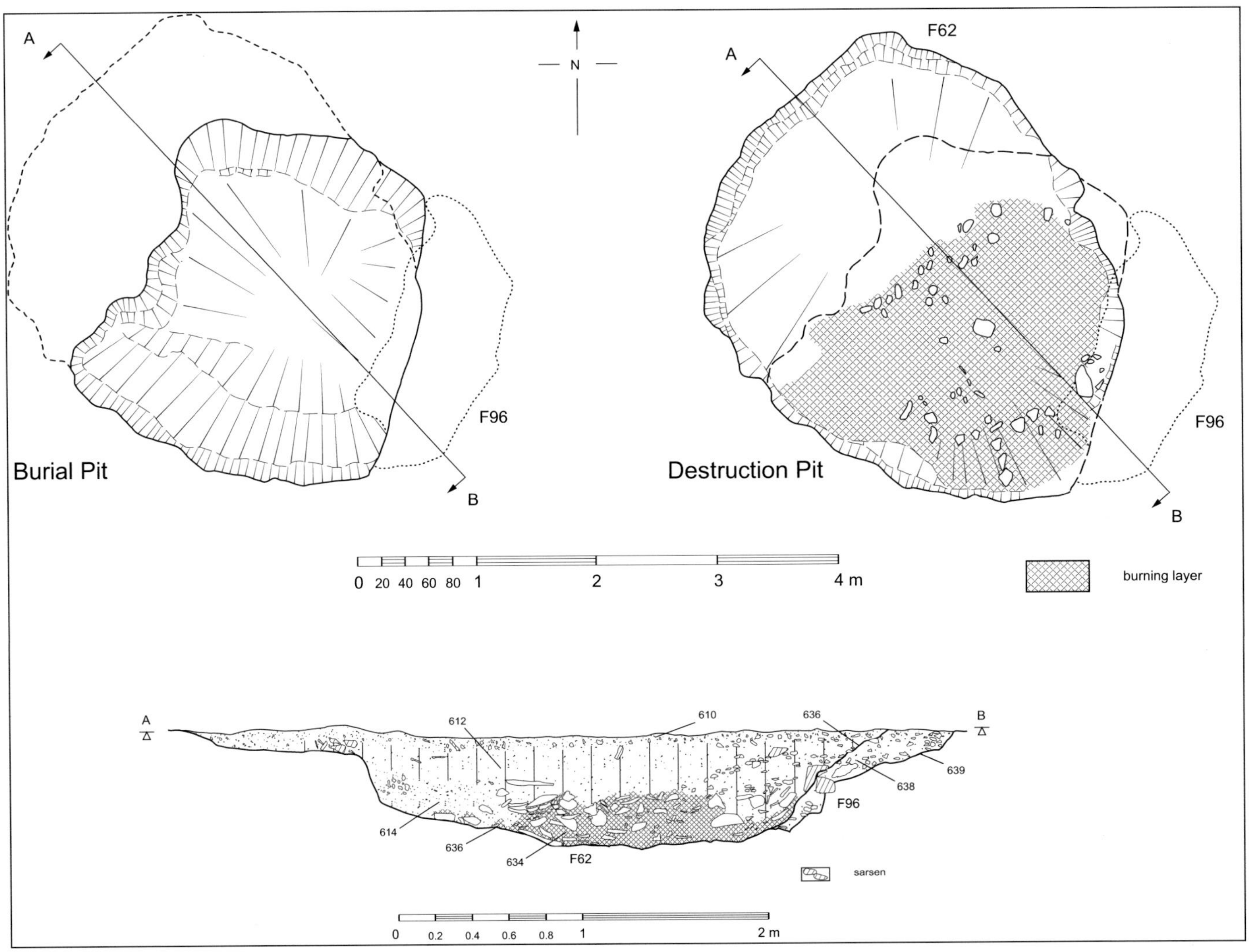

beneath the stone, one edge being effectively 'propped-up'.

As well as the sarsen two other deposits lay on the base of the burial pit. Running along the western edge was a wedge of very compacted brown silty clay [023], 0.12m thick at the wall of the pit and slowly narrowing until it disappeared 0.60m into the interior. This contained frequent fragments of chalk directly at the interface with the pit base. Finds included a bovine first upper molar, six sherds of pottery and four fragments of heavily corroded iron. The deposit is consistent with an area of ploughsoil that had tumbled back into the pit shortly after it was dug, being subsequently trampled.

In the north-eastern corner was a slump of stiff, brown silty-clay [025], 0.21m thick at the edge and extending 1.00m into the pit [025]. This contained frequent chalk lumps and sealed

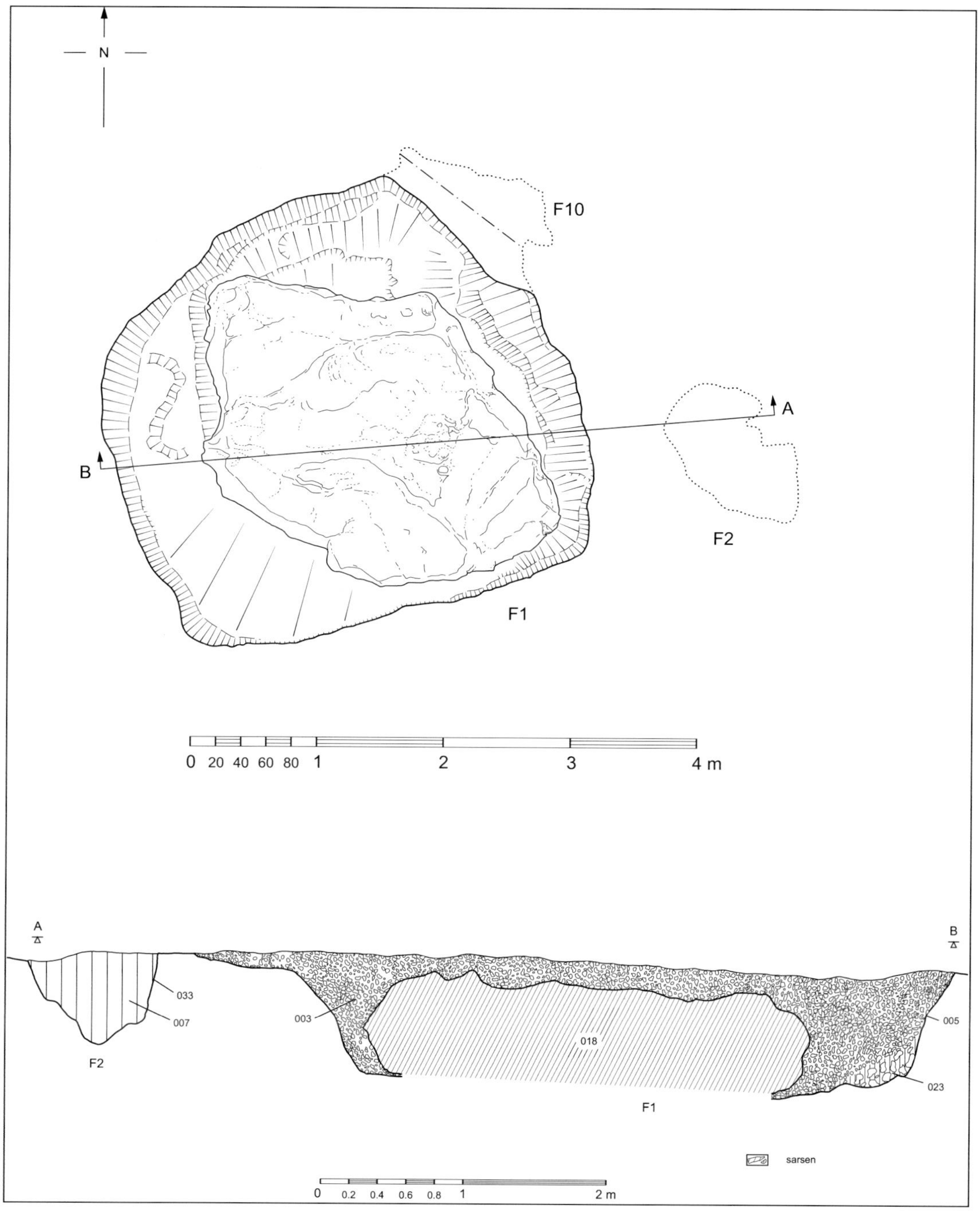

Figure 9.12. Stone burial pit F.1 (setting T1)

a sherd of green-glazed pottery that lay directly on the base of the pit. In turn this deposit was sealed by a thin layer (0.04–0.13m) of very compacted silty-chalk that contained a small piece of sarsen [024].

Sealing the stone, zone of trample, and area of slumping was a relatively uniform deposit of chalk rubble in a matrix of brown silty-clay [003]. Although compaction varied, being firmest against the sides of the pit and on its uppermost surface, this appears to represent a single, and presumably rapid, backfill event. Certainly no attempt was made to pack material into the void that existed beneath the sarsen. Finds included numerous flakes of flint, pottery, a fragment of brick/tile and four small lumps of sarsen. An animal burrow had disturbed this deposit at the southern end.

Running along the northern edge of the burial pit and into the north-eastern corner were the remains of the original stone-hole, F.10. As with settings L2 here and 4 of the Outer Circle, the creation of the burial pit had necessitated the digging away of almost the entirety of the stone-hole. In addition, the slump deposit on the base of the burial pit suggested that further disturbance had taken place during the toppling of the stone. What is interesting is that in this instance we have clear evidence that the toppling took place *after* the pit had been dug and was directed straight into it.

Excavations on the West Kennet Avenue

Excavations carried out in 2002 centred upon the single sarsen recorded by O G S Crawford as having been buried during the winter of 1921–2. Referred to hereafter as the Crawford setting, this stone was marked on the 1924 25 inch O.S. mapsheet and judged by Smith to correspond to the expected position of setting 63b according to her scheme (Smith 1965, 175) (Figure 3.1).

Crawford Setting (F.1)
F.1 first appeared as a large spread of light yellow-brown calcareous silt [005] within the natural soliflucted chalk gravel. This formed the fill of a steep-sided, flat-based ovate pit [004] which was over 1.00m deep, 2.10m wide and 3.40m long (Figure 3.5). The pit was aligned north-west to south-east. Context [005] contained plentiful angular flint, decayed chalk and coke inclusions, and was up to 0.34m deep. Beneath [005] was a layer of firm brown clay [020] which contained patches of loose decayed chalk. Plentiful charcoal, coke and coal were also found in this layer, which was up to 0.50m thick. After the removal of [020] a third fill [026] was revealed. This was a mixture of loose light brown silty clay and chalk rubble and was up to 0.70m thick. Context [026] also contained some coke and coal and at least one piece of brick. There are some slight indications of a stabilisation horizon between contexts [026] and [020].

In the base of the pit and sealed by the last fill [026] was a very large sarsen [031]. This stone appears to have been buried on one of its longer edges, sharing the north-west to south-east alignment of the pit. Complete excavation was not possible as safety considerations limited the depth of friable sediment which could be left unsupported in the edges of the pit.

Finds from the burial pits

The burial pits marking settings L2, L5 and L6 of the Beckhampton Avenue were remarkably free of material culture, only the heavily disturbed L3 burial pit producing any ceramic finds and the bulk of these from the ploughsoil fill. Not only were the burial pits clean in this area of the field, but test-pitting carried out in advance of the stripping of Trench 10 yielded only a single sherd of post-medieval Verwood-type ware. The logical conclusion to be drawn from this is that the quantities of pottery entering the ploughsoil in this western part of Longstones Field were extremely low. This is perhaps surprising given its long history of medieval and subsequent cultivation. It also contrasts markedly with the situation at the eastern end of the field, where excavations centred upon the T1 burial pit recovered 29 medieval sherds. Of these, 16 came from the burial pit itself with the remainder coming from the initial clean. This apparent gradient in ploughsoil pottery density across the field is most likely a reflection of increasing proximity to the extensive medieval settlement around Avebury Trusloe (Chapter 8).

Tr.	F.	Context	Ware	No.	Wt.	Comments
Longstones Field SW						
10	-	[001]	KVW (B)	1	3	Rim, very abraded
10	24	[404]	North Wilts oolitic	1	12	-
10	24	[404]	misc sandy	1	3	Abraded
10	23	[405]	Laverstock coarse	1	9	Abraded
11	-	[001]	KVW (B)	1	3	-
24	71	[800]	Laverstock coarse	1	12	Scratchmarked
24	81	[819]	Laverstock coarse	1	3	Scratchmarked
24	52	[844]	fine sandy	1	3	Glazed
24	81	[854]	Laverstock coarse	2	5	Scratchmarked
24	71	[801]-[829]	fine sandy	1	2	Glazed
30	-	[967]	KVW (B)	1	3	-
31	100	[901]	KVW (B)	5	6	-
34	-	[001]	North Wilts oolitic	1	4	Rim (jar?); very abraded
Avebury Trusloe						
1	-	[001]/[002]	KVW (A)	1	6	All from this group abraded
1	-	[001]/[002]	Laverstock coarse	1	24	Jar rim, finger impressed
1	-	[001]/[002]	KVW (B)	4	19	-
1	-	[001]/[002]	North Wilts oolitic	3	31	2 jar rims
1	-	[001]/[002]	West Wilts micaceous	1	5	-
1	1	[003]	KVW (B)	7	55	1 jar rim
1	1	[003]	misc sandy	3	15	1 with fine chalk or limestone inclusions
1	1	[003]	fine sandy	1	1	-
1	1	[023]	misc sandy	1	2	Rouletted + glazed (tripod pitcher?)
1	1	[023]	KVW (A)	2	4	-
1	1	[023]	KVW (B)	3	9	-
1	1	[025]	Laverstock fineware	1	10	Jug base, thumbed, glazed
1	1	[025]	misc calcareous	1	1	-

Table 9.2. Medieval ceramics from the Beckhampton Avenue excavations. KVW = Kennet Valley ware

Medieval pottery

Lorraine Mepham

The assemblage of medieval pottery from the Beckhampton Avenue excavations amounted to 47 sherds (250g). Overall condition is poor to fair; many sherds show high levels of abrasion, and this has hampered identification in some cases. Mean sherd weight overall is 5.3g.

The assemblage has been quantified within each context by ware type. In most cases this can be related to a known type or tradition, *e.g.* Laverstock-type coarseware, but in the case of some of the smaller, heavily abraded sherds identification could only be made on the basis of dominant inclusion type, *e.g.* miscellaneous sandy wares. Table 9.2 gives the full list of pottery by context. Totals by ware type are given in Table 9.3.

Ware Type	No. sherds	Weight (g.)
Kennet Valley Ware (A)	3	10
Kennet Valley Ware (B)	22	98
Laverstock coarse	6	53
Laverstock fineware	1	10
North Wilts oolitic	5	47
West Wilts micaceous	1	5
fine sandy	3	6
misc sandy	5	20
misc calcareous	1	1
Total	*47*	*250*

Table 9.3. Medieval pottery from the Beckhampton Avenue excavations; totals by ware type

The assemblage

The medieval assemblage contains examples from four ware types or ware traditions current in north Wiltshire and west Berkshire during the medieval period (11th to 14th centuries):

Kennet Valley wares (formerly known as Newbury groups A and B: Vince 1997): flint-tempered (Kennet Valley A) or flint-/chalk-tempered (Kennet Valley B) coarseware fabrics with a lengthy currency from at least the 11th century through to the 14th century, the B variants gradually superseding the A variants in the late 12th/early 13th century. These wares are widely distributed along the Kennet Valley west of Newbury as far as Devizes, and also across north Hampshire. Two production centres are known in the hinterland of Newbury (Birbeck 2000), and place-name evidence suggests a further production centre at *Crockerstrope* in the Savernake Forest near Marlborough (Vince 1997, 65). Petrological analysis of selected sherds from the Newbury area, north-east Wiltshire and north Hampshire supports the idea of a ware tradition encompassing several different production centres (Mepham 2000, 53–4). Most of the sherds are in the flint-/chalk-tempered (B) fabrics; the only diagnostic sherds are jar rims with internally and externally expanded profiles, a typical form in this ware type, dating to the 12th/13th century.

Laverstock-type wares: both coarsewares and finewares from the Laverstock tradition are represented here, the latter by a single sherd, the thumbed base from a glazed jug (Trusloe Trench 1, context [025]). Coarsewares appear to occur here only in jar forms (one rim, finger-impressed: Trusloe Trench 1, context [001]/[002]), and a few body sherds show the characteristic 'scratchmarking' common on 12th- and 13th-century vessels. Both coarsewares and finewares were manufactured at the 13th century Laverstock kilns (Musty *et al.* 1969), but the coarsewares have an earlier origin, being found in 11th/12th century contexts at Old Sarum and Wilton (Musty and Rahtz 1964; Andrews *et al.* 2000). Evidence from excavations within Salisbury indicates a currency for both coarsewares and finewares extending at least into the 14th century (Mepham in Rawlings 2000).

North Wiltshire oolitic wares: a few sherds, including jar rims, are present here. Wares tempered with oolitic limestone are found across north Wiltshire and south Gloucestershire. They were made, for example, at Minety; wasters from this site are dated to the 14th/15th century (Musty 1973), but the tradition clearly had earlier origins, based on the occurrence in the area of oolitic wares in earlier vessel forms, from the 12th century onwards (Vince 1984). The jar rims would be consistent with a 12th- or 13th-century date.

West Wiltshire micaceous wares: one sherd in a micaceous fabric, also containing, variously, patinated flint and degraded sandstone (?greensand) inclusions. Identification here is not absolutely definite, since this is small and undiagnostic, but it certainly bears at least a superficial resemblance to micaceous wares prevalent in west Wiltshire throughout the medieval period, with a distribution centring on Warminster, where documentary evidence suggests pottery manufacture in the Crockerton area (Le Patourel 1968; Smith 1997). The sherd is not closely datable.

Miscellaneous wares: nine sherds are either too small or insufficiently distinctive to assign to ware type. These include three sherds in a fine, sandy, oxidised fabric, two of which are glazed, probably deriving from glazed jugs of 13th or 14th century date (two from Trench 24; one from Trusloe Trench 1, context [003]). One other sandy sherd has rouletted decoration similar to that seen on 12th century tripod pitchers (Trusloe Trench 1, context [023]). Four other sandy sherds are completely undistinctive, as is a very small sherd in a calcareous (limestone-tempered) fabric.

Discussion

This small medieval assemblage has a broad potential date range of 11th to 14th century, although the emphasis appears to be on the 12th to 13th century. The ware types identified represent four of the major medieval ceramic traditions seen in north Wiltshire; all are seen, for example, in the large medieval assemblage from Alexander Keiller's excavations at Avebury (Jope 1999).

The condition of this material suggests that none represents *in situ* or primary refuse deposits – some of the assemblage does in any case derive from unstratified cleaning or topsoil contexts. Other sherds are likely to have been incorporated incidentally into feature fills, perhaps through the reworking of manuring scatters. The use of this material for dating is therefore to be viewed with some caution, although little of it is closely datable in any case.

Metalwork from the T1 burial pit

Graham Morgan

A small assemblage of heavily corroded fragments of iron was recovered from the excavation of setting T1 of the Beckhampton Avenue. These were x-rayed and subjected to limited mechanical cleaning in an attempt to identify and where possible suggest a date range.

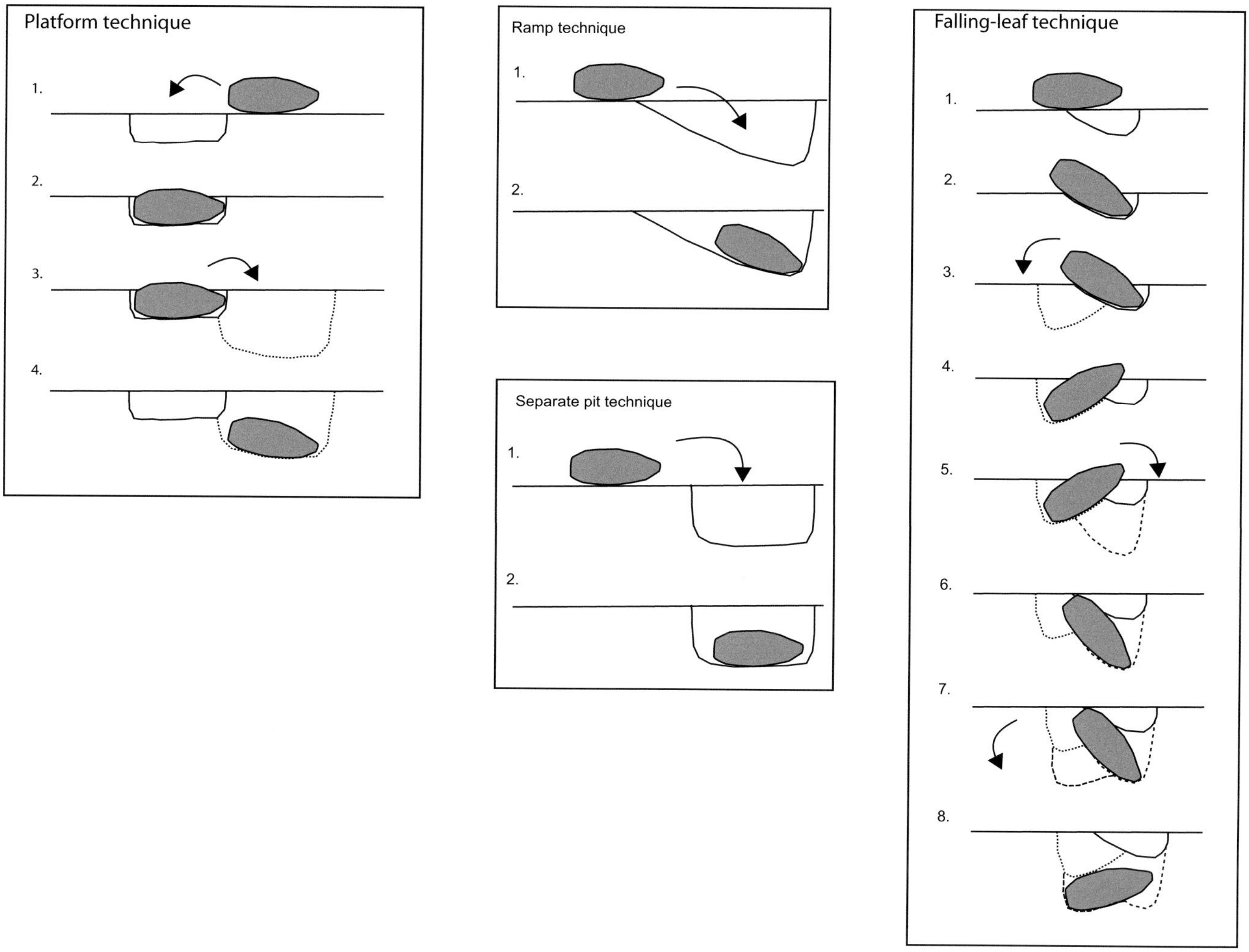

Figure 9.13. Techniques of stone burial

F.1 [003] Possible fragment of hand-made nail
F.1 [003] Hand-made nail
F.1 [003] Very small, triangular shaped fragment
F.1 [005] Possible fragment of hand-made nail
F.1 [023] Possible fragment of wire or hand-made nail

None of the objects were closely dateable; hand-made nails being produced from the Roman period up until the 20th century. The small triangular fragment from setting T1 is interesting as it was found embedded point-first into the solid chalk at the base of the burial pit. The most likely interpretation is that of a knife tip broken off during the digging out of the base of the pit into the compacted chalk.

Animal Bone

In total, only 32 bones and fragments were recorded from the stone burial pits in Longstones Field SW, of which only four were identifiable. All of these were from cattle and included a chopped rib fragment from the main fill of the L6 burial pit and a split tibia from a perforation in the L6 sarsen (identified by Fiona Coward). From the T1 burial pit there was a cattle molar and sheep/goat metatarsus, both recovered from the spread of topsoil trample on the base of the pit (identification by Anthony Gouldwell).

The practices of stone-burial

Combining the surviving detail from the Keiller excavations and the results gained by the current project a number of distinct methodological approaches to the burial of sarsens can be reconstructed (Table 9.4). In seeking to structure discussion, four stages have been proposed: digging the pit, toppling the stone, manoeuvring it into the pit and finally backfilling.

Digging the burial pit

On the basis of the excavated profiles, the

Setting	Technique	Morphology	Base	Stone-hole	Burial
Outer Circle (northwest quadrant)					
30	platform	shaped closely	flat	remnant in corner	complete
31	ramp	shaped closely	sloping	dug into one edge	complete
Outer Circle (southwest quadrant)					
4	separate pit	oversized reflecting stone	flat	dug into one edge	complete
5	separate pit	oversized reflecting stone (NB. reversed)	-	remnant in corner	projects into topsoil
6	separate pit	oversized reflecting stone	-	destroyed	projects into topsoil
7	falling-leaf	shaped at base	sloping	untouched	projects above turfline
9	falling-leaf	oversized reflecting stone	-	destroyed	complete
10	platform	oversized reflecting stone	-	destroyed	complete
12	separate pit	shaped closely	sloping	destroyed	projects above turfline
16	separate pit	oversized reflecting stone	-	destroyed	complete
19	disturbed	?	-	-	?
20	disturbed	?	-	-	?
21	disturbed	Keiller claimed identical to 22	-	destroyed	?
22	disturbed	Keiller claimed identical to 21	-	destroyed	?
24	separate pit	not shaped	-	moved	complete
Southern Inner Circle					
i	disturbed	?	-	untouched	?
ii	disturbed	?	-	adjacent	?
iii	separate pit	shaped closely	-	untouched	complete
iv	separate pit	not shaped	-	dug into one edge	complete
v	opportunistic	not shaped	rough	moved	complete
vi	separate pit	shaped closely	-	destroyed	complete
vii	separate pit	shaped closely	-	destroyed	complete
viii	separate pit	shaped closely	-	untouched	complete
ix	disturbed	?	-	destroyed	?
x	disturbed	?	-	destroyed	?
xi	disturbed	?	-	?adjacent	?
West Kennet Avenue					
29A	separate pit	shaped closely	flat	adjacent	complete
26B	separate pit	shaped closely *	-	-	complete
26A	ramp **	oversized reflecting stone	-	-	complete
25B	ramp	oversized reflecting stone	flat	destroyed	complete
25A	disturbed	?	-	-	?
24B	separate pit ***	shaped closely *	-	-	complete
20A	disturbed	?	-	-	?
18B	disturbed	?	-	-	?
18A	falling leaf	shaped closely	sloping	-	complete
16B	separate pit	shaped	-	untouched	projects into topsoil
15B	platform	oversized reflecting stone	sloping	-	complete
15A	separate pit	oversized reflecting stone (NB. reversed)	flat	untouched	complete
14A	separate pit	shaped	-	dug into one edge	complete
13B	separate pit	not shaped	sloping	destroyed	complete
13A	separate pit	shaped closely	-	-	complete
Crawford	separate pit	shaped	flat	?	complete
Beckhampton Avenue					
L2	separate pit	closely shaped	dished	dug into one edge	projects into topsoil
L3	disturbed	?	dished	-	?
L5	separate pit	closely shaped	dished	dug into one edge	projects into topsoil
L6	separate pit	not shaped	flat	dug into one edge	complete
L8	disturbed	?	dished	dug into one edge	?
T1	separate pit	not shaped	flat	dug into one edge	complete

* - one end of the pit had been deliberately enlarged.
** - this appears to have reverted to a falling-leaf when it was realised that after dragging the stone down the ramp it was not sufficiently deep.
***- stone was repositioned once in the pit.

Table 9.4. The characteristics of stone burial

digging of the pits appears to have been carried out in one of four ways (Figure 9.13). The first we can term the 'ledge' or 'platform' technique, where the initial stage was to dig a shallow pit adjacent to the long axis of the stone, large enough to fully contain it. The stone was then levered, dragged and/or pushed into this pit. Once in place a second, deeper pit was dug alongside, partly undercutting the edge of the first pit. Once this was of sufficient depth the stone was then manoeuvred over the resultant step and into the deeper pit. Like a staircase, this process could presumably have been repeated until the stone was deemed to be at a satisfactory depth, but in those cases where the characteristic stepped profile left by such digging is evident, one step appears to have been sufficient (settings 10 and 30 of the Outer Circle and 24b and 15b of the West Kennet Avenue).

A variation on this theme was the technique referred to by Keiller in his notebooks as the 'falling-leaf'. Rather than move the stone laterally into increasingly deeper pits, the stone remained largely in its fallen position. The tactic appears to have been to dig out an angled slot under one side of the long axis of the stone. When sufficiently deep the stone would then be tilted into the slot. Work would then commence on the digging of a second, deeper slot under the original resting position of the sarsen. As digging approached the bulk of the stone a supporting ridge of chalk could have been left in place and/or props used to prevent the stone from falling onto the excavators. Keiller interpreted setting 9 as a snapshot of an abandoned falling-leaf burial after precisely such an accident, the excavator busy straigh-tening and finishing the sides of the pit when the stone prematurely slipped. Once prepared, the stone would then be tilted into the second deeper slot and work would begin on deep-ening the original slot. The 'falling-leaf' description reflects the way that the stone effectively 'flutters' down into the ground, the number of iterations required to remove it from the topsoil dependant upon its size and bulk. In terms of profile, unless particular care was taken in propping and support during the final iteration, one would expect the base of the pit to slope along the long axis of the stone. Examples of falling-leaf burials are settings 7 and 9 of the Outer Circle and 18a and 26a of the West Kennet Avenue. Setting 18a is of particular interest as Keiller claimed in his excavation notebooks that the falling–leaf method had *not* been employed in this case. The very tight fit of the stone in the pit would support such a conclusion, making the *in situ* digging required to bury a stone in this manner extremely difficult. However, the surviving section drawing shows clearly the presence of opposed, sloping facets perpendicular to the long-axis of the stone, diagnostic of this method of digging (Figure 9.14).

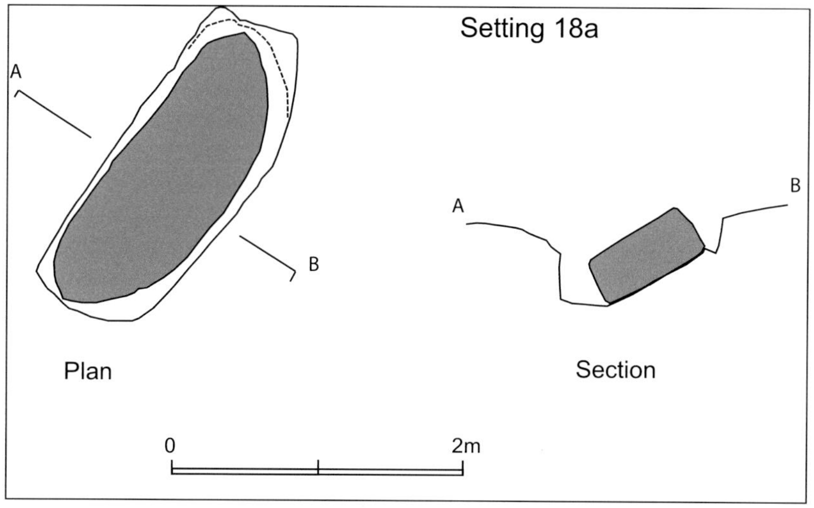

Figure 9.14. West Kennet Avenue setting 18A

The third technique can be termed the 'ramp' as it involved the digging of a sloping burial pit into which the stone could be slid or dragged. This ramp would presumably be dug from the surface, its length and gradient dependant upon the size and girth of the stone it was destined to accommodate. Two features distinguish this from an example of a falling-leaf burial where the initial stage proved sufficient to satisfactorily bury the stone. The first is the orientation with respect to the long axis of the stone. The second is the necessity of physically moving the stone down the ramp, giving the pit a distinctive plan form. To date the only examples are settings 31 of the Outer Circle and 25b of the West Kennet Avenue.

The final method involved the excavation of a pit at a distance away from the stone, the digging being completed before any attempt was made to manoeuvre or otherwise shift the sarsen. Once the pit had been completed the stone would then be manoeuvred into it. Although the bases of such pits occasionally slope, they lack the diagnostic plan and profile signatures of platform, falling-leaf and ramp burials.

The pits themselves seem to fall into three basic types. The first is cut very closely to conform to the shape of the stone, the latter fitting snugly within the final pit (*e.g.* L2, L5, 16b, 18a, 12, 29a, 31). The second is more generalised, approximating rather than closely following the shape of the sarsen and frequently over-cut (*e.g.* 4, 5, 6, 7, 9, 10, 16, 30, 15a, 15b, 25b, 26a). In the case of the third no concession was made to the shape of the sarsen (13b, L6, T1).

It is difficult to argue for any rigid pattern linking a particular technique of excavation to shape of pit. We might expect that in the case of the falling leaf method the pit would inevitably mirror the shape of the stone as it was dug directly around it. Likewise, in the case of the platform technique, the fallen stone was close enough to the pit to provide a template that could be used to ensure that excess digging was kept to a minimum. As to whether the pit was cut closely or oversize, this may simply reflect the need to create sufficient room for the excavators to work safely, particularly during the lower stages of the falling-leaf and platform methods. As a result we might expect the tolerance of pits dug away from the stones to be closer, as the excavators did not have to work around the bulk of the stone and/or supporting props. Balancing this, given that the stone could not be directly used as a template some mis-translation might be expected, leading to approximated or oversized pits. A good example is setting 13b of the West Kennet Avenue where a correction appears to have been made during the digging.

That such generalisations may be problematic is evident from setting 18a, a falling-leaf burial with little evidence of any concern to create a comfortable working space. What we can say is that in all of these cases there is a tangible sense that the pit and stone were intimately linked – the former was created solely for the purposes of containing the latter. In direct contrast we have the burial pits that do not bear any relationship to the stones they held. The clearest examples are settings 13b, L6 and T1. Frequently taking the form of generalised sub-rectangular cuttings, if the former burial pits can be regarded as bespoke creations, the latter are defiantly off-the-shelf.

As well as variation in shape, the pits differ with respect to depth and the regularity and neatness of the edges and base. One might assume that depth was a reflection of the thickness of the stone, however there are a number of examples of stones sunk either shallowly (and thus protruding above the turf-line or, more commonly, into the topsoil) or to an excessive depth. In considering this issue the Beckhampton Avenue burials are of particular interest. The deepest of the buried stones was setting L6, a particularly stocky sarsen with a folded 'organic' appearance and (like the Avebury Ring-Stone) natural perforations wide enough to push an arm through. Into one of the latter a curious deposit of animal bone had been inserted several centuries prior to the burial. This highly distinctive stone was clearly one that had attracted attention and may very well have been a named, perhaps efficacious, place in the landscape. It is possible that it was this very visibility that warranted a commensurately deep burial. If this was the case then it might also be worth considering the converse; very shallow burials afforded to sarsens that were socially 'invisible'.

Such peculiarly deep burials appear to have been rare – only eight of the 45 burials excavated exceeding 1.0m below the level of the chalk. Whilst such an interpretation of the stones special status may be convincing in the case of setting L6, it is difficult to sustain for any of the other deep burials. There are sufficient cautionary examples regarding the Avebury megaliths to illustrate that if you set out to explicitly look for distinctive features you will find them, whether they exist or not (*e.g.* Meaden 1999). Such an interpretation also appears to be countered by setting L5 which is every bit as distinctive as its perforated partner. The upper face of this stone had at one point been covered with a large zone of polish caused by the sharpening of stone axes. The surviving fragments were exceptionally smooth and glossy and evidence from a polissoir on nearby Lockeridge Down (Fowler 2000, 66–7) shows how striking such a surface can be when caught by the sun.[5] Despite this, the stone was buried shallowly enough for part to project into the ploughsoil.

As for the quality of the pit, this could reflect a host of factors from ability and expediency to aesthetics and standards. At one extreme we have pits such as L6 and T1 that are carefully cut with flat bases and vertical sides. At the other, we have the burial of setting *v* of the Southern Inner Circle, buried in what appears to have been a hastily scraped out area between two other burial pits.

Toppling the stone

At this point it is worth considering in more detail the process of toppling the stone, assuming it had not already fallen at a prior date. It is clear from his excavation notebooks that Keiller assumed that buried stones had either accidentally fallen long before burial had taken place, or were deliberately toppled as a direct prelude to burial activity. The weight of the sarsens, coupled with the often irregular bases and relatively shallow stone-holes means that stones would fall very close to the stone-holes, in many cases ending up in a position where the base lay directly over the stone-hole (what Keiller referred to as 'jumping' or 'kicking over'). Examples are setting 4 and setting 14 of the Outer Circle, the latter a recumbent stone that fell sometime after 1812 (Figure 9.15). Here the pointed base of the fallen sarsen covered most of the stone-hole, and had to be jacked up to enable the latter to be investigated. The close proximity of stone base to stone-hole can also be seen in the case of the much larger Longstones Cove setting (Adam) that fell in 1911 (see Gray 1935, fig. 1).

Looking at the position of the stone-holes in relation to the burial pits it is clear that in all cases the stones were buried very close to, if not directly over, their original standing positions (Figures 9.3 and 9.4). Of those pits fully excavated, in 13 cases the stone-hole was completely destroyed during the digging of the pit, with the truncated base visible in a further two. The burial pit had cut through the stone-hole on 12 occasions with only six burial pits separated from the stone-hole cut (three adjacent and three clearly separated).

That a second approach to the toppling of a stone may have been practiced is suggested by setting T1 of the Beckhampton Avenue. Here the sarsen was found sitting off-centre within a large, square pit. The sides of the pit were steep to vertical and base flat. Two features are of note. The first is that the stone-hole had been truncated along its long axis by the digging of the pit. The second is that the edge of the stone opposite the stone-hole had wedged firmly against the side of the pit before reaching the level of the base. This served to raise that end of the stone, leading to the substantial voids noted beneath the sarsen. Given the size of the pit, if the stone had been dragged or levered in from an already recumbent position, it would have been a straightforward task to have manoeuvred it into a more central position. The shape of the pit is also unusual in that no concession was made to the shape of the stone as would be expected if cut to receive an already recumbent sarsen. Taken together, these factors point to the possibility that the pit was dug up against a propped, yet still *standing*, sarsen. When the pit was ready the supports would have been taken away and the stone allowed to topple forwards into the pit – an efficient, if hazardous, undertaking.

Recognising such an approach depends upon being able to identify whether the original base of the stone lay directly against the remnant of the stone-hole. Unfortunately it can be ferociously difficult to ascertain with any confidence which part of any given stone originally served as the base. We have already mentioned staining that may relate to lichen growth on exposed surfaces. In addition, where the stone-hole remains largely intact, we can resort to a simple 'fitting the peg' exercise. Unfortunately, as discussed, intact surviving stone-holes are extremely rare.[6]

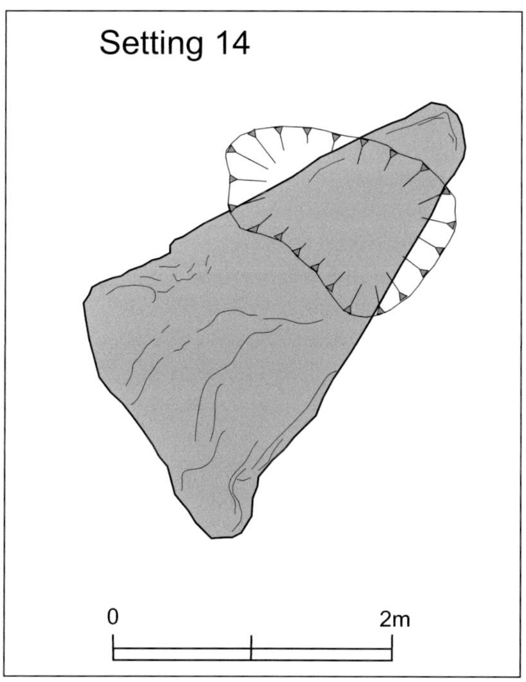

Figure 9.15. Setting 14 of the Outer Circle, Avebury.

Preparing the stone

With the exception of toppling, there does not appear to have been any deliberate preparation of the stones prior to burial. The main exceptions to this are settings L5, L6 and 18a. In the case of 18a chunks had been broken off prior to burial whilst in the case of L6 a wedge mark had been chiselled into it. In each case whilst it is clear that this took place at some point prior to burial, we do not know whether this was an intentional prelude or took place years, decades or centuries earlier. The insertion of the cattle tibia into the natural perforation passing through L5 is curious. If the perforation was exposed above ground then it is most likely that the plugging of this cavity took place shortly before the pit was back-filled, thus implying a conscious decision on the part of those undertaking the burial. This feature will be discussed in more detail shortly.

Manoeuvring stones into the pits and back-filling

With the exception of T1 (where the stages of toppling and manoeuvring may have been conflated), and the falling-leaf technique (where the only movement of the stone was the rocking to and fro required to bury it), fallen stones needed to be placed within the burial pits. This was most likely accomplished through a combination of pushing, dragging and levering and in the case of setting 16b of the West Kennet Avenue Keiller claimed to have identified crowbar marks on the edge of the burial pit.

That wrangling the stones into the pits was far from an exact science is suggested by the rare examples of stones sitting centrally within their burial pits and settings 5 and 15a, where the stones appear to have unexpectedly rolled, their shape a mirror image of the pits cut to contain them. In a number of cases the sarsens sit at an angle, frequently making contact with one or more edges; this is even observed in some of the oversize burial pits. It is interesting to note that in these cases there is no evidence that stone positions were adjusted once in the burial pits to make them more central. Nor was any attempt made to cut back the edges to ensure a better fit. This is perhaps most marked in the case of setting 9, where no attempt was made to either lever the stone off of the body of the supposedly crushed excavator or dig it out by cutting back the pit edge at this point. This is curious as it suggests some form of proscription was in place preventing any further interference once the stone had been laid to rest in its burial pit; once in and deemed deep enough the only activity permissible was backfilling.

There is no evidence from the Beckhampton Avenue burial pits of any significant period of time elapsing between the introduction of the stone into the pit and back-filling. Although there are thin layers of compacted trample (*e.g.* T1) there is no evidence of silting and weathering. As the often substantial voids beneath the stones attest, the back-filling was carried out from the surface with no attempt to pack soil and rubble under the stone. This was, however, a far from haphazard procedure as once the level had reached the base of the topsoil, care was taken to cap the pit with a highly compacted layer of chalk rubble. This implies that care was taken in digging the pits to ensure that the topsoil and subsoil were kept separate, and that in back-filling they were deposited in the correct order. The capping deposit made it extremely hard to recognise burial pits even after topsoil removal and cleaning. As Smith noted:

> 'Clean chalk rubble was rammed into the hollow above the stone and the whole levelled so that no trace remained of the operation. So meticulously was this done that burial-pits are often invisible even after the surrounding chalk surface has been scraped clean and extreme difficulty was sometimes experienced during Keiller's excavations before the sites could be detected.' (1965, 177)

This was certainly the case on the line of the Beckhampton Avenue where, excepting where parts of the stone protruded into the plough-soil, the relatively small remnants of stone-hole were identified more readily than burial pits.[7]

Summary: the practice of burying stones

As discussed earlier, at the simplest level burying a substantial sarsen might be expected to involve four clear stages. These are summarised in Table 9.5. A comparison with the principal techniques identified above is useful in highlighting the key differences between the approaches (Table 9.6).

The simple term 'stone burial' masks a wide variety of practice, with at least four basic techniques employed and considerable var-

Table 9.5. Stages in burying a standing stone

Stage	Activity
1	toppling the stone
2	digging the pit
3	manoeuvring the stone into the pit
4	backfilling

Technique	Suggested Sequence
Platform	1, (2 + 3 conflated), 4
Falling-leaf	1, (2 + 3 conflated), 4
Separate Pit	1, 2 , 3, 4 (toppling assumed to take place first to provide template for burial pit).
Toppled directly into pit	2, (1 + 3 conflated), 4

Table 9.6. Suggested sequence of stone burial events for techniques identified

Setting	Technique	Shape of stone
30	platform	irregular, barrel-like (thick)
31	ramp	irregular, tabular (thin)
4	separate pit	regular, tabular (thin)
5	separate pit	barrel-like (thick)
6	separate pit	irregular, tabular tapering at edges (thin)
7	falling-leaf	tabular (thin)
9	falling-leaf	regular tabular (thin)
10	platform	irregular, tabular (thin)
12	separate pit	irregular, tabular (thin)
16	separate pit	regular, tabular (thin)
24	separate pit	irregular, barrel-like (thick)

Table 9.7. Shape of stones of the Avebury Outer Circle in relation to burial technique

iation as to how they were executed. Stone burial involved a considerable input of time and labour. It was dangerous, difficult work; a complex choreography of supports, props, soil, stone, chalk and human bodies. Different methods also had their own inherent tempos and momentum. Contrast for example the separate pit and falling-leaf approaches. In the former the individual elements or stages could easily be separated and, if need be, undertaken at different times and by different personnel. In the case of the latter once the train of events had been set in motion by the toppling of the stone the work would have had to continue in earnest until the stone was buried.

One possibility is that the shape of the individual sarsens may have dictated the precise technique employed; on the basis of plan alone a case could certainly be made for the platform burials. All of the stones so buried are long and relatively narrow. Given that the falling-leaf method would require a large number of iterations to bury such a sarsen relying as it does upon the stone pivoting along its long-axis, the stepped approach of the platform method makes immediate practical sense. However, this is not exclusive, a variety of techniques were used to bury long narrow stones including the falling-leaf, and it is difficult to argue any convincing link between technique and stone shape for any of the other methods. The separate pit technique in particular appears to have been used on a wide variety of sarsens. It is difficult in practice to argue for any direct, convincing link between form and technique (Table 9.7).

The burial of setting 26a of the West Kennet Avenue is of particular interest as here those carrying out the burial had only resorted to the falling-leaf method after an initial ramp had failed to lower the stone to a sufficient depth. This is important for two reasons. Firstly it implies a degree of contingency and pragmatism. Secondly it illustrates that those responsible were drawing upon a repertoire of possibilities rather than slavishly adhering to a single prescribed practice.

Dating the burials

Following Stukeley, it was initially assumed by Keiller that the stone burials he encountered were relatively modern, dating to the late 17th – early 18th centuries (Keiller and Piggott 1936, 419–20). It was only when setting 9 of the Outer Circle of the henge was excavated that serious thought was given over to the possibility that these features could be significantly earlier.

The dating evidence we currently have for stone burials takes one of two forms. The first derives from observable stratigraphic relationships between pits and features such as graves, boundary ditches, destruction pits and buildings. Needless to say, the value of any such relationship is itself dependent upon the related feature being closely dateable. The second source of evidence is the material culture that was deliberately deposited, or accidentally incorporated, into the fill of the pits. As will become clear, the burial pits were remarkably clean of deliberate deposits excepting the sarsens they were dug to contain.

Stratigraphy: burials

There are four examples of burial pits that either cut through, or contain, deposits of human bone. The digging of the pit for setting 18b of the West Kennet Avenue had disturbed a shallow grave that had been placed close to the standing position of the stone. No grave goods or dating evidence were discovered in association with the bone. In contrast at setting 25b the pit disturbed a burial that appears to have been placed in an extension of the original stone-hole. That other burials may have been placed around this standing stone is suggested by finds of additional bones representing a total of three individuals and fragments of Beaker in the pit fill. A grave had also been truncated by the burial pit for setting 29a, where once again a body had been interred against the standing position of the stone. Some fragments of bone and Beaker pottery were recovered from the fill of this burial pit (Smith 1965, 209–10). It is clear that these burials are prehistoric and in dating terms tell us little more than the rather obvious fact that stone burial took some time after the stones were originally erected.

In the case of setting 9, the articulated skeleton of an adult male was found within the burial pit, sandwiched between the stone and the side of the pit. Found in direct association with the corpse were a pair of scissors, a buckle and a wooden handled probe (all iron) alongside three silver coins dated to *c.*1320–1350AD, with the earlier part of the range most likely (Ucko *et al.* 1991, 178). From the stance and position of the corpse, Keiller argued that he had been crushed to death whilst employed in burying the stone using the falling-leaf method, hard at work on finishing one of the sides of the pit when the propped stone slipped prematurely into the hole (Smith 1965, 177–80).

Since the rediscovery of the skeleton this interpretation has come under increasing scrutiny, with Pitts arguing forcibly that Keiller's original interpretation of the individual as a tailor is correct and that rather than crushed by the stone the individual was already dead when placed in the burial pit (Denison 1999; Pitts 2000, 126–34, pers. comm. 2006; Pollard and Reynolds 2002, 244–5). More recently, Edwards has suggested that the individual may in fact have been a shepherd, the scissors an essential tool for the removal of daggings (Edwards 2006). Whether accident or murder, tailor, surgeon or shepherd, this reinterpretation does not challenge the chronological assumption that burial and interment were contemporary. Although the pit fill surrounding the body was recorded as being more 'earthy' this appears to have been due to a deliberate dump of topsoil over the corpse; there is certainly no evidence in the excavation records or plan of the pit to suggest that the body had been buried in a separate cut.

Stratigraphy: boundaries

Relationships between burial pits and boundary features are relatively few, and the linear features cutting, or cut by, burial pits tend themselves to be poorly dated.[8] Perhaps the best example is setting 6 of the Outer Circle where a major boundary ditch had cut through the north-west end of the burial pit exposing the stone in the process. In the case of setting 4, a shallow lynchet was truncated by the burial pit. This appears to have been aligned upon the standing position of the stone suggesting that at some stage it was used as a marker in the laying out of a cultivation boundary. Unfortunately, though perhaps not surprisingly, the small portion of lynchet excavated produced no conclusive dating material.

On the line of the West Kennet Avenue the junction of a pair of perpendicular boundary ditches was aligned upon the standing position of setting 20a. The digging of the ditches cut into the stone-hole leading the stone (it is assumed) to eventually fall. At some time subsequent to this it was buried and then subsequently discovered and broken up. No dating evidence appears to have been recovered from the short stretches of these ditches excavated.

Stratigraphy: destruction pits

Fortunately, we have a number of burial pits that were subsequently dug out to enable the stone to be either dragged away or broken. Unfortunately, dating for the stone-breaking episodes, and thus the *terminus ante quem* they provide for burial, is generally crude (see Chapter 10). All we can say with any confidence is that the burning of stones 19–22 and *i* most likely took place sometime before 1719, with those of settings *ix*, *x* and *xi* after *c*.1724. The destructions through direct fracture of settings 20a and 25a of the West Kennet Avenue most likely date to the second half of the 17th century AD.

Stratigraphy: structures

In his excavation of the North-West Quadrant, Keiller noted that the burial pits of settings 30 and 31 were sealed beneath the foundations of buildings that predated the early 18th century. Setting 31 in particular is described as lying directly beneath the foundations of a square structure. Little information regarding these structures survives in the archives. They do not appear to have been planned prior to removal and are conspicuously absent from the notebook discussions and draft quadrant description. Interestingly, a detailed description was promised in a section of the projected monograph entitled 'Features of the Historical Period'. Unfortunately this was either never completed or the draft does not survive in the deposited archive. That Keiller did not consider them to be medieval is suggested by the lack of any mention of them in the 'Medieval' section, where all other features suspected of being medieval in date received full consideration. In light of this a more useful relationship is of setting 21 in the South-West Quadrant, where the burial pit truncated an earlier cess-pit. Keiller claimed that this had contained 12th-century pottery in its fill, though unfortunately Jope makes no explicit reference to this group of material in his report and as a result this dating has not been confirmed. Building upon the information presented above concerning the dating of the burning episodes, if Keiller's dating of the medieval pottery is correct we can place this burial in the period between the 12th century AD and *c*.1719.

In the case of setting 24, although Stukeley did not record the existence of the pond, he did note the presence of this stone, recording it as having fallen. The discovery of coins dating from the late 17th – early 18th centuries in the basal silts of the pond suggests that this burial took place after his last visit to the site in 1724. At a subsequent date, after the pond had been deliberately filled,[9] the buried stone was encountered during the digging of wall foundations and chunks of the upper portion were broken off to construct an abutting wall. If we accept a date of *c*.1800 for the filling of the pond this suggests that burial took place between *c*.1724 and *c*.1800.

Material culture

Although Keiller was selective, a considerable quantity of medieval and post-medieval pottery was retained from the 1930s excavations, including quantities of material from stone burial pits.[10] Small fragments of medieval pottery were found 'strewn' across the site and apart from some later Saxon sherds, almost all of this material dated to the 11th – 14th centuries. The sherds were largely confined to the topsoil and the presence of conjoining sherds found in different locations within (and in one instance between) quadrants of the henge interior lead Jope to conclude that they were the result of manuring activity (see also Smith 1965, 177). The absence of wares dateable to the later 14th century and beyond was seen as marking the date at which an earlier cultivated landscape of tofts and gardens reverted to pasture. That not all of the interior was cultivated intensively was suggested by the presence of a number of large, unabraded sherds within the assemblage (Jope 1999, 68–9, table 1).

The excavations of buried stones carried out by A C Smith and Lukis recovered around 50 sherds of what were described as 'post-Roman, mostly of Norman origin' pottery (Gray 1935, 103).[11] With regard to the campaigns directed by Keiller, the fills of almost all of the excavated stone burials of the Outer Circle contained residual fragments of 13th- – early 14th-century pottery derived from the surrounding topsoil. For example, the burial pits of settings 30 and 31 contained 18 and 16 sherds respectively. The clearest indication that this material was in a secondary context came from the burial pit of setting 6, where conjoining sherds were found within the fill of the pit and in the general topsoil of the cutting (Jope 1999, 69, table 1). To compound this, ceramics from the 12th to early 13th centuries are more abundant in the topsoil than later wares, resulting in a higher chance of earlier wares finding their way into burial pits. Jope illustrates this effect with the cautionary tale of Setting 9. This burial pit contained one 13th- and sixteen 12th-century sherds yet the coins found in association with the barber-surgeon place the burial in the early 14th century (Jope 1999, 65–69).[12]

Table 9.8. Radiocarbon dates from animal bone in the fills of stone burial pits

Laboratory Code	Context	Sample	Uncal. BP	Calibrated range (95.4% confidence)
Beta-140990	[426]	Bos rib	240±40	1510–1600AD (14.3%) 1610–1690AD (40.0%) 1730–1810AD (31.5%) 1920–1960AD (9.6%)
Beta-140991	[448]	Bos tibia	810±40	1150–1280AD (95.4%)

As a result it is difficult to approach the dating of the stone burials on the basis of pottery evidence alone; all we can say with confidence is that the burials post-date the deposition of the ceramics into the ploughsoil. As little pottery entered the topsoil after the reversion to pasture in the 14th century, Smith's claim on the basis of the pottery finds that none of the Avebury burials could be dated to later than the 14th century must be challenged (Smith 1965, 179).

The fullest assemblage recovered by the current programme of excavation relates to the burial pit of setting T1, and from its condition this pottery is most likely to have been incorporated into the fill of the T1 burial pit accidentally, part of a wider manuring scatter present in the surrounding ploughsoil. This interpretation is supported by the single piece of abraded Laverstock fineware that was found on the base of the pit directly beneath the zone of slumping and collapse that followed the toppling of the stone into the cavity. In dating terms, the medieval pottery recovered from T1 closely parallels that from Avebury, covering a broad range between the 11th and 14th centuries with a focus on the 12th to 13th centuries.

Radiocarbon dating

Other than residual pottery, finds from the fills of the burial pits are extremely rare, implying that in the vast majority of cases care appears to have been taken to ensure that the pits were back-filled with clean chalk rubble. As a result the deposits of animal bone from the L6 burial pit are of particular interest. A large piece of chopped cattle rib was embedded in the main body of the pit fill, sealed beneath the rammed chalk capping. In addition a split cattle tibia had been inserted within a perforation running through the sarsen. AMS dates were obtained for each of the bones (Table 9.8).

Beta-140990 is on a chopped cattle rib from the clean chalk backfill of the burial pit, and should, therefore, date the burial event. The later range of the calibrated span (1730-1810AD and 1920–1960AD) can be discounted on historical grounds. This distinctive perforated stone was not visible to Stukeley during his recording of the Beckhampton Avenue settings and although sporadic later burials did take place on the line of the West Kennet Avenue (see above), these were diligently recorded by the growing number of students of the site. This leaves the earlier part of the span, suggesting that this stone was buried some time during the 16th or 17th centuries.

As mentioned earlier, the cattle tibia is an extremely curious deposit. On the basis of associated worked flint it was assumed that this event took place during prehistory; a deliberate deposit incorporated soon after the stone was erected and thus able to provide a *terminus ante quem* for the construction of the Avenue. This is obviously not the case, and we are left with the implication that a somewhat unusual depositional event took place during the 12th or 13th century. Two scenarios are possible.

The first sees the bone packed into the cavity close to the time of burial. It seems unlikely that the tibia, clean soil packing and worked flint would not have weathered out of the perforation had the stone been exposed, either standing or recumbent, particularly given the minimum lag of 230 years between the events. As a result it is much more likely that the hole was plugged and sealed as part of the burial process; the soil packing and lithic material derived directly from the original stone-hole fill. The tibia is more difficult to explain. It may be evidence of an earlier deposit at the foot of the stone or an heirloom integral to earlier practices involving this particular sarsen and its distinctive perforations. The intentional removal of the stone may have also required removal of the paraphernalia associated with it and the role it played within contemporary folk-practice.

The second scenario assumes that the perforation lay close to the base of the stone when standing and was filled with the same clean soil as the remainder of the stone-hole. The tibia could than have been pushed down into the perforation from the surface, its presence going completely unnoticed by those involved in the subsequent toppling and burial. This latter explanation certainly removes the need to invoke heirlooms and long-lived folk-practices, but still leaves us with an equally odd depositional act requiring some form of explanation.

The final source of dating evidence for stone burials comes from coinage. We have already mentioned the coins found in association with the body in the burial pit of setting 9. One further coin was found in association with a burial pit; a worn and halved Short Cross penny most likely deposited between 1222 and 1237AD and found on the base of the stone-hole associated with setting 26a. Whilst this potentially dates the toppling of the stone, it is difficult to ascertain whether it dates the burial that followed. It is also unclear whether this was in a primary context given the extensive animal disturbance that had affected this feature (Smith 1965, 177).

Summary of dating evidence

Ucko *et al.* offer a concise and effective summary of the dating problems surrounding stone burial and the rather flimsy basis for many long-held (and oft-repeated) assumptions (Ucko *et al.* 1991, 177–81). Put bluntly, when they undertook their survey reliable dating evidence for stone burials was virtually non-existent. Whilst the current programme of excavation has added to our knowledge of stone burial as a practice, it has only resulted in the dating of one further burial event. That date is, however, highly significant.

Out of the 48 burial pits investigated through excavation since 1934, only four can be dated with any confidence. Two of these post-date Stukeley's record of the site, with some doubts existing as to whether the Crawford Setting had ever been a standing stone (Table 9.9).

Setting	Dating
9 (Outer Circle)	c.1320–1350AD
24 (Outer Circle)	c.1724–1800AD
L6 (Beckhampton Avenue)	c.1510–1690AD
Crawford Stone (West Kennet Avenue)	1921–2AD

Table 9.9. Dated stone burials

The presence of re-deposited 12th century or later pottery in the fills of many of the burial pits provides a general *terminus post quem* for the start of this process. The lack of any record of either buried sarsens or burial as an *active* process in the period between 1719 and 1724AD provides a *terminus ante quem* for the bulk of the burials. The recent suggestion of a possible Anglo-Saxon origin for such practices can be discounted as resulting from a confusion between the numbering schemes used by Keiller and Smith. Chaff-tempered sherds were found in the fill of the stone-hole of the *fallen* stone 7 of the North-West Quadrant as numbered by Keiller (Smith number 40), not the *buried* setting 7 of the South-West Quadrant (Keiller number 40) (contra Pollard and Reynolds 2002, 191–2). As a result whilst there is good reason to believe that stone 40 fell during the Anglo-Saxon period there is nothing to link stone burials to this phase.

With regard to specific methodologies, the lack of dating evidence makes it impossible to determine whether different techniques were in contemporary currency or whether they reflect development and change over time. What we can say is that the falling-leaf technique was certainly employed in the early 14th century and the separate pit technique in the 16th – 17th centuries. Keiller claimed to be able to distinguish between early (*i.e.* medieval) burials and late ones on the basis of the depth of the pit and care taken in its construction. Thus to Keiller, setting 9 was early and setting 7 late because part of the latter poked above the turfline, even though they were buried using the same technique. To support his claim Keiller argued that setting 7 had been marked as fallen by Stukeley in 1724 and Lukis and Smith in 1882. However, given that one part of the stone jutted proud of the turfline it is more than likely that in describing the stone as fallen they were referring to the projecting corner; indeed Keiller himself had referred to it as 'fallen' in his own pre-excavation plan (Smith 1965, fig. 67). There is then little convincing evidence to support Keiller's assumption that a pristine, methodical medieval practice slowly became diluted and corrupted over time. In fact the evidence from setting L6, argues the opposite – later burials could be as deep and well finished as the 14th-century example excavated by Keiller.

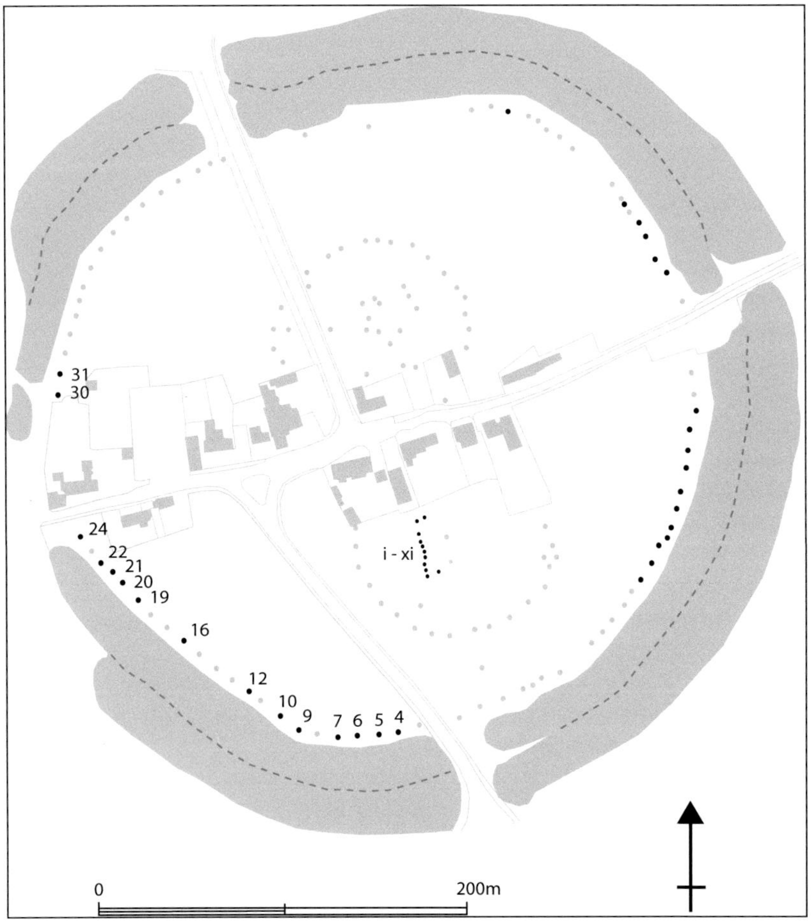

Figure 9.16. Overall distribution of burials at Avebury. Incorporates data © Crown Copyright/database right 2007. An Ordnance Survey/(EDINA) supplied service

The impact of stone burial

The distribution of buried stones within the Avebury henge has been reconstructed on the basis of excavated, parchmark and geophysical evidence (Figure 9.16). Due to the preponderance of excavation in the western half of the henge the resultant plan should be regarded as more reliable in this area. Although a wealth of information regarding buried sarsens is depicted upon the measured plan produced by Lukis and Smith (Figure 9.17), it proved extremely difficult to translate the locations recorded to contemporary scaled plans of the site.[13] As a result it has been used here to merely confirm the general existence (or otherwise) of burials in the unexcavated portions of the henge.

Even the most cursory examination of the distribution of stone burials within the henge reveals a marked clumping which in turn suggests a conscious effort on the part of those burying the sarsens to inter discrete and coherent blocks of stones. Although the fact that only a short stretch of the Beckhampton Avenue has been investigated makes the recognition of such patterns difficult, the same trend is evident in the distribution of burials along the line of the West Kennet Avenue. In each case the picture revealed is far from the 'intermittent pattern of burial – a few stones here, a few there' claimed by Smith (1965, 179). There is a pattern, but it is far from intermittent.

Given that the dates we do have for the activity bracket a minimum of 330 years this was clearly an extremely long-lived tradition. As for whether the practice of burial was sustained and systematic or more episodic, it is interesting to consider the number of standing stones that were actually buried. Looking first to the henge, with the exception of the small inner settings of the Southern Inner Circle and two stones of the Northern Inner Circle suggested by Lukis and Smith, burial seems to have focused upon the settings of the Outer Circle with a tendency to avoid the largest sarsens bracketing the entrances. In the western half, where excavation has been complete, a total of 13 out of a possible 39 stones were deliberately buried (33%). On the basis of geophysical and parchmark evidence, burial may account for a further 17 out of a possible 44 (39%) to the east, although this does not include burials that may have been subsequently dug out and destroyed, losing their distinctive geophysical signature in the process.[14] In the case of the avenues we can similarly examine the proportion of burials within the excavated portions. On the line of the Beckhampton Avenue, excluding the settings of the Longstones Cove, five definite (and one possible) stones were buried out of the 11 investigated (50%). The figures for the area of the West Kennet Avenue explored by Keiller are 15 out of 65 (23%).

If we treat these ratios as typical then we can gain a picture, albeit crude and hypothetical, of the scale of activity. Taking Smith's estimate of a total of 174 standing stones at Avebury (1965, fig. 70) as an approximation, we can envisage between 57 (33%) and 68 (39%) burials. Any estimate of the total number of stones making up either of the Avenues is fraught with difficulty, with previous estimates based upon assumptions of regularity in spacing and configuration that are difficult to justify in the light of new evidence. They do, however, provide an approximate upper threshold on stone numbers and for the purposes of the speculative exercise being carried out here, provide useful food for thought. Using the assumption of an average pair spacing of 25m and total length of 2.5km, a total of 200 individual settings can be suggested for the West Kennet Avenue (Pollard and Reynolds 2002, 101). In turn, we might expect a total of 100 individual settings along the line of the Beckhampton Avenue. If we then assume that the observed ratios on the excavated portions are representative, we might expect 46 (23%) of the West Kennet settings to have been buried and 50 (50%) of those making up the Beckhampton Avenue.

In stressing the speculative nature of this exercise the results are undoubtedly interesting, insofar as they point to a total of around 164 standing stones being buried over a period of at least 330 years. This does not suggest a particularly vigorous or sustained process; burials were rare events in the Avebury landscape. Indeed, taking the combined total of a little under 500 standing stones, if this had been a seasonal practice with a single sarsen buried every year, there would have been little surviving above ground by the middle of the 17th century for John Aubrey to have stumbled across.

The next key question concerns the tempo of stone burial: was this a gentle trickle or more episodic and erratic – punctuated bursts of activity spread over an appreciable period of time? The overall distribution certainly lends support to the latter. Further evidence comes from the burial of settings *i–xi* of the Southern Inner Circle and the single pit, along with transposed positions, of stones *v*, *vi* and *vii*. The latter three stones had to have been buried in a single episode. The careful way in which the remaining burial pits are aligned so as to respect one another and the line of the original settings also argues for a single planned event (Figure 9.5). Although it could be argued that the small size of these settings makes them unrepresentative, other clues can be found in the detail of the method used to bury selected sarsens and morphology of the resultant pits (Figure 9.18). The adjacent stones of settings 4, 5 and 6 were all buried using the separate pit technique, the pits dug oversized but respecting the shape of the stone. In the case of settings 21 and 22 Keiller deemed the approach taken to burial as being identical in each case.

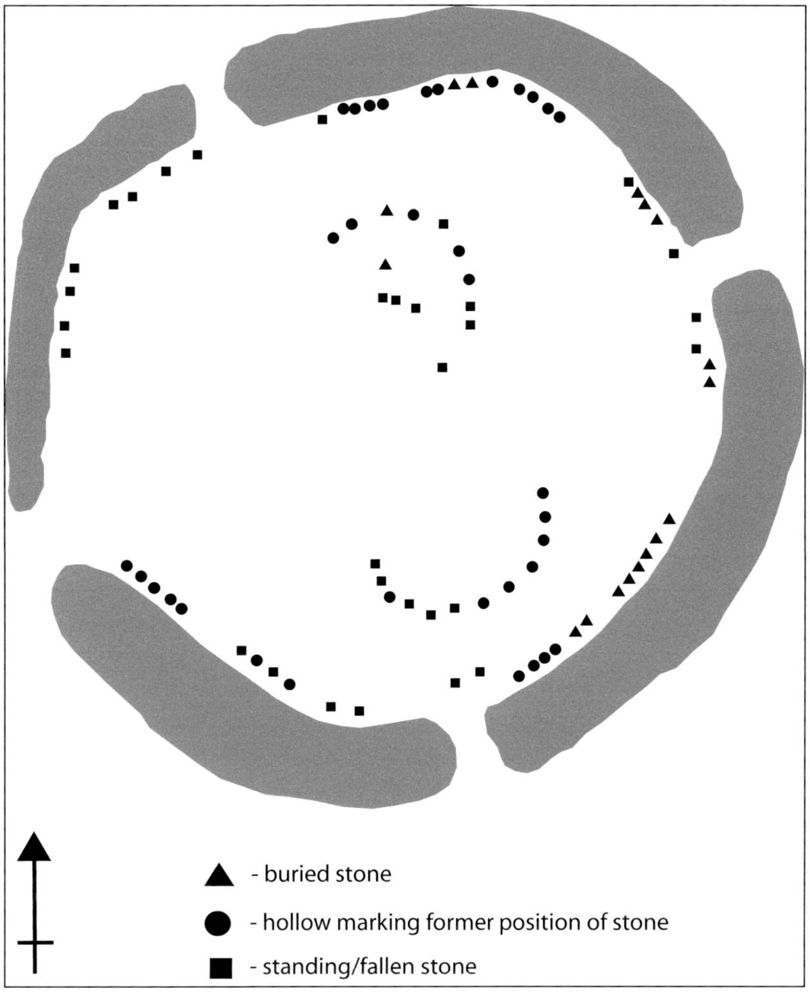

Figure 9.17. Plan of stones, buried stones and former stone positions at Avebury produced by Lukis and Smith (after Smith 1884, pl. V)

Motivations

Before considering the motivations that may have driven stone burial it is worth summarising what we now know of this practice. It was long-lived yet episodic, and far from piecemeal; groups of stones were being buried in clusters rather than individually, suggesting discrete bursts of activity rather than a gentle trickle. A number of techniques were employed that varied greatly in approach yet served to effect the same result – the complete removal of a stone from the landscape and its sealing beneath the topsoil under a solid cap of rammed and compacted chalk. Rather than points on a developmental sequence this suite of techniques appear to have been broadly contemporaneous – a repertoire.

Existing interpretations of stone burial have followed two distinctive paths, each shaped in large part by the assumption that stone burial was short-lived and tied to a particular juncture

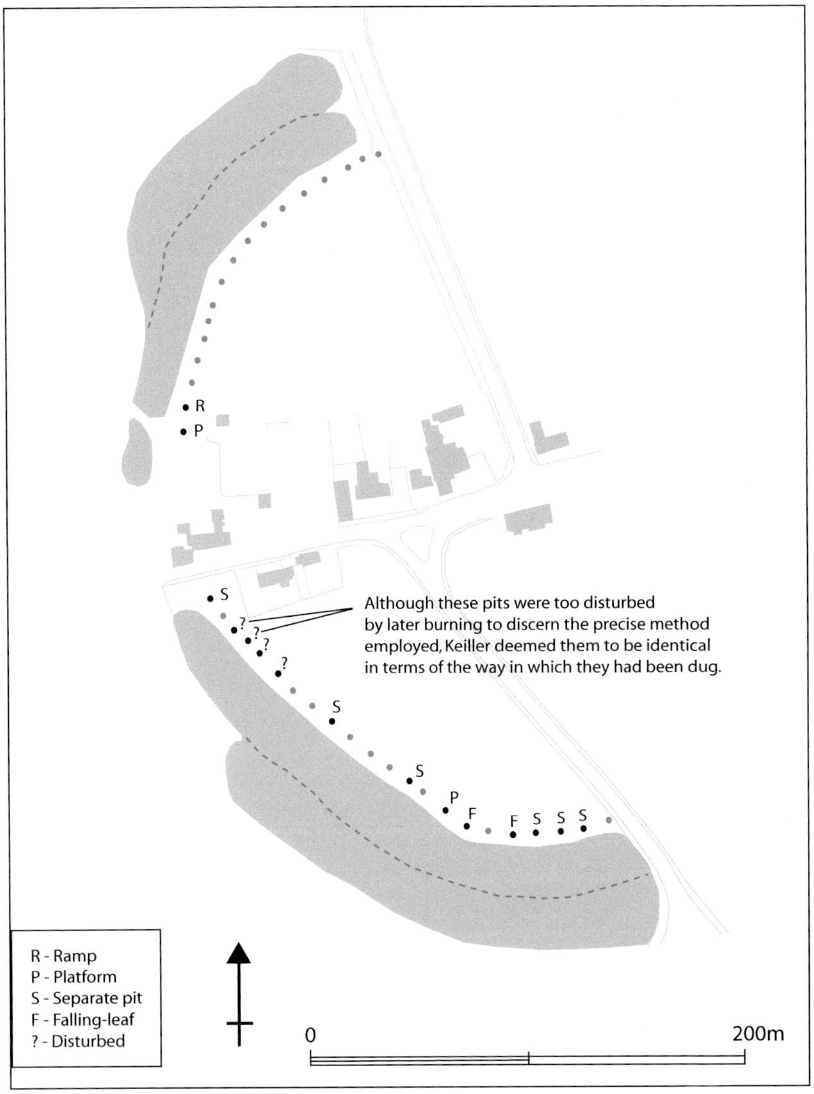

Figure 9.18. Spatial distribution of burial techniques at Avebury. Incorporates data © Crown Copyright/ database right 2007. An Ordnance Survey/ (EDINA) supplied service

in Avebury's long history. The first of these can be termed the *economic* explanation, linked to the assumption that all burials dated to the latter decades of the 17th century AD. The second might best be summed up by the term *superstitious* and is derived from a belief that all burials took place in the early 14th century AD.

Simple economics: burial for clearance

On the basis of the testimony of William Stukeley, itself drawn from local informants, the burial of stones was originally assumed to have been carried out to remove stones from the path of the plough. Stone burial was a form of field clearance, moreover one that took place shortly before stone destruction became the norm, a practice that appears to have its origins in the latter half of the 17th century (see Chapter 10). This interpretation certainly had currency in the 19th century (*e.g.* Long 1858b, 21–22) and was taken-for-granted by Keiller when he first encountered buried stones on the line of the West Kennet Avenue and within the North-West Quadrant of the henge.

There are several factors that support the interpretation of burial as a form of clearance. Firstly, by the early 18th century the villagers interviewed by Stukeley clearly *believed* that this was the case. Secondly, the morphology of the burial pits highlights the intention, if not always adequately executed, to ensure that the bulk of the stone was kept beneath the level of the ploughsoil. Thirdly, if we look at the distribution of burials, the clumping of stones can certainly be read as reflecting a desire to remove sarsens from discrete blocks of the landscape. Take for example areas 1 and perhaps 9 and 19 of the henge interior where stones were cleared from the partition boundary (Figure 9.19). The focus of burial upon the stones at the very perimeter of the interior (rather than deep within it) can also be understood as a practical response to the potentially cumbersome process of turning the plough at the end of a given strip.

Looking to the Avenues, in the case of West Kennet the bulk of the burials are clustered into two discrete, and largely contiguous, blocks. This strongly suggests a desire to create areas of land that were free of standing stones (Figure 9.20). Given that for much of their length the Avenues appear to have been running directly through intensively cultivated land we might well ask why, if clearance was the driving force, *all* of the stones were not buried? The excavations along the line of the Beckhampton Avenue are instructive in this regard (Figure 9.21). Settings L1–L6 are situated within a block of ridge-and-furrow aligned approximately N-S, all but L1 located on the ridges. Of these settings only three (L2, L5 and L6) were buried. The fact that L1 was not seems strange given its location within the base of a furrow. In the case of the second block of ridge-and-furrow (settings L7–L15) aligned approximately E-W, none of the stones were buried despite occupying a similar position within the body of a field to L1–L6. At this point we need to think carefully about the nature of medieval cultivation; in raising the issue of landscape-wide clearance there is a danger of focusing too closely upon the proverbial wood (the open field as a whole) at the expense of the trees (the individual strips within it). Given that each strip would potentially have been cultivated by a different villein, it could be argued that individual decisions for and against would have resulted in *precisely* such a pattern as that observed along the Beckhampton Avenue. It is unfortunate that we have no examples of either multiple burials or both burial and non-burial within a given strip to either challenge or support this.

In Avebury and along the West Kennet Avenue burial was concentrated into discrete blocks which suggest rather than a desire to rid the landscape of stones *per se*, the intent was to rid certain, well defined areas of the landscape of sarsens. In contrast, burials along the Beckhampton Avenue were more piecemeal, individual acts linked perhaps to the individual strips making up the open fields. Burial may well have been a sensible practical solution to the problem posed by megaliths that were deemed to be 'in the way'. This was time consuming and labour intensive, but perhaps less so than attempting to break the resilient stone into more manageable lumps. In considering the option of dragging, we must remember (in the case of the henge at any rate) that this was an area criss-crossed with boundary ditches, partitions and garden plots; effective obstacles to any potential escape route. Likewise, out in the fields, any stone would have to be dragged either along the length of a strip or across a number of strips (requiring at the very least intense and repeated negotiation with other villeins). Given the sheer weight, bulk and hardness of the stones, the notion of burial as a technology of clearance may well have had its attractions. As we will see below, it also has its problems.

Figure 9.19. Burials and boundaries. Incorporates data © Crown Copyright/database right 2007. An Ordnance Survey/(EDINA) supplied service

Challenging the clearance hypothesis

The first serious challenge to this interpretation came in 1938 with Keiller's discovery of the barber-surgeon, pushing the dating of burials back into the early 14th century, and his growing experience of the nature (and relative efficacy) of stone burials. In an illuminating diary entry reproduced by Ucko *et al.* (1991, 179) Keiller's foreman, the experienced excavator W E V Young, pointed out that buried stones posed more of a threat to ploughing than upright ones. Further to this, given the effort involved in burying a stone, the act would only be worthwhile if the small area of additional ground yielded was to be intensively and repeatedly ploughed. It is also worth pointing out that at sites such as Long Meg, Cumbria, medieval farmers appear to have been happy to plough through the megalithic settings without any attendant need to remove stones.

The clearance hypothesis depends in large part on the assumption that the interior of Avebury had been under the plough. There is in fact little evidence that it had ever been intensively cultivated. At the time of the burial of setting 9 the majority of the henge interior would have instead been under grass, the ploughing that did take place occurring in the 12th and 13th centuries (Pollard and Reynolds 2002, 241). If burial was for clearance then one would also expect the area showing the clearest evidence of ridge-and-furrow (the North-East Quadrant: areas 17–19 on Figure 9.19) to contain the greatest number of buried stones. This is not the case.

This objection can be strengthened if we consider the potential scale of clearance that

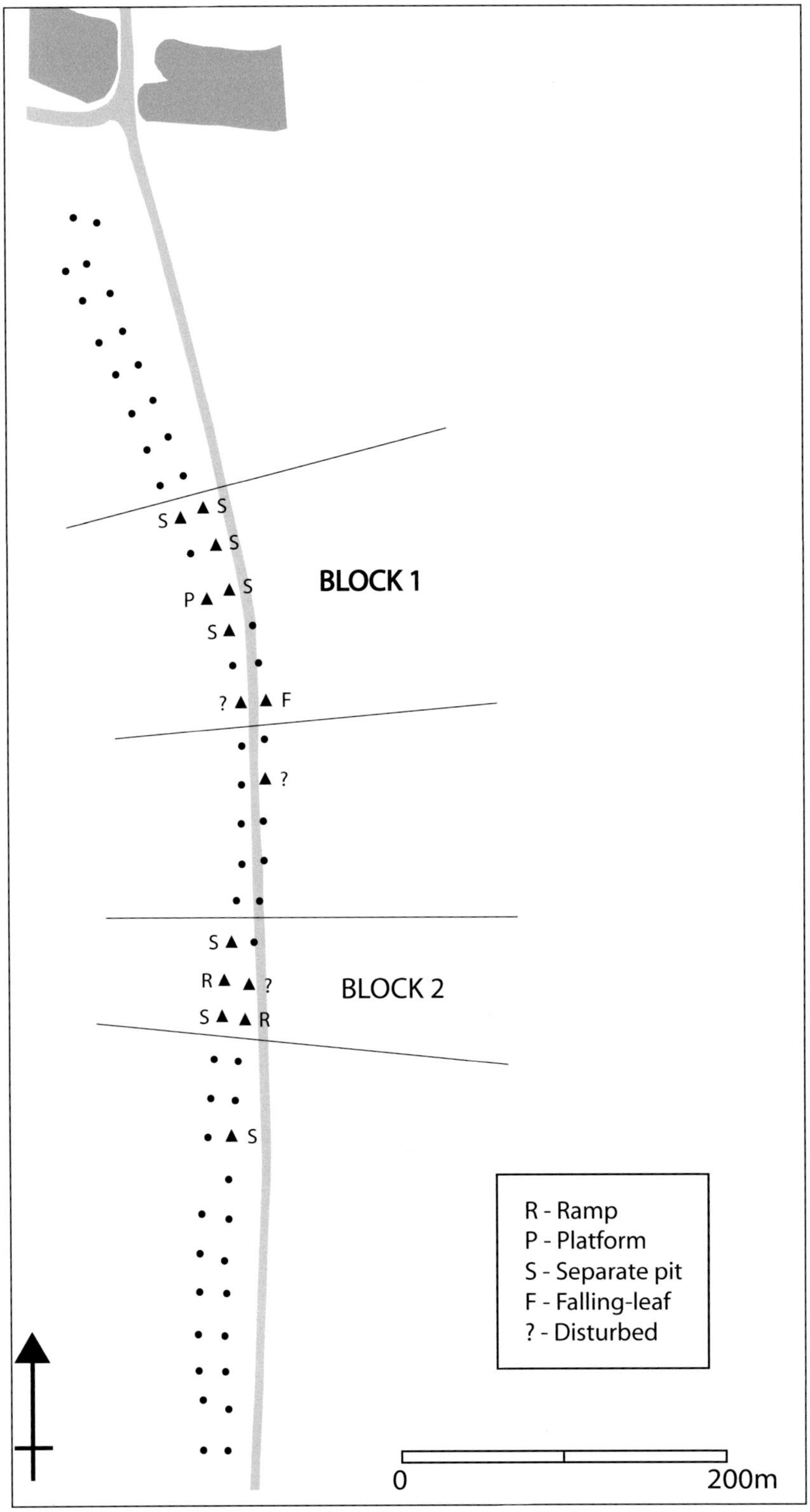

Figure 9.20. Spatial distribution of burial techniques on the line of the West Kennet Avenue

would have taken place in the Avebury landscape, and the concomitant need to bury sarsens. Put simply, if burial was an effective and accepted form of clearance there should be literally hundreds of buried stones in the dry valleys and out across the downs. Although the burial of at least one 'natural' sarsen is recorded in the 19th century (Smith 1965, 207, footnote 2) there is no evidence for a mass of earlier burials in the landscape around Avebury. The open area excavations carried out between 2002–3 in the sarsen-rich valley bottom at the sites of Falkner's Circle and the Crawford setting revealed no evidence for general burial. Ditto the area of the West Kennet palisades. Geophysical survey has also not revealed spreads of sarsen burials though it should be acknowledged that no large-scale geophysical surveys have been undertaken away from the monumental settings. Rather than burial, surveys at nearby Lockeridge have suggested that as late as the 18th and 19th centuries sarsens were instead being cleared into lines to delineate field boundaries (Fowler 2000, 68).

The question of why stones were not simply dragged away deserves further consideration. If clearance was the motivating force, and the internal complexity of the site a barrier to large scale movement of toppled stones then an obvious question is why were they not simply toppled into the ditch? Although it has escaped critical discussion, the way in which stones were kept out of the ditch during Avebury's later history is interesting. That other material *was* dumped into it is suggested by the cuttings made by Gray, which recovered quantities (not specified) of medieval pottery from immediately beneath the turfline and a layer of 'mixed silting' which extended to a depth of around 2.6m (Gray 1935, 112). Whilst this could conceivably reflect deliberate manuring the practicalities of cultivating (not to mention ploughing) the ditch would have been difficult.[15] The fate of the relatively small stones of the southern inner setting (*i–xi*) is also puzzling, as their relatively small size and uncomplicated form would have made it a simple task to carry or drag them away.

The final objection to the clearance hypothesis relates to the way in which the stones were buried. The ubiquitous provision of a rammed capping of chalk rubble makes little practical sense if the stone is already below the level of the ploughsoil, and conveys a strong sense that the sarsens were not so much buried as *sealed* beneath the ground.

The proverbial nail in the coffin comes from the barber-surgeon himself. Why would such a man be involved in routine field-clearance? Further, if an individual was accidentally killed

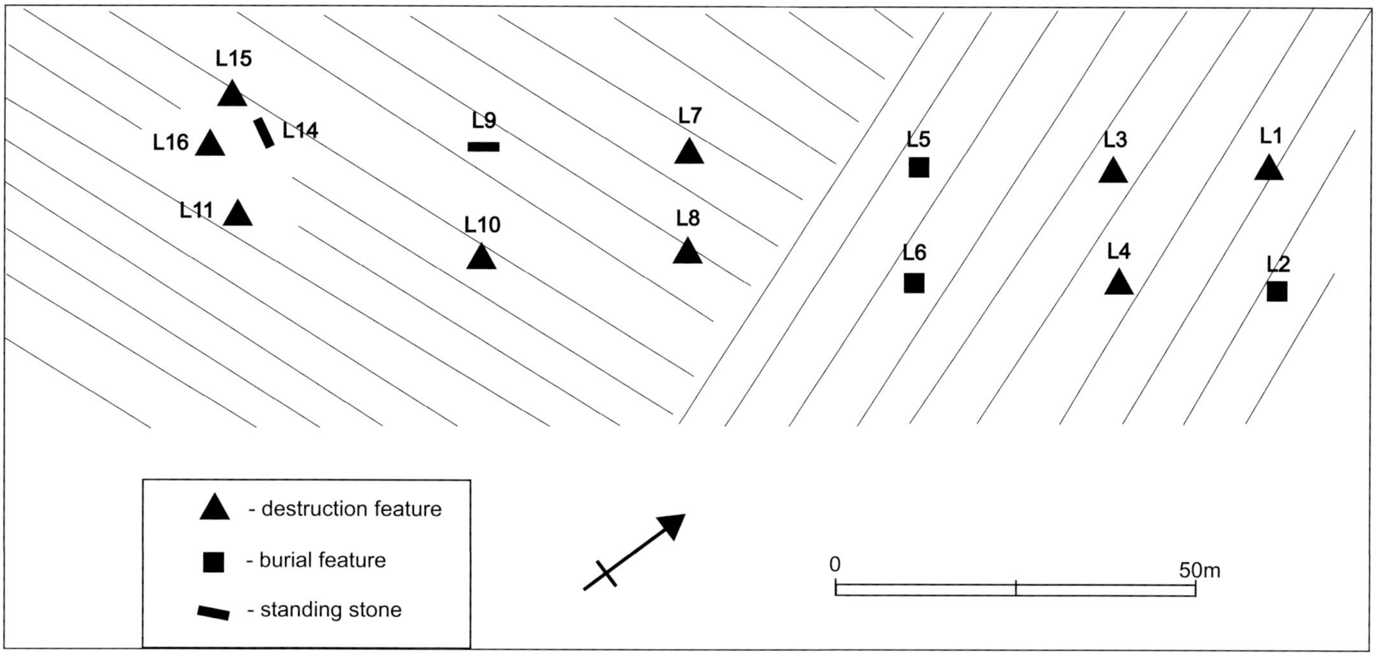

Figure 9.21. Beckhampton Avenue: burials and cultivation patterns in the south-west of Longstones Field

by a falling stone during such an episode why was the body not recovered from the pit and properly buried? Taken together, these factors prompted W. E. V. Young, to speculate that a modern economic mindset may not be the most effective way of approaching the rationale that lay behind stone burials.

Burial: a religious dimension?

> 'an anomalous result of having learnt so much concerning the victim of this accident was that this knowledge opened up a fresh problem. Why should a tailor, and moreover a man apparently not financially straitened, not, so to speak, "on the dole" have been engaged upon the task of burying a megalith? Here was no farm labourer removing a stone in order to facilitate ploughing. Nor indeed were any of these S.W. sector stones likely to interfere with agriculture much more than the deeply buried nos. 16 and 17 in the N.W. Sector, of which in this case one is irresistibly reminded. Have we here, and in the case of the adjacent early period burials of stones, examples of another reason for their removal, for instance, as suggested by W.E.V.Y. a collective penance imposed by the priory authorities? There is much to commend this idea to serious consideration.' (Keiller SW Sector Field notes, 31–2)

On the basis of the pottery evidence, Jope argued that whilst the process of burying the Avebury stones undoubtedly took years, it could have been completed within the space of a single decade (1999, 67). Combining this with the dating provided by the coin evidence, burial became a phenomenon of the early 14th century. Young's tentative association of the church with burial was reinforced by Smith (1965, 176–80) who cited a late 9th-century injunction of a council of Nantes in support of Church concerns about pagan worship taking place at sites such as Avebury. At the heart of Smith's interpretation is the claim that the 14th century was awash with superstition, and Avebury may have attracted practices deemed dangerous to the Church. To Smith, building upon the suggestion of Young, burial was Church-sponsored which explained in turn why somebody like a barber-surgeon or tailor was involved. This strand was developed by Jope who cited links between the devil and various elements of Avebury and its surrounding landscape. That superstition lay at the heart of this scheme is clear from Jope's claim that 'it would be surprising if so remarkable a monument as Avebury passed unheeded. There is no surviving medieval reference to the Avebury stones, but they may have given rise to superstitious practices, incurring ecclesiastical disapproval' (1999, 67). The precise nature of the Church response (*i.e.* how it was sanctioned and organised) was also considered. Given the scale of the undertaking, and assumed short timescale, it would have required more than the coaxing and encouragement of a parish priest. Nor would the essentially administrative alien priory have been likely to have wielded such influence. Instead Jope turned to routine village festivities such as wakes. He concluded his discussion with the evocative suggestion that '[i]n the deliberate burying of these stones there was probably a mingling of faith and superstitious apprehension at this fearful silent array' (*ibid.*).

Although presented in a tentative fashion, this explanation rapidly became an orthodoxy, gaining authority through repetition. This is perhaps most forceful in Burl's evocative account of stone burial at Avebury. Citing a lingering paganism in the area of Avebury, 'the Wiltshire peasantry, superstitious and conservative, continued in the ways of their forefathers ignoring the cajoling of Christian preachers with their foreign notions' (1979, 33). The fact that the Saxon church was constructed outside the circle is seen as 'recognising that Christianity was as yet too feeble to destroy the alien and evil strength of the stone circles inside' (*ibid.*). Citing the frequency of devilish names at the site (his chair, quoits and brand-irons can be found either within Avebury or in close proximity), a range of general references to witchcraft and folk practice were cited to link the site to activities in the 14th century deemed abhorrent by the Christian Church (*ibid.*, 36). Burl also popularised the link between the carved decoration on the late 12th -century font in Avebury Church to stone burial. Depicting what appears to be a bishop wounding a serpent this is argued to represent the triumph of Christianity over paganism being played out at this time in amongst the Avebury stones (*ibid.*, 35) (for details of the font see Pollard and Reynolds 2002, 256–7). Once again, the absence of pottery later than the 14th century was cited as a *terminus ante quem* for burial – it is a medieval practice 'at its height a few years after 1300' (Burl 1979, 37). Christianity is the engine driving stone burial, with specific events perhaps linked to annual fairs (*ibid.*, 37–8). Interestingly this interpretation has strengthened during the years since the first publication of Burl's seminal account: 'it' [*i.e.* the practice of burial] (1979, 37) becomes 'purification' in the second, revised edition of the text (2002, 34). According to Burl the beginning of the end for stone burial came with the death of the barber-surgeon – a potent reminder to the villagers of the perils of messing with powerful forces. The arrival of the Black Death effectively finished the practice (1979, 40).

This account has proved remarkably resilient despite the important work of Ucko *et al.* (1991, 180–1), which challenged this explanation on the simple grounds of the lack of any convincing evidence (supportive or with regard to dating) and the uncritical way the assumption that all burials were post-medieval had been replaced with the mantra that all burials were medieval.[16] The latter can be found in an undiluted form in the work of researchers such as Malone (1989, 90) and Bender (1998, 100–104), whilst calls to a vaguer, unspecified 'superstition' permeate other recent accounts. For example, drawing upon the case of the barber-surgeon and documentary evidence of a 13th-century murder at the henge (that of John the Spinner in 1282), Pollard and Reynolds have suggested that murders and disappearances 'generated a negative local folklore regarding the monument that could have prompted attempts at "cleansing" Avebury driven by a short-lived superstitious motivation' (2002, 245).

Problems with superstition and religion

A number of serious reservations can be raised with respect to this rationale. The new evidence regarding the dating of stone burials has revealed it to be a remarkably long-lived practice: it was clearly not limited to a single decade in the early 14th century. There are also serious inconsistencies in many of the interpretations tendered arising from the near total absence of convincing evidence. For example, in attributing burials to religious festivities, Jope omitted to consider why this only lasted a decade. Further, if burials took place during wakes our estimated total number of buried stones (*c.*174) implies a particularly bleak period for the village in terms of mortality.[17] Burl's account carries an air of finality and authority that is not supported by its evidential basis. There is also a circularity to the argument he presents: at one point the fact that pagan practices persisted is implied by the medieval burials, yet the burials are themselves explained as resulting from persistent pagan practices (2002, 29).

We have noted how the unusual case of the barber-surgeon is difficult to incorporate into any economic explanation. It is important to realise that he sits just as uncomfortably within religious or superstitious frameworks. Whether religiously sponsored or not, and whether a barber-surgeon, tailor or shepherd, the decision to leave the corpse in the pit is a remarkable one. Pollard and Reynolds have stressed how corpses left unburied in consecrated ground 'was a serious business in the middle ages' and reiterate how easy it would have been for people used to digging such pits to have dug the corpse out for appropriate burial (2002, 244).

As discussed by Ucko *et al.* (1991, 178–81), evidence directly linking the Avebury stones to practices deemed inflammatory by the Church is conspicuous by its absence. There does not appear to have been any Anglo-Saxon affinity for, or special attention paid to standing stones (as opposed to earthworks) (Pollard and Reynolds 2002, 192). This is perhaps illustrated at Avebury by the siting of what became Avebury High Street *along* the Beckhampton Avenue (Gillings and Pollard 2004, Chapter 6). The only early reference we do have to the stones, a 1307 charter reference recording the granting to Cirencester Abbey of a pathway between the church and the croft of one Johannis de la Stone, refers merely to 'the great old stones'. It is also difficult to link the various 'devil' toponyms to these events in any meaningful way as the wholesale linkage of the Devil with monuments appears to post-date the earliest burial, only gaining momentum from the late 16th century. As Hutton notes, there are no known cases of the Church dismantling a prehistoric monument due to pagan or satanic associations (cited in Bender 1998, 137–8). Further, it is unlikely that the surname 'de la Stone' would have been carried if it had dubious associations with the devil (Pollard and Reynolds 2002, 240–2). Grinsell has noted that areas rich in sarsen are commonly weak in folklore (1975) and Avebury is no exception, being notable for the lack of folklore associated with it (Harte 2006). In summary, we have little idea of medieval attitudes to the standing stones of Avebury, not least whether they saw them as in any way artificial or unusual. There is also no compelling evidence of any conflict between the medieval Church and what might be termed popular or folk religion.

The problem with explanations that foreground a generalised and non-specific notion of 'superstition' is that in the absence of evidence they are difficult to evaluate, and this is perhaps why they have proven so persistent. They draw upon the notion popularised in the 1970s (*e.g.* Dames 1976; 1977) that Avebury presents a puzzle to be unlocked, a singular prehistoric mystery that must be confronted and solved (Gillings and Pollard 2004, 186–7). The vagueness of terms such as 'superstition' makes them extremely malleable, particularly when they are combined with the widely held, yet largely erroneous, assumption that pre-Christian practices and beliefs survived into later periods in the form of popular folk rituals, memories and practices (see for example Hutton 1996; Harte 1998). The result is a heady and persuasive cocktail. Having established superstition as the driving force, the next stage is to then trawl historical accounts of the first half of the 14th century for likely catalysts or triggers for the beginning of the outbreak of stone burial.

To give an example of how such an interpretation can be constructed, it has been argued elsewhere that local inhabitants in the mid-19th century believed that sarsen stones grew out of the ground (Long 1858b, 29).[18] As a result burial represents an obvious solution to the problem of getting rid of an unwanted stone (for whatever reason) – you are simply putting it back from whence it came (Gillings and Pollard 2004, 132). To turn this into a plausible explanation for stone burial we merely need to assume that the same beliefs were held by their 14th century forebears, identify an historical crisis (trigger) and concoct a plausible 'folkloric' response. Following the famines that attended the agrarian crisis of 1315–17 (Goldberg 2004, 81–2), stones were 'replanted' in an attempt to restore fertility to the soil and ensure the harvest. By sealing them under a thick crust of compacted chalk they were deterred from resurfacing. The continuing failure of this strategy may have served to 'up the stakes' adding an additional, and highly potent fertiliser, to the last of the burials in the form of the barber-surgeon. With the end of the crisis came the end of stone burial. Shades of 'the Wicker Man', but not as far removed in spirit from existing explanations as some might think, and it will be interesting to see whether this explanation, designed merely to illustrate a point, in time gains authority.

Stone burial in the Avebury landscape

The new excavations have added critical evidence to our understanding of the processes involved in stone burial. We now know that the practice of burying sarsens may have spanned as much as four centuries, and explanations based upon the assumption of a discrete episode must be discarded. Likewise, the oft-repeated description of burials being carried out in a piecemeal, random fashion must now be revised. Our understandings of burial as a practice have also increased greatly, with a number of distinctive approaches recognised that seems to have formed a distinctive pool or repertoire that could be drawn upon in a flexible and pragmatic fashion.

Many, if not more questions remain stubbornly unanswered. In highlighting that burial was long-lived, the lack of dated examples sheds little light upon the tempo of this activity. Is this a slow, gradual, yet persistent process trickling across the centuries or are we seeing instead a dramatic phase of intensive stone burial taking place in the early 14th century followed by occasional, sporadic outbursts during the following four hundred years? The answer to this can only come with more excavated and dated examples.

With regard to motivation, the first point to raise is that given the longevity of the practice, is it reasonable to assume (or expect) that all burials were driven by the same rationale? To put this another way, should we expect the factors that prompted the first burials to have persisted in an unaltered form for four centuries, eluding comment or record during this time?

If a single rationale did drive the burials then we must regard stone burials as a carefully prescribed and carefully controlled practice – the only possible, or permissible, means of reacting to a specific circumstance or situation – practised only if and when prompted. This in turn raises questions as to how the knowledge was passed down and transmitted, and who would have been involved in such activities.

On the basis of the evidence assembled to date we would argue that burial should instead be seen as what might be termed an appropriate response – if a sarsen was deemed to be in the wrong place, for whatever reason, burial was the accepted way of dealing with it. This would certainly explain the rather contradictory evidence recovered to date and the problems encountered in furnishing a single convincing explanation. If a single rationale never existed, attempts to explain burial as a unitary phenomenon are always doomed to fail.

The circumstances that lead to the first stone burials are at present unknown, though the argument presented earlier regarding the size and hardness of sarsens should not be discarded uncritically. If the earliest stone burials did indeed take place in the early 14th century then they came at a time of change and transformation in the Avebury landscape. The evidence from the line of the Beckhampton Avenue as it crosses Butler's Field points towards a later 12th-century shift from sheep pasture to plough cultivation in this area (see Chapter 8). A century or so later within the Avebury earthworks the precise opposite appears to have been taking place, as a short-lived episode of ploughing and cultivation gave way to sheep husbandry. This was clearly a period of dramatic change and transformation and the decision to bury stones may well be bound up closely with this.

As to whether this was driven purely by the need to clear the land of obstructions or superstition (in any one of its myriad forms) is difficult to ascertain. We must be aware that the apparently rational requirements of activities such as clearance, and beliefs regarding the stones themselves, may not have been so clearly delineated, resulting in ostensibly utilitarian activities played out according to rules shaped by folk beliefs and practices. For example, the need to bury the stones beneath the level of the ploughsoil could be driven by the necessity of ensuring the stones did not hinder the plough, whilst the decision to cap the burials with rammed chalk, effectively sealing them below the ground, was a response to the fact that sarsens had the habit of 'growing up' to the surface if left unchecked.

In the course of this chapter we have reviewed the evidence for each of these explanatory pathways and shown how each fails to do justice to the full chronological range and nuances of practice that attended stone burial. For example, a convincing case can be constructed to support the idea of burial as a form of clearance, particularly along the line of the Beckhampton Avenue as it crosses the open fields. However, the same argument is less persuasive within Avebury itself, unless the rationale of clearance through burial can be articulated meaningfully in relation to sheep husbandry. It is perhaps easy to underestimate both the scale of sheep holding and its commensurate impact in terms of the landscape of Avebury (Smith 2005). Edwards has drawn attention to the sheer number of sheep on the manor during the 13th and 14th centuries, increasing from 250 around 1210 to 800 by 1324. Citing the fact that the earthworks of the henge were utilised as common pound in the 16th century, he has raised the possibility that this had originated much earlier, with at least parts of the base of the ditch utilised as a droveway during the medieval period and the South-West Quadrant a sheepfold (Freeman 1983, 87; Edwards 2006). While this would undoubtedly explain why stones were not simply toppled into the ditch (see above), it is still difficult to explain the observed stone burials taking place within the henge as resulting solely from the pressures of sheep husbandry. Providing shade from the sun and shelter from rain and wind, it could even be argued that the stones would have been a useful feature of the henge interior.

The question of why Stukeley thought burial was a relatively late process can be answered straightforwardly; some of them clearly were. In addition, as Smith suggested, the chance discoveries of buried stones would undoubtedly have taken place during ditch digging or agricultural activity (1965, 176).[19] Take for example setting 6 of Avebury's Outer Circle, a stone that that had been exposed in its burial pit by a later boundary ditch. It is clear from Stukeley that by the early 18th century his informants believed that burial was a means of clearing the land and by this stage it appears to have been carried out solely for this purpose; the late burial of setting 24 of the Outer Circle is a good example, carried out to remove an obstacle. It is interesting to speculate whether in this case the decision to bury was a result of the proscription on breaking prompted by Stukeley's campaigning (see Chapter 10) and the response of the villagers to revert to the 'old way' of doing things.

If we turn to the notion of Church-sponsored burial, fuelled by fear and superstition, weight is added to such an interpretation by the strange goings-on recorded at setting L6, which imply that this stone was afforded special attention when buried. However, no link need necessarily be drawn between the imperative to bury, and any possible acts of decommissioning with respect to the stone. The impending arrival of one may well have precipitated the other but otherwise no causal link need be inferred.

Likewise the barber-surgeon. Pollard and Reynolds have listed exclusions to the medieval prescription for burial in consecrated ground (women in childbirth, lechers, thieves, the cursed, and those who died suddenly, though not by accident or mishap) partly in an attempt to stress the unusual nature of such omissions and partly, one suspects, to suggest possible future lines of enquiry. On the basis of pathology, Pitts has suggested that rather than die as a result of accidental crushing, the individual was murdered and their body rammed into the stone burial pit in the window of time between digging and back-filling (2000, 133; pers. comm. 2006). This would account for the presence of the body and also clarifies the relationship between the individual and burial, one of convenient coincidence. If Pitts is correct, then the barber-surgeon is little more than a red-herring in seeking to explain the motivations behind stone burial.

Conclusions

Attempts to explain stone burial have gained considerable authority through repetition: first the economic rationale of Stukeley, followed by the mystical explanation first raised by W E V Young and popularised through the work of Smith and Burl. The latter has been characterised by a desperate search for documentary and other support, the most oft cited being the Nantes declaration and the decoration on the church font, neither persuasive.

The current excavations and archival research have challenged both the chronology and nature of this unique practice. Burying a stone was a complex process; a number of strategies were devised and drawn upon in a flexible and pragmatic fashion dictated in part by the specific target of the act, and the expertise and preferences of those carrying it out. It was also remarkably long-lived, spanning upwards of four centuries, and on the basis of the evidence assembled to date, episodic.

The challenge for future researchers is to shed light upon the origins of burial as a response, its tempo, and the motivations that fuelled the bursts of activity. If the origins of burial are at present unknown, by the early 18th century it was seen as one way of clearing the ground, and strong arguments can be made for extending this function back into the medieval period. However, not all burials make sense as acts of clearance in any rational-economic sense of the word and we must be wary of replacing one simplistic orthodoxy with another. What should be clear is that stone burial is worthy of detailed archaeological and historical study in its own right, being a key phase in the development of the Avebury landscape.

Notes

1 That this attempt at preserving the memory of these discoveries failed is evident from the press releases, newspaper headlines and general hyperbole that accompanied the 'discovery' of buried stones in exactly the positions recorded by Smith and Lukis by a National Trust geophysical survey team in 2003.

2 It is unclear whether this stone had been deliberately (as opposed to gradually) buried; although his published plan appears to show a carefully cut pit, no mention is made of such in the account and the drawing may simply record the edges of Passmore's trench. The shallow depth recorded (0.30m) also points towards a fallen stone.

3 Held within the Alexander Keiller Museum, Avebury.

4 A set of conversion tables are provided in the Appendices.

5 There are surviving patches of such polish on settings 4, 24 and 32 of the Outer Circle.

6 The suggestion from Keiller's surviving notebooks is that the process of identifying which end of the stone originally constituted the base was constrained by his interpretation of the stones falling into two basic shape categories, tempered by the assumption that all stones would conform to one or other of these basic types. Take for example setting 9 of the Outer Circle "Certain interesting considerations arose from the reerection of this stone. had it been placed in a position compatible with stability the sinister side near the face would have lain at an angle nearly equal to that of the dexter. The stone, thus reerected would have resembled in form no other known megalith at Avebury. After numerous variations of position had been undertaken, as is customarily done from the point of view of obtaining further experience, the stone was placed in such a position that the sinister side below the slope of the (higher) sinister angle was practically perpendicular. The highest point of the stone then pointed vertically upwards, and moreover, the line of a plumb bob held on this point passed then through the centre of the pointed base. Thus set, the stone took on the form of a typical B1 type. ..it was somewhat inherently unstable in this position, tending to fall towards the dexter side, but by no means to such a degree as not to be, relatively easily, counteracted by means of packing stones". A further example of this decision-making process concerns setting 4 (Keiller 43) (Keiller, unpublished, SW Sector Field Notebook).

7 In the case of setting L6 it took over two weeks of weathering before any distinction could be made between the chalk capping and surrounding natural.

8 This is compounded by the fact that they are often dated on the basis of the burial pits, on the assumption that these are all early 14th century in date.

9 The locals informed Keiller that this had taken place at the start of the 19th century (Keiller 1939, 230).

10 Unfortunately, beyond a brief comment to this effect by Jope, it is not clear how selection was carried out.

11 This material is recorded as having been deposited in Devizes Museum. As far as we are aware it has not been studied since Gray's cursory examination.

12 Although Jope's report is extremely useful, it was written in 1945 and only revised up to the projected publication date of 1965 when it was intended to make up part of Isobel Smith's monograph. The report finally reached publication in 1999, the introduction carrying the unusual caveat that the reader should approach the report 'as though published in 1965' (Jope 1999, 60). Unfortunately, there has been no further research on the Avebury assemblage nor critical appraisal of Jope's initial classification and interpretation in light of the advances in our understanding of medieval pottery that have taken place over the last 40 years.

13 A problem also encountered by Keiller. That the accuracy of this plan may be questionable is suggested by Keiller's note regarding setting 15 of the Outer Circle "although on Lukis' plan, so lauded by the admiring Smith, shows it nearly 5 times its actual distance from stone 34 (setting 13) – a glaring example of the gross inaccuracy of Smith and Lukis as surveyors".

14 This estimate is close to Lukis and Smith's claim to have revealed 15 burials on the eastern arc of the Outer Circle.

15 This said, it is worth noting that in places the top of the ditch fill does have a curiously level profile (*e.g.* South West Quadrant) that could be consistent with prior cultivation.

16 It is interesting to speculate whether Young would have appreciated the irony of this situation. It was, after all, his complaint in 1938 about how widespread the uncritical equation of burial with clearance had become that prompted consideration of a more superstitious motive (Ucko *et al.* 1991, 179).

17 To which supporters of the superstition/religion framework would no doubt point to the outbreak of the Black Death.

18 That this was widespread and persistent is suggested by the fact that Pepys had recorded precisely such a belief in his diary account of Avebury (Long 1858b, 11).

19 Following the discovery in 1999 of the buried stone at setting L2 of the Beckhampton Avenue, one of the ploughmen told us how he had known for years that there was a substantial stone buried in this location as he had felt the plough rise over it.

10
Stone-breaking

Destruction and depredation

That sarsen stones had been broken-down, worked and utilised for building purposes throughout the historic period is beyond question; even the most casual scrutiny of the oldest surviving structure in the village, the church, cannot fail to reveal the use of sarsen blocks in its 15th-century fabric. Indeed some of the early 17th-century structures still surviving in Avebury are notable for the use of sarsen in their primary constructional layers and those archaeological excavations that have taken place within the village have revealed evidence for the use of sarsen in wall foundations (Brentnall 1946, 180, footnote 2; Harrington and Denham 1986; Pollard and Reynolds 2002, 235–7, 255–7; Edwards 2003). Further afield, excavation at the church at Huish in the Vale of Pewsey, revealed the use of split sarsen slabs in the foundation layers of the 13th-century chapel (Thompson 1967, 59–60).

Despite this long history of sarsen exploitation, the late 17th century appears to mark a period of dramatic and rapid change to the physical fabric of Avebury and its avenues, affecting both earthworks and stones. Sometime between 1685 and 1695 the owner of Avebury manor, Ralph Stawell, had a substantial area of the earthwork to the immediate north of the western entrance levelled for the construction of a barn and planting of an area of trees. A subsequent episode of levelling and planting took place to the south of the western entrance sometime between 1721–4, linked to changes in ownership of the manor (Ucko *et al.* 1991, 170–2). Avebury's location astride the Marlborough-Bath coach road also appears to have had an impact upon the monument with the bank to the west of the southern entrance quarried in 1762 to provide material for the raising of the road level as part of a remodelling of the roadway (Smith 1965, 182; Burl 1979, 53).

Ad hoc **usage and the pragmatic breaking of stones**

With respect to the sarsens making up the various stone settings, both Aubrey and Stukeley recorded the pragmatic (and inventive) ways in which the villagers actively employed the stones. For example, Aubrey claimed that one of the stones had been converted into a pigsty or cattle stall, whilst Stukeley recorded a fallen stone of the Northern Inner Circle being regularly employed as a fish slab during market day (Ucko *et al.* 1991, 177). Certain of the standing stones also appear to have acted as important nodes within the complex and changing patterns of major field boundaries and more transient fence-lines within the circuit of the earthwork. In his excavation of the South-East Quadrant at Avebury, Keiller recorded how a narrow boundary ditch, containing sherds of 14th-century date, ran on a north-south alignment (marking the boundary between what would become pastures IX and X in the early 18th century) directly adjacent to the western edge of the base of Stone 102 of the Southern Inner Circle. Interestingly, when this line was later reinforced through the digging of a more substantial ditch, the latter was dug through the middle of the stone-hole, the stone having fallen to the west sometime subsequent to the digging of the original ditch (Keiller unpublished notebooks – cuttings 32(1) and (2)). In the case of the West Kennet Avenue, a number of linear boundary features were clearly aligned upon standing stones (Keiller and Piggott 1936, 421, fig. 2).

There was also an *ad hoc* carrying away and breaking of stones. Looking to the former, sarsens from the Beckhampton Avenue were used in 1701 to create a bridge over the Winterbourne stream (Burl 1979, 46). In the case of the latter, Aubrey recorded a stone at the start of the West Kennet Avenue falling in 1684 and breaking into two or three pieces (Fowles and Legg 1980, 37; Ucko *et al.* 1991, 101). Stukeley in turn related how an enormous stone flanking the northern entrance fell, broke into two pieces, and was subsequently broken up by the villagers through the use of wooden wedges (Stukeley 1743, 22, 24). That this was an unhurried undertaking is suggested by the comment made by Stukeley in his unpublished tour of Avebury that the Parish Clerk, Reuben Horsell, remembered it standing when he was a boy. As Horsell was recorded by Stukeley in 1724 as having 'known this country 40 or 50 year', was old enough to have fathered a son in 1693, and died on the 15th January 1727/8, this suggests the stone fell sometime in the 1670s (MS Gough Maps 231 f25v; Wiltshire Family History Society 2003). It was not eventually broken up and carried away until after the middle of 1722 as it appears on a prospect of the northern entrance dated to August of that year (Ucko *et al.* 1991, 204, pl. 64). It may have been that the sheer bulk of this stone deterred would-be stone breakers, but given that the far larger Obelisk was comfortably disposed of this seems unlikely. What is clear is that whilst the pieces of stone 47 lay broken on the ground a more urgent and focused period of stone breaking was gathering pace within and around the henge as sarsens were deliberately and systematically destroyed. This was not restricted to recently fallen stones or those lying recumbent; standing stones were pulled down and even stones that had previously been buried were dug up and shattered. It is to this episode of deliberate destruction that we now turn.

Documentary evidence for deliberate stone breaking

The first documentary evidence for the breaking-up of stones refers to the sarsen fields at Fyfield. It takes the form of a diary entry recorded on the 11th of November 1644 by the Royalist soldier Richard Symonds who had just marched to the area with the King's troops:

> 'a place so full of a grey pibble stone of great bignes as is not usually seene; they breake them and build their howses of them and walls, laying mosse betweene, the inhabaitants calling them Saracens' stones, and in this parish, a myle and a halfe in length, they lie so thick as you may goe upon them all the way. They call that place the Grey-weathers, because a far off they looke like a flock of sheepe.' (Symonds 1859, 151)

Further detail of this 'breaking' was provided by John Aubrey some 20 years later when he offered the following concise description of the process involved:

> 'I have verbum Sacerdotis for it, that these mighty stones (as hard as marble) may be broken in what part of them you please; without any great trouble: Sc. Make a fire on that [...] line of the stone where you would have it crack; and after the stone is well heated, draw over a line with cold water, and immediately give a knock with a Smyths sledge, and it will break like the Collets at the Glass house.' (Fowles and Legg 1980, 38)

At this point it is important to stress the difference between the breaking of sarsens generally, and the destruction of the settings that made up the fabric of the Avebury monuments. Whilst the buildings and boundaries that were a continual source of exasperation to Aubrey when he was undertaking his plane table survey may have involved sarsen in their fabric (and this is by no means certain), it is far from clear whether this sarsen had ever formed part of the monument. Likewise, Symond's brief mention was focused upon the natural sarsen trains present on Fyfield Down rather than elements of the monument complex.

In the case of the records of Aubrey, the only direct association between the burning process, house building and the standing stones of Avebury takes the form of a brief note regarding 'the Fractures made in this Antiquity for the building of those houses' and comment that the village houses were 'built with the Frustrum's of the Stones of this Monument', the latter deduction made on the basis that he could find no other immediate source of sarsen around the village (quoted in Ucko *et al.* 1991, 30, 166). Further evidence that Aubrey believed that assaults on the fabric of the monument were taking place comes from Edmund

Gibson's 1695 edition of Camden, which included information taken from Aubrey's unpublished manuscript:

> 'For a village of the same name being built within the circumference of it, and (by the by) out of its stones too.' (Gibson 1695, 111)

That a large number of standing stones had been removed from the monument by the time of his 1663 survey is clear from his surviving plans. What is less clear is whether these 'gaps' were the result of burial as opposed to wholesale destruction (see Chapter 9). It is important to acknowledge that Aubrey did not witness any stone destruction taking place, his proffered description coming second-hand as the qualifier *verbum sacerdotis* – 'on the word of a priest' – suggests. In his *Natural History of Wiltshire* (written between 1656 and 1686) the priest in question is identified as the 'minister of Aubury' [Avebury] (Aubrey 1847, 44), suggesting that Aubrey did at least ask-around.[1] The same could not be said of William Stukeley who appears to have embarked on what we would today recognise as a social-historical study of the processes of stone destruction. Although reliant principally upon interviews and related accounts, these came not solely from clergy or gentlemen, but in instances from the stone-breakers themselves. As well as discussing methods and motivations with those directly involved in the activities, he also appears to have witnessed at least one stone destruction taking place, resulting in a uniquely detailed record of the process (see below). What is more, in the case of Stukeley's records he was explicitly recording the destruction of stone settings rather than natural sarsen spreads.

Stukeley's written record adds weight and detail to the description recounted by Aubrey some 60 or so years earlier. The first stage was to dig a pit along the side of the stone with the aim of removing sufficient supporting earth to cause the stone to fall into the pit. Prior to actual collapse, boulders and large chunks of sarsen were placed in the pit to provide support, creating an airway beneath the bulk of the fallen stone to facilitate burning. Often the sheer bulk of the falling stone was sufficient to cause these supporting stones to break and shatter. In such cases enormous wooden levers were used to raise the stones to enable supports to be placed beneath them. Once supported, loads of straw were placed beneath the stones and fired to heat them up prior to the application of water and then a strike from a sledgehammer (Stukeley 1743, 15–16).

The Stukeley drawings

There appear to be two visual records of stone-breaking to accompany Stukeley's detailed written descriptions of the process. On the basis of archaeological support for some of the minor details present in his depiction, for example the distinctive iron rakes (Smith 1965, 181, fig. 66), the assumption taken here is that the depictions result from first-hand observation.

'An Abury Atto da fe 1724'

Since its first publication by Keiller and Piggott (1936, 419, pl. VI), the most frequently reproduced illustration is a black and white image entitled *'An Abury Atto da fe 1724'* (Bodleian Library MS. Gough Maps 231, fol. 5) (Figure 10.1).

Despite its frequent inclusion in narratives of Avebury, this image has until now escaped critical attention in its own right. This is unfortunate as it contains a wealth of detail about the precise mechanics of stone destruction. The first point of note concerns the scale of the burning pit, which is much larger than the stone held within it and has clearly been carefully dug, having neatly squared sides, a flat base and a ramp to facilitate access for both people and broken stone. Soil from the digging of the pit is heaped carefully to the right hand side and spaced sufficiently far back from the edge of the pit to prevent it collapsing

Figure 10.1. Stukeley's depiction of a stone burning 'An Abury atto da fe May 20 1724' (Bodleian Library MS. Gough Maps 231, fol. 5, reproduced by permission of the Keeper of Special Collections and Western Manuscripts)

back in. A pile of regular sarsen blocks are piled to the left of the pit, presumably broken stone that has been pulled clear of the conflagration. Although it is possible that this pile is of packing stones (particularly given the size of the sarsen being broken) the angularity suggests they have been broken. A few stray angular lumps are also visible around the perimeter of the pit.

The sarsen itself is shown as fissured and cracked, with the edge presented to the viewer broken and angular. Beneath the sarsen are three dark lumps that represent boulders placed beneath the stone to facilitate airflow, alongside tightly bound bales of fuel, most likely straw. What is clear is that the process of heating and breakage is dynamic rather than linear, with chunks of stone being broken off, removed and carefully stacked whilst fresh bales of straw were pushed into the blaze. The result is a gradual and progressive 'breaking-down' requiring constant and close attention. Evidence from the burning pit associated with the destruction of stone L16 of the Longstones Cove, showed how too much sustained heat could seriously weaken the sarsen, in the worst case reducing it to a pile of brightly-coloured sand. While this may have been less of a worry in the case of the extremely hard cortex, the stone-breakers would have wanted to avoid over-heating the freshly exposed faces. As a result we can imagine a continual state of flux with temperatures being gauged, burning straw bales repositioned, water applied, sledge-hammers pounded and chunks raked from the flames and soot.

Resting against the side of the pit are three tapering wooden levers, presumably the 'timbers 20 foot long and more' that Stukeley records as being used by a team of 20 men to lever up the stones to enable the support boulders to be inserted beneath (Stukeley 1743, 16). Other equipment includes twin-pronged rakes, poles, iron sledgehammers and flagons of water for wetting the heated stone, refreshment or both. The rakes are of particular interest as they do not appear to be adapted or co-opted farm-implements, Smith suggesting instead that they had been specifically manufactured by the local blacksmith for the purpose (Smith 1965, 180); a complex practice with its own specialised equipment.

In terms of personnel, a team of five men is depicted with some suggestion of seniority or ranking indicated by the full frock coats and hats worn by three of the breakers as opposed to the simple breech and blouse attire of the remaining figures. The former attire seems unusually 'dressy' for such an undertaking; we will return to the question of whether this depiction is of an everyday act or special performance later in this chapter. We can only assume that a larger workforce was involved in the digging out of the substantial hole.

Watercolour – date and provenance unknown

Reproduced by Burl (2002, pl. 10) this is essentially a mirror-image of what is presumably the same destruction event, as is evident from the number and poses of the figures and configuration of levers and tools.

Whilst the straw bales are more clearly depicted, the perspective has gone awry with respect to the ramp and the flagons relegated to a single vessel just creeping in at the bottom of the frame. Otherwise the careful stacking of spoil on one side and broken stone of the other is repeated along with the smoke and fissuring of the stone.

A poetical assault

The final, and perhaps most unusual piece of documentary evidence was discovered by Alexander Law in the Record Office in Edinburgh and relates to a 1725 commission from the Society of Antiquaries to the Scots poet, Allan Ramsay (Law 1969). Horrified at the stone-breaking being undertaken in Avebury by one Caleb Baily, the Society asked Ramsay to attack him in verse with the aim of shaming him into stopping.[2] The poem seems to have appeared in two versions and their titles are informative, as although taking place less than a year after Stukeley's last visit to Avebury, they imply a wholly new approach to the destruction of stones; the use of gun powder:

> 'The last Speech just before he hanged himself of Caleb Baily, who was Blawn Blind Breaking down with Gun Powder some curious Remains of Celtik Antiquity at Abery to mend a Park dike.'

> 'The Last Lamentation of ane Herostratian before he Hangd himself in a fitt of Horrour and Remorse for demolishing a Pice of curious antiquity to mend his Park wall, in which Barberous action making use of Gun Powder he was blown blind.'

Caleb Baily will be discussed in more detail later in this chapter.

Archaeological evidence for stone destruction

Circumstantial evidence of stone burning can be found in the earliest antiquarian accounts of digging at the site (for a summary of the various antiquarian excavations see Gillings and Pollard 2004). In his 1833 excavation at the Avebury Cove, Mr. Browne of Amesbury noted that 'Before the central one of the three, facing, (like the altar trilithon of Stonehenge) the north east, was placed the stone on which sacrifices were burnt. This I ascertained myself by digging, the place being still apparent where it lay, but now filled up with rubbish' (Long 1858b, 17).

The first excavation to link burnt debris to stone destruction (as opposed to druidical sacrifice) was carried out by A C Smith and William Cunnington between September 29th and October 5th 1865. In an attempt to elucidate the form and nature of the Avebury Cove they dug a series of trenches around the surviving stones. Here they recorded a 'quantity of black charred matter' containing 'numerous large flakes and chips of sarsen, covered with black charred matter and burnt straw, or other material' (Smith 1867, 211). Further excavations around the site of the Obelisk revealed large quantities of the same. Unlike Browne, the excavators directly associated the burning deposits with the stone destruction episodes that had been described by Stukeley (*ibid.*, 211–13). This is best illustrated in the case of the trench sunk into a depression in the surface of the ground where one of the stones of the Northern Inner Circle was conjectured to have stood:

> 'Here too we found a quantity of burnt and blackened chipped sarsens, as also many fragments of old-fashioned flat glass bottles, one nearly entire, of about the date 1700. This latter discovery was by no means remarkable, as an inn formerly occupied the spot where the farm house now stands in the yard adjoining, and jovial spirits may have demolished empty bottles a century and a half ago, as they sometimes do now: or Tom Robinson, so well denounced by Stukeley as the Herostratus of his day, and whose name is not endeared to the Wiltshire archaeologist, may have been a thirsty soul.' (*ibid.*, 212)

The major campaign of excavation undertaken at Avebury by Harold St. George Gray between 1908–1922, focused largely upon the ditch and bank. Only two stone settings were investigated, the area around the prostrate stone 102, and the curious cluster of three buried sarsens to the immediate east of the Cove (coded 'E' by Smith). No stone destruction features were encountered or investigated.

In her excavations at the site of the Sanctuary in 1930, Maud Cunnington encountered direct evidence of stone breaking. During excavation of the settings of the outer ring, she discovered that a number of stone holes had been deliberately enlarged (usually on the outside edge) with the bases covered in a burnt layer containing charred straw. In the fill of these holes and in the soil roundabout were numerous scorched pieces and fired flakes of sarsen. Although the published description is cursory, it seems to describe the practice of digging shallow pits directly adjacent to stones into which the sarsen could be toppled and burnt – it is unfortunate that no detailed record of these excavations remains. Fortunately, the unpublished diaries of the foreman of the Sanctuary excavation, W. E. V. Young, contain further relevant detail. On Tuesday 27th May 1930 Young made the following observations:

> 'Five stone holes of the outer circle were also excavated. These were of course very irregular in shape, the inner sides of the holes showed little disturbance, but the outer sides had been dug away into a sloping ramp, apparently when the stones were felled and carted away. In each of these sloping ramps there was a thick layer of black ash consisting of burnt straw, and a quantity of burnt flakes of sarsen.'

> '[discussing the outer stone circle and disturbances caused by the removal of the stones] The most interesting facts obtained are the methods employed by Green, Griffin and Co: in the destruction of these venerable monuments. In most of the holes one could clearly see how the stone was felled and broken up. Whichever way the stone was thrown a sloping ramp was dug towards the foot of the stone, and on this ramp we found a thick layer of pure black ash, composed mostly of burnt straw, full of burnt sarsen flakes of all shapes and sizes. Some of the chips measured from 6 to 9 inches in length.' (Young Diaries, Devizes Museum)

Of the stones destroyed by burning, Cunnington made explicit reference to settings 1, 2 and 41 (Cunnington 1931, 317, note 1) which, interestingly, appear to have been the only standing stones on the evidence of Stukeley's drawing of the site (made in July 1723). Two things are of interest here. The first is the fact that these are the stones of the circle that abut the West Kennet Avenue. Second is the fact that Stukeley makes no mention of stone *burning* in relation to the Sanctuary, recounting instead how Farmer Green dragged the stones of the Sanctuary away in two bursts of activity during 1724 (1743, 31).

Many more destruction features were encountered between 1934 and 1939 in the campaigns of Alexander Keiller. During his excavation of the West Kennet Avenue, Keiller excavated a total of 16 destruction features, 11 showing evidence of stone breakage through direct fracture and five of burning. The latter were identified on the basis of 'the blackened sides of pits dug beneath the prostrate stones, burnt fragments of sarsen and even piles of charred straw' (Keiller and Piggott 1936, 419). Likewise, in the course of his excavations within the henge at Avebury a total of 31 destruction features were excavated: 18 in the Outer Circle and 13 associated with the settings of the Southern Inner Circle. Of these 28 produced evidence of burning; 16 in the Outer Circle and 12 of the Southern Inner (contra Ucko *et al.* 1991, 181). As with the Sanctuary and West Kennet Avenue examples, the burning pits were found on excavation to contain masses of charred straw, flakes and 'scalings' of burnt sarsen, along with frequent finds of 17th- and 18th-century clay pipe (*ibid.*; Keiller and Piggott 1936, 419). Beyond this, very little information is given. In neither the interim reports (Keiller and Piggott 1936; Keiller 1939) nor the synthetic account of the excavations (Smith 1965) is any detailed discussion given over to the morphology of the destruction features, being content to describe them as 'shallow scoops' (*ibid.* 180). Where they appear in plan, for example with respect to the Obelisk and adjacent settings, they are only illustrated in a schematic form. Indeed the only detailed record presented comprises Smith's (*ibid.*) plates XXVIIb and XXXIVb.

This lack of interest in the 17th and 18th centuries is perhaps understandable given the archaeological standards and priorities of the day and the nature of the final monograph, published long after Keiller's death. However, Keiller's excavation notebooks and report drafts, complemented by a series of surviving plans and sections drawn by Stuart Piggott and Dennis Grant King, reveal not only a keen and active interest in the technologies of stone destruction, but a wealth of unpublished detail regarding the archaeology of these features.

The unpublished Keiller records

> 'These reconstructions of the dimensions of the stones will be found to agree very closely with its representations in Dr. Stukeley's drawings and surveys, and incidentally furnish a strong argument in favour of careful and accurate examination of burning pits, – relatively modern features apt perhaps to be regarded as possessing neither interest nor possible importance.' (Keiller Unpld. NW Sector Draft report, 12)

Two things are remarkable about Keiller's records of the destruction features he encountered during the campaigns of excavation carried out at Avebury. The first is that they were recorded at all. The second is the level of detail that was recorded, in many cases thorough structural accounts supported by meticulously drawn plans and sections.[3]

North-West Quadrant

The first destruction features encountered corresponded to settings 45 and 43, both of which had been standing during the period of Stukeley's visits (Figure 10.2). In the case of setting 43 a burning pit had been dug adjacent to the stone, separated from its base by an undisturbed strip of ground approximately 0.3m wide; left presumably to keep the stone upright and stable while the pit was being dug.

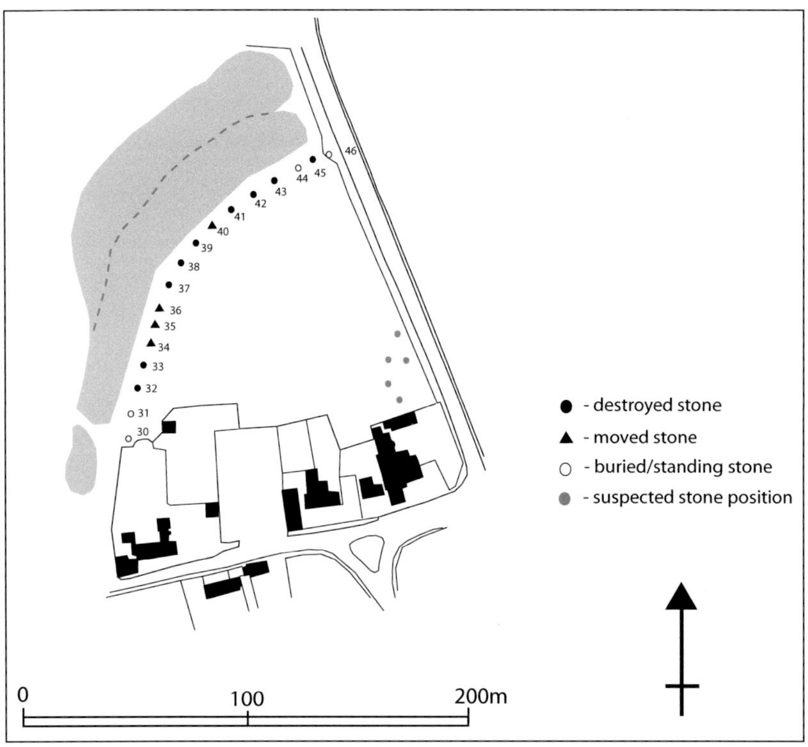

Figure 10.2. Destroyed stones excavated by Keiller in the NW Quadrant at Avebury. Incorporates data © Crown Copyright/database right 2007. An Ordnance Survey/(EDINA) supplied service

The pit extended 3.8m from the stone reaching a maximum depth of 0.88m below the level of the chalk. In digging the pit care had been taken to ensure that it was slightly too short (when measured out from the base) to contain the full length of the stone. Once the pit had been prepared, the next stage was to dig away the strip of ground down to the very base of the stone and then push it over into the pit. As the prostrate stone was too long for its intended receptacle, the uppermost part ended up resting on the furthest edge of the pit ensuring a cavity remained beneath to allow for fuelling and airflow. That heating took place was clear from the large quantities of broken sarsen fragments, ash and clumps of burnt straw found in the pit. This same basic procedure was followed at settings 38 and 39.

In the case of setting 45 an unusual sequence of fills was encountered in the burning pit, suggesting that in this case a different approach had been adopted. The base was covered in a deposit of pure black ash that was sealed in turn by a layer of compacted chalk rubble difficult to distinguish from the natural chalk. Above this rubble layer was the familiar deposit of ash and burnt sarsen fragments, sealed by a final layer of chalk. This implies two distinct episodes of firing, only one of which involved the breaking up of a sarsen stone. As it would have been difficult to have compacted the layer of chalk sealing the primary burning debris had the stone been lying in the pit, the initial fire may have been lit in an attempt to break a standing or leaning stone. When this failed, the base of the pit was consolidated in advance of a second, successful attempt that involved the deliberate toppling of the sarsen. It is unfortunate that the surviving plan and records do little to shed further light on this sequence.

A different technique was employed in the case of stone 37 where rather than dig a distinct burning pit, fuel appears to have been introduced beneath an already fallen stone by digging a series of scrapings and hollows along its length.

Not all stones were broken through heating, with settings 41 and 42 both destroyed by direct fracture. In each case a pit was employed but this seems to have been designed more to break the stone than contain the destruction. As with stone 43, a pit was dug adjacent to the standing stone but short of its full length. The presence of lever marks at the rear of the stone-hole show that it was then deliberately toppled over into the pit, however rather than end up suspended, when the uppermost part came to rest on the pit-edge it caused the back of the stone to break. The upper portion of the stone was then destroyed through direct fracture whilst the remainder was left in the pit where it was subsequently incorporated into a boundary bank. This could be read as a failed example of a burning identical in approach to that of settings 38, 39 and 43, the bottom half of the stone serving to fill the pit and prevent fuel insertion and airflow. However, the stratigraphy places these direct-fracture episodes appreciably earlier in the sequence than the burnings.

The sarsens marking settings 34, 35, 36 and 40 appear to have fallen naturally and rather than broken up, were instead manoeuvred into a line to form part of a field bank that also incorporated the lower portions of stones 41 and 42. The only damage inflicted on them was the chipping away of lumps that protruded from the face of the bank through direct fracture.

South-West Quadrant

Variety and variation were also evident in the SW Quadrant (Figure 10.3). In the case of setting 3 a very neat, rectangular burning pit had been dug adjacent to, but carefully respecting, the base of the standing stone. In contrast, the pit relating to the destruction of

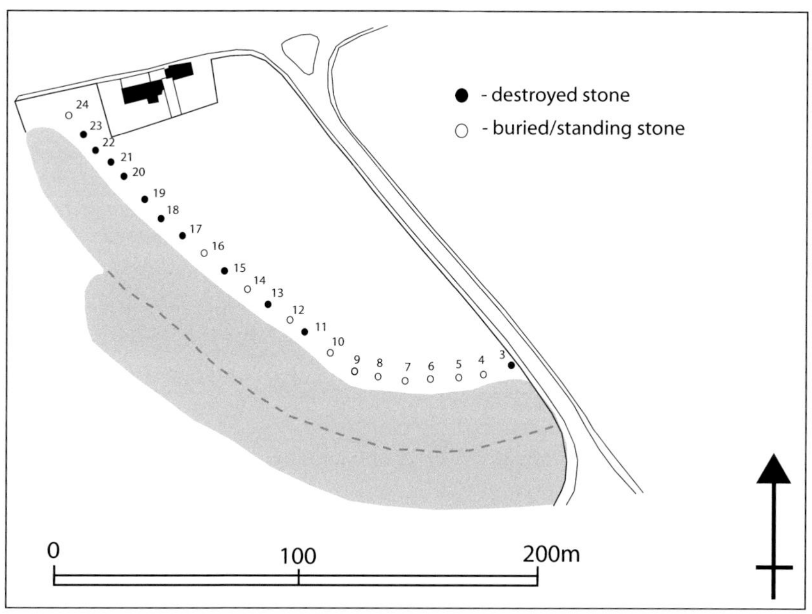

Figure 10.3. Destroyed stones excavated by Keiller in the SW Quadrant at Avebury. Incorporates data © Crown Copyright/database right 2007. An Ordnance Survey/(EDINA) supplied service

setting 11 took the form of a rough, shallow, oval, that had been cut around the base of the stone. At the opposite end of the pit to the stone-hole was a second smaller pit which contained a pile of packing boulders that presumably had been used to support the bulk of the stone after it had been toppled. At setting 15 the sarsen had been burned in a ramped pit similar to those described by Young at the Sanctuary.

In each of these cases, Keiller used the absence of burning debris from the lower stone-hole fills to argue that the stones had fallen prior to burial. However, this is difficult to sustain given the morphology of the pits, in particular the ramp, which seems expressly designed to cope with upright stones. It also fails to acknowledge the possibility of appreciable quantities of debris entering the stone-hole as the stone was toppled but prior to firing taking place. Needless to say there are no surviving section drawings to further elucidate these fill sequences.

More convincing evidence for the destruction of a recumbent stone came from setting. Rather than a discrete pit, a series of tunnels appear to have been dug beneath the fallen stone to permit fuel insertion and airflow, with a series of plinths and ridges left to support its bulk. This appears to have been a much more elaborate, and intensive approach than the simple scooping encountered in the NW Quadrant.

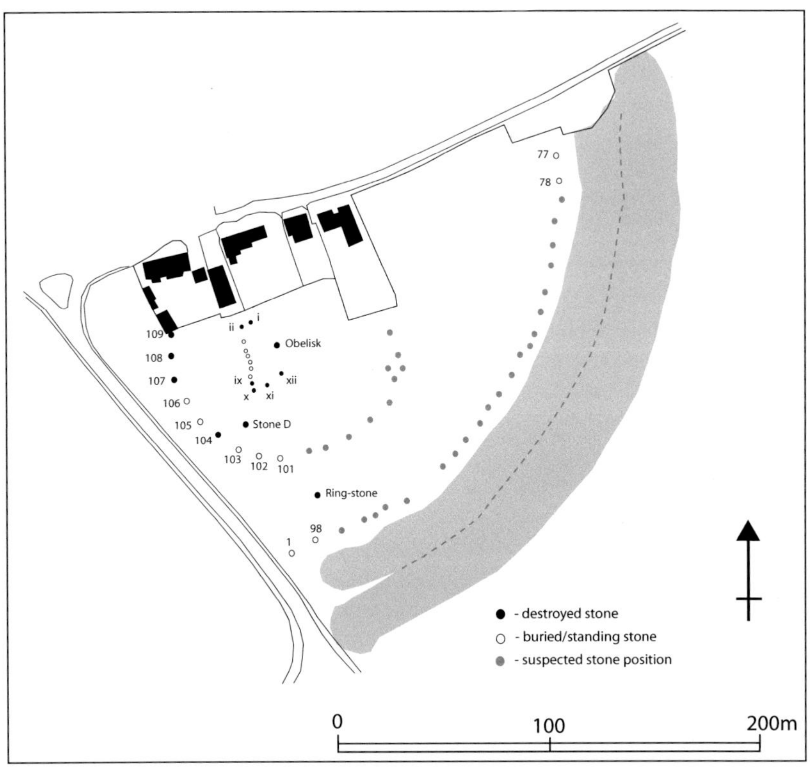

Figure 10.4. Destroyed stones excavated by Keiller in the SE Quadrant at Avebury. Incorporates data © Crown Copyright/database right 2007. An Ordnance Survey/(EDINA) supplied service

The destruction features associated with settings 17 and 18 were particularly unusual. In each case a relatively small but deep pit was dug adjacent to the stone-hole and densely packed with straw. In the case of 18 this had a conical form while for 17 a steep ramp was dug. In each case the pit was filled not only with burning debris but a large quantity of sarsen fragments resulting from direct fracture. Keiller's interpretation in each case was that the small pit size and densely packed body of fuel reflected an attempt to destroy heavily leaning stones; the inefficiency of this procedure evident not only in the stone-breakers resorting to direct fracture to complete the task, but also clumps of straw that had been too tightly packed to burn. The fact that although adjacent, different approaches had been taken to the digging of the burning pits, is strongly suggestive of deliberate experimentation.

Excepting the destruction pit of stone 23, which had been too badly damaged by subsequent garden activities to reliably record, the remaining stones (settings 19–22) had all originally been buried before burning took place. Although the relative depths of the original burial pits differed (ranging from 0.8–1.5m below the level of the turf) the same approach had been followed in each case. This was to firstly dig out the fill of the burial pit, before digging tunnels and cavities under the stone, leaving portions of the burial-pit base intact to support its bulk – an approach similar in many respects to that adopted in the case of the fallen stone 13.

South-East Quadrant

Four of the Southern Inner Circle settings investigated had been destroyed by fire (104,107,108 and 109) (Figure 10.4). Stone settings 104 and 107 had fallen and burning pits created by tunnelling out cavities beneath them. In contrast, very rough irregular pits had been dug to facilitate the burning of settings 108 (around the stone) and 109 (adjacent to it). A more complex sequence of events accompanied the destruction of the Ring-Stone where a very deep burning pit had been dug next to the stone, leaving a ridge of un-dug chalk in place to support it in the manner of settings 43 and 45 of the Outer Circle. Keiller presumed that the depth of the pit reflected the excessive thickness of the stone to be heated. In much the same way as Outer Circle settings 17 and 18, the deep-pit strategy was only partially successful, with a large chunk of the base of the stone left intact and filling the burning pit. A small gully was dug beneath this chunk in a second attempt to break it. That this failed is indicated by the presence of un-burned straw packed within it.

Looking to the internal settings of the Southern Inner Circle, stone *i* was found to have originally been buried before being discovered and burned (Figure 10.5). Surviving stones of this setting and the overall size of the burial pit suggest that this was not a particularly large sarsen. However, to facilitate the burning of this stone the same procedure was adopted as was used on the buried stones 19–22 of the Outer Circle. In practice a cavity, some 0.34m in depth, was dug beneath the stone as it lay in its burial pit, its bulk left supported on intact spurs of chalk. The resultant void was then filled with straw and the stone burned. In direct contrast to this elaborate and carefully choreographed activity, the destruction of stones *ix*, *x* and *xi* appears to have been much more pragmatic. These were burned in a single communal burning pit centred upon stone *x*. It appears that whilst digging the burning pit for stone *x* the burial pit for *ix* was discovered and the stone dug out and thrown into the existing pit. Stone *xi* likewise. In the case of setting *xii*, no burning took place, the stone being broken up *in situ* using direct fracture. This is attested by the complete absence of any burning debris and spread of 87 pieces of fractured sarsen covering an area of 2.4 × 1.5m to the south of the stone-hole. In the case of the central setting of the Southern Inner Circle, the Obelisk, a successive sequence of irregular hollows had been dug out beneath this enormous fallen stone enabling it to be gradually broken up from one end to the other.

As well as the way in which the heating of the stone showed variation there also appears to have been variety in what happened once the shattered sarsen fragments cooled. The pre-

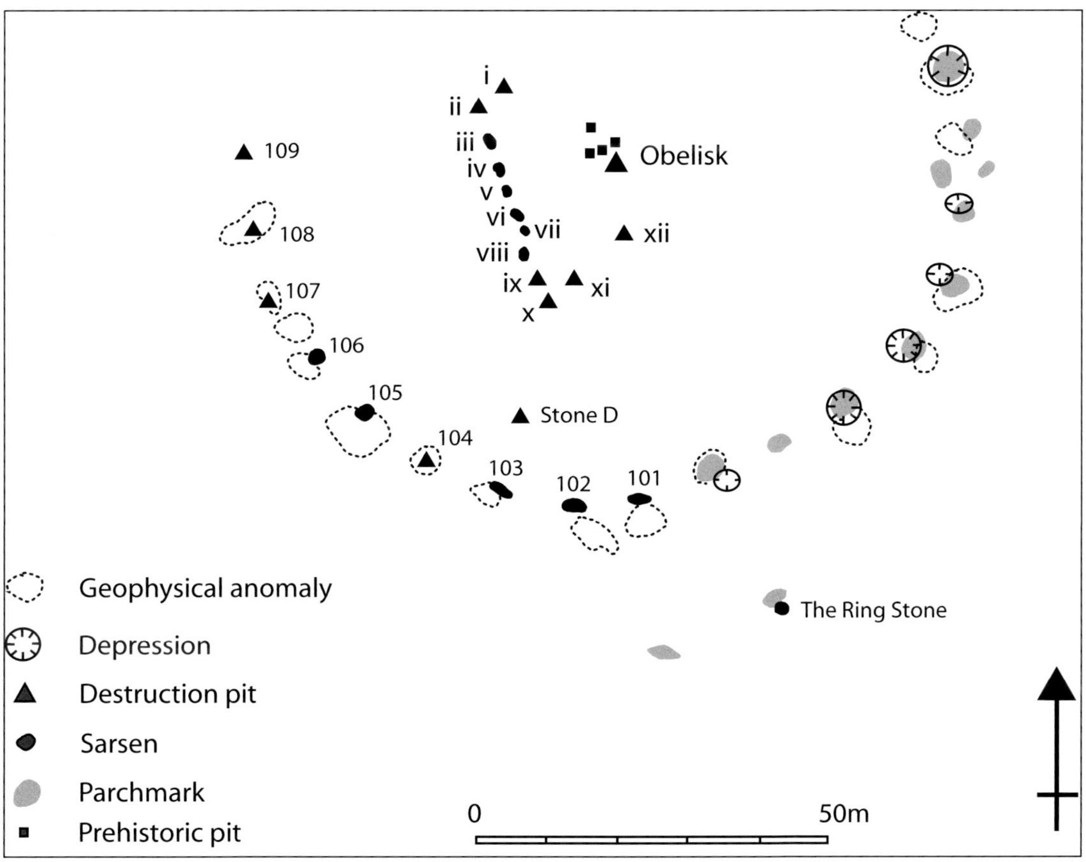

Figure 10.5. Detail of destruction features associated with the Southern Inner Circle at Avebury

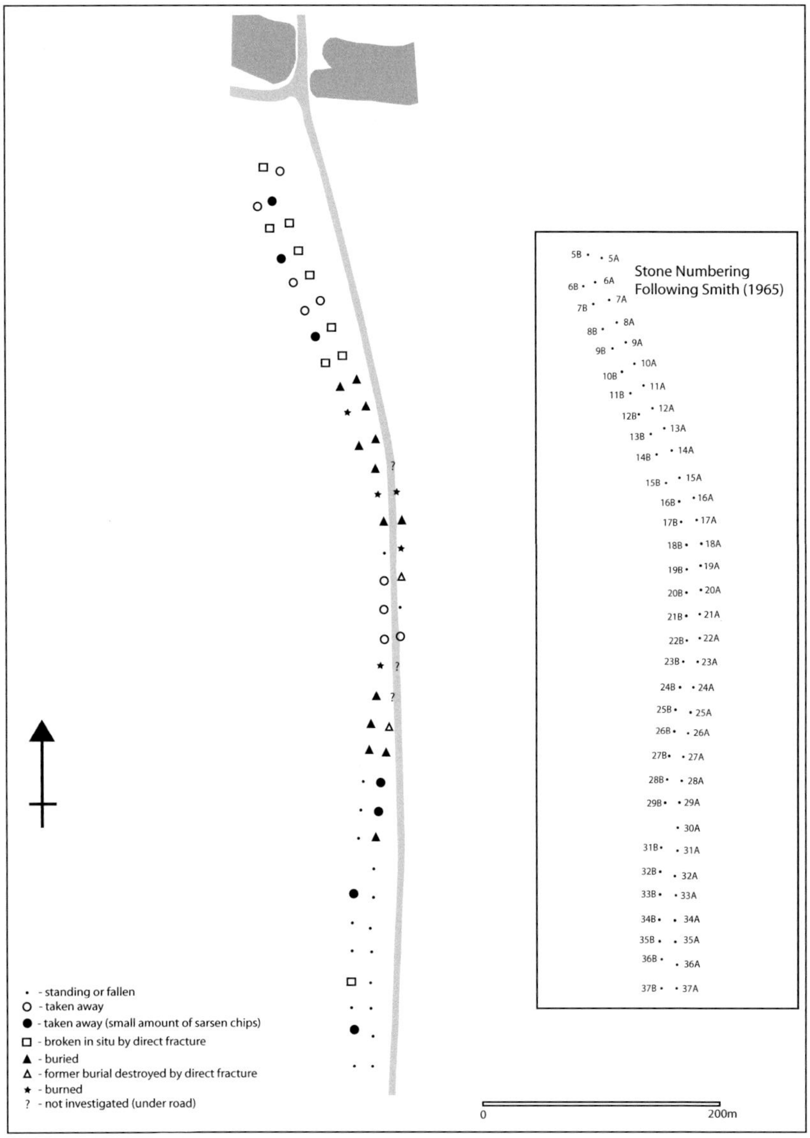

Figure 10.6. Destroyed stones excavated by Keiller on the line of the West Kennet Avenue

sence of sarsen flakes alone in the majority of burning pits excavated by Keiller suggests that the larger pieces of stone were removed and dressed elsewhere. However, in the case of the multiple burning pit of stones *ix*, *x* and *xi*, as well as the familiar burned and blackened flakes of sarsen, a quantity of unburned sarsen fragments were found in and around the burning pit. Keiller argued that these represented the trimming to shape of sarsen blocks on the spot as part of the general destruction process.

The West Kennet Avenue

Of the 66 settings excavated, a total of 32 revealed evidence for some form of destruction or deliberate relocation (Figure 10.6). Stone burning accounted for only five of the avenue settings with a range of strategies adopted. In the case of setting 23B a square pit was dug whilst the stone at 19A was burned by digging out rough scoops beneath it for the insertion of fuel. In each case the stone had previously fallen. With settings 17A and 17B more sustained diggings had been carried out beneath the stones leaving un-dug ridges of chalk to support the weight of the sarsen. More complex was the burning of stone 14B where a pit had been dug and the standing stone deliberately toppled on to it. Silting in the base of the pit suggested that it had been left for some time before the burning had been carried out as further digging beneath the stone was required before fuel could be inserted and lit.

Whereas direct fracture and the wholesale removal of stones appear to have been rare within the henge, on the line of the avenue they were by far the most common technique encountered affecting 27 settings. Three distinct types of feature relating to this process were encountered – empty stone-holes, stone-holes with very small amounts of associated sarsen debris (3.8–5.0kg), and stone-holes accompanied by large amounts of broken and flaked sarsen (between 14.1–209kg). Equating the first and second scenarios with the dragging away of stones to be broken in other locations, Keiller saw the third as reflecting *in situ* destruction of standing, fallen, and in the case of stones 25A and 20A, previously buried sarsens.

Clay pipes from the Keiller excavations

During his excavation of the SW and SE Sectors of Avebury during 1938 and 1939 Keiller discovered a number of clay tobacco pipes. Unusually for the time, and especially since this was ostensibly the excavation of a prehistoric monument, Keiller retained many of these, and 74 pipe fragments (31 from the SW Sector, 43 from the SE) are now held in the collections at the Alexander Keiller Museum, Avebury. No pipes are recorded from the NW Sector, either because they were not retained during that initial season, or because of a genuine absence from this part of the henge interior.

While the medieval pottery from Keiller's excavations has received study and publication (Jope 1999), little attention has been given to the early post-medieval finds, even though these have the potential to shed light on everyday social practices during an important period in Avebury's history. A ubiquitous component of many post-medieval ceramic assemblages, clay tobacco pipes are an important source of evidence, not least because they can be closely dated and are related to a very specific set of practices (principally tobacco consumption). The presence of clay pipe fragments in stone destruction pits along the Beckhampton Avenue suggested that their use and deposition might be closely associated with stone breaking: put simply they are the material culture of tobacco consumption by labourers directly involved in the destruction of megalithic settings. The Avebury pipes were therefore analysed with the following questions in mind:

- are finds of clay pipes related to the activities of stone destruction?
- if so, can they provide detail on the chronology of stone destruction?

The first question might be answered through a consideration of the context, and spatial and chronological distribution of clay pipes. If a demonstrable relationship existed, then the archaeologically-determined chronology of stone breaking could be matched against the documentary record given by Stukeley.

Catalogue

Note that nearly all the pipes comprise complete or substantially complete bowls, with few stem fragments being present within the collection. Stamp numbers refer to those given in D R Atkinson (1965, figs 1 and 2).

SW Quadrant

Cutting I

1. Thomas Hunt (stamp 12/13 on heel), 1660–1680.
2. Thomas Hunt (stamp 55 or similar on stem), 1685–1700.
3. No stamp, spurred bowl, 1690–1720.

Cutting I, burning pits

1–3. Thomas Hunt (stamp 1–4 on heel), 1660–1680.
4. Jeffery Hunt (stamp 24 on heel), 1650–1670.
5–6. John Greenland (stamp 71 on stem), 1690–1720.

Cutting IV, layer 1

1. Bowl with worn and undecipherable stamp, 1660–1680.
2. Heel fragment only, Thomas Hunt (stamp 1–4), 1660–1680.
3. Stem marked Thomas Hunt (stamp 45 on stem), 1685–1710.
4. Thomas Hunt (stamp 43–65 on stem), 1685–1710.
5. Richard Greenland (stamp 17 on heel), 1660–1680.
6. No stamp, spurred bowl, 1690–1720.
7. Spurred bowl, stamped JOHN—— on stem, possibly John Greenland, 1690–1720.
8. Spurred bowl, faint heart-shaped stamp on stem, 1690–1720
9. 19th century bowl with moulded decoration.

Cutting V

1–3. No stamp, spurred, elongated bowl, 1690–1720.
4. Stamped JOHN/-LEF (probably John Clefard) on heel, 1660–1690.
5. Thomas Hunt (stamp 10/11 on heel), 1660–1680.
6. Stem marked Thomas Hunt (stamp 45), 1685–1710.

'1938'

1. Early bowl, *c.*1620, with rouletting around lip.
2. Thomas Hunt (stamp 1–4 on heel), 1660–1680.
3–5. Richard Greenland (stamp 17 on heel), 1660–1680.
6. John Greenland (stamp 71–72 on stem), 1680–1710.
7. Ed Mills (stamp 89 on stem), 1680–1710.

SE Quadrant

Cutting 12(2)

1. Thomas Hunt (stamp 13 on heel), 1660–1680.

Cutting 41(1), burning pit, Stone 104

1–2. Unmarked bowls, 1660–1680.
3. Unmarked bowl, 1680–1700.
4. Thomas Hunt (stamp 44 on stem), 1685–1710.

Cutting 42(2)

1. No stamp, spurred bowl, 1680–1700.

Cutting 43(2)

1. No stamp, spurred elongated bowl, 1690–1720.

Cutting 53(3), layer 1

1–2. Thomas Hunt (stamp 13 on heel), 1660–1680.

Cutting 71 and 71b, layer 1

1. Thomas Hunt (stamp 13 on heel), 1660–1680.
2. Richard Greenland (stamp 17 on heel), 1660–1680.

'SE Sector'

1–17. Thomas Hunt (stamp 13 on heel), 1660–1680.
18–20. Thomas Hunt (stamp 1–4 on heel), 1660–1680.
21. Thomas Hunt (stamp 7 on heel), 1660–1680.
22. Thomas Hunt (stamp 11 on heel), 1660–1680.
23–24. Thomas Hunt (stamp 43–65 on stem), 1685–1710.
25. Bowl with unrecorded moulded 'HUNT' mark on side of body, 1660–1680
26–29. Richard Greenland (stamp 17 on heel), 1660–1680.
30. Thomas Widdos (stamp 73–74 on stem), 1710–1730.
31–32. No stamp, spurred bowls, 1680–1720.

Discussion

Nearly all the pipes with maker's marks come from Marlborough manufacturers (D R Atkinson 1965), especially the workshops of Thomas Hunt (active from 1667–1696; *ibid.*) and Richard Greenland. These are good quality pipes, well finished and usually clearly marked, perhaps as a sign of manufacturing pride. With very few exceptions, they were manufactured in the period 1660–1710, most perhaps belonging to the middle of that period. Unless a product of selective recovery, chronologically this is a very homogenous assemblage. That fragments of stem are absent in the collection demonstrates that Keiller was selective, to a degree, in his recovery. However, there is no reason to believe that he preferentially retained bowls of the late 17th and early 18th centuries, suggesting that the predominance of these is a true reflection of their presence during a particular phase.

There is the question of whether the clay pipe fragments have a direct relationship to the episodes of stone breaking. This seems quite likely for a number of reasons. First, the bulk of the pipes belong to a limited chronological horizon that corresponds closely with the known period of stone breaking (*i.e.* the later 17th and early decades of the 18th century). Second, several bowls are recorded as coming from stone burning pits in both the SW and SE sectors. Third, there exists in some instances a close relationship between the distribution of pipes and that of burning pits. For example, in the SE sector those pipes for which we have some form of context come from areas around destroyed stones: Cutting 12 relates to the position of the destroyed Ring-Stone, Cuttings 41 and 42 destroyed stones 104 and D; Cutting 53 close to the Obelisk; and Cuttings 71 and 71b destroyed stones 108 and 109. Few if any pipes appear to have been recovered from around the positions of standing or buried stones. The pattern is less convincing in the SW sector, where pipes are recorded exclusively from Cuttings I, IV and V. These correspond to the southern part of the Quadrant (stones 3–9), where only one stone had been destroyed through fire-setting (stone 3). No pipes are recorded from Cuttings VI–XVI where stone-breaking was concentrated.

There is a suggestion then that deposition of broken pipes took place within and around stone burning pits. Whether the pipes were used by stone breakers themselves and relate to specific destruction events is more difficult to determine. Many could be discards from nearby houses, deposited in hollows left by stone breaking; here the hollows becoming convenient receptacles for domestic rubbish. Nonetheless, stone breaking would have provided a ready context for pipe smoking, being a drawn out process that offered periods of waiting while the fire was building up. It was also a social event inasmuch as several individuals were involved, and the fires themselves provided a ready source of ignition for lighting tobacco. The homogenous collection of Thomas Hunt pipes from the SE sector is interesting in this respect; since they look like a batch of pipes bought in, used and deposited in a single event.

In terms of information that they might provide on the chronology of stone breaking, the later 17th- and earliest 18th-century date of most of the pipes corresponds to the historically documented phase of destruction recorded by Stukeley. However, Stukeley's dates for individual destruction events given in his frontispiece to *Abury* (Stukeley 1743) generally span the period 1700–1720. The artefactual evidence hints at earlier beginnings, perhaps in the 1660s–1680s. There is even some discrepancy between the two sources, seen in Stukeley's note that stones 18–21 of the Outer Circle were 'Taken away A° 1720', a date that is three decades or so later than many of the pipes from this area. The implications of this will be developed later in this chapter.

After Keiller

Following the excavations of Keiller, there were only sporadic archaeological encounters with stone destruction features until the present programme of survey and excavation. In 1942 and 1950 Young observed burning pits along the line of the West Kennet Avenue in trenches cut for water and oil pipes respectively. This was followed in 1957 by the excavation of burning pits associated with stones 72a and 72b and in 1958 and 1960 those relating to the destruction of 75b, 76b and 78b (Smith 1965, 207–8).

Stone destruction at Millbarrow

A group of features interpreted as stone burning pits were encountered during the 1989 excavation of the chambered long barrow of Millbarrow, located some 2.5km to the NNE of Avebury. In the area of the sarsen chamber, a stone-hole (F.442) was cut by a steep-sided pit with a scalloped base that contained charcoal and fragments of burnt sarsen (F.431). To the north of the chamber, in the vicinity of a possible façade, were two further features that were interpreted as destruction features. F.464 was a deep, sharply defined pit containing a thin layer of charcoal and some small fragments of sarsen. In contrast, F.406 was shallow with sloping sides and appeared to contain a succession of layers of burnt sarsen fragments and charcoal sealed by deposits of brown soil (Whittle 1994, 19–21).

Excavations on the Beckhampton Avenue 1999–2003

The excavations carried out by the current project on the line of the Beckhampton Avenue revealed a total of nine stone destruction features, six associated with the line of the Avenue itself and three with the settings of the Longstones Cove (Figure 2.36).

Setting L1 (F.21)

This was a roughly oval pit [403], 3.94 × 3.16m, up to 0.38m deep (Figures 10.7 and 10.8). The edges were very irregular, crudely and expediently cut, the sides shallow to moderate, merging with an uneven base. In places, the profile was slightly stepped, particularly on the south-east. A thin deposit of yellowish silty clay [406] on the base of the pit was interpreted as marking an area of *in situ* burning. Sealing this, the primary fill consisted of an extensive deposit of burnt sarsen fragments within a thin layer of fine charcoal or carbonised straw [402]. This deposit was largely confined to an oval spread *c.*2.0 × 2.2m, off-set to the north, and occasionally overlying a thin deposit of ploughsoil identical to the overlying layer [400]. A total of 106.5kg of small to medium-sized (0.02–0.30m) sarsen fragments and flakes were recovered, some displaying signs of burning. Clear patches of carbonised straw and charcoal were visible beneath the stones, their absence or lack of definition from some of the intervening spaces around the sarsen fragments suggesting differential exposure to weathering. Above the burning deposits was a compact brown clay loam ploughsoil [400] with occasional burnt sarsen and chalk pieces. Finds from this deposit were limited to two small pieces of brick and a fragment of clay pipe. Despite the full excavation of pit F.21, no evidence of the original stone-hole was located which is curious. It may be that the act of digging the burning pit and toppling the stone served to remove all traces. However, the particularly dry conditions that attended the excavation during the summer of 1999 made the recognition of negative features extremely difficult against the background of Coombe rock. As a result it has not been possible to determine the relationship between the burning pit and the original standing position of the stone.

Setting L3 (F.23)

As discussed in Chapter 9, the morphology of the feature is strongly suggestive of a stone burial pit (Figure 9.7) with the distinctive slump deposit sealing the base of the feature indicating that the buried sarsen had at a subsequent date been pulled from the hole. This is supported by the large number of iron nails recovered from the pit fills, presumably derived from the wooden frameworks and levers employed to haul the stone from its resting place. Along with the nails, fragments of clay pipe, pieces of iron fitting and a small amount of animal bone were recovered from the upper and lower pit fills along with sherds of medieval and post-medieval pottery. The latter was dominated by material dating from the 16th–19th century, including blue-transfer and brown-painted wares from the upper fill that date to as late as 1780–1820 AD. Only a single sherd of medieval pottery was recovered (a sherd of East-Wiltshire coarseware 12th – 14th century AD) which *may* relate to the original burial of the sarsen, but is most likely residual. No stone-hole was identified though the incomplete excavation of this feature (comprising two quadrants) precluded more detailed investigation.

Setting L4 (F.24)

F.24 was similar in character to F.21, being a shallow sub-oval pit [410], 5.40 × 4.00m, up to 0.33m deep (Figures 10.7 and 10.9). The sides

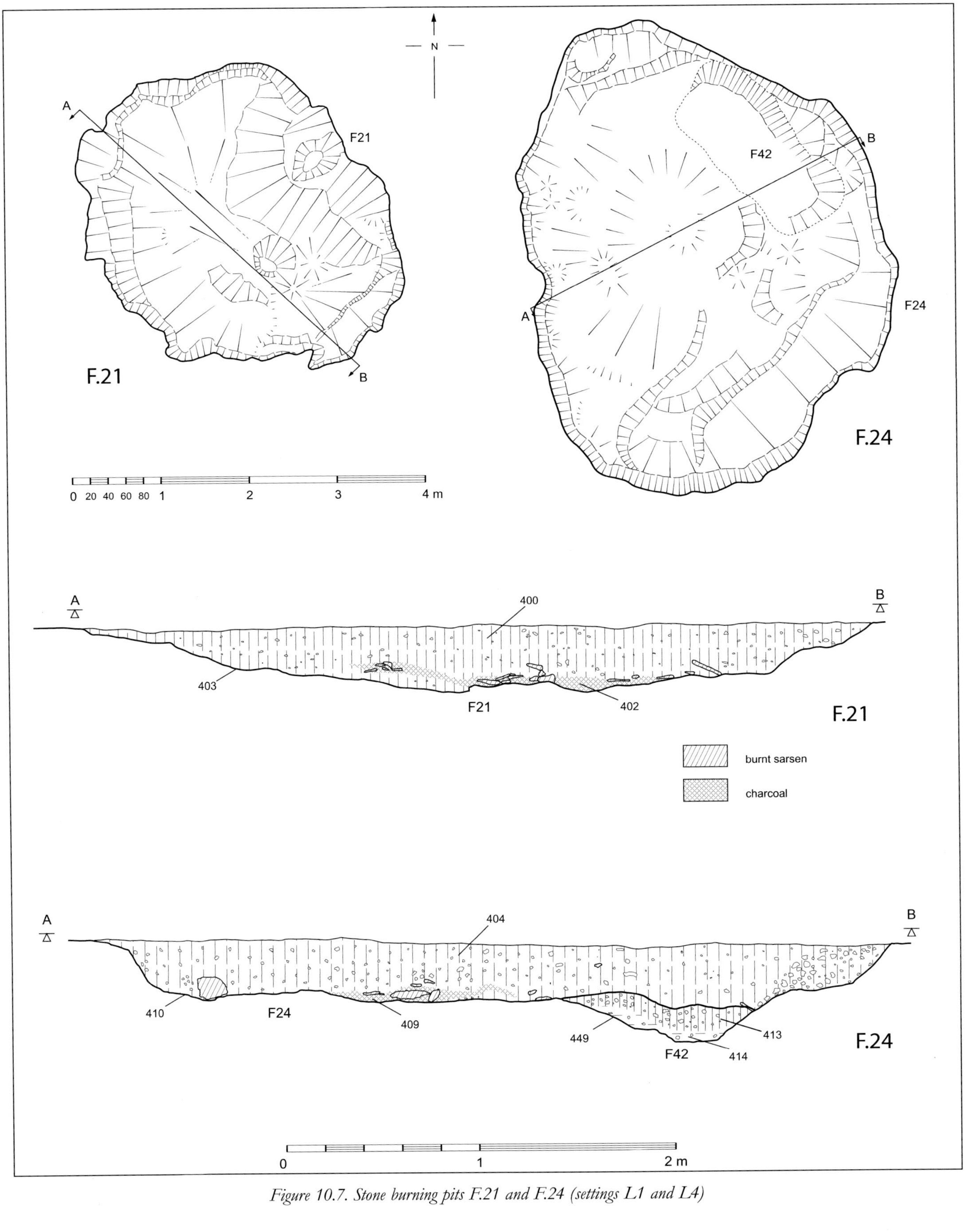

Figure 10.7. Stone burning pits F.21 and F.24 (settings L1 and L4)

were shallow to moderate, stepped merging with an uneven base. Whilst the edges of the feature were more regular than those of F.21, the base was equally irregular, being stepped and pitted in places with up-standing bosses of un-dug chalk. The pit had cut through the original stone-hole F.42. A thin lens of dark brown clay loam [415] occurred on the base of the pit towards its centre. This may represent a soil washed into the pit soon after it was dug. Over this lay extensive burning deposits [409], composed of burnt sarsen and charcoal or carbonised straw. These covered an area of 3.6 × 2.8m within the centre of the pit, from which came 136.5kg of small to medium-sized (0.02–0.30m) sarsen fragments and flakes. On the north-west side of the feature a chalk spread mixed with a light brown clay loam [408] sealed [409]. This in turn was overlain by [404], a compact brown clay loam ploughsoil, becoming much more chalky towards the base and sides. Flecks of charcoal and small pieces of burnt sarsen occurred in the base of [404], along with sherds of medieval (East-Wiltshire coarse and finewares) and post-medieval (Verwood-type ware, 16th–19th century AD) pottery. A stamped fragment of clay pipe stem was also recovered. As in the case of F23, the medieval pottery is most likely residual. In contrast to setting L1, the truncated base of the original stone-hole (F.42) was visible in the base of the burning pit towards its eastern edge.

Setting L7 (F.61)

Following removal of the topsoil this feature was visible as a distinct, almost circular (1.7m NS by 2.0m EW) area of heavily compacted, pale brown chalky silt [600] corresponding to a stone destruction pit (Figure 10.10).

The pit itself was shallow, sub-circular in shape (1.8 × 1.4m) and with a slightly dished profile sloping in towards the centre. Reaching a maximum depth of 0.2m, the surface of the cut was very soft, with a greasy texture and patches of yellow discolouration of the chalk [603]. This heat degradation of the base of the cut extended for a depth of some 0.07m into the natural. Directly sealing the cut was a thin layer of very loose burning debris [602], comprising abundant sooting and frequent inclusions of burnt sarsen. This layer varied in thickness from 0.01–0.10m and contained a fragment of stamped clay pipe stem. The final fill comprised the natural weathering deposit of ploughsoil visible upon removal of the topsoil [600]. Located directly adjacent to F.61 and, at least at this depth not cut into by the destruction pit, was the original stone-hole.

Setting L8 (F.62)

As with L7, the destruction pit was first revealed as a distinct area of mixed brown chalk-silt soil [610], containing occasional small fragments of burnt sarsen and flecks of sooting (Figures 9.11 and 10.11).

The cut of the destruction pit [636] was sub-rectangular in shape (3.7 × 3.0m) and appeared to define two distinct zones. The northern third of the pit was characterised by a platform, sloping gently down from north (depth 0.1m) to south (depth 0.2m). The cut then stepped down a further 0.1–0.2m to define a sub-rectangular zone with a slightly dished

Figure 10.8. (top) F.21 towards the end of excavation, showing basal spread of sarsen debris in partially excavated quadrants

Figure 10.9. (bottom) F.24 on completion of excavation. On the left is stone-hole F.42, cut through by the burning pit

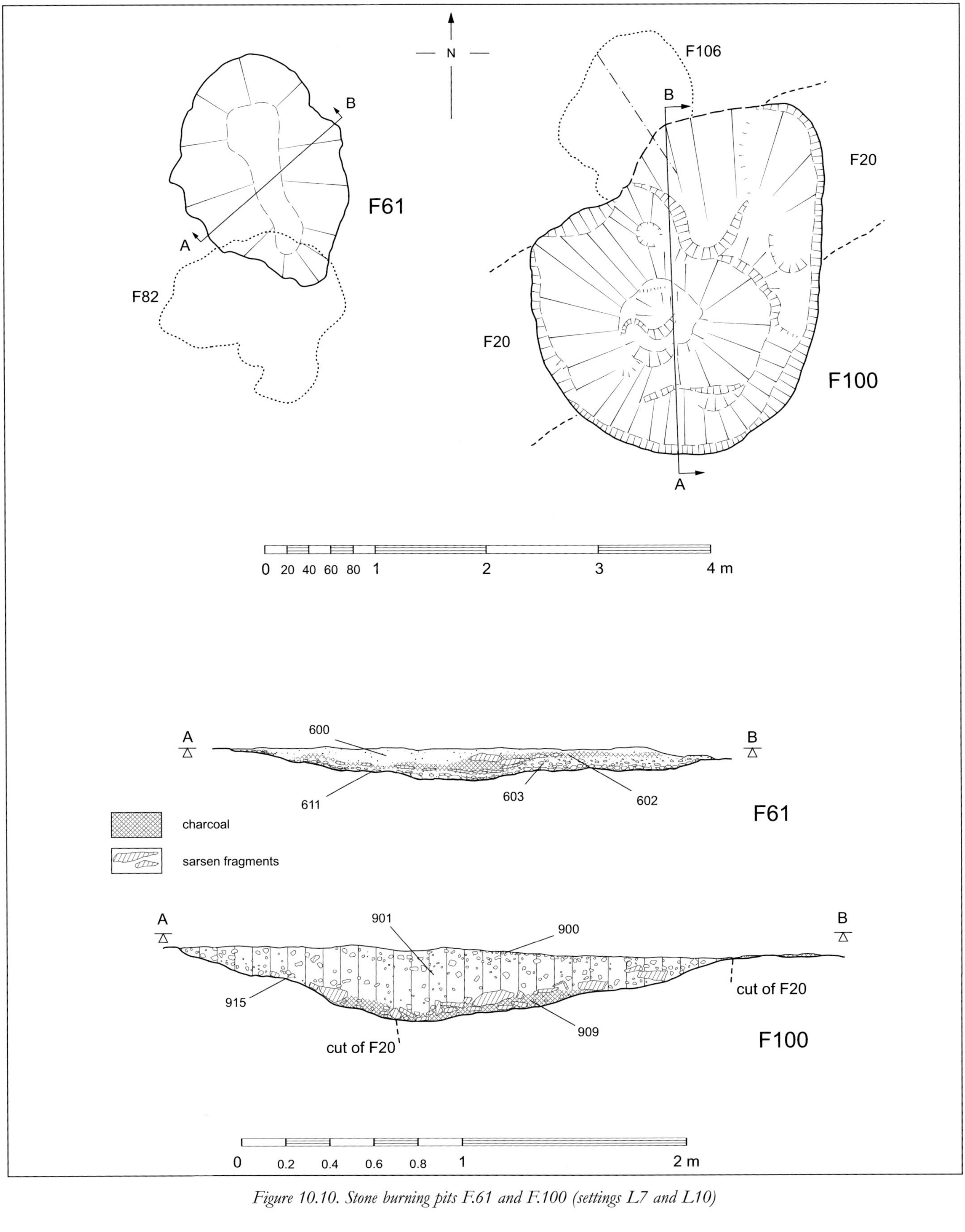

Figure 10.10. Stone burning pits F.61 and F.100 (settings L7 and L10)

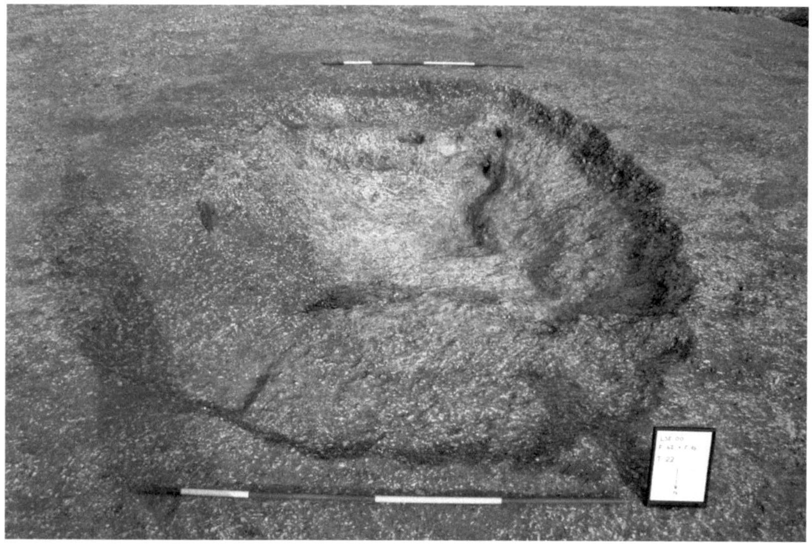

Figure 10.11. (top) Burial and burning pit F.62 on completion of excavation

Figure 10.12. (bottom) Stone burning pit F.100 under excavation, with basal spread of sarsen debris in situ. *The remaining stone of the Longstones Cove, 'Adam', in the background*

base to the south. The result is a distinctive stepped profile to the feature. Sealing the cut in the deeper southern area was a very thick, dense, layer of burnt vegetable matter, sooting and burnt sarsen [634].

The bulk of the burning debris was confined to the deeper southern section of the pit, though it did not completely fill the area, projecting a maximum of 2.0m from the southern edge of the cut. This left a clear gap of variable thickness between the step in the base of the cut and the mass of burning debris. Where evidence of burning debris was found in this gap it was as a thin, intermittent spread. Filling this gap between the thick zone of burning debris and the step in the base of the pit was a compacted block of re-deposited chalk [614]. This deposit directly overlay the cut and the thin, intermittent lenses of burning debris.

Overlying these deposits were two layers corresponding to the gradual, natural infilling of the pit. Sealing the burning deposit and redeposited chalk in the southern portion, and directly overlaying the gently sloping area to the north was a mixed silty brown layer. This comprised a weathered mix of chalk upcast, destruction debris and upper ploughsoil [612]. Two sherds of Roman coarse pottery were recovered from this deposit. This was in turn sealed by a relatively shallow upper fill of mixed, brown, chalky-silt with occasional fragments of burnt sarsen and areas of sooting [610].

In the area of the stone-hole (F.96) a number of small features were encountered that may be associated with the destruction episode. After removal of the burning debris [634] at the southern end of the destruction pit a large unburned sarsen stone was found resting upon an area of compacted natural [875]. This compacted area formed a distinct step directly adjacent to the rear of the destruction pit, with a gently rounded top. Cut almost horizontally into this step was a series of four, small, sub-circular features resembling truncated stake-holes. Two were located directly adjacent to one another cut into the rounded top of the chalk step (diameter 0.07m and 0.12m, depth 0.08m and 0.15m respectively). The remaining features comprised a further two hollows (diameter 0.08m and 0.1m, depth 0.11m and 0.12m respectively) aligned with the initial pair but this time placed vertically above one another and cut more into the face of the step. The regular linear placement, angularity and compaction of the chalk into which they are cut argues against animal disturbance and their orientation, lying almost horizontal rather than vertically, would rule out friction stakes associated with stone erection. It is also difficult to determine with any certainty whether the worked area of natural (forming the rounded step into which these features were cut) represents a component of the Neolithic stone-hole or excavations related to the subsequent toppling and destruction of the stone.

Setting L10 (F.100)

The southernmost of the avenue settings before the termination at the Longstones Cove, setting L10 was marked by a destruction pit (F.100) cutting into both the chalk natural and the upper fills of the late Neolithic enclosure ditch (F.20)

(Figures 10.10 and 10.12). Sub-oval, the cut [915] was 3.0 × 2.6m across, and up to 0.35m deep, regular in plan on the east, south and west, but 'scalloped' on the north up against the stone-hole. The latter might reflect working against a fallen stone. The sides on the east, south and west were very steep in their upper profile, then forming a shallow slope into an undulating base. A much shallower and more irregular profile existed on the north, and from this side a spur of un-dug chalk (in fact ditch fill) projected *c.*1.0m into the pit. This can be read in two ways. If the stone was standing it may reflect a deliberate attempt to not undermine or prematurely destabilise the sarsen prior to its controlled toppling, so leaving a 'platform' of un-dug material. If instead the stone was already recumbent, the irregularity of this side of the pit may reflect a partial undercutting of the fallen stone in order to facilitate the flow of fire and air under the megalith during fire-setting.

The earliest component of fill was a localised patch (*c.*0.4 × 0.2m) of compact olive-brown clay with numerous chalk pieces [914], situated on the south-eastern edge of the pit. Up to 0.05m deep, this filled a slight hollow in the base and edge of the cut. It is just possible that this represents the highly truncated base of an earlier feature. Extending from the western edge into the centre of the pit, and covering an area of 2.2 × 1.8m, was the burning deposit [909]. This comprised a very friable dark brown sandy loam with abundant angular sarsen flakes and fragments. Much of the debris was of spalls and smaller flakes, perhaps from dressing the stone, rather than larger irregular lumps which must have been removed. As such, the deposit was probably raked and sorted. Occasional 'mats' of carbonised straw occurred under some of the sarsen flakes. On the western side the deposit of sarsen flakes was densest and frequently sitting on a thin lens of carbonised straw. The interface between [909] and the base of the pit was not always clear, with some fragments of sarsen being 'pushed' or trampled into the natural and underlying ditch fill. Sealing much of the burning deposit was a compact pale grey-brown clay loam ploughsoil [901] with frequent small chalk pieces. Occasional fragments of sarsen and animal bone occurred within this. A thin lens of very chalky pale grey-brown silty clay [900] lay above [901], just to the north of the centre of the feature.

Cove setting L11 (F.52)

The episode of stone destruction was represented by an oval or circular pit, F.52 [804], of which only the western half was exposed and excavated. The pit was 5.4 × >2.5m in extent and up to 0.95m deep, regular in plan except on the south where the pit edge jutted-out to form a small sub-rectangular extension (Figures 10.13 and 10.14). Along its western edge the pit cut into stone-hole F.81. The pit sides were steep to vertical in the upper profile, becoming moderate to shallow and merging with an undulating base. On the south, coincident with the extension to the pit edge, there was a shallow sub-rectangular depression (*c.* >0.5 × >0.3m and 0.15m deep) set slightly back from the sides. Filled with layers of chalky dark grey-brown loam [855], [856], this could represent an earlier feature cut through by the pit; it is from this area that an iron spearhead and fragments of scale armour were recovered (see Chapter 7).

The fill sequence begins with a localised spread of stone destruction debris [822] roughly contained within the centre of the pit. Comprising a very dark grey-brown to black friable loam with much charcoal/burnt straw and sarsen fragments, this overlay an area of intense scorching on the pit base adjacent to the stone-hole. In places the sarsen fragments were reddened by heat and had even been reduced to a coarse sand; whilst to the north the burning debris included a dense fibrous mat of carbonised straw. This was followed by the deposition of a layer of brown clay loam containing chalk and sarsen fragments [820], distributed in a metre-wide band around the western and southern edges of the pit. Against the north-west edge was a lens of chalky mixed brown silty clay [853]. Overlying these was a pale olive-brown loam [851], fairly clean, containing only a little chalk, charcoal and fragmentary sarsen, perhaps representing a deposit of ploughsoil. In turn, this was sealed by a spread of sarsen destruction debris and orange-brown silty loam [844], 1.6m across and sited within the centre of pit. A large unburned sarsen boulder (probably a packing stone derived from the disturbance of F.81) lay within the middle of this. Finally, the upper pit fill was of layers of brown clay loam [821] and [805], the former containing a moderate quantity of chalk rubble probably derived from spoil generated in digging the pit.

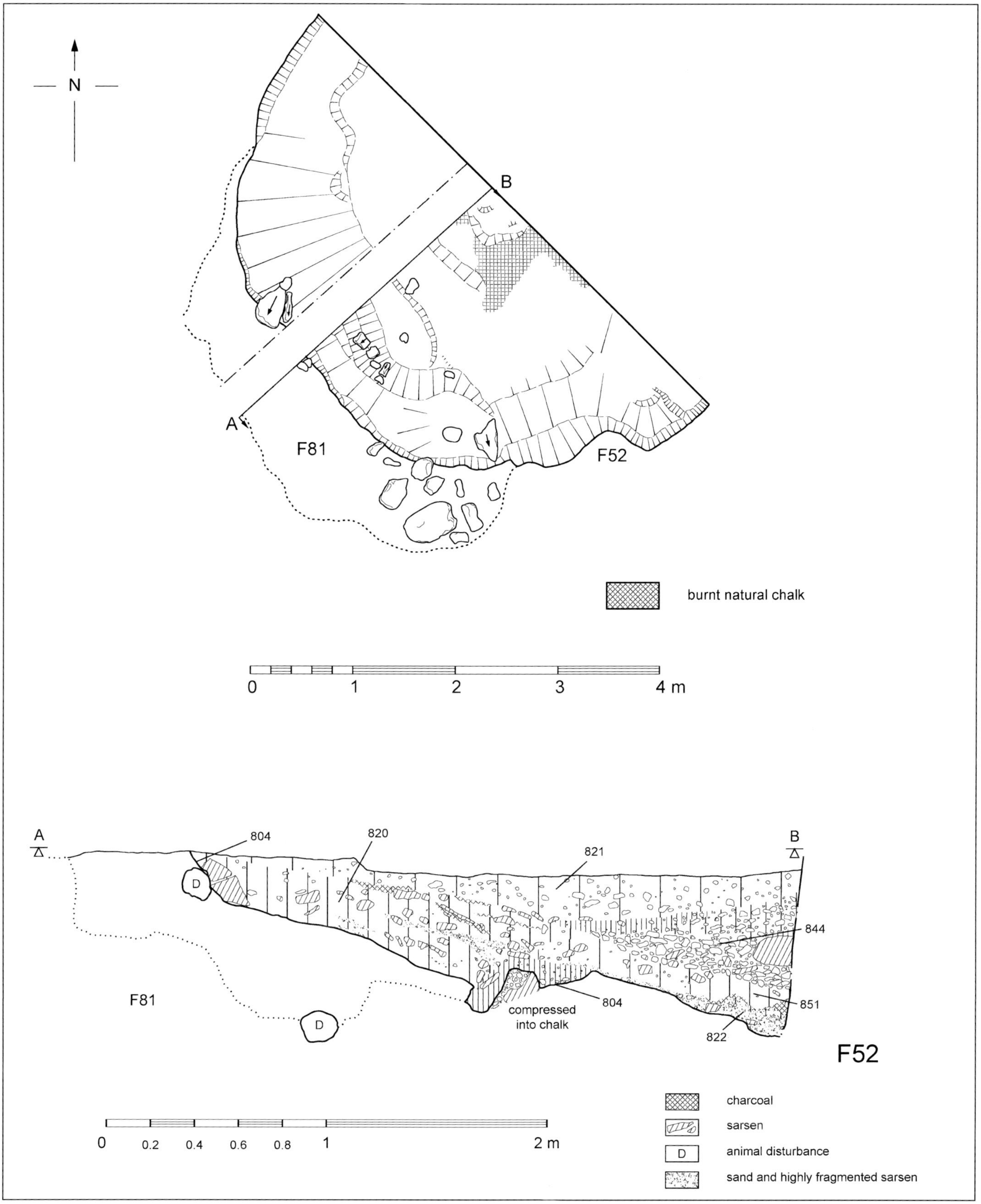

Figure 10.13. Stone burning pit F.52 (setting L16)

Cove Setting L15 (F.71)

The most substantial and unusual of all the destruction features, F.71 comprised a multi-lobate pit [803] with maximum dimensions of 6.4m NE–SW and *c.*6.5m NW-SE (Figures 2.67 and 10.15). Much of the southern half of the feature lay outside the excavated area. It was formed by an interconnecting arrangement of three deep sub-rectangular pits on the north-west, north-east and south-west, linked by a shallower central section. Each pit was in the order of 2.5–3.0m across, varying in depth from 1.0m on the north-west, to 1.8m on the south-west, and 2.1m on the north-east. The north-eastern pit had been taken down to a point below the base of stone-hole F.50 eradicating much of that feature.

The feature was regularly dug, with straight sides to the north-west and north-east pits, but slightly bowed on the south-west (and here the lower profile of the pit extends in a shallow bay out to the north). In the top 0.5m of the profile the sides sloped moderately, in many places cutting through the fill of the weathering hollow F.72. The sides then became very steep to vertical, terminating in a well defined junction with the base. The exception was on the west side, between the north-west and south-west pits, where a gently sloping shelf up to 0.7m wide, low down in the profile, ran for a distance of *c.*2.4m. This may have been constructed to ease access into the pit. The base, though tiered due to the differential depth of the individual pits, was in each section flat (Figure 10.16).

The pit stratigraphy displayed a very clear sequence of fills, beginning in the north-east

Figure 10.14. (top) Burning pit F.52 on completion of excavation (against far section), with associated stone-hole F.81 in the foreground

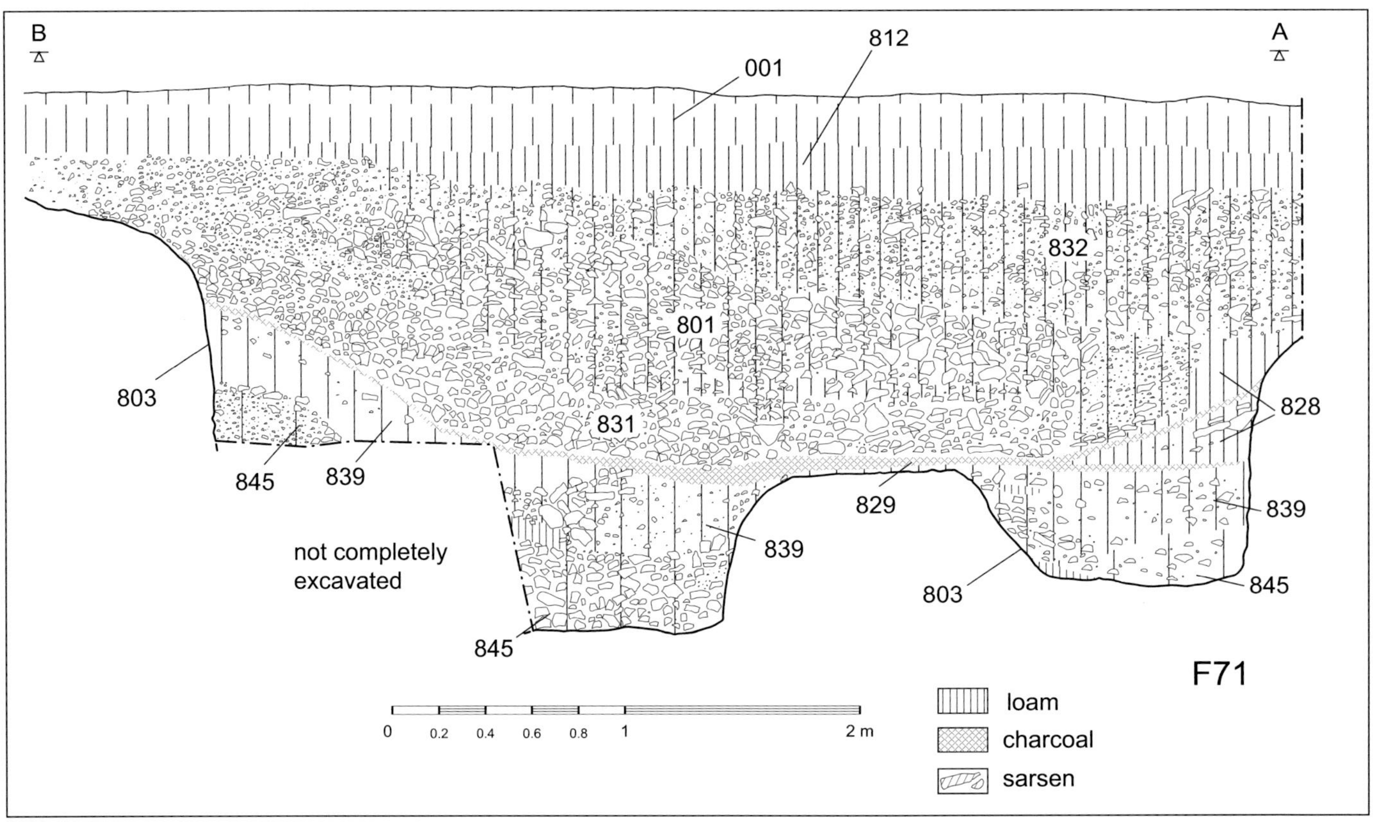

Figure 10.15. (bottom) Section of the massive 'furnace' burning pit F.71 (setting L15). For section location see Figure 2.67

and south-west pits with a layer of fairly pure loose angular chalk rubble [845], tipped from the outer sides, mixed with a pale grey-brown silty clay. Occasional lenses of silt ran within this. The chalk rubble was not a weathering deposit resulting from erosion of the chalk sides, as with most 'primary fills', but represented deliberate backfill. Above this were layers of pure brown clay loam with rare chalk pieces [839] and a brown clay loam with some small chalk and sarsen fragments [838]. Again coming in from the sides, these layers thinned-out towards the centre and were essentially restricted to the deeper north-east and south-west pits. Contexts [845], [839] and [838] are here interpreted as dumped deposits used to level the deeper sections of the destruction pit in order to create a level surface upon which the fire-setting could take place. Overlying these, and the base of the central and northern sections of the pit, ran a thin (up to 0.1m thick) but continuous burning deposit [829], corresponding to the actual stone destruction event. Thicker to the centre and thinning to the edges, this bifurcated on the west side sandwiching a thin lens of [828]. Staining the pit base and lower edges, this layer was black, almost pure charcoal, with occasional carbonised roundwood pieces. It included large amounts of angular sarsen flakes (destruction debris), some so heavily burnt that they were almost reduced to reddened sand.

Above the destruction layer were further infill deposits of chalk rubble: [831], [801] and [832]. [831] was a thick deposit of very loose and pure chalk rubble, made up of angular blocks with few voids between, thickest towards the centre of the feature. [801] comprised chalk rubble mixed with brown silty clay, and was restricted to the east and north sides of the pit, here filling it to the top. Compact in the top 0.2m, this became progressively looser with depth. Larger blocks of chalk occurred towards the base of the layer, pitched at various angles with frequent voids between. [832] made up the upper chalk backfill on the west side, overlying [801] and in places up to 0.65m thick. It comprised chalk rubble again in a brown silty clay loam, though discernibly more earthy than [801]. The slight hollow left by the digging and filling of the pit was sealed by a thin (up to 0.25m thick) layer of brown clay loam ploughsoil [812]. Given the size of this destruction feature very little pottery was recovered from the fills. All was restricted to the upper fill [801] and deliberate levelling deposits [838]; [839] and with the exception of a single sherd of East-Wiltshire fineware (12–14th century AD) was Roman in date.

Figure 10.16. Burning pit F.71 on completion of excavation

The north-western arm of the destruction pit F.71 cut through the remains of the original stone-hole, F.50, virtually obliterating it. All that survived were the very ends of the stone-hole on the north-east and south-west side, and here only the tops of the fill remained.

Cove Setting L16 (F.53)

Forming the southern setting of the Longstones Cove, this feature is the largest of the conventional stone burning pits encountered (Figures 10.17 and 10.18). Following removal of the topsoil it was clearly visible as a sub-circular spread of firm brown clay-silt [807], with a visible area of sooting and burnt sarsen flakes [825]. Full excavation was undertaken of two quadrants of the feature.

The destruction pit was sub-rounded (5.8 × 5.0m) and cut so as to form a ramp, sloping gently down from the surface of the subsoil at its southern edge to a maximum depth of 0.8m to the north where a clear step in the cut could be identified in its steeply sloping side. An interesting feature of this northern edge was a projecting 'promontory' of solid chalk natural with vertical sides extending from the base of the cut to the level of the step. The east and western sides were steeper and along with the base of the pit were very irregular [806].

Cut into the base of the destruction pit at

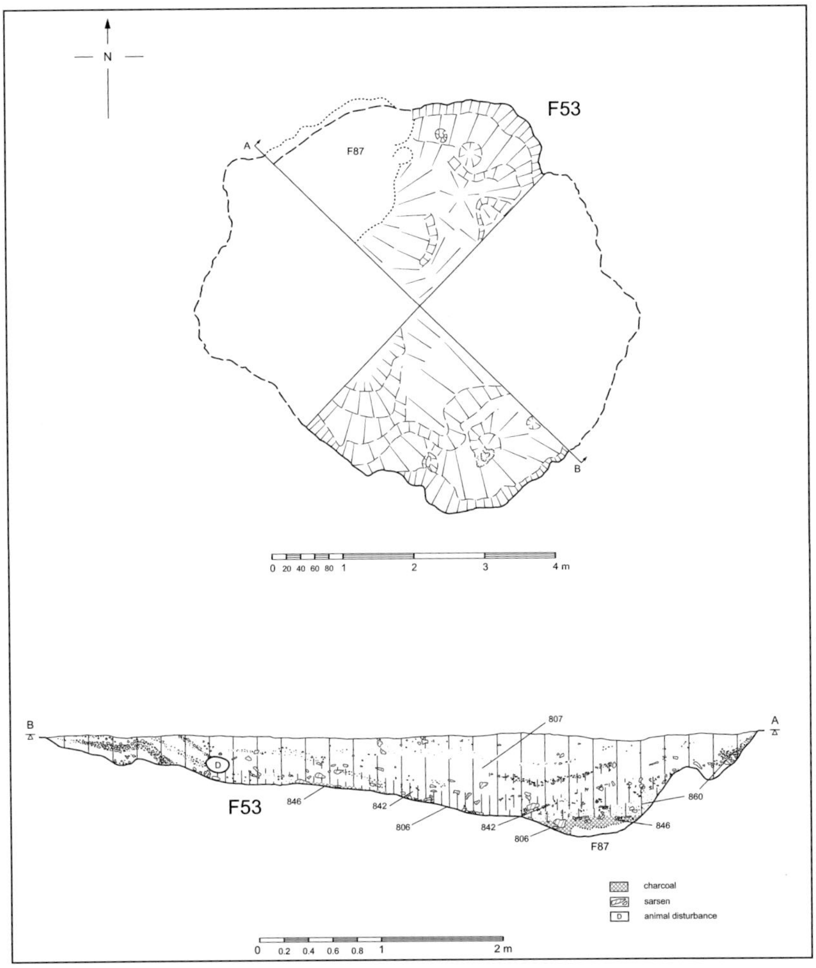

Figure 10.17. (top) Stone burning pit F.53 (setting L11)

Figure 10.18. (bottom) Burning pit F.53 under excavation. Note charcoal- and sarsen-rich basal deposits

the southern edge was a gently curving line of three shallow sub-circular depressions (typical diameter 0.2m) spaced at a regular distance of 0.8m. Filling these hollows was a chalk-free compacted brown clay-silt [868] containing numerous fresh flakes of flint. The hollow truncated by the section line also contained three rounded lumps of unburned sarsen. The only other find to come from this deposit was a fragment of heavily corroded iron. Sealing this deposit and extending for typically 0.6m from the edge of the cut was an area of moderately compacted orange-brown clay-silt containing frequent chalk lumps and fresh flakes of flint [861]. This deposit corresponds to an episode of collapse and slumping following the initial excavation of the feature but prior to any destruction activity.

Although not apparent in the section, at the northern edge of the destruction pit, directly overlaying the cut was a very thin and patchy layer of very compact orange-brown clay-silt containing numerous fresh flakes of flint and free of chalk [865], very similar to the [868] deposit identified at the shallower southern edge. Following the removal of [842] to the east of the stone-hole, two very shallow sub-circular depressions were revealed that could conceivably represent severely truncated post-settings.

The primary destruction layer took the form of a dense, black deposit of fibrous burnt vegetable material and frequent thin flakes of burnt sarsen [846]. The deposit completely covered the deeper basal areas of the burning pit. At the immediate northern edge of the destruction pit the burning debris [846] and clean silt layer [865] were sealed by a clear zone of slumping projecting at most 1.5m into the pit and comprising a compact brown deposit of numerous chalk lumps in a silty clay matrix [860]. Contained within this slump layer were frequent small flakes of flint and a substantial fragment of animal rib.

Sealing the burning deposit and slump layers was a very mixed, pale brown to dark grey-brown clay loam, the colour changes reflecting the decrease in chalk fragments and concomitant increase in sooting moving away from the edges of the feature toward the central portion [842]. This was in turn sealed by a firm, brown clay-silt with occasional chalk inclusions corresponding to a gradual infill of ploughsoil into the feature [807]. Visible at the surface of the subsoil at the southern edge of the pit and partially covered by this upper fill was an isolated area of burning debris, comprising a thin layer of sooting and burnt sarsen [825]. This directly overlay the slump deposit [861] and appears to correspond to post-destruction raking debris.

Adjacent to the northernmost edge of the cut of F.53 and truncated by the quadrant section are the surviving remains of the original stone-hole. Taking the form of an elongated oval depression aligned east-west [872], it is clear that the destruction pit was dug directly up to the body of the stone, removing almost the entirety of the southern edge of the stone-hole.

Excavations at the Falkner's Circle, 2002

Excavations revealed evidence of two features (F.6 and 7) linked to the post-medieval breaking of sarsen through burning (Figure 3.14).

F.6

This was the most substantial feature encountered during the excavation. It comprised a roughly circular pit [724], 3.6 × 3.3m and up to 0.9m deep (Figure 10.19). On the north and east sides the cut was regular and even, the sides being steep, with a step in the profile at a depth of *c.*0.5m, then sloping into a dished base. The western side of the pit was more irregular, both in plan and profile, with moderately sloping sides at the top, becoming steep to near vertical in the lower profile. The western edge proved very difficult to define in the upper profile where the distinction between fill and natural was hardly apparent. It is possible that the pit cut into an earlier feature at this point, but if so its extent could not be traced. The pit base and sides (especially on the west) were extensively fire-reddened, in some places turning the clayey sub-soil into brick-like lumps. The depth of the pit and its dished base suggest that it was cut *around* rather than *against* a presumably standing stone. There were no surviving traces of any stone-hole.

A complex sequence of fills was observed (Figure 10.20). The base was covered by a soft, black charcoal-rich and ashy soil [728] with abundant large pieces of burnt and fractured sarsen. The sarsen lay horizontal, in places several pieces thick. Abundant roundwood charcoal was present in this layer, some surviving as substantial pieces. This clearly represents a deposit formed through *in situ* burning. Above [728] was a compact orange-brown silty clay [727], containing charcoal flecks, small sarsen pieces and a thin lens of chalky gravel. This in turn was sealed by a compact chalk gravel with occasional charcoal

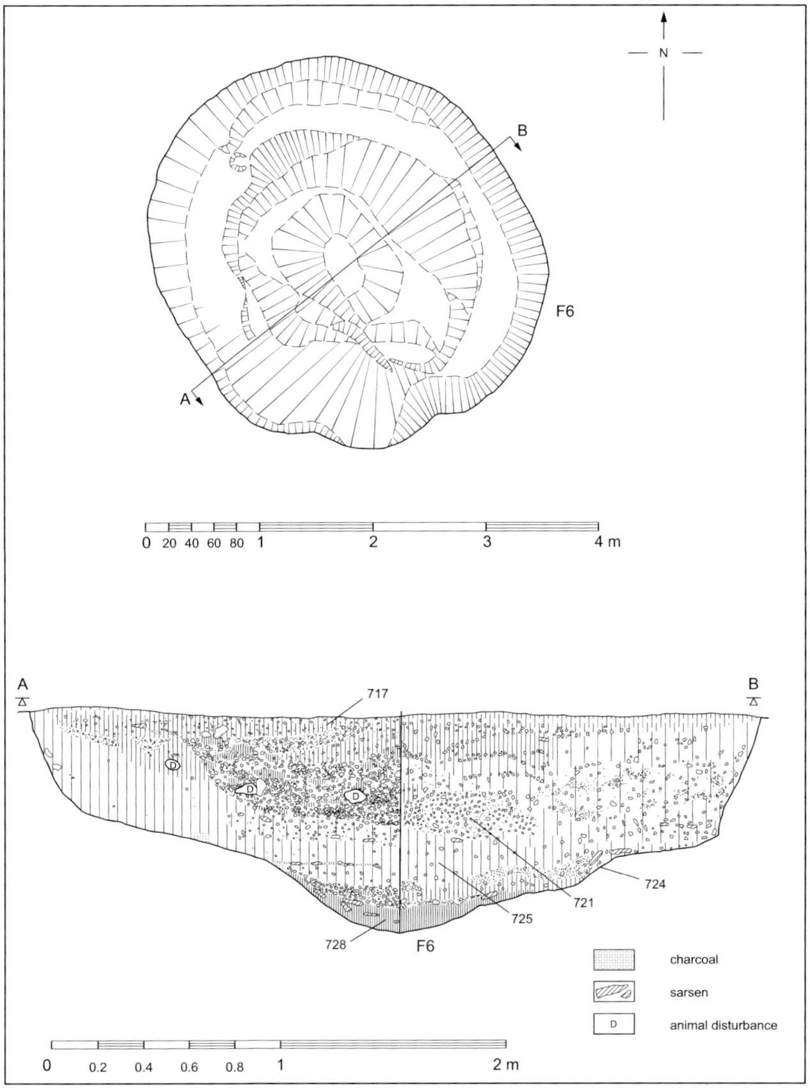

Figure 10.19. Falkner's Circle: stone burning pit F.6

Figure 10.20. Falkner's Circle: detail of fill in pit F.6

and sarsen [726], forming a thin lens running across the pit fill on the east side (no more than 0.02m thick), and a poorly sorted matrix of compact orange-brown silty clay with charcoal flecks and small sarsen pieces [725]. Sarsen was more abundant within this on the north side. This layer also contained blocks of clay with a pinkish hue caused by burning.

A second phase of burning and stone breaking may be represented by a loose black soil with abundant small sarsen pieces and patches of heavily burnt sandy clay [723], which was sitting atop [725] in a discrete area on the southern side of the pit. This was sealed by an orange-brown silty clay with some charcoal flecks [722], probably re-deposited natural, which was largely confined to the sides of the pit. The upper fills included a chalk gravel within a pale orange-brown silty clay [721], and an orange-brown sandy clay with charcoal flecks and small patches of fired clay [720]. Localised concentrations of roundwood charcoal and ashy lenses were present within [721]. Finally, a dark grey-brown silty clay [717] with small amounts of fired clay, charcoal and chalk pieces filled the top of the feature, spilling over onto the buried soil to the east.

Around 8.5kg of burnt and fractured sarsen came from the pit fill, much from the layers of *in situ* burning. All of this appeared to derive from the breaking of a single, presumably substantial, stone.

F.7

F.7 was a regularly cut oval pit [735], 1.4 × 1.0m across and up to 0.15m deep (Figure 3.18). It had been dug into chalky gravel and the clay fill of a solution hollow; the definition of the sides and base being difficult where it cut the latter. The sides of the pit sloped at a moderate angle, being shallower on the north and north-east, and merging with a dished base. The northern part of the pit was disturbed by animal burrowing. The basal fill comprised a thin lens of compact grey-brown silty clay [734]. Above this was a mixture of large roundwood charcoal, fractured sarsen and fire-reddened clay and chalk [733], representing the burning layer. This in turn was sealed by further layers of grey- to orange-brown silty clay [732] and [729], also containing charcoal and heat-fractured sarsen. At its south-west edge the pit cut through the original stone-hole, F.9 [737].

Medieval and post-medieval artefacts from the Beckhampton Avenue and Falkner's Circle

A range of early post-medieval artefacts was recovered from the stone destruction pits and the fills of contemporary cultivation furrows. This included ceramics, glass, clay pipe fragments and ferrous and non-ferrous metalwork. A large percentage of this material is likely to be derived, having entered the field as part of manuring deposits, then becoming incidentally incorporated into feature fills at a later date; this explaining the highly fragmentary and abraded condition of many pieces. Nonetheless, on the basis of their condition and relative ubiquity, several of the clay pipe fragments, pieces of ironwork, and perhaps some of the non-ferrous metalwork, might be seen as the material culture of stone-breaking. These are objects taken into the field to be used as part of the stone-breaking process (iron nails and fittings of wooden props or firewood), recreation practices (clay pipes), or which became inadvertently lost during the exertion of labour (*e.g.* buttons).

Post-medieval pottery
Paul Courtney

The post-medieval assemblage from the Beckhampton Avenue excavations is dominated by Verwood-type earthenwares, probably from the Dorset/Hampshire border. Three sherds (BSSW) could come from either Bristol or the Staffordshire area. Post-medieval imports include Raeren, Frechen and Westerwald stonewares. A total of eight fabrics were identified (Table 10.1):

PM1. Post-medieval 1. Verwood-type ware from Dorset/Hampshire border. Pink to buff fine sandy fabric with iron-speckled lead glazes. Mostly internally glazed forms sometimes with very thin wet-like glaze on exterior. ?16th–19th centuries.

BSSW. Bristol/Staffordshire Slipware. Coal Measures buff ware with red and white slip decoration. *c.*1680–1730.

FSW. Frechen stoneware. Sherd from speckled brown jug from Rhineland. 17th-century.

RSW. Raeren stoneware. Raeren small jug/mugs from Rhineland. *c.*1470–1550.

WdSW. Westerwald stoneware. Cobalt blue decorated jug. 17th–early 18th-century

PW. Pearlware. Industrial whiteware with blue tint in glaze. Plain, painted or transfer decorated. *c.*1780–1830.

DWW. Developed White Ware. Blue-transfer decorated. *c.*1830– present.

ES. English stoneware. Derby or Nottingham. 18th century.

Trench	Context	Fabric	Sherd no.	Notes
10	Test pit 3 [002]	PM1	1	-
10	F.21, [001]	PM1	2	DV (1 sherd)
10	F.23, [405]	PM1	6	Flatware
10	F.23, [405]	PM1	1	Sgraffito
10	F.24, [404]	PM1	9	Flatware
10	F.23, [434]	PM1	5	Flatware and hollow ware
10	F.23, [405]	PW	5	Blue transfer and brown-painted
13	[001]	PM1	1	-
14	[001]	PM1	1	-
15	[001]	PM1	1	Flatware
21	[001]	FSW	1	Poorly fired
22	[001]	WdSW	2	Jug
22	[001]	PM1	1	Flatware
23	[001]	PM1	1	Flatware
24	[001]	PM1	1	Flatware
24	[001]	PW	1	Plain rim
24	[001]	BSSW	1	Hollow ware, slip decorated
24	[807]	PM1	2	Flatware
24	[807]	RSW	1	Body sherd from small globular jug
24	F.50, [800]	PM1	1	-
24	F.52, [820]	RSW	1	Rim of small jug c.1475-1550
24	F.52, [820]	PM1	2	Flatware
24	F.52, [821]	PM1	1	flatware
27	[001]	DWW	2	Blue transfer decorated
30	[001]	PM1	1	Large bowl rim
30	[001]	BSSW	2	-
30	[001]	ES	1	-
31	[901]	RSW	1	-

Table 10.1. Post-medieval pottery from the Beckhampton Avenue excavations

Glass

F.23, [405]. Small fragment of pale green sheet glass. 1mm thick.

F.23, [405]. Small sherd of green bottle glass. Hand blown.

F.53, [842]. Small fragment of pale green sheet glass. 1mm thick.

F.62, [612]. Small fragment, probably bottle glass.

F.62, [614]. Tiny fragment, probably bottle glass.

Clay pipes

F.21, [400]. Small stem fragment. Bore diameter 1mm. Weathered.

F.23, [405]. Four pieces of stem, and a bowl fragment with a stamped heel. Reasonably fresh condition. Bore diameters 2.5–3.0mm. Stamp: TH-/MA-/HVN- (Thomas Hunt). Thomas Hunt worked in Marlborough from at least 1667 to 1696 (D R Atkinson 1965, 90). His pipes are extremely common within the region.*

F.24, [404]. Three pieces of stem, and one complete bowl with spur. Fresh condition. Two stem fragments refit to form a length of 114mm. One stem piece stamped THO/HVNT (Thomas Hunt); another W—/IA-/-ER- (William Frey). Bore diameters *c.*2.2–3.0mm. Bowl form *c.*1660–80. Judging from the distribution of his pipes, William Frey may have been based in Marlborough (D. R. Atkinson 1965, 91–2).*

F.52, [851]. Two joining halves of a bowl, one lightly burnt the other not. Long parallel bowl of *c.*1680–1700.*

F.53, [807]. Stem fragment. Bore diameter 4mm.

F.53, [842]. Stem fragment. Bore diameter 2.2mm.

F.61, [602]. Stem fragment. Bore diameter 3.0mm. Stamped IOHN/GRE – (John Greenland). Greenland's pipes have a local distribution, leading Atkinson to suggest that he was a Marlborough pipe-maker, active in the late 17th century (D. R. Atkinson 1965, 91–2).

F.62, [612]. Two pieces of stem, one 58mm long. Relatively fresh condition. Bore diameters 2.5–3.0mm.*

F.71, [801]–[829]. Six pieces of stem. Two groups of two (probably from different pipes) refit to form lengths of 66mm and 85mm respectively. Fresh condition. Bore diameters 2.0–2.5mm.*

In addition, five pieces of stem were recovered from ploughsoil contexts. Judging by the stem and bore thickness, all are of late 17th–early 18th-century date. Because of their size and unweathered condition, those pieces marked * are likely to be contemporary with the initial filling of the pits from which they came (*i.e.* they could be considered as 'stone breaker' pipes). These would suggest dates in the last quarter of the 17th century for the fills of pits F.23 and F.24, and a date perhaps closer to 1700 for F.52, which produced a typologically later style of pipe bowl. If decreasing bore diameter is taken as an indication of date, then pit F.62 might also fall within the last quarter of the 17th century (note comparable bore diameters from F.23 and F.24), while F.71 would be later; corroborating known documentary evidence of this stone's destruction in the 1720s. This will be discussed in more detail in the context of dating stone destruction.

Ironwork from settings L1–L4

Setting L1

F.21, [400]. Sub-rectangular sectioned rod, possibly the stem of a nail. Diameter 4mm, surviving length 40mm.

Setting L3

F.23, [405]. Eight nails with oval/sub-rectangular heads (6–13mm maximum dimension) and tapering rectangular-sectioned stems. Surviving lengths 25–60mm.

F.23, [405]. Rectangular-sectioned object with flat expanded end. Length 29mm.

F.23, [405]. Three pieces of iron plate. The largest rectangular, 65 × 35mm; the two smaller (55 × 29mm and 36 × 29mm), slightly curved along their lengths, are probably both from the same object. All look to be parts of straps, possibly hinge fragments.

F.23, [434]. Four nail fragments and a ferrous concretion. Nail stems with tapering rectangular sections (surviving lengths 12–30mm), heads squared/rectangular (none complete).

Setting L4

F.24, [404]. Two nails with rectangular heads and tapering rectangular-sectioned stems. Heads 11 × 6mm and 10 × 7mm, surviving lengths 27mm and 46mm.

F.24, [404]. Fragment of iron plate. 15 × 15mm.

F.24, [404]. Two fragments of highly corroded iron plate. 38 × 25mm and 27 × 20mm.

F.24, [409]. Two heavily corroded ferrous lumps. 50x 37 × 8mm and 39 × 35 × 12mm.

Fill of medieval plough furrow

F.28, [416]. Nail with oval head and a tapering rectangular-sectioned stem. Head 11 × 9mm, surviving length 44mm.

Discussion

Pits F.23 and F.24 stand out because of the quantity of ironwork present (17 and 7 pieces respectively), which is well above that expected from a 'background' noise created by manuring or other agricultural activity within the field. These two assemblages at least must be linked directly or indirectly to stone breaking. Nails comprise the most common object category, with fragments of iron strip and plate also being present. One possibility is that they were introduced as part of wooden props used to support stones during the felling and breaking process. Alternatively, they could have comprised fixtures and fittings of old doors or other domestic woodwork used as fuel in fire-setting. The nails are of medium to large size, above that used in furniture, and so more likely to derive from constructional woodwork or heavy-duty fittings.

Ironwork from settings L7–L16

Philip Macdonald and Philip Parkes

Topsoil finds

Tr.24, [001]. Nail with a small, damaged head and a tapering rectangular-sectioned stem. The tip of the stem is missing. Dimensions of head 8 × 7mm, surviving length 63mm.

Although typologically the nail could be of any date from the Roman period through to the early twentieth century there is no reason to suggest that it is of any great antiquity.

Tr.24, [001]. Spur fragment (Figure 7.5.7). Part of the arm of a spur consisting of a tapering rod, plano-convex in section, that is broken at its thickest end and which terminates at its narrowest end a now incomplete fitting consisting of two small rings arranged in a figure-of-eight. These terminal rings originally accommodated stud attachments for spur leathers. The form of the terminal suggests that the fragment is from a spur of 17th- or early 18th-century date. Length 44mm.

The wearing of spurs, even when not riding, became fashionable during the 17th and early 18th century. Although iron spurs of this date are usually plated with copper alloy, no trace of any plating survives on this example.

Setting L8

F.62, [614]. Irregular-shaped plate fragment, slightly curved towards one edge. Dimensions 37 × 34mm.

Setting L15

F.71, [829]. Rove. Incomplete and partially distorted rectangular-shaped rove with a central perforation. Dimensions 26 × 25mm.

Roves are rectangular or lozenge shaped perforated plates which combined with a nail to form a distinctive type of structural fitting known as a holdfast or clench bolt. Holdfasts are used to join two timbers; the nail is hammered through the timbers, the rove is then placed over the protruding end of the nail which is then hammered over. This arrangement prevents the nail from pulling back through the wood. As a type they are known from the Roman period through to the present day. Although commonly associated with shipbuilding, holdfasts are also associated with a range of timber objects and features such as doors, hatches and carts (Ottaway 1992, 618; Clark 1997, 159). Presumably, the rove was attached to old pieces of timber that were burnt as part of the destruction of the megalith.

F.71, [838]. Small trapezoidal-shaped plate fragment. Dimensions 17 × 13mm.

F.72, [814]. Nail with a flat, sub-rectangular head and a tapering, rectangular-sectioned stem. The lower part of the stem is missing. Dimensions of head 27 × 28mm, surviving length of nail 28mm.

Typologically, the nail could be of any date from the Roman period to the 19th century.

F.72, [814]. Fragment of a sub-rectangular sectioned rod, broken at both ends. Possibly part of the missing stem of the nail recovered from the same context (No.29) although the two fragments do not join. Surviving length 15mm.

Setting L16

F.53, [807]. Blade fragment (Figure 7.5.6). Blade fragment with two narrow, straight grooves cut into one face of the blade and running parallel with, and immediately below, its back. The back of the blade has a slight convex curve. The blade is embellished, on the same face as the cut grooves, with a stamped and inlaid 'maker's mark' which survives as an open semi-circle punctuated with radiating points (Figure 10.21). Probably part of a knife or a pair of shears. Surviving length 57mm, surviving width of blade 16mm, maximum thickness of blade 2.25mm.

Knives and shears are difficult artefacts to typologically classify and date, even when recovered complete, because of the inevitable changes to their original form caused by sharpening and wear; however, the cut grooves and the 'maker's mark' are both features which partially facilitate the dating of the Beckhampton blade.

The embellishment of blades with narrow cut grooves is not a common Romano-British phenomenon; Manning only illustrates one knife with a wide and shallow groove on one face of the blade (1985, 117, no.Q56, pl. 55) and none of the 103 knives he publishes in the British Museum catalogue have narrow grooves comparable to those cut on to the Beckhampton blade (cf. Manning 1985, 108–23). Early medieval examples of knife blades embellished with cut grooves are known from both the Coppergate excavations in York and a number of Anglo-Saxon contexts dating from the 5th to 6th centuries to the 9th to 11th centuries (Ottaway 1992, 579–81). Several examples of knives embellished in this fashion were also recovered from medieval London where the earliest example dated to the mid-13th century although the feature was most common on knives of 14th century date (Cowgill 1987, 17). Few assemblages of post-medieval knives have been published making comparison difficult; however, only one of the knives recovered during excavation of post-medieval deposits in Norwich had a narrow cut groove and this example may have been residually deposited (Goodall 1993, 128, no.835, fig. 94). Ottaway has speculated that the function of the narrow cut grooves was probably decorative although they may have indicated the quality of the blade or the maker's name in the same way as medieval Cutler's marks (1992, 582). Not all blades embellished with cut grooves were knives; two late 14th century pairs of shears from London were also decorated with grooves (Cowgill *et al.* 1987, 108, 111, nos.338 and 340, fig. 73).

The 'maker's mark' (Figure 10.21) is a more

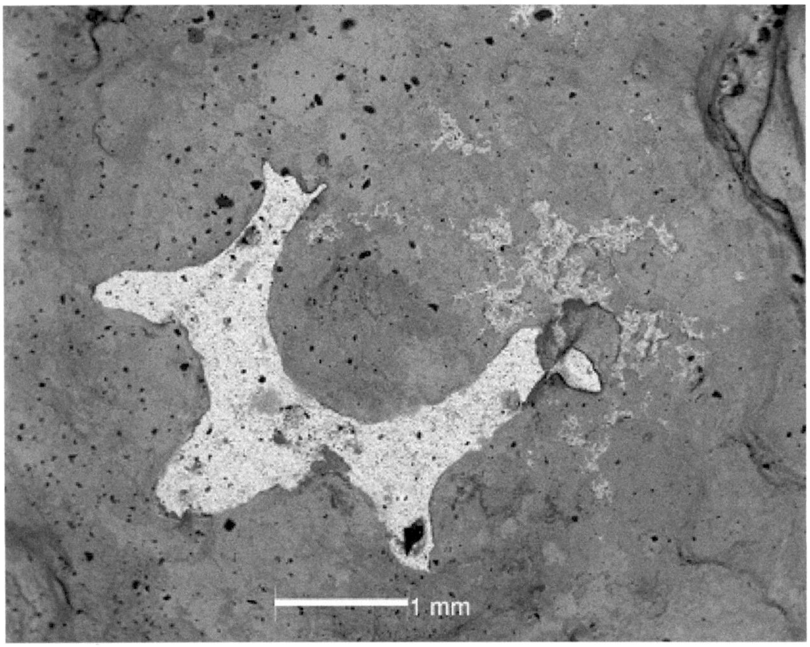

Figure 10.21. Inlaid 'maker's mark' on knife blade recovered from destruction pit F.53

useful dating indicator. The use of inlaid stamped marks is not a Romano-British or early medieval phenomenon. Maker's marks were widely used across Europe throughout the medieval and early post-medieval periods (Cowgill 1987, 20). The earliest maker's mark cited by Cowgill in her survey of blades from medieval London is of 13th-century date (1987, 20) although the phenomenon seems to be most popular during the 14th and 15th centuries. The use of makers' marks is not restricted to knife blades; for example, marks have been recognised on 12 pairs of shears from medieval London (Cowgill 1987, 17). Microscopic investigation suggests that the Beckhampton mark may originally have formed a circular, star-like motif. This star-like motif is paralleled by marks on three late 14th-century knives from London (Cowgill *et al.* 1987, 93, 97, 98, nos.104, 164, 176, figs. 6, 62) and it is not unreasonable to suggest a comparable date for the Beckhampton blade. Presumably, if correctly identified as medieval in date, the blade fragment was residually deposited in the 18th-century destruction pit. The Beckhampton mark was probably punched into the blade and then the inlay stamped into the impression cold. Analytical investigation indicates that the mark was inlaid with a copper-tin-zinc alloy (gunmetal). Interestingly, of the 47 medieval blades with inlaid marks analysed from London only one was inlaid with a gunmetal (Cowgill 1987, 24, table 5).

F.53, [807]. Nail with a small, damaged head and a tapering rectangular-sectioned stem. The end of the stem is missing. Dimensions of head 10 × 9mm, surviving length 53.5mm.

Although typologically the nail could be of any date from the Roman period through to the early 20th century there is no reason to suggest that it is of any great antiquity.

F.53, [807]. Amorphous ferrous fragment. Dimensions 20.5 × 16 × 15.5mm.

F.53, [842]. Fragment of a rectangular-sectioned rod, broken at one end and tapering to a point at the other. The rod is bent through two right angles towards its narrowest end so as to double back upon itself. Possibly the arm and middle section of a staple or joiner's dog. Surviving length 42mm.

Joiner' dogs are a form of staple used for joining two pieces of timber (cf. Manning 1985, 131). Comparable examples are known from the pre-Roman Iron Age through to the early 20th century.

F.53, [842]. Possible fragment of a heavily corroded nail with a damaged head and the upper part of a rectangular-sectioned stem. Of uncertain date. Length 13mm.

F.53 [842]. Fragment of a trapezoidal-sectioned tapering rod, broken at both ends. Length 26mm.

F.53, [842]. Amorphous ferrous fragment which thickens towards a curved edge. Possibly several smaller fragments corroded together. Dimensions 30.5 × 24 × 14mm.

F.53, [842]. Sub-spherical ferrous concretion, possibly a corrosion blister. Dimensions 13 × 11 × 11mm.

Non-ferrous objects

Fill of plough furrow

F.28, [416]. Small copper alloy plate with two perforations (*c.*1.5mm diameter). Fragmentary, but possibly of lobate form. Decorative or dress fitting? 11mm maximum dimension.

Setting L3

F.23, [405]. Circular plate from simple copper alloy button. Attachment loop missing. 17mm diameter. 17th/18th century?

Setting L11

F.52, [819]. Stamped base-metal button with four central thread holes. Traces of stamped decoration. 16mm diameter.

Setting L12

F.54, [824]. Small, amorphous fragment of copper alloy, possibly casting waste (identified by Macdonald and Parkes). Dimensions 11 × 8.5 × 6.5mm.

Setting L15

F.71, [801]. Copper alloy button. Domed, composite, with attached loop. 18mm diameter.

Animal Bone

Fiona Coward and Anthony Gouldwell

Post-medieval deposits (mainly stone destruction pits) produced 380 bones (Table 10.2). Sheep/goat and cattle are the most abundant domestic species represented. Horse, pig, and dog are also represented although at significantly lower percentages. A large carnivore species (probably fox or dog), lagomorph, frog, mole and unidentified small mammal remains were also recorded. However, much of this material was in excellent condition, markedly better than the condition evidenced by the main ungulate species, and is almost certainly recently intrusive.

Analysis of the destruction debris associated with Beckhampton Avenue setting L10

To shed more light upon the practice of stone breaking, the decision was taken to retain the full assemblage of sarsen from the destruction deposit of stone setting L10. In the case of previous stone destruction events the sarsen fragments were weighed and either re-buried or a representative sample of fragment 'types' was retained. The L10 debris was recovered by hand from context [909], F.100. The rationale behind retaining the full suite of discarded debris was to ascertain whether any further light could be shed upon the processes of stone destruction through analysis of the sarsen fragments. The exercise was structured around the following questions:

- How efficient was the burning process with regard to spalling and heat-damage (*i.e.* wastage)?
- Was there any evidence of the *in situ* hard-hammer trimming and shaping of blocks as argued by Keiller in the case of the multiple burning pit of stones *ix*, *x* and *xi* of the Southern Inner Circle, or was the initial dressing of stone blocks undertaken elsewhere as is implied by the historical accounts?
- Was the cortex preferentially retained on account of its extreme hardness and/or visual properties?

Approaching stone destruction debris

In the absence of any prior study of stone destruction assemblages or a sound body of experimental or comparative data, the first stage was to establish a series of debris types that could be associated with specific technological processes. This was in part a deductive process, thinking through the stages (and practical implications) of the process described by Aubrey and Stukeley. It was also partly inductive, looking at the range of recurrent diagnostic types present in the overall assemblage of stone fragments.

On the basis of the historical descriptions, the breaking of sarsen through fire-setting appears to have followed three basic stages. A fourth stage can be conjectured on the basis of Keiller's claim to have recognised what appear to be mechanically struck flakes in amongst recovered stone debris (Table 10.3). In terms of identifying specific 'types' of fragment, the approach taken has been to work within the general frameworks of lithic analysis, seeking to focus on the *chaîne opératoire* rather than any

Species	Post-medieval
Cattle	14
Sheep/goat	19
Pig	<1
Horse	1
Dog	<1
Large carnivore	10
Lagomorph	2
Mole	6
Unid. Small mammal	26
Frog	16
Bird	4
Total identifiable	*136*
Unidentifiable	*244*
% identifiable	*36*
Total	*380*

Table 10.2. Animal bone from post-medieval contexts on the Beckhampton Avenue: species representation

Table 10.3. Technological stages in fire-setting and working a sarsen

Stage	Rationale	Impact on stone
Toppling	Expose greater surface area to heating	Some initial fracturing *could* occur
Heating	Raise temperature of stone	Spalling of fragments from the surface of stone exposed to the heat
Sub-dividing	Reducing bulk of stone into manageable (useful) blocks through thermal shock and hard-hammer impact	Fracturing and shattering
Dressing (shaping)	Shape blocks into useful building (transportable) blocks	Hard-hammer shaping

Table 10.4. Types of sarsen debris resulting from stone destruction

Type	Description
Spalls	These are thin pieces of sarsen without faceting or other obvious indications of mechanical fracture. They tend to have feathered edges and uneven break surfaces. A relatively high percentage have cortex present and many show signs of sustained burning.
Crested Pieces	These are triangular in section and tend to have a length greater than twice the breadth. The majority appear to have been deliberately struck, most likely to remove distinctive ridges or corners.
Flakes	These are mechanically struck pieces that exhibit the characteristics of flakes. Many have bulbs of percussion (albeit often diffuse), platforms and facets on the dorsal face created by the removal of previous flakes.
Lumps	These are irregular pieces of sarsen, generally thick and angular, tending towards cuboid in some instances. Many are likely to have resulted from mechanical fracture.
Miscellaneous	A wide range of very irregular fragments that do not sit comfortably within the above categories.

Table 10.5. Destruction pit F.100: basic counts of sarsen debris. nr = not recorded

Fragment type:	Unburnt	unburnt cortex	burnt	burnt cortex	total	cortex total
Spalls	109	(2)	71	(39)	180	(41)
Flakes	113	(1)	62	(2)	175	(3)
Chunks	92	(1)	29	(2)	121	(3)
Crested	45	(3)	9	(5)	54	(8)
Misc.	243	(1)	60	(11)	303	(12)
Small fragments	nr	nr	nr	nr	918	(2)
Totals:	*602*	*(8)*	*231*	*(59)*	*1751*	*(69)*

Table 10.6. Destruction pit F.100: weights (in grams) of sarsen debris according to type, condition and presence of cortex

Fragment type:	unburnt	unburnt cortex	burnt	burnt cortex	total	cortex total
Spalls	6187	(367)	2453	(2288)	8640	(2655)
Flakes	14230	(836)	13159	(0)	27389	(836)
Chunks	14437	(1185)	4377	(364)	18814	(1549)
Crested	12527	(490)	2182	(5436)	14709	(5926)
Misc.	10261	(28)	4427	(216)	14688	(244)
Small fragments	nr	nr	nr	nr	2123	Nr
Totals:	*57642*	*(2906)*	*26598*	*(8304)*	*86363*	*11210*

notional end-product, whilst accepting the inherent crudeness and scale of the task of sarsen reduction being studied.

Following study of the assemblage of 1751 sarsen fragments, a total of four recurring fragment types were identified (Table 10.4). It should be acknowledged that a degree of overlap is inevitable between certain of the classes (*e.g.* flakes and spalls). It should also be remembered that in the absence of a strong body of comparative experimental data this 'process–based' classification is largely conjectural and subjective in nature. All of the material has been retained and archived should more refined schema emerge in time.

Quantifying the assemblage

With the exception of the smallest examples, the sarsen fragments were classified into types and then weighed and counted. As the material was not originally recovered through sieving, the decision was taken to only count and weigh the smallest fragments (in practice those below *c.*0.03m in maximum dimension) rather than attempt to classify them. As well as basic counts (Table 10.5) and weights (Table 10.6), dimensions were recorded for the four principal classes (a summary of this data is offered in Table 10.7).

In addition, all fragments were checked for the presence of cortex and evidence of burning. As well as illuminating the preferences of the stone breakers, study of the cortex was useful in shedding light upon the colour and texture of the original standing stone, factors that have been increasingly foregrounded in interpretations of megalithic monuments (*e.g.* Pollard and Gillings 1998; MacGregor 2002). On the basis of the cortical fragments present the sarsen appears to have been a deep reddish-brown with a surface richly textured with fossil root holes. Although reddish-brown sarsens are reasonably common at Avebury it is unclear in this case whether the colouration reflects the original colours of the stone when standing or is a result of the heating process – once again experimental work is needed to shed light upon this.

With respect to burning, the aim was to note any evidence of sustained heating and sooting. Whilst this appeared to be a straightforward task, it was complicated by the fact that the fragments (whether burnt or not) had been churned around in deposits containing considerable amounts of burnt straw and sooting, and had then been transported together in rubble sacks prior to analysis. While in most cases post-destruction surface sooting could be distinguished from the effects of sustained heating, in some cases clear distinction was difficult and some degree of ambiguity is inevitable.

The bulk of the recorded cortex (57%) is present on the spalls. If the assumption is made that these result from heat effects alone (*i.e.* lack any signs of mechanical fracture) this suggests a deliberate retention, rather than removal of cortex from the broken stone. This interpretation gains support if we look at the proportion of burnt cortex amongst the cortical spall fragments (95% of cortical spall fragments are burnt) which suggests that this surface material had been removed in an uncontrolled way as a direct consequence of heating. What is less straightforward to explain is the dominance of seemingly unburned spall fragments in the assemblage (see Table 10.8). This may be a distortion resulting from difficulties in distinguishing spalls and flakes, or it reflects processes of temperature-induced fracture away from the direct source of heat. At present, in the absence of any sustained experimental work this anomaly can only be noted.

Flakes are generated by direct fracture, for example the striking of a stone with a sledgehammer. The presence of an almost 50:50 split in terms of weight between burnt and unburned pieces suggests that this was taking place both in the fire and away from the heat source, or that struck flakes were making their way into the fire. The lower count of burnt fragments (implying much larger pieces) would support the assumption that they derive from the initial sub-dividing of the stone following the application of water. The remaining smaller flakes are best interpreted as resulting from subsequent on-site dressing.

The crested fragments and chunks are dominated by unburned pieces (*c.*76% and *c.*84% respectively), which suggests that they result principally from the shaping and working of stones away from the source of fire. However, it is interesting to note that the largest example of a crested fragment (364mm in length) was thoroughly burnt and sooted suggesting that some degree of control and preliminary shaping was being exerted during initial sub-dividing of the sarsen or that it was subsequently burnt. On the basis of this quantification exercise we can suggest a crude concordance between the reconstructed stages and fragment types identified (Table 10.9).

In attempting to shed light upon the

Type	minimum	maximum	mean	standard deviation
spalls (D1)	29	177	71	26
spalls (D2)	17	110	47	18
spalls (D3)	2	25	8	4
flakes (D1)	33	260	93	42
flakes (D2)	21	150	61	28
flakes (D3)	3	52	17	9
crested (D1)	53	364	116	51
crested (D2)	15	139	51	25
crested (D3)	8	82	35	16
chunks (D1)	28	160	75	32
chunks (D2)	17	157	45	21
chunks (D3)	11	100	28	14

D1 – dimension 1 (length)
D2 – dimension 2 (width)
D3 – dimension 3 (thickness)

Table 10.7. (top) Destruction pit F.100: dimensions (in mm) of sarsen fragments

Fragment type	Burnt examples by count	Burnt examples by weight
Spalls	39%	28%
Flakes	35%	48%
Chunks	24%	23%
Crested	17%	15%
Miscellaneous	20%	30%

Table 10.8. (bottom) Destruction pit F.100: summary of burnt proportions

Table10.9. Concordance of stages of stone destruction with debris types

Stage	Types produced
Toppling	Ideally none
Heating	*Spalls*, misc.
Sub-dividing	*Flakes*, chunks, crests, misc.
Dressing	*Flakes, chunks, crests*, misc.

Table 10.10. Comparison of surviving stone-hole dimensions

Stone	length	width	depth
L2	1.60m	0.90m	0.40m
L4	2.00m	0.80m	0.50m
L5	1.60m	1.20m	0.20m
L6	1.83m	0.90m	0.35m
L7	1.60	0.90m	0.55m
L8	1.60m	1.20m	0.55m
L10	1.40m	1.16m	0.30m

Stone	Destruction method	Weight
BA L1	Burning – rough pit	106.5kg
BA L4	Burning – rough pit	136.5kg
BA L10	Burning – adjacent pit	86.5kg
Avebury 17	Burning – upright	381.0kg
Avebury 18	Burning – upright	462.9kg
Avebury 104	Burning – tunnel	352.0kg
Avebury 107	Burning - tunnel	174.6kg
Avebury 108	Burning – rough pit	482.6kg
WKA 5B	Direct Fracture	25.6kg+
WKA 7A	Direct Fracture	178.7kg
WKA 7B	Direct Fracture	30.5kg
WKA 8A	Direct Fracture	16.8kg
WKA 9A	Direct Fracture	14.7kg
WKA 11A	Direct Fracture	14.1kg
WKA 12A	Direct Fracture	39.5kg
WKA 12B	Direct Fracture	14.1kg
WKA 14B	Burning – tunnel	178.3kg
WKA 17B	Burning – tunnel	69.4kg
WKA 23B	Burning – tunnel	24.7kg
WKA 25A	Direct Fracture	209.0kg
Falkner's F6	Burning – upright (required two burnings)	8.5kg

Table 10.11. Weights of sarsen debris from stone destruction pits

efficiency of the process we are faced with a paradox insofar as it is impossible to assess without some record of the original weight of the sarsen that was destroyed. One approach is to identify a proxy where the weight of the sarsen is known. For example, if we compare the dimensions of the stone-hole to those for the other excavated avenue settings we can see that the L10 stone was far from unusual (Table 10.10). There is certainly nothing to suggest it was as large as its surviving partner, Eve, which stands 3.3m high and reaches a maximum width of *c.*2.3m, and a better surrogate would appear to be one of the buried settings L2, L5 or L6. However, whilst the dimensions of the buried stones were recorded, the logistics of raising the stones from their burial pits for the purpose of weighing them proved prohibitive. Indeed weighed stones appear to be few[4] and it is difficult to treat those we do have (*e.g.* Cunnington's estimate of 17 tons for WKA 33A) as in any way 'typical' given the wide variety of stone shapes and sizes that characterise the Avebury settings. Our best estimate would be to place the L2, 5 and 6 sarsens in the order of five to ten tonnes.

A second approach would be to read the amount of debris as an inverse indicator of efficiency. This is problematic for much the same reason as any estimate of typical weight as we do not know the degree to which the amount of debris was a reflection of the size of the stone destroyed rather than efficiency of the process (Table 10.11). That it may well reflect the scale of the task rather than precise technique employed is suggested by the large amounts associated with the large stones of the Southern Inner Circle (104, 107 and 108). It may well be that this is a question that can only be addressed through a careful program of experimental replication.

Summary

Although it has not been possible to comment in any meaningful way on the question of efficiency, the classification and measurement of the L10 debris has shed important light upon the mechanics of stone destruction through heating. We know that cortex was not deliberately removed, the majority of cortex fragments resulting from the natural process of spalling during the heating of the stone. There is some indication that control was exercised during the initial splitting of the block to ensure that workable chunks of sarsen were liberated. The bulk of roughing-out work was undertaken in and around the pit, but away from the heat of the fire or after it had been allowed to go out.

Fuelling Destruction

So far we have looked in detail at the morphology and composition of both destruction pits and surviving debris. What has been missing has been any discussion of the conflagration itself and to this end charcoal was analysed from the remains of the fire-setting activity associated with settings L7 (F.61), L11 (F.53) and L16 (F.52) of the Beckhampton Avenue, and F.6 and F.7 of Falkner's Circle, in an attempt to shed light on the fuels employed.

Feature	Context	Sample	*Acer*	*Fraxinus*	*Quercus*	Salic-aceae	*Ulmus*
F.52	[822]	65	-	6r	-	2	-
F.53	[846]	75	1	6	1r	2	8
F.61	[602]	52	1	-	-	-	-

Table 10.12. Charcoal from post-medieval burning pits F.52, 53 and 61 of the Beckhampton Avenue

Charcoal from the Beckhampton Avenue
Rowena Gale

Identification was undertaken on three samples from stone destruction deposits:

F.52 (sample 65), F.53 (sample 75) and F.61 (sample 52).

Materials and methods

Bulk soil samples were processed by flotation and sieving. The flots were collected on a 0.5mm mesh and the residues retained on 5.6mm, 2mm and 1mm sieves. The resulting samples were scanned under low magnification and the charcoal separated from plant macro-fossils. Charcoal fragments measuring >2mm in cross-section were considered for species identification.

Sample 52 was sparse and contained only small fragments of charcoal, whereas samples 65 and 75 were also small but consisted of larger fragments. The samples were prepared for examination using standard methods (Gale and Cutler 2000). Charcoal fragments were supported in washed sand and examined using a Nikon Labophot-2 microscope at magnifications up to x400. The anatomical structures were matched to prepared reference slides.

When possible, the maturity of the wood was assessed (*i.e.* heartwood/ sapwood), and stem diameters and the number of growth rings recorded. It should be noted that measurements from charred material may be up to 40% less than the living wood.

Results

The charcoal analysis is summarised in Table 10.12 and discussed below. Group names are given when anatomical differences between related genera are too slight to allow secure identification to genus level. These include members of the Salicaceae (*Salix* and *Populus*). Where a genus is represented by a single species in the British flora this is named as the most likely origin of the wood, given the provenance and period, but it should be noted that it is rarely possible to name individual species from wood features, and exotic species of trees and shrubs were introduced to Britain from an early period (Godwin 1956; Mitchell 1974). Classification follows that of *Flora Europaea* (Tutin *et al.* 1964–80).

The anatomical structure of the charcoal was consistent with the following taxa or groups of taxa:

Aceraceae. *Acer campestre* L., field maple; *A. pseudoplatanus L.,* sycamore (see Discusion)
Fagaceae. *Quercus* sp., oak
Oleaceae. *Fraxinus excelsior* L., ash
Salicaceae. *Salix* sp., willow, and *Populus* sp., poplar. In most respects these taxa are anatomically similar.
Ulmaceae. *Ulmus* sp., elm

The taxa identified from F.52 (sample 65) included narrow ash (*Fraxinus excelsior*) roundwood and willow (*Salix* sp.) or poplar (*Populus* sp.). One fragment of ash stem measured 18mm in diameter and included seven growth rings. The stem appeared to have been felled during the late spring or early summer. Sample 75, from F.53, was more abundant and included relatively large fragments of oak (*Quercus* sp.), ash (*Fraxinus excelsior*), elm (*Ulmus* sp.), maple (*Acer campestre*) and willow (*Salix* sp.) or poplar (*Populus* sp.). The oak consisted of a wedge of roundwood which measured 15mm in radius and included seven growth rings. Charcoal deposits from F.61, although sparse, identified the use of maple (*Acer campestre*) or, possibly sycamore (*A. pseuoplatanus*).

Discussion

Relatively fast-grown roundwood was recorded in pits F.52 and F.53. Rough estimates of stem dimensions prior to felling suggest diameters of about 25mm and 45mm, respectively. The high ratio of oxygen available to surface area for narrow roundwood (compared to logs from wide billets) rapidly promotes high-temperature burning, but to maintain the highest possible temperatures the fuel needs to be constantly replenished. The sarsen stones from F.52 and F.53 are estimated to have been similar in size to the 'Adam' stone, *i.e.* about 4m above ground level, and the destruction of such vast stones by fire-setting must have consumed huge quantities of fuel. The spatial sequence of destruction of the numerous sarsens is unknown but may have been influenced by the availability and supply of fuel. Fuel debris from the pits was dominated by burnt straw but also contained food refuse (*e.g.* charred grain, peas/ beans). The straw would almost certainly have been used as a tinder to help ignite a blazing fire and as a fuel source, but it is not clear whether the domestic debris was also regarded as useful fuel or if the fire merely offered a handy opportunity to dispose of household rubbish.

The charcoal from the burning pits demonstrated that in addition to large amounts of straw, firewood was gathered from large tree species, including oak (*Quercus* sp.), ash (*Fraxinus excelsior*), elm (*Ulmus* sp.), willow (*Salix* sp.) or poplar (*Populus* sp.) and field maple (*Acer campestre*) or, possibly, sycamore (*A. pseudoplatanus*). Sycamore was introduced to Britain in *c.*1500 and gradually naturalised in most parts of the country (Mitchell 1974). The use of sycamore at Avebury in the fire-setting pits is probably unlikely but can not be ruled out. The conspicuous absence of shrubby species in these charcoal deposits may be specifically related to function.

The presence of fast-grown roundwood infers access to, and use of, coppice stems or poles from managed woodland (possibly on a seven year rotation), but further corroborative evidence is needed to verify this suggestion. The apparent felling of ash roundwood in the spring is also of interest since general practice dictates that timber and coppice is best felled when dormant (Edlin 1949). Spring-felled ash could imply that firewood was felled as it was needed, on this occasion immediately prior to the fire-setting event (indicating a late spring activity). Alternatively, wood felled in the late spring may have been left to season for later use. It is also worth noting that, unlike most species, ash wood can be burnt green (unseasoned) (Edlin 1949). Although we have no direct evidence of woodland management at Avebury, it is probable that, in common with most other settlements in England, coppicing was established at least by the Saxon period and possibly considerably earlier (Rackham 1986).

Charcoal from the Falkner's Circle

Ruth Young

Methodology

On site sampling comprised collection of between 10 and 15 litres of soil from selected features or layers. These samples were processed using an Ankara style flotation machine, with a minimum 300-micron sieve. All recovered material was sorted by hand, and identified using a combination of standard keys and reference material. Wood charcoal preparation and identification followed standard procedure, namely selecting a range of pieces $2mm^3$ and larger, splitting them according to transverse, radial longitudinal and tangential longitudinal sections, and examining them under magnification up to x100 (Dimbleby 1978; Thompson 1994, 20). Identification of wood charcoal was carried out using the keys of Ilic (1991) and Schweingruber (1978) alongside reference material.

Given the vast quantities of wood charcoal that were recovered from the stone-burning contexts, in marked contrast to the straw that dominated the Beckhampton Avenue pits, a sub-sampling strategy was implemented. For each sample, 50 wood charcoal fragments were examined and identified. If more than five different types were noted the intention was to then examine a further 20 fragments. In practice this second stage was not deemed necessary as in none of the samples did the number of wood species exceed five. With contexts such as [728] (the lower fill of the large burning pit F.6) where large amounts of wood charcoal necessitated the collection of more than one sample, 50 fragments were selected randomly from the total recovered fraction (*i.e.* 50 fragments in total were examined for the context). Although many of the samples were exceptionally rich in charred material, their functional origin was not in doubt. As a result, further extended investigation beyond an initial assessment was not deemed necessary.

Discussion

Table 10.13 lists the wood charcoal recovered from each sample whilst Table 10.14 records all the other plant macroremains identified. It is clear from the data that wood charcoal dominates the plant macroremains assemblage. This is perhaps not surprising given the nature of the features excavated, which were associated with stone destruction – a process unlikely to be related to food processing or preparation, or indeed permanent occupation. As a result the absence of any significant seed assemblage should not be surprising.

What is interesting is the marked difference that can be seen in the fuelling strategy employed in the Falkner's Circle destructions in contrast to that utilised at Beckhampton. In the latter examples a wider variety of wood species were employed along with substantial quantities of straw. That the fuel recovered and identified from Falkner's Circle is dominated by oak charcoal indicates that either a very different technology was being employed or that fuel was gathered on a purely opportunistic basis. F.6 at the Falkner's Circle certainly argues for the former, as does the fact that the vast majority of the wood charcoal pieces examined were whole or part twigs or small branches. Very little in the way of what would appear to be large branches or trunk wood was noted. This suggests that the wood used in the burning episodes was collected deliberately, and that the burners were preferentially gathering up certain sized pieces. The lack of distortion in the wood further suggests that it had been deliberately dried out before being burnt, as green wood tends to distort more than pre-dried wood (Figueiral in Fulford and Allen 1992). The dominance of oak also suggests that this type was being deliberately selected. Rather than simply collecting random pieces, oak was clearly the fuel of choice and the overall number of oak fragments suggests that it occurred in appreciable concentrations in the area at this time. There are other species present in this assemblage, but in very low numbers. This suggests that they may have been growing near the oak stands and fallen branches and twigs were gathered up along with the oak branches.

Species:	[717]	[721]	[723]	[728]	[733]
Hazel	3	-	6	-	-
Hawthorn	-	-	2	-	-
Ash	2	-	2	1	-
Ivy	-	3	-	1	-
Holly	-	-	-	1	-
Cherry	3	-	1	-	-
Oak	41	44	39	46	50
Willow	-	-	-	-	-
Yew	-	-	-	2	-
Unidentified	1	3	2	-	-

Table 10.13. Wood charcoal from post-medieval contexts at the Falkner's Circle

Species:	[717]	[721]	[723]	[728]	[733]
Fat hen	1	1	-	-	-
Speedwell	1	-	-	-	-
Cleavers	-	2	-	-	-
Dock	-	-	-	1	-
Bromegrass	1	-	-	-	-
Grasses	-	2	-	-	-
Barley	-	-	-	1	-

Table 10.14. Other plant remains recovered from post-medieval contexts at the Falkner's Circle

After the destruction

Having explored in detail the process of destruction it is useful to now consider what happened to the various types of burning pit after the reduction of the stone had been effected and the sarsen taken away. Once again Stukeley's records provide the earliest discussion of the fate of the destruction pits, where the vast majority appear to have been left open by the stone-breakers. Certainly the 'cavitys' were sufficiently visible to Stukeley to enable him to reconstruct the positions of destroyed stones. Otherwise a degree of neglect is suggested by his note that 'the places were notorious by nettles and weeds growing up' and comments that ash trees were planted in the cavities resulting from the destruction of some of the stones of the Southern Inner Circle (Stukeley 1743, 22, 24; quoted in Ucko *et al.* 1991, 272). Interestingly, the only mention of deliberate back-filling within Avebury concerns the claim that Thomas Robinson 'perfectly levelled' the ground following the destruction of stones of the Outer Circle (1743, 22). However, this referred to a contiguous line of nine or ten stones in the SE Quadrant that we now know to have been buried (see p. 333). A more useful comment concerns stones of the West Kennet Avenue that were seen by Stukeley prior to their destruction. Here he recorded 'their places fresh turf'd over, for the sake of pasturage' (*ibid.*, 30).

The archaeological evidence likewise supports the suggestion that in the vast majority of cases the pits were left to fill of their own accord or were put to pragmatic uses. We have already noted the recovery of numerous wine bottles by Smith and Cunnington in their excavation of a burning pit in the Northern Inner Circle. During his excavations on the Southern Inner Circle Keiller likewise made a number of discoveries that suggested the pits had not been immediately backfilled. In the fill of the multiple burning pit of stones ix, x and xi a mass of horse bone was recovered along with pottery dating from the 13th to 18th centuries. In the base of the burning pit of stone 109 of the Southern Inner Circle was a square cavity (approximately 1.5 × 1.0m) containing the burial of an adult carthorse. In each case these deposits were attributed to the proximity of the Pratt family's Tanning Yard and dated to the 19th century. Assuming this date to be correct, it suggests that sufficiently large and obvious hollows had survived into the 19th century to appear as attractive and suitable dumping areas. Indeed, the presence of stakeholes following the perimeter of the stone 109 pit suggests that the hollow resulting from the burning episode was deliberately fenced off.

In the case of settings L1 and L4 of the Beckhampton Avenue the destruction deposits were sealed by homogenous layers of plough-soil which seem to have formed slowly, perhaps as the result of repeated episodes of ploughing, since the charcoal-rich soil was 'washed' from around the sarsen fragments, only surviving underneath them. This pattern was repeated at setting L10 and, albeit on a smaller scale, at setting L7. In the case of the latter, following the burning and breaking up of the stone, all but the smallest flakes were removed and the pit once again left to naturally infill. In the case of the large pit associated with setting L11 of the Longstones Cove, once the larger pieces of sarsen had been raked up the gently sloping southern ramp the pit was not deliberately backfilled but instead left to fill naturally with a combination of ploughsoil and upcast.

The only destruction feature that produced conclusive evidence for deliberate back-filling following the stone breaking (as opposed to during the process as appears to be the case for setting L8) was the large furnace that had been constructed to burn setting L15. In this case the pit was fully backfilled with dumps of chalk rubble. The most likely explanation is a practical one, the back-filling a response to the sheer depth of the resultant hole and mounds of spoil generated by its digging.

The process of destruction

We can draw a number of conclusions from the surviving antiquarian, and earlier, evidence. The first is that stone breaking was already a well-established practice by the time Avebury was 'discovered' as an archaeological oddity in 1649. The second is that whilst stone breaking was taking place, and buildings and field walls were being constructed of sarsen in and around Avebury, the first direct (as opposed to anecdotal) association between destruction and standing stones comes with the records of Stukeley.

This has important implications for how we regard the process of stone breaking as there is a temptation to equate stone-burning solely with the destruction of standing stones. Instead we have to acknowledge that the practice originally developed in response to recumbent, partially buried sarsens out on the downs. The burning of substantial upright stones thus represents the enhancement and modification of an *existing* practice rather than wholly new development.

If we focus upon the detailed drawn record of Stukeley, in each of the depictions the suggestion is of a practice that was organised and efficient. It was also complex, labour-intensive and potentially exhausting. Put simply, those responsible have clearly 'done it before' and there is a distinct performative aspect to the event depicted, from the neatness of the pit to the scale of the sarsen chosen for destruction. There has been little discussion to date of the potential performance involved in a stone burning, particularly one taking place within the heart of a village. Burning a sarsen would always have been an event, but in the case of large stones the straw bales required to heat the sarsen would have resulted in a particularly dramatic (and smoky) conflagration. In the case of Avebury itself additional urgency, danger and spectacle would have been afforded by the sheer congestion of the site, both Aubrey and Stukeley documenting the buildings (with highly combustible thatched roofs), hedges, hay-ricks and boundaries that choked the interior. In this light it might be profitable to revisit the speculation of Smith and Cunnington regarding 'jovial spirits' after finding wine bottles in the burning pit of a stone of the Northern Inner Circle close to the site of the former inn. One might also suggest that the event recorded by Stukeley was unusual rather than routine. Even accepting Stukeley's frequent manipulation of scale to aggrandise the size of the Avebury settings (see Figure 4.2) the size of the sarsen and scale of the pit are clearly immense. This prompted Smith to suggest that the drawings depicted the burning of a buried stone (Smith 1965, 180, footnote 2), an interpretation which seems likely given the levers and depth of the burning pit as compared to the majority of such features excavated.

Assuming the two depictions represent the same event (and not an idealised or archetypal burning) it is tempting to speculate where this took place. The backdrop to the watercolour appears to be precisely that, an idealised downland scene complete with a scattering of barrows upon which the dramatic events are arranged. More interesting is the 'Atto da fe' image, where a ghostly standing stone is visible behind the pile of broken sarsen and plumes of smoke. This situates the event within one of the components of the monument and it may be interesting (though ultimately frustrating) to relate the date of the drawing to known date ranges for destruction based on documentary and archaeological sources and size ranges of stones surviving. The presence of a burial pit and lack of any adjacent sarsens of commensurate scale certainly rules out the huge settings of the Longstones Cove.

What is interesting is that in his written and drawn records Stukeley appears to be describing two very different techniques. Likewise Smith's published description of the process does not do justice to the actual variation encountered by Keiller. If we look in detail at the Beckhampton Avenue destruction events further evidence for variations in practice can be discerned. The burning pits marking settings L1 (F.21) and L4 (F.24) were shallow and irregular features: oval, between 3.16–5.40m across and up to 0.35m deep, with very uneven bases. The rough bases could be a reflection of expediency, as the diggers of the pit reached the harder chalk. It could also reflect practical considerations, an uneven base allowing for better airflow to the fire. In each case the basal fills comprised extensive spreads of flaked and burnt sarsen within a matrix of burnt straw and charcoal.

A very different pattern is seen at setting L8 where the destruction pit seems to have been dug in two stages. The original phase corresponds to the deeper southernmost area, comprising a sub-rectangular pit dug directly adjacent to and up to the base of the stone, destroying all traces of the stone-hole on the northernmost side. The stone was then toppled into the pit and burned, resulting in a concentrated zone of debris. The second phase comprised the digging of the gently sloping northern zone. This may have been to provide material to fill the gap between the burning zone and the lip of the original pit whilst simultaneously providing a ramp for hauling out the broken stone. Equally it could reflect two distinct episodes of activity. At some time prior to the early 18th century the stone was partially buried in a deliberately cut pit. That the surface of the stone projected beyond the surface by the 18th century is suggested by Stukeley's records (see below). At some point following this survey it was burned and broken up. It is at this point that the sloping northern portion of the exposed destruction pit was cut to facilitate the setting of fuel and subsequent removal of broken stone. It is also possible that the northernmost edge of the original burial pit, corresponding to the zone of re-deposited chalk, was cut-back at this time to increase the available working space. The highly irregular shape of this edge certainly supports such an interpretation.

Whether fallen or buried, the main problem in destroying stone L8 related to the introduction of adequate fuel beneath it to heat it to a sufficient temperature. Given the relatively small size of the stone suggested by the size of the destruction area, it is possible that hoists and levers were used to lift the sarsen to enable fuel and supports to be set beneath. This would explain the gentle downward slope of the stake-holes cut into the compacted chalk remnant of the original stone-hole. Following the stone burning, the over-cut area between the burial pit and platform was deliberately filled with re-deposited chalk to create a level platform for stone removal.

Moving on to the much larger settings associated with the Longstones Cove, the destruction of L11 involved the digging of a sloping ramp from the south directly up to the base of the stone-hole, effectively digging away its southern edge. The resultant wedge-shaped pit would serve to facilitate the removal of broken stone and the visible spread of burnt sarsen material at the surface on the southern edge lends valuable support to this interpretation. As with L1 and L4 the irregularity of the base of the burning pit could reflect the employment of a rather *ad hoc* digging strategy, or a much more deliberate attempt to ensure a flow of air beneath the stone once firing had begun. Once dug, the slumping of material along the southern edge suggests that the pit was left open for a period prior to actual stone destruction. At some point after this slumping the pit was filled with fuel and spacing boulders and the stone was toppled southwards into it. The clear step cut above the stone-hole to the north along with its post-setting most likely relate to this toppling event. The majority of the observed slumping at the northern edge of the pit appears to have taken place after the burning event and may well reflect a lack of stability in this steeper edge or a more conscious attempt to create a stable platform for the removal of stone once the firing had been completed.

One of the most interesting aspects of the L11 destruction was the curving line of hollows along the southernmost edge of the pit. Although situated an appreciable distance away from the stone-hole, it is tempting to see these features as representing the bases of truncated post settings associated with the original stone setting. The fact that they were truncated by the destruction pit and directly sealed by the slump deposit suggests that they predated the stone destruction episode. However, the irregularity of the base of the central hollow and clear evidence of animal burrowing in the upper fills may indicate that they are the result of later disturbance. This is certainly suggested by the piece of heavily corroded iron found in the base of the hollow containing the sarsen lumps.

The largest and most unusual of the burning pits was that associated with setting L15. This elaborately engineered pit represents an effective practical response to the challenge posed by a recumbent stone weighing over 50 tons. Too bulky to lever up and fire-set in the conventional manner, the solution adopted was to mine underneath the stone, leaving it supported on spurs of un-dug chalk, thus creating a void in which a fire could be set. Essentially, the pit became a furnace with the stone its 'lid'. The first stage of the operation involved digging the deep pits on the north-west, north-east and south-west, undercutting the stone by a metre or so on each side. These provided access and working space to allow further tunnelling, leading to the creation of a large void underneath the stone where the fire would be set. In order to maximise the surface area of the fire the deeper eastern and western pits were partially backfilled up to the level of the central section, thus creating an even base on which fuel for the burning could be spread. In the case of setting L16 too little of the burning pit was exposed to establish its form and character though the removal of the eastern side of the stone-hole and lack of disturbance to the west suggests a similar approach to that adopted for setting L11.

At the Falkner's Circle, in addition to the burning pits, a thick orange-brown sandy clay buried soil [701] was noted during excavation, extending across the eastern and southern part of the trench and filling a large natural hollow. An intermittent spread of fire-reddened clay and charcoal flecking [707] was traced over an area of *c.*10 × 4m within the centre of the buried soil. Restricted to its upper part, this most likely relates to episodes of post-medieval stone destruction otherwise attested by the destruction pits.

Variations in practice

From the information presented above it is possible to identify 11 distinct methods of reducing recalcitrant sarsens into manageable blocks of stone (Table 10.15). As with any classification, considerable variety exists within each of these destruction-types and a degree of overlap inevitably occurs. This most likely reflects the ways in which tried and trusted techniques and practices were interpreted, varying according to the precise mix of personnel involved, pragmatically with respect to the specific problems posed by any given sarsen, and of course temporally – this was after all a long-lived practice.[5]

Approaches to burning upright stones

There appear to have been five basic approaches to the burning of a standing stone:

The ramp technique

As described by Young in the case of the Sanctuary destructions and encountered at settings L11 (and possibly L16) of the Longstones Cove and stone 15 of the Outer Circle, this is clearly a technique developed to deal with the destruction of standing stones (Figure 10.22a). It involved the digging of a

Technique	Settings
Ramp	BA L11, L16 Sanctuary 1, 2, 41 (and 2 others) Avebury 15
Upright	Falkner's F6 Avebury 17, 18
Short-pit and lever	Avebury 3, 38, 39, 43, 45, ring-stone
Adjacent-pit	BA L7, L10 Falkner's F7 WKA 23B
Roughly-dug pit	Avebury 108, 109?, 11 BA L1, L4
Buried-stone	BA L8
Scoop	Avebury Obelisk, 37 WKA 19A
Tunnel	Avebury 104; 107; 13; 19, 20, 21, 22; I WKA 17A, 17B
Furnace	BA L15
Direct Fracture	WKA 34B, 12A, 12B, 11A, 9A, 8A, 7A, 7B, 5B Avebury 41, 42, xii
Dragging away	Sanctuary (remaining stones) BA L3 WKA 36B, 31B, 28A, 27A, 22A, 22B, 21B, 20B, 11B, 10A, 10B, 9B, 8B, 6A, 6B, 5A

Table 10.15. Techniques of stone destruction

sloping ramp from the surface down to the base of the stone-hole. The length and steepness of the ramp reflected the size of the stone and depth of stone-hole. Once the ramp had been dug the stone could be pushed over into the resultant pit, presumably on to boulders that had been placed there to support its bulk and allow adequate airflow beneath it. Given the need for the base of the ramp to support the weight of the stone during burning, it would have had to have been dug into the chalk natural rather than topsoil. Once burning and breaking had taken place the sloping ramp would then allow stone to be raked and hauled out of the pit. This may well be the technique described by Stukeley as typifying stone burning, where 'the method is, to dig a pit by the side of the stone, till it falls down' (1743, 15).

The upright technique

This is perhaps the most direct, if unimaginative, technique for destroying a standing stone (Figure 10.22b). What characterises it is that no attempt is made to topple the stone prior to burning. Instead a pit is dug around the base of the stone, filled with fuel and then ignited. The clearest example of this type of event was F.6 at the site of Falkner's Circle where a deep, almost circular pit surrounded the stone. That this approach may not have been particularly efficient is attested by the fact that two distinct fire-settings were needed to destroy the Falkner's stone.

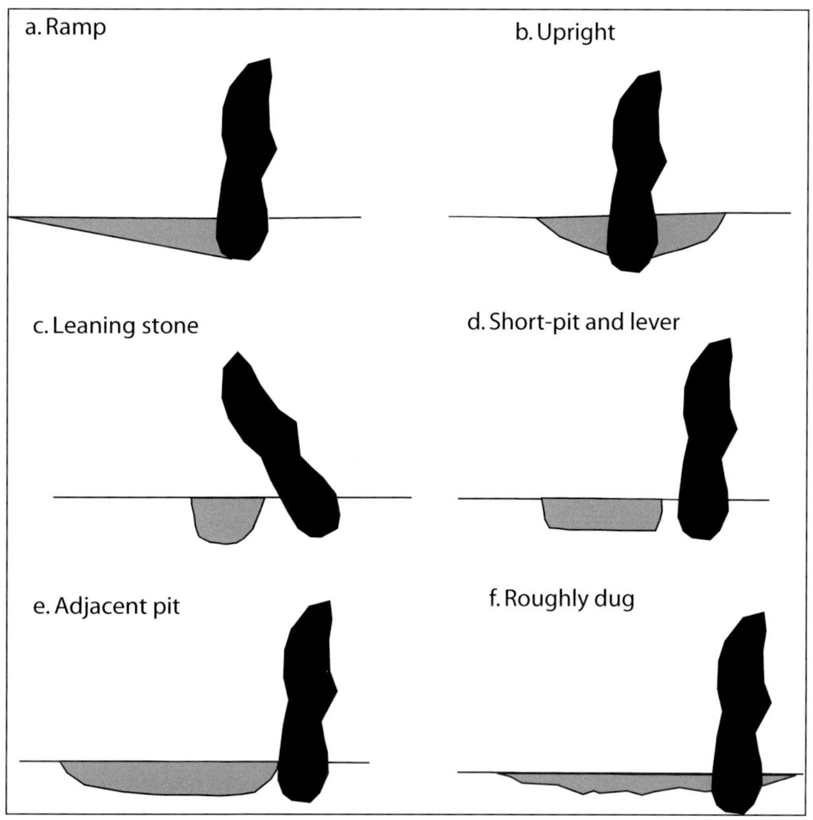

Figure 10.22. Approaches to the breaking of upright stones

Variations of this were encountered at settings 17 and 18 of the Outer Circle at

Avebury where deep pits were dug in an attempt to heat and break leaning stones without having to topple them (Figure 10.22c). As in the case of F.6, the process was inefficient insofar as the breakers had to resort to direct fracture to finally break up the sarsens.

THE SHORT-PIT AND LEVER TECHNIQUE

The approach adopted here was to dig a discrete burning pit adjacent to the stone but separated from its base by a ridge of un-dug ground, the latter acting as a retaining-wall to stop the stone from toppling (Figure 10.22d). The pit itself was carefully dug to ensure that it was too short to accommodate the full length of the stone. Once completed, the supporting ridge was dug away and the stone levered over onto the pit. Because the pit was too small, the far-end (*i.e.* top) of the stone would end up resting on the edge thus creating a cavity beneath for fuel and airflow. This technique was employed at settings 3, 38, 39, 43 and 45 of the Outer Circle.

To facilitate destruction of the Ring-Stone in the South-East Quadrant of Avebury an unusually deep burning pit was dug (1.5m below turf) for the stone to be toppled onto causing Keiller to ponder whether the stone itself was a particularly thick one. As in the case of settings 17 and 18 (see 'upright technique') the practice of digging very deep burning pits does not appear to have been particularly successful, a large chunk of the base of the stone remaining unbroken. As has been mentioned, despite the digging of a new gully under this chunk to get extra fuel beneath it, it could not be sufficiently heated (the gully remaining packed full of part burnt and unburnt straw). Rather than resort to direct-fracture the thwarted stone-breakers decided to bury it.

THE ADJACENT PIT TECHNIQUE

In practice a regular dish-shaped pit was dug adjacent to a stone, large enough to accommodate its fallen bulk and deep enough to provide a solid chalk base upon which to support its weight (Figure 10.22e). In the case of stones L7 and L10 of the Beckhampton Avenue a clear gap was visible at the level of the chalk between the cut of the stone-hole and that of the destruction pit, whereas at Falkner's Circle the pit dug to destroy stone F.7 cut into the stone-hole.

With the digging finished, the stone was then placed within the pit. Presumably boulders and fuel could either be laid on the base of the pit prior to the arrival of the stone or levers could be used to lift it once fallen to enable boulders and fuel to be placed underneath. What is unclear is whether the stones were actually prised and lifted from their stone-holes as part of the act of destruction (either before, during or after the digging of the pit) or were already lying prone. In the case of stone 23B of the West Kennet Avenue the stone appears to have fallen prior to being burned in its pit.

It is interesting to note that in the case of L7 and L10 surviving documentary evidence suggests stones that were either broken off to stumps or fallen and partially buried (L7, L10) and this technique may have been carefully tailored to the destruction of such stones.

THE ROUGHLY DUG PIT

Employed at setting 11 of the Outer Circle, 108 and possibly 109[6] of the Southern Inner Circle and L1 and L4 of the Beckhampton Avenue, this approach is characterised by the creation of a large, expediently dug pit with shallow sloping sides merging with an irregular base (Figure 10.22f). The pit appears to have been dug around the base of the upright stone, removing much of the stone-hole in the process; the stone was then toppled into the pit. As with the adjacent pit method it is unclear whether boulders and fuel were placed on the base of the pit prior to, or after, toppling. The presence of packing stones forced into the base of the burning pit of stone 11 of the Outer Circle seems to argue the former, though this is dependant upon the weight of the stone and relative compaction of the pit base at this point.

Approaches to burning recumbent stones

In much the same way as the ramp and adjacent pit methods appear to have been designed specifically to deal with upright standing stones, the stone-breakers also developed and refined a series of techniques to enable them to destroy stones that had fallen or been previously buried.

THE BURIED-STONE TECHNIQUE

One method of dealing with buried stones is illustrated by setting L8 of the Beckhampton Avenue (Figure 10.23a). In practice the fill of the burial pit was dug out and the pit itself enlarged to enable sufficient room for the burning to take place. Levers were then used to raise the stone enabling boulders and fuel to be placed beneath.

The scoop technique

This rather pragmatic technique appears to have been developed to facilitate the destruction of fallen or toppled stones with the minimum of excavation. In practice a series of scoops and scrapings were hollowed out along the edge of the fallen stone to enable fuel to be inserted beneath it (Figure 10.23b). Examples include the Obelisk, setting 10 of the Outer Circle and stone 19A of the West Kennet Avenue. The destruction of the Obelisk was unusual insofar as it was broken up gradually from the base to the top (over 6m) through a series of successive burning events. This was clear from the stratigraphy of the destruction pits, the upcast from the scraping out of burning hollows sealing the debris generated by the previous burning episode. This episodic 'nibbling away' at the bulk of the fallen stone may have taken place over an extended period of time.

The tunnel technique

A more elaborate approach to the destruction of a recumbent stone took the form of the creation of a series of airways and cavities beneath it, the bulk of the sarsen left supported by un-dug pillars and ridges of ground (Figure 10.23c). In the case of settings 104 and 107 of the Southern Inner Circle, this resulted in a distinctive cruciform plan as a series of channels were dug under the fallen stone to facilitate airflow. This was applied to stones lying on the surface (having fallen naturally or been deliberately toppled) and those discovered buried in earlier pits. Examples of the former include stone 13 of the Outer Circle and stones 17A and 17B of the West Kennet Avenue. When dealing with buried stones the tactic appears to have been to firstly remove the fill of the burial pit before digging down into its base to create tunnels and hollows beneath the stone (for example stones 19–22 of Outer Circle and stone i of the Southern Inner).

The furnace technique

The most sophisticated method for burning a fallen sarsen involved the digging of an elaborate furnace structure beneath it, the stone itself left to act as a 'lid' supported on un-dug spurs of ground (Figure 10.23d). The evidence from setting L15 of the Beckhampton Avenue shows that this required not only careful planning and organisation, but a large input of labour.

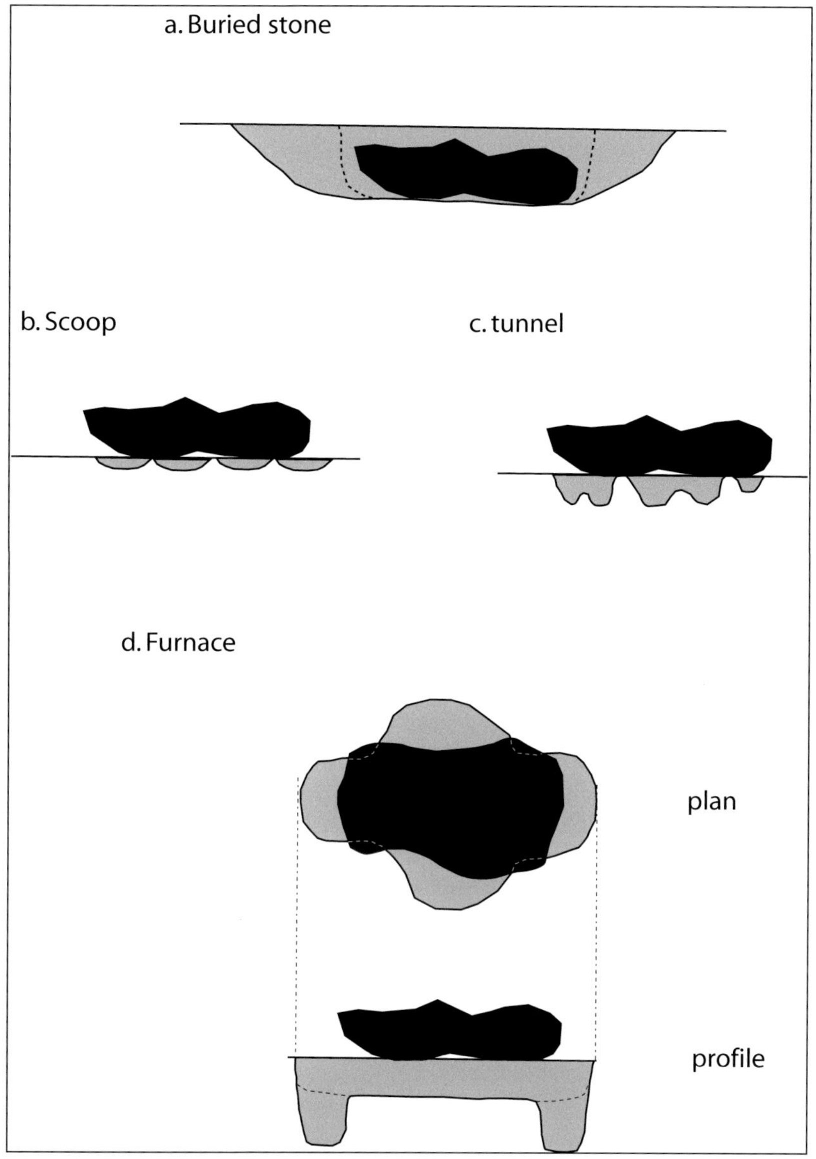

Figure 10.23. Approaches to the breaking of fallen stones

Direct fracture

Although stone-burning has perhaps captured the archaeological and historical imaginations, it is important to acknowledge that in some cases direct fracture (using iron wedges and presumably hammers) and the simple dragging away of stones accounted for more sarsens than fire-setting. As discussed earlier, this was certainly the case along the line of the West Kennet Avenue where 11 sarsens were broken up *in situ* using direct fracture. A total of nine of these appear to have been standing with a further two buried at an earlier date. Where detailed information survives regarding the destruction of the standing stones (eight cases), all were deliberately toppled prior to destruction, either through the excavation of a destruction pit that incorporated the stone-hole (settings12A, 12B, 11A and 9A), or through digging into the stone-hole and levering (8A, 7A, 7B, 5B). The most complex examples of direct fracture destruction took place on the arc of the Outer Circle and involved a variation on the short-pit and lever technique (settings 41 and 42).

Dragging away

On the line of the West Kennet Avenue the removal of stones to another location, either as an act of clearance or for breaking elsewhere, was also practised. This could result in low densities of sarsen chips and flakes (suggesting some limited direct fracture) or none at all. Of the 16 examples known a total of nine showed clear evidence of having been deliberately toppled prior to removal (stones 31B, 28A, 27A, 11B, 10A, 9B, 6A, 5A). At the Sanctuary, the bulk of the stones making up the settings were dragged away; and there is one example of a previously buried stone being dug up and presumably dragged away (setting L3 of the Beckhampton Avenue).

Further complications

It must be acknowledged that these are ideal types and there is an inevitable degree of blurring between some of the classes identified. For example, whilst the L15 construction is undoubtedly that of a carefully engineered furnace, in other cases it is difficult to distinguish between the tunnelling and furnace techniques; likewise the adjacent and roughly-dug pit techniques. To further complicate matters there are instances where more than one approach was adopted. Take for example stone 14B of the West Kennet Avenue. A circular pit was dug adjacent to the stone, removing much of the stone-hole in the process. The stone was then allowed to topple into the pit and then abandoned for a period sufficient for the original pit to silt up. At a subsequent date the project was continued, the silting necessitating the digging of a new pit under the stone to allow fuel to be inserted and air to flow. Direct fracture also appears to have been resorted to when firing failed to fully reduce a stone, as in the case of settings 17 and 18 of the Outer Circle. In the case of stone 24 of the Outer Circle a failed attempt to shatter the stone using iron wedges had taken place prior to the decision to bury it in the base of a pond (see Chapter 9).

There are also instances, such as the movement and incorporation of already fallen stones into structures such as field banks, that served to effectively remove the sarsens yet does not really constitute destruction.

What does this variation represent?

Having identified a series of discrete techniques, we are faced with the question of what they represent. One argument is that the techniques reflect the pragmatic challenges posed by specific stones. It is clear that different solutions were developed to break fallen as opposed to standing stones; the former drawing upon the experience gained out on the downs, the latter the result of improvisation and experimentation. It is also difficult to deny that some of the more spectacular and unusual techniques, such as the L15 furnace and sequential destruction of the Obelisk, were prompted by the specific challenges posed by a given sarsen. However, at any given time there appear to have been a range of options available for destroying a given recumbent or standing stone. As to whether these variations were a product of the gradual evolution and development of the techniques through time, or a reflection of the preferred techniques of individual groups requires careful consideration of the chronology of stone-breaking.

Dating the destructions

At first glance our dating for the destruction of the Avebury stones seems remarkably secure. Stukeley believed that the monument had been intact during the 16th century, claiming emphatically that not only had the destruction taken place within the 30 years up to his recording of the site but that:

> 'The custom of destroying them is so late, that I could easily trace the obit of every stone, who did it, for what purpose, and when, and by what method, what house or wall was built out of it, and the like.' (1743, 16)

Support for this is given in the careful

Year	Stones Destroyed
*c.*1694	Northern Inner Circle (1)
1700	Contiguous line of stones of the Outer Circle (9). Southern Inner Circle (2)
1701	Stones of the Beckhampton Avenue used to create bridge
1702	Stones of the Beckhampton Avenue close to western entrance (2)
1710	Southern Inner Circle (1-3)
1711	Stones of the Northern Inner Circle located in the street (3)
1712	Stones of Southern Inner Circle (5)
1713	Cove at Avebury (1) and ?Longstones Cove (1)
1714	Northern Inner Circle (1) and Beckhampton Avenue (3+)
1715	Northern Inner Circle (1)
1717	Northern Inner Circle (c.5)
1718	Outer Circle (c.3) and Northern Inner Circle (?1)
1719	Northern Inner Circle (3–4)
Sometime before 1720	Approximately 20 stones of the Beckhampton Avenue were broken sometime before 1720 by Farmer Griffin
1720	Outer Circle (1) and West Kennet Avenue (several)
1721/2	Northern Inner Circle (1)
1722	West Kennet Avenue adjacent to southern entrance (2)
1724	The Sanctuary

Table 10.16. Stukeley's time-line of stone destruction.

annotations on his famous frontispiece, recording dates that stones were carried away and/or destroyed. A tentative time-line of stone destruction based upon Stukeley's annotations is offered in Table 10.16.

The suggestion is of regular stone breaking spanning the period *c.*1694–1724, with a steady trickle of episodes punctuated by more sustained campaigns such as that taking place in 1700 and those affecting the Sanctuary and Beckhampton Avenue. Further evidence regarding the pace of destruction can be found in Stukeley's note that 'every year I found several of them [sarsens] wanting; but the places very apparent whence they were taken' (1743, 16).

Despite its detail, there is good reason to regard the veracity of Stukeley's records with a degree of suspicion. In a detailed analysis of the various drafts and notes that informed his final publication of the Avebury research, Ucko *et al.* highlighted a number of inconsistencies, commenting that his own notes were frequently either 'inadequate or self-contradictory' (1991, 182–3). A single example should suffice to illustrate this ambiguity. In his published discussion of the Outer Circle at Avebury, a line of 10 contiguous stones are recorded as having been destroyed by one Thomas Robinson (1743, 22). However, his unpublished tour originally recorded nine contiguous settings as having been destroyed (before being corrected to 10) and in his published frontispiece only nine are indicated as having been broken in this year by Robinson. To further confound this, in an earlier draft of the frontispiece (draft N) a continuous line of 12 stones are claimed to have fallen to Robinson in 1700 (Ucko *et al.* 1991, 272, pl. 32). This confusion regarding the precise number of stones destroyed by Robinson in 1700 might seem trivial if it were not for the fact that Aubrey's survey of 1663 showed the same area as empty of stones and campaigns of probing (Lukis 1881–3a, 151–3) and geophysical survey (carried out by the National Trust in 2003) revealed *buried* stones in the locations indicated by Stukeley. The claim that Robinson destroyed them in 1700 was a fiction.[7] Further, and as discussed earlier, the clay pipe evidence from Avebury suggests that destruction may have begun a decade or so before his inception date of 1694 and in one instance point to a date some three decades earlier than the 1720 recorded by Stukeley in his frontispiece.

Whilst this certainly calls into question the detail of his record and urges caution in the reader, his record is perhaps best thought of as uneven rather than fundamentally flawed and more reliable in its generalities than specifics. It is certainly the case that when combined with the results of excavation, Stukeley's drawings provide a useful *terminus post quem* for later destruction episodes. This is clearest in the case of Keiller's excavations along the western arc of the Outer Circle, where a close match between the documentary evidence and the sequence of destruction suggested by the stratigraphy of burning pits, field banks and ditches (Chapter 8) can be identified (Figure

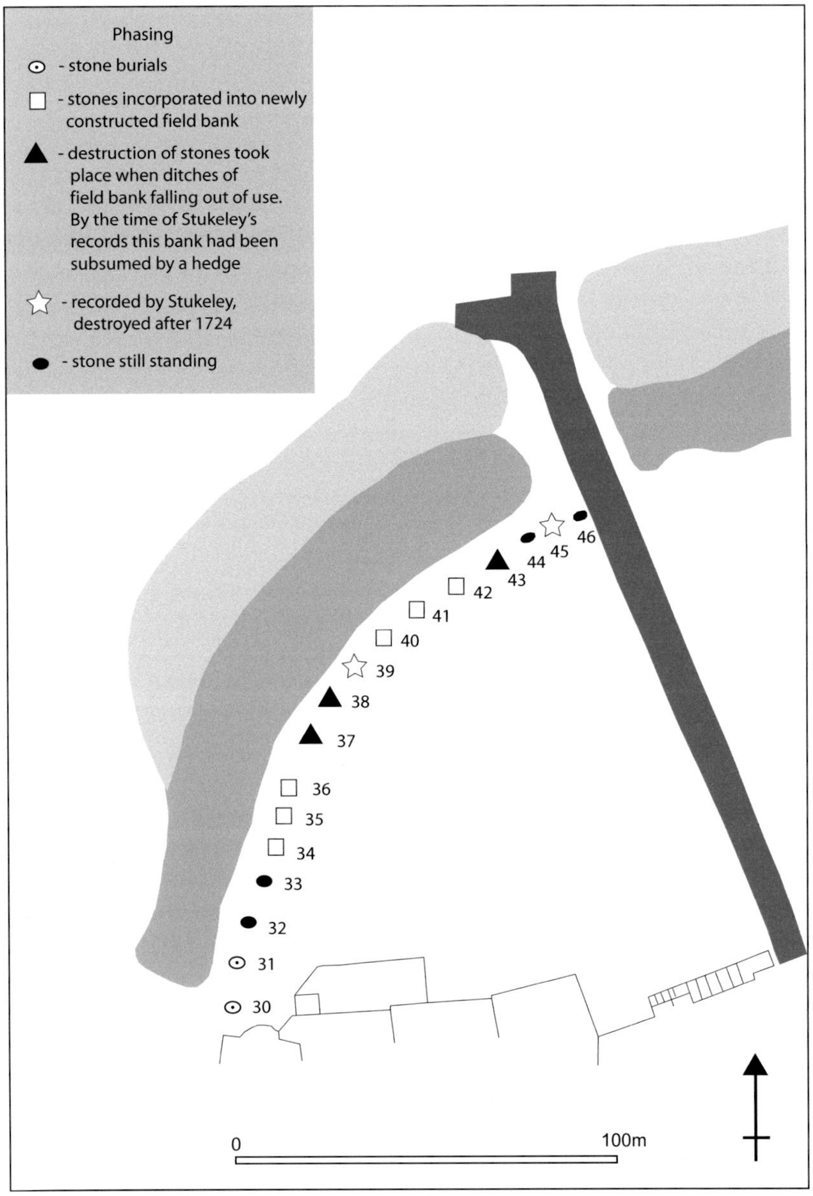

Figure 10.24. Phasing of stone destruction in the NW quadrant of Avebury. Incorporates data © Crown Copyright/database right 2007. An Ordnance Survey/(EDINA) supplied service

10.24). For example, the records of Stukeley (and for that matter Aubrey) are in agreement in recording settings 43 and 45 as standing by 1724, enabling us to date their destruction to a point after this with some confidence (Ucko *et al.* 1991, 233).

Looking to the Beckhampton Avenue settings, the ceramics recovered from the excavation of destruction features indicate at best a date between the 16th and 19th centuries. More refined dating comes from the documentary records and finds of stamped clay pipe (Figure 10.25). Stone L15 was lying fallen when Stukeley drew his plan on the 21st of May 1724 and was thus destroyed sometime after this date. Stones L11 and L16 were recorded as having been destroyed by Richard Fowler *c.*1717 (Stukeley 1743, 35). Although no stamped clay pipe fragments were recovered from these features, the presence of a wide-bore stem and later style of bowl would support the argument for a date around 1700.

In the case of stone L10 the surviving drawn records of this portion of the avenue are rather ambiguous; a stone in this position appears in some of Stukeley's drawings and not in others. In Gough Maps 231 f7v, a plan view of the avenue around Longstones Cove depicts L10 as an open (rather than filled) rectangle whilst in Gough Maps 231, 42 and Eng. Misc. b.65 f63 it is recorded as 'thrown down half buryed' and 'lying' respectively. In Gough Maps 231, 42, a perspectival drawing of the Cove looking from the south-east appears to record a stone in position L10 as 'thrown down half buryed'. In contrast, stone L10 is completely absent from MS Eng. Misc b.65 f109, f53, f58, f63 and Gough Maps 231 f223. The suggestion is of a fallen stone broken up *during* the period of his visits (*i.e.* between 1719–1724).

Settings L7 and L8 are consistently recorded in Stukeley's surviving drawings as fallen and partly buried, suggesting that destruction took place some time after 1724. Confirmation for this comes from the stamped clay pipe stem found in the L7 destruction pit. This was produced by the pipe-maker John Greenland who was manufacturing pipes from the late 17th and into the 18th century. Stem stamps appear late in his repertoire, perhaps during his period of residence in nearby Marlborough (1705–1736) (Atkinson 1980, 67–8).

More difficult are the L1, L3 and L4 destruction features. The absence of these stones from Stukeley's drawn records suggests that in the case of settings L1 and L4 destruction had taken place prior to his fieldwork. As we know that no effort was made to deliberately backfill and level the resultant burning pits and Stukeley recorded no depressions as marking their former positions (a practice undertaken with the Avebury settings) one can suggest a reasonable amount of time had elapsed between burning and recording. The presence of clay pipe dated to the period 1660–1680 suggests that these destructions had taken place in the third or fourth quarters of the 17th century.

In the case of L3, the presence of late 18th- – early 19th-century pottery in the fill of the

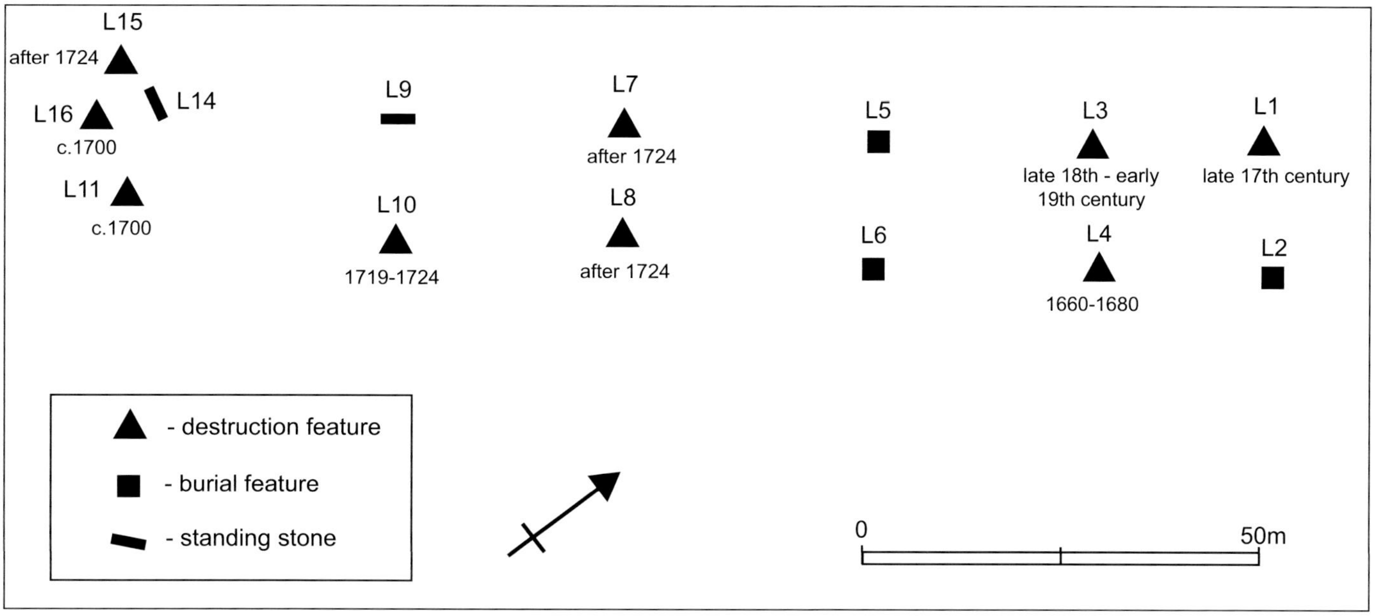

Figure 10.25. Dating the destructions on the line of the Beckhampton Avenue excavated in the south-west of Longstones Field

burial pit suggests that the stone had been dug out and dragged away long after the main period of stone-burning, perhaps as a result of the plough striking the shallowly buried sarsen. Other finds from the pit fill included a clay pipe bowl fragment with a stamped heel that had been manufactured between 1667 and 1696. If we accept a date in the last quarter of the 17th century for the burial of the stone this would account for its absence in Stukeley's records.

As has been discussed, the destruction events on the line of the West Kennet Avenue were of a rather different character, with wholesale relocation and *in situ* breaking preferred to fire-setting, particularly in the 200m stretch of avenue as it left the southern entrance of the henge. That this took place in the latter half of the 17th century is suggested by the documentary evidence. Aubrey had originally recorded the stretch of the avenue leaving the southern entrance of the henge as largely intact (Ucko *et al.* 1991, 186). In the description given in the 1695 edition of Camden, attributed to Aubrey's unpublished manuscript, the following is noted:

> 'From this place to West-Kennet is a walk that has been enclos'd on each side with large stones, only one side at present wants a great many, but the other is almost, if not quite entire.' (Gibson 1695, 111)

Careful study of Stukeley's drawings of the course of the Avenue such as the Panorama, drawn *c.*1723 (Piggott 1985, pl. 13) suggests that the stones had been removed by this date. Dating of the stone burnings (as opposed to dragging away/direct fracture) is more difficult. The only clay pipe evidence comprised a single broken and blackened example from the base of the second-phase 14B burning pit. Given the association between clay pipes and destruction seen elsewhere at Avebury, this absence is interesting and once again suggests a distinct episode removed from the main period of breaking.

A number of factors made the destruction episodes identified at the Falkner's Circle unusual with respect to previously excavated burning pits. First and foremost was the technology employed. Whilst F.7 was destroyed using the adjacent pit technique, F.6 was unique in the way in which the upright burning was effected. In both cases a very different fuelling strategy was employed to that seen elsewhere in the Avebury landscape, extensive use being made of roundwood as opposed to the more familiar straw. Two explanations can be offered to account for these anomalies. The first is that the Falkner's Circle destruction had taken place at a different time in the Avebury sequence. This is supported indirectly by the marked absence of any mention of the circle in the otherwise exhaustive records of Aubrey or Stukeley and the lack of clay pipes, implying that this distinctive destruction technology may have belonged to a very early episode of stone burning. The second alternative is that the destruction took place at the same time as the main episode of stone burning but was carried

Table 10.17. Radiocarbon determinations from late (post-prehistoric) features at the Falkner's Circle

Sample	Feature	Context	Measured Radiocarbon Age	2 Sigma calibrated results (95% probability)
Beta – 176547	6	[728[	140 ± 60 BP	Cal AD 1650 to 1950 (Cal BP 300 to 0)
Beta – 176548	6	[728]	260± 80 BP	Cal AD 1450 to 1710 (Cal BP 500 to 240) Cal AD 1720 to 1880 (Cal BP 230 to 70) Cal AD 1910 to 1950 (Cal BP 40 to 0)
Beta – 176549	6	[728]	210 ± 60 BP	Cal AD 1520 to 1580 (Cal BP 430 to 380) Cal AD 1630 to 1890 (Cal BP 320 to 60) Cal AD 1910 to 1950 (Cal BP 40 to 0)
Beta – 176550	7	[733]	280 ± 50 BP	Cal AD 1480 to 1670 (Cal BP 470 to 280) Cal AD 1770 to 1800 (Cal BP 180 to 150) Cal AD 1940 to 1950 (Cal BP 10 to 0)
Beta – 176551	7	[733]	380 ± 60 BP	Cal AD 1420 to 1650 (Cal BP 530 to 300)

out by a different, and distinctive, group of stone-breakers.

In order to explore this further a series of five conventional radiocarbon determinations were undertaken on samples of roundwood charcoal taken from the primary burning layers of F.6 [728] and F.7 [733]. The results are summarised in Table 10.17. We know that no stones were visible in these locations by 1840 when Falkner made his identification, and thus the outlying 20th century ranges can be excluded. Despite its unusual form, the F.6 destruction appears to have taken place during the main phase of stone breaking between the 17th and early 19th centuries. More surprising are the dates obtained for F.7 which span the early 15th to late 17th centuries, with the probability weighted towards the earlier part of that range. This is a conventional burning pit in terms of form but one that predates by an appreciable margin the destructions recorded at Avebury. It appears then that unlike the Sanctuary, Falkner's Circle did not disappear overnight, suffering instead a long and gradual process of demolition. All that remained after the destruction was a single stone embedded within (if not a key marker for) the tithing boundary and two recumbent stones lying amongst the general spread of sarsens present in the valley bottom. As a result it is perhaps no surprise that both Aubrey and Stukeley failed to recognise it.

Summary of dating evidence

In summary, the earliest stone burnings so far encountered appear to have taken place at Falkner's Circle, where some of the burnings pre-date those recorded at Avebury, but are interestingly not so far removed from the notes of Symonds and Aubrey. It is notable that the earliest destruction episodes seem to have taken place outside the Avebury earthworks, out along the avenues and in the adjacent dry valleys. It may well have been the case that these standing stones were regarded as part of the general sarsen spread that dominated the surrounding downland and that their destruction formed part of a general stone-breaking tradition. It is unfortunate that we have no documentary or archaeological evidence relating to the destruction of natural sarsens during the 17th century and earlier. We do not know the scale of the industry, or how it was organised; whether it was *ad hoc*, full-time or seasonal. We certainly have no information regarding the techniques and tools employed by these stone-breakers. As a result it is, at present, impossible to shed further light upon the evolution and development of practices as the focus of attention shifted to upright stones; needless to say, this would be a fascinating and challenging area for future research.

At this point it is worth mentioning Fowler's claim that stone-breaking through the use of iron wedges was taking place on Lockeridge Down as early as *c.*1199–1216. If true, this means that stones were being broken before the onset of burial (see Chapter 9), however there are good grounds to question this conclusion. The dating was on the basis of a halfpenny of King John found at a depth of 0.15m adjacent to a partly broken polissoir. Although an iron wedge was also found in this deposit the presence of 'half an iron horseshoe of late, or post-medieval date' at a depth of 0.2m suggests that some disturbance had taken place. This in turn throws doubt upon the assertion that 'this evidence seems to indicate active stone-breaking during the medieval period' (2000, 68). Whilst the presence of the coin certainly suggests that people were *visiting* this distinctive polished stone in the medieval period it is difficult to argue conclusively for breaking.[8]

Looking to Avebury, the Sanctuary and the avenues, if we combine the chronological evidence discussed above with the approaches identified a crude chronology for the key period of destruction can be suggested (Table 10.18).

Technique	Dating
Ramp	Middle phase
Upright	Early phase
Short-pit and lever	Late phase
Adjacent-pit	Middle phase
Roughly-dug pit	Early phase
Buried-stone	Late phase
Scoop	Late phase
Tunnel	Early phase
Furnace	Late phase
Direct Fracture	Early phase
Dragging away	Early and Late phases

Table 10.18. Phasing the stone destruction events

Early phase – pre 1719
Prior to Stukeley's visits stones were being incorporated pragmatically into other structures. They were also being destroyed in a host of different ways. Standing stones were burned in rough pits whilst tunnels were dug beneath fallen stones to allow heating to take place. The latter may represent the direct transplantation of a technique used and refined on the downs to destroy natural sarsens. Given the stone destroyed by Walter Stretch *c.*1694 had *fallen* may in part explain how the practice moved from the landscape into the henge, the latter representing no more (perhaps less) of a challenge to the stone-breakers than a large slab of sarsen on the downs. We might go further and cite the three upright burning attempts as transitionary – failed experiments in the breaking of standing (as opposed to recumbent stones). This had certainly occurred to Keiller in considering the unusual pits dug to destroy stones 17 and 18 of the Outer Circle.

As well as fire-setting, stone breaking was also carried out using direct fracture, with stones deliberately toppled onto or in pits before being broken up. This was most popular on the line of the West Kennet Avenue where it was accompanied by the wholesale dragging off of stones.

Middle phase 1719–1724 (Stukeley's tenure)
By this period a specific technique appears to have been developed to deal with standing stones. This involved the digging of a sloping pit, or ramp, from the surface down to the base of the stone-hole. Likewise the adjacent-pit method was devised to deal with smaller, part-broken and/or buried stones. The practice of dragging away stones was also practised in this period as is evident from the fate of the Sanctuary.

Late phase – immediately post 1724
A different approach was taken to the burning of standing stones with the ramp technique replaced by the short-pit approach, where stones were toppled on to pre-prepared burning chambers. The practice of tunnelling beneath fallen stones to facilitate burning appears to have been replaced by the much simpler practice of hollowing out scoops beneath the fallen stones, a process that was effective enough to destroy (albeit gradually) the enormous bulk of the Obelisk. That this was not the only technique in use for the destruction of large fallen stones is evident from the creation of the furnace at the Longstones Cove. Interestingly, this is the period when Caleb Baily is reputed to have begun to use gun-powder (Law 1969). If this is in fact the case (as opposed to poetic licence) then this would have involved a profoundly different approach to the slow, progressive heating carried out using straw and roundwood and it is difficult to see evidence for such an activity in the destruction features excavated to date.

Taken as a whole the practice of stone-breaking appears to have been a very long-lived one. Sarsens were being broken out on the downs from at least the early part of the 17th century and the fact that burning techniques were still being employed on the downs around Avebury as late as 1847 is attested by John Britton in a note within the Wiltshire Topographical Society's edition of Aubrey's (up until then) unpublished *Natural History of Wiltshire* (Aubrey 1847, 44). By this stage the process appears to have become more refined, involving the burning of strips of firewood laid along the required line of fracture to heat the stone prior to quenching and impact (Rupert Jones 1887, 123).

What is particularly interesting is that the dates obtained for the burning associated with F.7 of the Falkner's Circle are contemporary with or even earlier than that obtained for the burial of stone L6 on the line of the Beckhampton Avenue. This is of enormous importance to our understanding of the relationships between stone burial (originally thought to be exclusively medieval) and stone burning (thought to be exclusively post-medieval) particularly when we also consider the possibility that the burial of setting L3 of the Beckhampton Avenue may also have been late. As a result it is difficult to avoid the implication that traditions of burial and burning were, for a time, coeval.

With regard to the destruction of standing and formerly standing stones, whilst we may question the precise dates assigned to specific events (*e.g.* the inception date of 1694), it is difficult on the basis of the archaeological evidence examined to challenge the central tenet of Stukeley's argument – namely that the destruction of Avebury took place within a relatively tightly prescribed window of some 40 or so years centred upon 1700.

At this point it is useful to reconsider Aubrey's earlier record of stone burning and the destruction of megaliths to furnish building stone for the village. We have already suggested that the basis for Aubrey's link between stone-breaking and the Avebury stones (*i.e.* the absence of any stones in the area) lacked both conviction and an appreciation of the stone-breaking taking place in the broader landscape. However, a further factor might be worthy of consideration. Although Aubrey's plans of Avebury can be dated to the period *c.*1650–1666 he appears to have been compiling notes, revisions and addenda to his written manuscript at least into the 1680s (*e.g.* those regarding excavations around the Sanctuary) (Ucko *et al.* 1991, 30–35, 250). Given that the manuscript that has survived to the present day is the result of a recopying exercise carried out by Aubrey between 1685 and 1689, it is quite possible that comments regarding the destruction of standing stones were communicated to him (and incorporated into the text) some time after his survey of 1663. If this is the case then Aubrey and Stukeley might well have been describing the same events.

Techniques revisited

At this point it is useful to return to the wide range of techniques that were practiced by the stone-breakers. There is little evidence to support the notion of an increase in sophistication in the techniques over time (Table 10.18). This is not to say that some general trends do not emerge: for example, a gradual move away from the relative time-consuming approach of digging out cavities beneath fallen stones to simply scraping out scoops along their sides. It is merely to acknowledge that rather than any linear progression or evolution, there was a high degree of pragmatism in the choice of technique closely linked to the particular challenges posed by specific stones. An excellent example of this is the most technologically accomplished of all the recumbent stone-burnings so far encountered, the furnace at the Longstones Cove which took place at a time when scraping seems to have been the method of choice for dealing with such stones.

It appears that at any given time a variety of approaches were in currency, reflecting the preferences of individual stone-breakers spread across some three generations tempered by the specific challenges posed by individual sarsens. Put simply, if you wanted to break a stone you either heated it or broke it directly; how you went about the activity of fire-setting or direct fracture was in part a response to the particular circumstances and size of the stone, and in part what you had learned from your experience out on the downs or as part of a team working within the monument.

Which stones were destroyed?

As has been discussed in the context of stone burial, any attempt to carefully map the stones of the Avebury monuments that had been broken is fraught with difficulty. This is due to inconsistencies not only between the records of individuals such as Aubrey and Stukeley, but within their records (see Ucko *et al.* 1991). It is also a product of the lack of sustained excavation that has taken place on the stone settings within and around Avebury since the work of Keiller. As a result, whilst we can map the fate of individual stones with some degree of confidence in those areas that have been excavated, and speculate on the basis of geophysical survey results in the case of many others, for much of the monument we simply do not know.

Accepting the late burial of setting 24, if we assume that within Avebury burials preceded breaking, a reconstruction of the sarsens that would have been available to the breakers in the later 17th century can be tendered. This available 'pool' of sarsens has been plotted against the 1724 boundaries in Figure 10.26a. In Figure 10.26b the stones that were actually

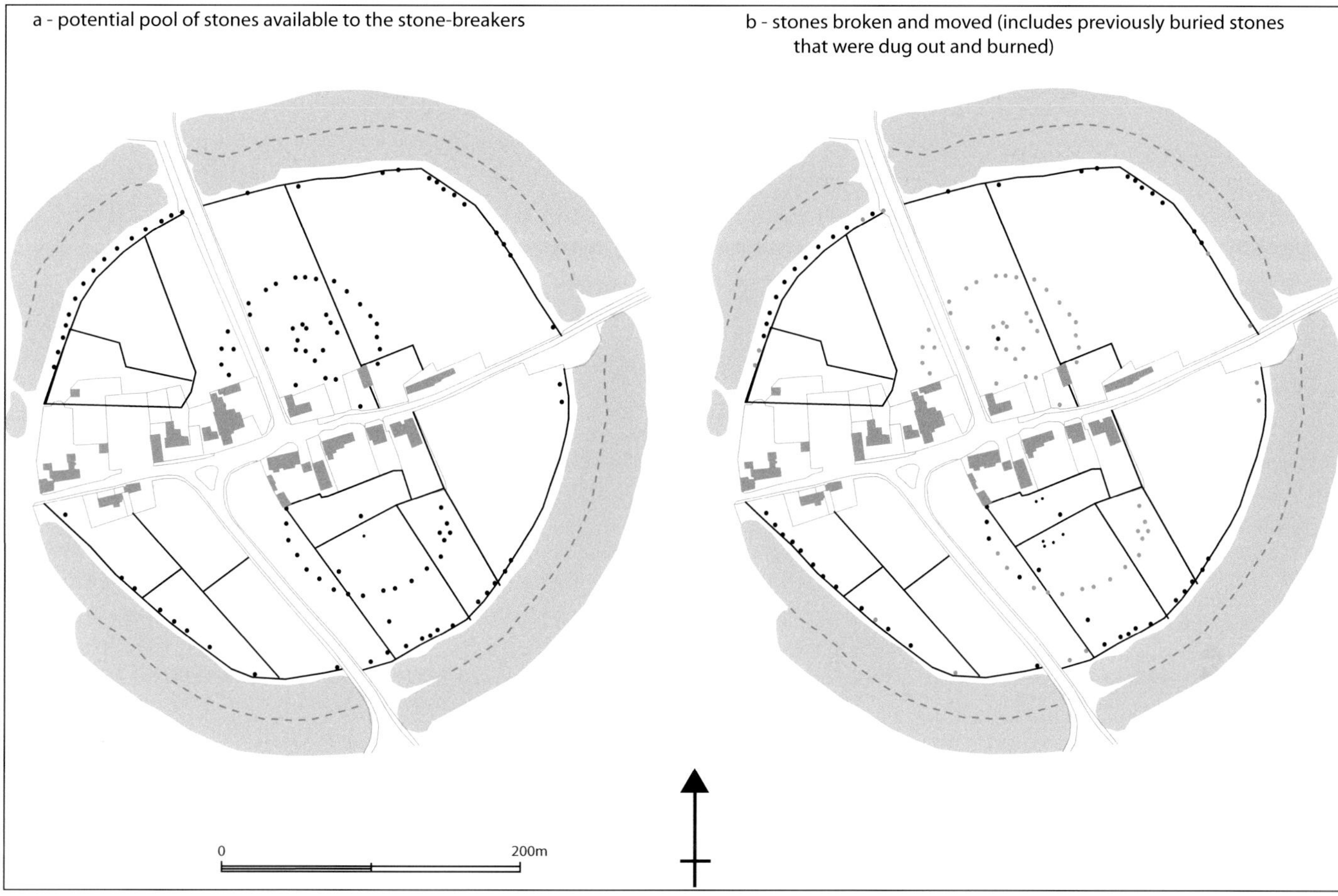

Figure 10.26. Actual stones broken at Avebury as compared to available pool of sarsens. Incorporates data © Crown Copyright/ database right 2007. An Ordnance Survey/ (EDINA) supplied service

destroyed have been indicated. The general picture is one of a concerted attempt to clear sarsens from the perimeter of the monument, leaving only a handful of isolated stones to mark the arc of the Outer Circle. Interestingly, but perhaps not surprisingly, the more massive stones that framed the original entrances appear to have been respected.

In terms of the overall pattern, it immediately becomes clear that whilst individual destructions may have been spread over decades, destruction is far from random, with destroyed stones concentrated in discrete clumps. This in turn argues for a process more episodic than sustained. Careful study of the techniques employed provides further support for this assertion, as in a number of cases adjacent sarsens were destroyed using the same technological approach and thus presumably during a single episode of stone destruction (Figure 10.27). This is most evident in the case of settings 16–46 of the Outer Circle. In contrast the destruction of settings 3–15 appears to have been more piecemeal. This may well reflect the character of earlier burial activity: in the South-West Quadrant the distribution of unburied stones was more sporadic whilst in the North-West very little burial had taken place leaving a coherent arc of sarsens to target. It is difficult to extend this to the interior settings given the paucity of excavation that has taken place.

Data for the avenues once again suggests strongly that stone breaking was focused upon discrete blocks of stones. This is clearest in the case of the West Kennet Avenue where a sufficient length has been excavated to reveal any such patterns (Figure 10.6). If we exclude buried stones from the picture there appear to be two major blocks of stone destruction. The first seems to have been concentrated upon the intact portion of the Avenue stretching from pair 5 to 12, and involved destruction through direct fracture and the dragging away of stones. The second block focused upon the remaining stones of settings 14 to 17, where fire-setting through the digging of cavities beneath fallen stones was the preferred method of breaking. If these distinctive blocks support the notion of two sustained campaigns of stone destruc-

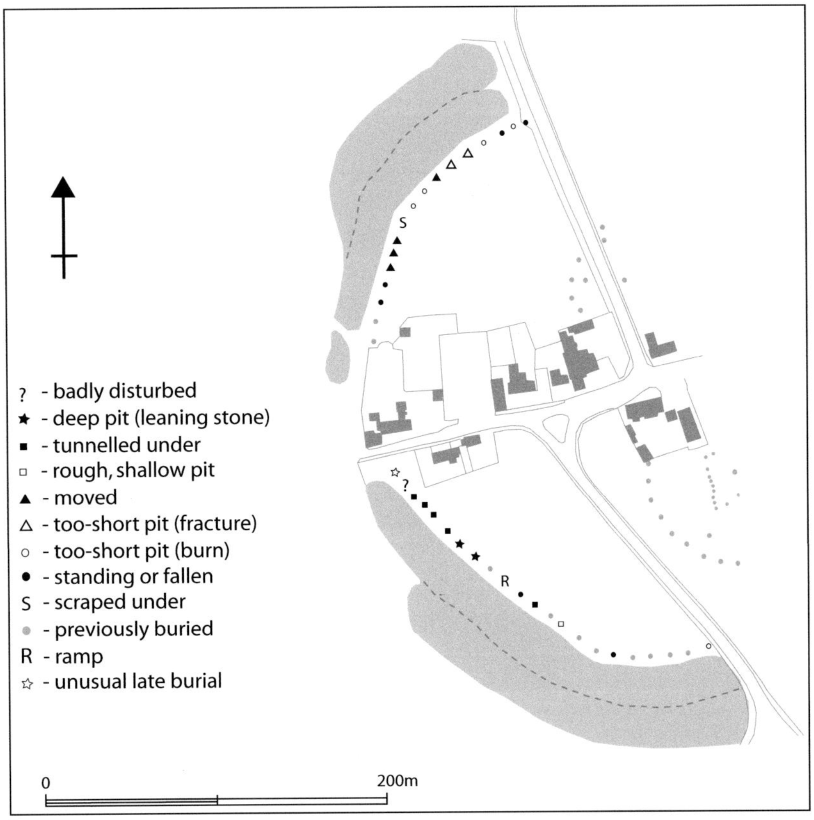

Figure 10.27. Distribution of Avebury destructions by technique. Incorporates data © Crown Copyright/ database right 2007. An Ordnance Survey/ (EDINA) supplied service

tion along the avenue line, then the more diverse range of techniques employed on the remaining settings investigated argues for more piecemeal, episodic destruction.

Given the relatively short stretch excavated, such broad spatial patterns are difficult to identify in the case of the Beckhampton Avenue. Overall they reveal a much less systematic destruction of non-buried stones in the vicinity of the Longstones Cove, beginning in the later 17th century and continuing after 1724 (Figure 10.25). That more systematic campaigns may have taken place is suggested by the documentary and geophysical evidence for the Trusloe end of Longstones Field. Stukeley's draft plans indicate that a reasonably intact portion of the avenue (in terms of stones either upright or fallen) crossed the field diagonally above Long Seas Lane at the time of recording (Bodleian MS Eng. Misc. b65 f109; f63), his only gap corresponding to the buried stone T1 located by geophysical survey and excavated in 2003. All of the stones making up this coherent stretch of the avenue were subsequently destroyed.

The pace of destruction

If any broad trends can be isolated from this it is of discrete bursts of sustained activity accounting for multiple stones in areas where appreciable numbers of standing or fallen stones were visible. This was coupled with more piecemeal destruction in those areas that had previously been subject to large-scale stone burial.

If we assume that the destruction of a stone took at most a week to effect, the overall timeframe of 40 years would suggest that stone destruction as a whole was not a sustained (*i.e.* year-round) or particularly vigorous process. As an example one need only consider the fate of the Obelisk, broken in a series of gradual stages. That it may in fact have been seasonal is suggested by two pieces of information. The first is Stukeley's reliance upon oral testimony. As we know stone destruction was taking place during the years he visited Avebury; the fact he did not record burnings directly (instead noting the pits left in their wake) suggests that the specific timing of his visits (with the exception of a May visit in 1719 taking place between June–August (Ucko *et al.* 1991, 42–53)) did not coincide with the preferred period of breaking. The second comes from the roundwood that was used to fuel some of the burning pits, which if felled only as required and burned green, indicates a date in late spring.

Who was breaking the stones and why?

So far we have attempted to characterise the activities and practices loosely grouped together as 'stone-breaking' and consider the timescale over which these activities had currency. What we have yet to consider is *why* stones were destroyed in this manner and why the apparent burst of activity that took place in the decades leading up to Stukeley's visits. Intimately bound up with this question is that of personnel and *who* was actually involved in the stone breaking. It is in attempting to shed light upon these questions that we find ourselves most reliant upon the surviving records of Stukeley, and it is perhaps with regard to this aspect of Avebury's history more than any other that *Abury* (Stukeley 1743) takes on the trappings of a canonical text.

With respect to guilty parties, in his published account Stukeley is emphatic, listing six 'cuvetous' local farmers and graziers whose names have since become synonymous with stone-breaking: Thomas Robinson, Farmer Green, John Fowler, Walter Stretch, Farmer Griffin and Richard Fowler. Between them Robinson was said by Stukeley to have destroyed some 40 sarsens with Griffin accounting for a further 20 (Ucko *et al.* 1991, 181). That this is not the whole story is clear from Stukeley's unpublished field notes (Appendix 1) which list a further group of people who were responsible for acts of stone breaking and vandalism. This included a lawyer, Mr Smith; the late parson of the local village of Winterbourne Monkton; and one Mr Boak. Stukeley also excluded from comment those responsible for the assaults that took place on the earthwork. Between 1685 and 1695 the then owner of the manor, Ralph Stawell, had an area of bank to the immediate north of the western entrance levelled and the ditch filled to facilitate the construction of a barn and tree-planting. If the former took place before Stukeley's first visit the same cannot be said of a subsequent episode of levelling and planting that took place to the south of the western entrance probably *c.*1722 when ownership of the manor changed once again (Ucko *et al.* 1991, 170–2). The impact of the latter was sufficient to cause Stukeley to revise draft plans of the site, yet prompted no explicit comment. Indeed, alterations by Sir Richard Holford prompted the following eulogy which appears to have been delivered without even the faintest trace of irony:

> 'All the way from the north round the top of the vallum on the other side of the ditch was leveld by Sir Rich[d] Holford whos name ought ever to be mentioned with honor and his memory dear to Antiquarians for his great care in preserving these glorious remains.' (Stukeley; Bodl. MS Eng. Misc. *c.* 323 p.120)

Stukeley lay the blame firmly at the feet of a small cabal of local men he identified as 'farmers'. He also appears to have exaggerated their involvement by attributing a number of missing stones to their actions that we now know had been buried long before and still lie beneath the turf of Avebury to this very day. He also placed an unreasonable emphasis upon Thomas Robinson as the notional head of the group, singling him out for particular ire. This is most evident in the drawn portrait Stukeley made of Robinson on the 22nd of July 1722. At some later date Stukeley had added the following captions to the drawing 'Ierostratus', 'Stone killer' and 'got his wife (an old woman above 50) with child'. By the time the portrait was published as an engraving in his *Abury* it had been altered almost beyond recognition through the addition of a sneer, smoking pyre and fluttery bat (Gillings *et al.* 2004, 153–4). He also, as was intimated earlier, attributed stone destructions to Robinson that we now know to have been buried.

Even his identification of the men as 'farmers' was a gross simplification as his group of stone-breakers included three publicans: Walter Stretch (Catherine Wheel at Avebury); John Fowler (White Hart at Kennet); Richard Fowler (Hare and Hounds at Beckhampton); and two minor land-owners (Griffin and Green) amongst their number (Edwards 2003; Gillings *et al.* 2004).

So why did Stukeley choose to focus his attack on these specific men when the reality suggests that stone destruction was a much more egalitarian undertaking? The difference between the two groups appears to be one of social class and standing. Those excused blame by Stukeley were all gentlemen, the accused in contrast were, to use a term of Stukeley's, 'miserable farmers'. This may reflect a deliberate strategy taken by Stukeley when it finally came to publication to contrast 'ignorant destruction' with the 'educated appreciation' of the local gentry. In this sense the disparity reflects little more than a process of careful academic selection on the part of the author. Another way of reading this evidence would be to argue that the damage inflicted by these latter 'stone-breakers' was of a wholly different character to that effected by Stukeley's original gang of six, and thus spared his ire by dint of the fact that their deeds were either thwarted or relatively small in scale. For example, Mr Smith only *attempted* to take away the stones of the West Kennet long barrow whilst the parson removed only a single, albeit large, sarsen from Millbarrow. Such a reading does not explain the absence of Mr Boak from Stukeley's diatribe. He was responsible for ploughing up one half of the Sanctuary, the compliment of which Stukeley was happy to attribute to Farmer Griffin (1743, 31). Nor does it explain why the name of Caleb Baily, the owner of the nearby manor of Berwick Basset, escaped comment by Stukeley at all. That around the year 1725, Baily was responsible for the wholesale destruction through burning of Avebury stones, can be gauged by the fact (as described earlier) that having described him as a 'goth' the Society of Antiquaries commissioned a poet to attack him in verse in an attempt to shame him into mending his ways (Law 1969). It is unlikely that Stukeley, a prominent member of the Society with a vested interest in such activities, would have been sufficiently ignorant to exclude it wholly from his later account.

The case of Thomas Robinson is a puzzling one. Over time Stukeley's dislike of Robinson grew and festered, resulting in his portrayal as the chief architect of destruction and it is difficult to know why this change of opinion took place. It may have been that Robinson was simply extremely good at stone-burning – a master, as it were, of his art – and perhaps not afraid to let everybody know it. It was Robinson after all who provided Stukeley with much of his detail. It could also have been personal, concerning matters that had nothing to do with stone-breaking.

As well as doubts about who was responsible for the acts, a degree of uncertainty also exists with regard to the motivations that lay behind the destruction of the Avebury sarsens. Stone breaking could clearly be a massive and expensive undertaking, involving a large amount of labour and materials. We have already discussed the scale of some of the burning structures and number of personnel involved. Thomas Robinson himself confessed to Stukeley that a stone burning could cost anywhere between 30 and 60 shillings, noting that two stones had cost £8 to destroy (Stukeley 1743, 15–16, 25).

At this point it is important to introduce a further complicating factor that makes the teasing out of any original motive fraught with difficulty. This is simply that the ultimate fate of any given stone may not reflect in any direct way the rationale behind its destruction. For example, a megalith may be destroyed as part of a process of re-organising boundaries and land clearance, the resultant stone generated then being used to build a field wall. In some cases these can be disentangled. For example, in the case of a section of the West Kennet Avenue Stukeley recorded:

> 'In the year 1720 I saw several stones just taken up there, and broke for building; fragments still remaining and their places fresh turf'd over, for the sake of pasturage.' (1743, 30)

Here the rationale appears to have been for building stone, the gain of grazing land a by-product. However in many cases it is much more difficult to unravel. Compare for example the published account of Walter Stretch's seminal stone burning:

> 'He exercis'd this at first on one of the stones standing in the street before the inn, belonging to the outer circle of the southern temple. That one stone containing 20 loads, built the dining room end of the inn.' (1743, 25)

with Stukeley's original discussion from 1722–24 making up part of his tour of the monument:

> 'The first he exercisd the base art upon, was one of the outer circle of the… Temple standing in the highway over against our inn, about 1694. Whilst it was upright in the road it surprizd the passengers among the rest, but falling down I suppose incommoded them by its bulk, this put him being the innkeeper upon practising upon it and probably some Traveller might help him to the unlucky hint.' (quoted in Ucko *et al.* 1991, 273)

What prompted Walter Stretch to destroy the stone? Was it a pragmatic act prompted by the need to unblock the entrance of his Inn by removing a recently fallen stone, the need to acquire sufficient building stone to enlarge his business, both, or neither? The surviving record is far from clear.

When he explicitly raised the question of motivation Stukeley claimed that the rationale for these acts was 'chiefly out of a covetousness of the little area of ground, each stood on' (Stukeley 1743, 15). This implies that in the majority of cases it was land that was of utmost importance rather than the stone itself. There is certainly circumstantial evidence to support this interpretation. For example, it may be no surprise that the area of the West Kennet Avenue that was most degraded was that directly adjacent to the henge where intensive agricultural activity was taking place (Keiller and Piggott 1936, 426), and the excavations of the Beckhampton Avenue in Longstones Field clearly revealed evidence of medieval and later ploughing. In contrast, in the case of Avebury itself such an explanation is hard to sustain. If the stone breaking was merely clearance for horticulture or agriculture then why were the majority of destruction pits abandoned to gradually fill with weeds or topsoil, or pragmatically with rubbish and trees? What is more, whilst a convincing case could be made for the fields traversed by the avenues, there is little evidence for intensive cultivation within the henge after the 14th century (Jope 1999), and we have already noted how at least some of the standing stones served as boundary markers in the organisation of the garden plots and orchards within the bank and ditch.

That this was not the only motivation is implied by Stukeley's use of the term *chiefly*, and throughout his records he makes frequent reference to destruction for the alternative purpose of liberating building stone (*e.g.* 1724, 24). This in turn has led a number of researchers to suggest a link between the intense burst of activity at Avebury and a general boom in building within the village during the late 17th and early 18th centuries (*e.g.* Malone 1989, 121–122; Ucko *et al.* 1991, 166). As with the suggestion relating to the freeing-up of land, there is evidence to both support and challenge this claim. For example, there are undoubtedly a variety of boundary walls and structures built from sarsen in and around the village that make it clear that a considerable amount of new building took place after 1650. We have also suggested that individuals such as Framer Griffin were preferentially acquiring land on the line of the Beckhampton Avenue (Chapter 8). Yet Stukeley went to great lengths to document the economic and structural downsides of such a strategy:

> 'They have sometimes us'd of these stones for building houses; but say, they may have them cheaper, in more manageable pieces, from the gray weathers. One of these stones will build an ordinary house; yet the stone being a kind of marble, or rather granite, is always moist and dewy in winter, which proves damp and unwholesome, and rots the furniture.' (Stukeley 1743, 16)

In light of Stukeley's stated motivations, his decision to portray the stone-breakers solely (and selectively) as farmers can perhaps be understood. By adopting this academic strategy (if strategy it is) the link between the principal motivation and named personnel becomes easily understandable and unquestionably 'tidy'. Any inherent contradictions, such as the above, can be attributed to the inherent irrationality (if not bullish stupidity) of the 'miserable farmers' perpetrating the acts, thus further strengthening his position.

It is only when we begin to look in detail at the historical and archaeological evidence that this neat equation begins to break down. The stone-breakers were not exclusively farmers and economic pressures fail to explain wholly the observed pattern and character of the destruction events. What then was driving the remarkable burst of stone-breaking that was focused upon the Avebury monuments in the decades around 1700? One possible line of enquiry emerged during the course of the programme of detailed archival research undertaken by Rick Peterson as part of the current project. The preliminary findings of this work have been published by the authors in an earlier article (see Gillings *et al.* 2004) and will be further developed here. At the same time, and wholly independently, research being carried out by the social historian Brian Edwards also began to foreground the importance of the same basic theme: this was religious non-conformism.

A religious dimension?

As long ago as 1979 Burl noted a relationship between the non-conformist chapel and the henge – the former not only located within the Southern Inner Circle, but constructed out of the remains of the very stones that formed its perimeter (Figure 10.28). The contrast between the meeting-house and the Anglican church could not be greater. Whilst the established church was located a respectful distance away from the fabric of the monument, the dissenting meeting house was fashioned out of it. Whilst he speculated that the zeal of Puritanism may have fired the hearts of the stone-breakers, that this was never followed up in any detail is perhaps a legacy of the status of stone-burning within narratives of Avebury – a shameful 'dilapidation' that comprises a sorry footnote in the sites ongoing history (Burl 1979, 46).

Of the principal stone-breakers identified by Stukeley both John Griffin and Thomas Robinson were active non-conformists, the former directly involved in the founding of the meeting-house (Dunscombe 1998, 7). If Stukeley's figures are to be believed these two individuals alone were responsible for the destruction of some 60 stones in and around Avebury. The prolific Caleb Baily, who escaped censure from Stukeley, himself made a bequest in 1749 'for the assistance of persons "who

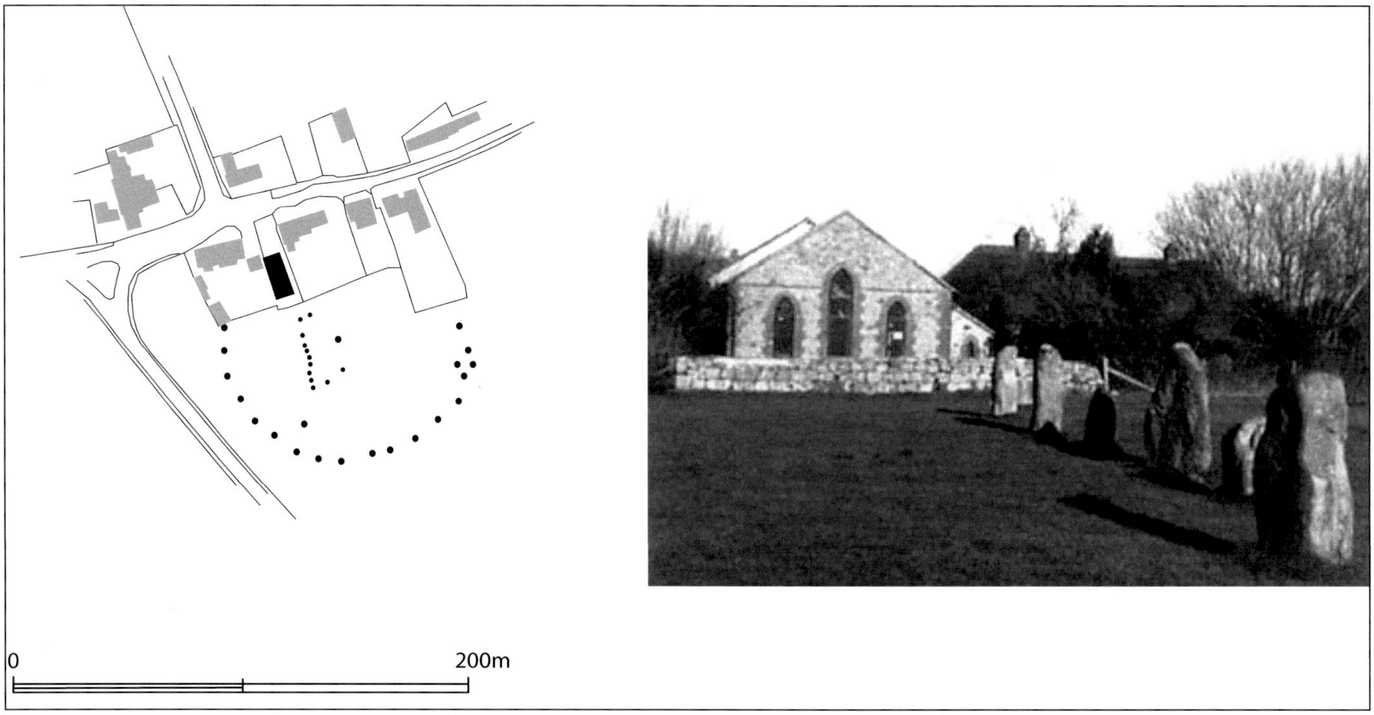

Figure 10.28. The location of the non-conformist chapel at Avebury. Incorporates data © Crown Copyright/ database right 2007. An Ordnance Survey/ (EDINA) supplied service

shall preach or study to be fit to preach to congregations of the Presbyterian, Baptist or Independent denominations'" (Reeves 1956, 123). This introduces the possibility that the spate of stone-breaking may have had a religious dimension (Gillings *et al.* 2004).

Non-conformity in the latter half of the 17th century

The period following the restoration of Charles II in 1660 was a particularly turbulent one for practising non-conformists, marked by ambiguity and intolerance as the government and parliament appeared to vacillate between toleration and persecution. Although the 1660 Declaration of Breda that accompanied the return of Charles II spoke explicitly of religious toleration, 1662 saw the introduction of both the Act of Uniformity and Corporation Act. The former demanded that all clergy accept the book of common prayer by the 24th of August, resulting in the expulsion of some 1760 ministers on what became known as Black Bartholomew's Day. The latter sought to bolster this by ensuring that religious and political undesirables were removed from positions of authority in the towns and boroughs and that loyal magistrates were in position to enforce it. This was followed in 1664 by the Conventicle Act which, feeding upon fears of rebellion, limited the size of non-conformist gatherings to five persons or less, threatening defaulters with fines and ultimately transportation. In 1665 the Five Mile Act served to further restrict ejected ministers by banning them from residing within five miles of their congregations or any corporate town. When the first Conventicle Act expired in 1668 non-conformist congregations were free to meet again, and the fact that they began to do so is suggested by the introduction two years later of a second Conventicle Act. As well as maintaining fines for offenders, this second act introduced financial incentives to people to inform upon non-conformists.

This first period of persecution ended in 1672 with the issuing of Charles II's Declaration of Indulgence. This permitted meetings providing they were open to all, held in a licensed, unlocked venue and the preacher was either a general preacher or had a license to preach either to that congregation or in that place. The peace was short-lived as from 1673 a second period of persecution took place beginning with the Test Act (which required all holders of military and civil offices to take the Anglican sacrament) followed by the recall of licenses for non-conformist meetings in 1675 with the withdrawal of the Indulgence. The prosecution of non-conformity would continue until James II's Declaration of Indulgence of 1687 and the Act of Toleration that followed the Glorious Revolution of 1689 (Hutton 1991; Harris 1993, chapters 2 and 5; Lancaster 1995; Spaeth 2000; Hutton 2004, chapter 5).

Acts of resistance?

The fact that the most intensive phase of stone breaking at Avebury took place during a period of intense persecution of non-conformists, and that some of the most prolific stone-breakers were non-conformists is highly suggestive. Rather than stone breaking purely for economic reasons could acts such as Farmer Griffin's acquisition of stretches of the Beckhampton Avenue embody more subtle undercurrents of resistance or defiance undertaken by a persecuted minority? Central to this argument is the suggestion that at this juncture the stones of the monument may have been inexorably linked in the minds of the local populace with the established church, through feast days and festivities. Memories of the visit of Charles II to the site may also have served to subconsciously link it in the minds of the non-conformists to authority in general and the Anglican Church in particular. This suggests that the decision to break the stones may have been a local reaction to wider events, and as much political and religious as it was economic.

Such a link between the church and the stones has been argued to lie in the re-issue in 1633 of the 'Book of Sports' by Charles I (Gillings *et al.* 2004). Originally issued by James I in 1617–1618, this volume sought to overturn puritanical Elizabethan proscriptions by defining a series of recreations (such as dancing, athletics, May-games, Whitson Ales and Morris dancing) that would be legal to undertake on the Sabbath. During the Civil War and after, advocacy of such activities became the mark of a 'specifically Stuart and Anglican' outlook (Marcus 1994, 153–4). Subsequently banned by the Long Parliament, maypoles served as a symbol of resistance to the republic (Hutton 1996, 236), and the Restoration brought with it a return to the popular recreations advocated by the Book of Sports. Maypoles in particular were used in the 1660s as part of a symbolic rejection of the Puritan past and Harris quotes Anthony Wood's account of the many maypoles set up in Oxford in May 1660, 'on purpose to vex the Presbyterians and Independents' (Wood, quoted in Harris 1993, 44). In light of this it is interesting to once more consider the location of the meeting-house with respect to the standing stones. Gray noted the use of the area in the centre of the Southern Inner Circle for the holding of fetes and erection of flagpoles (Gray 1935, 109, footnote 3), while Keiller's excavations discovered a number of early modern post-holes which were identified as marking the site of the village maypole (Smith 1965, 191). If this suggestion is true it means that the early meeting houses in the village, which seem to have been in Green Lane even before the construction of the current chapel around 1707 (Dunscombe 1998, 7), would have been sited directly adjacent to the area traditionally used by the parishioners as part of their May Day celebrations. It is also interesting to note that some of the earliest dates given by Stukeley for stone removal relate to megaliths adjacent to the chapel (Stukeley 1743, pl. I; Ucko *et al.* 1991, pl. 32–40).

Other events may also have contributed to the identification of prehistoric monuments with the Anglican parish. In August 1663 John Aubrey and Sir Walter Charleton persuaded Charles II, the Duke of York and Sir Robert Moray to visit Avebury, after a discussion at court about the site (Ucko *et al.* 1991, 25). Memory of this visit remained strong in Avebury: it was recorded by Pepys on his visit in 1668 and in more detail by Stukeley in the 1720s (*ibid.*, 26), who noted how Charles was remembered as having ridden into the yard of the Catherine Wheel to view the Cove (Stukeley 1743, 23, 43).

The everyday life of the village

Having raised the possibility of a religious dimension to Avebury's stone-breaking, care must be taken not to paint a very specific picture of Avebury in the latter half of the 17th century to support it; a representation shaped solely by the broad brush strokes of national political and religious history. To put this another way, there is a danger of projecting Avebury's current national importance back to the 17th century and interpret the ebbs and flows of village life entirely in terms of reactions to the national developments outlined above. That the modern day heritage-village bears little relation to the realities of Avebury in the 17th century we can be reasonably confident. As to the degree to which actions, practices and beliefs at the local scale mirrored the well-documented debates between government, parliament and the clergy, this is something we must investigate rather than assume.

What has become clear from the detailed historical studies that have been carried out, is that whilst sufficiently ferocious on paper, the impact on-the-ground of the various statutes outlined above could be seriously weakened by the failure of municipal and parish officials to implement and prosecute them (Lancaster 1995, 80). An excellent example of this can be seen in the case of the churchwardens. The incumbents of these parish offices were usually elected on an annual basis with one warden being proposed by the minister and one by the parishioners. As one of the tasks of the churchwardens was to present religious offenders such as non-conformists to the Archdeacons during their annual visitations, it could place these individuals in a sometimes difficult situation with respect to their friends, colleagues and neighbours (for a direct example see Smith 1982, 119; Lancaster 1995, 84–86; Spaeth 2000, 100–101). The solution that was frequently adopted was to preserve the peace by simply not presenting. Where there were a significant number of non-conformists amongst the parishioners it may even have been in their interests to ensure that a non-conformist was elected to the post to ensure that presentments were not made and Lancaster cites an instance of precisely this tactical behaviour (Lancaster 1995, 86). To investigate any relationship between conformity and stone-breaking therefore requires a much more subtle and detailed reading of the local evidence relating to non-conformity, persecution and village life in the period under question.

Another problem with non-conformism is the inherent fuzziness of the term and the danger of treating 'non-conformists' as a normative category. Terms such as 'non-conformist' and 'dissenter' appear to have been highly flexible, covering a wide spectrum of people and practices (Hutton 2004, 174). It has also been forcibly argued that whilst some Anglican clergymen and more radical separatists recognised a clear-cut dichotomy between conformity and non-conformity 'most parishioners saw shades of grey instead' (Spaeth 2000, 169). There appears to have been continual negotiation between what was officially prescribed and lay-practice, with the latter not fitting comfortably into either of these stark categories (Ingram 1995, 100). Barry Reay has elegantly argued that we need to think in terms of permutations rather than ideal types, noting how 'after 1660 the nonconformist sects were persistently troubled by adherents who returned to the restored Church of England when it came to marriage or the baptism of their children: the church was etched deep in the social fabric of the nation' (Reay 1985, 119).

This introduces problems in recognising non-conformity as Anglican ministers tended to characterise any deviation from rigid conformity as dissent or irreligion, when the actual reasons may be more prosaic (*e.g.* laziness or the lack of suitable clothing) or derive from lay understandings of avowedly conformist practices such as the receiving of sacrament (Ingram 1995; Lancaster 1995; Spaeth 2000). Indeed some researchers have argued that the concept of non-conformity itself only emerged after 1662 as a direct result of the narrow definitions of uniformity adopted by the Restoration church (Spaeth 2000, 255; Lancaster 1995, 38). As much of our knowledge regarding the presence and identity of non-conformists comes from the presentments made by clergymen the problem is a significant one.

It has to be recognised that the term represents a rather crude blanket-description that obscures considerable variety in the beliefs and degrees of separatism and divergence exhibited or extolled by individual groups. For example, a list of sects from 1656 lists 24 such groups ranging from the more familiar Presbyterians and Quakers to Swinskfeltrians and Soul-sleepers (Lancaster 1995, 167). This is further compounded by the tendency for collusion between groups such as Presbyterians, Baptists and Independents and the fact that a large body of so-called dissenters were extremely difficult to tell apart from the conformist church with regard to their beliefs and manner of observance. Indeed many non-conformists were equally happy attending both the Anglican church and non-conformist gatherings (*ibid.*, 22–3, 168). This is perhaps most clearly illustrated by the fact that many people identified as non-conformists or dissenters served as churchwardens as well as filling other parish offices (see Lancaster 1995, Chapter 4).

In the case of Wiltshire, the Act of Uniformity had resulted in the expulsion of 29 ministers, and a census of 1676 revealed that the county had the third highest population of non-conformists in the country and the second largest number of teachers (*ibid.*, 19). For Avebury, its position astride the main London to Bristol coach road and results of the Five-Mile Act of 1665 certainly resulted in it acting as a focus for non-conformity. The road served as an important conduit for ideas and individuals, leading to an increased concentration of dissenters in the areas buffering it (*ibid.*, 234). By geographical accident, its position five miles from the borough towns of Devizes, Calne, Marlborough and Wootton Bassett also made it an obvious focus for ejected preachers (Edwards 2003). In 1670 John Baker, who had been barred from his home congregation in Chiseldon, set up a chapel in Avebury where a congregation of 25 persons met close to the centre of the henge in a group of cottages. To give an idea of the scale of this meeting the number of practising Anglicans in the village at this time numbered 181. Other preachers such as Noah Webb, travelled from as far away as Hampshire to preach in Avebury (*ibid.*) and in 1707 a purpose built Chapel was constructed opposite the original cottages. Its success can be gauged by the size of the congregation in 1715, which numbered 130 (Dunscombe 1998, 3–8).

Having established the presence of a substantial non-conformist population in Avebury the next stage is to establish what kind of non-conformity they embodied. This is significant because different dissenting groups were persecuted to a greater or lesser degree (for example the Quakers) and held very different attitudes to the question of separation from the Anglican Church and participation at Anglican services. As a result the specific make-up of any group may have a bearing on the degree to which they might be expected to react against the established church, leading to the kinds of tensions and conflicts that may have prompted or fuelled the spate of stone destruction. Establishing the denomination(s) and internal organisation of Avebury's dissenters is extremely difficult due to the lack of surviving records from Wiltshire (Lancaster 1995, 159). A survey of 1669 rather unhelpfully described the dissenters of Avebury as 'of severall sorts' (*ibid.*, 169). More useful is a reference to the fact that the 'Presbyterian' (as opposed, for example, to Baptist, Quaker, Independent) meeting at Avebury did not apply for a licence after the Indulgence of 1672. Assuming this characterisation is correct, it enables us to speculate as to the nature of Avebury's non-conformism as Presbyterians were notable for their opposition to any strict separation from the established church. They also encouraged followers to attend Anglican Services and seek burial in the churchyard. The lack of any surviving Presbyterian records from the period has been argued to reflect the absence of any perceived distance from the wider parish community, and thus a lack of concern with documenting membership or meetings (Lancaster 1995, 159–83).

Evidence that Avebury's non-conformists were indeed of a more moderate persuasion can be found in a variety of sources. For example, Baptism records for St. James' Church record those of dissenters children well into the 1720s, including the offspring of prominent non-conformists such as Richard Baily, one of the founders of the meeting house (Table 10.19). A further founder member, John Griffin, is recorded as having served as a churchwarden from 1700–1701 (Waylen 1854, 436), and non-conformists John and Richard Fowler were publicans (White Hart at Kennet and the present day Waggon and Horses at Beckhampton, respectively) a profession unlikely to lend itself to the more ardent Puritan.

It is particularly interesting that a surviving presentment from Avebury entitled 'Avebury

Year	Dissenters	Anglicans
1696	2	0
1697	1	0
1698	2	9
1699	3	5
1700	4	5
1701	2	8
1702	5	10
1703	1	6
1704	0	13
1705	0	7
1706	4	9
1707	0	12
1708	3	15
1709	1	12
1710	3	5
1711	2	10
1712	3	7

Table 10.19. Children baptised at Avebury in the years when the label 'dissenter's child' was explicitly recorded

Sabbath Breakers 1682' presents not the group of villagers at fault but the individual Thomas Mortymer (presumably a churchwarden) for failing to present them despite acknowledging their defects to others (quoted in Dunscombe 1998, 6).

Dispute and persecution

This is not to imply that Avebury was free of any conflict involving the established church. Thanks to the detailed study of lay-clerical conflicts at Avebury carried out by Spaeth, we have an unusually detailed insight into the nature of disputes between the parishioners and incumbent Anglican clergyman in Avebury in the latter decades of the 17th century (Spaeth 2000).

The incumbent vicar of Avebury between 1671 and 1712 was John White, who appears to have combined a litigious nature with respect to tithe payments with a marked resentment of non-conformity. Following the purchase of Avebury Manor by Sir Richard Holford and the subsequent leasing out of the estate to tenant farmers, White embarked upon a suite of legal suits to recover tithe monies he felt owed to him. In 1695 he attempted to use the courts against a tenant of Holford named William Skeate, a man described by White as a dissenter who had set up a conventicle. In 1697 he filed an exchequer bill against nine Beckhampton men that resulted in the financial impoverishment of one Joseph Hayward who is identified as a dissenter in baptism records of 1696 and 1698. Whilst it is tempting to read direct persecution in this, it is important to acknowledge that White's ire was not solely directed at dissenters, with the litigious vicar equally comfortable suing conformists. A typical example is that of the tenant farmer John Rose who was sued in 1699 for failing to inform White that his tithe share of wheat was ready for harvesting. In 1700 White sent men of his own to harvest the wheat without Rose's consent with the resulting fracas leading to the farmer being charged with riot (*ibid.*, 134–41). As a result, his frequent resort to the courts appears to owe more to financial considerations and the need to recover tithes than any deliberate campaign of persecution.

This is not to deny that White disliked non-conformists intently, and a reasonable idea of the level of his hatred can be gained from his description of the 'hellish, factious, scandalous and schismatical conventicle set up in opposition to himself' (quoted in Spaeth 2000, 172). In 1698 he went as far as presenting the minister of the meeting house to the Bishop (*ibid.*). This certainly suggests that White himself felt under threat, and if his various legal manoeuvrings can not be read as evidence for direct persecution, his refusal to bury non-conformists certainly can. In 1710 White refused to bury Richard Bayly, one of the founders of the meeting-house, because of the latter's Presbyterian beliefs. The key question here is whether the actions of White were sufficient to galvanise the non-conformist congregation of Avebury into the kind of retributive action against their conforming neighbours that would result in the burning of stones. That the answer is no is suggested by the reaction of the ostensibly conforming parishioners to the actions of White. In the February following his failure to bury Bayly, the parishioners themselves tolled the bell and undertook the task of burying another non-conformist, Walter Alexander (*ibid.*, 201–2).[9] Rather than lead to any split between conformists and non-conformists, the combined effects of White's legal campaigns and strict attitude to dissent appears to have been to galvanise the entire parish in opposition to him.

Taken as a whole, the above evidence suggests strongly that Avebury's non-conformist population were little differentiated from their Anglican neighbours and unlikely to have been forced into, or resorted to, any unusual acts of defiance and/or resistance. In contrast Lancaster has recently argued that far from separation and fracture, the dominant characteristic of village life in this period was that of integration, with minor differences in religious belief less important than the maintenance of social cohesion. Amongst parishioners there is certainly no evidence for deliberate antagonism between conformists and non-conformists or any desire for hostility (Lancaster 1995, 24–5, 191–2). Although far from being a typical inhabitant of the village, the actions of the lord of Avebury manor, Sir Richard Holford, illustrate this well. In an impressive display of pragmatism he was able to instruct White to pay children who learned their catechism whilst drawing upon the direct testimony of non-conformist tenants (the Griffins) in protracted legal battles with the very same clergyman (Spaeth 2000, 92–3). We must also remember that not all of the stone-breakers appear to have been active non-conformists.

The danger of replacing one orthodoxy with another

To see stone-breaking solely as a manifestation of broader religious conflicts requires a strong, direct and recognisable link between the established church, its incumbent and the standing stones. Such evidence is difficult to find for Avebury. The presence of named stones both within the monument and spread across the downs, suggests that sarsens were embedded within the social life of the village and its surroundings, and that some at least may have been rich in folkloric association (Bowen and Smith 1977, 189). Although taking place some centuries earlier, the mere presence of a deliberately inserted cattle bone within a natural perforation in stone L6 of the Beckhampton Avenue suggests that certain individual stones could form the focus of activity and deposition. Other components of the Avebury landscape were likewise embedded within the religious calendar:

> 'The country people have an anniversary meeting on the top of Silbury-hill on every palm-sunday, when they make merry with cakes, figs, sugar and water fetch'd from the swallow-head, or spring of the Kennet.' (Stukeley 1743, 43–4)

However, it is difficult to see how such practices could be associated with any strict Anglicanism, certainly to the extent of rousing the Presbyterians of Avebury to such a degree they turned to the bonfires. Instead, the naming, and perhaps reverence, of certain stones can be viewed as an element of the 'folklorised christianity' that characterised much popular religious practice and embraced such dimensions as folk-remedies and astrology (Reay 1985, 111–17; Ingram 1995, 106–7; Reay 1998, 87). Rather than acts outside acceptable social and religious norms these would have been an integrated part of precisely the everyday social fabric that Lancaster has argued the non-conformists sought to maintain.

Returning to the question of the Book of Sports and proximity of the meeting-house to the site of the village maypole, whilst this spatial relationship has been argued to have led to a politically motivated assault on the stones as symbols of the Anglican parish (Gillings *et al.* 2004, 158) such an association requires careful consideration. Whilst oral testimony supported the suggestion that maypoles were danced around at this location in the early part of the 20th century, we have no evidence that this area served as the traditional location of the May festivities (Smith 1965, 204, footnote 1). The archaeological evidence for the area around the Obelisk suggests that it was crossed by a series of field-boundaries and Stukeley's own prospects show the location as rich in established trees, fences hedges and ditches. If this would not have posed sufficient challenge to even the most determined dancer, there was still the bulk of the fallen Obelisk to contend with. The final objection draws upon the point made earlier about direct action. If the maypole was causing offence then why not simply destroy the maypole? What is lacking is any convincing link between the standing stones and maypole, beyond the inevitable proximity of the latter to some of the former.

In considering the location of the meeting-house, to conjure up images of zealous non-conformists marching around the monument selecting the next stone for the pyre, or where best to erect a chapel so as to cause maximum offence to their conforming neighbours, is to project a rather idealised notion of 17th/18th century Avebury as a grassed, open, accessible area; Avebury as it is today not as it was in the period under study. This is to forget that the interior of the henge was *owned*, parcelled up and carefully fenced and bounded. The chapel was constructed in part of the gardens of the tenement of one Samuel Morris who had donated the land to the congregation (Dunscombe 1998, 7). To assume it was deliberately sited to disrupt maypole celebrations presupposes that Morris had this in mind when he acquired the property originally. In this sense the stones of the Southern Inner Circle may have been drawn to the construction of the chapel rather than vice-versa.

In the case of the visit of Charles II, the implication is that their subsequent destruction represents a veiled attack on the government and through it the orthodox Church. Such a suggestion is difficult to prove or disprove but the argument lacks conviction; the visit was certainly remembered yet once again the timing and nature of the gesture appear to make little sense (see below). Drawing any causal link between non-conformity and its persecution, and the episode of stone breaking is therefore difficult and the case is weakened further if we consider four final pieces of evidence. The first is that not all of the stone-breakers named by Stukeley (itself a selective list) were non-conformists. In the case of Walter Stretch, the proclaimed originator of the practice, there is no evidence at all to link him to any non-conformity (contra Edwards) and the presence of the grave-slabs of his son, George, and daughter-in-law embedded within the floor of Avebury church (close to the porch) could also be read as an argument for the Anglican credentials of this family.

The second piece of evidence concerns the nature of the act itself. If we accept that the non-conformist congregation of Avebury had wanted to protest or strike out against the Anglican church, then destroying the stones seems a rather cryptic and abstract way of doing so. Existing studies of the means by which parishioners expressed their displeasure at both church and incumbent clergymen have shown how direct and blunt such actions tended to be. These ranged from deliberate absenteeism and rowdiness during sermons, to the breaking of windows and other more visible acts:

> 'Thomas Chambers urinated against the pulpit of Norton Bavant church during divine service, a choice of location which was surely significant.' (Spaeth 2000, 17)[10]

The third factor concerns the timing of the events. If we accept Stukeley's 1694 as marking the beginning of the practice then why did it take 30 years from the Restoration for any act of resistance to take place? What is more, given the most concentrated period of persecution appears to have taken place between 1680 and 1686 (Lancaster 1995, 111), why did stone-breaking only take off some five or so years after the Glorious Revolution and Act of Toleration? In the case of Avebury, if the stones close to the village maypole caused such offence, why did it take around 30 years for them to be destroyed? Likewise, why was a period of 50 years allowed to elapse before one, and only one, of the Cove stones (stone III) was destroyed? The final, and perhaps most curious question, is if active non-conformity was a factor in the destruction of the Avebury stones, why was Stukeley silent on the topic? In his unpublished field notes and published *Abury*, he made absolutely no judgemental statement regarding non-conformists or their meeting-house at all. When the destruction of a stone to construct the latter is mentioned in the unpublished 'tour' of the site it is reported directly 'the next that was in the garden was destroyd to build the meeting-house' (quoted in Ucko *et al.* 1991, 279).

What is significant about the account reproduced in the 'tour' is that it was written during the period of fieldwork, not many years after. If Stukeley failed to recognise or acknowledge any religious subtext to the stone-breaking, then the stone-breakers (and villagers) he spoke to during his field visits were equally remiss, none feeling the need to raise it as an issue or concern. If we are to place interpretative faith in Stukeley's assertions we must be equally attentive to his silences.

The five-mile boomtown

Whilst at first glance the image of national debates and tensions being played out directly at the level of the village is beguiling, we need to be mindful of the slippery nature of non-conformity, the blurring of any rigid dichotomies in popular religious practice, and the importance to everyday village life of integration and accommodation. Failure to appreciate the nature of religious practice at the scale of the village runs the risk of achieving little more than the replacement of one broad, yet inadequate, orthodoxy (Stukeley's economics) with another (religious conflict).

A different explanation as to why stones were being burned and broken at Avebury in the late 17th and early 18th centuries has recently been offered by Edwards as part of a perceptive (and entertaining) critique of modern heritage concerns. Once again the link between stone destruction and non-conformists is highlighted, however the focus is very different. Whilst Edwards identifies the key stone-breakers as non-conformists, he stresses their status first and foremost as entrepreneurs and innkeepers. To Edwards, the role non-conformity plays in the destruction of the Avebury monuments lies not in any direct, religiously-motivated intervention, but instead in the changing fortunes of the village resulting from the various statutes passed. Avebury is very much a 'five-mile' village, witnessing a marked increase in population as a result of the Five Mile Act as it rose to prominence as a centre of dissent; the increased population creating a demand for clearance and house-building. Entrepreneurs such as Thomas Robinson were able to cater to this demand through stone breaking, clearing new pasture and constructing infill housing as part of the growing colonisation of the henge interior by dissenters (Edwards 2003, 1). As well as speculators such as Robinson the increased number of visitors also meant an increase in traffic through the site and the need for both road improvements and the provision and enlargement of facilities such as Inns. This, it is argued, was further compounded by the growth in quality and quantity of wheeled traffic between London to Bath (*ibid.*, 3). In this scenario the engine of change is the Five Mile Act and the resultant destruction of stones a quirk of geography. Whilst carried out in part by non-conformists, it was economically motivated and speculative in nature. At its heart is the assumption that an increased population brought with it increased demands for housing and produce.

Once again this explanation has both strengths and weaknesses. It is clear that the size of the dissenting congregation increased dramatically in the decades around 1700 and that both conformists and non-conformists were buying land in and around Avebury and opening new businesses. However, the suggestion that the non-conformists created 'a quite separate and distinct satellite community' once again fails to appreciate the importance of integration and difficulties in everyday practice of distinguishing conformist from dissenter.

Stone destruction and the parcelling up of the land

The accompanying argument suggesting that boundary changes precipitated by the growth of the 'chapel village' and the attendant remodelling of the henge interior resulted in stone destruction also needs further consideration. A careful study of the relationship between stone destruction, land ownership and tenancy would be of enormous value, however our understandings of the internal layout of late 17th century Avebury are limited by a lack of detailed sources and sustained archaeological investigation. Alongside Stukeley's famous frontispiece, surviving maps of the period take the form of an estate map of Avebury dated to 1733; the Inclosure map of 1794; a Tithe Map of 1845; and a sketch map of the area to the west of the Avebury earthwork from 1695 (see Ucko *et al.* 1991, 161–3, pls 46–9). Whilst informative these shed little detailed light upon ownership, and the ways in which the interior was partitioned in the 17th and early 18th centuries. Documentary sources are equally fleeting. We know that during 1724 and 1725 Caleb Bailey purchased land within Avebury (possibly pastures III and X) from George Stretch, presumably passed down from his father, Walter. Records also suggest that John Griffin owned land within the henge (Law 1969).

From the detailed analyses carried out in Chapter 8, it is clear that the post-medieval pattern of boundaries recorded by Stukeley followed closely an earlier medieval partition of the available space. If Edwards is correct in suggesting that the interior was further subdivided to create new plots and areas of pastures it is curious that this later re-organisation appears to have simplified, rather than affirmed (or further sub-divided) this earlier, more complex, system. If the post-medieval boundaries reflected a 'weeded' medieval pattern then this could well have resulted in surplus boundary markers and Stukeley's prospects and groundplot certainly shows sarsens embedded in the fence-lines as well as 'floating' within individual pastures. However the very presence of these floating stones in Stukeley's drawings argues against a concerted effort to clear them as part of any reorganisation process prompted by the Five Mile Act. Further to this, if stone destruction was motivated by land clearance and re-organisation, why was so much of the land thus liberated abandoned to weeds, nettles and rubbish?

Despite this, if we plot the field boundaries that were present in 1724 against the distribution of stones burned or otherwise destroyed, a convincing case can be made for linking at least some of the stone destruction to changes in ownership and re-organisation (Figure 10.29). The breaking of settings 41 and 42 of the Outer Circle, along with manoeuvring of stones 34–36 and 40, was undoubtedly bound up in the construction of a perimeter field bank, itself linked to the opening of the northern entrance. Further, if we combine the information relating to the method of destruction employed (and inherent phasing) a

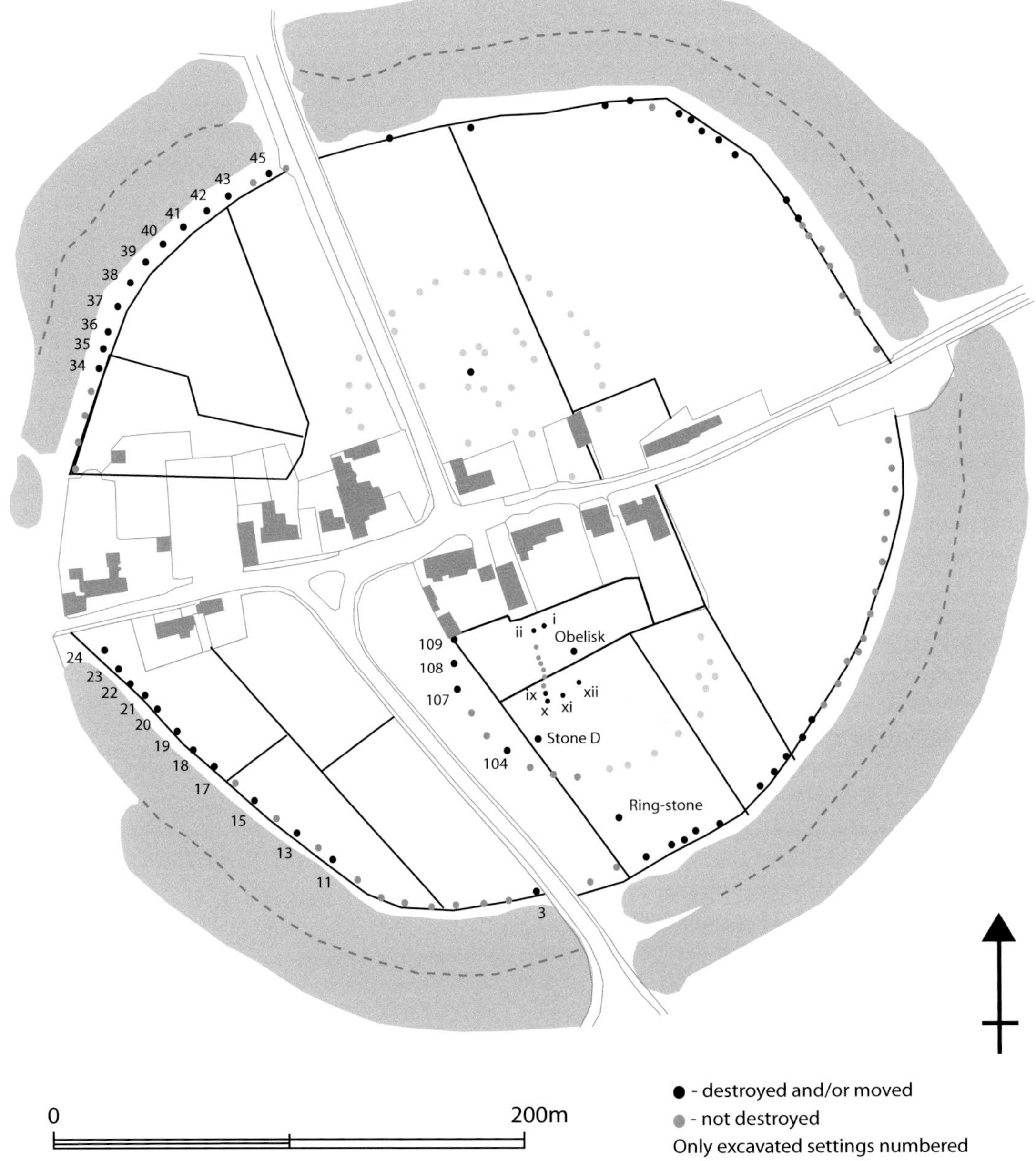

Figure 10.29. Destroyed stones and boundaries in Avebury present c.*1724. Incorporates data © Crown Copyright/ database right 2007. An Ordnance Survey/ (EDINA) supplied service*

convincing case can also be made for linking the late destructions of settings 37–39 to the purchase of pasture III by Caleb Baily; an act purportedly carried out to obtain stone for the repair of a boundary (Law 1969, 100). Beyond this it is difficult to relate blocks of destruction to individual plots. Instead, as was argued earlier, there seems to have been a broader concern with ridding the perimeter of the earthwork of standing and fallen stones. This appears to have been most driven, *i.e.* systematic as opposed to piecemeal, in the South-East and North-West Quadrants.

The argument that stone-breaking accompanied land clearance is perhaps more convincing beyond the immediate earthwork of the henge. In the case of the Sanctuary we know that ploughing followed the dismantling of the stone settings. Along the lines of both avenues geophysical, excavation and documentary evidence suggest that destruction events took place in areas of intensive, long-lived, cultivation.

The final element of Edward's suggestion that invites comment is the claim that the construction of the barn across the bank *c.*1694 can be seen as a proxy for agricultural improvements effected by farmers such as Green and Griffin in response to the explosion of the village (Edwards 2003, 4). Rather than growing agricultural surplus, it could be argued that the period between 1693 and 1700 was one characterised by bad harvests coupled with an increasing tax burden. That this impacted upon the villagers is suggested by the request made by the tenant farmer William Skeate for a rent reduction on account of 'the bad time and my losses' and no doubt explains some of the tithe disputes that plagued the vicar John White (Spaeth 2000, 77–8). Any increase in the intake and cultivation of land might therefore be read as much as a reaction to circumstances beyond the control of the village as its orderly expansion.

Conclusion: one rationale and one motivation?

Two things should be clear from the preceding discussions. The first is that any attempt to identify a single impetus for the episode of stone-breaking quickly becomes reliant upon a selective reading of the evidence and as a result is lacking in conviction. In much the same way as there has been a tendency to assume that the stones were originally erected according to a single coherent plan, there appears to be a similar temptation when faced with the question as to why they were taken down.

A wide range of people were involved in stone breaking and whilst straddling the decades around 1700, the practice appears to post-date the most active periods of religious intolerance and persecution. The archaeological evidence likewise points to variety and variation in the practices adopted. While they are all part of a general tradition of firing stones to effect fracture, there is little uniformity in its execution with many distinct strategies adopted. As a result we may have to concede that there may be a kernel of truth in all of the explanations so far tendered to account for stone destruction, with none able to account for all such events. Stones were undoubtedly destroyed to free-up land, others to provide building stone for the growing village. Whether directly, in the form of acts of deliberate iconoclasm, or indirectly through the expansion of the village, non-conformity may have prompted some of the stone breaking. Others may reflect secular, entrepreneurial urges on the part of local speculators, or more pragmatic considerations such as getting customers into an inn or loaded wagons through the village.

The Stukeley factor

As an observer and recorder Stukeley could not be described as either passive, objective or distanced, campaigning vociferously to halt the destructions. At this point it is prudent to raise the question of Stukeley himself and the role he may have played in the acts of stone-breaking he encountered. Once again highlighting the involvement of non-conformists in the burning of the stones, it has recently been suggested that Stukeley's protestations may have served to fuel the very fires he sought to extinguish (Gillings *et al.* 2004, 159). This is based upon the suggestion that Stukeley and his fellow objectors projected themselves (or were viewed) as staunch defenders of the Anglican faith, citing the fact that Stukeley was ordained in 1729 and that his most vocal supporter was the parish clerk Reuben Horsall.

Having stressed throughout this discussion the difficulty in identifying any religious tension sufficient to have led to a campaign of deliberate stone destruction in the late 17th century, this presupposes that one existed in the 1720s. Further, implicating Stukeley's religious convictions is teleological insofar as it anticipates his later ordination. Rather than representing the culmination of a long period of Anglican orthodoxy, recent studies of Stukeley's religiosity have highlighted the 'speed and drama' of his decision to become an Anglican clergyman (Hutton 2005).

If any explicit religiosity or theological positioning on the part of Stukeley can be dismissed it may still have been the case that his presence did lead to a late flourishing of stone-breaking. Assuming Stukeley's chronology is in essence correct, the practice of heat-fracturing standing stones originated in the late 17th century and the majority of stones destroyed within Avebury had been broken in the three decades prior to his visits.

> 'Just before I visited this place, to endeavour at preserving the memory of it, the inhabitants were fallen into the custom of demolishing the stones, chiefly out of covetousness for the little area of ground, each stood one. First they dug great pits in the earth, and buried them….After this, they found the knack of burning them.' (Stukeley 1743, 15)

In the case of the henge itself the practice may actually have been on the wane, the crucial period falling between the records of Aubrey and Stukeley. By the 1720s the attention of the stone-breakers certainly appears to have moved out of the henge towards the Avenues and sites such as the Sanctuary. In light of this it is interesting to speculate that the grandiose stone-burning he witnessed and illustrated was deliberately theatrical and laid on as much for his benefit as any other motivation; as much an illustration of 'how the seasonal burnings had been done' by the chief practitioners than the latest episode in an on-going, systematic process. Indeed his 'nannying' and endless objections may have actually rekindled interest in the practice within the henge leading to the subsequent destruction of stones such as the Obelisk and Ring-stone and the activities of Caleb Baily.

Conclusions: stone destruction in the Avebury landscape

Avebury's post-medieval history has been almost totally neglected by scholars, excepting historiographies of the personalities involved in its initial discovery and exploration and source criticisms of the records thus generated. This is perhaps most clear in the *Archaeological Research Agenda for the Avebury World Heritage Site* published by English Heritage and the Avebury Archaeological and Historical Research Group as recently as 2001. Purporting to be a comprehensive research framework, its resource assessment, research agenda and research strategy all end at AD 1500. Fortunately Avebury's history did not end in AD 1500 and, as a number of social historians and archaeologists are beginning to acknowledge, the developments that took place at Avebury over the course of the last 500 years are not merely critical to any understanding of its earlier history, but worthy of study in their own right. In this section of the monograph we hope to have drawn attention to some of this complexity through a comprehensive examination of the phenomenon of stone-burning. Through detailed archaeological study the process of stone breaking has been illuminated and the sheer variety of practices employed recognised. Archival and historical research has in turn shed light upon those engaged in such practices and the motivations that may, in various ways, have driven them. Two conclusions can be drawn from this. The first is that far from a regrettable 'dilapidation', stone-breaking represents a fascinating example of a now lost folk-industry and as a result deserves to be further investigated and researched. The second is that the broad tradition of breaking stones by heating them up was put into practice by many different people for many different reasons in many different ways.

One key question remains – why burning? How did burning come to represent the common-sense solution to the problem of an unwanted sarsen? The answer to this lies not in Avebury but out in the sarsen fields. At this point it is worth reiterating that the burning of substantial upright stones represents the enhancement and modification of an existing practice rather than a wholly new development. Perhaps it was originally the act of falling that changed the status of a stone, enabling a direct link to be drawn between megaliths and the natural sarsens 'growing' on the downs. Indeed it may be questioned whether the locals differentiated at all between standing stones and fallen ones, examples of both being inscribed with names and accruing folklore and meaning. In this case are there any grounds for assuming that those responsible were aware that they were destroying *something* at all? This may have been particularly acute in the case of monuments such as Falkner's Circle and parts of the West Kennet Avenue that drew upon both natural and artificially set sarsens in their structure.

The basic approach may already have been centuries old when it was applied to the stones at Avebury and to seek answers as to its origins and evolution we need to look beyond Avebury to the surrounding downland and valley bottoms. Although sarsen fields have been mapped, the 19th century industry documented, and suggestions of 17th–18th century stone breaking recorded during small-scale excavations on Totterdown (Fowler 2000, 72), earlier episodes of stone-breaking have not formed the focus of any sustained academic study or campaigns of structured excavation and investigation. As intimated earlier this would be an extremely productive area for future investigation, and the growing body of research into Improvement (*e.g.* Tarlow 2006) may offer a useful and productive context for further consideration of this phenomenon.

Postscript: stone burning today

During March of 2001 a stone-burning was recreated by a television crew for an episode of the short-lived BBC series *Time Flyers*. The stone had never formed part of any artificial setting and the exercise was in no way an experiment, controlled or otherwise; only a token attempt was made to replicate the precise technology employed and no attempt was made to quantify the efficacy of the process. Little more than an impromptu visual stunt, what is interesting is not the burning *per se*, but the reaction it engendered amongst observers of Avebury. In lively internet discussions the perpetrators were damningly referred to as 'stone-breakers' and an apology was demanded from the broadcasters of the episode. The spirit of Stukeley and the Society of Antiquaries of London clearly lives on.

Notes

1 In Long's opinion the clerical source was Parson Brunsdon of Mounckton (Long 1858b, 8).

2 It is indeed a sobering read for anyone contemplating a career in stone-breaking.

3 The numbering scheme adopted by Keiller in his original records (and interim publications) was completely revised by Smith in the monograph (1965). For example Keiller numbered the Outer Circle stones anti-clockwise from the northern entrance, Smith clockwise from the southern. The West Kennet Avenue stones were originally numbered individually from south to north, being subsequently grouped into pairs and numbered from north to south. In the current monograph all numbers have been standardised to the Smith scheme (see Appendix 3).

4 Given the care with which Keiller weighed destruction debris and packing stones, it is a reasonable assumption that some attempt at weighing the stones was carried out during re-erection. Although not located during the archival research carried out for the current project this information may still survive somewhere in the Keiller records.

5 There has been a tendency to regard the destruction of the Avebury sarsens as a short-lived, intensive episode. Whilst 40 years may represent the blink of an eye to the prehistorian, in the context of late 17th century history it is a substantial period of time.

6 This burning pit was not fully excavated by Keiller as it extended under a standing wall.

7 It is interesting to note that whilst we now know that the run of stones Stukeley claimed had been destroyed by Tom Robinson had in fact been buried, if we follow the arc of the Outer Circle to the immediate west there is a run of *c.*10 settings that appear as parchmarks yet lack the geophysical signature of burials. Stukeley failed to offer any dating evidence for these on his frontispiece and it may well be that these are in fact the stones destroyed by Robinson. Stukeley's error then was no more sinister than pointing to the wrong section of the circle.

8 The published synthetic report of this excavation lacks sufficient stratigraphic detail to further explore this issue; it would certainly be profitable to revisit the original excavation records.

9 White appears to have gained considerable pleasure from the fact that the villagers inadvertently buried Alexander with his head facing in the wrong direction (Spaeth 2000, 201).

10 A remarkable piece of academic understatement.

11
Burial and burning in context

Introduction: seeking parallels

To this point we have portrayed stone burial and breaking as a complex set of folk practices peculiar to the Avebury region. An important question concerns the extent to which this assumption is true; after all, neither megalithic settings nor sarsen scatters are unique to the Marlborough Downs.

In seeking to place stone burial and breaking in some form of context, it rapidly became clear that any attempt to examine all recorded instances of interference and/or destruction of megalithic settings was beyond the scope of the current project. Further, in seeking to find parallels for the activities at Avebury two problems quickly arose. The first was the tendency to view such activities solely through the lens of prehistory, regarding them as lamentable impacts upon the fabric of a previously pristine prehistoric stone setting. When encountered during excavation these events are described in terms such as *dilapidation*, *destruction*, *robbing* and *vandalism* and as a result are rarely afforded more than a passing mention. The second problem is that when instances of possible burial or burning have been encountered the immediate response has been to relate them uncritically to the events that took place at Avebury. In doing so the orthodox explanations that have held sway at Avebury – church-sponsored medieval burial, avaricious post-medieval destruction – are transplanted directly to the new context.

It is hoped that rather than closing a chapter of research, the latter sections of this monograph will serve to open one, acting as a solid foundation for further comparative studies and serving as a platform from which long-held assumptions, such as those outlined above, can be challenged. As a result, in seeking to identify possible parallels to the practices discussed in Chapters 9 and 10 discussion has focused upon a specific set of sources. The first comprises the unpublished archive of the Society of Antiquaries sarsen stones survey, a key component in their *Evolution of the Landscape Project*. The second examines a group of sites where the excavators, or later researchers, have cited a direct and explicit link between the features they have recorded and the incidences of burial and breaking that took place at Avebury. These comprise the henge sites of Stonehenge (Wiltshire) and the Devil's Quoits (Oxfordshire), along with a group of chambered long mounds known collectively as the 'Medway megaliths' (Kent). The final parallel, and perhaps most tantalising of all, is that provided by Stanton Drew, Somerset, a site visited by Aubrey and Stukeley who noted not only the presence of major stone settings but also acts of stone burial and breaking.

Burial and burning: a capsule summary

Before looking for possible parallels it is important to summarise what we now know about the practices of stone burial and breaking that took place in the Avebury landscape.

The earliest dated burial of a megalith appears to have taken place during the early 14th century, the latest during the 1920s and the umbrella term 'stone burial' masks a wide variety of practices. In the absence of reliable dates for many of the burials encountered it is difficult to determine whether these represent gradual changes in technique over time, the preferences of individual personnel, or pragmatic solutions to the specific problems posed by individual stones. Some combination of all of the above factors appears most likely. In terms of tempo, it is at present unclear whether stone burial took place gradually, perhaps one every other year or so, or in short sharp bursts, perhaps separated by decades if not longer. On the basis of the evidence assembled to date the latter interpretation is most persuasive. In terms of motivation, the arguments against utilitarian clearance and for a religious/superstitious imperative must now be re-evaluated. A number of the burials along the lines of the avenues make perfect sense as forms of strip field clearance, and the keystone of the religious explanation, the fate of the barber-surgeon, may be unrelated to the act of stone burial. Given the fact that burial, as a practice, was in currency for upwards of 400 years, a single, uniform and unchanging rationale seems unlikely and the difficulties we have in assigning a single explanation that fits all of the burials so far investigated reflects this. Instead stone burial is best thought of as the appropriate response to a stone deemed to be 'in the way' or 'in the wrong place' whether in respect to agriculture or everyday village life.

Our earliest dated stone destruction took place between the 15th and 17th centuries, though the evidence from sites such as Huish suggest that the breaking of sarsens for building stone may have been taking place in the wider Avebury landscape long before the practice was applied to the megalithic settings. What is clear is that far from distinct historic episodes the practices of burial and breaking were, for a time at least, coeval. If stone breaking more generally was a long-lived practice, the deliberate destruction of the Avebury settings appears to have taken place over a 40–50 year period centred upon 1700. Although stone-burning has captured the public imagination, a variety of techniques were used to render down or remove megaliths, ranging from simply dragging them away, to direct fracture and the construction of elaborate furnaces. As with burial the label 'stone breaking' covers an enormously varied set of practices and whilst some general chronological trends can be detected in terms of specific preference, there is a strong sense that stone breakers were drawing upon an established suite of techniques. What is clear is that rather than an innovation born solely out of a need to remove standing stones from the landscape, stone breaking was imported into this context from the surrounding downland where it was already well established. As with burial, the motivations behind the acts may have been varied and a single all encompassing rationale is difficult to sustain. Some were undoubtedly broken as they caused a nuisance, others for building and road improvements, others perhaps for more political reasons. What is clear is that by 1700 the accepted response to stones that had the misfortune of 'finding themselves in the way' had ceased to be burial and instead involved relocation and breaking.

The Sarsen Stones Project

Carried out between 1974–7 as part of the Society of Antiquaries *Evolution of the Landscape Project*, this initiative sought to record the location, status and context of all visible sarsen stones within the counties of Dorset, Hampshire and Wiltshire (for a general introduction see Bowen and Smith 1977). Although a brief summary was published in 1977 (*ibid.*) the compiled datasets remain in archive form in the Library of the Society of Antiquaries. A key component of the archive is the mass of field record sheets compiled for each individual stone, group or scatter encountered, along with summaries and annotated maps. As well as the status of the stones, the pro-forma recording sheets used by the project (termed 'Tally cards') explicitly set out to record evidence of breaking and/or working, including a question under the 'Description' category which encouraged consideration of 'Evidence for use, splitting or smoothing *etc*' (*e.g.* MS 953/4/2).[1] Although on the strength of the Tally cards reviewed this question was not always included, and when it was individuals interpreted it in a number of ways (when they bothered to address it at all), it was hoped that some evidence of activities such as burial and breakage may have been recorded.

The first stage was to identify sarsens associated with megalithic settings and explicitly recorded as having been buried, burned and/or broken. Mention of deliberate burial was limited to only two sites: Little Mayne, in the parish of West Knighton, Dorset (Tallycard WKH2), and Winterbourne Monkton in

Wiltshire. The former were suggested to comprise the remains of a stone circle, discovered by a local farmer during fencing operations. There was no confirmation of this interpretation or detail regarding the nature of these burials though the quantity of naturally occurring sarsens in the vicinity suggest that they were most likely geological. In the case of Winterbourne Monkton a group of sarsen slabs that had previously covered a series of prehistoric burials had been deliberately buried between 1854–5 'to avoid the plough' (Society of Antiquaries MS 953/1/2 p.12). In the case of burning and stone breaking, mention was likewise limited to a handful of sites. In the parish of Aldbourne, Wiltshire, Greenwell had recorded the presence of burned and heated chunks of sarsen within a series of cairns and round barrows (1890, 46, 50), however these were clearly primary to the construction of the mounds. The record of 'destroyed' sarsens at the site of a barrow in the parish of Westbury, Wiltshire, proved on closer inspection to refer to the mound rather than sarsens contained within it as originally noted by Colt-Hoare (1812, 54).

Otherwise the archive is silent despite recording over 699 individual sarsens, groups and concentrations (compiled from figures presented in MS 953/1/2). This is perhaps unsurprising given the focus of the project; the very presence of the stones in the archive (unless fortuitous discoveries) implies that they had escaped burial or wholesale destruction. One of the most interesting aspects of the project with respect to the current investigation was its sponsoring of two small excavations of natural sarsens on the Marlborough Downs, one partly broken, in order to explore the relationship between natural sarsens and the chalk subsoil and archaeological signatures left by later stone breaking technologies (Bowen and Smith 1977, 193–5). As discussed in Chapter 10, it would be extremely interesting to build upon this work looking more broadly at the archaeology of sarsen exploitation.

As a postscript to this appraisal of the Sarsen Stone Project archive, contact was made with the SMR for Buckinghamshire, a county with a direct link to the later sarsen working industries of the Avebury area. In the High Wycombe area of the county a specialised stone working industry had developed in the early 19th century centred upon a local variant of sarsen termed Denner Hill stone (Burtonwood 1995). Around 1850 one of the High Wycombe stone-masons relocated to the Avebury area and quickly established a very successful sarsen cutting business, replacing the rather haphazard stone burning techniques with the more efficient tools and techniques that had been perfected by the High Wycombe masons (King 1968). Despite the scale of stone-working that had clearly been taking place in the High Wycombe area in the 19th century, there appear to be no documented records in the county of stone burial, fire-setting or other forms of breaking (pers. comm. Julia Wise 2006).

'Wrecking' Stonehenge

> 'The post-Bronze Age story of Stonehenge is therefore essentially one of dilapidation, vandalism, occasional use, and restoration, its main role being as a tourist attraction.' (Cleal *et al.* 1995, 332)

At Stonehenge, Wiltshire, a number of stone settings had been removed from the Sarsen Circle, Sarsen Horseshoe and Bluestone Circle of the monument (*ibid.*, 167–255). In addition, a spread of bluestone chips in the so-called 'Stonehenge layer' has been interpreted as, in part, debris from the 'wrecking' of the stones, though the nature of this destruction, its inception date and duration is unknown (*ibid.*, 334–336). The excavations carried out by Atkinson in the 1950s failed to produce any convincing evidence for any medieval disturbance to the stone settings and there is only one feature suggestive of any major 17th /18th century removal of stones (*ibid.*, 338–9). It is therefore interesting to note that other than casual assaults inflicted by tourists seeking souvenirs, those convinced of the efficacy (medical or otherwise) of the fragments, and accidental vandalisms associated with fairs (held from 1680), the only explanation offered to account for the missing stones draws directly upon Smith's account of the stone burials at Avebury (Chippindale 1983, 44, 72). Despite the lack of any compelling evidence for medieval stone destruction at the site, let alone the deliberate burials that characterise medieval interventions at Avebury, the possibility is raised that the 'wrecking' may have taken place in the early medieval period in the context of 'religious fervour or pure superstition' (Cleal *et al.* 1995, 339). At the very least this implies some confusion between the episodes of burial and burning described by Smith.

The removal of stone settings clearly took place at Stonehenge along with the possible destruction of some of the stones. However we know little about the practices involved and even less about the dating of these events. As for motivation, discussion to date has been dominated by rather lazy analogies with Avebury.

The Devil's Quoits

The tendency to fall back upon Avebury and the orthodox account passed down by Smith (1965) and Burl (1979) is also in evidence at the site of the Devil's Quoits, Stanton Harcourt, Oxfordshire. Unlike Stonehenge, this is notable for having evidence of both stone burial and burning and to date offers the closest parallel to the Avebury settings.

The henge enclosed a circle of standing stones running around the perimeter. Excavation revealed that of an estimated 36 original settings a total of three were buried, three broken and 26 totally removed. Of the burials, one was known to have taken place in 1940 during the construction of a wartime airfield. The remaining examples appear to have been medieval, located either side of the eastern entrance to the monument (F.25 and F.28) (Figure 11.1). The F.28 burial pit seems to have been cut directly up to the standing stone which was then toppled into it, the base of the stone remaining within the orbit of the original stonehole (Figure 11.2a). That it was toppled directly into the pit rather than cut around is evident from the cavities and airspaces beneath the bulk of the stone (Barclay *et al.* 1995, 42–3). The suggestion is of a mode of burial similar to that of setting T1 of the Beckhampton Avenue, though here the pit appears to have been cut to reflect the shape of the stone it was destined to receive. The presence of primary silting down the sides of the pit indicate that it had remained open for some time either prior to (or after) the toppling of the stone. In direct contrast, the F.25 burial pit was dug adjacent to the stonehole and the stone had clearly been toppled prior to burial as in the case of the separate-pit burials seen at Avebury. Lever marks were evident at the ends of the stone-hole and one edge of the pit had clearly been damaged during the sliding in of the stone (Figure 11.2b). Unlike F.28, little attempt was made to shape the pit to reflect the shape of the stone. Interestingly the very edge of the latter pit was cut by a medieval plough furrow.

One of the megaliths was destroyed through fire-setting in a deliberately prepared pit, F.98. This took the form of an ovoid pit containing numerous pieces of burnt stone and showing evidence of burning on its south-west side (Figure 11.2c). Excavated by Grimes in 1940, this was described as being divided by 'a poorly defined transverse ridge, which was accompanied by two slight constrictions in the plan,

Figure 11.1. The henge and stone settings of the Devil's Quoits, Oxfordshire (after Barclay et al. *1995, fig. 6)*

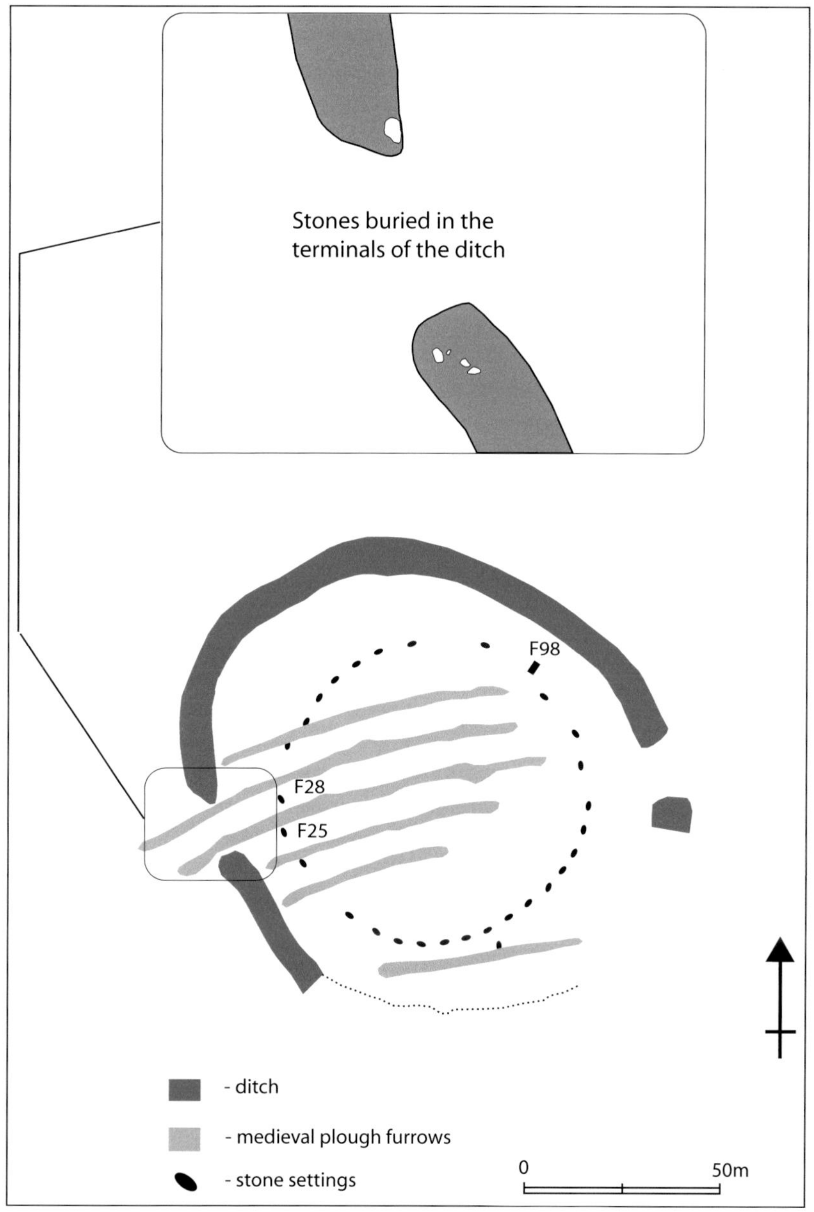

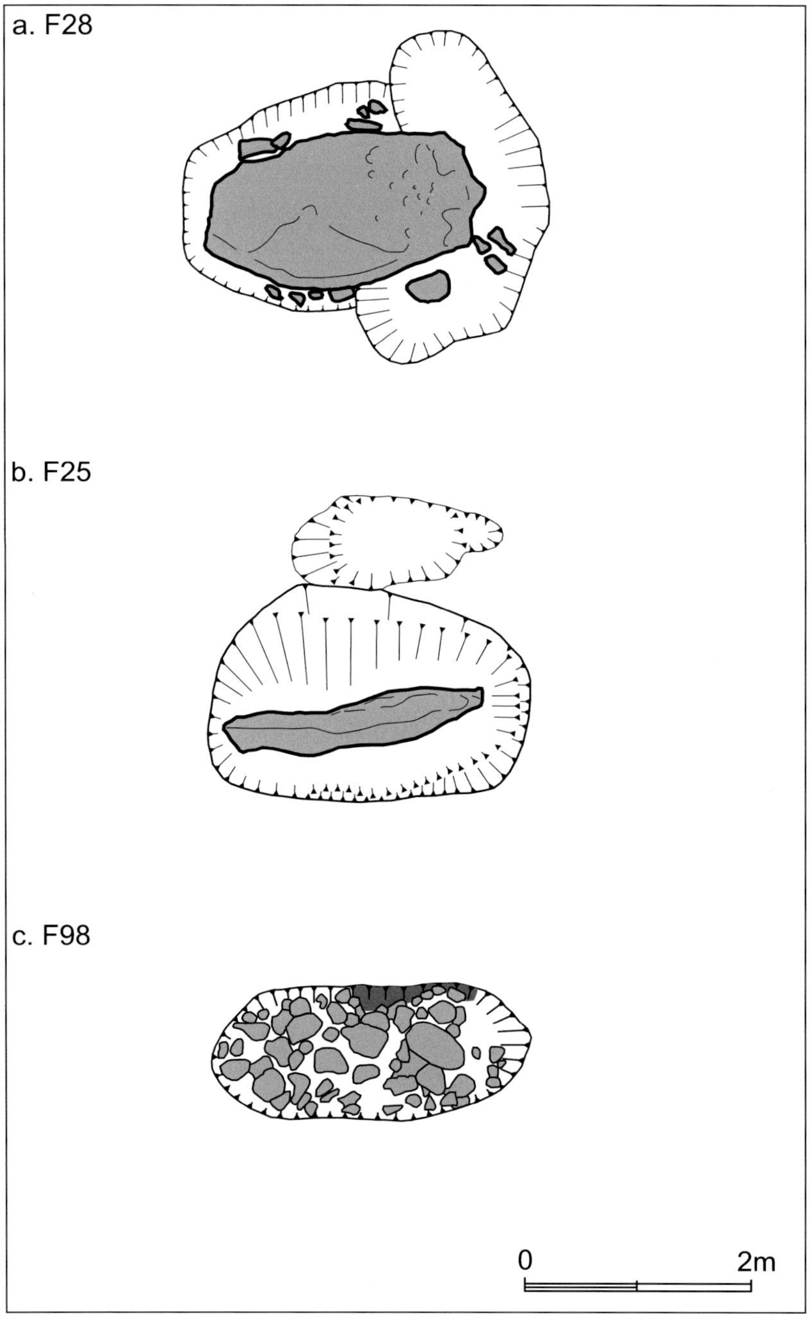

Figure 11.2. Settings F.28, F.25 and F.98 of the Devil's Quoits, Oxfordshire (after Barclay et al. *1995, figs 17, 24 and 25)*

suggesting that the hole had been dug in two parts' (Barclay *et al.* 1995, 42). As in a number of the Avebury examples, this may have been a deliberate attempt to ensure adequate airflow beneath the stone. The absence of any convincing traces of a stone-hole within the base of the pit and its position perpendicular to the arc of stones suggest that it had been dug at some distance from the original setting. As well as destruction of one stone through fire-setting a further two had been broken through direct fracture (F.158 and F.215), leaving stumps and fragments of broken stone in the remainder of the stone-holes. Of the 26 removed stones only empty stone-holes remained, some of which showed evidence of levering on their edges. A number of stones, presumably originating from the settings, were found in the ditch terminals of the western entrance, sealed beneath a layer of gravel possibly corresponding to a deliberate levelling of the surviving bank (Layer D). This layer contained 13th-– 15th-century pottery and was sealed by the medieval ploughsoil (Layer C) (*ibid.*, 23).

On the basis of the stratigraphy and pottery evidence it seems clear that the stone burials and dumping of stones in the ditch most likely took place in the 13th – 15th centuries and appear to focus around the western entrance of the henge, an area notable for the medieval plough furrows that run through and across it (Figure 11.1). In seeking to explain the rationale behind these burials, recourse is made once again to the familiar Avebury story, the stones being buried and destroyed as part of a response by the Church to unwelcome pagan activities. As with Avebury there is little to back up this assertion. Given the evidence from the Beckhampton Avenue, the burials could very well be related to deliberate clearance within the individual strips of an open field. The very different approaches taken to the burying of the stones may well reflect the fact that they stood in different strips and were, presumably, buried by different individuals; the deliberate placement of stones within the ditch a more pragmatic solution to the same problem.

The lack of stratification within the interior makes it difficult to unravel the sequence of burning, breakage and removal, though the linking of burning and breakage to the medieval period on the strength of the Avebury evidence reflects an accidental conflation of the events taking place at the latter site (Barclay *et al.* 1995, 43). Perhaps the most useful *terminus ante quem* is provided by John Aubrey who was only able to record three stones standing in the mid 17th century, suggesting that the destruction had taken place at some point prior to his visit. As for motivation the single burning pit is notable for the amount of stone left within it which includes a number of sizeable, regular blocks. This implies that the act was driven by a desire to eradicate the stone rather than break it down to liberate building material.[2] Likewise the substantial stumps left in the stone-holes of the fractured examples seem rather wasteful if the destruction was economically motivated.

Burial, breaking and the Medway megaliths

Located in the lower valley of the river Medway, Kent, is a group of sarsen built chambered long-mounds of early Neolithic date collectively termed the Medway Megaliths (Holgate 1981).

At the site of Addington the sarsens making up the main chamber of the monument appear to have been deliberately toppled and buried along with some of the kerbstones. Both Kit's Coty House and Coldrum also show evidence of kerbstones being toppled and sporadically buried (Ashbee 1993a, 65–6). Unfortunately of these sites only Kit's Coty House has witnessed modern excavation (1956) and publication of the latter amounts to little more than a brief note. As a result little in the way of detail regarding these activities survives beyond simple statements to the effect that stones were buried (*e.g.* McCrerie 1956, 251).

The only Medway megalith to have witnessed extensive modern excavation and full publication is The Chestnuts, excavated over a period of five weeks during 1957. In this case there was no evidence of any deliberate stone burial but instead a clinical dismantling of the monument fabric. The earthen mound surrounding the stone chamber appears to have been dug away in order to facilitate access, the chamber then being systematically cleared. As part of this process pits were dug at the base of some of the upright sarsens forming the walls of the chamber to hasten their collapse. What makes this assault interesting is its date; a group of almost complete pottery vessels and unabraded sherds found within the chamber and sealed beneath toppled stones, all point to a date in the late 13th century (Alexander 1961, 25).

Although the presence of quantities of abraded medieval potsherds in the ploughsoil suggested that the area had been intensively cultivated during the medieval period the failure to remove the toppled stones suggests that clearance did not drive this activity. Instead the positioning of the fallen stones argued strongly that the aim of the exercise was to get inside the chamber rather than topple stones for their own sake (*ibid.*, 26–7). This led the excavator to suggest that the late 13th-century dismantling of the monument was the result of deliberate treasure hunting. Citing a number of contemporary written sources from the Isle of Wight and Cornwall in support, he went on to speculate that the efficacy of the assault could indicate that a dedicated team of experts may have been responsible (*ibid.*, 25).

More recently Ashbee has disputed the grave-robbing element of this explanation on the grounds that the systematic dismantling seen at The Chestnuts was not typical of documented medieval and later barrow raiding (Ashbee 1993a, 64). Following the Avebury orthodoxy, he has argued instead that the dismantling of The Chestnuts in the late 13th century was prompted by Church displeasure at pagan activities taking place there. Building on Alexander's suggestion that the work was carried out by an experienced group, he embellished this by suggesting that an itinerant band of specialist wreckers may have been responsible, one of whom was to eventually meet his end crushed under stone 9 at Avebury (*ibid.*, 65). In an interesting extrapolation, and despite the lack of dating for the burials noted at Addington, Kit's Coty House and Coldrum, Ashbee extended this late 13th century date to all of these sites to create a distinct horizon of destruction in the history of the Medway megaliths that has little in the way of convincing evidence to back it up.

In terms of practice and scale the dismantling of The Chestnuts has little in common with the stone burials that took place at Avebury. Further, if a semi-professional gang of specialist monument breakers experienced in the dismantling of chambered long mounds were active, it seems strange that they ignored prominent examples of the latter such as West Kennet and Wayland's Smithy in favour of the Avebury settings. Whilst possible robbing was in evidence at both of these sites with some limited breaking of stones at the former, it is of a wholly different scale and character to the Medway examples (Peers and Smith 1921; R J C Atkinson 1965; Whittle 1991; Piggott 1962).[3] If the church-sponsored explanation is now difficult to sustain in the case of Avebury (see Chapter 9) on the grounds of a lack of any convincing supportive evidence, it is doubly difficult in the case of the Medway megaliths.

With respect to stone breaking, whilst there is clear evidence for the piecemeal destruction of sarsens during the 18th century and later, and of the use of sarsen as a building material in the wider landscape, there is little in the area of the Medway megaliths to parallel the activities witnessed at Avebury.[4] For example, convincing evidence for the breaking of sarsens through fire-setting is limited to rare (and unconvincing) indications of burning on sarsens at Lower Kit Coty's House and The Chestnuts. There is no evidence of the construction and use of burning pits nor of the use of fuels such as straw (Ashbee 1993a, 67). Perhaps most important in any consideration of deliberate stone breaking is the evidence of William Stukeley. Stukeley undertook visits to Kent *during* his period of recording at Avebury. For example, he made detailed records of the surviving stones of Kit's Coty House in 1722 and 1723 (Ashbee 1993a; 2001). That the Avebury monuments were at the forefront of his thinking whilst recording examples of the Medway megaliths is clear from the direct links he drew with the Avebury Cove whilst speculating as to the original form of Kit Coty's House (Ashbee 1993b). What has not been commented upon is the lack of any reference from Stukeley to any form of stone breaking taking place in or around these monuments or in the surrounding landscape. Given his experience at Avebury, if active destruction were taking place, he would surely have noted it.

In conclusion, despite the efforts of Ashbee to draw direct parallels between Avebury and the monuments of the Medway, on the basis of the evidence currently available there is little commonality between them.

Stanton Drew

At Stanton Drew, Somerset, is a complex of stone settings that comprise a stone circle (the Great Circle) of approximately 30 stones located within a ditched henge enclosure 135m in diameter. It is flanked by two smaller circles – the North-East (NE; 30m in diameter and comprising eight settings) and the South-South-West (SSW; 43m in diameter with between nine and 12 settings). Recent geophysical surveys have revealed nine concentric rings of pits (or possible post-settings) within the Great Circle, three concentric rings of pits within the SSW and a central arrangement of four pit-like features within the NE circle (David *et al.* 2004). From the north-east side of the Great Circle an avenue extended for 88m before joining a second stretch of avenue leaving the NE circle. Around 300m to the west-south-west of the Great Circle is a cove setting of three standing stones, the largest 4.4m in height (Burl 2000, 148; National Monuments Record).

What makes the Stanton Drew settings of interest here are comments made by both Aubrey and Stukeley regarding the fates of some of the stone settings during their early visits to the site. Aubrey recorded the Stanton Drew settings in 1664 (Fowles and Legg 1980, 67), a year after his detailed survey of Avebury. During a discussion of the stones he noted that:

> 'As hard as these stones are they make a skiff to breake them with sledges because they so incumber their good land, and they told me they are much diminished within these few yeares.' (*ibid.*, 46–7)

The suggestion is that stones were actively being broken up shortly before his visit. Given that the latter took place after his observations at Avebury (as is also evident from the parallels he draws between the avenues at each of the sites), his failure to mention any form of fire-setting (as opposed to direct fracture) is surely significant.

Stukeley visited Stanton Drew in July 1723, after he had completed several seasons of survey and record at Avebury. In describing the complex he commented that:

> 'The monument about ten years ago must have made a most noble appearance, because then perfect. It seems the nuns, and all the possessors of the estate, had left it untouched till a late tenant, for covetousness of the little space of ground they stood upon, buried them for the most part in the ground: he was justly punished, for the grass at this time will not grow over them, but withers, because there is not sufficient depth of earth.' (Stukeley 1776, 170)

He noted how buried stones could not only be detected by the parching of the grass growing above them but also by the distinctive sound they made when one knocked their boot heel against them and by 'thrusting an iron rod into the earth' (ibid.; 171). Recent earth resistance survey of the SSW circle has revealed at least one anomaly that is a good contender for such a stone burial (David *et al.* 2004, 353).

The parallels with his Avebury accounts are obvious, from the dating of the burials to a period a decade or so before his arrival, to the suggestion that greed for land fuelled the activity. Perhaps more interesting, given the records of Aubrey, is his failure to mention any form of sustained or organised stone-breaking, although he did note how unsuitable the stone was for building (1776, 171).

Taken together these accounts highlight two discrete episodes: one of stone-breaking through direct fracture taking place in the mid to late 17th century, followed by an episode of deliberate stone burial taking place around 1710. The failure of either commentator to mention the other activity further suggests that these episodes may have been relatively small in scale and duration, a conclusion supported by the number of stones surviving.

Though at first glance the implication is of an inversion of the traditionally posited 'burial to burning/breaking' trajectory, we have shown how at Avebury the two traditions were for a time coeval and the Stanton Drew episodes may well have fallen within this important transitional period. As a result the site has enormous potential to shed further light upon the character and chronology of these practices. Unfortunately, other than the records outlined above we have no further information regarding breakage and burial within the Stanton Drew settings. There has been no recorded excavation, either antiquarian or modern, and no attempt to ground-truth the anomalies revealed by the recent programme of geophysical survey (David *et al.* 2004). With its multiple circles, avenues, cove and suggestions of acts of stone burial and breakage, Stanton Drew offers many tantalising parallels with the Avebury monuments. In the absence of any sustained modern fieldwork these must remain for the moment merely tantalising.

Conclusions: a unique phenomenon?

Whilst the dismantling of megalithic settings during the historic period is attested at a number of sites (*e.g.* Burl 2000, 9–14) burial and fire-setting appear to be much less common, small in scale and invariably late in date. An example is the Victorian burial of stones at the circle of Fortinghall in Perthshire (*ibid.*, 246). Certainly no records could be found in the sources analysed of episodes of burial and destruction taking place at the same time as the events unfolding at Avebury.

Looking to the sites most often cited as parallels, on close scrutiny these have been shown to lack conviction. It is perhaps ironic that having witnessed prehistorians railing against the imposition of atypical models developed in Wessex upon the Neolithic of the remainder of the country, the same seems to have been quietly going on with respect to the medieval and later reception of monuments. Rather than explore the rationale behind these acts in their own right, we have too often seen instead the lazy importation of tenuous explanatory frameworks that are difficult to sustain for Avebury itself let alone any other context. Despite the lack of reliable dating evidence our best excavated parallel at present is offered by the Devil's Quoits, but when we consider the scale of activity taking place even this is far removed from the situation at Avebury. Stanton Drew may yet offer the closest parallels to Avebury but confirmation can only come with a sustained programme of excavation.

In conclusion, the burial and breaking of stone settings at Avebury remains for the moment a unique phenomenon. As with the analyses carried out in the present volume, medieval and post-medieval encounters with megalithic structures need to be analysed in their own right, treated as episodes in the ongoing lives of these structures as important in their own way as the events and practices that accompanied their inception. Parallels for the burials and burning seen at Avebury may well come to light, but they will require an attentiveness, openness and active appreciation of the archaeology of these later episodes if they are to be recognised.

Notes

1 A bundle of miscellaneous records including examples of completed Tally cards.

2 Grimes commented on the fact that, unlike sarsen, the conglomerate used to construct the stone settings would not have required the use of fire-setting to break it down. Noting evidence of burning upon blocks of the conglomerate stone used in the construction of Stanton Harcourt Church, he instead implied that fire may have been necessary to effectively purify stone derived from the circle

(Grimes 1960, 153). This is yet another interesting variation of the 'superstition' tendency discussed in Chapter 9.

3 It is perhaps worth noting that in the case of Wayland's Smithy, it was a fear that picnic campfires may inadvertently break the sarsens that prompted the excavations of 1919–20.

4 See for example the fate of the General's Tombstone, a megalith close to Kit's Coty House (McCrerie 1956, 252).

12
Antiquarian encounters with the Beckhampton Avenue

Avebury is fortunate insofar as a number of studies have been published exploring and documenting progressive antiquarian and archaeological encounters with the monument complex. The most thorough is that of Ucko *et al.* (1991). In their study of 17th and 18th century antiquarian investigations the authors produced a remarkably detailed, critical analysis of the first visits to, and records of, the site. In recent years this has, in turn, been supported by reflection and re-appraisal of some of the conclusions presented (*e.g.* Hutton 2005) as well as consideration of previously marginalised or neglected individuals (*e.g.* Peterson 2003). The same has also been true of formal archaeological interventions. These were first summarised by Long in an excellent series of articles for the *Wiltshire Archaeological and Natural History Magazine* (1858a, 1878) and subsequently by authors such as Gray (1935, 102–5), Smith (1965, 182–5), Burl (1979, 57–76) and most recently Gillings and Pollard (2004, chapters 8–10).

In light of this impressive corpus of work it is important to clarify from the outset the aims of this final section of the monograph. In considering the Avebury landscape as a whole, if we exclude the records of Stukeley and Twining, discussions of the Beckhampton Avenue have tended to focus upon the question of its existence (or otherwise) (*e.g.* King 1879; Lukis 1881–3a; Smith 1965, 216–7; Vatcher and Vatcher 1980; Ucko *et al.* 1991, 195–9). To his credit Long documented evidence whilst remaining undecided regarding its reality (1858b, 23–6), whilst Lukis (1881–3a, 152–5) dismissed it entirely and Burl (1979) and the Vatchers (1980, 41–2) asserted its presence without qualification.

Having established the definitive existence of the Beckhampton Avenue the time is ripe to compliment and enhance the existing corpus of work, filling gaps and developing strands that have previously been afforded only brief mention. This has taken two forms. In considering antiquarian encounters, the approach pioneered by Ucko *et al.* (1991) has been extended to the Beckhampton Avenue through a detailed analysis and transcription of Stukeley's surviving records.

In archaeological terms, the general ambiguities surrounding the existence of the avenue served to limit research into its course and settings. There was a very real failure to see the proverbial wood for the trees, the latter taking the form of a host of chance notes, observations and excavations carried out by Faith and Lance Vatcher during their tenure at the Alexander Keiller Museum. The small scale of all of these excavations, while confirming the presence of buried sarsens in particular areas, did nothing to resolve the more general question of the relationship of these sarsens to any wider monumental structure. In fact some of the stones excavated by the Vatchers, for example the stone discovered by the Beckhampton roundabout in 1967 (Vatcher 1969), lie beyond the termination of the Beckhampton Avenue and are presumably unconnected with it.

Thomas Twining's account of the Beckhampton Avenue

The first published record of the presence of the Beckhampton Avenue comes in a pamphlet published by Thomas Twining in 1732.

Twining was vicar of Chalfont in the Vale of Pewsey but we have no surviving records of precisely when he visited Avebury and saw the remains of the avenues. His publication had little impact on subsequent interpretations; where it was remembered at all, it was as an unreliable account. Twining gave a Roman date to the whole of Avebury and incorporated two further spurious avenues to recreate the complex as a landscape map of Roman Britain (Lukis 1881–3a, 154–5; Burl 1979, 51; Ucko *et al.* 1991, 37–9). However, Peterson (2003) has demonstrated that despite Twining's in-experience, which led him to some of his more dubious conclusions, his published field observations can all be linked to surviving landscape features.

In particular, as Burl (2000, 325–6) has noted, Twining might have provided a second contemporary voice to support Stukeley's (1743, 35; Bodl MS Gough Maps 231 f223) description of the Beckhampton Avenue:

> 'To the oblong Part of the Circus this Village [Beckhampton] joins.. ...the large Stones to the West, the Remains of the Discus now standing, are still call'd the Devil's Coits (Gale's Iter. p. 135) a term owing to the early Zeal of Christianity, both the discountenance all Resort to the Circus, (a Practice loudly decried by Tertullian, de spectaculis) and prevent the Damage such a Concourse of People must do in the Fields. Not that these two Stones were ever British Deities, as some Learned Men, without any Ground, have fancied; but a part of the Discus, as other Stones lying in the same field do shew, to justifie the Figure I have assigned the Whole.' (Twining 1723, 15)

Twining's recording of the name 'Devil's Coits' for the Beckhampton Cove resolves the ambiguity caused by John Aubrey's (Fowles and Legg 1980, 823) recording of a monument under the same name as lying to the south of Avebury. Stukeley and Twining were clearly recording the same monument, and both place it correctly in Longstones Field.

William Stukeley and the Beckhampton Avenue

Stukeley spent parts of two field seasons, in 1723 and particularly in 1724, attempting to understand the detail of the course of the Beckhampton Avenue. Drawings and notes which he made at this time and immediately afterwards survive in the Bodleian Library, Oxford, and provide valuable information both about the state of the monument in the 1720s and Stukeley's changing understandings of its form. The key figures have been reproduced below, together with a detailed discussion of their content.

Bodl. MS Gough Maps 231 f223, 320 × 193 mm, pen and wash (Figure 12.1)

This sheet seems to comprise a field drawing of a prospect together with a later interpretive modification below. The upper drawing is titled 'Prospect of the remains of long stone Avenue 14 July 1723. as I took it, from the top of an haycock.' It seems to have been drawn from north west side of Longstones Field, in the vicinity of SU 0888 6938, looking almost due south. The prospect takes in the area from Longstones long barrow in the west to Silbury Hill in the east. The drawing is assured and the treatment of the perspective and relief very convincing, especially in contrast to some of the engraved prospects in *Abury*. Several features are labelled: the present A4361 as 'Bath coach road'; the Wansdyke is shown near the horizon and labelled 'Wansd.' twice; 'Bekampton' appears above the village and 'St Anns hill' above Easton Hill. 'Longstone barrow' appears beneath that monument and 'barrow' above South Street.

Eight avenue stones are shown and the course of the avenue is indicated by a white gap in the wash. There is a recumbent stone on the north side of the avenue, several stone positions to the east of the group around the cove, possibly stone L1. Five stones are shown in the area around the cove: L7, L8 and L15 are recumbent; and L9 and L14 are standing. The most westerly pair of stones is shown im-mediately to the west of the boundary with Long Barrow Field and both are shown as recumbent.

On the lower half of the sheet is a pen sketch labelled 'The end of the Avenue'. Some detail of the west end of Beckhampton village has been transcribed from the upper drawing and labelled 'Bekampton'. A conjectural course for the avenue is shown passing through a pair of upright stones, curving to the north and west and terminating in a small double circle. The pair of uprights probably represent the stones Stukeley noted as removed by Richard Fowler in roughly this location. On the basis of this reconstruction Stukeley imagined the end of the avenue to be somewhere either

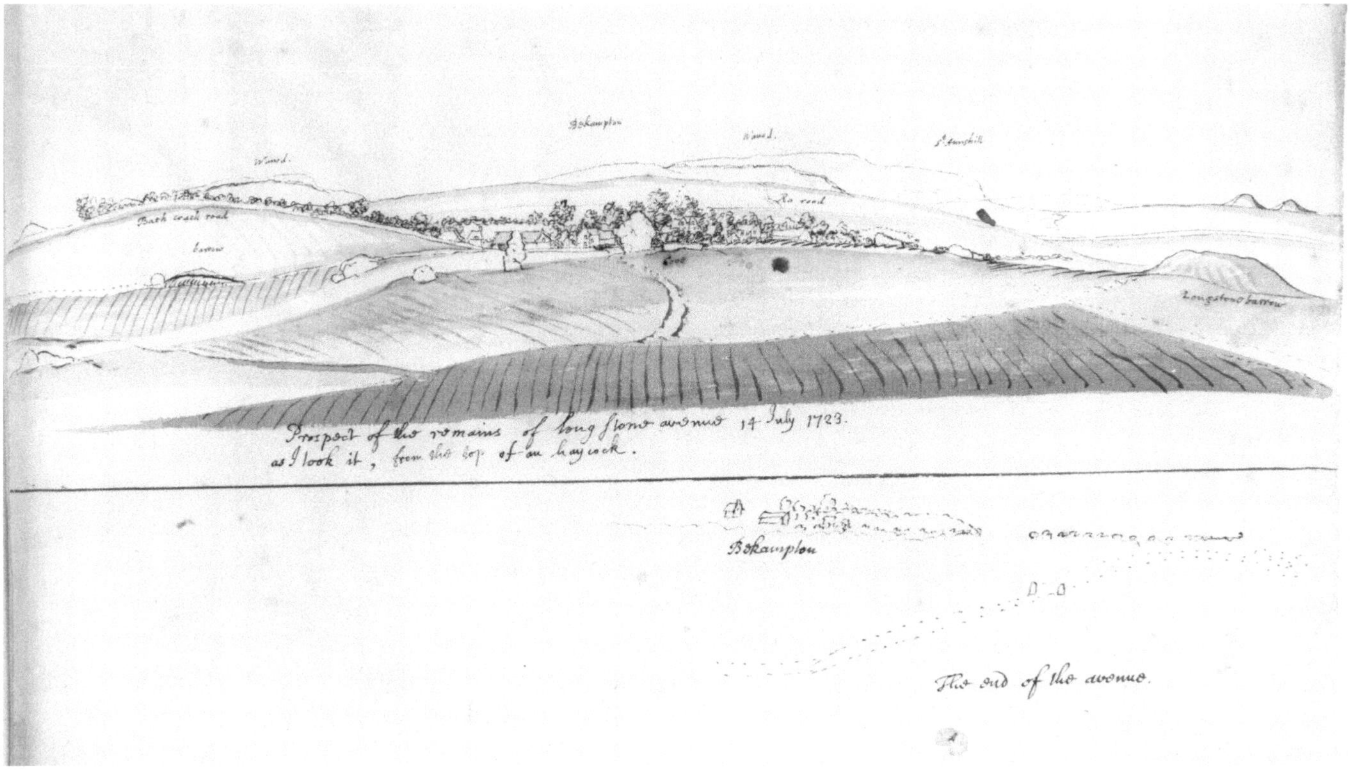

Figure 12.1. Stukeley's prospect of the Longstones from the north, drawn from 'the top of an haycock'. Bodl. MS Gough Maps 231 f223, 320 × 193 mm, pen and wash. Reproduced by permission of the Keeper of Special Collections and Western Manuscripts

beneath the A361 or in the northern part of Durran Field.

Bodl. MS Gough Maps 231 f7, 267 × 161 mm, pen (Figure 12.2)

This sheet comprises a number of different field notes and sketch maps. The lower half of the sheet has one continuous sketch map covering stone positions, roads and buildings from the west entrance of the henge to a point 600 feet beyond South Street long barrow. The map is less detailed as it moves west, with the east end of Avebury High Street at a considerably larger scale than the rest of the plan. Six buildings are shown to the east of the Winterbourne: the church; and buildings on the sites of the present Ashdown House; St Andrews Cottage; the Old Bakery; Rose Cottage and the Old Forge. West of the Winterbourne and south of Bray Street are two very small buildings which presumably represent stylised versions of Trusloe Manor and Manor Farm. To the west of these two buildings are five cottages and their associated gardens. North of Bray Street four buildings are shown: a substantial house on the site of the present Lower Acre and three cottages. Roads and field boundaries are shown in varying amounts of detail and with some indications of hedges. The Winterbourne bridge has been strongly emphasised. Several of the roads are labelled: Bray Street as 'From Calne'; what may be either Frog Lane or the current A4361 as 'Coach road to [illeg] Bath'; and Caitor's Lane as 'footway'. Bray Field and Trusloe Field are both labelled 'corn'. Linear measurements along the High Street, Bray Street and in some areas west of South Street long barrow, are given as numbers. If these measurements are in feet they are very accurate in those areas where they can be checked.

The line of the avenue follows Avebury High Street as far as the west corner of Rose Cottage, it is then shown passing to the north of the High Street through the grounds of Bridgemead, crossing the Winterbourne at the point of the present bridge and then running through the cottage gardens in the northern part of Trusloe Field. The line through Longstones Field is less clear but it appears to pass to the north of South Street. The stones are shown as open or filled rectangles. Moving westwards from the henge, a pair is shown as open rectangles in the west entrance, followed by a single open rectangle in the grounds of Fosse House. Beneath this stone is the note '1702 several'. There is a filled rectangle shown beneath the south west corner of Rose Cottage

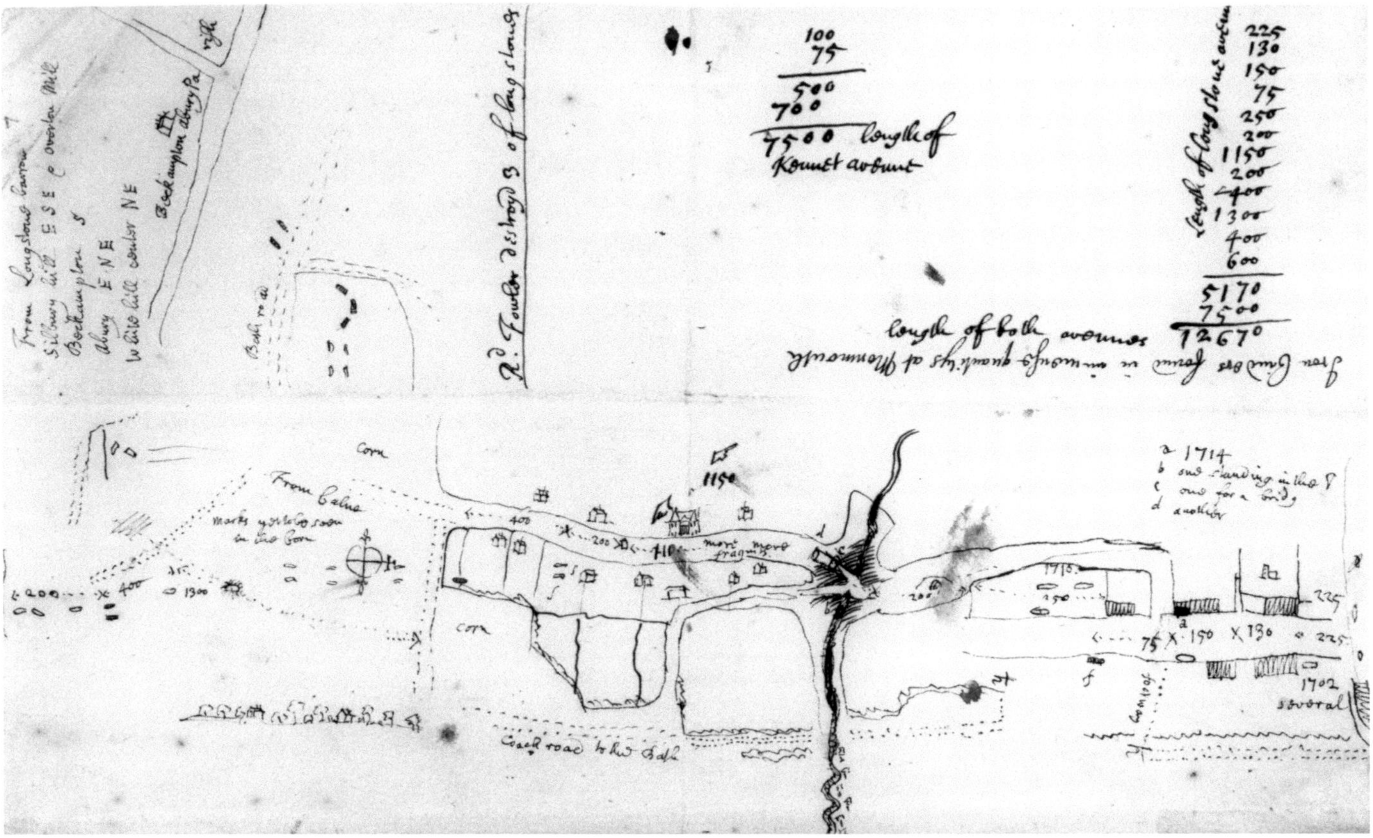

Figure 12.2. An early Stukeley field record of the course of the Beckhampton Avenue. Bodl. MS Gough Maps 231 f7, 267 × 161 mm, pen. Reproduced by permission of the Keeper of Special Collections and Western Manuscripts

and an open rectangle at an equivalent point on the south side of the High Street. The stone beneath Rose Cottage has the note 'a' beneath it, which is given the key '1714'. On the south side of the High Street, in the north western corner of the grounds of the present Harper's Cottage, is a filled rectangle with the single letter 'f' beneath it. Three stones are shown in the grounds of Bridgemead as open rectangles, two on the north side of the avenue and one on the south. Above these stones is the note '1710'. The letters 'b', 'c' and 'd' appear around the Winterbourne bridge and are given the key 'b one standing in the s', 'c one for a bridg' and 'd another'. At the east end of Bray Street the note 'more more fragments' appears. Two stones are shown as open rectangles towards the centre of the cottage gardens, both with the note 's'. A single filled rectangle appears on the south side of the avenue at the westernmost end of the cottage gardens. Three pairs of stones are shown as open rectangles in rather stylised positions. Above them is the note 'Marks yet to be seen in the Corn'. Six stones are shown in unclear locations to the west of South Street long barrow. Five appear to be on the north side of the avenue and one on the south. A number of distances are marked above the stones, presumably in feet. '1300' appears between South Street and the first stone, '400' between that stone and a pair shown as filled rectangles and the '200' covering the remaining three stones.

The top left corner of the sheet contains notes and another sketch map oriented at ninety degrees to the main sketch. The notes read: 'From Longstone barrow Silbury hill ESE and Overton Mill Beckhampton S Abury ENE White hill centre NE'. A separate note beneath the map reads 'R.[d] Fowler destroyd 3 of long stones'. The map appears to show the area around the Longstones Cove. Three roads are shown in outline: South Street; the trackway to the west of Longstones Field and the present A4. South Street is labelled 'Bath road' and a single building is shown south of the A4. The label 'Beckampton Abury Parish' also appears to the south of the A4. Nine stones are shown: L7–L10 as open rectangles; L14, L15 and L16 as filled rectangles and another pair, immediately inside Long Barrow Field as filled rectangles. On the remainder of the sheet are a number of notes and calculations. Upside down and immediately above the main map is the

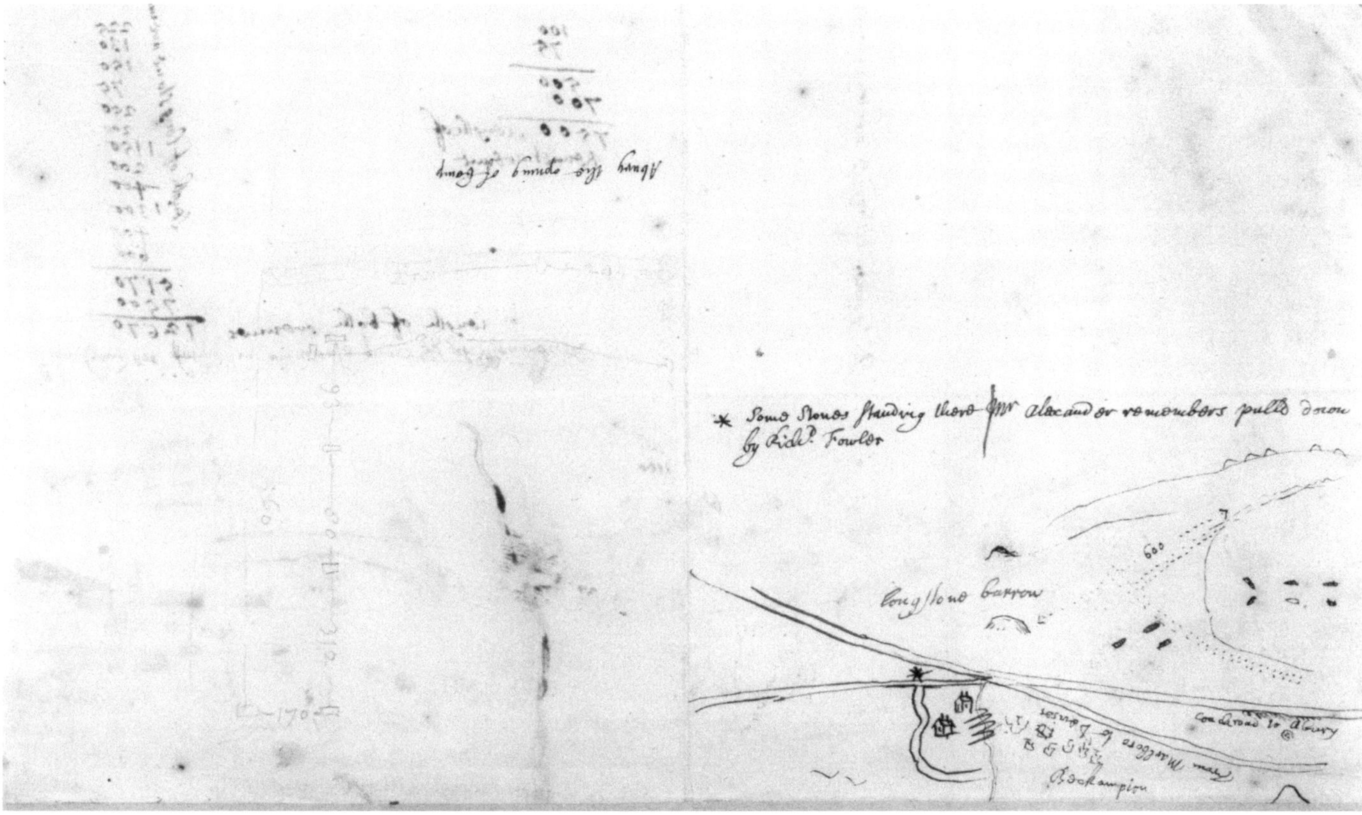

Figure 12.3. An early field sketch by Stukeley of the Longstones end of the Beckhampton Avenue. Bodl. MS Gough Maps 231 f7v, 267 × 161 mm, pen. Reproduced by permission of the Keeper of Special Collections and Western Manuscripts

note 'Iron Grinders found in immense quantitys at Monmouth'. Above this is a series of calculations regarding the length of both avenues. One column of figures is labelled 'Length of Long stone Avenue' and represents a summation of the measurements recorded on the main plan, given as 5170 [feet].[1] To the left of this the length of the West Kennet Avenue has been estimated by multiplying 100 by 75. The results of these two calculations have been added together to give a total, labelled 'length of both Avenues', of 12670 [feet].

Bodl. MS Gough Maps 231 f7v, 267 × 161 mm, pen (Figure 12. 3)

The reverse of the previous sheet includes another small sketch map which is almost certainly a field drawing. The map shows the western end of Longstones Field, Long Barrow Field and Beckhampton crossroads. Road detail is shown relatively schematically with the A4361 labelled 'coach road to Abury' and the eastern part of the A4 'from Marlboro to Devizes'. Two buildings are shown within Beckhampton village and the label 'Beckampton' appears below and to the right of them. A horizon line is shown towards the top of the map, probably indicating Windmill Hill, and providing a partial panoramic effect to the sketch.

Longstones long barrow is shown, and labelled. Silbury Hill and six round barrows are also shown, but without labels. Six avenue stones are shown around Longstones Cove, probably L7–L10, L14 and L15. Three stones are also shown immediately within Long Barrow field, two on the north side of the avenue and one on the south. With the exception of L10, shown as an open rectangle, all the stones are shown as filled rectangles. The distance from Longstones long barrow to the north west corner of Longstones Field is marked as '600' [feet]. To the north of the present A361 and opposite the junction with Beckhampton High Street is an asterisk, which is given the key 'Some stones standing there Mr Alexander remembers pulld down by Rich.[d] Fowler'. A single note separate from the sketch map, towards the top of the sheet, reads 'Abury the opning of Camp'.

Bodl. MS Eng. Misc. b 65 f53, 430 × 213 mm, pen over some pencil outlining (Figure 12.4)

This is a rather sparse sketch plan and is probably either a field drawing or an early

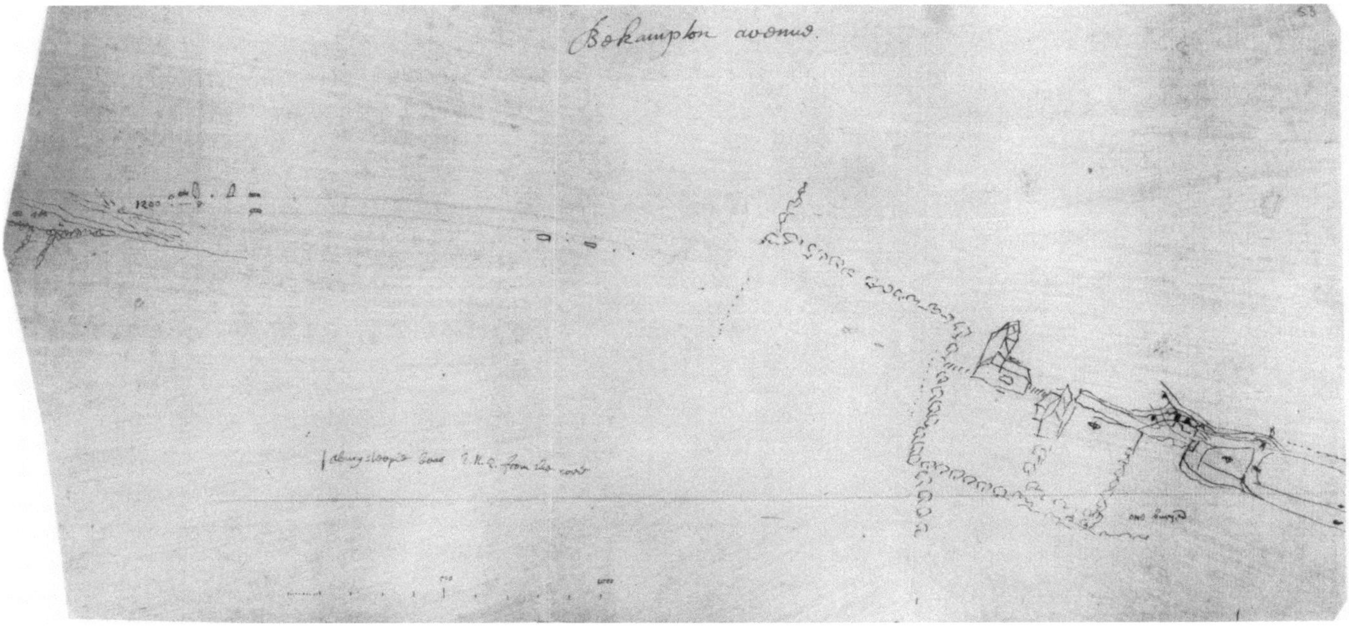

Figure 12.4. An early Stukeley field record of the course of the Beckhampton Avenue. Bodl. MS Eng. Misc. b 65 f53, 430 × 213 mm, pen over some pencil outlining. Reproduced by permission of the Keeper of Special Collections and Western Manuscripts

attempt to organise part of the evidence which would ultimately make up the 'triptych' drawing (Bodl. MS Eng. Misc. b 65 f109). The sheet is titled 'Bekampton Avenue' and has a scale of feet marked on the lower edge. The scaled plan shows the portion of the Beckhampton Avenue from 'Adam' (L14) and 'Eve' (L9) to the Winterbourne bridge in Avebury. There is a non-scaled westward extension showing the distance from L14 to what is presumably Beckhampton crossroads, this distance is marked as '1200' (feet). A note records 'Abury steeple bears E.N.E from the cove'. The plan shows two buildings only, both outbuildings of Manor Farm, Avebury Trusloe. One is clearly the barn which occurs on other plans in association with a pair of stones and the second building is a slightly smaller rectangular barn, slightly south and to the east of this. Hedge line and field boundaries are only shown around two rectangular fields to the south of the farm buildings and along the east and north edge of Trusloe Field, with a broken line indicating part of the west edge of Trusloe Field. Some road detail has been shown at the west edge of Avebury village and two bridges, one over the Winterbourne and the other over the drain on the east side of Butler's Field. In common with his other attempts at a map of this area, Stukeley has struggled with the shape and positioning of the Winterbourne bridge, redrawing it at least twice.

Seventeen stones appear to be shown, with a number of different conventions employed: stones are shown either as outline and upright, outline rectangles or as shaded rectangles. Upright outlines appear to relate to *in situ* stones as only L14 and L9 are shown in this way. Outline rectangles may refer to extant but fallen stones. L15 and L16 are both shown in this way, along with the stone pair associated with the Manor Farm outbuilding, two stones on the south side of the avenue in Trusloe Field and another two on the south side in Longstones Field. The filled rectangles may mark the positions of destroyed stones established by Stukeley from information given by local people. L7 and L8 are both shown in this way along with one stone south of the hollow way leading to Manor Farm from the east, one stone in Butler's Field, one stone on the east bank of the ditch between Butler's Field and the grounds of Bridgemead and a pair of stones around the current end of the High Street, to the west of Harper's Cottage and the Old Forge. There is also a note in the centre of Butler's Field 'one buryed' but it is not clear which stone this refers to.

Bodl. MS Eng. Misc. b 65 f58, 680 × 243 mm, pen and some wash detail (Figure 12.5)

A more detailed sketch plan, showing the avenue and landscape features between Manor Farm and the present Durran Farm in Beckhampton. Some foreshortening of the northern detail and a horizon has been used to give the

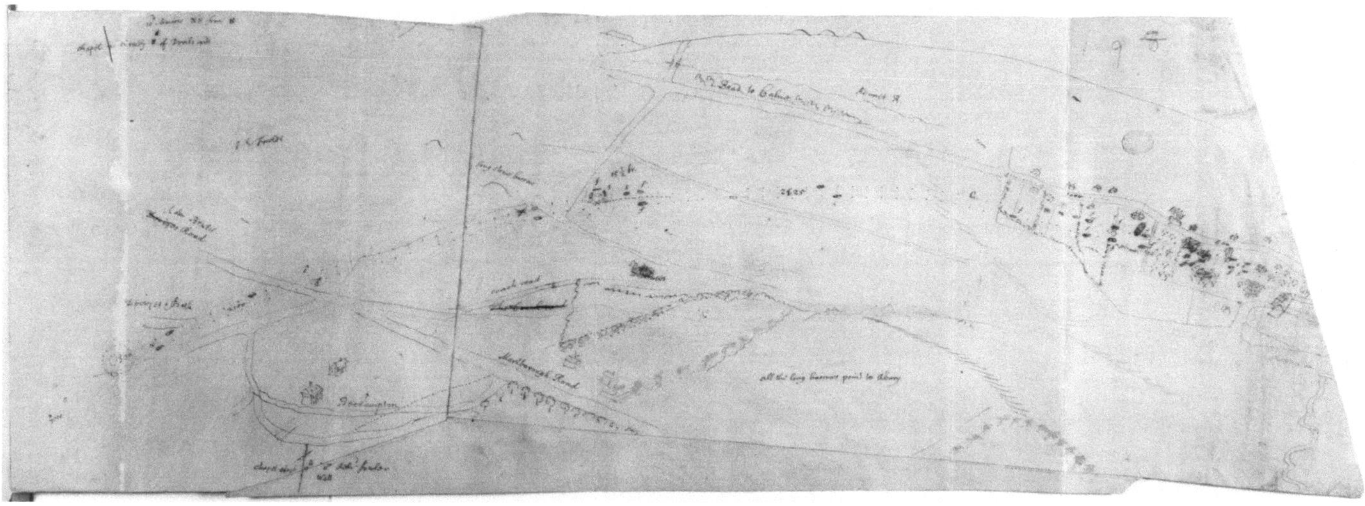

Figure 12.5. A preliminary reconstruction by Stukeley of the course of the Beckhampton Avenue. Bodl. MS Eng. Misc. b 65 f58, 680 × 243 mm, pen and some wash detail. Reproduced by permission of the Keeper of Special Collections and Western Manuscripts

suggestion of a panoramic view. No scale is given but a number of measurements have been added at various points on the avenue. This drawing appears to be an early attempt at a synthesis of various field sketches as part of the construction of Bodl. MS Eng. Misc. b65 f109. The plan shows the Manor Farm outbuildings and a row of what appears to be seven cottages associated with gardens in what is now the northern part of Trusloe Field. Eight buildings are also shown to the north of Trusloe Field, probably the seven cottages and Westbrook Farm which still stand in this location. A single building has been drawn in ink on the north side of the present A4, probably representing the Hare and Hounds inn. The position of this building has been modified in a wash addition and moved further east. Two reasonably substantial buildings are shown in Beckhampton village, north of the main street, neither of which seem to relate to any extant buildings. Hedges are shown in a few cases but field boundaries, road and track detail is generally shown by single lines. Hedges are shown around the cottage gardens in the north of Trusloe Field and surrounding the pasture behind the Hare and Hounds. Longstones and Long Barrow Fields are both shown, although the boundaries of Trusloe Field are less clear. There is some re-drawing and confusion in the road layout, especially south and west of Beckhampton. The 'field ways' through Long Barrow and Longstones fields are both shown. The A4 is labelled 'Calne Bristol ~~Devizes~~ Road' to the west and 'Marlborough Road' to the east of Beckhampton. The A361 is labelled 'Devizes and Bath' and the A4361 as 'coach road'. Bray Street is labelled as 'Road to Calne'. The Winterbourne is shown foreshortened flowing under Horslip Bridge and parallel to and north of Bray street, labelled 'Kennet R.' It re-enters the drawing in the south-east corner beneath Manor Farm. Some more general notes are also visible: 'corn' is written in the south-east corner of Bray field; 'longstones barrow' is labelled; in the top left corner of the sheet is a note which appears to read 'Chapel is directly 10^{d} – [illeg] NE from N of Devil's coits'; south of Beckhampton main street is a cross with 'chapel clost', 'wall' and 'Richd Fowler' written around it; finally, south of Longstones Field is a note 'all the long barrows point to Abury'.

Horslip and Longstones long barrows are both shown but South Street is not, although there is a suggestion of a pencil outline in approximately the right place. Three round barrows on the eastern edge of Windmill Hill are also shown on the skyline and two round barrows around the area of The Grange farm. Stones on the avenue are shown in two different ways, either as filled or open rectangles. In addition, some of the filled rectangles have the lower-case letters 'f' or 's' (presumably indicating fallen and standing stones) next to them. Conjectural stone positions have been marked with dots. The line of the avenue through Trusloe Field is shown as running through the gardens of the cottages lining Bray Street. Sixteen stones are shown in this area, all as filled rectangles, ten of which are marked as fallen. Two stones, one on either side of the avenue, as shown as filled rectangles in the centre of Longstones Field, with a single open

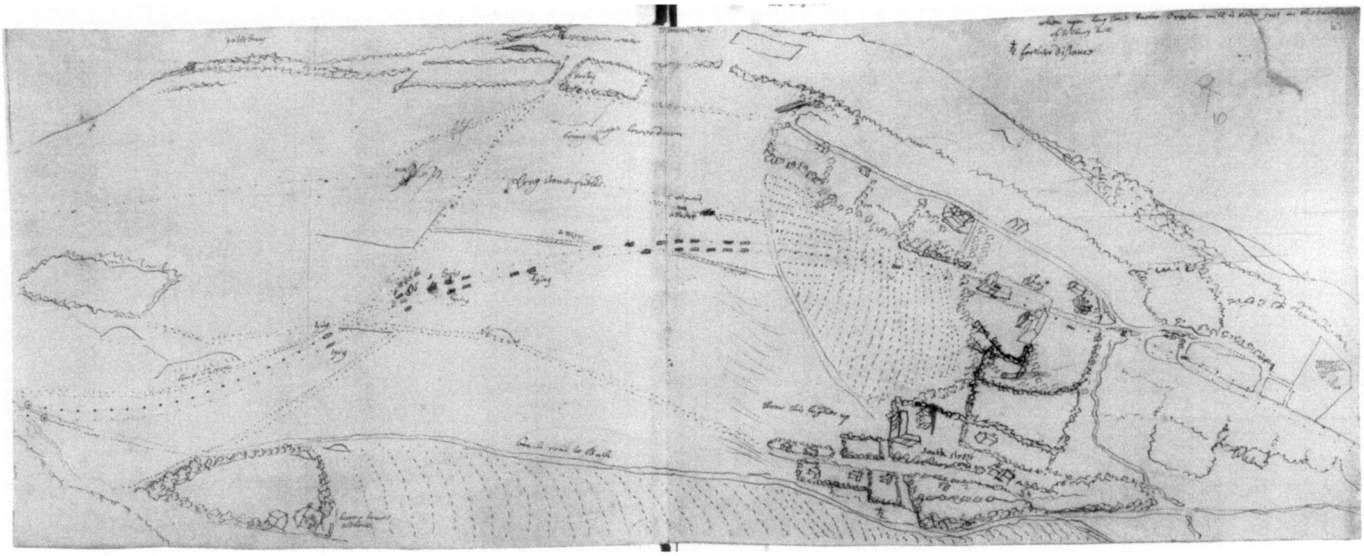

Figure 12.6. A developed reconstruction by Stukeley of the course of the Beckhampton Avenue. Bodl. MS Eng. Misc. b 65 f63, 600 × 238 mm, pen. Reproduced by permission of the Keeper of Special Collections and Western Manuscripts

rectangle on the line of the field way, seven stone positions further along the south side of the avenue. The figure '2125' is written in the centre of the avenue between these two sets of stones. A group of six stones are shown around the Longstones themselves, all except L16 as filled rectangles – although an earlier draft of the cove appears in a slightly displaced position as three open rectangles. Of these stones, L14 and L9 are labelled as standing and L7, L8 and L15 as fallen. '15½ br.' appears to the north of the cove. A pair of stones is shown as open rectangles four positions south of the cove, immediately inside Long Barrow Field, with the northern stone of the next pair shown in this way but subsequently deleted. The line of the avenue continues as conjectural stones to cross the A4 a little way to the west of Beckhampton crossroads. The final pair of stones before the road is marked with the symbol ♂, which is given the key 'R. Fowler'. One stone is shown between the A4 and A361 as a filled rectangle on the north side of the avenue. Two more stones are similarly shown, one on either side of the avenue, south of the A361. The figure '2100' is written in the centre of the avenue between these two stone groups. South of this is a conjectural double stone circle containing the number '300'. On this reconstruction the avenue presumably ended somewhere to the west of Durran Farm.

Bodl. MS Eng. Misc. b 65 f63, 600 × 238 mm, pen (Figure 12.6)
Another more detailed sketch plan showing the avenue and landscape features between the present Beckhampton House and Avebury church. Once again there is some foreshortening towards the top of the sheet and a horizon line to give some sense of a prospect. No scale is shown and no measurements are given as figures. This is very clearly not a field drawing but is a stage in the evolution of the field drawings towards the 'triptych' Bodl. MS Eng. Misc. b 65 f109. Only a selected number of buildings are shown. East of the Winterbourne the only building depicted is the parish church. The two Manor Farm outbuildings are shown in great detail with Manor Farm and Trusloe Manor shown slightly smaller, only three cottages are shown in the gardens in the north part of Trusloe Field and only a single building in outline north of Bray Street. There is a considerable amount of detail of buildings on either side of South Street: four cottages and associated gardens are shown to the south; to the north there is a larger building, which is probably the farm north of Frog Lane, and three cottages. The only other building shown is the Hare and Hounds in Beckhampton. The depiction of field boundaries is variable. In general hedges and plot boundaries are indicated, even in areas like Avebury where none of the associated buildings are shown. More detailed depictions of plot boundaries are given for the cottages in the north part of Trusloe Field and the area around the east end of South Street. Ridge-and-furrow has been shown by dotted lines in Trusloe Field and south of South Street. More field boundaries are shown towards the top of the plan than in earlier versions. The road layout is shown with

more assurance, although a substantial swing to the west has been introduced in the south end of the field way through Long Barrow Field, probably in order to put a smooth curve in this portion of the avenue. Labelling is less profuse than on some earlier drafts: 'Yatesbury' and 'Horslip' are written in the appropriate locations near the top of the sheet. South Street is labelled where it passes through Avebury Trusloe and the A4361 as 'Coach road to Bath'. Within Longstones Field 'a mere' is marked in three separate locations and the field itself is labelled 'Long stone-fields'. Two engraver's instructions are visible in Longstones Field: 'bring [illeg] lower down' in the north west corner and 'throw this higher up' in the south east corner. 'hare and hounds alehouse' is written by that building and 'long barrows' by Longstones long barrow. In the top right corner of the sheet is the note 'when upon long stone barrow Overton mill is seen just on the south side of Silbury hill.', beneath this is the symbol '*ћ*' and the key 'farther distance'. This symbol appears in the plan between the cottages south of South Street and the current A4361.

Three long barrows are shown: South Street; Longstones and Horslip. South Street is shown with eight small upright sarsens surrounding it. Six round barrows are visible: two next to the A4361 behind the Hare and Hounds; one between Longstones long barrow and The Grange; and three on the eastern slopes of Windmill Hill. In this drawing the line of the avenue has been quite substantially altered from previous drafts. It is now shown as continuing on the line of Avebury High Street though Manor Farm yard and then across Trusloe Field and to the south of the cottage gardens. The dense concentration of stones previously recorded in the cottage gardens seems to have been transposed to the section within Longstones Field. Within Long Barrow Field the avenue follows the sweep introduced in the path of the field way to take it to cross the A4 at a point considerably further west than earlier drafts. Additionally there are traces of an alternative line, shown largely as conjectural, which runs across the more northern portion of Longstones Field and into Grange Field. Stones are shown as filled or open rectangles. A single stone is shown on the north side of the avenue as a filled rectangle at the south west corner of the grounds of Bridgemead. A single stone on the south side of the avenue is also shown as a filled rectangle, to the south of the trackway leading to Manor Farm. A pair of stones are shown as filled rectangles beneath the northernmost of the two Manor Farm outbuildings. There is only a single stone shown in Trusloe Field, a filled rectangle on the south side of the avenue. The two separate courses become visible within Longstones Field. A single stone is shown as a filled rectangle on this northern course, probably on the southern side of the avenue, with the note 'removed' above it. There is a group of 13 stones in the eastern part of the field on the southern course which are very similar in arrangement to those shown in the Trusloe Field cottage gardens on earlier drafts. Working from east to west these are: two stone pairs; a single stone on the south side; two stone pairs; a single stone on the north side; another single stone on the south side; a single stone on the north side; one conjectured stone position and another single stone on the north side. Of these stones four are shown as open rectangles, the remainder as filled rectangles. Three stone positions to the west of this group are two filled rectangles on the south side of the avenue, the easternmost of which has the note 'lying' to the right of it. Of the excavated stones, L5, L6 , L7 and L8 are shown as filled rectangles, with the note 'lying' above L7 and below L8. L9 is shown as a smudged attempt at drawing the upright stone, with the letter 's' above it. L14 is drawn as a standing stone with another 's' to the right, L15 and L11 are shown as filled rectangles (with the letter 'f' above L15), while L16 and an additional stone within the cove are shown as open rectangles. Above the cove is the note '15½ f. br.' Four stone positions to the south west of the cove, in the upper part of Long Barrow Field, a pair of stones are shown as open rectangles. The note 'lying' appears above and below the pair. The conjectural stone positions at the point where the avenue crosses the A4 have been circled, presumably to indicate that Stukeley believed these stones to be the ones he recorded elsewhere as removed by Richard Fowler, but there is no note of this on the drawing. Stukeley appears to have begun to place the cove on the conjectured upper line of the avenue in the northern part of Grange Field, but this has then been deleted.

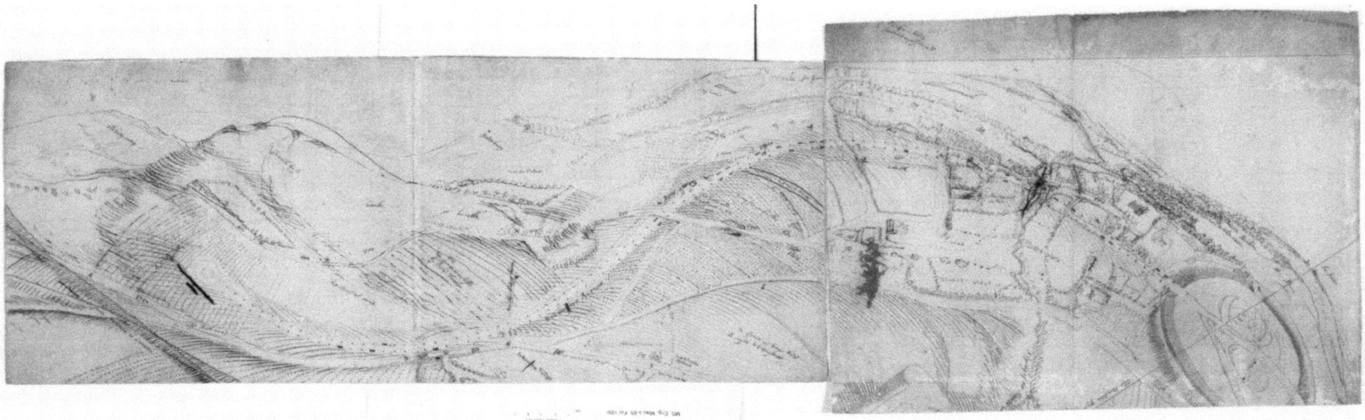

Figure 12.7. Stukeley's reconstructed prospect of the Beckhampton Avenue. Bodl. MS Eng. Misc. b 65 f109, 1021 × (max) 300 mm, pen and wash. Reproduced by permission of the Keeper of Special Collections and Western Manuscripts

Bodl. MS Eng. Misc. b 65 f109, 1021 × (max) 300 mm, pen and wash (Figure 12.7)

This drawing formed part of the 'triptych', with Bodl. MS Eng. Misc. b 65 f44, which covered the whole complex as Stukeley saw it. The drawing pulls together all of the details noted in the field drawings and earlier drafts described above and covers the landscape and monuments between Avebury itself and the point where the Roman road crosses the present A361. Perspective effects and several horizon lines have been used to make this drawing more of a panoramic view and less of a plan, although an outline (and unlabelled) scale has been added in the top left corner. A few more buildings have been shown than in earlier drafts but many are either missing or shown only in outline. No buildings at all are shown within the henge itself. Within Avebury village the church, great barn and Avebury Manor are shown, along with buildings in the block between Church Walk and the High Street and a building on the site of the present Old Forge. No buildings are shown on the south side of the High Street. Buildings shown in Avebury Trusloe include Trusloe Manor, Manor Farm and its two outbuildings. Two of the buildings north of Bray Street are shown and three of the cottages in the northern part of Trusloe Field. South of Frog Lane and South Street five cottages are shown, while north of the road there are three further cottages and one larger farm with outbuildings. Apart from distant views of Monkton, Broad Hinton and Yatesbury churches, the only other buildings shown are the Hare and Hounds and a single building north of the main street in Beckhampton. The depiction of field boundaries is relatively detailed. In general hedges and plot boundaries are indicated, the main exception being within the henge itself. Ridge-and-furrow has been shown by dotted lines or wash lines on most of the fields in the foreground of the panorama. There is much more detail approaching the horizon lines than was the case in earlier drafts. The road layout is shown relatively clearly and the distortion of the path of the field way through Long Barrow Field has been partly corrected. The smooth curves of the avenue have been preserved by a more subtle distortion of the overall perspective. Labelling is profuse and the labels can be divided into a number of categories. The following place-names are present: 'Oldbury camp'; 'Cherill hill'; 'Yatesbury'; 'hare and hounds Alehouse'; 'Bekampton Village'; 'Horslip gap'; 'Long Stone fields'; 'Windmill hill'; 'Monkton' and 'Br. Hinton'. Many of the roads are labelled: the A361 as 'The Bath road'; the A4 as 'The Bristol road'; the A4361 as 'Coach road'; Frog Lane as 'South street'; and a continuation of Bray Street as 'road to Calne'. Some land-use information is given: 'heath' in several locations and 'A mere' indicating a pond near Horslip. A line through the north circle cove in the henge is labelled 'The Meridian pass[truncated]'.

Four long barrows are shown: Millbarrow; South Street; Longstones and Horslip. South Street is shown without the standing sarsens visible on Bodl. MS Eng. Misc. b 65 f63. Up to 29 round barrows are visible: the increased numbers from earlier drafts being accounted for by the groups around Fox Covert, south of the A361 and towards Winterbourne Monkton. The avenue follows Avebury High Street at its eastern end and then takes the same broad line as in Bodl. MS Eng. Misc. b 65 f63, although fewer stones are depicted and the conjectural upper line is omitted. The western end is placed as a conjectural double circle just east of Harepit Lane. Stones are shown either as filled rectangles or as perspective drawings of standing stones (L9 and L14 only). Annotations and measurements appear along the course of the avenue. Beginning at the western entrance of Avebury henge, there are two stones shown on the north side of the avenue. There is then an interval of four conjectural stone pairs, together with a note to the engraver 'shorten this interval by one'. A pair of stones is shown on either side of the High Street, at the corner of Church Walk, followed by another stone on the south side of the avenue. The next conjectural pair has the date '1710' written above it. Two stones are shown on the northern side of the avenue, one at the south east corner of the present grounds of Bridgemead and one, two stone positions further on, immediately to the east of the Winterbourne. Repeated re-drawing of the Winterbourne bridge has confused the issue in this area but there appear to be no further stones shown on the east bank. The letters 'a' and 'b' appear, to the north and east respectively of the bridge, and a key at the top of the drawing gives: 'a. laid for a bridg' and 'b. standing upright in ∇'. West of the bridge a single stone is shown on the north side, followed by a pair straddling the trackway to Manor Farm. In the pasture to the south is the note 'shorten one or two'. Three stone positions further west is the pair of stones beneath the Manor Farm outbuilding. The figure '700' also appears in the centre of the avenue. A single stone is shown on the south side of the avenue in Trusloe Field. On the east side of Longstones Field there is a group of seven stones. The join of two sheets occurs here and it is possible that some detail, including a possible stone pair has been lost in a repair. A pair of stones is followed by two on the north side of the avenue, one on the south and another on the north. There is then a gap of one stone position and then another stone on the north side. The figure '1900' appears in the avenue at this point and the letter 'A'. The letter 'A' also appears to the north of the line of the avenue. A key towards the bottom of the drawing reads: '12 stones are buryd there [illeg] to [?] Longstones'. L5, L6, L7, and L8 are shown as filled rectangles, with L9 and L14 drawn as standing stones. L15 is shown as a filled rectangle and the note 'The Cove calld Long Stones or the Devils coyts'. There is a gap of three stone positions before the next pair, which are shown as immediately to the south of the northern boundary of Long Barrow Field. No other stones are shown in this field, although the last conjectural pair has been circled and the note 'two stones demolishd by Rich[d] Fowler' added. The next pair of stones shown straddles the present A361 immediately to the west of the junction with Beckhampton High Street. This pair is shown by Stukeley as lying off the line of the avenue, the northern stone of the pair aligned with the south side of the avenue. Five stone positions further west a single stone is shown on the north side of the avenue and the southern stone of the next pair is also shown. Three stone positions on from this is the last stone shown on the avenue, a single stone on the south side. Next to the conjectural double circle at the end of the avenue a two-line note has been heavily erased. The words 'The Temple...' can be made out at the beginning of this note.

Bodl. MS Gough Maps 231 f217, 271 × 175 mm, wash with some pen detail (Figure 12.8)

While this drawing looks like a landscape prospect it is so stylised and so much contemporary detail is missing that it seems likely that it was not drawn in the field. It shows the view west from the Longstones cove towards Fox Covert. The drawing is titled 'A View of the valley at the end of Bekhamton Avenue from the Cove 26 May 1724'. The only other labelling is the letter 'A' which appears above Fox Covert and is given the key 'where was the end of Bekamton Avenue'. No 18th-century features are shown apart from an indication of the trackway on the west edge of Longstones Field and a small enclosed copse around the present location of The Grange.

Fifteen round barrows are shown in the general vicinity of the Fox Covert group with another two shown on a spur of Hemp Knoll and a single barrow behind the present site of The Grange. The only long barrow shown is Longstones. The course of the avenue is marked as a pair of wash lines and seven stones are shown in total, all recumbent apart from L9 and L14. L9 is in the immediate foreground and appears to have been added after the rest of the prospect had been drawn. The distance between L9 and the cove appears to have been foreshortened to an unrealistic degree. L14 and L15 are shown in the cove, two attempts have

Figure 12.8. Stukeley's prospect of the Longstones Cove, looking south-west towards the Longstones long barrow. Bodl. MS Gough Maps 231 f217, 271 × 175 mm, wash with some pen detail. Reproduced by permission of the Keeper of Special Collections and Western Manuscripts

been made at representing L15, one partly overlying the other. A pair of recumbent stones are shown in a position roughly corresponding to those plotted immediately within Long Barrow Field on other drawings (see above) and a further pair have been added at some distance beyond Longstones long barrow and presumably intended to represent those which Stukeley noted elsewhere as having been destroyed by Richard Fowler.

Summary of Stukeley's observations on the Beckhampton Avenue

Stukeley's data on stone positions and former stone positions is not consistent between the various field and interpretive drawings (Figure 12.9). Taking only those stones which are consistently reported by Stukeley in the same positions we can identify some 18th-century evidence to add to the results of more recent excavations. The four stones which Stukeley saw himself seem to have been one on the corner of the present Harper's cottage and three stones around the Longstones Cove (L9 'Eve', L14 'Adam' and L15). The positions of stones he had reported to him as recently destroyed include some which lie within the excavated portion of the avenue (L3, L7, L8, L11 and L16). They also include a stone on the south side of the High Street, immediately to the west of the henge entrance, a pair on stones straddling the High Street level with the Old Forge, a single stone east of Manor Farm, another pair beneath the former barn at Manor Farm, and a single stone in the centre of Trusloe Field. All of these stones would fall on the line both of the avenue as reconstructed by Stukeley and the stones excavated as part of this project, in Longstones Field and by Wessex Archaeology (Wessex Archaeology 1998) immediately to the west of Avebury.

Beyond the Longstones Cove Stukeley's observations are more problematic. The pair of reported stones at the border of Longstones and Long Barrow Fields are the only pair consistently shown in the same position. The stones reported as destroyed by Richard Fowler further south have been given a wide variety of positions. In part this is due to Stukeley's redrafting of his evidence as his ideas about the location of the end of the avenue changed. The Vatcher's discovery of a buried stone to the west of Beckhampton roundabout indicates that some sarsen burial took place in

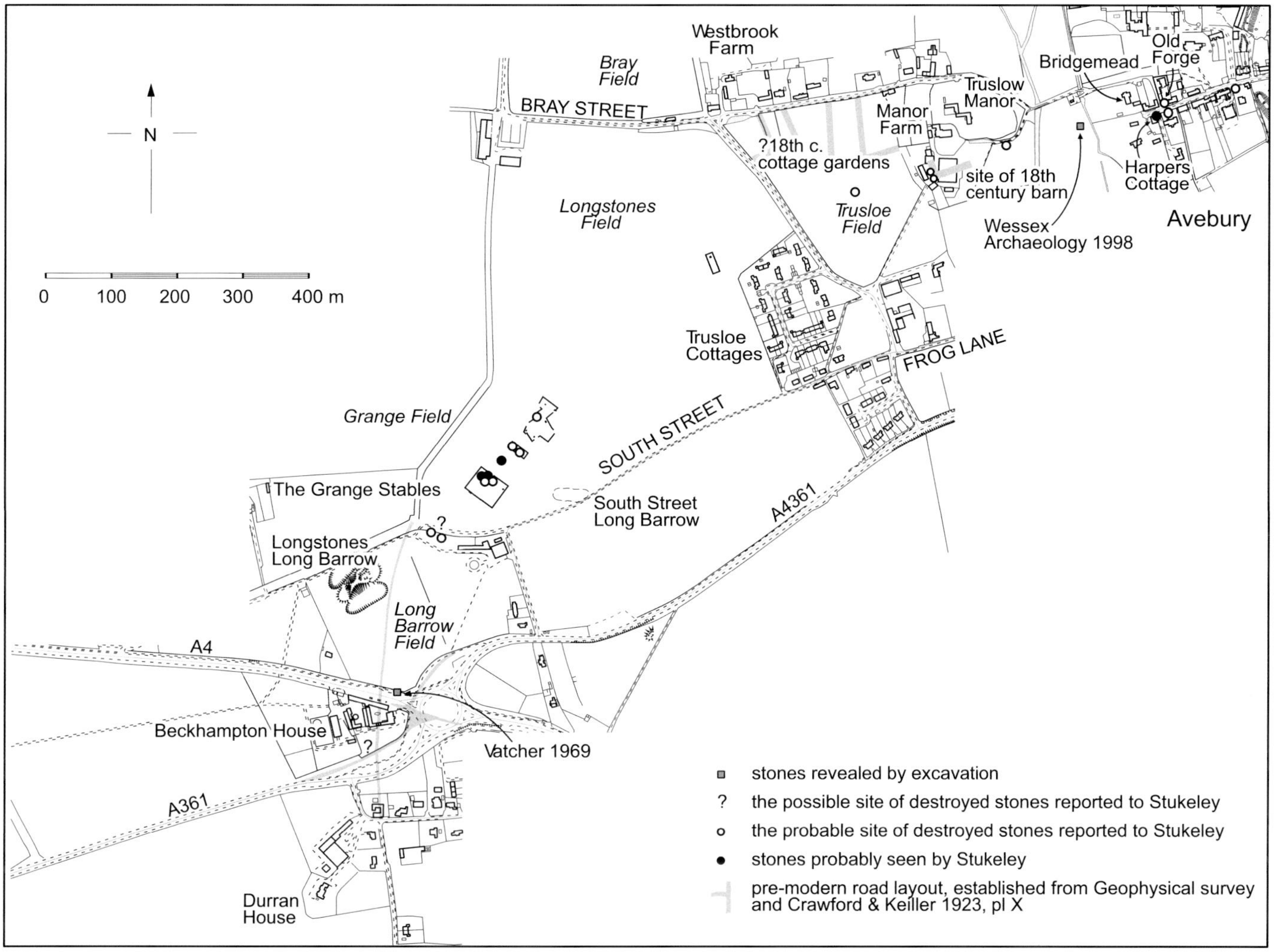

Figure 12.9. Summary of Stukeley's observations on the Beckhampton Avenue

this area (Vatcher 1969), but it is unlikely that any of the stones reported to Stukeley beyond the cove ever formed part of the Beckhampton Avenue.

Note

1 It should be noted that Stukeley's figures do not add up as presented, the total should be 5090.

Appendix 1: Stukeley manuscripts relating to the Beckhampton Avenue held in the Bodleian Library. A summary list and transcription of notes

Figures from Stukeley 1743 are referred to using the published Table numbers. Engraver's proofs for these Tables are listed only if they carry subsequent amendments. Drafts of Table I in Stukeley 1743 are referred to using the letter system of Ucko *et al.* 1991. Breaks or illegible material are indicated by the use of square brackets. Material which has been lined through in the original has been underlined in the transcript.

MS Gough Maps 229 f5 v: small fragmentary view of Silbury from the south with Avebury directly behind and the restored Avenues shown as single lines. The end of the Beckhampton Avenue is missing. Wash.

MS Gough Maps 229 f26 v: view of Avebury from the south, a very free pen and wash drawing which shows the circle and West Kennet Avenue as stones but the two sides of the Beckhampton Avenue as curved lines. Presumably postdates the drawing on the front of the sheet 'done July 1723'.

MS Gough Maps 229 f105 v: fragment of draft T of Table I showing part of the western entrance. Added to a sheet of paper to enable Stukeley to finish a field drawing of Stonehenge dated Aug 1722, dating draft T to before this date.

MS Gough Maps 229 f115 v: draft of a drawing of the end of the Beckhampton Avenue showing the two stones removed by Richard Fowler, draft version of what became Table XXIV.

MS Gough Maps 229 f207: version of Table XXIV dated 1724.

MS Gough Maps 229 f208: version of Table XXIV dated 1724.

MS Gough Maps 229 f213: proof of Table XXIII 'A Prospect from Abury Steeple' amended in ink.

MS Gough Maps 231 f2: page of notes

'when the sun was half darkened which was at 6 a clock there was a plain circular rain bow which lasted but seemd to grow gradually more in diam.'

'total at 35' after 6'

'lasted 3 ½'

'many urns found in the barrows E. of avon. they are frequently found in the sides of the barrows.'

'It seems very likely that W. Kennet village was the residence of the high priest here & tis the finest place in the world for contemplation tis surrounded on all hands with hills especially to the North & East most open westw[d]. the head of the Kennet & all the other springs conct thro it on the southside from the w. & such waters as flow eastw[d]. meeting the rising sun are reckoned most wholesome the widest prospect is westw[d] & that not far. but this will tempt one to walk out upon the hill tops & then we have what view we please. methinks theres something in the air which the great men have breathd before us that contrivd a work of such excessive granduer. upon the tops of every hill before us we view the Vast barrows of all sorts & bulks the monum[ts]. of our predecessors & that prompts us to make of the little of life to consign our memory at least to a longer date than these large monuments. this manner of burial is highly to be admird & one would think they exceeded us in the hope of an after life that took such care of their remains as if the immatial part should again come to reclaim & to distinguish its dissolved ashes. & the dignity of human nature is well regarded in it that should be distinguished from the parts of matter which have not been animated with a rational principle. I find the eclipse was but very short at Abury & Marlburgh & we were not far from its northern limits at Haradon hill. Hara is an old Irish appelative I suppose & perhaps the name of the pson [illeg] in that barrow. it seems not unlikely that the king concernd in founding Stonehenge is buryd in that calld the Kings barrow or Aurelius his barrow. tis a very large one & old & on the highest hill & perhaps from some traditional respect [illeg] has distinguished that for the [illeg] intment of Ambrosius who in greatest probability was buryd in the Cathedral of old Sarum. the end of the bekamton Avenue lys before a vast valley divided into many branches whence the company parting might severally take such course as toe their respective dwellings over the finest downy turf that can be. here are but 4 archdruids tumuli about Abury *i.e.* long ones & the paucity seems to prove the thing. there is but two at Stoneheng beside the little one I opend we find some of them dispersd about in several other parts of the kingdom generally very large & often not near any temple being buryd in the country where they livd. I remember not above half a dozen that I have seen one towards Shaftsbury, near chichester near the Soar Nottingh. Iulabers, Kits coty house, its likely there have been temples near.'

MS Gough Maps 231 f3 page of notes

'bearings from the barrow in the corner of Fowlers past. 26 May 1724. Longston long barrow 278 the barrow above it by the past. 279. the barrow on Cheril hill 280. Yatesbury 308. cove of bek 310½ horslip l barr 335. Windmill hill 345 [illeg illeg] 34. Abury Steeple 41. Windmill oh 79 overton mil 115, Silbury 117 The great divided barrow 220. the road end in the valley by ☿ [mercury, presumably the end of the Beckhampton ave] 244. oldbury 274 At Longston cove I set the sights of the instrum. To the entrance of the Avenue into abury which is just on the right hand of Abury steeple the opposite point looked most directly down the valley of the *manes*. The n. point of the mean(?) line being 58½. The stone of the cove standing is most precisely set e & w but with the common variation to the right. The line of the bekampton Avenue runs directly in the line from NE to SW at Abury but with the common variation of 6[d]. The former I suppose found at Kennet but the cove was more [illeg] somewhat than that line. So that the work [illeg illeg] line is a S[illeg] of all the places I saw from the valley of ☿ just by the bank that runs from the corner of the road to the ro.[man] road. Below the corn [?cove] and downs looks the most like evening or sunset for quite round you see just the tips of the barrows as that upon Cheril hill the gr[eat] one by the pasture above ☿ Longston long barrow, Abury steeple & Silbury as it were sinking beneath the mountain tops dropping into the nocturnal horizon a poet might certainly form a fine description from it. The variation is truly but 6[d] Not 7[d]. 26 May 1724 The true n. point goes over Gr[eat?] [illeg illeg] at Silbury It is but 7[d] more than y[r] 6 S. from E. turning the compass the opposite way I find the line where the Bekampton Avenue terminates runs from Silbury to the most western barrow of the western group So that the two [illeg] are defined by 7[d] more southwards than Abury base line that is the line passing through Silbury Hill upon the e & w. 6[d] difference from the (?)true Bekampton Avenue therefore infallibly terminates at the end of the road. Where I drew the circular [illeg]. Abury work is doubly formed from the eastern [illeg]. This day I find as my best solution that ☿ was at that very place I paced along the ro. road from Silbury [illeg] is full 6000 f & I think more somewhat if not 7000. Long Stones l barrow head points to the N.E. precisely 6[d] variance as usual not the cove but by accident. Silbury certainly has a parapet about it as soon as you mount the high ground going across from South Street to the w entrance from horslip you see the purpose and direction of the Avenue. Long Stones cove pointing directly to the utmost end of the valley below. the hills to the right & the left which open themselves very finely like wings Cheril Hill and the great ridge whereupon stands Oldbury to the right, Fowler's Hill & St Ann's to the left, these goe strait forwards

& by their successive differences diminish to the eye in [illeg] and sight to the utmost extremity with an awful yet of lovely appearance especially in the evening L. Stone L. barrow head much damaged with digging chalk out of it & perhaps stones. is Weedon from Guy *i.e.* the [illeg] hill? as soon as I saw longstone cove I found it the interval of 50 stones from Abury I conjectured there must have been another such at Kennet Avenue & measuring very nicely I found at the 50th stone an on line vacancy that its upon an [illeg] & at that very place the road crosses the Avenue whence theres no room to doubt from symmetry [illeg] but that there was a cove too. The stump of the stone on this side is left by the [illeg] of the cove. The architects [illeg] that tho' they took the admirable method of diversifying by [illeg] these vast porticos & going sometimes up sometimes down sometimes of a declivity on one side then on another yet being of such along the way well thought it fit to give it this fine break in the middle by a cove.'

MS Gough Maps 231 f5: 'An Abury Atto de fe 20 May 1724' wash.

MS Gough Maps 231 f7: a sketch map in pen and ink of the Avebury end of the Beckhampton Avenue giving measurements to stone positions and dates of removal, including crop mark evidence from west of the Winterbourne. More details on f7 v.

MS Gough Maps 231 f9: notes, including: 'Mr Holford at the anchor tavern chancery lane, one great stone lay in the middle of the road before the inn for many years which they broke at last another behind the meeting house which was burnt.'
'Landlord at the White hart [*ie John Fowler*] says the head lay northward in the barrow they dug up. Mr Smith a lawyer in W. Kennet lives in monument yard and desires to take away the stones of S long barrow to make a bridge, over the Kennet. Esq[r] Landsdown is his uncle. of the lawer.'

MS Gough Maps 231 f12: 'View of the progress of the bekampton Avenue 29 May 1724' pencil and wash which shows stone positions to the east of the cove.

MS Gough Maps 231 f22: draft Q Table I

MS Gough Maps 231 f23: draft O, Table I.

MS Gough Maps 231 f24: draft P, Table I.

MS Gough Maps 231 f25 v: notes probably made after 24th May 1724, including: 'tis remarkable that all this holy country has no snakes tho' all the country round abounds with them nay at Lockeridge many & yet they never reach up the Kennet to Overton [illeg illeg] at Marlborough Savernake Forest. At Byknoll beyond Gr. hinton a ro. camp. Mr Boak plow[d] up overton Hill tho' land is Mr Saunders late Mr Tuckers. Ruben Horsal has known this country 40 or 50 year & neither he nor the oldest man alive has ever heard of a snake being seen [illeg]. what I admire that they don't come up the valley through Overton when they are so plentiful at Lockeridge.'
and;
'The barbarous massacre of a stone here with leavers & hammers sledges & fire is as terrible a sight as a Spanish Atto de fè. The vast cave they dig around it the hollow under the stone like a glasshouse furnace or bakers oven the huge chasms made through the body of the stone, the straw, the faggots the smoak the prongs and the squallor of the fellows looks like a knot of devils grilling the soul of a sinner'

MS Gough Maps 231 f32: proof of 'A prospect from Abury Steeple' amended in ink.

MS Gough Maps 231 f33: various wash sketches including an elevation of 'Adam' and the arms of 'Cha. Tucker Esq[r] a lover of Abury Antiquitys.'

MS Gough Maps 231 f34: draft U, Table I.

MS Gough Maps 231 f34 v: pen sketch map showing Sarah Nalder's house and the vicarage. This names the path by the vicarage as 'Caiters lane', see also MS Gough Maps 231 f47 v.

MS Gough Maps 231 f36 v: notes including: 'In order to observe the better the <u>temple of mercury and the mound(t) at the bottom</u> termination of the Bekampton Avenue, there are upon the low part of the downs half a mile W. of Bekampton 9 barrows very ancient of different modes all in a row from SW to NE & one by the side upon the top of that highest and most to the NE you see overton Hill just on the S side of Silbury. in the valley a little nearer Bekampton more towards the left among the corn between the Bath road <u>where</u> before it crosses the roman road & the Bristol road going up Cheril Hill was the said <u>temple or</u> termination of the Avenue a little south of a square enclosure up on the Bristol road. these 10 barrows seem set oblique on purpose to be seen from this temple. from this temple a fine valley runs in a strait line with Silbury and overton hill forwards to the summits S of oldbury which I walked up this after noon [illeg] you see the whole country to the Bath & the Welsh hills beyond the Severn & so along by the sort of cliff by broad hinton on the right hand quite to the hakpen going to barbary ca. the great number of barrows here regards this temple. tho' the country N of Abury seems not high yet it is really very high as is plain by the vast descent that way by highway and Broad hinton into the north part of Wiltshire. The prospect from these hills is so immense that the [illeg illeg] is lost in a mist the eye cannot reach it. This shows the tract of ground here abouts the highest in all England.'

MS Gough Maps 231 f 42: pen and wash 'Longston cove prospect as lately 21 May 1724'.[1]

MS Gough Maps 231 f42 v: rough pen sketch of the Longstones as they were in 1724, showing only L9 and L14.

MS Gough Maps 231 f46: pen and wash 'A circular view of the termination of bekampton Avenue May 26 1724'

MS Gough Maps 231 f46 v: pen and wash 'A circular view from the spot of the temple at the end of Bekampton Avenue May 26 1724' This version shows the 'temple' as two rough circles and indicates that Stukely was still occasionally considering the end of the Beckhampton Avenue as a circular temple at this date.

MS Gough Maps 231 f47 v: notes (later than 1723) including:

'What Mr Twining calls Titus Style is Caitors lane and style, by the parsonage at Abury & is a path from the church into the fields but relates no more to Silbury hill from which it is a mile distant than Turn-Style.'

'Holford bears a dog p.s. a. at bolonè a fefs g.

Tucker v. on a band engraild a. 3 hearts g.'

MS Gough Maps 231 f56: rough pencil and wash outline of avenues and henge as a serpent.

MS Gough Maps 231 f57 v-f58: draft R, Table I.

MS Gough Maps 231 f217: pen and wash 'A view of the valley at the end of Bekhampton Avenue from the Cove 26 May 1724.' This shows stone L15 as fallen to the north of the cove but still *in situ* and appears to be a field drawing, contradicting MS Gough Maps 231 f 42. L9 has been added later and appears too close to L14.

MS Gough Maps 231 f220: proof of Table XXV 'A view near the spot of the Temple at the end of Termination of Bekampton Avenue July 19 1723' amended in ink.

MS Gough Maps 231 f223: pen and wash 'Prospect of the remains of long stone Avenue 14 July 1723 as I took it, from the top of an haycock.'

MS Gough Maps 231 f 241: pen and wash portrait of Thomas Robinson surrounded by a palimpsest, along the lower edge is a sketch plan in ink of Avebury High Street from the present Red Lion to the car park. Above the portrait in dark ink 'Gripple diminutive of Grip α γλυφος ή. l p r. and to the right of it in a similar ink the lable 'Tho. Robinson Asbury 1722 26 July' beneath the portrait, also in a dark ink, 'Ierostratus'. Added subsequently in a paler ink after the name 'Stone-Killer' and beneath the date 'got his wife (an old woman above 50) with child'

MS Gough Maps 231 f 241v: draft ink drawing of a circular view from a point on the Beckhampton Avenue somewhere SW of Beckhampton, probably one of the suggested terminii. Outline only.

MS Gough Maps 231 f243v: notes:

'Capt. Madoc informs me of a fine mosaic pavemn^{t}. found at Caerwent which the owner knocked in pieces for fear it should be chargabl to him with people coming to see it. & of 2 statues of fine ro. work coloss pportion found at Chepstow wch the people destroyed. Raddon belw Marlboro Abury seems dominated from the road in antient British times belw. thos 2 places over the downs for there was no road from overton hill till the romans made it. the druids barrow overlooking W. Kennet is certainly part cut away for the ro. road. tis curious to behold how well turned the [?]curvings are considering it must be done by guess for tis impossible to find a radius of length enough to strike such arks & over such unequal ground & the founders seem to have purposely obscurd the design of their scheme by the intersection of the two hills so that at Silbury you can see only both extremities of the Avenues [?]& the town of Abury nor can you see any of the Avenues for its whole length & the turnings & drift of it is only to be found out by judgement & observation & taking the bearings to lay it down in plans. first describe the Avenues plainly then illustrate their curvity & natural figure &ct the places of the two stones are discernable upon the green bank below the two streams of monkton brook by the bridge & so thro' Mr Griffins y[d].'

MS Gough Maps 231 f244v split into two sheets by a contemporary fold, upper sheet: pen outline panorama showing Longstones Cove with L16, L15 and L14 labelled a, b and c respectively, title 'From Silbury Hill July 26 1722' and notes 'the Cove south side one of the Long Stones was fell down a corpse bones was found under it when the Landlord of the Hare & Hounds took it away (burning it) it containd 15 load a. the stone b. fallen c. standing R[d]. Fowler.' The bone should have been beneath L16 on this account, and may go with the Roman ironwork recovered from there in 2000. Lower sheet: portrait of Stukeley sleeping by Gerald van Gutch with title 'Aliquando bonus dormitat Homerus.', notes in Stukeley's hand 'From Abury Church Silbury hill S. Overton hill SE by S. Long Stones SW by W'

MS Gough Maps 231 f245v: pen and wash drawing of Avebury without houses or stones and with only West Kennet and Beckhampton entrances in bank. View from Millbarrow presumably intended to be its ancient state. Title 'Town of Abury', notes beneath 'from the meridian line in monkton fields. where a surprizing regularity in nature appears & well regarded by the founders. Abury is enclosed on all sides with hills but towards the north. which seems to indicate in their philosophy the immense voyd beyond the works of nature.'

MS Gough Maps 231 f248v: notes 'bearings from kennet Avenue cove May 29 1724 whitehill spot 20 gr. single barr. on hakpen 59 64 barrow I opend 86 90 ½ 130. overton mill 130½. E. kennet barr. 138½. the line connecting Silbury & Kennet aven. cove is 16[d] N. of W. being 253 life is nothing but fluids moving by heat in an organised body heat op[?er]ates by communicating its own motion & the canals direct it as the banks of a river. furzes l. barrow is in the line from 4 barrows to the single barro w. of S. long barrow the ro. road from overton hill towards Marlborow is 82 towards Silbury 270. at Overton hill Silbury is 11. variant from true e. & w. point bein 281 the base line therefore is 275. & that passes a little S. of oldbury ca. furzes l. barr. [illeg] is 252. Kennet aven. cove 312. I found a very fine flint impressed [illeg] an oyster shell Ruben Horsal has one with a fishes head & two fins and found a very fine flint [?]ochinus which he gave to parson [?]Thorold. a round barrow flaggd with stones belw. the 2 pastures under whitehill & the 5 barrows towards abury the ro. road by ☿ runs 263. the line connecting beckampton cove & Silbury is 122. the Titan princes lived in thrace & Macedonia the grecians used the calendar of the eastern greeks of Asia minor & troy & carryd it into Italy. renewed by [illeg]. by the Julian calendar we may find adding the days difference in the year Cesar altered it we may [illeg] the time when the 7th of april fell on our day. the line connecting bekampton cove & entrance into Abury goes up to the strange causeway on hakpen n. of the London road. tis so contrived that at Silbury bekampton Cove and Kennet cove goe off at an angle of 120 d. or 3[d]. of a circle. bekampton Avenue tminus no doubt must be brought down so far into the valley that the westn group may appear & it may be pointed out by the central place of the appearance of thos barrows or the ridg on which they stand. twas very great skill in geometry that could lay down the ground so nicely where every great part is entirely hid from the other or but obscurely visible & to be found out by trigonometry & such accurate instrum[ts]. as we use nowadays & the turning the more these half of Abury circles towards the east pbally for convenience of the [illeg] of the two temples has created some small irregularity as it seems me in the bekamton Avenue for that goes out somewhat from the diagonal line therefore outs Abury more upon the full west but really upon consideration tis done with most incomparable dexterity & phaps more out of desire than necessity to avoyd too much formality as was the manner of the antients. & in a circular work more liberty of this sort may be taken & so far from creating any offence to a [illeg] eye that it entertains it with more satisfaction & delight as in the managem^{t}. of the obliquity of the entrance into S^{t}. Pauls, the eye sees much more of the sidelines than if it had been direct. & can give a better guess at the remaining parts than otherwise by the natural perspective every one is master of. that have knowledg of architecture or made any observation of things in this work tis matter of great surprize that they could accommodate it so well to the country. at Kennet aven. cove you see before you the barrows under whitehill theres a most delightful concavity under that hill where the 2 great pastures are. theatrical opening to the west. in plowing up this spring a field enclosed by the w. entrance out of Abury they took up a large stone found [illeg]. Several little reliques of seemingly old works of stone before the druids house.

MS Gough Maps 231 f259: two pen and wash prospects, upper 'A Group of Barrows on the side of the valley above Beckampton', lower 'A Group of barrows upon Overton hill'.

MS Gough Maps 231 f266: pen and wash drawing of Beckhampton Cove from the east showing a depression in the position Stukeley usually gives for L11 and the note 'the stone opposite to Long Stone Cove was broke by Farmer Griffin about 7 year agoe'.

MS Gough Maps 231 f279v: map of churchyard of St James' in ink, draft only, notes 'Hospes ad ociidnas quicumq advenevis oras Wiltoniae fig videre cupis prima novus genetrix salutantes limina Alria sublini prospicit alina fede suppostam mirare moleui'

MS Gough Maps 231 f283: pen and wash drawing of view towards Silbury from Avebury church 'Prospect from Abury Steeple.'

MS Gough Maps 231 f314: large sheet used twice in landscape orientation. Lower part (probably earliest) pencil and wash drawing (uncompleted) of original form of the circles with many Britons chariot racing &ct, note 'the two Avenues are a quadrant exactly different in the circumference'. Upper part (probably latest) pen drawing of 'prospect of Kennet Avenue from the Druid's tumulus'

MS Gough Maps 231 f325: pen and wash drawing 'a general view of Abury and adjac^{t}. Country July 26 1722.'

MS Gough Maps 231 f326: pen and wash drawing 'A prospect of Abury from the north point.'

MS Eng. Misc. b. 65 f13: pen and wash drawing, large fold out panorama centred on Silbury, 'A General Prospect of Abury. July 26 1722.'

MS Eng. Misc. b. 65 f13v: drafts in ink of drawings linking the form of the Avenues to the shape of Silbury.

MS Eng. Misc. b. 65 f18: large pen and wash draft S, Table I.

MS Eng. Misc. b. 65 f18v: a draft in ink of the drawing linking the Avenues and Silbury by form, notes 'this is the true scheme of the formation of the work at Abury [illeg] is learnt how Silbury is the model of the mausoleum of the temple Silbury pportion both including and is included by it which is such a curiosity in geometry as is not easily paralleld. the reason why they formed not Silbury of that neat form pportion [illeg] earth sufficient stability & even after so many ages some great flaws in it are slid down not long agoe. we see natures self seldom gives a less to hills tho made of solid chalk and nothing other than rocks will stand more precipicious.'

MS Eng. Misc. b. 65 f23: pen and wash draft V of Table I.

MS Eng. Misc. b. 65 f31: pen and wash drawing 'Iconography of the temple at Abury in its perfection.'

MS Eng. Misc. b. 65 f31v: fragment of pen and wash draft of Table I.

MS Eng. Misc. b. 65 f33: pen and wash draft N of Table I, showing three fallen stones in the village on the Beckhampton Avenue.

MS Eng. Misc. b. 65 f44v: lots of notes, now all scored through 'to take in all the beautys of abury we must widen our imagination & think with the antients & behold the most stately strife betw. art & nature

Major rerum mihi nascitur ordo

the Avenues are well contrivd for tho they run in a valley yet never along the lowest ground but with a declivity from them to the bottom that the rain may never lodge. the grand meridian opens northw^{d}. very advantageously a fine moderate rise directly in front upon which is the great archdruids sepulchre on each hand a high hill windmill hill & the corner of hakpen calld whitehill that easternmost is highest to keep off the keen winds which are indeed sharp at this place the air [illeg] very fine but the delicate Zephyrs have more free introduction by that end of the horse-[illeg] or oldbury hill being much farther removd indeed the architects here have at first well contrived their scituation and plotted as it were with nature that tis hard to say whether they have suited their building most to the place or the [?]flias contrived to cooperate with them. for tis just as one have laid out a site for a magnificent palace where the [illeg] house is bounded but at a reasonable distance but when the season invites to take a tour abroad for health & pleasure, surmounting any of the hills presents us with an unbounded prospect which if we had at home that pleasure & temptation to exercise is lost.

some countrys have health, wealth & pleasure allotted in parcels & nigardly proportions but this enjoys them all in boundless pfusion the richest grass stards in the medows in extravagant length [illeg words] over the downs give the sweetest [illeg words] to the sheep very fat in the dryest [illeg] the pastures appropriate for the [illeg] animal & the delight of the Britons the horse the fields are strong with marly sulphur for corn & the grateful variety of ground for [illeg] or travelling or park is beyond compare.

upon Windmill hill the horizon opens very precisely beyond Abury northwards Cheril hill & Hakpen make the two equidistant wings I observe the barrows upon Hakpin hill & others here are set in the [illeg] not upon the very highest part of the hills but upon so much of the declivity or edge as that they make app. as above to thos below the valley in the Avenue. this valley along which goes Kennet Avenue is a lovely one declining on both sides equally & makes the approach of the Avenue along it extraordinary magnificant. a barrow on the meadow edg above on the left hand near the hedg the top coverd with stones set in a ring the southern edg of it is plowd away from the long barrow at E. Kennet is a charming prospect to the R. Kennet, overton hill & so the whole length of Kennet Avenue well nigh to abury along which I suppose after lustration in the river & cutting down branches about the meadows here they went in the procession. the field road in Kennet Avenue turns thro' the Avenue just on the very spot where the cove stood. both, the Avenues are contrived to run in valleys so that they are theatrical their whole length the pomp going along em showing to best advantage upon sides of the hills, the valley too of Bekampton Avenue seems to wind its self on purpose to humor the Avenue. so there is a regular valley between Abury & Silbury. from that stone in the [illeg single letter] side of the entrance of Kennet Avenue into Bekampton by the ditch side they have been pilfering ever since I knew the place every year some great parcels being knockd off yet much remains. last year a wooden wedg was drove into the stone at the w. entrance & still left, this stone of a most surprizing quantity fell down of its self one side of the chalk being wore away that supported it by the road for its set on a tip end. the fall broke it into two & left a great chasm the strolling for relaxed minds upon these downs is the most agreable exercise & amusement in the world especially when you are every minute struck with some new piece of wonder in antiquity. the neat turn of the huge barrows wraps you up into a contemplation of the [illeg] of life & passage from one state to another & you meditate with your self of the sake & for [illeg] of the barrows psonages who has took care of their ashes that have rested so many ages..[incomplete]

MS Eng. Misc. b. 65 f53: pen map of Beckhampton Avenue in the village and out to the cove, title 'Bekampton Avenue.'

MS Eng. Misc. b. 65 f58: pen measured sketch map of Beckhampton Avenue in Avebury and out to a terminal placed in Beckhampton.

MS Eng. Misc. b. 65 f63: pen, measured map/ prospect of Beckhampton Avenue in Avebury and out to a terminal placed at Fox Covert.

MS Eng. Misc. b.65 f68: pen and wash drawing 'A View from the spot of the Temple at the end of Bekampton Avenue July 19 1723.', note 'Et regum cineres extructo monte quiescunt.'

MS Eng. Misc. b. 65 f83: pen and wash plan

'The entrance of the Avenues into the Temple at ABURY.'

MS Eng. Misc. b. 65 f93: pen and wash map of Avebury and environs 'The Scenography of the Country about Abury.'

MS Eng. Misc. b. 65 f98: pen and wash drawing 'Prospect of Abury from the North'

MS Eng. Misc. b. 65 f103: pen and wash drawing 'A Prospect of the north side of Abury 12 July 1723.'

MS Eng. Misc. b. 65 f109: pen and wash drawing, the Beckhampton arm of the triptych, with the Avenue ending slightly short of Fox Covert as a temple.

MS Eng. Misc. b.65 f109v: several sheets joined to make the triptych, one sheet has pen version of the Silbury/Avebury Avenues relationship drawing (see also MS Eng. Misc. b. 65 f13v and f18v). Middle sheet has on its lower half a pen and wash drawing of 'the western group of barrows at the end of Bekampton Avenue 21 May 1724' and above this half a page of notes 'the reason why urns & bodys are found together is [illeg] they had phaps kept the ashes to be buryed along with them, dying before as was the case of the 2^{d}. I opend at Stonehenge double where the womans ashes pbably being a beloved wife was kept till her husband dyd. 6000 f. from Silbury to end of Bekamton Avenue. the eastern end of the under group is of a particular family the 4 barrows are made & set together with great exactness and conformity. & show some relation in that age no doubt well understood. the very barrows whether single or in groups appear to have a regular design [illeg] & the very ground and prospect was not neglected for these their eternal habitations. I have lamented that so many of them have been pfanely opend & their bones dispsd by vulgar hands without any use or doctrine gatherd therefrom & their sacred remains freqtly dispersd about the plowd lands like common manure & with the same intent. several I opend I was disappointed in when designd only to retrieve their customs & restore them to their pristin glory carefully recomposing the venerable remains.'

'31 May 1724 we dug out of the barrows of the S. group found a bit of an urn red without & black within as if not burnt quite thro. much black wood ashes and flint seeming to have been burnt. bits of the urn black. a larg bit of the neck of the urn black without red within. the crutches[?] as they calld em which they found (Tho. Griffin) are crocks or earthen ware. large bits of coal we found. no sign of bones when we had dug down to the surface so that doubtless there were consumed. tis a flat old barrow the ☿ is in a line with the most westn barrow & Silbury from the most eastn you see Overton hill & the place of ☿ at the corner of the last arable on the right.'

Note

1 'As lately' in this instance refers to a period a least seven years earlier than the date on the drawing, before the removal of the cove stones around L14.

Appendix 2: The social and economic relationships between individuals named by Stukeley within early 18th-century Avebury

The information collated below was derived from Tithe and Inclosure documents (WRO 184/4) held in the Wiltshire and Swindon Record Office, Trowbridge.

Baily

Richard Baily attested on 19th May 1764

Fowler

William Fowler attested on 22nd February 1756
John Fowler attested on 11th March 1756

Griffin

Tenancy between **John Griffin**, yeoman son of **Peter Griffin** and Sir **Richard Holford** dated 9th October 1703

John Griffin attested on 30th April 1709

Peter Griffin appointed **Richard Holford**'s Gamekeeper on 12th November 1736

'Oct 25 1741
Then received of Farmer **Griffin** the sumr of Seventy four Pounds & ten shills in part of rent.
By [illeg]
Rich. Holford'

'We **Peter Griffin** & **Mary** his Wife do hearby Certify that the late **Richard Holdford** Esqr deceased, his wife, her mother Mrs Metcalfe & her sister Miss Sarah Metcalfe were at Avebury Eight weeks in the year 1741, and that they were told by the three maids that were with them whilst at Avebury, & by Edward the Man Servant, that Mrs Metcalfe, mother to Mrs Holford, paid them their wages, & that they lookd upon themselves as Servants to the said Mrs Metcalfe, & that during both the aforementioned times whilst the aforesaid Persons were at Avebury, **Richard Holford** Esqr bore the whole expense of Housekeeping in maintaining them all, as appears by the bills that were delivered by us to the said **Richard Holford** & allowed in part of Rent, as witness our hands at Avebury this sixteenth day of November 1742.
Peter Griffin
X The Mark of **Mary Griffin**
Witness M Cardonnel
Richard Baily'

'Received the 16th Novem: 1742 of **Peter Griffin** One Hundred, & Twenty four Pounds in part of arrears of Rent due to my late Brother **Richard Holford** Esqr for the Estate at Avebury – **Staynor Holford**
Witness
M Cardonnel'

Holford

I ye sd John White do agree & promise that I will put forth & dispose of ye 14l above mentioned that Sr **Richard Holford** gave to my younger children to the best benefit & advantage of my sd children when I have an opportunity and will pay the sums accordingly, witnesse my hand John White 2nd October 1701 (also witnessed by **Will** and **Emanuel Skeate**)

'Janr 1713/4
Then measured and divided Silborough Meadow in the Tything of Beckhampton and Parish of Abury
Between Sr **Richard Holford** Kt: Mr **Richard Green**: & **Wm Smith** into equal parts as followeth...
...John Overbury
Devizes'

Susanna Holford attested on 18th October 1718 and 22nd June 1719 – paying bills by writing to her banker Mr Nichols

Staynor Holford attested on 19th May 1764

Nalder

John Nalder attested on 19th May 1764

Phelps

John Phelps attested on 30th April 1709
William Phelps attested on 30th April 1709

Pope

'**Farmer Pope**' attested on 30th April 1709

Smith

'Memorandum
2d October 1701
That by mediation of Mr **William Smith** of Calston & others I Sr **Richard Holford** Kt have been prevailed on to accept and receive of Mr John White Vicar of Avebury for my Costs in the suite against him ye sume of forty pounds, and for that he seemes to be sorry for what is past & that he was ill advised & promiseth for the future to live more neighbourly & peaceably, & on his part to avoid all kind of misunderstandings I have as a demonstration of my friendship submitted to give, & do now give to his seven younger children forty shillings a piece, and to Miss Mary White his eldest daughter fifty three shillings & three pence which do make up fifteen Guyneas & halfe a Guynea being 16-13-3 and I do desire & direct the sd Mr John White do permit his eldest daughter to enjoy & dispose of her 2-13-3 to her own use as she shall think fit, & that he do put forth ye other 14l for the benefit of his younger children.
Witnesse my hand **Richard Holford**

Tooker

'Whereas I **Charles Tooker** of East Kennett in the County of Wilts Esqr. have sold and Conveyed to Sr **Richard Holford** of Lincolns Inns in the County of Middx knight the Parsonage Impropriate and Free Chappell of Backhampton in the said County of Wilts and Two farms there comonly called Goddards and Truslows Farmes and all the Lands Meadowes pastures and appurtencances thereto belonging and also four Tenements there And all the Estate right title and [illeg] I had therein or thereto which said impropriation and Farmers are now in Lease for four years by me made to Richard Carswell Yeoman whereof upwards of two years is yett to come at the Rent of Two hundred and [illgc] pounds per anm. payable half yearly But I not now having with me the Counterparte of the said lease nor any of the Counterparts of the Leases of the said four Tenements or Cottages I the said **Charles Tooker** doe hearby Undertake promise and agree to and with the said Sr **Richard Holford** his heirs Executors and Administrators that I will within one month next produce and Cause to be Delivered to the said Sr **Richard Holford** the Counterparte of the said Lease Undefaced and Unaltered And that I will when desired by the said Sr **Richard Holford** or his Assignes procure the severall owners of the said Tenenements or Cottages to Attone and to become Tenants to the said Sr **Richard Holford** his Heirs or Assignes Witness my hand this eighteenth day of December Anno Dm one Thousand Seven hundred and ten
Char Tooker'

Appendix 3: Concordance between the Avebury stone numbering schemes adopted by Keiller (unpublished excavation records) and Smith (1965)

Avebury stone numbering schemes

In bringing Keiller's excavations to publication, Smith found it necessary to renumber all of the stone settings excavated and recorded during Keiller's fieldwork seasons. Whilst the numbering scheme adopted by Keiller worked perfectly in terms of labelling features that were excavated and recorded, it was not flexible enough to facilitate the overall reconstructions and interpretations carried out by Smith (1965: 175). To give an example, Keiller's numbering of the West Kennet Avenue settings began at 1 with the southernmost setting he investigated. Settings were then numbered sequentially from this point up until the southern entrance of the henge (stone 66). Smith's scheme was to number not individual stones but discrete pairs (using 'A' and 'B' to indicate whether the stone lay on the east or west side of the avenue) starting at the southern entrance of the henge and increasing as one moved south, enabling settings beyond those investigated by Keiller to be accommodated into the sequence.

In the case of Avebury's outer circle, Keiller numbered anti-clockwise from the northern entrance while Smith numbered clockwise from the southern. The southern Inner Circle stones were numbered from 100 by Smith once again running clockwise from the southern-most setting. The 'Z' prefaced numbering scheme used by Keiller for the settings around the Obelisk were replaced by Roman numerals.

To minimise potential confusion, and aid future researchers in relating the archival records to published accounts of the site based upon the scheme adopted by Smith, the following conversion tables are offered.

West Kennet Avenue					
Keiller	Smith	Keiller	Smith	Keiller	Smith
1	37B	31	22B	61	7B
2	37A	32	22A	62	7A
3	36B	33	21B	63	6B
4	36A	34	21A	64	6A
5	35B	35	20B	65	5B
6	35A	36	20A	66	5A
7	34B	37	19B		
8	34A	38	19A		
9	33B	39	18B		
10	33A	40	18A		
11	32B	41	17B		
12	32A	42	17A		
13	31B	43	16B		
14	31A	44	16A		
15	30B	45	15B		
16	30A	46	15A		
17	29B	47	14B		
18	29A	48	14A		
19	28B	49	13B		
20	28A	50	13A		
21	27B	51	12B		
22	27A	52	12A		
23	26B	53	11B		
24	26A	54	11A		
25	25B	55	10B		
26	25A	56	10A		
27	24B	57	9B		
28	24A	58	9A		
29	23B	59	8B		
30	23A	60	8A		

Avebury Outer Circle			
Keiller	Smith	Keiller	Smith
1	46	31	16
2	45	32	15
3	44	33	14
4	43	34	13
5	42	35	12
6	41	36	11
7	40	37	10
8	39	38	9
9	38	39	8
10	37	40	7
11	36	41	6
12	35	42	5
13	34	43	4
14	33	44	3
15	32		
16	31	A	A
17	30	B	B
18		C	C
19			
20			
21			
22	24		
23			
24	23		
25	22		
26	21		
27	20		
28	19		
29	18		
30	17		

Southern Inner Circle	
Keiller	Smith
1	109
2	108
3	107
4	106
5	105
6	104
7	103
8	102
9	101

Inner settings of Southern Circle	
Keiller	Smith
Zx	i
Z1	ii
Z2	iii
Z3	iv
Z4	v
Z5	vi
Z6	vii
Z7	viii
Z8	ix
Z9	x
Z10	xi

Bibliography

Adkins, R. and Jackson, R. 1976. *Neolithic Axes from the River Thames.* London: British Museum

Albarella, U. and Serjeantson, D. 2002. A passion for pork: meat consumption at the British late Neolithic site of Durrington Walls. In P. Miracle and N. Milner (eds.), *Consuming Passions and Patterns of Consumption*, 33–49. Cambridge: McDonald Institute

Alexander, J. H. 1961. The excavation of the Chestnuts Megalithic Tomb at Addington, Kent. *Archaeologia Cantiana* 76, 221–34

Allen, M. J. 1997. Environment and land-use; the economic development of the communities who built Stonehenge: an economy to support the stones. In B. Cunliffe and C. Renfrew (eds.), *Science and Stonehenge (Proceedings of the British Academy 92)*, 115–44. Oxford: Oxford University Press

Allen, M. J. 1998. Landscape and landuse reconstruction: looking forward or looking back. In A. Woodward and J. Gardiner (eds.), *Wessex Before Words: some new research directions for prehistoric Wessex*, 15–17. Salisbury: Wessex Archaeology

Allen, M. J. 2000a. High resolution mapping of Neolithic and Bronze Age chalkland landscape and land-use: the combination of multiple palaeo-environmental analyses and topographic modelling. In A. Fairbairn (ed.), *Plants in Neolithic Britain and Beyond*, 9–26. Oxford: Oxbow Books

Allen, M. J. 2000b. Soils, pollen and lots of snails. In M. Green, *A Landscape Revealed: 10,000 years on a chalkland farm*, 36–49. Stroud: Tempus

Allen, M. J. 2001. Research agenda, palaeo-environmental. In A. Chadburn and M. Pomeroy-Kellinger (eds.), *Archaeological Research Agenda for the Avebury World Heritage Site*, 34–8, 54–7. Salisbury: English Heritage and Avebury Archaeological and Historical Research Group

Allen, M. J. 2005. Considering prehistoric environmental changes on the Marlborough Downs. In G. Brown, D. Field and D. McOmish (eds.), *The Avebury Landscape: aspects of the field archaeology of the Marlborough Downs.* 77–86. Oxford: Oxbow Books

Allen, J. R. L. and Fulford, M.G. 1996. The distribution of South-East Dorset Black Burnished category 1 pottery in South-West Britain. *Britannia* 27, 223–83

Andrews, P. 2006. A middle to late Bronze Age settlement at Dunch Hill, Tidworth. *Wiltshire Archaeological and Natural History Magazine* 99, 51–78

Andrews, P., Mepham, L. and Seager Smith, R. 2000. Excavations in Wilton, 1995–6: St John's Hospital and South Street. *Wiltshire Archaeological and Natural History Magazine* 93, 181–204

Armour-Chelu, M. and Andrews, P. 1994. Some effects of bioturbation by earthworms (Oligochaeta) on archaeological sites. *Journal of Archaeological Science* 21, 433–43

Ashbee, P. 1993a. The Medway Megaliths in perspective. *Archaeologia Cantiana* 111, 57–111

Ashbee, P. 1993b. William Stukeley, the Kit's Coty House and his coves. *Archaeologia Cantiana* 112, 17–24

Ashbee, P. 2001. William Stukeley's Kentish studies of Roman and other remains. *Archaeologia Cantiana* 121, 61–102

Ashbee, P., Smith, I. F. and Evans, J. G. 1979. Excavation of three long barrows near Avebury, Wiltshire. *Proceedings of the Prehistoric Society* 45, 207–300

Ashmore, P. 2000. Dating the Neolithic in Orkney. In A. Ritchie (ed.), *Neolithic Orkney in its European Context*, 299–308. Cambridge: McDonald Institute

Astill, G. 1988. *The Countryside of Medieval England.* London: Blackwell

Atkinson, D. R. 1965. Clay tobacco pipes and pipemakers of Marlborough. *Wiltshire Archaeological and Natural History Magazine* 60, 85–95

Atkinson, D. R. 1980. More Wiltshire clay tobacco pipes. *Wiltshire Archaeological and Natural History Magazine* 72, 67–74

Atkinson, R. J. C. 1957. Worms and weathering. *Antiquity* 31, 219–33

Atkinson, R. J. C. 1965. Wayland's Smithy. *Antiquity* 39, 126–33

Atkinson, R. J. C., Piggott, C. M. and Sandars, N. K. 1951.

Excavations at Dorchester, Oxon. Oxford: Ashmolean Museum

Aubrey, J. 1847. *Aubrey's Natural History of Wiltshire.* Trowbridge: Wiltshire Topographical Society

Barber, M. 2004. Mount Pleasant from the air: cropmarks old and new at the henge enclosure near Dorchester, Dorset. *Proceedings of the Dorset Natural History and Archaeological Society* 126, 7–14

Barber, M., Field, D. and Topping, P. 1999. *The Neolithic Flint Mines of England.* London: English Heritage

Barclay, A., Gray, M. and Lambrick, G. 1995. *Excavations at the Devil's Quoits, Stanton Harcourt, 1972–3 and 1988.* Oxford: Oxford University Committee for Archaeology

Barclay, A., Lambrick, G., Moore, J. and Robinson, M. 2003. *Lines in the Landscape: cursus monuments in the Upper Thames Valley.* Oxford: Oxford Archaeology

Barclay, G. J. 1999. Cairnpapple Revisited: 1948–1998, *Proceedings of the Prehistoric Society* 65, 17–46

Barclay, G. J. 2005. The 'henge' and hengiform' in Scotland. In V. Cummings and A. Pannett (eds.), *Set in Stone: new approaches to Neolithic monuments in Scotland*, 81–94. Oxford: Oxbow Books

Barker, C. T. 1985. The long mounds of the Avebury region. *Wiltshire Archaeological and Natural History Magazine* 79, 7–38

Barrett, J. 1994. *Fragments from Antiquity: an archaeology of social life in Britain, 2900–1200BC.* Oxford: Blackwell

Barrett, J. 1999. The mythical landscapes of the British Iron Age. In W. Ashmore and A. B. Knapp (eds.), *Archaeologies of Landscape*, 253–65. Oxford: Blackwell

Barrett, J. C., Bradley, R. and Green, M. 1991. *Landscape, Monuments and Society.* Cambridge: Cambridge University Press

Bayliss, A., McAvoy, F. and Whittle, A. W. R. 2007. The world recreated the date of Silbury Hill. *Antiquity* 81, 26–53

Bayliss, A., Whittle, A. and Wysocki, M. 2007. Talk about my generation: the data of the West Kennet long barrow. *Cambridge Archaeological Journal* 17 (51), 85–101.

Bell, M., Fowler, P. J. and Hillson, S. W. (eds.) 1996. *The Experimental Earthwork Project 1960–1992.* York: Council for British Archaeology

Bender, B. 1998. *Stonehenge: making space.* Oxford: Berg

Bewley, R., Cole, M., David, A., Featherstone, R., Payne, A. and Small, F. 1996. New features within the henge at Avebury, Wiltshire: aerial and geophysical evidence. *Antiquity* 70, 639–46

Birbeck, V. 2000. *Archaeological Investigations on the A34 Newbury Bypass, Berkshire/Hampshire, 1991–7.* Salisbury: Wessex Archaeology

Birks, H. J. B., Deacon, J. and Peglar, S. 1975. Pollen maps for the British Isles 5000 years ago. *Proceedings of the Royal Society of London* 189, 87–105

Bloch, M. 1995. People into places: Zafimaniry concepts of clarity. In E. Hirsch and M. O'Hanlon (eds.), *The Anthropology of Landscape: perspectives on place and space*, 63–77. Oxford: Oxford University Press

Boast, R. 1997. A small company of actors: a critique of style. *Journal of Material Culture* 2, 173–98

Boessneck, J. 1969. Osteological differences between sheep (Ovis aries Linné) and goats (Capra hircus Linné). In D. R. Brothwell and E. Higgs (eds.), *Science in Archaeology*, 331–58. London: Thames and Hudson

Boivin, N. 2004. From veneration to exploitation: human engagement with the mineral world. In N. Boivin and M. A. Owoc (eds.), *Soils, Stones and Symbols: cultural perceptions of the mineral world*, 1–29. London: UCL Press

Booth, P. 1996. 'Pottery and other ceramic finds' in Mould, C. M, Excavations at Oxford Road, Bicester. *Oxoniensia* 61, 75–89

Bowden, M. 2005. The middle Iron Age on the Marlborough Downs. In G. Brown, D. Field and D. McOmish (eds.), *The Avebury Landscape: aspects of the field archaeology of the Marlborough Downs*, 156–63. Oxford: Oxbow Books

Bowen, H. C. and Fowler, P. J. 1962. The archaeology of Fyfield and Overton Downs, Wilts (interim report). *Wiltshire Archaeological and Natural History Magazine* 58, 98–115

Bowen, H. C. and Smith, I. F. 1977. Sarsen stones in Wessex: the Society's first investigation in the evolution of the landscape project, *Antiquaries Journal* 57, 185–96

Bradley, R. 1975. Maumbury Rings, Dorchester: the excavations of 1908–13. *Archaeologia* 105, 1–97

Bradley, R. 1984. *The Social Foundations of Prehistoric Britain: themes and variations in the archaeology of power.* London: Longman

Bradley, R. 1993. *Altering the Earth: the origins of monuments in Britain and continental Europe.* Edinburgh: Society of Antiquaries of Scotland

Bradley, R. 1998. *The Significance of Monuments: on the shaping of human experience in Neolithic and Bronze Age Europe.* London: Routledge

Bradley, R. 2000. *An Archaeology of Natural Places.* London: Routledge

Bradley, R. 2002. *The Past in Prehistoric Societies.* London: Routledge

Bradley, R. and Chambers, R. 1988. A new study of the cursus complex at Dorchester on Thames. *Oxford Journal of Archaeology* 7, 271–89

Brannand, M. and Taylor, M. 2003. The survey and excavation of a Bronze Age timber circle at Holme-next-the-Sea, Norfolk, 1998–9. *Proceedings of the Prehistoric Society* 69, 1–84

Brentnall, H. C. 1946. Sarsens. *Wiltshire Archaeological and Natural History Magazine* 51, 419–39

Bridges, E. M. 1978. *World Soils.* Cambridge: Cambridge University Press

Britnell, W. 1982. The excavation of two round barrows at Trelystan, Powys. *Proceedings of the Prehistoric Society* 48, 133–201

Brown, A. G. 2000. Floodplain vegetational history: clearings as potential ritual spaces? In A. S. Fairbairn (ed.), *Plants in Neolithic Britain and Beyond*, 49–62. Oxford: Oxbow Books

Brown, T. 1997. Clearances and clearings: deforestation in Mesolithic/Neolithic Britain. *Oxford Journal of Archaeology* 16, 133–46

Browne, H. 1833. *An Illustration of Stonehenge and Abury.* Privately printed

Bullock, P., Federoff, N., Jongerius, A., Stoops, G. and Tursina, T. 1985. *Handbook for Soil Thin Section Description.* Wolverhampton: Waine Research Publishers

Burl, A. 1979. *Prehistoric Avebury.* New Haven and London: Yale University Press

Burl, A. 1988. Coves: structural enigmas of the Neolithic, *Wiltshire Archaeological and Natural History Magazine* 82, 1–18

Burl, A. 1993. *From Carnac to Callanish: the prehistoric stone rows and avenues of Britain, Ireland and Brittany.* New Haven and London: Yale University Press

Burl, A. 2000b. *The Stone Circles of Britain, Ireland and Brittany.* Yale: Yale University Press

Burl, A. 2002. *Prehistoric Avebury.* Second edition. Yale: Yale University Press

Burl, A. 2004. A.D. Passmore and the stone circles of north Wiltshire. *Wiltshire Archaeological and Natural History Magazine* 97, 197–210

Burtonwood, G. 1995. Denner Hill Stone: Unpublished report for Buckinghamshire County Museum Archaeological Service

Byron, R. (ed.) 1935. *A Shell Guide to Wiltshire: a series of views.* London: Architectural Press

Canti, M. G. 2003. Earthworm activity and archaeological stratigraphy: a review of products and processes. *Journal of Archaeological Science* 30, 135–48

Carmichael, D. L., Hubert, J., Reeves, B. and Schanche, A. (eds.) 1994. *Sacred Sites, Sacred Places.* London: Routledge

Case, H. 2004. Circles, triangles, squares and hexagons. In R. Cleal and J. Pollard (eds.), *Monuments and Material Culture. Papers in honour of an Avebury archaeologist: Isobel Smith*, 109–19. East Knoyle: Hobnob Press

Chippindale, C. 1983. *Stonehenge Complete.* London: Thames and Hudson

Clark, J. 1997. Medieval ironwork. In S.T.Driscoll and P.A.Yeoman (eds.), *Excavations within Edinburgh Castle in 1988–91*, 154–62. Edinburgh: Society of Antiquaries of Scotland

Clarke, D. L. 1970. *Beaker Pottery of Great Britain and Ireland.* Cambridge: Cambridge University Press

Cleal, R. in prep. The pottery from Wyke Down. In M. Green, M. Allen and C. French (eds.), *Neolithic and Bronze Age sites on Cranborne Chase*

Cleal, R. M. J. 1995. Pottery fabrics in Wessex in the fourth to second millenia BC. In I. Kinnes and G. Varndell (eds), *'Unbaked Urnes of Rudely Shape': essays on British and Irish Pottery for Ian Longworth*, 185–94. Oxford: Oxbow Books

Cleal, R. M. J. 2005. 'The small compass of a grave': early Bronze Age burial in and around Avebury and the Marlborough Downs. In G. Brown, D. Field and D. McOmish (eds.), *The Avebury Landscape: aspects of the field archaeology of the Marlborough Downs*, 114–32. Oxford: Oxbow Books

Cleal, R. M. J., Allen, M. J. and Newman, C. 2004. An archaeological and environmental study of the Neolithic and later prehistoric landscape of the Avon Valley and Durrington Walls environs. *Wiltshire Archaeological and Natural History Magazine* 97, 218–48

Cleal, R. M. J. and Montague, R. 2001. Neolithic and Early Bronze Age. In A. Chadburn and M. Pomeroy-Kellinger (eds.), *Archaeological Research Agenda for the Avebury World Heritage Site*, 8–19. Salisbury: Wessex Archaeology and English Heritage

Cleal, R. M. J., Walker, K. E. and Montague, R. 1995. *Stonehenge in its Landscape: twentieth century excavations.* London: English Heritage

Coles, B. 1992. Further thoughts on the impact of beaver on temperate landscapes. In S. Needham and M. G. Macklin (eds.), *Alluvial Archaeology in Britain*, 93–9. Oxford: Oxbow Books

Colt Hoare, R. 1812. *The Ancient History of South Wiltshire.* London: William Miller

Colt Hoare, R. 1821. *The Ancient History of North Wiltshire.* London: Lackington, Hughes, Harding, Mavor and Jones

Connah, G. 1964. Excavations at Knap Hill, Alton Priors, 1961. *Wiltshire Archaeological and Natural History Magazine* 60, 1–25

Connerton, P. 1989. *How Societies Remember.* Cambridge: Cambridge University Press

Cooper, N. J. 1998. Pottery Supply to Roman Cirencester. In N. Holbrook (ed), *Cirencester: the Roman town defences, public buildings and shops*, 324–50. Cirencester: Cotswold Archaeological Trust

Courty, M. A., Goldberg, P. and MacPhail, R. 1989. *Soils and Micromorphology in Archaeology.* Cambridge: Cambridge University Press

Cowgill, J. 1987. Manufacturing techniques. In J. Cowgill, M. d. Neergaard and N. Griffiths (eds.), *Knives and Scabbards*, 8–39. London: HMSO

Cowgill, J., de Neergaard, M. and Griffiths, N. 1987. *Knives and Scabbards.* London: HMSO

Crawford, O. G. S. 1923. Notes on field-work round

Avebury, December 1921. *Wiltshire Archaeological and Natural History Magazine* 42, 52–5

Crawford, O. G. S. and Keiller, A. 1928. *Wessex from the Air.* Oxford: Oxford University Press

Crump, T. 1990. *The Anthropology of Numbers.* Cambridge: Cambridge University Press

Crutchley, S. 2005. Recent aerial survey work in the Marlborough Downs region. In G. Brown, D. Field and D. McOmish (eds.), *The Avebury Landscape: aspects of the field archaeology of the Marlborough Downs*, 34–42. Oxford: Oxbow Books

Cummings, V. and Fowler, C. (eds.) 2004. *The Neolithic of the Irish Sea: materiality and traditions of practice.* Oxford: Oxbow Books

Cummings, V. and Whittle, A. W. R. 2004. *Places of Special Virtue: megaliths in the Neolithic landscapes of Wales.* Oxford: Oxbow Books

Cunnington, M. E. 1913. The re-erection of two fallen stones, and discovery of an interment with drinking cup, at Avebury. *Wiltshire Archaeological and Natural History Magazine* 38, 1–11

Cunnington, M. E. 1926. Notes on recent prehistoric finds. *Wiltshire Archaeological and Natural History Magazine* 43, 399–400

Cunnington, M. E. 1929. *Woodhenge.* Devizes: Simpson

Cunnington, M. E. 1931. The Sanctuary on Overton Hill near Avebury. *Wiltshire Archaeological and Natural History Magazine* 45, 300–35

Dames, M. 1976. *The Silbury Treasure.* London: Thames and Hudson

Dames, M. 1977. *The Avebury Cycle.* London: Thames and Hudson

Darvill, T. 1997. Ever increasing circles: the sacred geographies of Stonehenge and its landscape. In B. Cunliffe and C. Renfrew (eds.), *Science and Stonehenge (Proceedings of the British Academy 92)*, 167–202. Oxford: Oxford University Press

Darvill, T. 2005. *Stonehenge World Heritage Site: an archaeological research framework.* London and Bournemouth: English Heritage and Bournemouth University

David, A. 1999. *Beckhampton, Nr Avebury, Wilts: draft report on geophysical survey May 1999.* Ancient Monuments Laboratory, Unpublished report

David, A. 2000. *Beckhampton, Nr Avebury, Wilts: draft report on geophysical survey May 2000.* Centre for Archaeology, Unpublished report

David, A., Cole, M., Horsley, T., Linford, N., Linford, P. and Martin, L. 2004. A hidden Stonehenge: geophysical survey at Stanton Drew, England. *Antiquity* 78, 341–58

David, A., Field, D., Fassbinder, J., Linford, N., Linford, P. and Payne, A. 2003. 'A Family Chapel…. to an Archdruids Dwelling': an investigation into the stone circle at Winterbourne Bassett, Wiltshire. *Wiltshire Archaeological and Natural History Magazine* 96, 195–205

Davies, P. and Wolski, C. 2001. Later Neolithic woodland regeneration in the Long Barrow ditch fills of the Avebury area: the molluscan evidence. *Oxford Journal of Archaeology* 20, 311–17

Degerbøl, M. and Fredskild, B. 1970. The urus (Bos primigenius Bojanus) and Neolithic domesticated cattle (Bos taurus domesticus Linné) in Denmark. *Det Kongelige Danske Videnskabernes Selskab Biologiske Skrifter*, 1–177

Denison, S. 1999. Lost skeleton of 'barber-surgeon' found in museum. *British Archaeology* 48, 4

Dimbleby, G. 1965. Post glacial changes and soil profiles. *Proceedings of the Royal Society of London* B, 355–62

Dimbleby, G. 1978. *Plants and Archaeology.* London: Paladin

Dimbleby, G. W. 1976. Climate, soil and man. *Philosophical Transactions of the Royal Society of London* 275, 197–208

Dimbleby, G. W. and Evans, J. G. 1974. Pollen and land-snail analysis of calcareous soils. *Journal of Archaeological Science* 1, 117–33

Dunne, C. M. 2003. Neolithic structure at Drummenny Lower, Co. Donegal: an environmental perspective. In I. Armit, E. Murphy, E. Nelis and D. Simpson (eds.), *Neolithic Settlement in Ireland and Western Britain*, 164–71. Oxford: Oxbow Books

Dunscombe, H. 1998. *Avebury: a five mile chapel.* Avebury: Avebury Chapel

Dyer, J. F. 1964. A secondary Neolithic camp at Waulud's Bank, Leagrave. *Bedfordshire Archaeological Journal* 2, 1–15

Eagles, B. N. 1986. Pagan Anglo-Saxon burials at West Overton. *Wiltshire Archaeological and Natural History Magazine* 80, 103–20

Earl, G. and Wheatley, D. 2002. Virtual reconstruction and the interpretative process: a case-study from Avebury. In D. Wheatley, G. Earl and S. Poppy (eds.), *Contemporary Themes in Archaeological Computing*, 5–15. Oxford: Oxbow Books

Edlin, H. L. 1949. *Woodland Crafts in Britain.* London: Batsford

Edmonds, M. 1999. *Ancestral Geographies of the Neolithic: landscape, monuments and memory.* London: Routledge

Edwards, A. and Horne, M. 1997. Animal bone. In A. W. R. Whittle (ed.), *Sacred Mound, Holy Rings: Silbury Hill and the West Kennet palisade enclosures: a later Neolithic complex in north Wiltshire*, 117–29. Oxford: Oxbow Books.

Edwards, B. 2003. Changing Avebury. *3rd Stone* 47, 44–58

Edwards, B. 2006. *Public history parallels of the official history of prehistory.* Unpublished paper delivered at 'The Cultural Reception of Monuments' conference, Bristol 6th–7th April 2006

Ellis, C. 2004. *A Prehistoric Ritual Complex at Eynesbury, Cambridgeshire.* Gressenhall: East Anglian Archaeology

Evans, C. 1988. Acts of enclosure: a consideration of

concentrically-organized causewayed enclosures. In J. Barrett and I. Kinnes (eds.), *The Archaeology of Context in the Neolithic and Bronze Age: recent trends*, 85–96. Sheffield: J.R. Collis Publications

Evans, C. 2004. Unearthing displacement: surrealism and the 'archaeology' of Paul Nash. In C. Renfrew, C. Gosden and E. DeMarrais (eds.), *Substance, Memory, Display: archaeology and art*, 103–17. Cambridge: McDonald Institute for Archaeological Research

Evans, C. and Hodder, I. 2006. *A Woodland Archaeology: Neolithic sites at Haddenham.* Cambridge: McDonald Institute for Archaeological Research.

Evans, J. G. 1968. Periglacial deposits on the chalk of Wiltshire. *Wiltshire Archaeological and Natural History Magazine* 63, 12–26

Evans, J. G. 1970. Interpretation of land snail faunas. *Bulletin of the Institute of Archaeology* 8–9, 109–16

Evans, J. G. 1971a. Durrington Walls: the pre-henge environment. In G. J. Wainwright and I. H. Longworth (ed.), *Durrington Walls: excavations 1966–1968*, 329–337. London: Society of Antiquaries of London

Evans, J. G. 1971b. Notes on the environment of early farming communities in Britain. In D. D. A. Simpson (ed.), *Economy and Settlement in Neolithic and Early Bronze Age Britain and Europe*, 11–26. Leicester: Leicester University Press

Evans, J. G. 1972. *Land Snails in Archaeology: with special reference to the British Isles.* London: Seminar Press

Evans, J. G. 1975. *The Environment of Early Man in the British Isles.* London: Elek

Evans, J. G. 1978. *An Introduction to Environmental Archaeology.* London: Elek

Evans, J. G. 1990. Notes on some Late Neolithic and Bronze Age events in long barrow ditches in Southern and Eastern England. *Proceedings of the Prehistoric Society* 56, 111–16

Evans, J. G. 2003. *Environmental Archaeology and the Social Order.* London: Routledge

Evans, J. G. and Jones, H. 1979. Mount Pleasant and Woodhenge: the land Mollusca. In G. J. Wainwright (ed.), *Mount Pleasant, Dorset; excavations 1970–71*, 190–213. London: Society of Antiquaries of London/ Thames and Hudson

Evans, J. G., Limbrey, S., Mate, I. and Mount, R. 1993. An environmental history of the upper Kennet valley, Wiltshire, for the last 10,000 years. *Proceedings of the Prehistoric Society* 59, 139–95

Evans, J. G., Pitts, M. W. and Williams, D. 1985. An excavation at Avebury, Wiltshire, 1982. *Proceedings of the Prehistoric Society* 51, 305–20

Evans, J. G. and Smith, I. F. 1983. Excavations at Cherhill, North Wiltshire, 1967. *Proceedings of the Prehistoric Society* 49, 43–117

Fisher, P. F. 1991. The physical environment of Cranborne Chase. In J. C. Barrett, R. Bradley and M. Hall (eds.), *Papers on the Prehistoric Archaeology of Cranborne Chase*, 11–19. Oxford: Oxbow

Fitzpatrick, E. A. 1993. *Soil Microscopy and Micromorphology.* Chichester: Wiley.

Flood, R. J. 1986. *Seed Identification Handbook.* Cambridge: National Institute of Agricultural Botany

Foster, A. 2001. Romano-British burials in Wiltshire. In P. Ellis (ed.), *Roman Wiltshire and After: papers in honour of Ken Annable*, 165–77. Devizes: Wiltshire Archaeological and Natural History Society

Fowler, P. J. 2000. *Landscape Plotted and Pieced: landscape history and local archaeology in Fyfield and Overton, Wiltshire.* London: Society of Antiquaries of London

Fowler, P. J. and Blackwell, I. 1998. *The Land of Lettice Sweetapple: an English countryside explored.* Stroud: Tempus

Fowler, P. J. and Evans, J. G. 1967. Plough-marks, lynchets and early fields. *Antiquity* 41, 289–301

Fowles, J. and Legg, R. (eds.) 1980. *John Aubrey's Monumenta Britannica (parts 1–2).* Shelbourne: Dorset Publishing Company

Freeman, J. 1983. Selkley Hundred: Avebury. In D. A. Crowley (ed.), *Victoria County History of Wiltshire*, 86–104. Oxford: Oxford University Press

French, C. and Lewis, H. 2005. New perspectives on Holocene landscape development in the southern English chalklands: the upper Allen Valley, Cranborne Chase, Dorset. *Geoarchaeology* 20, 109–34

French, C. and Pryor, F. 2005. *Archaeology and Environment of the Etton Landscape.* Peterborough: Fenland Archaeological Trust/East Anglian Archaeology

French, C. A. I. 1988. Aspects of buried prehistoric soils in the lower Welland valley and the fen margin north of Peterborough, Cambridgeshire. In W. Groenman-van Waateringe and M. Robinson (eds.), *Man-made Soils*, 115–30. Oxford: British Archaeological Reports

French, C. A. I., Lewis, H. A., Allen, M. J. and Scaife, R. G. 2001. Palaeoenvironmental and archaeological investigations on Wyke Down in the upper Allen valley, Cranborne Chase, Dorset, England. Interim summary report for 1998–9. *Proceedings of the Dorset Natural History and Archaeological Society* 122, 53–71

Fulford, M. G. and Allen, J. R. L. 1992. Iron-making at the Chesters Villa, Woolaston, Gloucestershire: survey and excavation 1987–91. *Britannia* 23, 118–191

Gale, R. 1990. Charcoals. In J. Richards (ed.), *The Stonehenge Environs Project*, 252–3. London: English Heritage

Gale, R. 1996. Charcoal from the Pond Field barrow. In A. B. Powell, M. J. Allen and I. Barnes (eds.), *Archaeology in the Avebury Area, Wiltshire: recent discoveries along the line of the Kennet Valley Foul Sewer Pipeline, 1993*, 19. Salisbury: Wessex Archaeology

Gale, R. and Cutler, D. 2000. *Plants in Archaeology.* Kew: Westbury and Royal Botanic Gardens

Garwood, P. 1999. Grooved Ware in southern Britain: chronology and interpretation. In R. Cleal and A. MacSween (eds.), *Grooved Ware in Britain and Ireland*, 145–76. Oxford: Oxbow Books

Geddes, I. 2000. *Hidden Depths: Wiltshire's geology and landscapes*. Salisbury: Ex Libris Press

Gell, A. 1992. The technology of enchantment and the enchantment of technology. In J. Coote and A. Shelton (eds.), *Anthropology, Art and Aesthetics*, 40–63. Oxford: Oxford University Press

Gell, A. 1998. *Art and Agency: an anthropological theory*. Oxford: Clarendon Press.

Getty, R. 1975. *Sisson and Grossman's The Anatomy of the Domestic Animals*. London: W.B. Saunders Company

Gibson, A. 1992. Possible timber circles at Dorchester on Thames. *Oxford Journal of Archaeology* 11, 85–91

Gibson, A. 1999. *The Walton Basin Project: excavation and survey in a prehistoric landscape 1993–7*. London: Council for British Archaeology

Gibson, A. 2004. Round in circles. Timber circles, henges and stone circles: some possible relationships and transformations. In R. Cleal and J. Pollard (eds.), *Monuments and Material Culture. Papers in honour of an Avebury archaeologist: Isobel Smith*, 70–82. East Knoyle: Hobnob Press

Gibson, A. 2005. *Stonehenge and Timber Circles*. 2nd edition. Stroud: Tempus.

Gibson, E. 1695. *Camden's Britannia: newly translated into English, with large additions and improvements*. London: F. Collins

Gillings, M., Peterson, R. and Pollard, J. 2004. The destruction of the Avebury monuments. In R. Cleal and J. Pollard (eds.), *Monuments and Material Culture. Papers in honour of an Avebury archaeologist: Isobel Smith*, 139–63. East Knoyle: Hobnob Press

Gillings, M. and Pollard, J. 1999. Non-portable stone artefacts and contexts of meaning: the tale of Grey Wether (www.museum.ncl.ac.uk/Avebury/stone4.htm). *World Archaeology* 31, 179–93

Gillings, M. and Pollard, J. 2004. *Avebury*. London: Duckworth

Gillings, M., Pollard, J., Peterson, R. and Wheatley, D. 2002a. *Excavations at Beckhampton, 2002*. Universities of Leicester, Newport and Southampton, Unpublished report

Gillings, M., Pollard, J. and Wheatley, D. 2002b. Excavations at the Beckhampton Enclosure, Avenue and Cove, Avebury: an interim report on the 2000 season. *Wiltshire Archaeological and Natural History Magazine* 95, 249–58

Gingell, C. 1992. *The Marlborough Downs: a later Bronze Age landscape and its origins*. Devizes: Wiltshire Archaeological and Natural History Society

Gingell, C. J. and Montague, R. 1996. *The Cove, Avebury Henge Monument*. National Trust, Avebury Estate Office, Unpublished report

Goddard, E. H. 1894–96. Notes on objects from a Saxon interment at Basset Down. *Wiltshire Archaeological and Natural History Magazine* 28, 104–8

Godwin, H. 1956. *The History of the British Flora*. Cambridge: Cambridge University Press

Godwin, H. 1975a. *The History of the British Flora*. 2nd edition. Cambridge: Cambridge University Press

Godwin, H. 1975b. History of the natural forests of Britain: establishment, dominance and destruction. *Philisophical Transactions of the Royal Society of London* 271, 47–67

Goldberg, P. J. P. 2004. *Medieval England: a social history 1250–1550*. London: Arnold

Goodall, I. H. 1993. Iron knives. In S. Margeson (ed.), *Norwich Households: medieval and post-medieval finds from Norwich Survey excavations 1971–78*, 124–33. Norwich: The Norwich Survey and Norfolk Museums Service/East Anglian Archaeology

Gosden, C. 2001. Making sense: archaeology and aesthetics. *World Archaeology* 33, 163–7.

Gosden, C. and Lock, G. 1998. Prehistoric histories. *World Archaeology* 30, 2–12

Gowlett, J. A., Hall, E. T. and Hedges, R. E. M. 1986. The date of the West Kennet Long Barrow. *Antiquity* 60, 143–4

Graves-Brown, P. 2000. *Matter, Materiality and Modern Culture*. London: Routledge

Gray, H. S. G. 1935. The Avebury excavations 1908–1922. *Archaeologia* 84, 99–162

Green, M. 2000. *A landscape Revealed: 10,000 years on a chalkland farm*. Stroud: Tempus

Greenwell, W. 1890. Recent researches in barrows in Yorkshire, Wiltshire, Berkshire etc. *Archaeologia* 52, 1–72

Grigson, C. 1982. Porridge and pannage: pig husbandry in Neolithic England. In M. Bell and S. Limbrey (eds.), *Archaeological Aspects of Woodland Ecology*, 297–314. Oxford: British Archaeological Reports

Grigson, C. 1999. The mammalian remains. In A. W. R. Whittle, J. Pollard and C. Grigson (eds.), *The Harmony of Symbols: the Windmill Hill causewayed enclosure*, 164–252. Oxford: Oxbow Books

Grinsell, L. 1975. Folklore of sarsens. *Evolution of the Landscape Project: Newsheet* 2. Society of Antiquaries MS 953/1/1

Guilloré, P. 1985. *Méthode de Fabrication Méchanique et en Séries des Lames Minces*. Paris: Institut National Agronomique

Gunter, J. and Roberts, V. 2005. *Geophysical Surveys Spring 2005: Avebury World Heritage Site*. University of Bristol, unpublished report

Haggarty, A. 1991. Machrie Moor, Arran: recent excavations at two stone circles. *Proceedings of the Society of Antiquaries of Scotland* 121, 51–94

Hallam, E. and Hockey, J. 2001. *Death, Memory and Material Culture.* Oxford: Berg.

Hamilton, M. and Whittle, A. 1999. Grooved Ware of the Avebury area: styles, contexts and meanings. In R. Cleal and A. MacSween (eds.), *Grooved Ware in Britain and Ireland*, 36–47. Oxford: Oxbow Books

Harding, J. 2000. Later Neolithic ceremonial centres, ritual and pilgrimage: the monument complex of Thornborough, North Yorkshire. In A. Ritchie (ed.), *Neolithic Orkney in its European Context*, 31–46. Cambridge: McDonald Institute for Archaeological Research

Harding, J. 2003. *Henge Monuments of the British Isles.* Stroud: Tempus

Harding, J. 2006. Pit digging, occupation and structured deposition on Rudston Wold, eastern Yorkshire. *Oxford Journal of Archaeology* 25, 109–26

Harding, P. 1988. The chalk plaque pit, Amesbury. *Proceedings of the Prehistoric Society* 54, 320–6

Harrington, P. and Denham, V. 1986. Excavations at Avebury 1982. *Wiltshire Archaeological and Natural History Magazine* 80, 217–21

Harris, T. 1993. *Politics Under the Later Stuarts.* London: Longman

Harte, J. 1998. Folk memory. *3rd Stone* 31, 5–9

Harte, J. 2006. *Inside the Devil's Chapel: fear and the supernatural in the folklore of prehistoric sites*, Unpublished paper delivered at 'The Cultural Reception of Monuments' conference, Bristol, 6th–7th April 2006

Haselgrove, C. 1997. Iron Age brooch deposition and chronology. In A. Gwilt and C. Haselgrove (eds.), *Reconstructing Iron Age Societies*, 51–72. Oxford: Oxbow Books

Haycock, D. B. 2002a. *Paul Nash.* London: Tate Publishing

Haycock, D. B. 2002b. *William Stukeley: science, religion and archaeology in eighteenth-century England.* Woodbridge: Boydell Press

Healy, F. 1996. *The Fenland Project Number 11: The Wissey Embayment: evidence for pre-Iron Age occupation.* Gressenhall: East Anglian Archaeology

Healy, F. 1997. 'Site 3, Flagstones' and 'Neolithic and Bronze Age. In R. C. Smith, F. Healy, M. J. Allen, E. L. Morris, I. Barnes and P. J. Woodward (eds.), *Excavations Along the Route of the Dorchester By-pass, Dorset*, 27–48, 283–91. Salisbury: Wessex Archaeology

Herne, A. 1988. A time and a place for the Grimston bowl. In J. C. Barrett and I. A. Kinnes (eds.), *The Archaeology of Context in the Neolithic and the Bronze Age: recent trends*, 9–29. Sheffield: J.R. Collis Publications

Hodder, I. 1982. *Symbols in Action.* Cambridge: Cambridge University Press

Holbrook, N. and Bidwell, P.T. 1991. *Roman Finds from Exeter.* Exeter: Exeter Archaeological Reports

Holgate, R. 1981. The Medway megaliths and Neolithic Kent. *Archaeologia Cantiana* 97, 221–34

Holgate, R. 1987. Neolithic settlement patterns at Avebury, Wiltshire. *Antiquity* 61, 259–63

Holgate, R. 1988. *The Neolithic Settlement of the Thames Basin.* Oxford: British Archaeological Reports

Hornsey, R. 1987. The Grand Menhir Brisé: megalithic success or failure. *Oxford Journal of Archaeology* 6, 185–217

Hubbard, R. N. L. B. and Clapham, A. 1992. Quantifying macroscopic plant remains. *Review of Palaeobotny and Palynology* 73, 117–32

Hughes, G. and Crawford, G. 1995. Excavations at Wasperton, Warwickshire, 1980–1985. Introduction and Part 1: the Neolithic and Early Bronze Age. *Birmingham and Warwickshire Archaeological Society Transactions* 99, 9–45

Hutton, R. 1991. *Charles the Second: King of England, Scotland and Ireland.* Oxford: Oxford University Press

Hutton, R. 1996. *Stations of the Sun: a history of the ritual year in Britain.* Oxford: Oxford University Press

Hutton, R. 2004. *Debates in Stuart History.* Basingstone: Palgrave Macmillan

Hutton, R. 2005. The religion of William Stukeley. *Antiquaries Journal* 85, 381–94

Ilic, J. 1991. *CSIRO Atlas of Hardwoods.* Bathurst, NSW: Crawford House Press.

Ingram, M. 1995. From reformation to toleration: popular religious cultures in England, 1540–1690. In T. Harris (ed.), *Popular Culture in England,* c. *1500–1850*, 95–123. London: Macmillan

Johnston, R. 1999. An empty path? Processions, memories and the Dorset Cursus. In A. Barclay and J. Harding (eds.), *Pathways and Ceremonies: the cursus monuments of Britain and Ireland*, 39–48. Oxford: Oxbow Books

Jones, O. and Cloke, P. 2002. *Tree Cultures: the place of trees and trees in their place.* Oxford: Berg

Jongerius, A. 1970. Some morphological aspects of regrouping phenomena in Dutch soils. *Geoderma* 4, 311–31

Jope, E. M. 1999. Medieval pottery from Avebury. *Wiltshire Archaeological and Natural History Magazine* 92, 60–91

Jundi, S. and Hill, D. 1998. Brooches and identities in first century AD Britain: more than meets the eye? In C. Forcey, J. Hawthorne and R. Witcher (eds.), *TRAC 97: Proceedings of the Seventh Annual Theoretical Roman Archaeology Conference Nottingham 1997*, 125–37. Oxford: Oxbow Books

Keiller, A. 1939. Avebury: summary of excavations 1937 and 1938. *Antiquity* 13, 223–33

Keiller, A. n.d. *Reports on cuttings I–XV and XXVI.* Unpublished typescript report, Alexander Keiller Museum, Avebury

Keiller, A. and Piggott, S. 1936. The recent excavations at Avebury. *Antiquity* 10, 417–27

King, B. 1879. Avebury – the Beckhampton Avenue. *Wiltshire Archaeological and Natural History Magazine* 18, 377–83

King, N. E. 1968. The Kennet Valley sarsen industry. *Wiltshire Archaeological and Natural History Magazine* 63, 83–93

Kinnes, I. 1979. *Round Barrows and Ring-Ditches in the British Neolithic.* London: British Museum

Kinnes, I. 1992. *Non-Megalithic Long Barrows and Allied Structures in the British Neolithic.* London: British Museum

Kirkham, G. 2005. Prehistoric linear ditches on the Marlborough Downs. In G. Brown, D. Field and D. McOmish (eds.), *The Avebury Landscape: aspects of the field archaeology of the Marlborough Downs*, 149–55. Oxford: Oxbow Books

Kubiena, W. L. 1938. *Micropedology.* Ames: Collegiate Press

Lancaster, H. 1995. Non-conformity and Anglican dissent in Restoration Wiltshire, 1660–1689. Unpublished Ph.D. thesis, University of Bristol

Latour, B. 1993. *We Have Never Been Modern.* Hemel Hempstead: Harvester/Wheatsheaf

Latour, B. 1999. *Pandora's Hope: essays on the reality of science studies.* Cambridge, MA: Harvard University Press

Law, A. 1969. Caleb Baily, the demolisher. *Wiltshire Archaeological and Natural History Magazine* 64, 100–6

Law, J. and Hassard, J. (eds.) 1999. *Actor Network Theory and After.* Oxford: Blackwell

Le Patourel, H. E. J. 1968. Documentary evidence and the medieval pottery industry. *Medieval Archaeology* 12, 101–26

Lewis, A. L. 1891. On the Wiltshire circles. *Journal of the Anthropological Institute of Great Britain and Ireland* 20, 277–88

Lewis, H. 2002. An investigation of ancient cultivation remains at Hengistbury Head Site 6, Christchurch, Dorset. *Proceedings of the Prehistoric Society* 68, 83–102

Lewis, J. 2005. *Monuments, Ritual and Regionality: the Neolithic of northern Somerset.* Oxford: British Archaeological Reports

Limbrey, S. 1975. *Soil Science in Archaeology.* London: Academic Press

Limbrey, S. 1978. Changes in quality and distribution of the soils of lowland Britain. In S. Limbrey and J. G. Evans (eds.), *The Effect of Man on the Landscape: the lowland zone*, 21–7. Oxford: Council for British Archaeology

Long, W. 1858a. Abury. *Wiltshire Archaeological and Natural History Magazine* 4, 309–363

Long, W. 1858b. *Abury Illustrated.* Devizes: Bull

Long, W. 1878. Abury notes. *Wiltshire Archaeological and Natural History Magazine* 17, 327–35

Longworth, I. H. 1971. The Neolithic pottery. In G. J. Wainwright and I. H. Longworth (eds.), *Durrington Walls: excavations 1966–1968*, 48–155. London: Society of Antiquaries of London

Longworth, I. H. and Cleal, R. 1999. Grooved Ware gazetteer. In R. Cleal and A. MacSween (eds.), *Grooved Ware in Britain and Ireland*, 177–206. Oxford: Oxbow Books

Longworth, I. H., Wainwright, G. J. and Wilson, K. E. 1971. The Grooved Ware site at Lion Point, Clacton. *British Museum Quarterly* 35, 93–124

Loveday, R. 1998. Double entrance henges – routes to the past? In A. Gibson and D. Simpson (eds.), *Prehistoric Ritual and Religion*, 14–31. Stroud: Sutton

Lukis, W. C. 1881–3a. Report of the prehistoric monuments of Stonehenge and Avebury. *Proceedings of the Society of Antiquaries of London* 9, 141–57

Lukis, W. C. 1881–3b. Report on the prehistoric monuments of Wilts., Somerset and South Wales. *Proceedings of the Society of Antiquaries of London* 9, 344–55

Lynch, F. and Musson, C. 2004. A prehistoric and early medieval complex at Llandegai, near Bangor, North Wales. *Archaeologia Cambrensis* 150, 17–142

Mabey, R. 1998. *Flora Britannica.* London: Chatto and Windus

MacGregor, G. 2002. Making monuments out of mountains: the role of colour and texture in the constitution of meaning and identity at recumbent stone circles. In A. Jones and G. MacGregor (eds.), *Colouring the Past*, 141–58. Oxford: Berg

Malim, T. 2000. The ritual landscape of the Neolithic and Bronze Age along the middle and lower Ouse Valley. In M. Dawson (ed.), *Prehistoric, Roman and Post-Roman landscapes of the Great Ouse Valley*, 57–88. London: Council for British Archaeology

Malone, C. 1989. *Avebury.* London: Batsford

Maltby, M. 1990. The exploitation of animals in the Stonehenge environs in the Neolithic and Bronze Age. In J. Richards (ed.), *The Stonehenge Environs Project*, 247–9. London: English Heritage

Manby, T. 1974. *Grooved Ware Sites in Yorkshire and the North of England.* Oxford: British Archaeological Reports

Manning, W. H. 1985. *Catalogue of the Romano-British Iron Tools, Fittings and Weapons in the British Museum.* London: British Museum Publications

Manning, W. H. 1995. Scale armour (lorica squamata). In W. H. Manning, J. Price and J. Webster (eds.), *Report on the Excavations at Usk 1965–1976: the Roman small finds*, 14–15. Cardiff: University of Wales Press

Marcus, L. S. 1994. Politics and pastoral: writing the court on the countryside. In K. Sharpe and P. Lake (eds.), *Culture and Politics in Early Stuart England*, 139–60. London: Macmillan

Martin, L. 2004. Falkner's Circle, Wiltshire: Report on Geophysical Surveys, 2002 and 2003. *Centre for Archaeology Report No. 4/2004.* London: English Heritage

McAvoy, F. 2000. The development of a Neolithic

monument complex at Godmanchester, Cambridgeshire. In M. Dawson (ed.), *Prehistoric, Roman and Post-Roman Landscapes of the Great Ouse Valley*, 51–6. London: Council for British Archaeology

McCrerie, A. 1956. Kit's Coty House. *Archaeologia Cantiana* 70, 250–1

McOmish, D. 2005. Bronze Age land allotment on the Marborough Downs. In G. Brown, D. Field and D. McOmish (eds.), *The Avebury Landscape: aspects of the field archaeology of the Marlborough Downs*, 133–48. Oxford: Oxbow Books

McOmish, D., Riley, H., Field, D. and Lewis, C. 2005. Fieldwork in the Avebury area. In G. Brown, D. Field and D. McOmish (eds.), *The Avebury Landscape: aspects of the field archaeology of the Marlborough Downs*, 12–33. Oxford: Oxbow Books

McSparran, C. 2003. The excavation of a Neolithic house in Enagh Townland, Co. Derry. In I. Armit, E. Murphy, E. Nelis and D. Simpson (eds.), *Neolithic Settlement in Ireland and Western Britain*, 172–5. Oxford: Oxbow Books

Meaden, T. 1999. *The Secrets of the Avebury Stones: Britain's greatest megalithic temple.* London: Souvenir Press

Mepham, L. 2000. Enborne Street and Wheatlands Lane: medieval pottery. Unpublished report

Mercer, R. 1981. *Farming Practice in British Prehistory.* Edinburgh: Edinburgh University Press

Meskell, L. 2004. *Object Worlds in Ancient Egypt: material biographies past and present.* Oxford: Berg

Meyrick, O. 1955. The Broadstones. *Wiltshire Archaeological and Natural History Magazine* 56, 192–193

Mitchell, A. 1974. *A Field Guide to the Trees of Britain and Northern Europe.* London: Collins

Mount, R. 1991. An environmental history of the Upper Kennet river valley and some implications for human communities. Unpublished PhD thesis, University College Cardiff

Murphy, C. P. 1996. *Thin Section Preparation of Soils and Sediments.* Berkhamstead: AB Academic Publishers

Murray, A. S. and Wintle, A. G. 2000. Luminescence dating of quartz using an improved single-aliquot regenerative-dose protocol. *Radiation Measurements* 32, 57–73

Musty, J. 1973. A preliminary account of a medieval pottery industry at Minety, North Wiltshire. *Wiltshire Archaeological and Natural History Magazine* 68, 79–88

Musty, J., Algar, D. J. and Ewence, P. F. 1969. The medieval pottery kilns at Laverstock, near Salisbury, Wiltshire. *Archaeologia* 102, 83–150

Musty, J. and Rahtz, P. A. 1964. The suburbs of Old Sarum. *Wiltshire Archaeological and Natural History Magazine* 59, 145–51

Neal, D., Wardle, A. and Hunn, J. 1990. *Excavation of the Iron Age, Roman and Medieval Settlement at Gorhambury, St. Albans.* London: English Heritage

Needham, S. P. 2005. Transforming Beaker culture in north-west Europe: processes of fusion and fission. *Proceedings of the Prehistoric Society* 71, 171–217

Noble, G. 2006. *Neolithic Scotland: timber, stone, earth and fire.* Edinburgh: Edinburgh University Press

O'Hanlon, M. 1989. *Reading the Skin.* London: British Museum

Oswald, A., Dyer, C. and Barber, M. 2001. *The Creation of Monuments: Neolithic causewayed enclosures in the British Isles.* Londona: English Heritage

Ottaway, O. 1992. *Anglo-Scandinavian Ironwork from 16–22 Coppergate.* York: Council for British Archaeology

Palmer, R. 1976. Interrupted ditch enclosures in Britain: the use of aerial photography for comparative studies. *Proceedings of the Prehistoric Society* 42, 161–86

Parker Pearson, M. 2000. Ancestors, bones and stones in Neolithic and Bronze Age Britain and Ireland. In A. Ritchie (ed.), *Neolithic Orkney in its European Context*, 204–214. Cambridge: McDonald Institute

Parker Pearson, M. 2004. Earth, wood and fire: materiality and Stonehenge. In N. Boivin and M. A. Owoc (eds.), *Soils, Stones and Symbols: cultural perceptions of the mineral world*, 71–89. London: UCL Press

Parker Pearson, M., Pollard, J., Richards, C., Thomas, J., Tilley, C., Welham, K. and Albarella, U. 2006. Materializing Stonehenge: the Stonehenge Riverside Project and new discoveries. *Journal of Material Culture* 11, 227–61

Parker Pearson, M. and Ramilisonina 1998. Stonehenge for the ancestors: the stones pass on the message. *Antiquity* 72, 308–26

Parslew, P. 2004. *Beckhampton: time present and time past.* East Knowle: Hobnob Press

Passmore, A. D. 1926. Avebury: a new stone in the Kennett Avenue. *Wiltshire Archaeological and Natural History Magazine* 43, 341–3

Payne, S. and Bull, G. 1986. Components of variation in measurements of pig bones and teeth, and the use of measurements to distinguish wild from domestic pig remains. *ArchaeoZoologia* 2, 27–65

Pearsall, D. M. 1989. *Paleoethnobotany: a handbook of procedures.* San Diego, California: Academic Press

Peers, C. R. and Smith, R. A. 1921. Wayland's Smithy, Berkshire. *Antiquaries Journal* 1, 183–198

Peterson, R. 2003. Thomas Twining's Roman Avebury. *Wiltshire Archaeological and Natural History Magazine* 96, 210–13

Phillipson, D. W. 1994. The significance and symbolism of Aksumite stelae. *Cambridge Archaeological Journal* 4, 189–210

Philpott, R. 1991. *Burial Practices in Roman Britain: a survey of grave treatment and furnishing A.D. 43–410.* Oxford: British Archaeological Reports

Piggott, S. 1935. Stukeley, Avebury and the Druids. *Antiquity* 9, 22–32

Piggott, S. 1939. Neolithic pottery from Hackpen, Avebury. *Wiltshire Archaeological and Natural History Magazine* 48, 90–1

Piggott, S. 1948. Destroyed megaliths in North Wiltshire. *Wiltshire Archaeological and Natural History Magazine* 52, 390–2

Piggott, S. 1962. *The West Kennet Long Barrow: excavations 1955–56.* London: HMSO

Piggott, S. 1964. Excavations at Avebury 1960. *Wiltshire Archaeological and Natural History Magazine* 59, 28–29

Piggott, S. 1985. *William Stukeley: an eighteenth-century antiquary.* London: Thames and Hudson

Pitts, M. W. 2000. *Hengeworld.* London: Arrow

Pitts, M. W. 2001a. Excavating the Sanctuary: new investigations on Overton Hill, Avebury. *Wiltshire Archaeological and Natural History Magazine* 94, 1–23

Pitts, M. W. 2001b. *Hengeworld.* London: Arrow Books

Pitts, M. W. and Whittle, A. W. R. 1992. The development and date of Avebury. *Proceedings of the Prehistoric Society* 58, 203–12

Pollard, J. 1992. The Sanctuary, Overton Hill, Wiltshire: a re-examination. *Proceedings of the Prehistoric Society* 58, 213–26

Pollard, J. 1995a. The Durrington 68 timber circle: a forgotten late Neolithic monument. *Wiltshire Archaeological and Natural History Magazine* 88, 122–5

Pollard, J. 1995b. Inscribing space: formal deposition at the later Neolithic monument of Woodhenge, Wiltshire. *Proceedings of the Prehistoric Society* 61, 137–56

Pollard, J. 2005. Memory, monuments and middens in the Neolithic Landscape. In G. Brown, D. Field and D. McOmish (eds.), *The Avebury Landscape: aspects of the field archaeology of the Marlborough Downs*, 103–14. Oxford: Oxbow Books

Pollard, J. and Cleal, R. 2004. Dating Avebury. In R. Cleal and J. Pollard (eds.), *Monuments and Material Culture. Papers in honour of an Avebury archaeologist: Isobel Smith*, 120–9. East Knoyle: Hobnob Press

Pollard, J. and Gillings, M. 1998. Romancing the stones: towards a virtual and elemental Avebury. *Archaeological Dialogues* 5, 143–64

Pollard, J. and Reynolds, A. 2002. *Avebury: the biography of a landscape.* Stroud: Tempus

Pollard, J. and Ruggles, C. 2001. Shifting perceptions: spatial order, cosmology, and patterns of deposition at Stonehenge. *Cambridge Archaeological Journal* 11, 69–90

Powell, A. B. 1994. Newgrange – science or symbolism. *Proceedings of the Prehistoric Society* 60, 85–96

Powell, A. B., Allen, M. J. and Barnes, I. 1996. *Archaeology in the Avebury Area, Wiltshire: recent investigations along the line of the Kennet valley foul sewer pipeline, 1993.* Salisbury: Wessex Archaeology

Pryor, F. 1974. *Excavation at Fengate, Peterborough, England: the first report.* Toronto: Royal Ontario Museum

Pryor, F. 1998. *Etton: excavations at a Neolithic causewayed enclosure near Maxey, Cambridgeshire, 1982–7.* London: English Heritage

Pryor, F., French, C., Crowther, D., Gurney, D., Simpson, G. and Taylor, M. 1985. *The Fenland Project, No. 1: archaeology and environment in the Lower Welland Valley.* Cambridge: Fenland Project Committee/East Anglian Archaeology

Rackham, O. 1986. *The History of the Countryside.* London: J M Dent

Rappaport, R. A. 1968. *Pigs for the Ancestors: ritual in the ecology of a New Guinea people.* New Haven and London: Yale University Press

Rawlings, M. 2000. Excavations at Ivy Street and Brown Street, Salisbury, 1994. *Wiltshire Archaeological and Natural History Magazine* 93, 29–37

RCHME 1979. *Stonehenge and its Environs.* Edinburgh: Edinburgh University Press.

Read, H. (ed.) 1934. *Unit One: the modern movement in English architecture, painting and sculpture.* London: Cassell

Reay, B. 1985. Popular religion. In B. Reay (ed.), *Popular Culture in Seventeenth Century England*, 91–128. London: Croom Helm

Reay, B. 1998. *Popular Cultures in England 1550–1750.* London: Longman

Reeves, M. E. 1956. Protestant nonconformity. In R. B. Pugh and E. Crittall (eds.), *The Victoria History of Wiltshire, vol. 3*, 99–149. London: Oxford University Press

Renfrew, C. 1973. Monuments, mobilization and social organization in Neolithic Wessex. In C. Renfrew (ed.), *The Explanation of Culture Change: models in prehistory*, 539–58. London: Duckworth

Renfrew, C. 2003. *Figuring it Out: the parallel visions of artists and archaeologists.* London: Thames and Hudson

Rhodes, E. J., Bronk-Ramsey, C., Outram, Z., Batt, C., Willis, L., Dockrill, S. and Bond, J. 2003. Bayesian methods applied to the interpretation of multiple OSL dates: high precision sediment age estimates from Old Scatness Broch excavations, Shetland Isles. *Quaternary Science Reviews* 22, 1231–44

Richards, C. 1996. Henges and water: towards an elemental understanding of monumentality and landscape in late Neolithic Britain. *Journal of Material Culture* 1, 313–36

Richards, C. 2004a. A choreography of construction: monuments, mobilization and social organization in Neolithic Orkney. In J. Cherry, C. Scarre and S. Shennan (eds.), *Explaining Social Change: studies in honour of Colin Renfrew*, 103–13. Cambridge: McDonald Institute for Archaeological Research

Richards, C. 2004b. Labouring with monuments: constructing the dolmen at Carreg Samson, south-west Wales. In V. Cummings and C. Fowler (eds.), *The Neolithic of the Irish Sea: materiality and traditions of practice*, 72–80. Oxford: Oxbow Books

Richards, C. (ed.) 2005. *Dwelling Among the Monuments: the Neolithic village of Barnhouse, Maeshowe passage grave and surrounding monuments at Stenness, Orkney.* Cambridge: McDonald Institute for Archaeological Research

Richards, C. and Thomas, J. 1984. Ritual activity and structured deposition in later Neolithic Wessex. In R. Bradley and J. Gardiner (eds.), *Neolithic Studies: a review of some current research*, 189–218. Oxford: British Archaeological Reports

Richards, J. 1990. *The Stonehenge Environs Project.* London: English Heritage

Richards, J. and Whitby, M. 1997. The engineering of Stonehenge. In B. Cunliffe and C. Renfrew (eds.), *Science and Stonehenge (Proceedings of the British Academy 92)*, 231–56. Oxford: Oxford University Press

Roberts, I. 2005. *Ferrybridge Henge: the ritual landscape.* Morley: Archaeological Services WYAS

Robertson-Mackay, M. E. 1980. A 'head and hooves' burial beneath a round barrow, with other Neolithic and Bronze Age sites, on Hemp Knoll, near Avebury, Wiltshire. *Proceedings of the Prehistoric Society* 46, 123–76

Robinson, H. R. 1975. *The Armour of Imperial Rome.* London: Arms and Armour Press

Roe, D. and Taki, J. 1999. Living with stones: people and the landscape in Erromango, Vanuatu. In P. J. Ucko and R. Layton (eds.), *The Archaeology and Anthropology of Landscape*, 411–22. London: Routledge

Rupert Jones, T. 1887. History of sarsens. *Wiltshire Archaeological and Natural History Magazine* 23, 122–54

Schoch, W. H., Pawlik, B. and Schweingruber, F. H. 1988. *Botanical Macro-remains.* Berne: Paul Hapf Publishers

Schweingruber, F. H. 1978. *Microscopic Wood Anatomy.* Teufen, Switzerland: F.Fluck-Wirth

Serjeantson, D. 1996. The animal bones. In S. Needham and T. F. Spence (eds.), *Runnymede Bridge Research Excavations, Volume 2: refuse and disposal at Area 16 East Runnymede*, 194–233. London: British Museum Press

Sharples, N. M. 1991. *Maiden Castle: excavations and field survey 1985–6.* London: English Heritage

Shortt, H. d. S. 1937–39. Objects belonging to Mr. Seamark, The Shrubs, Newtown, Tisbury. *Wiltshire Archaeological and Natural History Magazine* 48, 351–2

Simpson, W. G. 1981. Excavations in field OS124, Maxey, Cambridgeshire. *Northamptonshire Archaeology* 16, 34–64

Smiles, S. 2005. Thomas Guest and Paul Nash in Wiltshire: two episodes in the artistic approach to British antiquity. In S. Smiles and S. Moser (eds.), *Envisioning the Past: archaeology and the image*, 133–57. Oxford: Blackwell

Smith, A. C. 1867. Excavations at Avebury. *Wiltshire Archaeological and Natural History Magazine* 10, 209–16

Smith, A. C. 1884. *British and Roman Antiquities of the North Wiltshire Downs: in a hundred square miles round Abury.* Devizes: Wiltshire Archaeological and Natural History Society

Smith, I. F. 1965. *Windmill Hill and Avebury: excavations by Alexander Keiller 1925–1939.* Oxford: Clarendon Press

Smith, I. F. 1974. The Neolithic. In C. Renfrew (ed.), *British Prehistory: a new outline*, 100–36. London: Duckworth

Smith, I. F. and Simpson, D. D. A. 1966. Excavation of a round barrow on Overton Hill, North Wiltshire. *Proceedings of the Prehistoric Society* 32, 122–55

Smith, N. 2005. Medieval and later sheep farming on the Marlborough Downs. In G. Brown, D. Field and D. McOmish (eds.), *The Avebury Landscape: aspects of the field archaeology of the Marlborough Downs*, 191–201. Oxford: Oxbow Books

Smith, R. W. 1984. The ecology of Neolithic farming systems as exemplified by the Avebury region of Wiltshire. *Proceedings of the Prehistoric Society* 50, 99–120

Smith, R. W. 1985. Prehistoric human ecology in the Wessex Chalklands with special reference to the valleys. Unpublished PhD thesis, University of Southampton

Smith, R. W. 1997. *Excavations at Emwell Street, Warminster: the early economy and environment of a Wiltshire market town.* Salisbury: Wessex Archaeology

Smith, W. 1982. A select account of the private papers of Bishop Seth Ward in the Wiltshire Record Office. *Wiltshire Archaeological and Natural History Magazine* 76, 115–22

Soffe, G. 1993. A barrow cemetery and other features recorded by air photography at Beckhampton, Avebury. *Wiltshire Archaeological and Natural History Magazine* 86, 142–57

Soffe, G. and Clare, T. 1988. New evidence of ritual monuments at Long Meg and her Daughters, Cumbria. *Antiquity* 62, 552–7

Spaeth, D. A. 2000. *The Church in an Age of Danger: parsons and parishioners, 1660–1740.* Cambridge: Cambridge University Press

Spyer, P. 1988. Introduction. In P. Spyer (ed.), *Border Fetishisms: material objects in unstable spaces*, 1–11. New York: Routledge

Startin, W. 1982. The labour force involved in constructing the causewayed enclosure. In H.J. Case and A.W.R. Whittle (eds), *Settlement Patterns in the Oxford Region: excavations at the Abingdon causewayed enclosure and other sites*, 49–50. Oxford: Council for British Archaeology and Ashmolean Museum

Startin, W. and Bradley, R. 1981. Some notes on work organisations in prehistoric Wessex. In C. Ruggles and A. Whittle (eds.), *Astronomy and Society in Britain during the period 4000–1500 BC*, 289–96. Oxford: British Archaeological Reports

Stone, J. F. S. and Young, W. E. V. 1948. Two pits of Grooved Ware date near Woodhenge. *Wiltshire Archaeological and Natural History Magazine* 52, 287–306

Stukeley, W. 1724. *Itinerarium Curiosum.* London

Stukeley, W. 1743. *Abury: a temple of the British druids, with some others described.* London.

Stukeley, W. 1776. *Itinerarium Curiosum.* 2nd edition. London

Swanton, M. J. 1973. *The Spearheads of the Anglo-Saxon Settlements.* London: Royal Archaeological Institute

Swanton, M. J. 1974. *A Corpus of Pagan Anglo-Saxon Spear-types.* Oxford: British Archaeological Reports

Symonds, R. 1859. *Diary of the Marches of the Royal Army during the Great Civil War (edited by C.E. Long).* London: Camden Society

Taçon, P. S. C. 1991. The power of stone: symbolic aspects of stone use and tool development in western Arnhem Land, Australia. *Antiquity* 65, 192–207

Tarlow, S. 2006. *The Archaeology of Improvement: Britain 1750–1850.* Cambridge: Cambridge University Press

Theodoratus, D. J. and LaPena, F. 1994. Wintu sacred geography of northern California. In D. L. Carmichael, J. Hubert, B. Reeves and A. Schanche (eds.), *Sacred Sites, Sacred Places*, 20–31. London: Routledge

Thomas, J. 1991. *Rethinking the Neolithic.* Cambridge: Cambridge University Press

Thomas, J. 1993. The politics of vision and the archaeologies of landscape. In B. Bender (ed.), *Landscape: politics and perspectives*, 19–48. London: Berg

Thomas, J. 1996. *Time, Culture and Identity: an interpretive archaeology.* London: Routledge

Thomas, J. 1999a. An economy of substances in earlier Neolithic Britain. In J. Robb (ed.), *Material Symbols: culture and economy in prehistory*, 70–89. Carbondale: Southern Illinois University Press

Thomas, J. 1999b. *Understanding the Neolithic.* London: Routledge

Thomas, J. 2004. The later Neolithic architectural repertoire: the case of the Dunragit complex. In R. Cleal and J. Pollard (eds.), *Monuments and Material Culture. Papers in honour of an Avebury archaeologist: Isobel Smith*, 98–108. East Knoyle: Hobnob Press

Thomas, N. 1955. A Neolithic pit on Waden Hill, Avebury. *Wiltshire Archaeological and Natural History Magazine* 56, 167–71

Thomas, N. 1964. The Neolithic causewayed camp at Robin Hood's Ball, Shrewton. *Wiltshire Archaeological and Natural History Magazine* 59, 1–27

Thompson, J. 1994. Wood charcoals from tropical sites: a contribution to methodology and interpretation. In J. G. Hather (ed.), *Tropical Archaeobotany: applications and new developments*, 9–33. London: Routledge

Thompson, N. P. 1967. Huish Church: excavations of the original foundations and an early chapel. *Wiltshire Archaeological and Natural History Magazine* 62, 51–66.

Tilley, C. 2004. *The Materiality of Stone.* Oxford: Berg

Tilley, C., Hamilton, S., Harrison, S. and Anderson, E. 2000. Nature, culture, clitter. Distinguishing between cultural and geomorphological landscapes: the case of hilltop tors in south-west England. *Journal of Material Culture* 5, 197–224

Tomber, R. and Dore, J. 1998. *The National Roman Fabric Reference Collection: a handbook.* London: Museum of London Archaeology Service

Tutin, T. G., Heywood, V. H., Burges, N. A., Valentine, D. H., Walters, S. M. and Webb, D. A. 1964–80. *Flora Europaea.* Cambridge: Cambridge University Press

Twining, T. 1723. *Avebury in Wiltshire, the remains of a Roman work, erected by Vespatian and Julius Agricola during their several commands in Britanny.* London: J Downing

Ucko, P. J., Hunter, M., Clark, A. J. and David, A. 1991. *Avebury Reconsidered: from the 1660s to the 1990s.* London: Unwin Hyman

van Vuure, C. 2005. *Retracing the Aurochs: history, morphology and ecology of an extinct wild ox.* Sofia-Moscow: Pensoft Publishers

Vatcher, F. d. M. 1969. Avebury: Beckhampton Avenue. *Wiltshire Archaeological and Natural History Magazine* 64, 127

Vatcher, F. d. M. 1971a. Site file AV71, Site B, Marlborough-Ramsbury Drainage, Trusloe. Alexander Keiller Museum, Avebury

Vatcher, F. d. M. 1971b. Site File AV71, Site C, Paradise Garden. Alexander Keiller Museum, Avebury

Vatcher, F. d. M. and Vatcher, L. 1980. *The Avebury Monuments, Wiltshire.* London: HMSO

Vera, F. W. M. 2000. *Grazing Ecology and Forest History.* Wallingford: CABI Publishing

Vince, A. G. 1984. The medieval ceramic industry of the Severn Valley. Unpublished Ph.D. thesis, University of Southampton

Vince, A. G. 1997. Excavations at Nos. 143–5 Bartholomew Street, 1979. In A. G. Vince, S. J. Lobb, J. C. Richards and L. Mepham (eds.), *Excavations in Newbury 1979–1990*, 7–85. Salisbury: Wessex Archaeology

von den Driesch, A. 1976. *A Guide to the Measurement of Animal Bones from Archaeological Sites.* Cambridge, Mass.: Harvard University, Peabody Museum

Wainwright, G. J. 1971. The excavation of a Late Neolithic enclosure at Marden, Wiltshire. *Antiquaries Journal* 51, 177–239

Wainwright, G. J. 1972. The excavation of a Neolithic settlement on Broome Heath, Ditchingham, Norfolk. *Proceedings of the Prehistoric Society* 38, 1–97

Wainwright, G. J. 1979. *Mount Pleasant, Dorset: excavations 1970–1971.* London: Society of Antiquaries of London

Wainwright, G. J. 1989. *The Henge Monuments: ceremony and society in prehistoric Britain.* London: Thames and Hudson

Wainwright, G. J. and Longworth, I. H. 1971a. *Durrington Walls, excavations, 1966–1968.* London: Society of Antiquaries of London

Waterson, R. 1990. *The Living House: an anthropology of architecture in south-east Asia.* Oxford: Oxford University Press

Waton, P. V. 1982. Man's impacton the chalklands: some new pollen evidence. In M. Bell and S. Limbrey (eds.), *Archaeological Aspects of Woodland Ecology*, 75–91. Oxford: British Archaeological Reports

Waton, P. V. 1983. A palynological study of the impact of man on the landscape of Central Southern England. Unpublished PhD thesis, University of Southampton

Watson, A. 2001. Composing Avebury. *World Archaeology* 33, 296–314

Watson, A. and Keating, D. 1999. Architecture and sound: an acoustic analysis of megalithic monuments in prehistoric Britain. *Antiquity* 73, 325–36

Waylen, J. 1854. *A History Military and Municipal of the Town of Marlborough.* London: John Russell Smith

Wessex Archaeology 1998. 11Kv cable refurbishment Avebury, Wiltshire: archaeological watching brief. Salisbury: Wessex Archaeology Report 41688.1

Wessex Archaeology 2000. LSE99 Avebury: palaeo-environmental assessment. Salisbury: Wessex Archaeology Report 47777.1

Wessex Archaeology 2001. LSE00 Avebury: assessment of charred plant and charcoal remains. Salisbury: Wessex Archaeology Report 47777.2

Whittle, A. W. R. 1990. A model for the Mesolithic-Neolithic transition in the upper Kennet valley, north Wiltshire. *Proceedings of the Prehistoric Society* 56, 101–10

Whittle, A. W. R. 1991. Wayland's Smithy, Oxfordshire: excavations of the Neolithic tomb in 1962–62 by R.J.C. Atkinson and S. Piggott. *Proceedings of the Prehistoric Society* 57, 61–101

Whittle, A. W. R. 1993. The Neolithic of the Avebury area: sequence, environment, settlement and monuments. *Oxford Journal of Archaeology* 12, 29–53

Whittle, A. W. R. 1994. Excavations at Millbarrow chambered tomb, Winterbourne Monkton, north Wiltshire. *Wiltshire Archaeological and Natural History Magazine* 87, 1–53

Whittle, A. W. R. 1997a. Remembered and imagined belongings: Stonehenge in its traditions and structures of meaning. In B. Cunliffe and C. Renfrew (eds.), *Science and Stonehenge (Proceedings of the British Academy 92)*, 145–66. Oxford: Oxford University Press

Whittle, A. W. R. 1997b. *Sacred Mound, Holy Rings. Silbury Hill and the West Kennet palisade enclosures: a later Neolithic complex in north Wiltshire.* Oxford: Oxbow Books

Whittle, A. W. R., Atkinson, R. J. C., Chambers, R. and Thomas, N. 1992. Excavations in the Neolithic and Bronze Age complex at Dorchester-on-Thames, Oxfordshire, 1947–1952 and 1981. *Proceedings of the Prehistoric Society* 58, 143–201

Whittle, A. W. R., Davies, J., Dennis, I., Fairburn, A. and Hamilton, M. 2000. Neolithic activity and occupation outside Windmill Hill causewayed enclosure, Wiltshire: survey and excavation 1992–3. *Wiltshire Archaeological and Natural History Magazine* 93, 131–80

Whittle, A. W. R., Pollard, J. and Grigson, C. 1999. *The Harmony of Symbols: the Windmill Hill causewayed enclosure.* Oxford: Oxbow Books

Whittle, A. W. R., Rouse, A. J. and Evans, J. G. 1993. A Neolithic downland monument in its environment: excavations at the Easton Down long barrow, Bishops Cannings, North Wiltshire. *Proceedings of the Prehistoric Society* 59, 197–239

Wiltshire Family History Society 2003. *The Bishop's Transcripts and Parish Registers of Avebury: baptisms and burials 1607–1837.* Devizes: Wiltshire Family History Society

Woodward, A. and Woodward, P. 1996. The topography of some barrow cemeteries in Bronze Age Wessex. *Proceedings of the Prehistoric Society* 62, 275–91

Woodward, P. J., Davies, S. M. and Graham, A. H. 1993. *Excavations at the Old Methodist Chapel and Greyhound Yard, Dorchester, 1981–1984.* Dorchester: Dorset Natural History and Archaeological Society

Young, W. E. V. 1950. A Beaker interment at Beckhampton. *Wiltshire Archaeological and Natural History Magazine* 53, 311–27